F. W. Newman

A Dictionary of Modern Arabic

F. W. Newman

A Dictionary of Modern Arabic

ISBN/EAN: 9783741180408

Manufactured in Europe, USA, Canada, Australia, Japa

Cover: Foto ©Andreas Hilbeck / pixelio.de

Manufactured and distributed by brebook publishing software (www.brebook.com)

F. W. Newman

A Dictionary of Modern Arabic

A DICTIONARY OF MODERN ARABIC.

BY

F. W. NEWMAN,

EMERITUS PROFESSOR OF UNIVERSITY COLLEGE, LONDON.

VOL. II.

LONDON:

TRÜBNER & CO., 8 AND 60, PATERNOSTER ROW.

1871.

ANGLO-ARABIC VOCABULARY.

ABASE, *v.a.* waḷḷuṣ.
Debase, rcaṣil. Degrade, eṣill.
Depress, hebbuṭ, nezzil.
Humiliate, kaxxuṣ.
Disgrace, xicn. Lower, ṣcffil.
Subduo, kaḷḷuṣ, akḷuṣ.
— ṛayyiṣ, dawwik, ғ.
Reduce, ikfuḷ.
CONQUER. BAFFLE. DISPARAGE.

ABATE, *v.a.* cṣquṭ, ṣlotṭ.
Attenuate, ariqq, raqqiq.
Damp (fire), akmid.
Deduct, oṇṣom, jchhi, в.
Diminish, ṣaṭṭir, qallil.
Discount, ṭokṛom, в.c.
  oṇṣom, iqṭaṣ.
Lessen, naqquṣ. Lighten, kaffif.
Lower, ikfuḷ, kaffuḷ.
Moderate, oḷbot.
Quell, eziel, zewwil.
Bridle, zemmim.
Calm, ṛawwiq. *Confine,* oṇjor.
Disable, ṣajjiz. *Stop,* auqif.

ABATE, *v.n.* inqaṣ, iṣnaṭ.
— (as wind), ihda, ṛallin.
— (as fire), okmod.
— (as zeal), oftor, ifxal.
— (as courage), wchen ychin.

Grow Blunt, Dull, eill.
Cease, zél. *Decay,* uṣṛub.
Decline, ohbot, zoul.
Decrease, qill, kiff.
Fall off (lessen), kiṣṣ.
Fall, waqaṣ ṣṇqaṣ. *Flag,* iṣterki.
Intermit, inqaṭuṣ.
Grow Puny, teṣâṣṛar.
Remit, *v.n.* coff, lien.

ABIDE, *v.n.* iṣteqirr.
Continue, *v.n.* iṣlemirr, ṣall, ӹ.
— (in series), tewâla'.
Dwell, oṣcon.
Endure, *v.n.* ḷâṛin, oṣlob.
Keep at,   ) admin,
Do Habitually,) iṣtedmin.
Last, doum, dâwim, iṣtediem.
Linger, ilbaθ.
Persevere, wâẓub, temâda'.
Remain, ibqa'. Stick to, lézim.
Stay, aqicm fie, maṣ; *vulg.*
  iṣteqicm. Wait, uṣtebir.

ABODE, *s.* maqarr, maqâm.
Asylum, melâṣ, menâṣ.
Domicile (Homestead), maurun.
Dwelling-place,) meṣcen,
Habitation,   ) maṇall(a).
Home, waṭan, 4.

1

House, dâr, bait, 3.
Hovel, koyy, 3. Hut, ccuk, 4.
Place of hospitality, maẊaif.
Lodging, menzil.
Refuge, melja', Shelter, mâ'wa.
Residence, maqran.
Resting place, marîll, maŊaᴛᴛ.

Abound, *v.n.* be plentiful: ceϴor yceϴor: teceϴϴer.
Be Copious, tewâfar.
Be Exuberant, ofzor.
Overflow, be Redundant, aficẊ.
Superabound, tezekkar.
Teem? ratrut, b. Foisonner.
Swarm? ixfa', b. Fourmiller.

Abstain, *v.n.* suff, coff, izhed, —san.
Contain oneself, temessec.
Controul oneself, teflabbes.
Debar oneself, uflteми min, inqatus san.
Dispense with (Be Content without) isteρni san.
Forbear, uflteriz min.
Forego, otroc, iqnas san.
Refrain, tewarras.
Restrain, Withhold, oneself, imtenic; floux nofsec min.
Shun, jânib; ijtenib min.

Account, *v.a.* ustidd, sodd min jomla, nozzil-oh menzilat.
Appraise, ϴemmin.
Calculate, oflsob, aflyu.
Cipher, \} orqom;
Score, / octob el flusêb.
Consider (Scan?), tefarras.
Dun, Call to Reckoning; flâsib.
Deem, Repute, flassib.

Estimate, soum.
Reckon, Count, södd. Think.

Admit, *v.a.* (lit.) adkil, dakkil.
Harbour, \} uflwi, ufltewi cala.
House, /
Entertain, Ẋuif. Shelter, 'éwi.
Lodge, enzil, seccin.
Receive, lûqi, istaqbil.
Welcome, isterflub bi, teraflflab bi, fic.
Go out in mass to Welcome in, ufltafil fic.

Adorn, *v.a.* zeyyin.
Accoutre (Rig), 'ehhib.
Apparel, (Busk), lafflq.
Array, Attire, icsi, cosi.
Beautify, Grace, jammil, flassin.
Bedizen oneself, tebarraj.
Betrick, Trick up, Deck (with jewels, etc.), xannif, xantif.
Clothe, Dress, elbis.
Crown (with garland), cellil.
Decorate, Ornament, zekrif.
Embellish, \} etfluf bi, tefflluf.
Enrich, /
Embroider, ᴛarriz (*v.p.* i.).
Enamel, \} zewwiq.
Emblazon, /
Enchase, rayyus.
Equip, aiudd. Fit up, waẊẊub.
Furnish, Garnish, jebhiz.
Make Gay, bêhi.
Invest with robe of office, qallid.
Paint, Colour, lawwin.
Polish, oyqol.
Set off (invest with grandeur), flaffil, b. x.
Variegate, waxa' yaxi.

ANGLO-ARABIC VOCABULARY. 3

ADVERSE, *adj.* moɛruɖ.
— (wind), ſâliɛ.
Adversary, kaɣuim.
Opposed to. mokâlif.
— (mutually), motekâlif.
Opposite, moqâbil, moſlâʌi.
Contrary, moɾâyir.
Contradictory, naqieɖ, monâqiɖ.
Contrarious, mokâɣum, mokâbuɖ el ɛaql.
Hostile, ɛadawiey.
Inimical, motebâɾuɖ.
Incompatible, motenâfi.
Repugnant (mutually), moɖâdid, motenaffir.
AVERSE. CAPTIOUS. HEADSTRONG.

ADVISE, *v.a.* ɛour *or* axier ɛalaihi bi.
Admonish, inɣaſl.
Awake, Arouse, *fig.* nabbih.
Counsel, afrun-oh bi.
Dissuade, rajjiɛ ɛan (see DISINCLINE).
Exhort, waɛoɔ yaɛuɔ.
Persuade, Convince, aqnuɛ.
Prompt, laqqin.
Recommend, isteſlɛin.
Remind, ʌeɛɛir.
Suggest, fɛɛir, auſlu.
Urge, ſlarrij ɛalaihi bi'en.
Warn, eſlʌir, ſlʌʌʌir, min, ɛan: ſlarris min; enʌir.
BID. INCITE. INFORM.

AGE (of one man), ɛômr, ɛinn.
Elderhood, xaiba, xaikouka, B.
Old Age, cobr B.; ɛibr el ʌinn.
Manhood, marjalieɣa.
Maturity, ictihêl.

Youthful Prime, xoboubieɣa.
Boyhood, ɣubâ.
Childhood, ɣuɾɾ.
Infancy, ɾofoulieɣa.
Primogeniture, bocourieɣa.
Maidenhood, bicêra, betoulieɣa.
Birthday, ɛuid; yaum el mielâd.

AGGRIEVE, *v.a.* eɛie ɛala'.
Abuse, Illuse, behdil, xanyir, B.
Afflict, ibteli.
Annoy, 'eʌʌi, 'êʌi, iv.
Bereave, iſjaɛ, fajjiɛ fie.
Concern (Grieve), ocroθ, ɛcriθ, *v.p.* viii.
Deject, kaffla, xajjib.
Depress (fig), hobbuɣ, ocrob.
Deprive, aɛdim, aſlrim.
Distract (the head), ɣaddus.
Distress, aɖjir, ɖajjir, ɖâyiq.
Grieve, *v.a.* aſlzin, ſlaɛɛir.
Harass, etɛub, arʌi, s.
Infest, xaɾɾib.
Injure, Wrong, uɔlim.
Maltreat, ɛannif.
Molest, neɛɛid ɛala', nêɛid.
Oppress, aɖuim, isteɖuim, xêdid.
Overload (crush under burdens), elhid.
Outrage, ifteri ɛala'.
Pain, 'ellim, wajjiɛ.
Persecute, uɖraſlud.
Pester, jêɛir. Sadden, seudin.
Torment, ɛaʌʌib.
Tyrannize, } jour ɛala',
Domineer over, } ojbor, ajhir.
Usurp, teɛadda' ɛala'.
Vex, Mortify, ɾomm, exɛul, zeɛɛul.
Worry, ɛâɛiɛ, kâxin.

Wound (pain), amǔuǐ.
DISTURB. ENRAGE. HURT. SPOIL.

AGREE, v.n. (be consistent), see also ALLOW, COVENANT.
Accord with, ittefiq bi.
Agree with (resemble), flâci.
Consist with, wâfiq.
Coincide, terâbaq.
— (Fit) with, râbiṭ.
Comport with, intali ɛala'.
Consort with, nêsib.
Concur, tewârad, x.
Concur concerning, ajmiɛ ɛala'.
Correspond, ɜâhi, insi*?
Compare, v.n. xâbih, axbih.
Compete with, 'wêzi.
Conduce to, 'ewwil ila'.
Conspire to, afɜu ila'.
Match with, lâyim.
Be at one, ittefiud.
Resemble, mêθiL FIT.

ALLOW, v.a. ajiez, jawwiz.
Accede, Agree to, wâfi ila'.
Accept, iqbal.
— iqtebil, isteqbil.
Acquiesce in, istesrif bi.
Admit of, Permit, Agree to, istebiefl. Adopt, ittekia.
Assent, qoul bi, istejieb, ajieb ila'.
Authorize (a deed), fialliL
— (a person), seyyib.
Approve, istefisin, istefili, istaywib.
Compromise, v.n. terâɜa'.
Concede, ismaɛ lɛho bi.
Comply with, TÂwiɛ.
Conform to, tewâfaq bi, imtoθil bi.

Consent, irɜa' bi, ɛan.
— irtaɜu. Empower, welli.
Entrust (a person), fawwuɜ.
Humour, sêyir.
Indulge, rakkuy, sêhil, ɛawwiɛ.
Give Leave, i'ɪen lɛho bi.
Go Along with, te'êtɛ. — têbiɛ.
Permit, sêmifl, ismafi lɛho bi.
Submit to, ikɜaɛ li.
Suffer, ufitemil.
Tolerate, esrifl, serriɛl.
Yield to, inqied li.
Vouchsafe, tefaɜɜal; ɛajifl, sejjifl.
Wink at (delinquency), jawwiz, tejawwez fie.

ALONE, wafid (with suffix pronoun).
Isolated,   } monfarid,
Insulated, } motefarrid.
Lone, Lonely, } wafidâni,
Lonesome,   } motewafiud.
One, wâfiud ('efiad).
Only, adj. wafiuid.
Retired, nêzifi, montezifi; kilou, F.
Sequestered, monɛazil, mostezil.
Single, farad, fɪɪɪ, F.
Singular, mofrad.
Solitary, fârid, faroud, firâdiey.
Unique, faried.

AMAZE, v.a. aries, behhit, †ibhet. v.p. bohit, inbehit.
Astonish, ɛajjib, v.p. v. x.
Astound (strike down), idhix, adhix; v.p. vii.
Confound, iɜhil, ɛahil, v.p. vii.
Make Giddy, dawwik.

ANGLO-ARABIC VOCABULARY. 5

Strike Dumb, iſſlum, ikris.
  v.p. istesjim.
Perplex, aſluir, ſlayyir, *v.p.* v. i.
Pose, Poze, ɼoff.
Puzzle, icbaſl, *v.p.* v. ; aswuy,
  v.p. viii.
Surprize, icbis sala', idhem, ʀ.
Stun, ikras, *v.p.* vii.
Stupefy, kabbil.
    CHARM. DAZZLE.

AMBASSADOR, sofier, 6.
Embassy, sofâra.
Agent, weciel, 6.
Chargé d' affaires, Political Agent, mostémad.
Commissioner, mâmour, 12.
Emissary, dasies, 11.
Envoy, resoul, 10, wâſid, 7.
The Legation, el mâmourieya.
Nuncio, *pop*. eltxie.
Plenipotentiary, *adj*. mosteqill.

AMUSE, *v.a.* farrij sannoh.
— *oneself*, teselle' ; teceyyaſ, ʙ. telchhe', iltehi; tenezzeh, tafarraj ; tefesseſl.
Amuse (deceive by delay), mâtul. CHEAT.
Comfort, selli. Divert, lchhi.
Divert from, lêhi san, lâsub san (see Divert). Please, asjib.

ANGER, *s.* ɼaẓab.
Agitation, aẕturâb.
Choler, Ire, ſlanaq.
Displeasure, ɼobn (aic), ʙ.
Frenzy, sirsêm.
Fierceness, ɼaxmara.
Fury, sosâr. Huff, θêra, θoura.
Ill-temper, qahr, ʙ. (Spleen).

Indignation, sckaт, sokтa.
Irritation, ſlared.
Madness, jonoun.
Outburst, ɼâyila, 12.
Passion, kolq, tekalloq.
Resentment, ɼall. Rage, hcijân.
Vexation, ɼamm. Wrath, ɼaiz.
    GRIEF.

ANGRY, ɼaẕbân.
Choleric, ɼaẕoub, ɼuẕabiey.
Cross, faqsên. Annoyed, zeslân.
Displeased (Splenctic?), mon- qahir. Furious, sesrân.
Fierce, moteɼaxmir, 3.
Gloomy, mecroub, cerieb?
Indignant, sêkiт.
Irritated, moſlterix, ſlardân sala'. Passionate, kolqâni.
Offended at, xâmir min, ʙ.
Sad, moseudan, moteseudin.
Rabid, celbân, mecloub, mos- teclib. Sullen, maſlsour.
Raging, hêyij, heyyâj.
Wrathful, moɼtêz.
CRUEL, ILLNATURED, MAD, EN- RAGE, RAGE.

ANIMAL, *s.* ſlaiwân, 2.
Beast (wild), waſlx, 3 ; (tame) dâbba, *pl*. dawâbb.
Tame Beast, waſlx 'enies, waſlx dajoun *or* dâjin.
Fierce Beast, sebos, 5 ; waſlx cêsir *or* xâri *or* jâriſl, 12.
Shy Animal, ſlaiwân xârid.
Domestic Animal, ſl. 'ehliey, beitioy, jouwiey.
Bird, тâyir, тair, 3.
Brute, behiema, 11.
Creature, maklouq, 2.

Quadruped, ʌét el arbaε, ғ.
Reptile (as lizard), dabieb.
— (as scorpion), hêmma, *pl.* hewâmm. Fish, semec, 4.
Vermin, flaxara, 2.
Insect (*Bestiola*), dowaiba, 2.
Shell-fish, vadaf, 4.
Animalcule, flöwaiyan.

Antelope, (*gener.*) el baqar el wañx; raxâ, *pl.* arxâ; gabi.
— Persian, ɣazél.
— Arabian, el aryel, 11; el gabi el raxieq.
— Numidian, yañmour, 11.
— Nyl Ghau, el yañmour el moñajjal.
— Abyssinian (the Madoqua), yañmour el molouc.
Giraffe, zoráfa. Derr.

Antiquity, qadâma, qadiemieya, el qadiem, ʙ.
Yore, qidm (qodm) ʙ.
Antiquities, ê'θêr; êθêr qadiema.
Cavern, maɣâra, 11.
Coins, mescoucêt.
Chapel, nâwoua, ναός.
Medals, sclûñuit.
Pillar, εâmoud, 12.
Ruin, yabâb; — *pl.* karâbât.
Sculpture, tavwier.
Temple, heicel, 11.
Urn, qâroura.

Ape, qird, 3. Baboon, maimaun.
Monkey, secdân. Satyr, nisnês.

Apples, toffañ(a).
Pear, najâɣ(a), armoud, comeθra'.

Pine Apple, qaxra (σтεσм); εain el nês (*ananas*).
Quinces, εefarjal.

Arch, *s.* qinrara, 11; qaus, 4; flaniey, *pl.* flanâyâ, ʙ.
Arcade, εuqd, εaqâda, qabous, ʙ.
Arched Opening, rawâqa.
Arched Recess, iewân.
Arch of Window, râqa.
Arch of Door, flunâya.
Corner Stone, rocn, 4.
Cornice, Vault, qauvara.
Column, duεma, daεâma, 11.
Dome, qobba, 5.
Pillar, εömda, 10; εâmoud, 11; εamoud, 8; darεc, ʙε.
Roof, seqf, 3.
Stonework, Vault, qabou.

Argue, *v.n.* barhin εan.
Altercate, teflâjaj, toqâwal.
Analyse, favvul.
Contest, tekâɣam, kâɣum.
Contradict, nâquí.
Controvert, xâjir, texâjar.
Debate, tecêlom, teλêcer.
Demonstrate, auλuñ.
Doubt,   ) mâri,
Impugn,) imtori flo.
Discuss, tcbûñaθ, ibñaθ, bûfluθ εan. Demur, irtêi.
Dispute, *v.n.* tεjâdal.
Examine, nâzur fle, istobɣur.
Infer, entij, istentij.
Object, εâruí, uεteruí.
Maintain, temeεεeo bi.
Plead, uñtijj εala.
Oppose, kâlif fle.
Plead for, nâλul εan.
Reason, teεaqqal, tedabbar.

Prove (Serve as Proof), istedill sala. Refute, ûâjij.
Wrangle, teûânaq, tenêzeq. CAVIL.

ARISE from, uûyal min, injim san.
Come about (from), tc'êto, toûawwal.
Grow out of, onxou min, inxi min. Issue from, oxdor min.
Result from, intij min.
Spring from, ATlas min.

ARM, s. salad, 4.
Armpit, 'ubT, 4.
Forearm, sésud, 12.
— Airâs, 8, or pl. aaros.
Bone of Forearm, zend.
Elbow, mirfaq, 11, AL
— suois, 3, Ds.
Protuberance at Wrist, cês, 4; cous, 9.
Wrist, musyam, c. —baus, 4, B.
— mafyul (konqat) el yed.
— rosf (4) el yed.

ARMS, siláû, 8. Weapons of War, sôddat el ûarb.
Sword, seif, 3. Cutlas, sérour.
Sword Edge, ûosêm.
Cimetar, yaterân.
Dagger, Dirk, kanjar.
Broadsword, xácirieya.
Poniard, midass, cemmiys, (bonyâr), De Br.
Sheath,) riláf.
Scabbard,) rumd.
Case,) qiráb, 2.
Lance, romû, 4, 5.

Missile, mirmâya.
Spear, kaxt, 3.
Dart, misrâq, zerâqa.
Javelin, ûarba, 10, 5.
Bayonet, zerâya.
Arrow, seûm, 5; noxxâb(a), ncbl(a). Shaft, jaried.
Bow, qaus, pl. qisioy.
Bowstring, weler, 4; qinâb.
Quiver, jasba, 5; miklâya (bag).
Crossbow (engine), minjanieq.
Sling, miqlás, 11. GUN.

ARMOUR, sôdda modajjija, jonna, 10. Shield, tars, 3.
Breastplate,) dirs, 3.
Corslet, Cuirass,)
Coat of Mail, zerd, zerdieya.
Ring of the Mail, zerda.
Helmet, kouae, 10.
Leather-buckler, daraqa, 10, 5.
Escutcheon, mijann, B.
Belt, ûammâlet el seif.
Sash, zonnâr, wixâû.
Plume, jiqqa. Crest, xouxa.
Feather, riexa, su.

ARMY, sasoer, 11; jond, 3.
A Host, jaix, 3.
A Force, qouwa, 2.
Troops, jonoud.
A Soldier, jondiey, sascericy.
National Guard, ûâßsa 'ehlicya.
Infantry, maxxâya, B.; payâda, o.
Cavalry, kiyâla, forsên, sewâri.
Artillery, raupajieya.
A Regiment, jambora, 11.
— eláî (πομπή?)
A Legion, Tábour, 12; ôrte, B.

A Battalion, boulouc, farioq, c. x. 10.
Brigade (Flag), liwâ, 8.
Band, fuuj, 4; cerdous(c), 11, b.
Corps, jouq, 4; jauqa.
Troop, zomra, sorba.
Company, jamâsa.
Small Company, xirAima.
Detachment, firqa, 10.
File (of troops), mutraq, 11.
Guards, ſlorras, xorar.
Advanced Guard, moqaddama, solâf. Reserve, radicf.
— moteqâsudien.
Garrison, xiſlna? râbita?
— moſlâfaza.
Auxiliaries, najda.
Reinforcement, mosêsada.
Expeditionary Corps, ziſlâfa.
Van, ralieſa, 11.
Rear, ʒahr (ظ). Flank, ſôrʌ?
Troop of Horse, } cetieba, f. x.;
Squadron, } ceθieba, râbonr, jamâsat kiyâla. War.

Arraign, v.a. tâlib-oh bi.
Accuse, ithim, ethim.
— pop. ixteci ſala'.
— iqrif ſala' (v.p. viii.).
Advocate, Maintain, eθbit, θebbit, onʒor.
Adjudge, Award, oſlcom li.
Appeal, râßs, isteſieθ.
Attack, Impugn, ntsan bi.
Charge with, iθlib-oh bi.
Condemn, dien, dâyin.
Criminate, 'êθθim, istêθim.
Defend (in law), lâdid san, ſlâmi san.
Decide against, ijzim ſala'.

Demand Bail, istecfil.
Exact, istcufi, ilzem, qarrut ſalaihi. Dun, ſlâsib.
Indict, mâſluc, qâʌu.
Litigate with, kûʒam, lâjij, telâjaj.
Plead for, Vindicate, nâʌul ſan.
Prosecute, ſlâcim, istêθim?
Recriminate, v.n. telâwam, tetêhem.
Sentence, iqʌu, oſlcom, ſala'.
Sue at law, dâsu, iddaſu ſala'.
Summon, istoſlʌur, istedſu.
Blame.

Arrange, v.a. inʒum, naʒʒum.
Disembarrass, ſellic, b.
Disentangle (hair), ſorriſl.
Regulato, rettib.
Set in order, reccin, onsoq, neſsiq. Set even, sewwi.
Set in row, roʒʒ.
— in rank, ʒaff, ʒafʒof.
Lay in Strata, inʌud.
Sort, } waffiq,
Assort, } rabbiq, waʌʌub?
Place Symmetrically, hendim, laffiq. Set. Govern.

Aspect, talsa. Mien, hieʒa.
Appearance, ʒâhir.
Countenance, moſlayyâ (seat of shame).
Exterior, Outside, kârij.
Face, wejh, 8.
— (flat side) raſſla.
Figure, xecl. Form, ʒoura.
Lineaments, seſlana, c.
Look, View, manʒar, 11.
Manner.

Ass, ḥumâr, pl. ḥamicr.
Donkey, jaḥx, 5.
She-Ass, *ctên, 10; ḥumâra.
Mule, baṛl, 5. She-Mule, baṛla.
Ass's Colt, corr 5.
Wild Ass, farâ*, 5.
Zebra, coir, 3, 4, ʏ.; zerd, ʙ.

Assemble, v.n. (For v.a. see Gather) uḥtcâl.
Associate, v.n. tcsâxar.
Congregate, v.n. (as animals) teserrab, te*ejjal.
Convene, v.n. intcdi, iltêm, incaqid.
Gather, v.n. ijtemic.
Meet (by accident), v.a. lâqi, yâdif.
— v.n. telâqa', iltaqi, tayâdaf.
Rally, v.n. inceθib, teceθθeb.
Rendezvous, Tryst, tetemmax, Bɢ.; uḥtexid, inḥaxid.
Frequent.

Attack, v.a. uḥmil cala'.
Assail, iṛtêl.
Assault, iftic, ḥârib.
Dart upon, inzcriq cala'.
Dash at, ibrux ḥe; (as cavalry) inquḍḍ cala'.
Fling oneself at, inḥaaif, irtemi cala'. Fall upon, auqus ḥe.
Foray against, aṛier cala'.
Impugn, utcan bi.
Invade, tecaddâ cala'.
Maraud against, oṛzou.
Prowl against, cuiθ ḥe.
Pounce, Spring, wcθeb ycθib.
Run down, iqteḥum, iqḥam.
Rush upon, ihjim cala'.
Spring upon, utḥr, youl, cala'.

Swoop (as bird or cavalry) inquḍḍ cala'. Sally, obroz.
Encroach, Rob, Jump, Run.

Augur, v.a. tcfâ*el bi.
Bode, Forebode, tcxâ*em bi.
Betoken, Portend, carrif bi.
Divine, iftcḥ fâl.
Guess, uḥzir, ḥazzir.
Foretell, Predict, anbi*.
Omen, terayyar bi, — cala'.
Presage, wêhim ?
Prognosticate, tenabba'.
— (by stars), najjim.
Promise, Predict, wacad yacad bi.
Warn of, enair. Denote.

Averse, motecerrih.
Disinclined,) monêcif.
Indisposed, (mostencif.
Reluctant, (nafour (shy).
Unwilling,) motenaḥr.
Disgusted with, qârif can.
Adverse, Headstrong, Disincline.

Awl, s. mibkax.
Auger, miθqab.
Bodkin, mikrêz.
Gimlet, bariema (corkscrew).
Punch, minkez.
Probe, misbâr, mijass.
Surgeon's bodkin, miel, 4.

Babble, v.n. olṛou.
— as brook, baqbiq.
Clack, jasjis, θerθir.
Drivel, Maunder, bajjiq, ikṛal.
Fable, tekarraf, ikterif.
Gabble, sallic (jaw).
Gibber,) ḥasḥus, barrum (in
Jabber,) brogue), orron, ilcen.

Prate, cêci. Rant, hêti cala'.
Rattle (gabble), irɾi.
Rhodomontade? dardix.
Romance, mohyuy, ɒ.
Spout (Rave), ihai.
Twattle, ihaor, karrif.
Boast, Chat, Talk, Stammer.

Back, s. ẓahr, ḷ, 3.
Shoulder, cctif, 4.
Blade Bone, mancif.
Spine, ɳasec, silsilct cl ẓahr.
Vertebra, fiqr(a).
— faqâr(a), karaz(e).
Waist, kayr, 3. Loina, yolb, 4.
Side, jánib, 12.
Buttock, felce, 10; ridf, 4.
Breech, *ist, ɾaiz, (Seat) maq-
 ɾad. Posterior, dobr.
Pelvis (basin), ɳauẓa, ɾaur el
 jauf el esfel.
Hip, wiric, 4. — ɳarqafa.
Croup, ɾajoz, 4.
Rump, cefel, 4. Body.

Bad, adj. radi. Base, reẓicl.
Captious, lajouj.
Cheap, rakuiy. Cruel, qâsi.
Defective, nâquy.
Dirty, wesik, darin.
Dreadful, mokawwif.
Excessive, zêyid.
False, mozowwar.
Fanciful, kayoul.
Foolish, aɳmaq. Greedy, xarib.
Headstrong, ɾanicd, jamouɳ.
Hurtful, moẓurr.
Idle, cesoul, ccalûn.
Ill-natured, coxir.
Lavish, fayyûẓ. Lewd, fèsiq.
Light-minded, sekief el ɾaql.

Mad, majnoun.
Painful, mo*ellim. Proud, ɾâli.
Rash, mojêzif. Rough, ᵬoxin.
Shameful, faẓuis.
Stingy, bakicl. Timid, heyoub.
Unjust, janif.
Unpleasant, cerieh.
Useless, bâtuL. Weak, ẓauif.
Wretched (person), xaqicy.
Bad (gener.), radi.
Ill, sou* (before noun).
Evil, sie*y, ẓemicm.
Worse, arda', anjes.
Abandoned (person), kâsir.
Audacious, fâjir, fujour.
Blasphemous, mojaddif, tajdieɳ.
Corrupt, Vicious, fêsid.
Criminal, *cɵicm.
Culpable, moauib.
Damaged, moktill.
Degenerate, mostchjin.
Depraved, maɾcous.
Faulty, maɾour, mesyoub.
Foul, fâɳux. — baxies (fetid).
Fraudulent, meccêr.
Hideous, qabicɳ (ugly).
Guilty, mojrim.
Heinous mecroub.
Impious, cêfir, cofriey.
Infamous, mojarres.
Iniquitous, bâɾi, pl. boɾâyâ.
Knavish, ɾuxxâx.
Loathsome, xanics.
Malicious, xinnier.
Mischievous, mouẓi.
Nefarious, xirrier.
Outrageous, mofteri.
Rascally, ɳeràmicy.
Sinful, ᵬâru, mokru.
Vile, reẓiel (vicious).

ANGLO-ARABIC VOCABULARY. 11

Villainous, xariex.
Ungodly, tâliſl.
Wicked, kabieθ.
Wretched (state), bâyis.

BAFFLE, v.a. aſlbut? ſallib.
Balk, Disappoint, kayyib.
Cripple, Frustrate, kabbil.
Defeat, hezzim. *Disable*, satrul.
Discomfit, akzil.
Disconcert, olkom.
Dodge, telawwa'. Elude, imraſ?
Fail (a friend), okaol.
Foil, Frustrate, abtul.
Leave in the Lurch, aklif.
Parry, uscis. Rout, cessir.
Thwart, sâcis. CHEAT,
CONQUER, DISTURB, REPEL.

BAG, s. jawâl, txawâl.
Budget, yörru, 10.
Bundle, robra. Pouch, jorâb, 9.
Pocket, jaib, 3, 5.
Fob, sôbb. Purse, cies, 4.
Travelling Bag, korj, 4.
Leather Bag, saiba, 5.
Wallet, mizwad (Coffee bag, B.).
Portmanteau, jamadân.
Nosebag (for horse), miklâya, muslaf.
Shot-pouch, muvfana.
Skin for water, joud, ziqq, qirba, 2, 10.
Sackcloth, miſl, 4.
Hair Sack, kaixa, 10.
Sack for gruin, sadl, 4.
— xecêra, 6, 8, 11. ſarâra, 11.
— jaulaq, 11. — tollies, 11.
Sack, zecieba, 11.
Satchel, sôdaila, 11.

Skin for oil, honey, Larf, 3, B.
Rice Sack, farad rozz, B.
Coffee Sack, tarad (?) bonn, B.

BANK (of river), xatt, 3.
— sief, 4 (or COAST).
Shore, xâtu, 12.
Strand, Laffa, 2.
Berg, Outmost Bank, jorf, 4, x. B. Alluvium, B. (weeds marking high-water line?).
Opposite Bank, el qâtus.
Further Bank, el sadwat el qoxwâ.
Edge, taraf, 4 (BORDER).
Side, jânib, 12; yaub.
Reach, Dend, maſluid.
Winding, lawâ.
Meandering, tesawwaj, tesriej, tcurieb.

BANNER, liwâ, 8.
Colours, bandicra.
Flag, sinjâq, 11.
Standard, salam, 4.
Streamer, bairuq.
Unfurling . . . naxr. . .
Pennant, Pendant, râya.

BARK, s. Peel (crust), qixr, 3, B.
Rind, liſlâ, qorûfa, x.; qirrûf?
Husk, Sheath, ſimd, 4.
Pod, Hull, karroub, karnoub.

BARREL, s. Cask, barmiel, 11.
Dutt, Hogshead, betlieya, 11.
Great Wine Vessel, bâtuya, 12.
Tun, Vat, dann, 5.
Water Butt, qurruil, D* BT.
Cask, ⎱ boux, AG.
Keg, ⎰ wâriel, D* BT.

Bucket of leather, dalou, *pl.* dolâ. Pail, rülba, 10.
Tin-pail, satal, 3.

Base, Vile, rcaicl.
Abject, rariefl, dárir.
Beggarly, faqâyiricy.
Cheap, rakiey. Common, doun.
Despicable, monhên.
Grovelling, aclicl.
Humble, kânic, motewâlur.
Ignoble, } sefil, acfil,
Low, } sofliey, soflâni.
Mean, daniey, 8.
Paltry, kasica.
Peddling, qaxif (*shabby*).
Petty, flaqier (contemptible).
Poor, Miserable, mescien.
Servile, Slavish, ward, 4.
Sordid, qaair (*dirty*).
Sorry, Scurvy, necid.
Submissive, kalour.
Vulgar, hemjiey, sawâmiey, souqiey. Trivial, zoqâqiey.
Bad, Stinoy, Shameful.

Basket (round), qoffa, 10.
Fruit Basket (Pottle), maqraf.
Cheese Basket, xanada.
Limber Basket, zenbicl, 11.
Hamper? wicêf. Crate, qafav.
Pannier, maflmil, qarral.
Maund, mixanna.
Beehive Basket, selle, 2, 10.
Bin (Basket), sebad.
Deep Tray (Bowl), qavea.
Chest, vandouq, 11.
Meat Tray, rabieqieya.

Bath (warm), flommâm, 2.
Bath Apron, muflzem, 11.

Towel (gencr.), minxafa, 11.
Bath Towel, foutn, 10.
Clout, } mimsefla,
Duster, } roqsa, 5.
Toilet, } mendiel, 11.
Kerchief, } maflrima, 11.
Napkin, pexciera.
Soap, râboun. Sponge, sefinja.
Comb, moxt, 4.
Brush, forxa, forxâya.

Battle, *s.* qitêl, monâtele.
Bloody Battle, melflama.
Combat, masrace, mosêrace.
Single Combat, birêz, mobâraze.
Engagement, monâwaxa.
Skirmish, couna, s.
Expedition, tejrieda.
Fight, waqsa, 2, 11.
Diversion, mofâlata, moxâfala.
Sally, hojoum, karaja.
Skirmishing, molârama.
Foray, Inroad, fâra, içâra.
Raid, ráziya.
Tournament, morâsana.
Stratagem, ceid el flarb, mecieda, fluila, moflâyala, moflârafa.
Blockade, moflâvara.
Fortifying, taflyuin, taqwieya.
Escalade, xaelaqa, xacbata.
Attack, fetc, hojoum.
Assault, çâyila, içtiyâl.
Defence, flurâse, teterros.

Bay (of sea), *s.* joun.
Cove, jouna. Creek, kaur, 5.
Bight, Gulf, corfez.
Gulf, Channel, kaliej.
Sound, sebika? Straits, cziqqa.
Frith, Estuary, boucâz, 11.

BEAT, v.a. uÁrib, oÁroh.
Bang, Slam, oydom.
Box, v.n. telécem.
Butt (as ox), inrafl.
Buffet, Cuff, olcom.
Cane, Thrash, qallim li.
Clap (hands, wings), yaffiq.
Dash, v.a. olrom.
— v.n. (as waves), telâram.
Drub, irzes, B. (iryas?).
Fence (in sport), v.n. terâsan.
Flap (wings), rafrif.
Hit from afar, ayuib.
Kick, Beat against, okbor fle.
Knock, orroq.
Lash, ojlod, ilfas.
Pat, olrox, (c.) ilrafl?
Punch, Poke, zoqq.
Ram, docc. (PUSH.)
Slap, olros, uyfiq. Strike, doqq.
Strike down, adbix.
Dash the limbs about, tekâbar, iktebur.
Tap, Wave hand, rabrub.
Throw (in wrestling), uyras.
Whip, Bastinado, oxmor, oxmor salqa, B.; oxbor (o.*Rap*).
— on nape of neck, uyîas.
BREAK, CRUSH.

BEAUTIFUL, *adj.* jemiel.
Braw, Brilliant, béhi.
Bright with washing, wâÁu, wâÁuiy. Cleanly, náqiey.
Comely, wexiem.
Elaborate, mocellaf, motccellif.
Elegant, garicf, mostemlifl.
Fair, yabicfl.
Fine, zciyin, zeyin.
Gaudy, motcbéhi.

Gay, zéhi, mezhou.
Goodly, melieñ (*elegant*).
Gorgeous? mozekraf.
Graceful (refined), xélebicy.
Handsome, flasen.
Neat, menzoum, montézum.
Ostentatious, motefâkir.
Pretty, cowaiyis, flösein.
Shapely, yaiyir.
Smart, Smug, motezêyin.
Spruce, motewâÁa.
Prim? zoraiyif.
Sightly, dignified, wajich.
Symmetrical, mohendam.
Well-moulded, motayawwir.
Splendid, } fâkir,
Superb, } moftekir.
Tawdry, jaffak, Aou jakka, B.
Tidy? nazâyifley.
Trim? xâmir, ximmier.
In Trim, moxammir.

BED, *s.* Bedding, farx(a), 5, 10.
Bedroom, boit el naum.
Cemetery, marqad, 11 (Bedroom, F.). Cradle, mehd, 3.
Bedstead, serier, 8; tekt (3) el farx. Recess with bed, maÁjas, 11.
Canopy of bed, mizalla, bexkâna. Blind, xitérn.
Curtain, pardâya (SCREEN).
Gnat Curtain, nâmousieya.
Mattress, mirrafla.
Housing, rörrafla.
Coverlet, pirâ, 8.
Counterpane, luflâff, 10; milflafu, 11.
Wrapper, milaff.
— of wool, flurùm, 9.

Blanket, ûurâm abyaẑ.
Sheeting, molâ'.
— xarxouf, (ᴀʟ).
A Sheet, melâya, xarxoufa, 11.

Bee, *s.* naûla.
Sting, maibar, zebân, saqy, xance. Drone, dabbour.
Wasp (Hornet), zenbour, 11.
Hornet, xafour?
Swarm, Hive, sirb, 4; sorba.
Comb, Hive, cowâra, cowwûra, 11. Honoy, sasel.
Hive (Box or Basket), cowâra, kalieya, kalûya, *pl.* kalûyâ.
Comb with honey, xohd.

Belly, batn, 3.
Viscera, fawûd, 8; fowwâd.
[Lifeblood, mohja, 10.]
Lungs, riya, 2. Heart, qalb, 3.
Lobe of heart, } cirx, 3.
Paunch, }
Pericardium, xiŕâf.
Spleen, taûûl. Liver, cibd, 4.
Bile, yafrâ. Gland, lauze.
Kidney, colwa, 11.
Stomach, muxda, 10.
Bowel, musn', 4.
Intestine, mayrân, 11.
Entrails, aûxâ. Midriff, ûujâb.
Membrane, ŕixâ, 8.
Peritoneum (enclosing lower viscera), yufâq.
Womb, raûm, 4.
Bladder, meθêna (biwûla, ᴀᴀ.).
Gall, morra.
Gall-bladder, marâra.
Rectum, sorm.
Abdomen (internal), jaufa.
Anus, majsar, maqsada, kâtim.

Belt, *s.* (of leather) cemar.
Belt, Zone, minтaqa, 11.
Girdle, Girth, Scarf? ûazêm (of *silk?*)
Shoulder-belt, ûamiele, 11; ûammâlet el scif.
Embroidered Belt, ûuyâya.
Sword-belt, } wixâû, 8, 11.
Sash? }
Sash, Girdle, zonnâr.
Waist-strap, sebte.
Waist-band, dicce, 10.
Apron, muûzem, miezer.

Bid, *v.a.* doll; ausuz ila (wasaʀ, yasaz), fie. *Advise,* axier.
Despeak, dâric, tedârec.
Charge, wayyu, anyu.
Command, 'mor ('emar) bi.
Commission, *v.a.* wellij.
Direct, arxid, seddid.
Enjoin, ofrod sala.
Prescribe, farriz salaihi.
Govern.

Big, ûokm, ûakiem, c.
Bulky, θekien, cebier el ûajm.
Burly, badien, badin.
Cumbrous, ŕalies.
Fleshy, molaûûum.
Gigantic, safricticy.
Corpulent, tekit? (*six* ʙ. *bis;* Gros). Colossal, sauniey, ʙ.
Plump, morabrab, ʙ.
Large, Great, cebier.
Large, Wide, wesiee.
Thick, semiec. Huge, jesiem.
Broad, Thick, Excessive.

Bind, *v.a.* sayyub.
Bandage, *v.a.* ûammid.

Belt, ßazzim, zennir.
Braid, oĂfor, Ăaffir.
Brace, Strain, rannib.
Chain, zenjir.
Clog, cestic, saqqul.
Fetter, qayyid. Gird, uĂzim.
Halter, orson, arsin.
Knit, ojdol. Knot, ocqod.
Shackle, xeccil? saqqul.
Swathe, oqmot.
Swaddle, qammut.
Tether, oxcol? Tie, orbot.
Tighten, xidd, yörr, qannib, ßazziq.
Trammel, labbic, oznoq, ezniq.

Bird, râyir, tair, pl. toyour, tair.
Bird of Prey, tair jâriß, 12; t. cêsir, 12.
Birds of Passage, t. qawâtus, t. sawâbir, t. ʒawâsun.
Waterfowl, t. ma²ieya.
Eagle, nesr, 3.
Crane, corcie, 11.
Owl, boum(a). Duck, batt, 3.
Diver, sawwâs, 11.
Poultry, farrouj, 11.
Pigeon, yamâm(a). Crow, qâq.
Parrot, dorr(a), 2, 10.
Swallow, kottâf. Plover, forfor.
Game-birds, t. el yaid.
Warblers, yawâdiß.
Small Bird, soxfour, 11 (as sparrow); — towair.
Young Birds, fark, 3, 5.
Brood, fuqse. — (eggs hatched at a time), ßôĂna, qorqa, b.
Covey, ʒauy, 9.
Beak, minqâr. Wing, janâß, 8.

Feather, riexa, ни.
Down, zepab, ziff.
Crest,) xouxa, jomma,
Comb,) tôrra, sörf, 4, в.
Wattle, sönqafa.
Crop, ßauyala. Egg, baiĂa, ни.
Gizzard, qaunaya, 11.
Maw, jirrieya. Pouch, jorâb.
Nest (in tree), söxx, 5.
— (in rock), wecr, 4; wecn.
— (of sitting bird), maßĂan.
Cage (Crate), qafy.

Bite, v.a. soĂĂ. Browse, irtes.
Champ, uslec. — (bridle), lonc.
Chew, imĂaʃ. — the cud, ijtirr.
Clench (the teeth), ecizz sala'.
Crunch, oqrox, qarqix.
Gnash, yörr bil esnân.
Gnaw, sardix. Graze, irra'.
Grind (teeth), qarqut bi.
Munch, omrox, maʃmiʃ, naʃniʃ.
Nibble, Nip off, oqroĂ.
Sting (as serpent), ilses, ildaʃ, usquy. — (as flea), oqruy.

Black, adj. oswad.
Blackened, moscwwad.
Blackish,) sowaid,
Swarthy,) osciyid.
(Nigrescent), moswidd.
Coal Black, faßuim, oswad faßum.
Raven Black, adlem, oswad ʃirbieb.
Dark, ßâlic (see Brown).
Jet Black, oswad ßâlic.
Dark (as night), ßâlic, moĂlim, ʃaiyim.
Dusky, qâtim, sâtim, satim.
Gloomy, adjan. Murky, midjân.

Dismal, moseudan, motesendin.
Dun, adkan, adeen.
DULL BROWN. COLOURS.

BLAME, v.a. loum.
Animadvert on, ozmor fie.
Attack, Impugn, utran sala'.
Carp at, tejennâ sala'.
Censure, Disapprove, aomm.
Charge (Tax, Reproach with), iθlib-oh bi. Chide, sâtib.
Complain, ixteci, texecce'.
Condemn, wannib.
Criticise, naksia.
Decry, istehjin.
Denounce, héti sala', qoum sala'.
Dispraise, ocaol.
Expostulate,) oxtob, texat-
(Remonstrate),) teb (sala').
Inveigh (Storm), flaxxic sala'.
Object to, encir salaihi xai°a°.
Rebuke, wabbik
Reprimand, intebir, inher sala.
Reprobate, istaqbifl, istakbiθ.
Reprove, sazzir.
Scare by shouts, ozjor (Hiss off).
Scorn (Reproach), iθrib, v.a. or with sala'. Scold, jâdil.
Threaten, heddid, teheddad.
Wrangle with, teflânaq mas.
— flâniq.
ABBLION, CAVIL, DEFAME, DISHONOUR, DISPARAGE.

BLOW, v.n. (as wind), hobb.
— softly, insim? onxor nesiem.
— hard and cold, infafl.
Huffle, Whiffle, fluff? hiff; *ger*. flaficf? hefief.
Bellow, sujj, *ger*. sajiej.
Blare (Puff), ishcj?

Bluster, usyuf.
Fan, Blow in Gusts, insif.
Roar, iqyuf, *ger*. qayuif.
Whistle, nyfur. SOUND.

Blue, *adj*. czraq.
Bright Blue (eye), axbel, x.
[But *Fauve* Fallow in B.]
Blueish, mozriqq.
Indigo, coflicy.
Violet, monûwix (menwiex?) banefsojicy.
Purple, arjawân, forfier, birfier.
Azure, semâwicy.
Made Blue, mozerraq.

BOAST, v.n. jéhi.
Talk Big, fulliз, xafiflur.
Brag, faxxir, okrot.
Bluster, *lit*. usyuf, *fig*. texazran.
Brave, v.a. tejâser sala', tejehram sala'.
Bully, terehdal sala'.
Challenge, irmi ibâfla sala'; istedsu lil maidûn.
Dare,) istehtir,
Defy,) tchêter, sala'.
Plume oneself, tebûhê, tefûkar, onfok rouflec, tezekwar bi.
Swagger, tesajban, tcoebbar, tesâzam, tebchraj, tefatraf.
Strut, tebakter, tobafdad.
Vaunt, iftekir, tefakkar, lehwiq, jokk, ijmak? ijfak?

BODY, *s*. jesed, 4; jism, 4.
Trunk, badan, 4. *Head*, rû°s, 3.
Limb, jûrifla, 12. *Eye*, sain, 3.
Cheek, kadd, 3. *Mouth*, fomm, 4.
Tooth, sinn, 4. *Throat*, flalq, 3.
Neck, raqaba, 5. *Arm*, safad, 4.

ANGLO-ARABIC VOCABULARY. 17

Hand, yed, *pl.* eyâdi.
Finger, uybae 11.
Breast, sadr 3. *Loins,* salb 4.
Back, ḍahr 3. *Belly,* baṭn 3.
Leg, sêq 9, 2.
Foot, rijl 6, *or pl.* arjol.
Groin, arnima, B. (arbina?).
Bone, salm ḷ, 5.
Hair, sacra, nu 3.
Body (also), badan 4.
Body of beast, joθθa 10.
Corpse of man or beast, dº.
Remains (corpse), silou, *pl.* axlâ.
Body (Person) of man or woman, jism 4.
Carcase, Carrion, jiefa 10, 4.

Boil, *v.n.* iḷli.
Bubble, Gurgle, baqbiq.
Effervesce, four, tekammar.
Rumble, Seethe, zemzim.
Scald, *v.a.* osmoṭ.
Simmer, tectic.
(Boil out, Break out in the skin, faqfiq.)

Bone, salm ḷ, 5.
Little Bone, sâxiq.
Dry Bone, rimma 10.
Splinter of bone, saguyat salm.
Projection of a bone, sinsin 11.
Spine, flaseo. Socket, maqsara.
Vertebra, fiqra nu, faqâra nu, karaze nu.
Knuckle, cesas 5, ṣôqda 10.
Dib, Ankle-bone, cesb 4, 5.
Rib, ḍulʕ 3, 4.
False Rib, sarsouf 11.
Breast Bone, qass 3.   Body.

Book, *s.* citêb 10, mayfiaf 11,
sifr. (Ancient, Sacred) Book, Codex? zibr 3. Tome, jezou.
Blank Book, dafter 11.
Pocket Book, dafter el jaib.
Volume, mojellad (*bound*).
Cahier, bâb; corrêse 11.
Pamphlet, Tract, coteib.
Newspaper (Leaf), yafluifa 11.
Page, yaffla 10. Chapter, ayflâfl.
Division, Part, fasl 3, qism 4.
Verse (of Bible, etc.), êya 2.
Section, jozʼ, daste?
Paragraph, siqqa 3.
Copy of a work, noska 10.
Review, tayaffofla 2.
Periodical, mieqâtieya.
Miscellany,) majmouʕ 2.
Magazine,) daste?
News, waqâyiʕ.
Map, kârṭa, kâriṭa, c.
Letter, mectoub 11.
Dispatch, risêle 11.
Translation, terjama.
Annotation, taqyied.
Margin, bêmix 12, flâxiya 12.
Scrap (Extract), nobʕe 10.
Summary, kolâya.
Index, Catalogue, fihrise 11.
Preface, koṭba. Printing, tabs.
Introduction, moqaddama.
Binding, tejlied.
Appendix, ḍamiema.

Booty, *s.* ṛaniema, ṛazwa, yaṛma (*Turk*).
Spoil, seleb 4.   Prey, fariese.
A Prize (in war), iqtcrama, oeseb
Plunder, nehb, nehieba.
Game, said. Sport, qarf
Venison, qanieya.

2

ANGLO-ARABIC VOCABULARY.

Sportsmen, *ehl el qayf.
Quarry (animal pursued), тarieda, daricce.

BORDER, s. nâfluya 12.
Bound, fladd 3.
Boundary, Term, mofladda.
Limit, fig. zarf 3, fladd 3.
Frontier, tokm 3.
Brim, flâffa (Edge).
Brink, flâfiya 11. Rim, тâra.
Margin (of book), hêmix 12.
Strip (of linen), cinâra, x.
Hem, cefâfa. Ridge, fûrib 12.
Selvage, cenâr, cienâr, в.
Edge, тaraf 4 (BANK).
Ledge (Raised Edge), θenieya, в.
Side, jânib 12, vaub, jiha 2.
Skirt, flâxiya 12. Lappet, ʌeil
Flap, cenaf 4 (FRINGE). [3, 4.
Strip (of cloth), xiqqa; (of plaster), jolba 10.

BOUGH, s. foyn 3, 4.
Small Bough, ʃayna.
Branch, farsa 3.
Graft, ʃira, ʃara 4, 5.
Sapling, ʃariese, fesiele 11.
Layer? тerriez, kalf 3.
Sucker? surq 3. Sprig? ʃarz 3.
Twig? xasnoun 11, в.
Sprout, Scion, fark 3, 4, 5.
Stalk (as of cherry), culâqa.
Withe, Flexible rod, xaтb 9.
Branches, danâkiex.

Box,   } qirûb 2.
Case,   } damanjân 2.
Chest, Trunk, vandouq 11.
Money Chest, seflflâra 11.
Casket, Canteen, bextekte.

Coffer, kozeina.
Pomatum Box, floqqa.
Tray, misnada. (Bowl), qaysa.
Wooden Box, sôlba. BASKET.

BRAVE, adj. jariey.
Active in assault, fêtio 7.
Alert, qaiyim, fâyiq, nebieh.
Ardent, flâmi.
Audacious, fâjir, в.
Bold, Daring, jêsir, jesour.
Chivalrous, fadâwiey.
Courageous, xajies, xojâs.
Dauntless, } ʃâzi,
Intrepid, } ʃazêwiey.
Determined, ʌou jezm.
Energetic, flamies, aflmes.
Enthusiastic, hêyim.
Firm, θebiet, mostcqirr.
Gallant? jaʌes 9, jaʌsân.
Hardy (Masculine), fafll 3.
Heroic (Valiant), baтaliey.
Impetuous, ʌou baтx, vawwâl.
Prompt (Forward in bravery), mobâriz, miqdâm; motejêair.
Spirited, dûyib, ʌou himma.
Stern, Fierce, bêsil.
Resolute, mâyis, в.; ʌou sazêma, mostczim.
Venturesome, mokâтur.
EARNEST. RASH.

BREAD, kobz 4; saix (Eg.).
Bran (Brown Dr.), koxcêr.
Crumb, lobb.
Crust, qixra, qixfa.
Thin Crust, qoxaifn.
Cracknel, qarqixa 11.
Biscuit (Square), boqsomât.
Rusk, qarqouxa.

Scone, raɟief 8, 9.
Ring cake, ccɛce.
Roll, Bun (Bolus), qorɣ 4.
Crumpet, kɛtuifa 11.
Unleavened Br. *Pastry*, fɑтuir.

Break, *v.a.* icɛir, *v.p.* vii.
— up, ceɛɛir, *v.p.* ᴠ.
— off, *v.a.* foↃↃ.
— open, baɛɛuj.
— (the law), teɛadda ɛala'.
— (a treaty), oncoθ, onqoↃ, koun.
Burst, ifqaɛ, ifqaˣ.
— *v.n.* ifqiɛ.
Chap, *v.a.* ofror, *v.n.* vii.
Cleave, iflaɛ, ifliq.
— (wood), ifraɛ.
Crack, oxrot?
  ixɛar, *v.p.* vii. (*sic* ʙ.).
Fracture, uↃtrum, Ↄaттum.
Hack up, hexxim.
Pick, Break up (ground), uɛziq.
Rip up (by violence), ibɛaj.
Shatter, ↃaɛↃaɛ, ordok.
Shiver (Split), xaqxiq.
Smash, obroɛ, iqɣum?
Snap, uↃtrum. —(a rope), iqтaɛ.
Split, xoqq, *v.p.* vii. ifxak, ʙ.
Wrench (Sprain), mâlik.
Wreck (Split) a ship, ixtir ɛ.;
  iqɣum, of wind.
  Cut, Tear, Crush.

Breast, Front, *s.* ɣadr 3.
Breast Bone, qaɣɣ 3.
Bosom, ↃuↃn 4.
Breast of woman, nehd 3.
— of any female, θeda, *pl.* eθdie.
Teat, Dug, bizz 5.
Nipple, Ↄulma 10.

Top of Breast, } zewar
Bottom of Throat, }
  (esp. in animals). Body.

Breathe, *v.n.* tenaffes.
Expire, Respire, *v.n.* rodd el
  nefes?
Inspire, *v.n.* istenfis? ijʌib el
  hewâ.
Gasp, inhej, ilhed (*sic* ʙ.).
Heave (the bosom), tenehhed.
Pant, ilheθ, ilhej.
Suck in (breath), isↃab el hewâ.
Suffer Asthma, orbou.
Wheeze, tenaffaθ?

Bridle, *s.* lijâm 8.
Bit, fecc (4) el lijâm.
Rein, ɛunâu 8, ɛorɛ 4.
— dezcien, ᴀᴘ.
Snaffle, Ↄaçema 2, x. тxaralja, ᴀᴘ.
Chain Curb, silɛilet el lijâm.
Ring Curb, Ↄalaqat el lijâm.
Camel's Bridle, zimâm 8.
— Nose-ring, kizêma 5, 11.
Halter, miqwad, raɛen.
— raxma, ᴀᴘ.
Iron Headpiece, reɛɛêu, ᴀᴘ.
Strap, ɛcir 3. Thong, qâyix.
Tie, Band, ribât 10.
Martingale, selcbend, ᴀᴘ.
  ɣariema, ʙ.
Bridle, *v.a.* cljim, lajjim, zomm,
  zemmim. Check, icbaↃ.
Controul, iczum.
Curb, okzom, iqmaɛ.
Hold in, oↃbot. Rein, aɛunn.
Pull up sharply, oxnoq.
Restrain, irdaɛ, warriɛ.
  Abate, Stop.

BRIGHT (as colour), zêhir;
(as day), nawir, naiyir.
Brighter, ezher. Gay, bêhi.
Brilliant, bêhir, mozhir.
Clear, râyiq, ŷâfi.
Fresh of Colour, naδuir.
Gay or Light of Colour, zêhi.
Flashing, lâmiε, ιου raunaq.
Glossy, Glittering, ιου barieq.
Lucid, jeliey. Lustrous, lammiε.
Luminous, moδuiy, naiyir.
Pellucid, ιaffâf. Serene, ŷâflu.
Refulgent, monier, monawwir.
Resplendent, barrâq.
Fresh and Florid (of a man),
ιaλλ, ραδυιλ. PURE, SHINE.

BRING, *v.a. vulg. imperative* jieb;
better, bêt, *f.* hêti, *pl.* hèlου;
aflair (present), aurid.
Bring in, on; ojlob.
Bring about, isteflyul.
— back, aruid, rajjis.
— off, ιaheb bi, (*go off with*).
— up or to, auιul.
— up, Bear, rabbi, enxi.
— abreast, qarrur.
— forward, Promote, aqdim.
CARRY.

BROAD, carieλ. Ample, mottesis.
Extensive, madied, motemaddid.
Large, wêsir. Spacious, fesiefl.
Roomy? mobafibufl, ν.
Vast, rafluib. Wide, wesies.
— spreading (tree), warief.
BIG. FLAT.

BROOM, *s.* micnese 11.
Besom, micsefla.
(Shoe) Brush, miqamms.

Whisk, } miqaxxa, secâfa,
Fly Flap, } minaxxa, micexxa.
(Hair) Brush, (Clothes) Brush,
— forxa, Bg.; forxâya, ap.;
broxiema, Β.

BROWN, *adj.* esmar.
Brownish, semarmar, Β.
Embrowned, mosmirr, oamarâni.
Brunet, somair, Β.
Whity Brown, aŗbar.
Dark B. esmar flâlic, zerzouriey.
Tan, Tawny? aŗbes.
Sandy, rimâdiey.
Dove Coloured, faktêiey.
Hazel, bondoqiey.
Dark Chesnut, adbes (treacle-coloured ?).

(Large) BUILDING, Fabric,
bonyân. Barrack, qarla.
Caravansery, kân.
Corn Exchange, sêflat el
flôboub. Edifice, rumâra.
Exchange, majlis el tijâra.
Factory, cerkân 11.
Hotel, Inn, fandaq 11, locenda.
Hospital, kastekâna.
Kiln, qamien 6.
Palace, serâi, serâya.
Shop, doccên 11.
Store, Depôt, maflarra 2.
Tavern, flânout 12, miekâna.
Town-hall, maflcema 11.
Warehouse, makzen 11.
Wine-shop, kammâra 11.
CHURCH, FORTRESS.

BUNDLE, ŷôrra, robra; boqja, c.
Bale, marbat; bâla, c.
Truss, flôzma. Pack, farda, c. κ.

ANGLO-ARABIC VOCABULARY.   21

Package, mayarra, ɛub⁴, pl. aɛbâ.
Packet, } xodda 10,
Faggot, } jorze.
Parcel, rizma 10. SHEAF.

BURN, v.a. oɔroq, v.p. viii.
 v.n. burn clear, baybuy.
Broil, ixwi. Char, imɔax ?
Consume, imɔaq ; see DESTROY.
Fry, iqli. Glow, v.n. buyy.
Heat, v.a. ɔurr, eakin.
— (an oven), oejor.
Kindle, ejjij, weijij, (qied) auqid, wallic ?
Light (up), ixɛal, axɛul ; elhib, aɔrim. Parch, xalwuʈ.
Roast (chesnuts, etc.), jammir (corruptly, qammir).
Scorch, xayyit ; v.p. xieʈ :
 v.a. (as sun) xawwib, B. AL
Singe, xaɛwuʈ. Scald, oɛmoʈ.
Simmer, tectic. Toast, ɔammuy.
Warm (cherish), daffi.
   SHINE, BOIL, COOK.

BUSINESS, s. xoɣl 4.
Affair, 'emr 3, ɔâje 2, qaɛuiya, pl. qaɛâyâ.
Concern (in trade), ɔurfa 10.
— (of production), ɛanɛa 10, ɛanâɛa 11.
Occupation, xoɣl 4.
Drudgery, mihna, mehêna, dauqaɛa. Service, kidma.
A Profession, ɛanɛa 10.
Trade, cêr 2. Work, camel 4.
Dealing, moɛâmala.

CALL, v.a. indá' : vulg. indah.
Call aloud by name, ixɛaq.
Name, ɛemmi.

Cite, odɛou, istedɛu.
Summon, isteɔɔur.
Call out, Proclaim, nâdi.
Call on, Visit ; ɛour, morr bi, ʈöll bi, fout ila' ɛand.
Call for, Deserve, istedɛu, isteɔuqq.
Call on (for aid), isteɣieθ, isteɛuin, isteɛuiɛ, istenjid, istenyur.
Call to account, ʈâlib.
— at law, ɔâcim.
— for money, ɔâsib.
Call to witness, xehhid, istexhid.
   ARRAIGN.

CALM, v.a. rawwiq.
Abate, Damp, akmid.
Appease, reccin. Hush, seccit.
Assuage, Sooth, larruf, lâʈuf.
Allay, Alleviate, } kaffif,
Lighten, Relieve, } rayyib.
Blunt, Dull, ecill, echim ?
Lull, nawwim (nayyim).
Mitigate, Quiet, escin, seocin.
Pacify, ɛâliɔ. Soften, layyin.
Recruit, rammin, B.
Smooth, mehhid, weθθir.
Still, ehdi, heddi.
Tranquillize, Compose, raffih ?
   COMFORT.

CAMELS (gener.), 'ibl.
Two-humped C., dohêmij.
One-humped C., jemal 5.
Male d⁰., baɛnir, pl. abâɛur.
Female —, nâqa, pl. nouq.
Young —, qâɛoud, ɔawâr.
Dromedary, hejien 10, B.
Hump of C., ɛenâm 8, ɔadba.
Foot (Pad) of C., koff 5, manɛem 11.

Camel's hair, wabar.
Cry of C., aruit, b.
Back of C., ŗârib 12, metn 5.

CAMP, s. mocascer, cörJu, b., aurdie, c.
Arsenal, torsckâna, torsêna, raupakâna, kaznat el silâfi.
Barracks, qazla.
An Entrenchment, kandouq 11.
Fortifications, tefiȳuinât.
Camp of defence, mocascer waqiey.
FORTRESS, WAR.

CAP, s. (in general) qallouse.
Skull Cap, tâqieya 12.
(Sweat Cap,) saraqieya 12.
Red Fez Cap, callebaux 11, tarbanz 11.
Cap with dangling tip, rarbaux maxmout.
Conical Cap, qabas, qabbasa, qabouca; qobaica.
Hair Cap, round or pointed, qalbaq.
Cylindrical Mitre, qâouq 12.
Stuffed Cap, qâouq, tenbaqieya.
Other forms of Cap (Hat), rantour 11, rorrour 11.
Night Cap, esqoufiya, tekfiefat el rê's.
European Hat, barnaita.
Tiara? colâya, bexla.
Turban, camâma 5, 11, loffa, xâxa, xâxieya.
Cowl, } railisên (tippet?).
Hood, } rantour? (domino?).
Head Band, ruvâba, rabra.
Pointed Cap, } qalansowa.
Mitre (Helmet), }

CAPTIOUS, mowaqqis.
Cavilling, monâqir, monâqix.
Contentious, ladoud.
Contrarious, mokâlif, mokâvum.
Disputatious, mocêbir, motecêbir.
Litigious, lajouj, mufijâj.
Quarrelsome, mojâdil, monêzic.
Quibbling, moxêcil.
Sceptical, momteri.
ADVERSE, CAVIL, HEADSTRONG.

CAR, s. marceba 2.
Cart, naqâla (vehicle).
Coach, sarabâna. Truck, jarâr?
Chariot, marceb 11, s.
Carriage, cerouse, AP.
Wain, Car (gener.), caraba.
Railway Car, marceba bokârieya
Driver, sewwâq, sêyiq.
Groom, sêyis.
Wheel carriage, sajala.
Wheel, sajala; jark, B.
Pole of coach, noxxâbat el sajala; jarrâr; mijarr.
Axle, miflwar, seffoud 11.

CARESS, v.a. wadwid.
Allure by stealthy glances, ŗannij. Cajole, dâhin.
Assume Intimacy with, dâmij.
Coax, nâŗix. Coddle, râkuv.
Court (a woman), fiâli.
Dance attendance on, dehliz cala' Flatter, mâliq, malliq.
Fondle, dallil. Ogle, fizil.
Play the Gallant to, zabbib, tezarraf bi.
Pet, sêyis, tewaddad ila'.
Sooth, larruf, lâruf, telarraf bi.

Wheedle, flâyil, tefiâyal sala'.
Woo, otxoq c.
CHEAT, DECOY, CONCILIATE.

CARPENTER, najjâr. Tools, êlêt.
Awl, mibkax. Axe, fê's 3.
Chisel, esmiel. Pincer, mêsic.
Hammer, mirzeba.
Nail, mismâr 11. Saw, minxâr.

CARPET, (gener.) bisêr 2, 8, 10.
— or Matting, nosoj.
European C. ranfase, tenfase 11, Ap. also, ecliem 11, flaml 3, cibâya, B.
Tapestry, nesieja 11.
Shaggy Rug, zonliya, Bg. sillieya?
Carpet, Rug (or Cushion) for prayer, sojjâda.
Rush Matting, flaynira 10.
Strip of Matting, nakk 10.
Cane Mat, bâriya 12.
Upholstery, nojond.
Printed Drugget, namaT 5, 4.

CARRY, Bear, v.a. uflmil.
Lift, irfas. Carry, oxqol, Ap.
Carry arms, onqol cl silâfl.
Carry, Transport, onqol.
Transfer, flawwil.
Convey, ausul, aurid.
Carry, Impel, flammil.
Carry across, cabbir (?).
— away, onxol, axiel, v.p. vii.
— off, irfas, iAheb bi (go off with).
— down, nezzil, afldir.
— up, calli, aysud.
— in, adkil; or say, Go in with.
— (out), (lit.) akrij, (fig.) ajri.
Carry oneself, Behave, osloc.

CAST, v.a. irmi, iqaif bi.
Dart, irxaq, ozroq bi.
Drop (it to me), ixlafl, Ap. uTrafl.
Fling, uflaif (also Elide).
— horizontally, zitt, Bg.
Pelt, râxiq. Stone, orjom.
Shoot, qawwiy (tic?).
Shoot, Squirt, naxxib.
Throw, oxlof, Ap. B.
Toss, zojj (Brandish).
Pitch up, farr, Bg.
Cast away, uTrafl, daxxir.
Cast down (eyes, face), oTroq.
— (gener.), aflbiT, elqi.
— (down precipice), warrut.
Cast out, oTrod, oTrox, inbiA bi.
Cast off, daxxir, elqi sannec.
Cast (earth or grain) upon, heyyil, ehiel; also hiel, B.
Cast up (a sum), oflsob.
Cast up, out (vomit), oTrox.
Cast in a mould, oscob, isbic.
Cast into (misfortune, auqus bi.
Cast oneself on (a person), fig. Taff calaihi.

CAT (gener), sinnaur 11.
Common Cat, qiTT 5, 10, qiTTa, also hirr, hirra, c.
Lion, 'esed 3. Cub, xibl 3, 5.
Lioness, lebouwa 2, 10.
Tiger, nemir 3, 4.
Panther, habr 3.
Leopard, sebenda'.
Ounce, Cheeta? railes 11.
Lynx, Caracal, fehd 3.
Tusk, nâb, pl. enyâb.
Claw, miklâb 11, kalb, c.

CATCH, v.a. (a ball, a hare) olqof, ilqaf.

Catch (by surprise, *opprimo*), odhom, fâja'; icbis cala'.
Catch (overtake), oqfox, ilflaq, adric.
— (outrun), tafârat.
— (up sounds), telaqqaf.
Snap up, ucfiq.
Arrest, ucfiq, oqboš; iqbuš cala'.
Capture, istê'sir.
Clasp, taxabbaθ bi (see Cling).
Clutch, oqfox, oqboš.
Grasp, oqmor. (GRIPE.)
Pull out (a thorn), ontox, B.
Catch one's Foot in, texarbaq, texarqal. Seize, oqboš.
Scramble for, tebâhax cala'.
Snap at, obhox [ohbox, c.].
Snatch away, ikTuf.

HOLD, KEEP, TAKE.

CAUSE, *s*. sebab 4, culla 10.
End in view, râya.
Goal, Mark, *fig.* caruš 4, carušniya.
Butt, Target, hedaf, hidfa 10.
Means, wâsita, tarieqa 11, 2, wasâta 11, weaiele 11.
Motive, bâcuθ(e) 12.
Object, corša. *Purpose*, qayd.
Occasion, mê'rab 11.
Reason, moujîb(a) 11.
Pretext, culla 10.

CAVERN, *s*. maçâra 11, câr(a), *pl.* acwâr.
Cave, Grotto, cehf 3.
Den, Hole of serpent, johra 10.
Lair, wajâr, marbaš.
Hole (of rock pigeon), noqba 3.
Small Cavern, cowair.

CAVIL, *v.n.* nâqir, lodd, naqix.
Bother, zehhiq (B. vétilleur).
Carp at, tejenna' cala'.
Catch (by question), coff.
Be Disputatious, lijj calaihi fie.
Equivocate, wâlis.
Prevaricate, dâlis ? dallis.
Gloze, 'ewwil. Pervert, uccis.
Pick in pieces, nakxis.
Quibble, xêcil.
Twist, Misinterpret, flarrif.
Sophisticate, flâwil (*garble* ?).
Wrangle, cêbir.

BLAME, CRITICIZE.

CEASE, *v.n.* zêl; ifraç min.
Desist, iklux, otroc; ucdal can; tenêzel can (*sic* B.); caddi can (*sic* B.).
Discontinue, } inqaTac can,
Intermit, } oftor min.
Leave off, tekalla' can.
Remit, coff can.
Stop, *v.n.* tewaqqaf, intehi min.
Pass away, ibrafl.
Fail, ifni, infid.
Retire (from business), teqâcad.

ABATE, LEAVE.

CELLAR (Pantry, Bread-room), celâr, cerâr.
Corn-cellar, maTmoura.
Wine-cellar, qabou el nebica.
Summer Cellar, sirdâb 11, xerxemieya, B.
Garner, anbar, anbâr 11.
Store place, maxkar, mexheb.
Magasine, makzen 11.
Icehouse, meθlaja.
Larder, beit el ma'ouna.
Safe, flowâTa. Dairy, libâna.

CEMENT, s. paste, lizêq: (crushed tile), kâfaqie, karâsêni, B.
— (of sand, etc.), madar.
Glue, ґarî. Gum, romґ.
Gum of pine, rulc, ruloe.
— ammoniac, qanâ waxaq.
— sandarac, sendarous.
— tragacanth, cetiera, c.
Mastich, lâqouna, marraci.
Mortar, tebâxier.
— (of mud and straw), siyâs.
Plaster (for wound), lezqa; (for wall), jibs, jibsruin, jurr (Gypsum).
Size, Isinglass, siries.
Solder, liflâm. Varnish, dihên.
PITCH.
CEMENT, v.a.
Consolidate, olflôm.
Glue, ґarri. Gum, rammiґ.
Paste,) elvuq, lavvuq,
Stick,) elziq, lezziq.
Solder, seiria, B. Weld, ortoq, X.
Cement, fig. olflôm, ocqod.
Plaster, omdor, maddir. JOIN.

CERTAIN (thing), 'ecied.
Sure, moflaqqaq, min yaqien.
Evident, lâyifl. Obvious, ẓâhir.
Visible, mostaẓhir.
Well-known, masloum.
Notorious, Celebrated, xebier.
Manifest, bâyin, baiyin, mobayyan.
Perspicuous, Clear, wâẕufl.
Signal, belieґ, aґarr 9.
Signal proof, borhên sêтus.
CLEAR.

CHAIR, s. oorsi 11.
Rocking Chair, corsi hessês.

Stool, escemle (σκαμνί).
Turn-Stool, corsi dawwâr.
Arm Chair, randaliey, B.
Footstool, maura.
Bench (gener.), roffa 10.
— (of wood), docce 10, tekte 3.
— (of stone), marraba 11.
Sofa, diewân, pl. dawâwien.
— sedala (from Latin?).
— namraq, eriece, su, 11.
Couch, mottecê. Throne, carx.
Cradle, Throne, serier 3.
Sedan? naqqâla.

CHAMPAIGN, Field (open country) falâ, badou, el bâdi, bâdiya.
Upper Country, rasuid.
Table land,) serτ jebal, B.
Plateau,) baqâs, X.
Highland, Wold, Fell, rabwa', pl. roba'. Lowlands, esêfiL
Expanse, tefessofl, imtidâd.
Rural place, mabdau.
Cultivated country (rus), rief 4.
Cavern, maґâra.
Declivity, fladour.
Defile, maduiq. Desert, qafr.
Excavation, faflt. Farm, Laica 5.
Field (enclosed), flaql 3.
Forest, ґairal 11.
Grain, flöboub. Herb, baql 3.
Grass, flaxiex 11.
Land, barr, 'erâ.
Mountain, jebal 5.
Sheaf, flôxma. Stable, ekour.
Summit, acla'. Vale, qâs.

CHANGE, v.a. ibdîl, baddil, uflrif.
Alter, ґayyir. Barter, dâoix.
Exchange, bâdil.

Change (money), oṣrof.
Convert into, ḥawwil, aḥuil.
Pervert, uṣcia.
Transform, } iqlib,
Metamorphose, } imsek.
Reverse, iqlib, qallib.
CHANGE, v.n. teṛuyyar, teḥarraf.
— (be Fickle), teqallab.

A CHANGE, ṣarf 3, ṣârifa 12.
Alternation, ṣôqba 10.
A Reverse, inqilâb, necba 2, neceb 3.
A Revolution, teqallob.
A Vicissitude, nâyiba 12.
Alteration, taṛyier 11.
— (for worse), inḥurâf.
DISASTER.

CHARM, v.a. fig. ixces.
Bewitch, irqa'.
Captivate, istemlic, isbi qalboh or saqloh.
Enrapture, iṣrul, aṣrul.
Entrance (Preoccupy), saḥil.
Enchant (lit. or fig.), iaḥar.
Fascinate, ṛalsim.
Ravish, } heyyim,
Rapture, } ehiem.
Transport, oalob el saql.
I am transported, râr saqli.
DELIGHT.

CHAT, v.n. teḥâce'; ihaer; olqox (Syria).
Chatter, ilṛaṭ. Tattle, nimm.
Gossip, tesêmir, tenâjâ.
Prattle, tenâdam.
Whisper, tebetbet, weswis, teweswea. BABBLE,
SPEAK, STAMMER, TALK.

CHEAP, rakiev. Inferior, doun.
Common (inferior), sâmmiey.
Dowdy, Shabby, moteqaxxif.
Homely, Coarse, qabâ.
Indifferent, moseccej, n.
Mean, daniey. Rubbish, rafax.
Moderate in price, mohewwad (Accommodating).
Ordinary, sâdiey, ustiyâdiey.
Poor, Sorry, wâṭu.
Tawdry, jaffâk?
Trumpery, hezil. BASE.

CHEAT, v.a. ṛoxx, ibkas.
Cheat by pretexts, sallil; (Shuffle off, tesallal).
Cheat by temporizing, mâṭul.
Befool, ṛaxxim. Belie, cêaib.
Beguile, lêhi (HOAX).
Betray, koun. Delude, ṛorr.
Cajole, dâhin (Butter).
Catch (by subtlety), ṛoff.
Circumvent, dâkil, odkol sala', ḥâwil. Connive at, ḥâbi.
Cozen, terâwaṛ bi, râwiṛ.
Deceive, ikdas.
— (mutually), tckâtel.
Defraud, omcor.
Dissemble, dâji, ibhet.
Dodge, telaulau, wârib.
Dupe, cêyid, cied (?).
Elude, omroṛ, isteṛwi.
Equivocate, wâlia.
Evade, tclawwa'.
Fabricate, uṣnas.
Play False to, iṛdar bi.
Falsify, zewwir.
Feign, Forge, izṛil.
Forswear oneself, uḥnaḏ.
Impose upon, iṛlib (sala').

Juggle, secbir sala'.
Machinate, v.a. uñtêl.
Outwit, icbis (Surprise).
Overreach, iotenif, v.; irbin, rabbin, arbin, rêbin, x.
Plot, cemmin li.
Practise upon, } iltemis.
Tamper with,
Prevaricate, dâlis?
Swindle, dallis.
Scheme against, teñâraf sala'.
Trick, lâsub, dâsub, ramir, mêziñ. Caress, Decoy, Counterfeit, Hide.

Cheek, s. kadd 3.
Cheekbone, ojna, wejna 2, 4.
Dimple, rammâse.
Face, wejh 3. Jaw, fecc 4.
Jawbone, madara.
Under Jaw, Chinbone, ñanec 4.
Wrinkle, raána.

Child, weled 4. Babe, rufi 4.
Sucking Child, rufi raluic.
Nurse, Midwife, dâya.
Embryo, janien.
Weaned Child, faruim, faruil, c.
Family.

Chisel, s. eamiel.
— (sculptor's), minñar.
— (fine), minqâr.
Graver, minqâx?
Turner's Chisel, mikrât?
Gouge, mikrama.
A Groove, tekriem.
A Fluting, tekruir.
Carpenter.

Choke, v.a. (in drinking), †ixraq, xardiq.

Choke (in eating), rozz, ariyy.
— (with plenty), daqqir.
Cloy, abxim, v.p. vii.
Disgust, arsi, rañßum.
Encumber, olkom (vic b.).
— orboc, rabbic.
Overfeed, zehhiq (choke?).
Sicken, Surfeit, sukim, seddim.
Smother, römm. Stifle, farrus.
Stop up, sodd. Strangle, oknoq.
Suffocate, iqras el nefes,rammim el qalb. Fill, Confuse.
Choke, v.n. izwar; be crop-full?
— with laughter, ifqas min (split with); breathe with difficulty, isheq.

Choose, v.a. (pick), naqqi, intaqi; onmox; iktêr.
— (will), aried.
Elect, inrakîb, urrafi.
Prefer, mezzi, êθir, auθir, istêθir. Single out, afrid.
Select, ofroz, ijtebi, istarfi.

Church, ceniese 11.
Abbey, dâyir θ, or pl. doyoura.
Chapel, masbed.
— (ancient), nâwous 12.
Convent? vanmas(a).
Cell of monk, zêwiya 12.
— qillâya 11.
Conventicle, } majmis.
Synagogue,
Mosque, mesjad 11.
Chief Mosque, jâmis 12.
Spire, } maisena 11.
Steeple, } menâra 11.
Temple, heicel 11.
Tomb of Saint, mesêr.

CITY, *s.* mediena 10, 11.
Metropolis,) el cásuma 12.
Capital, } dâr el flôoouma,
dâr el saltana, qâsudat el
milo, mostcqarr (maqarr) al
milo, serier el melio.
A Chief City, muyr 4, 5.
Thorp, qarya, *pl.* qora' *or* qaráyá.
Borough, oefr 3, 5.
Hamlet, qayaba.
Canton, belad 5.
Town, belda (9?).
Township, sâyifl.
Quarter, flâra (maflalla).
Precincts, diyâr.
Environs, flawâli.
Suburb, xâfluya 12.
A Mart, bandar 11.
Farm, Village, xaica, 5.
Region, bilâd 9.
Parish, flaiy, *pl.* aflyâ.
Country Parish, flâra barrâhieya.
Small Town, bolaida.

CLASP, *s.* mixbec.
Anklet, kalkâl. Bead, karaze,
Armlet, muxâad.   [su.
Bracelet, siwâr 8.
Brooch, xamxa.
Buckle, ebziem 11.
Button, zorra 4.
Jewel, flolie (jauhera).
Set Jewel, yuira, moráf.
Ring, flalaqa 2.
Ear Ring, Pondant, qorr 3, 4.
Nose Ring,   } xonf 3.
Ring at *top* of ear,
Spangle, rafiefla, barq.

CLEAR, *adj.* yâfl, rafley, râyiq.
(See BRIGHT).

Distinct (as voice), jehier,
baiyin, fâriz.
Lucid, mofvufl, yariefl.
Limpid, qarâfl. *Pure,* rêhir.
Pellucid, jeliey, xaffâf.
Open (as a road), moselleo,
mosazzel.
Unmixed, sêdifl. CERTAIN.

CLERGY, eclierous.
Bishop, oscof 13.
Archbishop, morrân.
Pontiff, flubr. Priest, oêhin.
Patriarch, barrieo 13.
Abbot, riyies el dair.
Friar, rêhib 8 (*pl.* rohbân).
Nun, rêhiba.
Monk (Solitary),) motewafl-
Hermit,   } flud; sêyih
Anchorite,   ) 7, *sic* B.
Devotee, flabies 6.
One under Vow, nâair, zêhid.
Prelate, imâm, *pl.* eyimma 8.
Chief Priest, qammay 13.
Pastor, qasies 3, 6, 9.
Curate, kouriey.
Deacon, xammâs 13.
Preacher, wâruz. Liturgy, raqs
Priesthood, cehnout.   [3.
The Order (of Clergy), rafma.
Formulary, rotba 10.
Rule of Faith, qânoun el iemân.
The Faith (Creed), el dien.
Religion, diyâna.
Enactments, raqâyid.
A Ceremony, monseo 11.
Diocese, abraxieya.

CLEVER, xâtur. Able, lausecuiy.
Accomplished, taqin.
Acute, Keen, achien.

ANGLO-ARABIC VOCABULARY. 29

Adroit, †sâyiq (sic n.).
Alert, qaiyim.
Apt, Ready, labiq.
Artful, moßârif.
Competent, 'ehil.
Cool-headed, yâßu.
Crafty, marin. Cunning, dâhi.
Clear-sighted, bayuir.
Deft, Shrewd, ßâaiq.
Discriminating, fâriz.
Experienced, kabier, (Tried) sayyâr. Expert, nußrier.
Intelligent, fehiem.
Ingenious, elmasuiy.
Inventive, mobdi.
Knowing, sârif. Learned, sâlim.
Prompt, Quick, laqin, darrêc.
Refined? oeiyis. Skilful, mêhir.
Sagacious, aeciey.
Subtle, modaqqiq.
Sly, Wily, moûtêl.
Smart, Wideawake, nebieh.
Versatile, motemehhir, motayarrif. INDUSTRIOUS, PRUDENT, EARNEST, ELOQUENT.

CLOTH, Stuff, qomâx 8.
Web of Cloth, loßma *(woof)*.
Texture, ßuyâce. Nap, wabar?
A piece of Cloth, têb 4.
Woollen Cloth, jouk, milf.
Raw Cloth (calico), kâm.
Calico, xier. Canvas, jinfâs.
Cotton Cloth, qoruiniey.
Printed Cloth, boyma.
Printed Drugget, namar 5, 4.
Camlet, mokayyar.
Goat's hair Cloth. sâbâ'.
Felt, labad, lobâda, coxâya.
Holland, kaix.

Haircloth, sebad.
Kersey, Serge? miaß.
Wool and Silk mixed, xâli, n.
Oil-Cloth, moxammas.
Damask, moxjar.
Muslim, xâx, mouyoliey.
Dimity, bafteh Hindiey.
Crape, barinjaq.
Loom (for weaver), naul; (for lady), minsej. WOOL. SILK.

COAST, s. xâtu 12.
Beach, Strand, qaif 3, n.
Cliff, kaif? ecêm, 'ecme.
Shore, sêßul 12.
Road for ships, marse' 11.
Watering-place, maurida 11.
Water's Edge, ßâffat el mai.
High-Water Line? jorf 4.
BANK. WATER.

COAT, s. sōbâya, *pl.* sobi' or sobâwât. Spencer? qabâ.
Cape (short cloak), sabâ.
Kirtle, farmala, n.
European Coat, beale.
Frock Coat, oertêcieya.
Jacket, cebbond, cebbout.
Corslet, dorrâsa.
Jerkin? Doublet? miltiyân.
Cowl, cerdoun, yâbouja.
Vest, Bodice, zieboun.
Waistcoat, yadrieya.
Cloth Pelisse, beniex.
Fur Pelisse, farwa, oore 2.
Wrap, molteßaf.
Cloak, maxlaß. Mantle, ridâ.
Hooded Cloak, bornos.
Outer Cloak, fauqânieya.
Tippet? railisên.
Collar, yâqa, zieq, kanâq.

(Loose) Collar, rauq 4.
Sleeve, comm 4.
Lining, barâna. Cuff, rodn 4.
Pocket, jaib, 3, 5.
Breast Pocket, ṡōbb, siyâle, s.
Dress.

Coffee (liquid), qahwe.
Coffee beans, bonn.
Tea, txâi, xâi. Teapot, xâidân.
Dregs of Coffee, tonwa.
Biggin, becraj.

Coin, mescouce 2, ṡōmla.
Die for Coin, sicce 10.
Medals, selâfluit (Kayat).
A Medal, qouna, o. b.
Currency, mosâmala.
Silver Coin, ṡōmla fuXXieya.
Bullion, Ingots, sebâyic.
An Ingot, scbiece.
Mint, ȧarbakûna.
Cash, naqd 3. Ducat, dienâr.
A Para, fils 3, muxrieya 2, 11, al
Piastre, ṛarx, qarx, 3.
Drachma, dirhem 11.
Dollar, riyâla, ṣu.
Franc, france, ṣu.
Pound, liebra, liera sterliens.
Commerce. Money.

Cold, s. bard. Hail, barad.
Small Hail, rurr. Dew, nodâ.
Chilliness, borouds.
Intense Cold, zemherier.
Freshness, rarâwa.
Moisture, rorouba.
Damp, nadi, nadâwa.
Evening Dew, rull 5, bs.
Mildew, tarwief, ṡōfouna.

Colours, adj. and subs.
Black, a. eawad, s. sewäd.
Blue, ezraq—zorqa.
Brown, esmar—somra.
Green, akXar—koXra.
Grey, axheb—xohba.
Red, aUmar—flōmra.
White, abyaX—biyâX.
Yellow, arfar—rōfra.

Comfort, v.a. selli.
Condole with, sazzi.
Console, wesi. Rest, arieU.
Relieve, arbiX min (?).
Dissipate (grief), farrij san.
Solace, jâbir. Calm.

Commerce, s. matjar.
Coin, mescouce 2.
Company, Partnership, xarâce.
Debt, dain 3. Money, darâhim.
Intercourse, mokâlara.
Rich, adj. ṛaniey 8.
Revenue, s. maflvoul 2.
Traffic, tijâra. Traffic, v.n. tējir.
Wealth, ẓerwa.

Companion, s. rûfllub 4,
    mosâflub.
Accomplice, saqied, mosâqid.
Ally, flalicf, moteflâlif.
Assessor, qasuid, Colleague.
Associate, moqârin.
Acquaintances, masârif.
Coadjutor, motesâwin.
Colleague,   } zemiel 6.
Work-fellow,
Comrade, rafieq 6.
Consort, qarion 4.
Courtier Guest, jelies 6.

ANGLO-ARABIC VOCABULARY.   31

Confederate, moterâhid.
Friend, vadieq 4, 6, θ.
Dear Friend, moḵubb, ḵabieb θ, rodaiyiq.
Intimate Friend, kaliel 9.
Familiar, 'eniec, 'êlif 4.
Fellow (like), meθiel, naʒuir, xabieh.
Counterpart, xaqieq, wizên, râq?
Contemporary, mosâyar.
— (of same age), tirb 4.
Guest and Lodger, neziel.
Maid of Honour, jeliese.
Kinsman, nesieb, qarieb.
Messmate, nadiem 6.
Partner, xariec 6, 4.
Rival, raqieb.
— (in trade), ḵarief.

A COMPANY (mercantile), jamɛuiya, xarâce.
Partnership, xirce, moxârace.
A Meeting (of a Company), jamɛuiya.
A Committee, jamɛuiya, ɛömda.
Executive Committee, el ɛömdet el sâmila.
Share, ḵuyya 10.
Allotment, sehm 4.
Shareholder, mosêhim.
Instalment, taqɛieṛ.
Call for money, qiṣṛ 3.
Net Profit, maḵryoul 2.
Distribution, teuzieɛ.
Division, iqtisêm.
Portion, qisma, naxuib.
Profit due, el fâyidat el mosteḵaqqa.
Account, ḵusêb.   Audit, faḵy.
INTERCOURSE.   COMMERCE.

COMPARE, v.a. (as in poetry), meθθil, xabbih bi, li.
— (also), râbiq bein, ɛâdil bein, qâyis, sêwi, uɛmel maɛdal.
Match, qârin.   Collate, qâbil.
Confront (bring together), wâjih.
EQUAL, VIE.

COMPEL, v.a. uârurr, arɛim.
Constrain (fig. and lit.), ɛaɛɛif.
Coerce, iqher, ecrih.
Drive to, elji ila'.
Force, îrub ɛala', uʒlim.
Impel, uḵmil, ḵammil.
Necessitate, aḵwij ila'.
Oblige, elzim.
Overpower, ojbor, ajbir li.
Require of, râwid.

CONCILIATE, v.a. isteɛruf, hêwid, il'em, v.   Court, sêyir.
Cultivate (observe), dâri.
Insinuate oneself into, dâkil.
Propitiate, yâliḵ.   Soothe, lâruf.
Persuade, istemicl.
Win over, istemlic.
Gain, ictesib.
CARESS.   DECOY.   KIND.

CONDIMENT (Seasoning), tebil 12.
Anchovy, sinâmoura.
Capers, qabbâr.   Oil, zeit.
Cruets, qizḵ, pl. teqâzieḵ.
— ebâzier.   Savoury HERBS.
Cruet-stand, miqzeḵ.
Lees of Grapes, jozcina.
Lees of Sesame, cosb.
Mushroom, forr 11, ɛöxx el rorâb.   Mustard, kordal.
Pepper, fulful.   Salt, milḵ.
Pickle, mokallal; melouḵa.

Sauce, ṭaraṭōur (sic p.).
Tartar of Wine, ṭarruīr.
Tomatoes, banadoura.
Truffle, cemâ, cemâya.
Verjuice (of grape), ḥuṣrim.
Vinegar, kall.
Side-dish, ṭabkâna?

Confine, v.a. uḥbiṣ.
Besiege, ḥâṣur.
Blockade, oṣdom (barricade).
Coop up, Hem in, } oḥgör, oḥrör, uḥṭaṭ.
Shorten, Limit, } oqṣör, qaṣṣūr.
Constrain, ṣaṣṣif (treat rudely).
Compress, izniq, loẓẓ.
Constrict, ẓenniq.
Cramp, fig. ḥarrij.
Cripple, fig. kabbil.
Crowd, ẓeḥlum, cebbiṣ.
Cut off, Intercept, } iqṭaṣ, kâẓim.
Fence in, ozrob? ẓerrib.
Fasten up, iṭliq, aṭliq.
Dam up, sodd. Pen up, oḥgor.
Shut off, Detain, ḥouṣ.
Shut in, up, oḥjor.
Fetter, Shackle, qaṣṣid.
Hamper, Straiten, ẓayyiq ṣala'.
Pond up, oḥjoẓ. Stint, qarmuṭ.
Tether, oxcol. Trammel, labbic.
Bind, Press, Stop.

Confuse, v.a. ṣarbiq.
Bewilder, kawwiṣ, v.p. vii.
Cloak, labbiṣ, iltebiṣ.
Complicate, aṣuiṣ, ṣawwuṣ; xarcil (trip up).
Confound (a person), ibheṭ.
Disorder, lakbuṭ.

Distract (bother), oṣjoq, vaddaṣ el rê's.
Embarrass, } ṣanqil.
Encumber, } ṣarqil.
Entangle, } xarcil.
Embroil, xabbic, xarbic.
Tangle, Entangle, Implicate, } kardiṣ, ḥabbiṣ,
(morally), abliṣ, xâbic.
Engage, } olboc, labbic
Preoccupy, } orboc, rabbic.
Perplex, aḥuir, ḥayyir.
— xawwiṣ, xaṭṭil el bâl.
Pose, Puzzle, ṭoff, icbaḥ.

Disturb.

Conquer, v.a. ifteḥ, iṣlic, temellic ṣala', uẓūr bi.
Master, } isteuli ṣala',
Overmaster, } oṣṭou ṣala'.
Overmatch, fâruṭ, teṭallab ṣala'.
Overpower, iqwa' ṣala', ojbor.
Prevail, iṭlib ṣals'.
Subdue, akḥuṣ, iḥtij?
Subjugate, aṭuiṣ (sic), ṣekkir (set to task).
Triumph, intaṣur, istaẓhir (?).
Vanquish, iqher.

Baffle. Exceed.

A (political) Constitution, tenẓuima.
Political Institutions, tenẓnimât siyêsieya.
Responsibility, moṭâlaba.
Personal Rʳ mes'youlieya ẓakṣuiya.
Responsible Minister, weẓier moṭâlab.
The Public, el jomhour.
Public Opinion, râi al ẓaṣb.

ANGLO-ARABIC VOCABULARY. 33

The Opposition, el mosárada.
A Party, ‏)‎ ḥuzba, rabs,
A Faction, ‏)‎ firqa.
Factiousness, mocêbara.
Party Spirit, mosâyaba.
Affairs, 'omour, mayâlifl.
A Business, flâja 2.
Claims, dasâwi. POLITY.

CONSULT (mutually), v.n. texâ-war, te'wâmar, ittemir.
Confer, tekâbar, tedûwal, teflâce', teaêcer.
Deliberate (together), tefûwal.
Hold Interview, tewâjeh.
COVENANT. THINK.

CONTRIVE, v.a. aujid, yânus.
Compose, 'ellif, yannif.
Concoct, Hatch, lafflq.
Construct, hendis.
Create, anxi, okloq.
Devise, ikterus. Invent, afldiө.
Fabricate, uyrapus.
Innovate, abdus, ibtedus.
Machinate, iktcliq.
Brood over, oảmor fle, aảmir sala', uflṭaảun.
Cause, sebbib, cewwin, yayyir, sallil. Occasion, aujib.

Cook, v.a. oτbok.
Boil down, Decoct, uττabik.
Boil (water), ṛalli.
Stew (meat), ealiq, osloq.
Make Broth, usmel maraqa.
Bake, uτhi. — (bread), ikbiz.
Broil, Roast in oven, ixwi.
Roast, Scorch, jammir (vulg. qammir). Toast, flammuy.
Singe, xalwuτ, xacwuτ.

Dry in sun, qaddid.
Heat (the oven), osjor.
BURN. BOIL.

COOKERY, τubâka, τabk.
Cooking vessel, muτbak.
Kitchen, maτbak.
Cook's knife, sêτönr 12.
Bill, Hatchet, bolτa 10.
Meat-hook, collâba.
Gridiron, moyabbas, B.
— scerdal, cerdiele, AL
Iron Spit, seffond 11.
Wooden Skewer, seik 4.
Dish of cooked food, τabiek.
Side dish? τabkâna.

CORD, String, marse nu 4.
Twine, Thread, kaiτ 9.
Rope, flabl 4, 5.
Packthread, dobâra.
Cable, qily 4. — gômana, C.
Mooring rope, mirse', seleba, B.
Noose, fakk 5.
Slip Knot, xaniera. NET.

COUNCIL, s. el xoura', s. diewân, pl. dawâwien.
Privy Council, diewân kâyy.
General C.—diewân sâmm.
Diet (Bund), sörba.
Parliament, el majlis el asla'.
Standing Committee, jamsuiya moflaccima.
House of Representatives, majlis el nowwâb el cibâr.
Congress (in Europe), majmis el wofedâ el kâyya; majmis sâmm. Assembly, maflfil.
Board, majlis. Meeting, jamâsa.
Convention, iltiyâm.

3

Deputation (?), eōmda (leading men, spokesmen).
Legislative Body, jauq qaδwiey; diewân el ixtiràc el asla'. POLITY.

COUNTERFEIT, v.a. zéfiL
Adulterate, } karbut,
Vitiate,   } istebdil.
Coin, yöuf. Corrupt, efaid.
Disguise, neocir, baddil.
Garble, fūlit, flarrif, flâwil.
Alter, fayyir. Forge, izfil.
Imitate, qallid.
Fabricate, uvnac.
Falsify, zewwir. Pervert, uscis.
CHEAT, CHANGE, CONFUSE, CONTRIVE, DEFACE, SPOIL.

COURT (or dynasty), daula, pl. dowal.
Throne, carx, serier 8.
Crown, têj 9, icliel 11.
Diadem, mixwâà 11 (turban, x.); cuyâbat el melic, b.
Accession —, irtiqâ ila' el carx.
Demise (of the Crown), irtiflûl ila' el jinân.
Palace, scrâi, serâya, qayr molouciey.
Procession, maucib.
A Solemnity, uflitifâl.
Official Costume, melbous (11) resmiey.
Act of Allegiance, mobâyaca.
Homage, imtiêêl, temeêêol.
A Liege (of Crown), morâwic, têbix, 4 or pl. tebaca.
A Subject, racniya, pl. racâyâ.
Submission, Reverence, koλous.

Etiquette of precedence, tartieb resmiey. POLITY.

COVENANT, v.n. tesâhod.
Agree, v.n. ocqod, uched.
Ally, v.n. tewâθaq.
Band together, teflazzeb.
Bargain, tesêwam.
Contract, toxâruT.
Cabal,   } tesâvab,
Conspire, } ustayub, cala'.
Coalesce, tcdâmaj cala'.
Combine, ijtcmic bí.
Complot, texâwar.
Confederate, tcflâlaf.
League, terâbuT.
Promise, wacad yacud.
Stipulate, istelzim? oxroT.
Undertake, iltezim.
Unite, v.n. itteflud.

CRANE (bird), corcie 11.
Argala,   } el corcie el
Marabou, } xakm.
Ibis,   } boulouja,
Stork,   } laqlaq 11.
Heron, doncola (dongola), belxoun.
Numidian Crane, roranouq 11.
Bittern, Bellower, cajjâj.
Spoonbill, abou milcaqa.
Cormorant, esfaroud.
Flamingo, noflâf 9.
Pelican, rakm.

CRIME, jaram 4, jariema.
Delinquency, kaʂr.
Fault, ᴀenb 3. Guilt, 'iθm.
Misconduct, ʒalâla.
Misdeed,   } meséya.
Misdemeanour, }

Malversation, iséya.
Neglect, ʕoflân.
Offence, jinâys. Plot, cemien.
Felony, qabâfla 11.
Sin, karâ, kâruya, pl. karâyâ.
Trespass, zella (False step).
  MISTAKE. FRAUD.

CRIMINAL, mojrim.
Accomplice, mosâqid.
Bandit, mosâyub.
Brigand, luyy 3.
Confederate, ɦalief.
Culprit, meawoum.
Delinquent, kâsir, ʕâɦl.
Culpable, jâni, jânif?
Felon, qabieɦ. Guilty, 'eθiem.
Highwayman, qârus el rarieq.
Peculator,) iʕtelia,
Poacher,) iktelia.
Offender, mokrui, a. sâyîb, B.
Plunderer, néhib.
Ringleader? saqied.
Robber, sélib. Rascal, ɦarâmi.
Marander, ʕâzi.
Thief, sériq, serrâq.

CRITICIZE, naksis.
Discriminate, ifriz, afriz.
Distinguish, mayyiz.
Reprove, osaol. Sift, ʕarbil.
Review, teyaffaɦ.
Scrutinize, daqqis ala', ifɦay.
Pass Strictures on, ɦarrir sala'.
Taunt, Satirize, ohjou, ihji.
  ABUSE, CAVIL, ARRAIGN.

CROUCH, v.n. lit. (as dog on bosom), irbul.
Cringe, teseffel.
Cower, tewâlas.

Lie Flat for concealment, ilbad, telabbad.
Lurk in shortened posture, tecarfas.
Squat up (as dog), aqsui.
Squat on heels, obroc.
Sit as tailor, qarfix, qarfuy.
Stoop, oɦbou (uɦbi), teɦabba'.

A CROW, (gener.) qâq 9.
Pie? Daw? xaqrâq 11.
Raven, ʕorâb 8, 9. Rook, ʕodâf
Carrion Crow, zêʕ 9.   [9.
Starling, zorzour 11.
Magpie, saqsaq, saqqate, abou zerieq.
Chough, el zêʕ el aɦmar el sêq.
Jay, el ʕorâb el mozewwaq.
Corn Crow? ʕorâb el zers.

CROW, v.n. insab. Cackle, céci.
Carrol, ʕarrid. Chatter, ilʕar.
Caw, Scream, insaq.
Chirp, zeqziq, rettil.
Clang, Jar, Screech, yaryur.
Cluck, oqroq. Coo, ihtif(moan).
Croak, niqq, naqniq.
Cry (Crow), yuiɦ.
Call (as cuckoo), izsaq.
Hiss, fuɦɦ. Quack, saqriq.
Drum, Boom, Rattle (as crane), uyliq.
Twitter, waтт, tewarwar.
Warble, nâʕi.
Buzz, wizz, wuzz. —wezwiz.
Hum, zinn (donn, dandin?).
  CRY, SING, SCREAM.

CRUEL, qâsi. Atrocious, fâɦux.
Austere, Severe, yârim.

Barbaric, Vulgar, hemij, hemjiey. Brutal, waſhziey.
Fierce, Stern, ſhådd, bêsil
Hardhearted, jåß.
Harsh, Unfeeling, } qåʒuſl, ʙ. qåsiſl?
Furious, secrân.
Grim, sábis, sabous, bêail.
Inhuman, Merciless, } faʒuiʒ, faʒʒ.
Rigorous, sanief, sönsiey.
Savage, mouſlux.
Stern, Scowling, jehim, ʙ.
Truculent, ᴀou ɾaxmara, moteɾaxmir. Trenchant, qåᴛuɾ.
Violent, Severe, motesatrif.
Uɴᴊusᴛ, Aɴɢʀʏ, Mᴀᴅ, Iʟʟ-ɴᴀᴛuʀᴇᴅ, Pʀouᴅ, Rouɢʜ.

Cʀusʜ, v.a. doxʜ, daxdix.
— (metals), irʒas, ʙɢ.
Batter, raåruʒ (Break up).
Bray, osſlön. Break, icsir, cessir.
Bruise, roʒʒ (Break up).
Comminute, raqqiq.
Crack, v.a. ixsar, ʙ. oxʀoᴛ?
— up, hexxim.
Grind up, uᴛſlan.
— (in handmill), ojʀox.
Mash (by weight), saffis.
Mash, Mix, Mess, okbos.
Pound, osſlön.
Smash, ohʀos, ʙ., saqqis, furqis, ʙ.
Squash, ihxim? ixdak, ordok.
Rub to powder, Pulverize, } nassum, idhec? isſlaq.
Shatter, ʒoᴛʒus.
Stamp on (Paw), olbor.
Thresh, Tread by ox, } dous, odros, ʙ.

Trample, idsas [vulgo (male?) odhos, oſldos].
Tread down, ocbos, cebbia.
Bʀᴇᴀᴋ, Pʀᴇss.

Cʀʏ (aloud), v.s. ʒuiſl, ʒawwit.
Bawl, jasjus?
Brawl, saᴛsuᴛ, ɾaᴛɾuᴛ.
Cry out (a person's name), izsaq.
— with joy, hinn, henhin? hellil, ʙ.
Clamour, Chatter, ilɾaᴛ.
Groan, ('enn, pres. yawinn).
Lament, teſlasser.
— te'ewwaf (cry Af).
— te'ewwah (cry Ah).
— teſlayyaf (cry ſlaif).
Hoot at, ɾåɾi sala'.
Hum (as crowd), ʒujj, donn.
Huzza, ʒelquᴛ, tehellel, s.
Pule, waᴛᴛ, tewaᴛwaᴛ.
Shriek, inſlub, inteſlub.
Sigh, te'êwah. Scream, sayyuᴛ.
Sob, ixheq (hiccup), tenehhed (heave the bosom).
Shout, oʒrok. Moan, nouſl.
Skirl, uʒſlal. Storm, ſlaxxic.
Spout, Rant, hêti.
Wail, welwil.
Wailing, s. mâ'tem 11, s.
Weep, ibsi, dammus.
Whoop? hembim. Yell, ʒiet.
Sᴘᴇᴀᴋ, Sᴄʀᴇᴀᴍ, Souɴᴅ, Cʀow, Gʀɪᴇᴠᴇ.

Cuᴘ (wine glass), cê's 3, cêse, pl. ciyâs.
Tumbler, Goblet, qadaſl 4.
Broad Cup, Saucer, ᴛås(e).
Tin-cup, tenece ɴu.

Tankard, coub 4, bouqâl, o.
Mug, cobbâya. — ceile, AL
Small Coffee Cup, finján 11.
Outer Cup to d⁰., ӡörfa 10.

UTENSIL.

CURDLE, v.n. roub.
Cake, v.n. teqarray.
Clot, tecebbab, tesaqqad, ustaqid.
Crust, v.n. qaxxir, o.
Congulate, tejabban.
Foam, iṛṛi, ezbid, rayyim.
Thicken v.n. (as milk), ikθer, tekaθθer.
Grow Solid, injamid, tejammad (jomid, o.).

CURL, v.a. (hair) ozlof, jaccud.
Bend, ilwi. Crimp, Plait, ecwi.
Curl up, Roll up, Dogs-ear, Rumple; aacbil.
Twirl, Twine (Wind) up, iftil.
Coil, lnwwi.
Twist, Screw, obrom, barrim.
Roll round, loff, laflif.
Wrap up, cobb (sic B.), (make into a ball?). Crook, cawwij.
Curve, oflnou (uflni).
Arch, qawwis. Double, rabbiq.
Fold, utwi. Crumple, jaslic.
Rumple, Ruffle, marmut.
Crease, sajjir, ṛuḽḽun.
Wrinkle up, cerrix, cermix.
Frizzle, ceswic. Knot, osqod.
Loop, carwi?
Reef, ⎱ qatrub,
Tuck up, ⎰ xammir.
Reel, v.a. cewwif, sellic.
Turn, adier, satruf.
Roll (the eyes), dawwir.

CUSHION, s. tecêya.
Bolster, wisêd. Bedding, râq 2.
Pillow, mikadda (murdaṛa?).
Small Pillow, kodaidieya.
Hassock for back, misnad.
Under-cushion, maqsad.
Ring-cushion, liwâya.
Mattress, mutrufla, AL — of sofa, martcba, B.
Housing(undercloth AL)torrâfla.
Hassock (or carpet) for prayer, sojjâda. BED.

CUSTOMARY, mostêd.
Familiar (object), mêlouf, masloum, mênous.
Ordinary, uctiyâdiey.
Common, sâmmiey.
Conventional (Usual), mashoud.
Habitual, mostesmal.
Established, resmiey.
Regular, qânouniey, morrarid.

CUT, v.a. uqtas.
Cut away, fig. ozrom.
Chip (stone), inflat.
Chop up, xaqniq?
Chop off, bott. Chap, oftor.
Carve, Dissect, xarrifl.
Clip, qoyy, qayquy.
Cleave, iflac, ifluḽ.
— iḽiq; ifras.
Fell (trees), ibrafl.
Gash, flözz, oxrot?
Graze, hiff. Hack up, hexxim.
Hash, Mince, ofrom.
Hew (wood), ifras, najjir.
Lop (trees), Poll (trees), icsefl, qallim. Mangle, xarmit.
Nib (a pen), qott.
Notch, flozz, iθlim, ofroḽ, ifllar.

Pare, ibri; (too close), qarrut
ṣala'.
Prune, zebbir, вaẓẓuf (ḅ) el
xajar. Rend, mezziq.
Retrench, ijzim.
Rip (the belly), ibẓaj.
— (a sewing), oftoq, fettiq.
Saw, onxor. Scarify, xarrut.
Scratch, ikmix.
Scrape off the skin, iqḷaṭ.
Shape, Cut out, ṣayyul.
Shave, uẓlaq; (with chisel),
okrot? oxrot (?) oxrot (?).
Shear (wool), jozz.
Slash, xarrim, xaraim.
Slice up, flatḷut. Slit, oxrom.
Split, xoqq, xaqxiq.
— (open), baṣṣuj.
Wound, ijraḷ.
BREAK, PIERCE, PRICK, TEAR.

DAMSEL, jâriya 12.
Girl, Maid, bint δ, ibna.
Lass, fetiya. Wench, ṣubieya.
Maiden, bicra, betoul, bint, bicr.
Nymph, flôuriya, c.; jinnieya,
в. (*fairy*).
Virgin (eccles.), ṣaârâ 11.
Young woman, xâbba, *pl.*
xawâbb.

DAPPLE, *v.a.* naqqix, naqwix.
Checquer (with black and
white), xaflwir.
Mottle, raqqut.
Speckle, nemmir.
Spot, baqquṣ. Streak, barqix.
Streak with white, fawwif.
Stripe, qallim. [s.
Variegate, waxxi? waxa' yaxa',
GREY.

DARE, *v.n.* tejêser, tejarra',
ijteri, istejri.
Adventure, *v.a.* jêxif bi.
Endanger,) ɾarrir, oxroẕ li
Imperil,) kaṭar.
Hazard, qâmir (play pranks
with). Risk, *v.a.* kâṭur bi.
Venture, *v.n.* tevadda'.
ENDURE, OPPOSE, STRIVE.

DARKNESS, ẕôlma ḅ, 10, ẕalâm.
Night, leil, *pl.* liyâli.
Evening Dusk, ɾaṣaq.
Midnight, nuṣf el leil.
Evening Twilight, xafoq.
Shade, faiy.
Shade, Screen, ẓull.
Dusk, qotma, ṣôtma.
Obscurity of night, dajou, dojya.
EVENING. BLACK.

DATES (dry), temr 4, qaṣba, ɴᴜ.
Fresh ripe date, balaḥa, ɴᴜ,
ɾoṭab 5.
Dates boiled and dried, kolâl, ʙs.
Green Date, râmik.
Date in boxes, ṣajwa.
Cluster (of Dates), ximrâk,
zebâṭa, ɴᴜ, ṣarjoun 11.

DAUB, *v.a.* ṣekmuṭ.
Bedabble, lawwiṭ.
Bemire, waflflul, ṭayyin.
Bespatter, ṭarrux, †aṭrix, ʙ.
Besmear, îlṭak, ṣaccir.
Blur, loce, o.
Dab, Mess, okbor.
Muddle, Paddle, kabbur.
Dirt, Dirty, weṣaik.
Discolour, ceddir *or* efṣik *or*
ṣebbil el laun. Dye, oɾboɾ.

Defile, Pollute, dannis, najjis.
Plaster (a wall), layyis, ʙ.ᴄ.
Plaster, Smear, Overspread, ᴀᴛli, odhon.
Soil, ᴛabbuꜱ (*also* Mould, Train).
Spot, baqquꜱ.
Stain, Distain, kaʃʃub.
Sully, ꭗien, ꭗayyib.
Tarnish, ecbi. Taint, aꭗdi.
Confuse. Mix.

Dawdle, terákaꭗ, tebârâ, tewâna'. Dally, telebbe'.
Delay, *v.ꜰ*. te'ekkar ꭗan, teꭗawwaq ꭗan.
Idle, *v.ꜰ*. tecésel (ꭗan).
Lag, obröu, qaꭗꭗur.
Linger, ilbaθ. Lounge, inʃajuꭗ.
Loiter, temehhel, istcʲkir.
Neglect, ehmil, tehêmel ꭗan, aꭗfil, teꭗâfel ꭗan.
Temporize, mâᴛul.
Play the Sloven, telêceꭗ.
Be in Vacation, ibᴛal.

Day (24 hours), yeum, *pl.* eiyâm.
— of light, nehêr 2.
Full Daylight, ʃöfla, ʃaflwa.
Noon, ʃöhr ♭.
Afternoon, caꭗr (2 to 4 o'clock).
To-day, elyeum.
Yesterday, 'emꭗ.
To-morrow, *ꜱ*. ꭗad, ꭗadwa.
— *adv*. ꭗadaⁿ.
Day before yesterday, auwal 'emꭗ.
Day after to-morrow, baꭗd ꭗadiⁿ.

Deal (out), *v.a.* qaꭗꭗim, aqꭗim bain. Allot, aqruꭗ, cꭗhim.
Apportion, Rate, aqꭗuᴛ, qaꭗꭗuᴛ.

Cut up, Detail, afꭗul, faꭗꭗul.
Dispense, Dole out, iqteꭗim.
Distribute, wezzuꭗ.
Divide, ofroq, farriq ꭗala'.
Part, *v.a.* baꭗꭗul.
Portion, *v.a.* ojzou, jezzi.
Share, *v.a.* flaꭗꭗuꭗ.
— *v.ꜰ*. (mutually) tesêhem bi, ꭗêhim-oh bi.

Dear (in price), ꭗâli.
— (beloved), maflboub.
Fondly Loved, maꭗꭗouq.
Esteemed, Rare, caziez.
Costly, moθmin? moθemman?
Precious (metal), θemien.
Valuable, ᴀou qiema.
Choice, nafies. Select, montâqi.
Cherished, flariez.

Debt, *ꜱ*. dain 3. Loan, qarʒ.
National Debt, el qarʒ el'ehliey.
Indebtedness, istedâna.
An Engagement (debt), teꭗahhod 2.
Debtor, madyoun; ꭗariem, ʙ.
Creditor, ꭗariem, ᴄ., modayyin, madâyinieꭗ.
Debenture) senad 4,
(Warrant),) ꭗenada.
Exchequer Bill, ꭗenada ꭗala' el kaz(ie)na.
Treasury Scrip, auráq kaz(ie)na.
Withdrawing, Calling in (of bank notes), insiflâb.
Bill of Exchange, softeja 11; boulꭗa (*i.e.* polizze).
Bank Note, qâꭗima 12.
Checque, Conveyance, flawâle.
Receipt for money paid, rajꭗâ, woꭗoul, ꭗenad 4.

Promissory Note, serci 11.
Bond (Bill due), temessoo.
Deed, racc 3.
Falling Due, istiflqâq.
Presentation (of hill), icdâ, tédieya.
Payment, dafɛ, wefâ, icfâ.
Deferred Instalments, teqâsier mo'wejjala.
Mortgage, Pledge, rehn.
Thing Pledged, marhoun, mortehin.
Interest, Profit, fâyida 12.
Interest, fâyuʌ 12, o.n.
Rate of Interest, susr el fâyuʌ or fâyida. Usury, ribâ.
Discount, isqât, flasm.
Stopping of Payment, tewaqqof ɛan dafɛ. Depreciation, qatɛ.
Financial Pressure, moʌâyaqa mâlieya.

Decay, v.n. uɛrub, wehe' yehi.
— fig. isqat, ohbot.
Decline, zoul, inqay.
Fall off, fig. kaɛɛ, kiɛɛ.
Mould, v.n. }
Grow Mouldy, } teɛaffan.
Pine, uʌna', inseqim.
Rot (as bone), rimm.
— (as wood), tokk.
— (as meat), inxafl, b.
— (as clothes), ihterâ'.
— (as fruit), ɛayyin (d. bis).
Spoil, v.n. intezis, infeɛid.

Decay, v.a. esqut, auhi.
Corrode, ilflaɛ; 'oocl yêcol 'col.
Corrupt, afɛid. Decompose, flöll.
Disintegrate, ifɛek.
Dissolve, ʌcwwib.

Make Mouldy, ɛaffin.
Rot, chri', anxifl.
Sap, aɛrub. Spoil, inzɛɛ.
Hurt, Destroy.
Flag, v.n. Deform.

Decide, v.a. (another's cause), ifɛul, ofzor; iqraɛ, bott, ijzem bi.
— for (prefer), rajjifl.
— against; pass sentence, judgment on; ijzem, oflcom ɛala'.
This Decides me, héʌo yomielni; causes me to incline.
Decide for oneself, v.n. bott el râi flo 'emr.
Adjudge, oflcom li.
Award, ixraɛ li.
Determine, v.a. oktom (ɛɛal).
Pronounce upon, ufltim ɛala'.
Settle, Conclude, amʌu, anhi.
Sentence, iqʌu.

Declivity, fladour.
Acclivity, yaɛöud.
Abyɛɛ, hêwiya. Chasm, houwa.
Cleft, falaq 4, falfl.
Crevasse, xaqieqa, xaqiefa.
Coomb, wehda 5.
Defile, maʌuiq 11. Dell, joura.
Descent, hebour.
Dingle, falaq 9, ifjiej ?
Gap, xarm 3. Glon, zenqa.
Gorge, kâniq 12.
Gulley, ʌinâb 11.
Mountain side, yaub el jebal.
Mountain pass, maɛbar 11, θɛfr 3, ɛörqoub 11.
Precipice, warra, mehleɛ 11.
Ravine, mehwa' 11, mehwâya.
Slope, mail. Steep, modaʃldier.

ANGLO-ARABIC VOCABULARY. 41

A Subsidence, mesqaт.
Verge? liɟf (lowest slope of hill).

DECOY, v.a.
— wellif, в. (for 'ellif?').
— ikdas (deceive).
— sawwid (familiarize).
Allure,) ruɽɽib, saxɹiq,
Lure,) ɹammiq, xawwiq.
Attract, ijʌib, istɔjieb.
Amuse, lehhi ; cheat by delay,
 mâтul.
Bait, Entice, aɽwi, isteɽwi.
Beguile,) lâsub,
Lead Astray,) isteʌull.
Divert from, lêhi san, xâɽil san.
Ensnare, Entrap, râwiɽ, kâtil.
Dazzle, fig. abhil.
Debauch, fandil.
Entrap, auqis or waqqis fle fakk.
Flatter with false hope, waqqis,
Inveigle,) jawwin, в. [в.
Involve,) (deepen!).
Misguide,) aʌull, ʌallil,
Mislead,) tewwih, ʌayyis.
Seduce, ezill.
Stimulate (and Allure), ɽozz.
Tempt, imteɟlun, imɟlan, iɟtin.
CHEAT.

DEER, pl. mehê.
Buck, eiyâl, 11 (pl. eyâyiel).
Stag, söfɽ, ɽ.
Red Stag, el eiyâl el aɟlmar.
Hind, ʌauna?
Fawn, raxâ, pl. arxâ ; kaxf(a),
 pl. kixafa.
Hart, rie'm 4, pl. ar'âm.
Fallow Deer, el rie'm el axqar ;
 el eiyâl el axqar.

Roebuck, gabi 5. Doe, gabiya.
Young Roe, xâdin.

DEFAME, v.a. xannis.
Asperse, orjom (pelt with stones),
 xannir, x. Backbite, iɽtêb.
Blaspheme, jaddif sala'.
Brand, jarris (by public exhibi-
 tion of a criminal).
Curse, ilsan.
Decry, ozjor (hoot off, hiss off).
Discredit, Impugn, iθlim ɹuitoh,
 qallil ɹuitoh, mezziq surʌob,
 kassir surʌob, oɟlsom min
 surʌuhi, oтsоn flo surʌuhi,
 ikriq nâmôusoh.
Misrepresent, iqaif fle ɟaqqibi.
Slander, Calumniate, waxa yaxi ;
 waxxi bi, sala' (Colour ?).
Sting, fig. ilsec.
Tattle against, nimm sala'.
Traduce, ithem.
BLAME, DISPARAGE, DISHONOUR.

DEFECTIVE (in body), masour.
Bald, aylas. Bare, ajrad.
Blind, asma'. Dumb, akres.
Crippled (in arm), ectes, afxal.
— (in foot), afras.
Deaf, атrax, ayamm.
Humpbacked, aɟdab.
Lame from birth, asraj.
Left-handed, axwal, asser.
Leprous, abras. Maimed, ajdas.
Mangy, aqras. One-eyed, aswar.
Paralytic, maflouj (on one side).
Rickety, ecseɟl, cesieɟl.
Snubnosed, afras.
Squinting, axwes.
— (slightly), ajher.

Deform, v.a. cawwir.
Corrupt, afsid. Damage, kassir.
Destroy, follix. Disguise, neccir.
Deprave, uscis. Disable, catTul.
Disfigure (make ugly), xannis, semmij, xawwih, sayyib, baxxis. Distort, imsok.
Impair, akill bi. Mar, soqqut.
Pervert, iqlib, flarrif can.
Ruin, ikrib. Vitiate, karbut.
Spoil, satTul, inzcs.
Waste, aowwib, ctlif. Decay.

Delay, v.a. 'ekkir.
Adjourn, Prorogue, amhil.
Ask Adjournment, istemhil.
Defer (to a fixed date), 'ejjil.
Put off (a creditor), matul.
Protract, abru, istobru.
Retard, sawwiq. Stop, auqif.
Postpone, uflaif.

Delight, v.a. abhij, behhij, oflbor.
Gladden, sorr, cairr.
Gratify, arda'.
Divert, Relieve, farrij.
Please, obsot, asjib, axriß, 'enniq, 'òniq.
Rejoice, v.a. farrifl.
Move, Excite (generally with joy), atrib. Joyful.
Delight, s. ibtihêj.
Gladness, sorour. Glee, flòbour.
Joy, farafl, farfla.
Emotion (generally pleasant), tarab. Pleasure, inbisât.

Deliver (from), kalluy, istekluy, min. Exempt, acfl can.
Clear, Free (a place), sollic.
Let Escape, anji, najji.

Set at large, seyyib, sorrifl.
Liberate, astiq. Release, aTliq.
Relieve (the mind), ariofl, farrij.
Rescue, onqoa, anqia, intòx.

Demand, v.a. oTlob. Ask, is'cl.
Ask back, isterjis, isteridd.
Demand before a judge, teqâxâ.
Demand (in Pol. Ec.), istemidd, istcflàur. Dun, flâsib.
Exact, ilzom, istoufi, râwid-oh sala' xai'. Extort, belluy.
Require, istelzim.
Arraign, Inquire.

Denote, v.a. 'exxir (sketch, B.).
Beckon (Blink, Wink), ifmis.
Betoken, sarrif bi.
Appoint, Define, sayyin.
Allude to, aumi ila'.
Advert to, axier ila'.
Designate, wescm yosim.
Distinguish, mayyiz.
Hint at, icni can.
Imply, cenni. — fehhim bi.
Indicate, usni.
Mark out, sallim, bayyin.
Signal, Make Sign, irmiz.
Augur, Intend, Show.

Dense, adj. (as stone or wood) solb, movmad, ccθies.
— (as fog), sâqid, clotted.
Thick (as fog or forest), ceθicf.
— (as flock of birds), motecceθθib.
— (as weather), mosabba'.
Compact, molezzcz, moctenis.
Solid, mecion, jolied. Stout.

Deny, v.a. oncor.
Make flat Denial of, Give the Lie to, ceaaib.

Abjure, aůrim (*deprive, forbid*).
Contradict, nâquů.
Decline (not accept), i'bâ.
Disavow, tenĉcer.
Discard, oszol, daxxir (*abandon*).
Disclaim, Disown, tebarrâ min.
Object to, encir.
Recant, ijůad. Renounce, orfůů.
Refuse (not grant), ibkal salaihi (*i.e. grudge* to him).
Reject, irtidd (Disappoint, Refuse), kayyib.
Retract, Recant, irjas fie.

DEPART, *v.n.* iaheb, ebsad, iɟrab.
Budge, Stir, *v.n.* tecelcel (*sic*), teůarrec.
Decamp, irůal, terazzel.
Drop to the rear, Fall back, injirr ila' warâ.
Part from, Part with, fâriq; ifteriq san.
Pass (as time), imůu.
Recede, inseůub.
Recoil, tedâfas, irjas ila' warâ.
Remove, *v.n.* intaqil.
Retire (to distance), tebâsad, inteziů. — (to privacy), ikteli, tefarrad, iktelij, F.
Retreat, welli, tewellâ; (milit.) irjas.
Retrograde, teqahqar. [san.
Separate, *v.n.* iůral san, ifterij
Take yourself off! inqalis, B.
Vanish, zieů, zouů.
        Go. WANDER.

DESERT, qafr 5; xaul AL falâya, *pl.* fal°a.
A Barren, jarad, jorda.
Wilderness, baur, erů bawâr.

Pathless tract, 'erů sâqoul 12.
A Solitude, kalâ.
Open (uncultivated) land, barr, bedou, bâdiya.
Steppe, vaůrâ 11, mâfâze 11, F.
Level Desert, faifâ 11, F. 5, 3, X.
Desert with mirage, lammâsa.
Mirage, serâb. Sand, raml 5.
        CHAMPAIGN.

DESIRE, *v.a.* orɟob bi, fie; temennâ.
Aspire to, nâfis.
Be Ambitious of, ibri, ibtcri.
Covet, utmar fie.
Crave, osxom, tesaxxam.
Be Eager for, oůroy sala'.
Be Enamoured of (Gloat over?), inxaɟif bi, ixɟaf bi hewâ; inseusiů.
Hanker after (flesh), iqram, istarmus.
Hope for, orjou, o'mol, 'emmil.
Hunger after, ihbi cala'.
Gape after, oxkoy. List, roum.
Long for, ixtêq, texawwaq, touq ila'.
Lust after, texehbe.
Have a Mania for, tehêfat.
Pant after, ilhij bi.
Be Entangled (in love), Inoculated with, inbelix bi, B.
Will, nried, xâ°. Wish, ixtehi.
Yearn after, telehhef ilâ'.

DESTROY, *v.a.* abied, bayyid, ehlic, fellix.
Annihilate, imůaq, *vulg.* lêxi.
Blast,   ) inůas,
Blight,) ix'em sala'.
Blot out, imůu.
Consume, afni, ʌewwib.

Cut off, aqruś, ikterim.
Decompose, ifsek.
Demolish,) hodd,
Pull down,) ohdom.
Depopulate, abier, bawwir.
Desolate, dammir, odmor.
Devastate, karrib.
Dilapidate, hewwir, v.p. hour.
Disintegrate, Rot, astub.
Dismember, ifteris.
Dispeople, aqfir.
Efface, utmis, utlis.
Exhaust, Expend, xafflt, anfid.
Exterminate, otrod.
Extirpate, qarrim, iqlas.
Eradicate, isté'yul, ijtefl, ijteflu.
Kill by fatigue, mawwit, chlic.
Quell, Quench, ehmid.
Shatter (a building), śaśśus, (*but* aesais, k.).
Ravage, ikrib. Ruin, etsus.
Spoil, souf, inzes.
Waste (Throw away), dahwir.
 KILL. DEFORM. DECAY.

DEVOTE, *v.a.* (vow) onaor li.
— (appropriate), kayyuy, oyrof.
— (oneself to), tewellas bi.
Be Absorbed in, tebafiflar fic, tesammaq fie.
Be Addicted to, inhemic bi.
Give Adhesion to, uctayum mas.
Apply oneself to, lêzim, admin, istedmin, xai'a", tesarraś li, f. incibb sala', jodd fic, usteni bi, ijtebid fie.
Be Bent upon, insacif sala'.
Be Engaged in, inxabic bi, ixtebic bi, oxboo el saql.
Be Given to, tesêrâ, invubb sala'.

Be Preoccupied with, iltebic bi.
Occupied upon, mowellaj bi.

DEVOUR, *v.a.* istcrut.
Bolt down, ozlot, souf, esicf.
Eat gluttonously, ixterih.
Eat ravenously, kimm, intehim.
Gobble up, olqom, ilteqim.
Gormandize, ilher, teraffes, utwi (Tuck in ?), b.
Gulp down, ilfafl.
Guttle, óxmot (*pop. ?*), *lit.* perhaps, Whip off, Whisk off.
Prey upon, ifteris, suiθ fie, f.
Snap up, telaqqaf, ilqaf, laqqif.
Swallow, ibtelus, telchhem, iltehim.
Be Greedy for food, ilhif, clhif.

DIG, *v.a.* oflfor.
Dig up, Rake up, onbox.
Dig for (Delve, Mine), ibflaθ, istebfluθ. Bore, oθqob.
Burrow, tejafiflar.
Carve, Grave, onqox.
Hollow, jawwif. Mine, ifflay.
Mine (in milit. sense), usmel lofm.
Pick with axe, usziq.
Pierce, Break through (a wall), onqob.
Sap? astub. Scoop, jawwir.
Scollop, qawwir. Trench, ifflat.
Excavate, ifflar (faflflar, sculptor). PIERCE.

DIKE, Dam, sedd 3.
Embankment, carma 10.
Floodgate, Sluice, zeriebat el mâi. Mole, Bar, flâjiz 12.
Pier, jisr li marâcib.

Quay, rayyat aljâr.
Sea-wall, Breakwater, } rarf, rayuif.
BANK, COAST.
Dip, v.a. irmis.
Dive, v.n. irtus, rous.
Douse, Duck, v.a. rott.
Drench, ballil, balbil.
Drown, rarriq. Dye, orbor.
Deluge, töuf sala'.
Moisten, Damp, rarrub, naddi.
Overwhelm, ormor.
Plunge, v.a. rawwut, arier.
Soak, inqas. Steep, ustun.
Sop, isqi. Souse, v.a. rattus.
Swamp, v.a. rawwuy.
Wet, boll, naywil? PLUNGE.

Dirty, darin, vulg. wesik (nasty)?
Filthy, qasir (sordid).
Foul, fâllux. Grimy, fâllum.
Greasy, zefir. Smutty, dâsur.
Gross, semij (LEWD).
Impure, Unclean, dania, najis.
Turbid, cedir, moteceddir, sacir, mosaccer, sejies.
— makbout, c. (trampled).
Muddy, raflul (turbid).
BASE, SHAMEFUL, DULL.

Disable, v.a. sattul.
Benumb, kaddir.
Cripple (in arm), cettis.
— (in foot), faxxi.
Debilitate, almi, wehhin.
Derange, marmut, B.
Disqualify, artij sala'.
Emasculate, kanniê.
Effeminate, nassum.
Enervate, akmil, B.

Enfeeble, esqim.
Exhaust, xafflt, B. kawwir.
Incapacitate, sajjiz san.
Impair, akill bi.
Lame, asrij, fayyus.
Lop, ecaifl, oessifl.
Maim, ijdas. Mar, seqqut.
Mutilato, kabbil.
Stupefy, Palsy, akdil, kattul.
Weaken, alsuf.
BAFFLE, DESTROY, DISTURB.

DISASTER, nafls, moyuiba 11.
Calamity, dâhiya (terror).
Misery, Woe, bolâ (bilwa, belwa'), belieya, pl. belâyâ 14.
Misfortune, nocês? nallöuse.
Misadventure, } flâdiê 12.
Mischance, } xâ'ma, B.
Bale, Ruin, ters. Relapse, necse.
A Bane, Pest, êfa 2.
An Embarrassment, belxa, B.
A Plague, Žarba.
A Trial (pain), muflo(a) 10, ibtilâ. Harm, Hurt, larar.
A Mischief, eaê, eaieya.
Damage, Loss, kosrân, kisêra.
Detriment, iktilâl.
A Nuisance, wabâl.
Casualty, saral 4.
Woes, Afflictions, tebârieil.
GRIEF, CHANGE.

DISEASE, Illness, maral 4.
Ailment, soqm 4.
Indisposition, dasbala, B.
[Rather Aesbala?]
Disorder, texwiex, lakbara.
Ailment, sulla 10.
An Affection, influrâf el mizêj.
Indisposition, sulla 10.

Malady, dâ'.
Fit, Paroxysm, borflâ, wasce.
Relapse, necba 2, 3.
Acute Symptoms, sawârul flâdda.
Chronic state, flâl mozmin.
(Special Diseases.)
Ague, rajief.
Apoplexy, hemda, secte.
Asthma, nefß, rabou.
Boil, dommila 11.
— of Aleppo, flabb el sena.
Cancer, seratân, écila, nêsour, rasâya.
Cholera, sousa, hieĺa, texwiera.
A Cold, istihwâ.
Colic, qaulanj, maṛv, moṛûv, maṛiev (*Gripes*).
Coma, hecr. Consumption, sill.
Cough, sosâl, sosla, ceflfla.
Diarrhœa, ishêl, insibêl.
Dropsy, istisqâ, flaban.
Dysentery, nesief.
Elephantiasis, josêm.
Epilepsy, vars. Flux, siyâl.
Eruption, Tafila, B. Tafra 2.
Erysipelas, flamou, flömra.
Fever, flömma'.
Hot Fit, flomêm.
Gangrene, sarba.
Gout, gout (*sic*), da' el molouc.
— (in feet), naqrea.
Gravel, flaywa.
Headache, vodâs.
Hiccup, xehqa, flazouqa, carb, B.
Inflammation, iltihêb.
— of liver, cobâd.
Issue, karáj. Leprosy, bary.
Jaundice, yaraqân.
Lethargy, sobât. Mange, jarab.

Measles, flayba, flarsên, B.
Obstruction, mânis.
Ophthalmia, ramad, samax, samay. Palsy, fâlij, kalâs.
Piles, bawâsier, *sing*. bâsour, bâyour. Plague, tâsöun.
Pleurisy, jirsêm, birsêm, sêt el janb; jonâb, K.
Rheum, raxfl, sosêm.
Rheumatism, flaẍâr, B.
Ringworm, qawaba 11.
Scrofula, varâja, dâ' el konâsier.
Scurvy, escorbout.
Small Pox, jodariey.
Spasm, texannoj.
Ulcer, qarfl(a) 3.
— in mouth, flalâ, qilâs.
Volvulus, toflajflôr, B.

TUMOUR.
(Results of Disease.)
Debility, ẍanâ.
Emaciation, intiflâl.
Fading, icmidâd.
Flaccidity, terahhol.
Leanness, ẍawa'. Pain, 'elem 4.
Paleness, comouda.
Smart, wejs 4. Torpor, cesel.
Wasting, xoflöub.

DISHONOUR, *v.a.* ihtic, ifẍafl.
Abash, Shame, akjil, kajjil.
Affront, akzi, xannir, K. xantur, K. xanyir, B.
Curse, ilsan. Disgrace, surr.
Insult, tcwaqqafl sala'.
Outrage, ifteri bi, sala'.
— behdil. Stain, xien.
Profane, dannis, najjis.
Rail at, sobb, sêbib.
Reproach, xammit, iôlib.

Revile, ɛayyib ɛala'.
Upbraid, ɛayyir ɛala'.
Vituperate, oxtom, xêtim.
ABASE, BLAME, DEFAME, DISPARAGE, LAUGH.

DISINCLINE, v.a. Indispose; aʃluid ɛan, ezieṛ ɛan, emiel ɛan, uyrif ɛan.
Disaffect, Revolt, v.a. ecrib-oh fie.
Disgust with, aqrif ɛan, qarrif ɛan; (sic vulgo. B. qu. for ʃarrif?) TaʃΩum.
Divert from, xâṛil ɛan.
Draw off from, ejniʃl ɛan, ʃlarrif, uʃlrif ɛan.
Dissuade from, rajjuɛ ɛan.
Estrange from, jannif, naʃʃr ɛan.
Set one against, rodd ɛan, yodd ɛan.
Warn against, anair ɛan, ʃlaair ɛan.
Withhold (Stop) from, mânuɛ ɛan.

DISPARAGE, v.a. istekiff.
Belittle, istayṛir.
Contemn,) uʃltaqir, oʃlqor,
Despise,) istchien.
Decry,) isterail,
Depreciate,) istorkuy.
Deride, ohzou bi.
Derogate from, ibkeɛ (oʃlɛom min ɛurʒubi).
Detract, weceɛ yccis, wecois, aucia.
Discredit, ikfaʒ or iθlim ruitoh; iqdaʃl. Disesteem, izdori.
Neglect, ehmil.

Scorn, isteʃlqir.
— (baseness), tecèram ɛan.
Slight, ehien, ɛêbil?
Spurn, oxlof, o.
Underrate, istehjin?
Vilify, reaail. ABASE, BLAME, DEFAME, DISHONOUR, LAUGH.

DISTRACTION, laboɛ.
(Bother, pop. ɛajqa.)
Confusion,) lakbara,
Disorder,) cerceba.
Irresolution, kabla.
Puzzle, Stupor, ʃluira.
Perplexity, texwicx el bâl, lauɛa, o.

DISTURB, v.a. aqliq, qalliq, qalqil, uɛcer. Afflict, barriʃl bi.
Agitate, uʃturr, marmir.
(Bother, pop. osjoq.)
Derange, uʃlrif el mizêj.
Disarrange, marmot, marmit.
Discomfort, ezɛul, zeɛɛul.
Discompose, xawwix, ɛala'.
Disquiet, izɛaj, ezɛuj, naʃṛuy; v.p. ohdoɛ, B.
Distract, yadduɛ el râ'ɛ.
Disorder, lakbuy, daɛbil.
Displace, ɛazzil.
Incommode, θaqqil ɛala'.
Offend, xoqq ɛala'.
Trouble, collif.
Upset, oercib, qallib. SHAKE.

DIVER (bird), ṛawwâɛ, ṛayyuia, ṛammâɛe.
Albatross, batrôɛ, el bayy el dakm.
Little Auk? qauqieɛ.
Gannet, timm. Gull, nouraɛe.

48   ANGLO-ARABIC VOCABULARY.

Goosander, baττ el semeo.
Fulmar? baττ el baſlr.
Kingfisher, janqala, mêzour.
Petrel? baττ el nau.   DUCK.

DIVIDE, *v.a.* aqsim, qassim.
Analyse,   ) ſlöll, ſlallil,
Resolve,   ) ofroq.
Detach,   ) foyy,
Disconnect,) ofroq,
Disjoin,   ) farrik bain.
Dissever, Sever,) boττ,
Sunder,   ) afriz.
Dissociate, Disunite, ifγul.
Dialocate, kalluſ, kalwiſ.
Dismember, ifteris.
Dissect, xarriſl.
Decompose, iſsek.
Disintegrate, aτrub.
Disengage,   ) ifteſl,
Disentangle,) sellie,
Clear, Free,   ) scrriſl.
Insulate,) ofrod, afrid,
Isolate,   ) farrid, jarrid.
Loosen, arki. Partition, uſljib.
Separate, Part, jezzi, barsuâ.
Unfasten, Untie, ſlöll, oncoθ.
Undo, focc, iklaſ. DEAL.

Do, *v.a.* uſmel.
Accomplish, onjoz, anjis.
Achieve, iqân.
Complete, temmim, etimm.
Consummate, do to perfection, etqin.
Discharge (a duty), ifraſ min.
Enforce, ajri, amân.
Execute, anfiλ. Fulfil, isteucub.
Finish,   ) kalluy, ſalliq,
Conclude,) anhi, oktom.
Perform, iſcal. Perfect, cemmil.

DOCUMENT, waraqa, *nu.* 4; cöhda, xiqqa? Acquittal, woyoul.
Act, Deed, yaco 3.
Bill, calâma. Receipt, rajcâ.
Bond (now due), temesoc.
Charter, destour? cöhda?
Clause,   ) mâdda, *pl.* mawâdd.
Article,)
Credentials, Patent, manxour.
Decree, flöcm 4. Pact, xaττ 3.
Diploma, firmân 13.
Edict, marsoum 11.
Endorsement,) qabâla, c.
Acceptance,)
Immunity, mocâfâyn.
Imperial signature, roſrû.
Letters Patent, ʿemr xarief.
Passport, Clearance, barâʾaL
Privilege, mezieya 14.
Signature, imλâ.
Ticket, teacira.
Warrant,   ) senad,
Debenture,) senada.
Warrant,   ) cuhdân, κ.
"Caution,")
        LAW, DEBT.

Doa, celb(a) 5.
Watchdog, ccelb nâröur 12.
Mastiff, darwês 11, celb jocfiaicy.
Hound, celb yaidicy, celb λâri.
Boarhound, zeſr, zcſſâriey.
Greyhound, hejraſ, selâqa, celb selouqicy.
Whelp, jurou, *pl.* ojrou *or* jirâ.
Puppy, colaib.
Nail, Claw, ĝâfir 12.

Door, Gate, bâb 9 or *pl.* abwâb.
Portal, biwâbs.

Little Door, bowaib.
Wicket in Gate, kauka.
Door-post, rijl el báb.
Threshold, sateba 4.
Lintel, sateba fauqânieya.
Pannel, lauɧ 4.
Leaf of door, musras.
Hinge, musraf, Prov. mofayyala, ᴀʟ nezmâda, ʙɢ. mixbec, ʙ. jarour, saqab el báb, c.

Doubtful (thing), recciey, moxtebih.
— (doubting), mortieb.
Abstruse, mostaqya'.
Ambiguous, ᴀou masnayain.
Apocryphal, moncer.
Arduous, θaqiel.
Complex, moqterin.
Complicated, motexarcil.
Confused, molakbar.
Contested, morieb.
Crabbed, sawies.
Difficult, rasb, rasier, mostaysub, motcrassir.
Disputable, raibiey.
Enigmatic, mosamma'.
— (Riddling), ramziey.
Entangled, motcxarbic, motesarbiq. Equivocal, lobaiey.
Intricate, motcxeccil.
Knotty, mosaqqad.
Obscure, moſlaq, mostaſliq.
Occult, moktefi, kaifiey (*clandestine*).
Perplexing (question), moxcil.
Profound (dº), ſawies ʙ.
Questionable, moxeccec.
Recondite, moltebis, molabbes.
Subtle, daqieq.

Transcendental, rafies.
Uncertain, mauhoum.
Unknown, majhoul.
Vague, mobhem.
Various, mofannan.

Dʀᴀᴡ, *va* isɧab.
Drag, Tug, Lug, jarjir.
Tow, xaɧтut.
Pull, jorr. (See Pull.)
Trail, zeɧɧuf, ezɧul. ᴇɴ ixɧot.
Attract, ijᴀib. Import, ojlob.

Dʀᴇᴀᴅғᴜʟ, mokawwif.
Dread, Dire, makouf, makief.
Appalling, ᴀêsur.
Awful, mories, mehieb.
Deadly, momiet.
Destructive, mobied.
Dismal, mouɧlux.
Dreary, moseudan, moceddar.
Fatal (deadly), mohlic.
Fearful, } hêyil, mehoul,
Frightful, } mohewwil.
Formidable, } mohêb.
Redoubtable, }
Horrible, Horrid, moxtemâ'iz.
Mortal (disease), qâtil.
Shocking, faȝuis.
Terrible, morsub, mofeȝȝis.
Pᴀɪɴғᴜʟ, Hᴜʀтғᴜʟ.

Dʀᴇss, *s.* libs. Clothes, θiyâb.
Costume, melbous 11.
Fashion, zeiy. Garb, cism.
Garment, Vesture, } coswa,
Raiment, Apparel, } cisê.
Mourning Habits, ɧudâd.
A Suit, raqm. Uniform, râqim.
Gown, θeub, *pl.* θiyâb.
Cap, qabas. *Coat*, sôbâya 10.

4

Belt, cemar. *Shawl*, xâle 2, 9.
Shirt, qamier. *Shoe*, fluɛê 8.
Trowsers, libês 8. *Veil*, sitr 3.

DRINK, *va* ixrab.
Drain (medicine), tejarras.
Gulp down, ilfaſt.
Guzzle, tecabbab.
Fuddle, zeffir.
Quaff, qarbis, easief.
Rince the mouth with, temaſ-maſ. Gargle, tefarfar.
Sip, Sup,) orxof, mozz,
Suck,) mezziz.
Swallow, ibtelus, iblas.
Swill, sôbb. Tipple, teccyyaf.

DRINK, *s*. xorba, xaráb.
Beer (white with millet), bouze.
European Beer, foqâs, *vulg.* biera.
Barley-water, xarâb el dorâ?
Chocolate, xôcôlâte.
Coffee, qahwa. *Milk*, flalieb.
Lemonade, liemonâda.
Mead, xarâb el sasel.
Nectar, raſluiq, ccuθer, tesniem, xarâb Selsebiel.
Negus, raſluiq?
Sherbet, xarbèt, B.
— of raisins, koxâf.
Tea, txâi, xâi.
Wine, kamr; *vulgo*, nebieɛ (*toddy*), *antiqu.* modâm.
Water, mâi.
Ale, Porter, miar.
Arrack,) earaq,
Brandy,) saraqiey.
Liquorice, sous.
Rum, rom, roum.

DUCK, barra 3. Drake, barr.
Goose, wezze (auxe).
Gander, wezz.
Eider Duck, wezz el ziff.
Swan, bajas, baxas.
— ardaſ, arſaſ. — foun, qoufi.
Goosander, barr el semec.
Pelican, rakm, seqqâ. DIVER.

DULL (of colour or edge), cêll, ccliel.
Dim, cêaif (*i.e. in eclipse*).
Dark, moſlim, ſlâlic, faiyim (*cloudy*). Dingy, cêliſl.
Dowdy,) modassar,
Dirty,) modaffar.
Dun, adkan, adcen, dokânicy (BLACK).
Dusky, salim, qatim, sâtim, qâtim, mostim.
Faded, moccmmad.
Faint, nâvul. Tarnished, cêbi.
Muddy, Cloudy, raſlul.
Pale, mozafran. Turbid, cedir.

DWELL, *vn* oscou.
Abide, doum, dâwim.
Colonize, *va* sammir.
vn tewarran, isteurun.
Be Fixed, isteqirr.
Inhabit, temecceu flo (Be Established in).
Reside, iqrun. Sojourn, omcoθ.
Settle in, istemain flo, tobellad.
Stay, *vn* nqiem fie, *vulg.* istaqiem fie.
Lodge, *vn* inzil. Tarry, iθwi.
Find Shelter, i'wi, to'ewwâ.

EAGLE, near 3. Condor, rokk?
Vulture, sôqâb 9.

ANGLO-ARABIC VOCABULARY. 51

King Vulture, qaxɛam.
Griffin Vulture, ɛanqâ.
Falcon, ɣaqr, *pl.* ɣöqor 10.
Royal Falcon, xâhien 12.
Kite, ɦudâya, xouɦa.
Goshawk, ɛorrâq.
Hawk, bâz θ, 2.
Buzzard, el bâz el moterehhil.
Sparrow-hawk, bâxiq 12.
Kestrel, ɣoqaira, nabbĕɛel hewâ.

EARNEST, *adj.* ʌou himma, homâm.
Anxious, mahmoum, Xâjir, maxjar.
Ardent, ɦâmi. Eager, ɦariɣ.
Energetic, aɦmaɛ, ɦamioɛ, xehiem. Hearty, qalbioy.
Enterprizing, najid, sĕɛu.
Impassioned, xajiey.
Intent, raɣuid. Spirited, dâ'ib.
Solicitous, mohtimm.
Truehearted, ɣadicq.
Pathetic? hêyim.
Vehement, xadied.
— (Excited), hêyij.
Zealous, ɢayour. SINCERE, INDUSTRIOUS, PRUDENT, CLEVER.

EARTH, *s.* 'erx, torâb.
Brick, ʀoub(a), ojorra, B.
White Cement, tellieɛ.
Chalk, ɦawwûr, ʌʟ ɦaura, B.
Clay with sand, ɣalɣal.
Clay, ʀuin. Crockery, fakkâr.
White dº· leban el ɛaaêr.
Gypsum, jibɛ, jibɛien, jifɣuin, juɣɣ. Lime, cilɛ, jier, Bɛ.
Quick Lime, noura.
Marl, tebâxier. Mortar, kâfaqie.
Plaster, jier, jibɛ (xied?).

Potter's clay, raʃal, ɛejjiel, torâb el fakkâr.

At EASE, } mortêɦ,
In Repose, } mosterâɦ.
Calm, sêcin. Still, rêcin.
Comfortable, motchenni.
Confident, moumin.
Quiet, Tranquil, mormâ'in.

EFFACE, ɛa aɦni, ʋʀmiɛ, uʀlia.
Annul, abʀul. Blot out, imɦu.
Cancel, oxʀob.
Erase, Scratch out, karrux.
Expunge, orɣod (*sic* B. *bis*; Biffer, Rayer), inɛek (abolish).
Obliterate, ɛaffi, *vp* indariɛ.
Make Obsolete, daθθir, *vp* i. vi. vii.
Rub out, ɦöcc. DESTROY.

EFFORT, *s.* muɦna 10, ɛeɛui, *pl.* mesêɛu.
Adventure, taɣaddie, mokârara.
An Adventure, wâqiɛa, *pl.* waqâyie. Attempt, tehejjom.
Attention, dairan el bâl, B. ustinâ, uɦtirêɛ, iltifêt; inɛucêf.
Earnestness, himma, iɦtimâm, jidd. Pains, cedd, ɦarɣ.
Endeavour, mejhoud, jehd.
Enterprize, ɛazm, ɛazêma.
Exertion, moɛânâya, ijtihêd.
Care, Forethought, ɛunâya.

ELEMENT, ɛônɣör 11. *Fire*, nâr 9.
Water, mâ', *vulg.* mûi, *pl.* miɣâh, amwâh.
Earth, 'erx, *pl.* 'erɑ̃ɑ̃u.
Air, howâ, *pl.* ehwiya.
Heat, ɦarr. *Cold*, bard.
Rain, maʀar 4. *Frost*, jelied.

Wind, rieß, f. 4.
Thunder, raed 3. *Mire*, laröuk.

ELEPHANT, fiel 3, 4.
Proboscis, zcloume, barröum, korröum (*snout*).
Ivory, sâj.
Rhinoceros, karruit; cercend, cercedân (*unicorn*?).
Hippopotamus, 'erd, в. barnieq.

ELOQUENT, favuiñ, belief.
Fluent, таliq, naтuq, leain, c.
Garrulous,   ) qawoul.
Loquacious,   ) qawwâl.
Talkative,   ) laqqâx, *Syria*.
Dictatorial, Pedantic, ɾalbâwi.
Glib, motelehhij.
Long-winded, sefouc.
Voluble, miqwâl, misfêc.
Voluminous (writer), mocθir, micθêr. Gushing, monbacuq.
Wordy, Verboso, cilmâni.
Sounding (*orator*), râliq, muylâq. Loud (clear), jehicr.
Harsh-voiced, yakib.
Shrill and Sweet, rakiem.
Impassioned, xajiey.
Various (in style), motefannin.
Expressive, nabbâr.
Impressive, scwwâr, mo'eθθir.

ENCROACH, tcrâwal.
Invade, afier sala', icbis.
Make Inroad, tejarrâ.
Poach, iɾtelis.
Trespass, tesaddâ.
Usurp, jour sala'.   ATTACK.

ENDURE, ra oybor sala', qâsi.
Bear, va teñammal, isteñmil.
Breast, kâwiẕ, qâwim.

Brook (Swallow), tejarrac.
Confront, tewâjch.
Digest (evils, etc.), esiet.
Last out, Outlast? ẕâyin в.
Encounter, Stem, sâruẕ.
Sustain, aτuiq sala'.
Withstand, Undergo, cêbid.
OPPOSE, DARE.

ENRAGE, ra aɾẕub, ɾaẕẕub.
Anger, va añniq.
Chafe, va auɾir, ajiex.
Enfrenzy, iacar, secrin.
Exasperate, eakur.
Fret, va ñarrid.
Gall, añrix, ñârix [saqqir].
Harass, sâcis.   Incense, aɾioȝ.
Infest, xaɾɾib. Infuriate, seraim.
Irritate, ecied, в. (*sic*).
Madden, jannin.   Pester, jêcir.
Pique,   ) inci, enci,
Provoke,) necci.
Pick a quarrel with, Provoke to combat, uñterix bi.
Rouse, Stir up, heyyiq.
Ruffle, kaxxin. Tease, naaniA.
Treat with Scorn, nêcif.
Vex, ɾomm, aɾimm, ɾizz sala' (*prick at*).
Worry,) tehêrax sala'.
Bait,) teñârax sala'.
INCITE, DISTURB.

EQUAL, va sêwi.
Balance (equal), wêzin.
Match (equal), qârin, râbiq.
Vie with, sâdil.

ERR, та ẕull.
Blunder, tcɾâfel, osθor (*stumble*).
Miss, ruiñ.   Mistake, iɾlaт.

ANGLO-ARABIC VOCABULARY.

Offend, esie, xoqq sala'.
(*guiltily*) eanib bi.
Overlook (not see), oshou.
Slip (morally), sill.
Stray, Xuis.
Wander (in mind), ihai, têwih.

ESPECIAL, Special, kayöuy.
Characteristic, wayfiey.
Partial, joz'iey.
Particular, mofrad.
Peculiar, makyöuy, moktuyy bi.
Principal, kâyy.
Specific, Peculiar, koyöuyuiy.

ESPECIALLY, lâsieyima.
Principally, kâyyate^n.
Peculiarly, koyöuya^n.

ESTABLISH, Stablish, alleim, flaccim. Erect, onyöb.
Assure, 'eccid, weccid.
Attest, Avouch, eθbit, θebbit.
Build up, xayyid.
Confirm, aqirr, qarrir.
Consolidate, warrud, elflum.
Constitute, aqsud, ijsal, nazzum.
Corroborate, 'eyyid, ewied.
Create, anxi. Define, sayyin.
Enact, lxras, sonn sonna.
Make Firm, weθθiq.
Fix, orcoz. Fortify, meccin.
Ground, Found, 'essis.
Initiate, abdi (*open*).
Implant, ofroz.
Institute, walas yalas.
Intensify, xaddid.
Ratify, yâdiq sala', saqqid, sâqid.
Root, Ground, araik.
Set up, aqicm, qawwim, *vp* oqicm. Steady, reccin.

Strengthen, qawwi.
Testify, Witness, qorr bi, ixhed.
Verify, flaqqiq, rafiflufl.
SET. GOVERN.

ESTIMATE, oflzor, qaddir.
Account, ustidd.
Appraise, θemmin.
Calculate roughly, ijtezim.
Compute, oflsob.
Conjecture, kammin.
Consider, tefarras. Also Tefarras bi, *suspect*.
Opine, oftdos. Scan, farzin.
Price, Rate,) sessur, soum,
Value,) séwim, qawwim.
Survey, komm. THINK.

EVENING, mesê, mafribieya, sehera B. Sunset, mafrib.
Yester-eve, el leilet el bârifla.
Sunsetting, foroub *or* fiyâb el rams.
Evening twilight, xasoq.
Evening dusk, raseq.
Hour after sunset, saxâ.
From 4 to sunset, saxieya, ayuila 11 x. DARKNESS.

EXCAVATION, faflt, B.
Ditch, flöfra.
Furrow, katt 3, telem 4.
Moat, kandaq 11.
Hole in ground, Hollow, noqra.
Pit (as for gravel), flafiera.
Pit (deep well), jobb 10.
Well, bier 4.
Ridge of Furrow, fârib 12.
Trench, okdoud 11.
Tank, Pond, borce 10.

Public Tank, qaʃɾal, ʙ.
Cistern in house, sehriej.

Exceed, ʋɑ jâwiz, oɾdou,
zied ʃala', ocboɾ ʃala'.
— ʋn tejâwaz, afɾiʈ, axiʈʈ.
Run to excess, oɾlou fie.
Go ahead, osboq, tɛqoddam ʃala'.
Surmount, anieʃ ʃala'.
Surpass, tɛʃâwat, tɛʃâɾaʈ, ibras.
Transcend, tɛʃaddâ.
Outdo, fouq ʃala'.
Overdo, afɾiʈ fie, xiʈʈ fie.
Overtask, ʃarhid, ʙ.

Excessive, zêyid.
Enormous, mofɾaʈ.
Exorbitant, motɛjâwiz.
Extraordinary, kârij el ʃâda.
Extravagant, moxiʈʈ.
Extreme, motenêhi.
Inordinate, kârij ʃan el fladd.
Immense, sazuim.
Redundant, lâyuʎ, zokaricy.
Superfluous, fâʎul, faʎoul.
Plentiful. Wonderful.

Excellent (person), faʎuil,
fiʎul? — (thing), jaiyid.
Capital, sazuim. Choice, naficɛ.
Consummate, mottâqin, ablaʃ
ma yecoun.
Eminent, monief.
Prime, ʃâl, kâriq (sic).
Exquisite (Pure), zeciey.
Firstrate, afʎal.
Honourable, mocram, motecer-
rim. Illustrious, bêhir.
Noble, xarieʃ, najieb (nabial?).
Original, badiɛʃ.
Perfect, cêmil, mocemmal.

Pre-eminent, ʃôlwâ'iey, mota-
qaddim. Select, montâqi.
Splendid, fâkir.
Supereminent, qiddiem.
Superexcellent, eʃɾâ.
Superfine, rafieʃ.
Superior (man), bâɾiʃ.
Very Superior, } mifʎâL
Transcendent,
Superlative, afʎal ma yecoun.
Surpassing, ʃâyiq, motɛʃâɾiʈ.
Grand, Generous, Excessive.

Excretion (medical t.), istifɾaɣ?
korouj el mawâdd, birâz.
Secretion, raxfl.
Dripping from nose, zocêm.
Earwax, middat el êaên.
Excrement, } makraj,
Fæces, } birâz.
Humour, kalaʈ 1. Bile, yaʃɾâ.
Gall, morra. Chyle, cielous.
Chyme, ciɛmous.
Matter, midda, qaifl.
Phlegm, balɣam.
Scurf, flazêz, hibrieya (fiue).
Saliva, rieq, roʎâb, lema' ʙ.
Foam at mouth, loʃâb.
Spittle, tufl, bizêq, bouʃâq.
Sweat, ʃoraq. A Tear, damʃ 3.
Urine, baul. Refuse, ʃ.

Exercise, ʋa (the mind), mar-
rin; (a horse), jarrid (ʙ. sic).
Accustom, sawwid ʃala'.
Chasten, ʃazzir, heᴀᴀib.
Discipline (troops), qarnuʃ.
— (oneself), irtâʎ.
Educate, 'eddib, raxxifl ʃala'.
Familiarize, 'ênis, ʋp x.
Habituate, admin? ʋp x.

Instruct, karrij, afrun.
Drill, darrib kala'.
Train, rouḍ, rawwuḍ.
Study, odros.
Teach, sallim, darris.
Practise (an art), māris, istedmin (admin, x.).

Expel, *va* otrod min.
Banish, anfi. Exile, sercil.
Cashier, Discard, oszol, sazzil.
Dismiss, Divorce, aṭliq.
Dispossess, anhuḍ, iklas min.
Eject, idfas min, armi bihi san.
Exterminate, inzes, iqlas, min.
Extirpate, istêṣul, qarrim.
Pull out, Push out, akrij, ralluc, railus, b.
Reject (harshly), mozz, b.
Remove, *va* xiel, axiel.
— to distance, absud, bassud.
— put aside, naḥḥu.
— transport, onqol.
— pump off? inzefl.
— (trundle off), cerril, b.
Rid oneself of, Get Rid of, eziefl, zewwiḥ.
— eziel (cause to cease).
— eshib (cause to depart).
— tekallū min.
Scare away, isteflzz.
— (by shouts), ozjor.
Supersede (an officer), ustefi san, istersfi san.
Sweep off (as a wave), onxol.

Explain, *va* [away], 'ewwil.
Clear up, abien, bayyin (*declare*).
Comment on, ixrafl.
Define, sayyin, sarrif.
Dilate on, eshib.

Elucidate, auḍuḥ.
Enlighten (a person), efhim.
Expatiate, tefāyaḥ.
Expound, sabbir san.
Interpret, terjim.
Paraphrase, fessir.
Teach (a person), sallim; fehhim, **B.**
Translate, istekrij. Say.

Extract, *va* istekrij.
Draw out, Pull out, iqlas.
— (teeth), iqbas, **B. sic.**
Elicit, istexkib (milk or blood).
Evoke, istedsu.
Extract (from a book, letter, etc.), iltaqir, lakkuy.

Eye, sain 3 *f.* Eyelid, jufn 3, 4.
Eyebrow, hājib 12.
Eyeball, ḥadaqa 4.
Eyelash, xasr el jufn, hodb el sain (*fringe*).
Orbit of eye, maḥjar 11, **v.**
Pupil, boubou, bawabbou.
Iris, dâyir el boubou.
Outer angle of eye, liḥâz.
Inner —, mâ'q, mouq.

Fall, *vn* waqas yaqas.
Fall back, Drop, isqaṭ.
Fall down, ibbuṭ.
Fall in (as roof), ikḥs.
Fall in with, rādif, lāqi, waqas yaqas ileihi.
Fall in one's way, present itself, ismaḥ, **v.**
Fall suddenly, karr.
Fall (in ruin), hour, tehewwar, (in death), ifrus.
Fall out, *Happen*, waqas.

Fall, Pitch upon, aʀuîb.
Fall (as thunderbolt), ifqis.
Fall headlong, tewarrat.
Drop, Slip from the hand, töﻻﻻ, ialet.
Pounce, Swoop, ihwi.
Fall off, Become less, kass.
Fall out, *Quarrel*, inɾabin mas.

FALSE (thing), mozewwar.
Affected, moʀannas.
Artificial, uʀrunâsuiy.
Bastard, Spurious, ʀabīk.
Counterfeit, seɾel.
Calumnious, qadaɦey.
Fallacious, moɷull.
Fictitious, taʀnieɦey.
Imitative, taqliediey.
Liar, céʌib. Made up, sameliey.
Perfidious, kâyin.
Perjured, ɦâniθ.
Slanderous, nammâm, nammiey.
Traitor, } ɾaddâr,
Treacherous, } ɾadour.

FAMILY, ɕaila.
Household, 'ehl el beit.
Father, 'ab, 'abou, *pl.* 'abâ.
Mother, omm, *pl.* ommebêt.
Parent, wâlid(a).
Son, ibn, *pl.* abnâ; †ben, *pl.* benien; najl.
Daughter, bint 5.
Brother, âk, akou; *pl.* âkâ, ikwâ, ikwân.
Sister, okt, *pl.* akawêt.
Grandfather, jadd 3, 4.
Grandmother, jadda, nâna, c.
Grandchild, ɦaɦd(a) 11.
Ancestors, } selef 4, 6.
Predecessors, }

Eldest Son, el bicr 4.
Orphan, yetiem 4, 11.
Widower, 'ermel 11.
Widow, 'ermela 11.
Heir, wâriθ 6.
Uncle (patruus), ɕâm, (avunculus) kâl.
Aunt (amita), ɕamma, (matertera), kâla. NATION.

FANCIFUL (person), kayoul, motekayyil; (thing), kiyâliey, tekayyoliey.
Fantastic, makyoul.
Capricious, mozentur, ɦalâtiey.
Conceited, moktêL
Crazy, malʀöux (MAD).
Drivelling, mokarrif.
Ideal, teʀawworiey.
Imaginary, wehmiey.
Imaginative, motewehhim, moʀawwariey.
Queer? maxɕöur, в.
Superstitious, moweswes, moteweswis.
Whimsical, hewâ'iey.
LIGHTMINDED, FOOLISH.

FAR, baɕuid. Afar, baɕuidaⁿ.
Aloof, little way off, boɕaid.
Distant, seɦuiq, nayiey, ʀ.
Remote, qâʀu, ʌarieɦ c. moteqâʀu, montêθ? ALONE.
Retired, nêziɦ, monteɕiɦ.
Uttermost, Outmost, aqʀa'.
Withdrawn from, monɦâs ɕan.

FARM, s. ʌaisa 5, mesrasa 11.
House (*gener.*), beit 3, maɦall 2.
Storehouse, makzen 11.
Barn, xouna 10, jorn.

Granary, horie, *pl.* ehrâ.
Garner, 'anbar 11.
Byre, marâfl.
Stable, marbaт 11; (of horses) ekour.
Shed, dara', в. (асrа'?).
Cowhouse, uтabl.
Sheepfold, flaтnira.
Pen, zerieba 11.
Barn-floor, 'andar 11.

Fат, *adj.* semicn 5.
Corpulent, badien, jesiem.
Fleshy, lañuim, molafIflum.
Greasy, dahicn, modhin.
Gross, Rank, semij.
Oily, dohniey.
Plump (B), morabrab [Sleek?].
Plump (K), rabiez.
Plump-barrelled (horse), ṭalies.
Paunchbellied, baтun, mobтun, mocrix.
Stout, tekit? (в. Gros). Bio.

Fеar, ва kâf (kift) min; ikxi, ер viii.
Be Agitated, ijzes, inkuAA.
Be Alarmed, irhib.
Apprehend, ofldos (*sic*).
Be Disquieted, ohdos (*sic*).
Collapse (Be Crushed in heart)? uâjar, teJajjar.
Cower, тâтâ. Dread, irtесub.
Crouch, Cringe, temescen.
Be Dismayed, welch yclih.
Despond, okmod, texajjab.
Grovel, tewâJaс. Quail, ojbon.
Suspect, ittehim.
Be Timorous, wajal yajil.
Be Terrified, iſzес.
Tremble, Frighten.

Fеar, *s.* kauf, makâfa, kaifa.
Agitation, uTurâb.
Alarm, dehwa в. wejal 4.
Apprehension, kaxya, kaxyân.
Awe, Aеsar. Confusion, bilbâl.
Commotion, iktibâт.
Consternation, indihêl.
Cowardice, jabâna.
Despondency, komoud? xajab, xojoub. Dismay, dehxa.
Disquiot, qalaq, qalqala, hodas.
Disturbance, inziсâj.
Dread, rosb, rasba.
Fright, heul 4, rehba.
Horror, wehra в.
Panic, kiAAa, ittilêh, tewelloh.
Poltroonery, nadála.
Stupor, flaira.
Suspicion, tekawwox.
Terror, fizs, fezес 4, fezca.
Timidity, kajl, fexal, в.
Tremour, rajſa,rajafân, irjâſ 11, rasx, irtisâx.
Uneasiness, jezес.

Ferret (*gener.*), surse, ibn сurs. (tame ferret), sariese, kaттâf el fenec (rabbit-catcher), F.
Civet Cat, quт el zibâd.
Ermine, qâqoum.
Genet, zerdawâ.
Ichneumon, } nems 3.
Mangouste, } zeqzêq.
Marten, qarqaJôun.
Tree Marten, таllâс el xajar.
Polecat, } gurbân :
Stoat, } el qarqaJôun el
Skunk, } qaаir.
Brown Sable, sommour.
Weasel, dalaq.

Fetter, *s.* qaid 3, 4.
Clog, oostec. Buckle, ebziem.
Foot Rope, } cuqâl 10,
Shackle, } cöqla, xicêl.
Spike for picketing, sicce 10.
Iron stake, kâzouq 12.
Staple, rezze. Ring, flalaqa.
Strap, scir 3. Thong, qâyıx.
Tother, flujâr.
Trammels, zinâq.

Field, *s.* (open country), faλâ.
Croft without trees, flaql 3.
A Fallow, xarêqi, 'erλ mortêflo.
Sown Field, mezraca 11.
Pulse Field, maqTun 11.
Lawn, rets 3. Meadow, marj 3.
Park, } fluyûr, flazuirn,
Enclosure, } flacr, flâcoura,
zerieba, ɾuit mozcrrab.
Hedged Paddock, mesieja.
Pasture, marca' 11.
Prairie, mesraſi 11, martes 11.
Walled Garden, fladicqa 11.
Public Garden, bostên 11.
Private Garden, jonaina 11.
Flowery plain, rauλa, *pl.* riyâλ.
Savannah, baqca 5, raqma.
Forest.

Fill, *vs* melli, imla*.
— to the brim, } arfill,
(Overfill), } raffifl.
Choke, daqqir, sodd.
Cram, zcffir.
Freight, Man; ixflan.
Fill Full, afcum, xaflflun.
Glut, seddim (in Polit. Econ.), daqqir.
Gorge, Overfeed, raffla.

Pack, cabbi.
Sata, Satiate, axbic, xabbic.
Stuff, oflxou, uflxi.
Replenish, okros, Rg. *vp* vii.

Fine, *adj.* (superfine), rafles;
(showy), ecijin, bêhi; (gay), zêhi, mezbou; (subtle), da-qicq; (as powder or fur), nâcum; (as a blade), ʌe'yicl, rebief, morbif.
Delicate, raqicq, nêzic.
Elegant, zarief, meziey.
Refined, (t)xelebi.
Sleek? lcmies. Soft, lniyin.
Smooth, amles.
— of cheek, 'esicL
Soft and Smooth, weθier, r.
Beautiful.

Finger, *s.* uybar 11.
Ring Finger, binyur 11.
Little F., kinyur 11.
Fore Finger, sebbâba.
Tips of F., anâmiel, binân.
Thumb, abhem 11, bêhim 12.
Knuckle, cecas 5, cöqda 10.
Nail, ʒufr 4, λâfir 12, ḅ.

Fire, *s.f.* nâr 9.
Artificial Fire, waqied.
Flame, lebb, lehicb, lisên el nâr.
Brand, ʒarma 10, xocla 10.
Blaze, wejja.
Smoke, dok(k)ân.
Spark, xarâra 10.
Live coal, jomra 10, bayya, ʌı.
Soot, xaflflâr, B. xoflwâr, c.
— (in air), hebâb, sewâd.
Fuel, florâqa. Steam, bokâr.
Vapour, bawâk.

ANGLO-ARABIC VOCABULARY.   59

Fishbone, élét el nâr.
Flint, qaddâfl, rawwán, AL ralbouk, &c.
Steel, zenâd, qidâfla.
Tinderbox, miqdafl.
Tinder, yôufân.
Touchwood, qâ'ou.
Match, cönd cibriet.
Bellows, minfak 11.
Coalrake, muflrec.
Poker, miscar.
Shovel, misflâya, miqlab.
Tonga, milqât. —xabbâθ 11, x.

Fireplace, Hearth, manqid.
Firegrate, mijmara.
Firebox? cênoun.
Drazier, minvab, &c.
Chafing Dish, minqal, AL
Stove, wojâq 2 (*Turk*).
Hearth, mostcuqid.
Fender, flâjiz lil nâr.
Oven, forn 4.
Furnace, etoun, eθoun 2.
Forge, tennour.
Clay Furnace, cour 4, 0.
Kiln, qamien jicr.
Chimney, madkana.
Censer, Fumigator, mibkara.

Fish, s. semec(n) 3, 4.
Small Fish, somaice.
Fin, zecnifa, jenâfl el semec.
Fishbone, flasec.
Gills, nakxoux.
Scale, fils, 3. — qixra (*crust*).
—flarxafa. Sprat? besèrieya.
Whale (Large Fish), *gener.*
flout 9. Chub, xâl 9.
Shark, karráf? qirx.

Gudgeon, qâboudie.
Herring, fesiek.
(Sardine?) zence.
Mackarel, isqamri.
Perch, tewiena, x.
Red Perch, zerboun.
Trout, semec Eriewân, semece monaqwaxa. Whiting, bouri.
Shad, vaboufa, xâbil, ».

Fit, *adj.* lâyiq.
Adapted to, kalieq li.
Apt, 'ehil li, motc'ehhil.
Affinity, te'ehhol.
Appropriate, monêsib.
Suited, } vâlifl li,
Snitable, } mowâflq.
Well assorted, kâyil, mootoli.
Worthy, jadier bi, en. Useful.

Fit, *va* 'ehhil, labbiq.
Accommodate, yeassir.
Adapt, waflq. Accoutre, 'ehhib.
Adjust, flarrir, asdil.
Apply, rabbiq, râbiq sala'.
Appropriate, kayyny.
Arrange, } reccin, nazzum.
Range, *v.a.* } sewwi, rettib.
Attach, qayyid. Equip, acudd.
Furnish, jehhiz.
Fit up (a shop), wazzub.
Prepare, Dispose? hcyyi, wâflq.
Govern.

It Fits, *v.* yakiel.
Befits, yenbari.
Becomes, } yejmol,
Beseems, } yelieq, yelbaq li.
Behoves, wajib yejib; yesouf li.
Comports with, yantali sala'.
Is Meet, yayufll.

Is Right, yaflaqq ealaic.
Suits, yonêaib.

FLAG, *on* isterki, uẢwi.
Dry up, *on* inxaf.
Droop, iaqat, ifxal, uẢni.
Decay, wehe yeuhi.
Fade, obrox, icmad?
 (with sun) iclaß.
Faint, wehen yehin, wena yeni.
Pine, inacqim, isteqim.
Swoon, ifxa (yafxa' ealaic), ifma, ifba.
Wither, iẢbal, inhezil.
Waste, *on* sell.
 TIRE, THIN, WEAK.

FLAT, *adj.* meetöuß, mobattat.
Even, sewiey, mosêwi.
Level, motemehhid, momehhed, mosemhed, a.
Plain (Plane), sehil, sêbil.
Smooth, lemies, amles, weθier.

FLEET, *s.* Navy, xowan, dounanmâ.
Ship of War, marceb ßarbiey.
Merchantman, marceb tijâriey.
Fireship, ßarrûqa.
Steamship, seßenet el bokâr.
 vulgo also, marceb el nâr.
Steampacket, vâpour.
Man of War, xauna, *pl.* xowan.
Armament, cumâra.
Squadron, ostöul 11 (στόλος).
Ship, marceb 11.
Vessel, qayêse, 11.
Galley, Barque, seßena 10, 11.
Gunship, seßena midfacuiya.
Ship of the line, qabaq 2.
Frigate, frefäта. Brig, briec.

Galleon, ẓaliyoun (Egypt).
Sloop of War, jafna ö (Barbary).
Barge, xakröur(a) 11.
Lighter, mâxiwa, ag.
Cutter, ßlouce 11.
Shallop, zeuraq 11.
Pinnace, vandal 11.
Yacht, State-Barge, folc 10.
Gondola, qanja 10, qanjiya, barxa ö.
Rowing Galley, ẓorâb 9.
Wherry, qâyiq 12.
Ship's Boat, qârib 12.
Nile Boat, dahcbieya.
Skiff, macdiya.

FLOUR, Meal, *s.* тaßuin.
Finest Flour, daqieq, cemâja, zehr el daqieq.
Brown Flour, coxkêr.
Bran, nakâl, rodda?
Dough, Paste, cajien.
Paste of Pie, raqâq.
Leaven, kamier(a).
Starch, naxâ.

FLOW, *on* ijri (*run*), isfaß, vubb.
Dash (as water), kirt, isßc?
Dribble, texalxal. Drop, oqтor.
Drip, *on* teraxxaß.
Flood, rouf cala', fuiẢ, urfaß cala'.
Gush out, infajir, indaßq.
Leak, wecef yecif.
Melt, *on* sieß, ẢOub.
Ooze, inßd, iari, inẢuß, nizs.
Pour, *on* ihтul, invubb.
Run off, Ebb as a single wave, inẢab. Splash, *on* kirr.
Scud (as tears), iarif?
Spirt, *on* onfor, inẢak?

ANGLO-ARABIC VOCABULARY. 61

Spout, inbaɛ, onbot.
Sprinkle, roxx. Squirt, naxxib.
Stream, sieL
Swamp, ta ɾawwuy.
Trickle, irɛaf, ibtul (as tears).
Poua.

Flower, *s.* zehra 3, 2.
Rose, ward(a) 2.
Dog Rose, jol nisrien.
Sweet Briar, nisrien.
Lily (*gener.*), zenbaq.
Jasmine, yesmien. Iris, sousên.
Violet Pansy, benefsej.
White dᵒ·? kicri.
Wallflower, kieri, b., manθour ayfar.
Pink, Carnation, mikmalieya.
Clove Pink, qoronfol.
Tulip, kizêma. Crocus, corcom.
Geranium, ibrat el râsu.
Poppy, kaxkâx.
Convolvulus, leblâb.
Bluebell, Hyacinth, jarse.
Jonquil, qatmir bouliya, b.
Narcissus, narjies.
Hyacinth? Lavender? sonbol 11.
Anemone, xaqieq nasmâni.
Marjoram, marzencoux, flabec el fiel.
Sunflower, cerâr; dawwâr el xams; tonaum; yamriyoumô,
Asphodel,) sierês,   [b.
Daffodil, } barwâq.
Honeysuckle, zehr el sasel.

Fly, *s.* ᴀobâba *nu, vulgo* dobbâna *nu.* Meat Fly, zenbout.
Mosquito, nâmous 12.
Small Sand Fly, baqqa *nu.*
Gnat, basöula *nu.*

Midge, barɾaxa *nu.*
Gad Fly (Hornet), zonbour 11.

Fly, *vs* tuir; (as small insect), terayyar, terâyar.
Flit, tóuf, iᴀrif? Flutter, rafrif.
Flit, Float, Flutter (as sport of the wind), okfoq fil hewâ, qaddif (b. *sic*).
Fleet (pass rapidly), imtelis? ijâl? Hover, flöum.
Soar, flalliq (*in circles*), isteqill?

Follow, ta itbas (etbis, f.).
— (a master), ittebis, tetebbas.
Accompany, yâflub.
Attend, râfiq. Ensue, otlou.
Chase, otrod, târid.
Hunt, yuid, uytêd, iqnuy, iqtenuy.
Hunt down, oqfox.
Hunt for, fettix.
Overtake, ilflaq.
Pursue, odroc, dâric.
Push hard after, icrix.
Run at, iqtoflum.
Track out, iqtefi, teqaffû.
Imitate, Seek, Attack.

Food, *s.* qout 4. A *Meal,* 'ecla.
Bread, kobz. *Milk,* flalieb.
Meat, loflm. *Meat Dish,* tabiek.
Herbs, boqoul. *Roots,* josour.
Pulse, mûx. *Grain,* flöboub.
Greens, kaxrawât. *Gourds,* qars.
Onions, basaL *Fruit,* fêcihe 12.
Plums, kauk'. *Dates,* temr.
Nuts, jauz. *Mulberries,* tout.
Grapes, ɛunab. *Oranges,* bortoqâl.
Apples, toffâfl. *Poultry,* farrouj.
Spices, bahêrât. *F'lour,* taḍuin.

Condiment, tâbal 12.
Grease, zefer.   *Soup*, xauraba.
Sweets, ɲölawâ.
Pudding, faloṇae.
Pastry, maṛjoun.
Victuals, ṛaix, ṛaixa, maṛâx.
Eatables, mêcoul 2, ʽecl.
Viands, ⎫ raṣâm.
Meats, ⎭ maraṣum.
Side Dishes? rabkanêt.
Aliment, ɼiaê.   Supplies, miera.
Provisions, zewâḍa, mouna, ma-
 ʼouna, maṛouna, temawwon.
Stores, ᴧckiers 11.
Fodder, salaf.

Foolish, aɲmaq, ɲamqiey.
Absurd, *Blind*, ṛamâwicy.
Cracked, Crazy, hêtir, maɩroux.
Doltish, ⎫ belied,
Stolid, ⎭ mabloud, c.
Fatuous, raqis, B. qalɲɩaa, B.
 ṛabieʀ 11, B.
Halfwitted, heffêt.
Ignorant, jêhil 6, jehoul, moe-
 tejhil.
Imbecile, eblch, mohtclis.
Inexperienced,Inexpert,ɼaxiem.
Silly, ehbel, B. behloul 11,
 arṣan, c.
Stupid, ɼabiey, kâθir,majdoub,B.
Fanciful, kayoul.   *Idle*, ceslân.
Lightminded, ràyix.
Headstrong, lefout.
Mad, majnoun.   *Rash*, mojêzif.

Foot, s.f. rijl, pl. arjoḷ.
Footsole, qadam 4.
Instep, qadam 4 (sic).
Heel, ṛaqab 4.

Anklebone, ceṛb 4, 5.
Tendon Achilles, ɼörqoub.

Forest, s. ɼaiᴛal 11.
Holt, ɲurx 3, 4 (*antiqu*. ɲaraja).
Wood, ɼaiʎa 5.   *Grove*, maxjar.
Plantation, maɼris 11.
Covert, ɼâba *nu*.
Bosk, daɼla *nu*, madɼal.
Brushwood, *Scrub*, ṛöqoul,
 ɲasec, B.
Bush, ⎫ zeur,
Thicket, ⎭ zeur ṛâxu, ṛuiʀ?
Jungle, ʼejma 10.
Glade, manfaᴧ 11.
Lawn, retṛ 3.
Cane Brake, maqʀab.
Arbour, ṛaricxa.
Orchard, Croft, ɼaiᴛ.

Forgive, oɼṛor ila', li.
Apologize, usteair.
Excuse from, uʀfaɲ ṛan.
Exempt from, uṛfi ṛau.
Remit, Condone, sêmiɲ.
Pardon, uʀfaɲ li.

Fortress, s. ɲuʀn 3.
City Wall, sour 4, 9.
Tower, borj 3.   *Castle*, qaʀʀ 3.
Citadel, qalṣa 5.
Palace, scrâi, seràya; jauṣeq.
Edifice, cumâra.
Fabric, bonʀûn.
Battlement, cernec B. xorrâfa.
Barbican, faʀuil.
Rampart, mitrês 11.
Moat, kandaq.
Lighthouse, Steeple,menâra 11.
Pinnacle? Minaret? xorfa 10.

Fraud, meer, caid.
Cheat, Cheating, ɣixx.
Craftiness, marûna.
Cunning, dahê*. Deceit, kodɛa.
Deceitfulness, kadieɛa, kadâɛa.
Delusiveness, ɣorour.
Imposture, ɣobn, ɣabiena, tejbien, tezwier.
Trick, flnila, maflûla.
Trickery, uſtiyâl, moflârafa, morâwaɣo, moqâmara.
Wile, Guile, ɣadra.
Wiliness, Guilefulness, Treachery, ɣadr, taɣdier.

Frequent, ca teraddad ɛala'.
— (society), ɛâxir, ïktelur mac.
Haunt, êlif.
Betake oneself to (a place), istaqbil (teqabbal) ila'.
— (by preference), wâθir, teflarra' ila'.
Be Found in, olfi fie, iv. vp.
Recur to, râjiɛ.
Repair to, roud fie.
Take Refuge in, ilja ila', ilteji ila'. Resort to, intêb.
Have Recourse to, tejâwa, f. uɛmid ila'.
Range over, joul fie.
Make for, oqɣöd ila'.
Seek Shelter, isteari, ĉwi ila'.

Frighten, v.a. kawwif.
Affright, akicf.
Agitate, uɛrarib, koll, ep vii.
Appal, iaɛar. Awe, ehicb.
Damp (courage), afxil, foxxil.
Daunt, afziɛ, fezziɛ.
Discourage, akmid.
Dismay, ajziɛ, fezziɛ.

Intimidate, kaxxi.
Scare, hewwil.
Scare away, wellih, axrid, xarrid, istefizz.
— (by shouts), ozjor.
Startle, naffir; jaffil (fajjil, B.).
Terrify, arɛub, ruɛɛub, orɛob.
Unman, Cow, ajbin.

Fringe, s. hoddûb (pl. of hédib).
Flounce,) sejaq, c. (?)
Festoon ?) sijûf.
Frill, coxcex, tocriej.
Edging,) colfa,
Trimming,) ɛödda.
Tassel, xarrâba 11.
Tuft, kuɣl 10, aowâba.
Lace,) tekriema,
Network,) xabieɛe.
Embroidery, rurâz, zeiya, B.
Braid, Tissue, flabec.

Frost, s. jelied. Ice, bouz.
Hard Frost, qars ? saqieɛ.
Icicle, ɛöθnoun bonz.
Snow, θelj 3. Hail, barad.
Flake of Snow, roqɛat θelj.
Fine Hail,) xurr,
Hoarfrost,) xofxâf.
Hailstone, ɣuqɛa ? siqɛa ? qorx bouz (lump of ice).

Fruit, s. (gener.) θemar 4, 5.
Table Fruit, fêcibe 12.
— maiwa, Bg.
Bunch, ɛanqoub 11.
Cluster, ximrâk. Nosegay, bâqa.
Stone of Fruit, ɛajwa, c.
Pip, bizra 3. Pulp, xaflm.
Kernel, niwâ*, niwâya.

Core, Marrow, lobb 3.
Pith, qalb, jommâr, B.   FOOD.

FRUIT TREE, xajara moθmira.
Banana, Plantain, mouz.
Date tree, nakla.
Its fruit, temr.   Its fibres, lief.
Elder, senboq, senbouqa, seb-
 bouqa, kamân, bielesên; *vulgo*
 xajar el belesên.
Indian Fig,   ) xabr,
Prickly Pear,) xöbbaira.
Sycamore, Wild Fig, jommaiz.
Olive, xajarat zeitoun.
Vine, dâliya 12.
Vine leaf, ɼalfaq 11.
Grapes, sanab.
Vine-pole, seumêo 11, mesmêc.

FUEL, *s.* ßörâqa, c.
Kindling (as paper), mieqâd.
Firewood, ßaTab.
A Log, qorma 10, 11, ßaraba.
Faggot, jorze, ßâzima.
Charcoal, faßm.
Pit coal, faßm 'erχuiy.
Live coal, jomra, bayyat nâr.
Embers, melle.   Ashes, rimâd.
Cinder, xöußeya, AL

FUNERAL, *s.* jinêze.
Coffin, têbout.
— (of sultan), qobba.
Hearse, naqâla (*cart*).
Pallet? nasx.   Obsequies, jihêz.
Bier, maßmil, serier 8 (*sedan*).
Procession, nßtifâl.   GRAVE.

FURNITURE, eθêθ.
Ware, mazrouf.   Goods, rizq 4.
Tackle, Equipage, xödda.
Chair, corsi 11.   *Carpet,* bisêr.

Chest, xandouq 11.
Cushion, tecêya.   *Bedding,* ßrâx.
*Lamp,*qandiel 11. *Screen,* ᴧorwa.
Table, mâ'ida 12.
Utensil, zarf 8.

GAME BIRDS, röyour el xaid.
Pheasant, qaij(a).
Partridge, ßajal(a).
Francolin,   ) dorrâj,
Snite,   ) dorroj.
Grouse? qarâ.   Snipe, bicêsoun.
Woodcock, dojâj el 'crâ.
Beccafico, towainiya.
Ousel, Coot ? tefolloc.
Crake, tefolloo el barr.
Quail, sommona, sommâna
 (farra, *Kasrawan*).
King Quail, selwa, naßj.
Tragopan (*ceriornis,* horned
 pheasant), cerawân.
Water hen, dojâj el mâi.
Purple Coot, borhên.

GATHER, *va* [For *vn* see AS-
 SEMBLE.]   Collect, ijmas.
Accumulate,) χömm.
Concentrate,)
Agglomerate, orcom, *vp* vi.
Assemble, aßßl, *vp* viii.
Associate, xa câxir.
Cluster, lomm. Group, lamlim.
Congregate, oßxod ? *vp* viii.
 vp inßaxir, intedi.
Convene, isteliem, *vp* viii.
Convoke, odxöu, osqod.
Cull, Crop, iqruf.
Glean, qoxx, laqqur.
Heap up, cewwim, cewwir,
 ceddis, cerdis.
Pick, Pluck, ijni.

ANGLO-ARABIC VOCABULARY.   65

Pile up, sarrim.
Rally, ceθθib? ocθob?
Reassemble, oῆxor? x.
Sum up, ajmil, ӡömm.
Summon, isteῆλur.

GENERAL, *adj.* mojtemis.
Generic, jinsiey.
Collective, ijmâliey.
Common (property or road), sâmm. — (pest), samiem.
Comprehensive, xâmil.
Prevalent, ţâlib.
Public (right), jomhouriey.
Universal, sömoumiey.

GENEROUS, ceriem.
Very Generous, micrâm.
Beneficent, moosum.
Bounteous, } jawwâd.
Bountiful, } mennân.
Charitable, moῆsin.
Large handed, mojzil.
Large hearted, wêsis el yadr.
Lavish, fayyâᾱ. Liberal, sekiey.
Magnanimous, } motecêrim,
Highsouled, } sâli el himma.
Munificent, webhêb, rezzêq.
    GOOD, EXCELLENT, KIND.

GET, *va* } ῆayyul,
Procure for oneself, } istaῆyul.
Get (bring on), ojlob, *vulg.* jieb.
Get (earn), ictesib.
Get (win), uӡfar bi, tсţallab sala', nâl (nilt), tewaqqas sala'.
Get (curry off as booty), iţtenim, fouz. Acquire, iqni, iqteni.
Alight on, uῆyal sala'.
Attain, iblaſ ila'.

Bespeak, } dâric,
Provide, } tedâreo.
Enjoy, Possess, ῆöuz.
Gain, irbaῆ, icsib.
Find, wajad yejid, *vp* wojid.
Obtain, uῆӡu bi.
Possess, ῆöuz, imlic.
Become Possessed of, imtelic, temellec bi.
Take Possession of, istemlic, isteῆwiz sala'.
Win by stockjobbing, râbiῆ.
— by usury, râbi.

GIVE, *va* aстu. — back, rodd.
— forth ; see Emit, SUPPLY.
— over ; see CEASE.
— in to, tesâтa.
— in, *on* yield; ῆotт, lien.
Afford, nojjim, aurid, ajdi.
Appropriate, koyy bi, kuyyoy.
Bestow, imnaῆ.
Endow (a college), waqaf yaqif; auqif, anῆq?
Endue, kawwil. Hand, nâwil.
Grant, weheb yehib.
— ismaῆ leho bi. — ctῆuf bi?
— aῆsin ila', ecrim ila'.
Impart, xâric-oh bihe.
Lavish, ibdil, sebbiſ?
Present, ehdi, eddi.
Vouchsafe, orzoq, monn salaihi bi, ansum salaihi bi.

Go, rouῆ. Come, jie, 'eti.
Go aside, inхorif.
Go away, DEPART, iaheb.
Go back, irjas. Go before, osboq.
Go across, morт, osbor.
Go by, fout, imᾱu.
Go round, dour.

5

Go up and down, joul; see **WANDER.**
Go up, uṣɛad, ʊтlɛc.
Go down, inzil, uɴdir, inɴadir.
Go on, forward, teqaddum, inbari ғ.
Go out, ʊтlɛc, okroj.
Go near, iqdim, odnou min, iqtorib min.
See Betake oneself.
WALK, RUN, HASTE, DEPART.

GOATS (gener.), masz.
A Single Goat, maszeʼ.
He-goat, teis 3.
She-goat, ṣanze, masẑêyṣ.
Kid, jadie 9.
Goatsʼ down, teftiec.
Chamois,   ) teitel, badan,
Mountain-goat,) arwieya 11,
ṣanz jebaliey, teis jebaliey.

GOOD, adj. тaiyib, melieɴ.
Better, akyar, kair, aɴraʼ.
Brave, xajiec.   *Clever*, xôтur.
Earnest, homâm. *Grand*, juliel.
Eloquent, faṣuiɴ.
Excellent, fuẑuil, jayyid.
Generous, ceriem.
Happy, moṛbouт.   *High*, ɛâli.
Industrious, xehiem.
Joyful, mofriɴ.   *Just*, ɛâdîl.
Kind, raʼouf.   *Nice*, тaiyib.
Nimble, raxieq.
Pleasant, ʼenieq.
Plentiful, wâɴr.   *Pure*, тâhir.
Prudent, raxied. *Quick*, seriec.
Religious (person), duiyin.
Rich, ɣuniey.   *Right*, ɣâyib.
Sincere, ṣodieq.   *Useful*, nâɴc.
Benign, kaiyir.

Refined, moheᴧᴧeb, ociyiᴧ.
Well-bred, edieb, edoub.
Well-behaved, moɴtexim.
EXCELLENT.

GOODS, rizq 4.   Wares, silcᴧ.
Articles, emtica, from *sing.*
  metêc.   Chattels, eθêθ.
(Household) Stuff, qomâx.
Moveables, ecɛaf. Gear, jihêx 8.
Upholstery, najd.
Property, mûl *pl.* amwâl.
Merchandize, baẑâca 11.
Small Ware, kordâ, *pl.* -awâт.
Store, ᴧekiera 11.
Supply, miera 10.
Possession, Estate, mulc 4.
FURNITURE.

GOURD, qarɛa, xijr вg.
Pumpkin, yaqтuin.
Long Purple dᵒ bâdinjân.
Squash ? cousâ.
Cucumber, kiyâr.
Rough dᵒ ɛajour.
Long dᵒ tesrouᴧ.
Girkin, ẑoṛbous 11.
Melons, buтuik.
Unripe Melons or Girkins, faqqous.
Water Melon, jabûᴧ, ᴧɪ
[Pumpion ?] raɣɣu, вg.
Pomegranate, rommân.

GOVERN, ʊa oɴcom (judge).
Administer, sous.
Appoint, ɛayyin.
Arrange, nuggum.
Controul, icgum.
Destine, qaddir.
Direct, arxid, seddid.

Dispose, dabbir.
Dispose of, Dictate to, tayarraf bi.
Enact,) ixras.
Institute, } onyob.
Legislate,) sonn sonna.
Establish, 'eyyid.
Guide, ihdi, chdi.
Hold in, oǎbor. Invest, qallid.
Install, waȝȝuf.
Manage, adier. Ordain, orsom.
Organize, reccib.
Prescribe, farriz salaihi.
Post, Station, nayyub.
Present to office, wajjih.
Regulate, wâfiq, rettib,
Register, qayyid.
Reign, temellec. Settle, reccin.
(Dominate), tesellat sala'.
Rule, isteuli sala'.
Superintend, bâxir.
Tyrannize,) jour,
(Domineer), } tefarsan, ojbor.
POLITY, SET, BID.

THE GOVERNMENT, el ñöcouma.
Administration, idâra.
Politics, Policy, siyêse.
The Executive? } el ǎabâra.
High Police, }
The Ministry, el nazra, arcên el daula.
Post of Minister, wezêra.
A Minister, wezier 6.
Overseer of Finance, nâzur el mâliya.
Prime Minister, el wezier el aczam; yadâratoh.
Privy Councillor, serieriey.
Secretary, cêtim el sirr.
The Chief Secretary of the Embassy, el cêtim el awwal li esrûr el sofûra.
Holder of the Privy Purse, 'emien el yörrat el homâyounieya.
Board of Finance, majlis el mâliya.
The Cabinet, el majlis.
The Exchequer,) majlis el
The Treasury, } kazna, kaznat el mâliya.
The Civil Service, el melcieya.
The Service, el kidma.
The Soldiery, el cascerieya.
Civilians, el medniey.
The Military, el casceriey.
The Guard, el xorra.
Commander of the Guard, wâli el xorra.
A Functionary, mowaȝȝuf.
Counsellor, moxier.
OFFICERS, POLITY.

GOVERNOR, wâli, waliey 8.
Judge, ñâcim. Pasha, bâxâ' 2.
Judgment Hall, mañcema.
Lieutenant Governor, motesellim.
Viceroy, nâyib, *pl.* nowwâb.
Vicegerent, qâyim maqâm, qaimaqâm.
Ruler, moteyarrif.
Administrator, modier.
Leader, Prefect, qâyid, *pl.* qowwâd.
Magistrate, qâǎu, *pl.* qoǎǎâ.
Sheriff, ara' 2.
Mayor, xaik el belda.
Alderman, xaik *pl.* maxâyik.
Military Governor? Minister of

War? moxier el mocascer
[*counsellor of the camp*. Ctf.
renders it Governor-General].
Palatine (kind of viceroy),
 kadicwi? esp. of Egypt.
Chamberlain, flâjib 7.
Constable, jilwâz 13.
Serjeant, qawwâs (*archer*).
Beadle, txâ'oux.
 OFFICERS, POLITY.

Gown, θeub, *pl.* θiyâb.
Robe, qonbâz. Petticoat, fistên.
Dress robe, qaftên, xâya, mo-
 yabbafa.
Stole, barraxien, *pl.* barârix.
Outer Gown, Smock, qabâ.
Quilted Frock, jobba.
Shirt, qamier 9, 8, 10.
Woman's Gown, montêna.
A Wrap, molteflaf.
Surplice, teunieyn, *pl.* towan,
 citouna κιθων, χιτων.

GRAIN, *s*. Corn, floboub.
A Grain, flabba, qamfla.
Seed Corn, taqâwa, taqwiya 11.
Winnowed Grain, doriek?
Seed, zerc. Pip, bizr, bizra.
Crop, falla 4, 5.
— mausim (season) 11.
Cut Crop, xokar?
Harvest, flaxâd.
Yield, mafixoul 2.
Wheat, flunta, qamfl.
Best Wheat, borr.
Maize, dora, dorâ, ꜱorra.
White Maize, dorâ Xâmiey.
Yellow Maize, dorâ Muxriey.
Millet, ꜱorra boiXa.
— flabb el xarâniq.

Barley, xacuir. Rye, jâwidâr.
Oats, karral, xauflân, horto-
 mân ᴀʟ
Rice, rozz (arozz).
Seaame, simsim.
Panicum, dokn.

GRAND, jaliel.
Great (*lit.*), cebler 5, (*fig.*)
 ꜱaʒuim 5.
August, Aweful, mohieb.
Illustrious, bêhir.
Imperial, homâyouni.
Lofty, Sublime, sêmi, seniey.
Mighty? fakiem.
Majestic, majied.
Respectable, Portly, mobajjal.
Reverend, mowaqqar.
Right Honourable, mocaʒʒam.
Splendid, fâkir. Stataly, fairân.
Stupendous, ꜱajjâb.
Superb, mofakkir, moftekir.
Venerable, moflteram.
 EXCELLENT, EXCESSIVE,
 BIG, HIGH, PROUD.

GRAPES, ꜱunab.
Purple Gr. ꜱönnâbiey.
Unripe Gr. flayrim, cixmix,
 qixlemix. Raisins, zebieb.
A Vine, cerma 3, dâliya.
Sultanas, cixmix.

GRASS, *s*. flaxiex 11.
Blade, xetle 3. Herb, ꜱöxb.
Sea Weed, qaxx el baflr.
Herbage, celâ, χιλος.
Tare (in corn), ziewân.
Milfoil, barbarâ.
Clover?) ribba, föyya.
Lucerne?) qorr, yaunaja.

Fern, serkas, bitâria.
Nettle, qariev? Moss, osonna.
Thistles, qarrab?
Chickweed, rufllob.
Grass cut for horse, qavuil.
Tuft, Clump of Grass, quyl 10.
Hay, θian. Lucerne, barsiem s.
Straw, tibn. Stubble, qaxx.
Turf, Green sod, kiλra.

GRAVE, s. torba.
Tomb, qabr 3.
— of saint, mezêr.
Burying Place, ⎫ maqbara.
Tombstone, ⎭
Sepulchre, maqbar, madfan, madfana.
Cemetery, marqad 11, mehjas F. marâfl (resting place; also *stable*). Catacomba, lofläud.
Sarcophagus, lafld 3.
Burying place of a Mohammedan hero, maxhod? [but in GN. maxhed is the bier or hearse of the Sultan].
FUNERAL.

GRAY, Grey, *adj.* axheb.
Brindled, monaddar.
Checquered, sarranjiey.
Dappled, moxaflwar.
Freckled, abrax. Piobald, ablaq.
Mottled, monaqwax.
Speckled, monaqqar, moneccet.
Spotted, arqar, arqax, elâjib?
(ܐܪܩܛ n. Bariolé).
Spotted as leopard, monemmar.
Silvery, fuλλuiy.
Streaky, mobarqax.

Striped black and white, arqam.
Striped *pink*? axcel. COLOURS.

GREASE, s. zefer (any rich food).
Grease, Fat, dasem.
Tallow, Ghee, dohn.
Lard, Suet, xaflm.
Dripping, ruqrâq, rorâfa?
— sacêr (lees). Olive oil, zeit.
Lees of sesame, cosb.
Oil of sesame, sieraj.
Butter (salt), semnn nu.
— (fresh), zobda nu.

GREEDY, xarih, xarhên.
Covetous, râmis, mostccθir.
Craving, qârim, moqterim.
Eager for, flaricy ralo'.
Famished, melhouf.
Gluttonous, molhif, nessêf.
Hungry, jausân.
Predatory, moçtêl.
Rapacious, kâtuf, karrâf, çâvub.
Ravenous, nehim, menhoum.
Starving, hebyân.
Voracious, 'ecoul, 'eccêl, lehoum, milbêm, mosterur.
DEVOUR, STINGY, UNJUST.

GREEN, *adj.* akλar.
Greenish, mokλurr.
Verdant, mokaλλar.
Intensely Green, akλar fládiq o.
Bright Green, flstéqiey.
Dark Green, auraq.
Olive Green, zeitouniey.
Verdigris coloured? zinjâriey.
Black Green, adhem. COLOURS.

GREENS (eatable herbs), kaλrawêt. — lafiana s. λαχανα.

Cabbage, coronba ʀʌs.
Head of Cabbage, malfouf.
Cauliflowers, qarnabicт.
Broccooli, zenbouт 11, qaliebêt.
Asparagus, helyoun.
Spinach, esbânij, isbânik.
Artichoke, ɖarxouf ʙ.
  'erʎuxauce, ᴀʟ. Food.

Grief, s. ɖözn. Chagrín, xajab.
Affliction (state of bereavement), fajâsa.
Affliction (suffocating grief), ɾoyya 10 ʙ.
Agitation, uʎturâb.
Anguish, ɖayar, ɖöyra.
Anxiety, ʎöjra, hcmm 3.
Care, Solicitude, sanâ, ɾunâya.
Concern, ictirêθ.
Disquietude, texwiex, hedas.
Distress, ʎuiqa, ʎaiq.
Emotion, xajou. Sadness, cê'bn.
Gloom, Melancholy, scud.
Mortification, iɾtimâm.
Perplexity (Stupor), ɖaira.
Regret, te'essof.
Sorrow, cerab, corba, corâba.
Trouble, inzisâj. Pains, sanâ.
A Trouble (grave affair), mohimma 2 s.
Vexation, ɾamm.
Vexatious affair, belxa ʙ.
Woe, belâ, belieya 14.
  Anger, Disaster, Grieve, Wretched.

Grieve, vs. See Aggrieve.
Grieve vn ɖzen sala'.
Ache, wajas yajis; tewajjas.
Smart, imʎaʎ (sic).
Deplore (sing Dirge), irθi li.

Be Dejected, ikɖs.
Be Concerned, icteriθ.
Lament, teɖasser.
Moan, nouɖ. Mourn, ondob.
Regret, Rue, iɾteqid, te'essof.
Repine, inɖayur c. inqahir ʙ.
Be Pained, i'lem, te'ellem.
Be Sad, teseudan.
Sigh, tɔ'êweh.
Sorrow, icterib. Cry.

Gripe, vs cerbix
Grasp, ocbox, ecbix.
Pinch, ocmox, ecmix.
Clutch, Extort, oqmoт.
Grapple, sarbax, karmax ?
Clench, yörr. Nip, oqrox.
Clip,   ) ecizz sala',
Grip,   } ontox,
Pinch,) qarruʎ sala'.
Clasp, texabbcθ bi, inxabiθ bi (inxabuт biʙ.), texanqax sala'.
Cling to, tcrarbax fie, tekarmax fie, tecerbax bi, tecebbax bi, cerbix li, tecelleb bi.
Cling to, incemix ila' ʙ.
Hold to, inmesic ila'.
Hold by, temessec bi, temeoccm bi, tenaxxab bi.
Tighten, xidd, qannîb.
Wring, uɖziq, ɖazziq.
  Catch, Hold, Press.

Groin, s. kinn (konn) el wirio; arniba, arnima, ɖâlib 12 ʙ.
— (more classical), ɾabn θ, maɾbin 11, rofɾ.
Os sacrum, sajb. Coccyx, ɾibb.
Anus, maqsadn, kâtim 12 ʙ. ᴘ.
Fundament (Seat), maqsad.
Pubes, câna, pl. söwan.

Grow, *vn* inxâ, intcxi; *fig.* izdâd.
Grow up, onmou, inmi; teraqqâ.
Bud, bozz, barcum.
Bloom, zehhir, ocqod el zehr.
Blossom, nawwir.
Burgeon, cemmim, tezerrar.
Germinate, } zerric B.
Shoot, Sprout, } onbot, nabbit.
Thrive, yuflfl, teracrac.
Flourish, izkar.

GUARD, *va* uflric, isteflris sala'.
— afiriz, ikfir.
Convoy, } raffir, ŗâfir,
Escort, } kaffir.
Cover, ŗaTTu (oclou F.).
Defend, ufimi, flâmi can, dâfic
can; flarris-oh, flaaair-oh, min.
Keep, o̱ifoʒ, waqqi.
Keep eye on, hcmmin sala'.
Patrol, keep ward, côss.
Patronize, ajier (*rio*) B.
Preserve, ucyum.
Protect, waqa yaqi, waqqi can,
itleqi.
Save, Spare, flâfiʒ.
Screen, aêri (dâri B.).
Secure, êmin, yöun.
Shelter, êwi, uflmi.
Tend (the sick), dâri, côul.
Watch, onror, ikfir.
Watch over, wâcu.

GUN, *s.* micflala, bârouda 12,
bondiqieya 11.
Musket, tofence.
Pistol, Tabanja, farad.
Rifle, bârouda mobarrama.
Battery, baTarieya, madâfic
mojehbezo B.
Cannon, midfac 11.

Howitzer, mihrês 11.
Mortar, hewân 4.
Firearms, esliflа nârieya.
Cannon Ball, Taub 4.
Ball, jolla 10 (coura D. BT.).
Bullet, rayâyâ (bondoqa, D. BT.).
Shot, qowây (qowês).
Small Shot, kardaq, raxx.
Slugs, ruxx kanin.
Bomb, Shell, bomba, qonbara.
Powder, bâroud.
Priming, aekiera.
Cartouch, qarrâs; foxcet bâ-
roud; fouxice; cömâr bâroud.
Cartouch box, beit bâroud.
Stock of gun, qondâq el bârouda,
kaxab el micflala B.
Barrel, mâyöura 12 (*tube*).
Breech, baurima.
Muzzle, fomm?
Pan of gun, jorn, fâliya.
Touchhole, borma B.
Trigger, raqqây (*dancer*).
— zinbarec (*watch-spring*).
Guard at trigger, setêr.
Hammer, miqlab.
Cock, dicc, tecc.
Cock with hammer (?) jaqmaq,
xaqmaq, zenâd. FIREIRONS.
Sight of Gun, niexân 11.
Percussion Cap, qabac.
Wadding, lobda.
Ramrod, mideco.
Bayonet, zeŗâya, flarba 5.

HAIR, *s.* xacra 3 BU.
*Horse*hair, sebieb, zebab.*
Bristles, holba, BU.
Beard, liflya, *pl.* liflа'.
Bearded Chin, aaqon 3.

Shag on Face, ⎫
Whisker? ⎬ scbab *
Downy Beard, zcṛab.
Fine Down, zoṛaib.
Bird's Down, ziff.
Eyelash, hodb el rain.
Moustache, xârib 12.
— xanab 2 *pl.* xawânib к. в.
Cat's Moustache, moŝêl ?
Lock of hair, wafra ʀ.
qöʒʒa, maqyöuy в.
Tail of hair, jomma.
Hair in mass, limma, lomma.
Tuft of hair, xarrâba 11.
— qonbara. Curl, jaɛda.
Front curl, тöттп.
Topknot, ṛorrn. Tress, jadiele 11.
Braid, ẋaira 3, ẋaθera 11.
Ringlet, ṛadiera 11 в. zêlif c.
ɲalqat (10) xaɛт, koyla 10 в.
(*tuft*?).

Hammer (of iron), mirzeba.
Sledge Hammer, muттaqa.
Joiner's Hammer, jácouj ᴀʟ.
Hammer of firelock, miqlab, jaqmaq (Gun).
Mallet, doqmâq ᴀʟ.
Rammer, Thumper, miejana.
Wooden Bat or Mallet, midaqqa, *pl.* madâqq.

Hand, *sf.* yed, *pl.* eyâdi, cidi.
Fist, qobẋa, el yed el maтbouqa.
Back of hand, qifâ el yed, ẋahr (ظ) el yed.
Hollow of hand, ceff (3) el yed.
Palm, râɲ(a). *Finger,* uybas 11.

Happen, *vn* uɲdaθ, yuir li, ijri li.
Befal, *vs* ayuib, *vn* uɲval.

Chance, nydif, ittcɓq.
Come about, teɲawwal, te°êtâ.
Fall out, waqas yaqas.
Occur (by ill-luck), ucraẋ.

Happy, maṛbouт, moṛtebuт.
Auspicious, maimoun.
Blessed, mobâreo.
Fortunate, sesuid, meaɾöɛd.
Lucky, bakieт, mabkouт.
Prosperous, nâjiɲ, mofliɲ.
Successful, fâyiz, mowafɓq, moqbil.

Harbour, *s.* miena, *pl.* ma°in.
Basin, ɲuuẋ, *pl.* ɲuyâẋ.
Dock, bont в.
Sea Port, escole 11 в.
Stairs, Landing Place, escele.
Stocks for ship, sqâla c.
Naval Mart, bandar 11.
Pier, jiɛr li marâcib.
Quay? rayf, rayuif (Breakwater).
Road for ships, marso' 11.
Watering Place for ships, maurid 11.
Port, forda ʀ. Dike.

Harness, *s.* ɾöddat *or* ᴛaqn el kail. Trappings, rakt.
Saddle, for riding, serj 3.
Bridle, lijâm 8. *Whip,* miqrasa.
Fetter, qaid 4, 3. *Car,* saraba 2.
Horse-collar, zinâq.
Horseshoe, nosl.

Hasten, Haste, *vn* isteɛjil, ezmis, inhaẋ bi, bâdir.
Bustle, *vn* iktabiт.
Fidget, teqalqal. Hurry, ihras.
Scamper, herwil.

Scud, tezeꟼlif.
— as ship, injac ʙ.
Scuffle, oꭇꭇof, dabbio.
Speed, esriꭇ, iꭇꭇam ?
Urge, Press on, ꭇn sêriꭇ.

Hate, va icrah, istaqbiꟼ.
Abhor, omqot. Detest, obꭇoꭇ.
Abominate, istcbxiꭇ.
Decline, va i'bû, izꭇal ꭇan.
Be Disgusted, ibxaꭇ, tccerrah min, oqrof, teqarraf ꭇan.
Be Ashamed of, ikjal bi.
Disdain, ⎫ i'naf;
Scorn,   ⎭ istenciꭇ, tecêram, ꭇan.
Dislike, ꭇuif, ꭇâf, istecrih.
Execrate, ilꭇan.
Loathe, islexniꭇ.
Take Offence at, tenaꟼꟼay li ʀ. ixmir min.
Revolt from, inꭇr ꭇan.
Shrink from, ixmâzz ꭇan, teqazzez, teqazqaz, min.
Shudder at, iqxaꭇrir.

Head, s. rê's 3.
Skull, jomjoma 11.
Cranium, qaꟼf 4.
Pericranium, semꟼaq 11.
Crown, l'atc, hêm, hêma.
— yâfouq, nâfouq, omm el rê's.
Brain, dimâꭇ.   Marrow, zouz.
Marrow (brain), mokk 4.
Spinal Marrow, nokâꭇ.
Eye, ꭇain 3.   Temple, yödꭇ 4.
Ear, 'oan 4, 5.   Nose, 'enf.
Nostril, minkâr 11.
Mouth, fomm 4.   Chin, ꭇaqon 3.
Cheek, kudd 3.
Bridge of Nose, qaꭇabat el 'enf.

Headstrong, adj. jamoêꟼ.
Conceited, moktêl.
Contumacious, motenamrid.
Disobedient (son), ꭇaqouq.
Factious, fettên, ꭇou ꟼtnâ, jaubalétiey.
Froward, naqq ʙ. moqil ? ʙ.
Heretical, mâriq, molꟼud.
Mutinous, raꭇyûn.
Obdurate, jûꟼ.
Obstinate, mârid.
Obstreperous, ꭇâyuf.
Pert, Petulant, Saucy, seꟼeh.
Pertinacious, moꭇurr.
Perverse, monqalib.
Rebellious, motemarrid.
Refractory, mokâbir el ꭇaql.
Restive, ꟼaroun. Restless, qaliq.
Self-willed, ꭇanied.
Stiffnecked, lcfout.
Stubborn, ꭇâꭇu, ꭇayyân.
Turbulent, moꭇejjis, motexawwix.
Tumultuous, xaꭇoub, mixꭇâb.
Unbridled, fâlit, sêꭇib, hêmil.
Uncontrouled, motcꭇatris.
Unruly, xomous.
Untractable, waqieꟼ.
Violent, Intemperate, ꭇanief.
Wild, motewaꟼꟼux, (xaroud, nafour).
Wayward, sênir ꜰ.
Wilful, maixoum ?
Wrong-headed, ꭇabiey.

Heat, s. ꟼarr, ꟼarâra, sokouna.
Sultriness, ꟼamâwa, ꭇatm ꜰ.
Scorching heat of sun, xaub ʙ.
Summer heat, qaiꭇ.
Haziness, cedara, iktibâl.

Haze, xabwara? samâ ᴋ.
Mist, icûherr.   Fog, ḍabâb(a).
Drought, naxâf.
Aridity, qoḥöula.
Dust, ḡabâr, ḡabra ᴀʟ.
— safâr, ṣafra ʙɢ.
Fine Dust, hebwa.
Motes in sunbeam, hebâ.

Hᴇᴀᴠᴇɴ, semâ' 2.
World, donyâ. Globe, cor'a.
Sky, jawou.   Zone, mɪɴᴛaqa.
Quarter of H. kâfiq 12.
Sun, xams 3.   Moon, qamr 4.
Star, najma 3, ceuceb 11.
Firmament, falec. Pole, qᴏᴛb.
Vault of H. qobbat el semâ.
Zenith, semt el rê'a, auj el semâ.
Horizon, 'ofq, 'efâq.
Equator, kᴀᴛᴛ el istiwâ.
Milky Way, el majarra, 'omm el semâ, ᴛarieq el lebâna, ᴛarieq el tibn, doraib el tebbâna.

Hᴇʟᴘ, va essuf bi, sêsuf.
Aid, ṣôun, asuin, sâwin.
Ask aid, istesuin.
Abet, anjid, nâjid.
Advocate, ᴏebbit.
Assist, ouʏor.   Avail, ᴀᴛuil.
Back up, ḍâhir ḷ.
Bolster up, seccij.
Countenance, } woffiq,
Favour,   } ḥaʒʒu.
Forward, } maxxi,
Promote, } aqdim.
Promote (sale or circulation), rawwij.
Patronise, ajisr.

Prop up, esnid, sênid.
Prosper, najjih. Succour, aṭieᵭ.
Reinforce, sêsnd.
Ask Succour, isteṛieᵭ.
Uphold, Support, sâḍad.
Vindicate, Plead for, nâḍul san.
    Sᴜᴘᴘʟʏ.

Hᴇʀʙ for food, baql 3.
Potherb, sobzewa c.
Roots (esculent), joṣour.
Pulse, mâx c.   — qaᴛâniey.
Greens, koḍra 5, kaḍrawêt.
Onions, baṣal.
Spices, fonb, (in food) qiʒḥ.
Potherba, sobzewêt.
Endive, hindiba.
Succory, xiccurieya.
Celery, cerafs bostêni.
Parsley, baqdounis c. cerafs.
Watercress, qarra, jarjier el mâi.
Cress, raxâd.   Lettuce, kass.
Fennel, xomra.
Skirrett, ceráwieya, aciseroun.
Chervil, aᴛrielel.
— cozbara kaḍrâ.
Purslain, forfuḥuin.
— rijlâ, ḥauc ᴋ.
— el baqlat el ḥamqâ.
    (Savory Herba, qiʒḥ.)
Mint, nasnâs.   Savory, sester.
Spearmint, namâm.
Sage, mariemiya.
— sélibieya, el naṣama, qawwiese ᴅ.
Thyme, ḥaxâ ᴅ.
Wild Thyme, kalindrâ.
Rosemary, ᴛôbsiterân.
— icliel el jebal.
Anise, xibitt.   Fᴏᴏᴅ.

(Medical Herbs.)
Aconite, boix.
Camomile, bàbounaj, aqßawân.
Cyperus, socâda.
Elleborine (B), zermouze, damxaqieya.
Hellebore, karbaq.
Hemlock, zauceràn.
Hyssop, zoufâ. Rue, sedâb.
Hopa, flaxiexat el dienâr.
Mallowa, kabieze 11.
Sorrel, ßömmâï, ßömmaiï в.
Sea Holly, xeuc el baßr.

HIDE, vn ikſa' (ep yokfa'), iȼba', istekß. Abscond, tewârâ.
Lie Hid, ikteß, tckoffâ.
Lie in Ambush, icman, tecemman, terawwaf, orbot (sic в.) irbaɣ? terabbuɣ.
Lurk, iktil, tekattel.
Lie in Wait, orɣod, teraɣɣad.
Skulk, iknie. Sneak, indies.
WATCH. KEEP.

HIDE, ea ikß, akß.
Bury (corn in pit), utmir.
— (a corpse), idfin.
Conceal, octom.
Cover, fatru (oclou ɣ.).
Cover up, tömm (stop up, fill up).
Cloak, fig. labbis, oɼxou, aɼxi.
Entomb, oqbor. Screen, aêri.
Mask, fig. ostor.
Secrete, Hoard, kabbi.
Shroud, lit. ceffin, fig. idfin.
Suppress, idsaa sun?
Veil, ußjab. KEEP.

HIGH, adj. câli, fig. motecâli.
Lofty, caliey, xâmik, xêhiq.

Sublime, sêmi, seniey.
Elevated (or Subtle), raflec.
Prominent, lit. nêti, lit. or fig. bâriz.
Supernal, salawiey.
EXCELLENT, GRAND, PROUD.

HOLD (fast), ea imsic.
Keep hold, amsic bi.
Hold (contain actually), ußwi, ußtewi cala'.
Hold (contain potentially), wescs ycsic; sês.
Hold (one's breath), ußbis cala'.
Hold in, oïbor (GOVERN, CONFINE).
Hold up, Lift, irfac.
Hold up, Uphold, sâïud (HELP).
Hold back, off, down (see STOP).
Handle, moss. Embrace, sâniq.
Comprize,   ) teïammon cala',
Comprehend,   ) ixtemil cala', oxmol.
Detain, Retain, ßôux.
Encompass, ictenif.
CATCH, GRIPE, KEEP.

HONOUR, ea ecrim, cerrim.
Admire, tecajjab min, isteßli, istesgum (overrate?).
Cultivate (Lat. observo), dâri.
Dignify, bajjil в. с. x.
Elevate (in Rank), irfac, (Raise) raqqi.
Be Enthusiastic for, hiem hi в.
Esteem, acuzz. Exalt, calli.
Glorify, fakkir, majjid, amjid.
Magnify, caggum.
Aggrandize, fakkim.
Praise, oßmod (theol.); imdaß, messi.

Prize, istejied, terannam, isternim.
Promote (in station), aqdim.
Regard, ustebir.
Respect, unterim (sic B.).
Revere, Venerate, waqqir.
Signalize, Make Signal, novy talaihi.
Tend (pay attention to), rásu.
Value (set value on), nûfis, tenâfes fie.
Welcome with high honour, istenjib.

HORSE, s. Ωuyân 2, 8, 10.
Horses, kail, koyoul.
Cavalry, kiyâla, forséu.
A Steed, Charger, jawâd.
A Stud, Ωalba, r. tawâla B.
Bloodhorse, Ωuyân 'cyuil, co-Ωuil, coΩuilân.
Racing Stud, Ωulbat el sibâq.
Nag, Hackney, Roadster, cediex 10.
Palfrey, Ambler, rehewân.
Mare, farea 3, 4, 9.
(Filly) foraise. Foal, felwou.
Colt, mohr, pl. mihêra.
Beast for riding, recouba, marcoub (a shoe!).
Packhorse, } zêmila 12 B₁.
Sumpter horse, } culgo, dâbba, pl. dawâbb (beast).
(Parts of Horse.)
Mane, sórf 10.
— masrufu (place of mane).
Crest (of stallion), cêhil 12.
Withers, Ωâric, Ωauree.
Ridge of back, xinkâb?
Rump, cefel 3. Croup, cajoz 4.

Shoulder, mancib 11.
Barrel, joΘΘa 10, badan 4.
Belly (interior), jauf.
Flank, Rib ? ðulz 3, 4.
Hip, Ωurqafa B. Leg, qàyima 12.
Foreleg, airâs, pl. earoe.
Forefoot, yed, pl. eyâdi.
Hindfoot, rijl, pl. aijol.
Hough } cerzöub,
(bend of leg), } zörqoub.
Pastern, beit el xicêl.
Fetlock, rosf 4, zorr 4.
Hair at Fetlock, Θonna 10 B.
Horse-hair, ecbieba, zebab.
Horsetail, acil (lappet).
Forelock, nâyuya 12.
Solid hoof, Ωâfir 12.

Hot, adj. Ωarr; vulg. especially of culinary heat, sokn.
Hot, fig. Ardent, Fervid, Ωâmi.
Scorching, Suffocating, moxawwib. Lukewarm, fêtir.
Sultry, ratim. Muggy, wakim.
Stinging, } leaaês,
Peppery, } Ωurricf.
Pungent, xaaicy, Ωâdiq.
Warm, act. dâfi (cherishing), pass. dufyân.
Torrid, ramid. Arid, qâΩul.
Parched, Singed, xâyir.
Dry, yabis, yâbis, nâkif.

HOUSE, dâr, pl. dour.
Arch, Ωunâya. Cellar, celâr.
Door, bâb 9, or pl. abwâb.
Kitchen, marbak. Lock, râl 2.
Laundry, marsila? Roof, seqf.
Room, beit 3, ouda 2, 10.
Window, xabbêe 11.
Area, Ground Plot, sêΩa.

ANGLO-ARABIC VOCABULARY. 77

Yard, } vaßa 3.
Inner Court, } ßaux al.
Story, rabaqa. A Flat, daur 4.
Stairs, darj. Gallery, mamxa'.
Staircase, sellem 11 (*ladder*).
Lobby, Passage, dchliez.
Corridor, tarma, Bg.
Cloister ? rawâqa.
Veranda, } xebnaxien, Bg.
Balcony, }
Arched Recess, iewân.
Balustrade, darabzoun.

HURT, *va* àörr.
Damage, kassir, naqquy.
Impair, akill bi, wecis yecis (*detract*).
Incommode, θaqqil sala'.
Infringe upon, iθlim bi.
Pain, ellim, wejjir, aujir.
Pinch, Stint, nécid, neccid sala'.
Ruin, ikrib. Spoil, inzes.
Wrong, sou* ila', esie sala'.
AGGRIEVE, DECAY, DEFORM, DESTROY, DISTURB.

HURTFUL, *adj.* moðurr.
Baleful, } tesnis, motsus.
Pernicious, }
Baneful, wabiel.
Calamitous, sajous.
Damaging, moksir.
Detrimental, mokill.
Disastrous, } naßus,
Sinister, } menßöus.
Ill-omened, mex*oum, *vulgo* maixoum.
Mischievous, mouai.
Noxious, aou êfa.
Poisonous, mosimm.

Ruinous, Wasteful, mollif.
DREADFUL, PAINFUL.

HUSBANDRY, Tillage, ßurâθe, fîlâßa.
Tilled land, felloußa 11.
Plough, mußrêθ 11.
Oxen and Plough, faddân 8.
Ploughtail, lisên el faddân.
Ploughshare, sicce 10.
Yoke, nier.
Reaping tool, mußyad.
Digging tool, mußfar (SPADE).
Sickle, minjal. Scythe, miklâ.
Pruning hook, xafra.
Hoe, Pick, miszeqa.
Harrow, θels, *vulgo* mislasa (also *trowel*).
Flail, midaqq, miðrab (ðarbac.).
Roller, mindarounu (milêse c.).
Watering pot, } miraxxa.
Waterer, }
Winnowing Shovel (*vannus*), mirfax, miarâya (minsef c.).

IDLE, *adj.* ceslân, cesoul.
Careless, molchêwin.
Dawdling, motewâni, motebâtru.
Dilatory, lâbiθ, motesawwiq.
Forgetful, motenêsi, nessé.
Heedless, ĝâfil. Helpless, kâmil.
Inert, kâdir. Languid, saxil.
Inattentive, mohimil.
Indolent, molerehhil.
Lazy, cêhil. Listless, rakou.
Leisurely, motemehhil (also, Long-suffering).
Negligent, mornffil.
Poltroon, tinbal.
Remiss, moterâkus.
Slothful, motecêsil.

Slovenly, } lecis,
Sluttish, } motelécis
 (also, Temporizing B.).
Slow, baruis. Sluggish, belied.
Sottish, sátul.
Spiritless, qaliel el himma,
 qaliel el marouwa.
Supine, monáājis.
Tardy, mobru, wakricy (*belated*).
Trifler, motelchbi, subbieϴ.

ILLNATURED, rodi el nicya.
Atrabilious, seudâni (choleric).
Austere, Stern, sârim.
Crabbed, motobarrim.
Cross-grained, sawuiy.
Envious, ϑayŏud.
Ferocious, xaris.
Fretful, ϑardân.
Imperious, qâhir (*also* Pettish).
Irascible, raŏub.
Malicious, kubieϴ, xionier.
Morose, nâxif (*dry*).
Peerish, uccid. Snarling, cexir.
Perverse, monqolib.
Quarrelsome, monêzis.
Querulous, xcoicy.
Snappish, Petulant, monâqir.
Spiteful, ϑaqoud, maqit, mob-
 tḟri sala'.
Surly, Dogged, mosafrar.
Testy, Touchy, } xosticy,
Queer, Crusty, } mosxout B.
Unfeeling, Heartless, jâõ.
CAPTIOUS, CRUEL, HEADSTRONG,
 ROUGH.

IMITATE, ca iqtedi.
— sluvishly, wáḟid.
Ape, qallid.

Follow close, têbis, tetebbas.
Resemble, ϑâci, teqayyaL
Ilc-present, onqol. FOLLOW.

IMPROVE, *os* ajied, juwwid.
Ameliorate, } ϑayyun,
Better, } rayyub.
Amend, ayluϑ, yulluϑ.
Benefit, afied. Perfect, ccmmil.
Chasten, PUNISH, sazzir.
Correct, asdil, saddil.
Consummate, atqin.
Polish, Prune (style), heaaib.
Rectify, ϑaqqif, qawwim,
 yaϑϑuϑ, soddid.
Redress, céfi (*recompense*).
Refine, Purify, zeei.
Reform, *eddib. Ilctrieve, dâwi.
Repair, Patch, rommim, ramrim.
Train, roud, rawwud, darrib,
 *ellif. EXERCISE. ADORN.

IXCITE, *ca* ϑarrud, istcϑueϴ,
 aḟri sala'. — ϑuϴϴ, ϑaXX.
Animate, ϑammi, nukki.
Arouse, } aϑeq, aqicm.
Rouse, } anϑud, istcnhuJ.
Awakên, eshir, nabbih; aiqas,
 youquz; yaϑϑu (*to sobriety*).
Fill with Ardour, } istchimm,
 or Vchemence, } aϑmis.
Drive (*lit. or fig.*), souq.
Encourage, xajjis.
Excite, ϑarrie. Fret, ϑarrid.
Exasperate, ϑarrix.
Impel, ϑammil ilu'.
Inflame, ruḟib (*with desire*).
— (*with fierceness*), arḟi.
Inspirit, naxxut.
Instigate, heyyij.
Invite, istedsu. Kindle, eϴier.

Precipitate (one into), qaḍḍum.
Prompt, laqqin.
Reanimate, ansux.
Stimulate, Spur, rozz, ohmoz.
— mutually, ḍāzir.
Stir up (to tumult), xawwix a.
Urge (a horse, etc.), ajhid.
Whet, ḍaddid.
ADVISE, DECOY, ENRAGE, PRESS.

INCREASE, va zied, zeyyid.
Augment, anmi. Add, aẑuif.
Aggrandize, fukkim, saggum.
Aggravate, θaqqil.
Enlarge, cebbir.
Intensify, xaddid.
Enhance, salli.

INDUSTRIOUS, sesuiy, vonsa' c.
Active, samoul. Alert, qaiyim.
Assiduous, molēzim.
Attentive, monsacif, moqayyad, moteqayyid. Busy, xaṭṭūl.
Diligent, jēhid, mojtchid, mojēhid.
Energetic, xehim, ḍamies.
Enterprizing, sāzim, nadb, nojjād, mindabâ.
Laborious, xiṭṭiel.
Painstaking? Ḍaruiv, mosteni.
Persevering, mowâgub, mostemirr, modâric.
Persistent, modāwim.
Plodding, oedifl, māḍun, ou muḍna. Prompt, fāyiq.
Sedulous, mojidd.
Stirring, ḍuric.
Strenuous, jurhēm.
Thrifty, mowaffir.
Wideawake, ncbieh, ḍâṣiq.
EARNEST., NIMBLE.

INFORM, Tell (a person), va akbir, kabbir.
Acquaint, aelim, axcur.
Advertize, aslin.
Apprize, aτlis-oh sala'.
Certify, ḍuqqiq.
Direct, Guide, doll, ehdi.
Indoctrinate, faqqih.
— waṭut yaṭut.
Instruct, afied.
— (in science), karrij.
Notify, xarrif-oh san.
Prompt, laqqin. Warn, nabbih.
Teach, sallim, darris.
ADVISE, PUBLISH, SAY.

INK, ḍubr. Inkstand, muḍbam.
Inkhorn, dawâya, pl. 10 dawa'.
Sandbox, mirmala.
Blotting Paper, waraq tenxief.
Wafers, borxân.
Sealing wax, locc.
— xams lil katm.
— xams oḍmar (eswad).
Seal,) mehr,
Signet, } τâbis,
Ring,) kâtim 12.
Seal (impression), katm.
PAPER, PEN.

INNATE,) ṭariezioy,
Inborn, } maṭrouz.
Constitutional, jibilliey, majboul.
Essential, aētiey, jauheriey.
Genuine, ḍaqieṭiey.
Immanent, lēbid, lēzim, moltaḍum.
Indigenous, motlad c. motebellid.
Inherent, lēzib, mottaḍud bi.

Instinctive, Inbred, kolqiey.
Native, beladiey, bilâdiey.
Natural, ᴛabieᴄuiy, ᴛabᴄuiy.
Racy, Racine, 'eyliey.
Sterling, doᶠri ᴀʟ ᴛoᶠriey?

Iɴǫᴜɪʀᴇ, istekbir.
Cross-examine, imteflun.
Ask Explanation, istefair.
Interrogate, istefhim.
Question, isteᴄlim.
  Aꜱᴋ. Sᴇᴇᴋ.

Iɴꜱᴇᴄᴛ, dowaiba.
Crawling Insects, kixâx.
Animalcule, flöwaiyan 2.
Ant, namla, ɴᴜ.
Bee, naflla, ɴᴜ. Bug, fiafoee 11.
Beetle, joᴄl, konfese 11.
Butterfly, farâxa, ɴᴜ.
Flea, barᴦouθ 11.
Fly, ᴀobâba, ɴᴜ. 8.
Louse, qamla, ɴᴜ.
Scorpion, ᴄaqᴍb 11.
Spider, ᴄancebout 11.
Tarantula, ritteile.
Tick of sheep, qarâda, ɴᴜ.
Vermin, flaxurat.

Iɴꜱᴇʀᴛ, adkil, aulij.
Drive in (*a ɴᴀɪʟ*), ᴄammiq, ᶠawwuᴛ, beyyit.
Enter (in a book), qayyid, dawwin. Inject, bokk.
Insinuate,) dàkil, does ᴠᴘ vii.
Slip in,   ) idflax, ᴠᴘ vii.
Interlace, flabbic.
Intercalate, odroj fie, darrij, ᴠᴘ vii.
Interlard, okboy fie.
Interpolate, flaxxi fie.

Introduce, dakkil, dammij.
Intrude upon, idmaq ᴄala', dammiq.
Thrust in,) oflxor ᴠᴘ vii.
Poke in (B.),)

Iɴꜱᴜʀʀᴇᴄᴛɪᴏɴ, Rovolt, qauma.
Insurgent, moqâyim.
Rebellion, temarrod.
Outbreak, ᶠâyila 12.
Outburst, intixâb.
Sedition, Hostility, fitna.
Schism,) moxâqqa,
Secession,) infuyâl
Anarchy,) faᴄa' ᴋ.
Disorder,) iktilâl.
Riot, texeᶠrob.
Tumult,   ) θêyira 12.
Excitement,) iθêra 2.
Confusion, belbela 11, bilbâl.
Onset, fetc. Fray, mokâyama.
Din of fray, maᴄmaᴄa.
Uproar, heuxa, dauxa, ᶠauxa, ᶠauᶠa, joxxa. Wᴀʀ.

Iɴᴛᴇɴᴅ, Mean, inwi.
Appoint, sayyin.
Brood over, oᴅmor, aᴅmir.
Debate, irtêi viii.
Decide, ᴠɴ uftim ᴄala'.
Design, oqyöd.
Destine, aqyud; qaddir li, ᴄala'.
Determine, ᴄɴ yammim nefᴄeo, yammim ᴄala'.
Hasten to, Be about to, ezmiᴄ.
Meditate to, ihtimm bi, homm bi, ᴄala'.
Persist in, ayurr ᴄala'.
Plan, dabbir. Plot, cemmin li
Prepare to, istesudd, aᴄudd nefᴄeo. Project, teqaʀʀad.

Propose, Purpose, aszim sala'.
Resolve, uštemid sala', osmod sala'.
Scheme ǝgninst, teŭâraſ, teŭâyal, ralɒ'.
Undertake, bâxir fle.   THINK.
INTERCOURSE, kolta, mokâlota, iktilât.
Acquaintance, marrifa.
An Amour, suxra mas.
Communing, mofâwaḋa.
Companionship, moyâŭaba.
Company, yüŭba.
Comradeship, morâfaqa.
Connection, salâqa.
Dealings, mošâmala, tayarroſ.
Familiarity, 'olfa, istienês, mowênese.
Intimacy, indimâj, tedâmoj.
Partnership, ixtirêc, moxârace.
Relation to, with; tasalloq bi, intiseb, monêsсba.
Relations with, mowâyala, mokûlata.
Relationship, nesba, ielâf.
Society, mošâxara, ittilâf.
Traffic, tijâra.

INVERT, ra iqlib.
Intervert, orcos.
Reverse, arcis, uscis.
Pervert, Distort, imšek.
Overturn, cercib, qallib.
Upturn, cobb.
CHANGE, DEFACE, COUNTERFEIT.

JAR, zier 4. Wine Jar, qolla 10.
Small Jar, deccouja, barx 3 B.
Great Wine Jar, bâтuya 12, kâbiya 12.

Urn, Water Jar, jarra, tiefâr, bestouqa 5, 10 B.
Two-handled Jar, qarrâba.
Amphora, zelsa 10.
Vase (antique), qâroura.
Vessel, 'êniya 12, farâs 2 B.
Porcelain Bowl, soltânieya B.
A Cooler, barrâda, matarieya, hexxa, B. *vulg*. xorba.
Gallipot, martebân.
Metal (?) Vessel, mâsoun 12.
Earthen Pan, mâjour 12.
Earthen Pot, qayarieya.
Butter Pot, dabba.
Cream Dish, mizbad 11.
Milk Vessel, muŭlab 11, ŭâloub.
Pan for Curdling Milk, mirwab.
Pot of Pomatum, ŭöqqat dihên.
UTENSIL. Jva.

JEWEL, ŭölie (*cut*?), jauhera 11 (*uncut*?).
Precious Stone, ŭajar θemien or ceriem.
Agate, saqicq Yemêni.
Amethyst, jemset, cerechên, jabellaqoun c.
Beryl, ŭajar csraq.
Carbuncle, behrimân, yâqout jamriey.
Chrysolite? zebarjad.
Crystal, bellaur.
Coral, morjân, bosd.
Cornelian, (Garnet?) saqieq.
Diamond, elmâs.
Emerald, zebarjad, zomorrod.
Garnet, lasl, ŭajar Sielûn.
Hyacinth, esmanjouni, ŭajar Yemêni, yâqout Kâqâ.
Jasper, yaxim, yayb.

Onyx, caqieq? jczs c.
Opal, mehê.
l'earl, dorra 10, loulowa, pl. lâli.
Ruby, behrimân (carbuncle), yâqout aflmar, lasl (cornelian? garnet?).
Sapphire, raficr, yaqout ezraq.
Topaz, yaqout arfar.
Turquoise, fairouze(j).
Gold, &eheb. Gold dust, xaar.
Gold wire, tiel.
Precious ore, tibr.
Silver, fuxxa.
Quicksilver, ziebaq.
Ivory, sâj, sinn el fiel.
Amber, cehrobâ, cchromân.
Talc, tölq, ceuceb el 'erd.

Jocose, moherrij.
Buffoon, qaxmar, meskara, kalbouy.
Facetious, Pleasant, fecieh.
Humourous, moskin (c. sic, bis).
Ironical, hezwiey n.
Jocular, hezil. Lively, forih.
Sarcastic, mursân, teheccomiey.
Jovial, zehrâwiey.
Satirical, noctiey, hejawicy.
Sportive, mézifl.
Witty, rafiec el caql.
    Joyful, Laugh.

Join, ra wayal yayul; wayyul bi.
Add, aduif, zied fiehi bi.
Affix, elziq, lezziq.
Agglutinato, layyuq.
Annex, elfluq.
Append, calliq fie.
Associate, câxir, râfiq.
— xâric, axric.
Attach, Tackle, qayyid.

Blend, oklot.
Combine, kallut, waffiq.
Connect, auyul, wayyul.
Concorporate, alflöm, elflum.
Compact, meccin.
Couple, oxboc fie (hitch on).
Dovetail, caxxiq.
Incorporate with, xümm ila'.
Match, Couple, iqrin, qârin.
Mingle, Mix, imzej, oklot.
Subjoin, raddif.
Unite, 'efflud, wafaq yafiq.

Joyful (persou), mesrour; (event) mofrifl, moxirr, mofarrifl.
Blithe, flâbir.
Cheerful, baxoux, baxxâx, maxroufl el kâtur.
Delighted, mobtehij.
Glad, farifl, farflân.
Jocund, faroufl, mifrâfl.
Jolly, maklous (or Dissolute).
— zékir, zekkâr (exuberant).
Jovial, zehrâwiey el tabc.
Jubilant, mutrâb.
Merry, baflboufl.
Pleased, mabsout.
Touching, Impassioning, motrib.

Judge, s. flâcim.
— (religious), mofti.
Magistrate, qâxu, pl. qoxâ'a.
Counsellor, moxier.
Advocate, mobâxir.
Attorney, weciel el dacwâ.
Accuser, tébim.
The Accused, el moqterif, el methoum.
Prosecutor, moddacu cala'.
Defendant, moddusâ calaihi.

Arbitrator, weciel ɛōrɓey.
Witness, xâhid 3.
A Bribe, raxwa. Law.

Jɛo, Ewer, 'ibrieq 11.
Two-handled Jug, dauraq 11, dawaic в.
Handle of jug, ɛörwa 11 (*loop*).
Pitcher, bcllây 11.
Cruise, injânâ.
Washbason, таxт 3.
Small Jug, Milk Jug, couz 9.
Coffee-pot, becraj 11.
Teapot, xaidân.
Flagon, ѕelâⱭɑiya.
Flask (Retort), qomqom.
Decanter, bellaura.
Black Bottle, soudâya.
Stopper, Bung, sedâda.
Glass Bottle, xiexa в.
Vessel of common Glass, qozêze; qaniele, qaniena, qinniena al
Liqueur Bottle, ɛanbarieya.
Oil Cruise, modhon, midhen ?
Phial, Vial, ⱭÖnjour ғ. (ⱭÖnjoud, ᴋ.).
Cruet, Bottle, kanvar в. miqzeⱭ.
Jar. Utensil.

Jump, *vв* notт. Bound, onzou.
Caper, teⱭanⱭal.
Clear (Leap across), ᴛaff в.
Curvet, teqanᴛаr.
Dance, irquy. Frisk, irɛay.
Frolic, Rollick, imraⱭ.
Gambol, naᴛnuт.
Hop, uⱭjil. Jig, teⱭanjal.
Leap, iqflz, iqmiy, iqmis ғ. iqmis c. Play, ilɛab.
Pounce (as lion), weθeb yeθib; (*also* leap s.)

Prance, jallil. Rear, xobb.
Romp, taᴠaᴛran. Shy, ijⱭl.
Skip, ozfon. Sport, telebhê.
Spring, uᴛɓr, uᴛmir.
— at, yöul, inɛeriq, indafis, inⱭaʌiſ, inᴛabiɛ, — ɛala'.
Start, inɓr.
Swoop upon, ibwi, inyami, inquⱭⱭ, ɛala'. Run, Attack.

Just (person), ɛadiel, ɛâdil, ɛudil.
Just (thing) ; see Right.
Considerate, rawiey.
Equitable, monyuf.
Fair, mosdil.
Moderate, moqtayud.
Reasonable, moteɛaqqil.
Right, Ɑaqqâni, yâyib.
Righteous, moqsuт.
Straightforward, sedied ? yayoub?
Truthful, yadieq, yâdiq.
Upright, mosteqiem.
Virtuous, yâluⱭ. Good, Prudent, Religious, Sincere.

Keep, *vs* oⱭfoz.
— (stick to), Ⱡzcm, lêzim.
Keep safe, Preserve; waɛa' yaɛu ; auɛu ; aⱭriz, istaⱭria.
Detain, Ɑöux.
Garner ? oⱭcor, uⱭtecir.
Harvest, oⱭyöd, uⱭyud.
Hoard (in Pol. Ec.), yammid.
Hoard, Secrete, kabbi.
Hold in, Keep in, uⱭbia.
Engross, Ɑawwuт ɛala'.
Imprison, osjon.
Retain, Ɑöux, imɛic ɛandec.
Reserve, abqi, afⱭul, faⱭⱭul, isteƒⱭul.

Save up, ſlâfiʒ; uſltefuʒ bi; teſlaffaʒ ɛala'.
Store up, oʌkɒr, iʌʌekir.
Keep Stores, tezchheb, teſlawwaj, temawwan.
Treasure up, icnez.
Warehouse, okzon, iktezin.
HOLD. GUARD. HIDE. GATHER. SPARE.

KETTLE, ɾollâya (*boiler*; *teaurn*); gôgam (*sic*) ᴬᴸ
Boiler (as of steam engine), ſlalla 10 (c. ʙ.).
Cauldron, qazên 10.
Copper, kalqien 11.
Baking Pan, tâwa, tôwaiya ᴬᴸ
Frying Pan, râjin 12, miqlâya, laſlauqi ʙ.
Heater, Boiler, miskana.
Saucepan, qidra 10, 3.
Pipkin, borma 10.
Stew Pot, tenjara 11 ᴬᴸ
— dost, 3.

KILL, ɛa oqtol.
Butcher, Cut the throat, inſlar.
Massacre, ijzir.
Sacrifice, Slaughter, iʌbaſl.
Strike dead, armi. CRUSH, CUT, DESTROY, PRICK, PIERCE.

KIND, *adj.* ſlanoun.
Accommodating, mohêwid.
Affectionate, wadoud.
Benevolent, ra'ouf.
Benign, kaiyir.
Bland, molâtuf.
Civil, Urbane, cciɣis.
Compassionate (God), ſlannân.
Complaisant, moṡėyir.

Courteous, Gracious, ɛʌruf, ɛʌrouf, monɛʌruf, moteɛʌrruf.
Debonnaire, baxoux.
Delicate, Tender, raqieq.
Enduring, ɣabour.
Forgiving, ɣaſouſl, ɛaſouw.
Friendly, Kindly, ſlöbbiey.
Gentle (beast), damieė.
Goodnatured, Easy (person), moṡ́hil. Lenient, semouſl.
Longsuffering, motemebhil ʙ. (*also* Dilatory).
Loving, moſlubb.
Lowly, Meek, wadieɛ.
Merciful, raſluim (raſlmân, raſlöum). Mild, laruif.
Patient, moto'enni, mostêni.
Peaceable, sėcin.
Pitying, Sympathetic; xaſleq, xaſouq. Placable, ɾaſour.
Placid, ſlaliem.
Pleasing, Agreeable, 'enieq.
Quiet, Tranquil, morma'in.
Sociable, momtezij, rifâqieɣ.
Warm-hearted, xauqieɣ.
Well-behaved, ⎱ moſltoxim,
Well-bred, ⎰ 'edieb, 'edoub.
GENEROUS. GOOD.

KING, melic 3, meliec.
Queen, melice, meliece.
Prince, Chief, qaddâm.
Emperor, kâqân, xâhin xâh, imperâtôr.
Sovereign, ⎱ solrân,
Potentate, ⎰ kân.
Petty Sovereign, moteselrun.
Petty King, moleic.
Hetman (Chief, President), faikomân.

Despot, solrân morlaq.
Realm, Territory, molc 4, milc 4.
Reign (in date of time), cahd 3, molce? Royalty, mâlicicya.
Kingdom, memlece 11 (*theolog*. melcout).
Sovereignty, temelloc.
Sovereign Power, solra.
Domination, tesellor.
Dynasty, daula, *pl.* dowal.
POLITICS.

KINGDOM, Realm, memlece 11.
The United States, el wilâyât el mottcfluda; el mamêlic el mojtemica.
The American Dominion, el maxaikat el Amiericieya.
Territory, molc, milc 4.
Empire, selrana.
Hereditary Fief, mêlicêna.
A Country, bilâd 9, coura *ws*.
A Possession, flauze.
A Government, wilâya 2.
A Province, 'eyâla 2.
A Department, cumâla 2, *also* caml 4. Fief, iqrâca 2.
A Prefecture, } sinjâq 11,
Military gov᷾. } liwâ 8.
A District, } maqûraca.
County, Shire, }
A Jurisdiction, qaḍâ.
A Circuit, Circle, dâyira 12.
Districts, } arjâ, F.
Regions, } nawâflu.
Appanages, tewâbic.
Strips of Territory, arrâf.
Confines, flödoud.
Frontier, Limit, tckm 3.
POLITICS.

KITCHEN, marbak.
Fire, nâr 9, *fem*.
Fireirons, êlêt el nâr.
Fireplace, mouqid.
Fuel, florâqa.
Scullery, marsêl.
Washtub, Laver, lecen, mirsel.
Sink (Stone or Earthen washtub), mircen 11.
Pump, röromba.
Clout, mimsefla.
Broom, micnese.
Dustpan, foroxkâna ᴀɪ.
Metal Sieve, rirbâl 11.
Fine Sieve, minkal 11.
Flour Sieve, daqqâq.

KNIFE (for table), sicciene 11.
Butcher's knife, sêrour.
Surgeon's knife, mous, 4.
Razor, mouse' 11, mous cl flalâqa.
Clasp knife, murwa' 11.
Penknife, mibra'.
Lancet, mifyad, naxter c.
Blade, noxla 5.
Handle, nuyâb, yed.

LAD, adult youth; fetc' 9.
Stripling, yâfâc.
Young Man in prime, xâbb 4, 7, 10. Boy, rabi 9.
Boy growing up, moterarric.
Bachelor, sazib 4.
Groom, guardsman, rolâm 8, 9.
Groom, stable boy, sèyis.

LAMP (instr. of light), muxbafl.
Table Lamp, qandicl 11.
Oil Lamp, mesraja.
Hand-lamp, sirâj 10.

A Light (as candle), λau 8.
—(grand, brilliant light), nour 4.
Flambeau, mixcal, xaϲuiIa.
Brand, Torch, λarma 10.
Lantern, fânous.
A Lustre,   ⎫ najfa,
Chandelier,   ⎬ θorya,
Hanging Lamp,   ⎭ terieya.
(Wax) Candle, xamϲa 3.
Candlestick, xamϲadân.
Socket of d⁰, rûba, *ш*.
Wick, fetiele 11.
Snuffer, minτaf; miqaʏʏ or miqraλ el xamϲa.
Extinguisher, moτfa'.
Olive Oil, zeit.
Oil of Sesame, sieraj.

Lake, boЛaira 11.
Tarn, θeɾb 4, 5.
Pool, borϲe 10.
Pond, ɾadier 6, 10, manhel.
Basin, Лauλ, *pl.* 5, Лuyâλ.
Reservoir, mesqâya.
Marsh, torϲa 10 (fresh).
Morass,   ⎫ baτuiЛ 11,
Water Hole, ⎬ abraЛ 5.
Lagoon, Salt Marsh, ϲebika 5.
Fen, heur 4, 5.
Swamp, naqâϲa, manqaϲa, mostenqiϲ mâi.
Slough, Sludge, rouba.
Quagmire, ɾawwâr.
Dog, waЛЛa, *ɴш* mauЛal; τuin 4.

Land (terra firma), barr 3.
Desert, qafr.
Champaign, el bedon, faλâ.
Main Land, ⎫ el barr el 'eʏuil,
Continent, ⎬ *or* el mottaʏul.

Land, soil, 'erλ.
— earth, mould, toràb.
— region, iqliem 11.
— ground, Лaλuiλ.
— estate, qâϲ, ϲaqâr.
— country, bilâd 9.
Tract of world, ʏoqϲ.
Tracts, regions, arjâ ʏ.
Clime, qoτr 4. Zone, minτaqa.
Island, jeziera 11.
Isthmus, lisên (8) el barr, berzek 11.
Promontory, xinâk?
Cape,   ⎫ râ'ϲ,
Headland,   ⎬ ɴenab el barr.
Ness, Лarf el barr.   KINGDOM.

Laugh, *ɴ* uλЛec, teλâЛec.
— rudely, qahh, qahqih.
Banter, berrij. Giggle, cetcit.
Play Buffoon, tekalbaʏ.
Burlesque, ⎫ iqlib, imϲek,
Caricature, ⎬ oϲzoj ?
Deride,   ⎭ teleϲϲiz,
Make Fun of, temelϲiz ϲala'.
— Grimace, barnix, telaulaq.
Play Farce, taqaxmar.
Gibe, temaxqaϲ, temaxϲeh.
Insult, oxtom, xêtim.
Jest, hϲaair, hϲzzir.
Joke, ihzel. Lampoon, neϲϲit.
Leer at, Лawwiq *b.* (izwar *c.*).
Mock at, ⎫ ϲekar min, bi;
Jeer,   ⎬ temeϲkar ϲala'.
Rally (banter), hêziJ.
Ridicule, maxxiq, ihzir, ϲelak.
Satirize, ohjou, hejji (*ϲpell!*).
Sneer at, heϲϲim.
Sport with, imzeЛ maϲ, mêzuЛ, dâϲub, lâϲub.

Scoff at, kalboy (see Buffoon).
Taunt,) istehzi bi,
Twit,) ibze'.
Titter, teqahqah.
Trick (at play), vs fâmir.
    Dishonour.

Lavish, adj. bûail.
Expensive (in habits), moarif, minfâq.
Prodigal, mobair, mobaaair.
Profuse (person), fayyâl.
Wasteful, motlif, modahwir.
    Generous.

Law, xariexa 11.
Lawsuit, dasswâ 11.
Judge, Ωâcim 7.
Crime, jaram. Criminal, mojrim.
Sentence, Ωöcm 4.
Document, raco 3.

Lawful, Ωalâl (rubet.).
Allowed, jâyiz, me'aoun.
Permitted, morakkay.
Free, Open, mobâΩ.
Legal, Legitimate, xarruiy.
Proper,) moyaΩΩaΩ?
Justifiable,) vâyib.
    Fit. Right.

Lay, vs Ωött, olqi.
— hands on, imaio,
    (eccles.) waΔos (yaΔas) yedain.
Lay hold of, tcmessec bi.
Lay down (Pay, Sacrifice), sellim.
— up (money), rammid. Keep.
— in (stores), tezchheb.
— down (Prescribe), sayyin, farris. Govern. Say.
— over (Reserve), abqi, uΩaif.

Lay low, Δajjus, elqi sala' el 'erΔ.
— before (Present, Propose), osroΔ, aurid. — open, icxif.
— out (Develop, Arrange), waΔΔub.
Lay (tax) upon, cellif.
— together, lomm, ijmas.
    Gather.
Lay Eggs, bieΔ; auΔus baiΔ.
    Set.

Lead, vs qoud, uΩmil ila'.
— vs, take the lead; teqaddam, tesebbaq, tayaddar.
Conduce to, 'ewwil sala', afΔu, iqΔu, sala'.
Conduct, fawwit, wayyul, au-yul, xayyus,
Direct, seddid, arxid.
Dispose to, heyyi ila'.
Indispose to, uyrif san.
Guide, ehdi, doll.
Incline, vs rajjis, amiel, mayyil.
Induce, odsou (call).
— anjib (make obligatory).
Influence, imlic saqloh, istemlic.
    Incite, Compel, Advise.

Leaf, waraqa, nu 4.
Blossom, naur, nu, nawwâr.
Bud, xirr 4, zorra nu 5, sain 3.
Bloom of fruit, wabar.
Flower, zehra, nu 3.
Follicle? Calyx? cimm 4.
Germ, lobloub 11, jounabad Bg.

Learn, tesollam.
Be Aware, idri, tcfarran.
Become Aware, ynir wâΩq sala'.
Apprehend, adric, telaqqan.
Ascertain, Ωaqqiq, 'eccid, aiqin.

Attain, uτlas sala'.
Comprehend, ifτunbi, li, ictenih.
Be Conscious of, uʃljis bi.
Detect, ecxif san, ictexif.
Discern, xouf.
Discover, istenbuτ.
Discover a novelty, isteʃldiθ.
Feel, ʃlass. Find (to be), elfi.
Know, uτrif, uslem.
Perceive, ixsar bi, istcεxir bi, ixteliq sala' B. ʃlöss bi B.
Prove by trial, iktebir.
Study, darris.
— (a profession), tekarraj.
Understand, iʃhem, ilqan; waqif yaqif sala'.

LEATHER, jild 3.
Russian Leather, 'edicm 10.
Morocco, sektiyân.
Red Leather, ʃlaur.

LEAVE, ra otroc, kalli.
Abandon, daxxir B.
Bequeath, otroc, kallif.
Desert, zéyil.
Forsake, Relinquish, objar.
Neglect, ehmil, aφfil.
Leave off, ifraφ min, inflcc.
Let, kalli, das (before Verb).
Leave out, Omit, uʃlaif.
Pass by, fout, elφi K.
Quit, Clear off from; oklou san, min; tejarrad san B.
Vacate, tekalla' san, min.

CEASE, DAWDLE.

LEG, séq 2, 9. Thigh, fakd 4.
Ham, barn el séq.
— lobbat el séq.
Knee, rocba 10.

Kneepan, raxfa B. felcet el rocba.
Inside of Knee (poplas), musτaf el rocba.
Calf, laʃlm el séq, scmânet el rijl B. bâτ el séq (sic) c.

LEWD, Unchaste, sûhir.
Animal, adj. ʃlaiwâniey.
Bestial, behiemiey.
Carnal, Lustful, xehiey, xehwâniey.
Debauched, monhemic (sic B.), [addicted, absorbed in].
Dissipated, mofandal.
Dissolute, Incontinent, kalies.
Immoral, Corrupt, fêsid, fêsik?
Impudent, waqieʃl 5.
Impure, najis. Hardened, jâfi.
Immodest, fêsiq.
Lascivious, Libidinous (animal), xabiq. Lecherous, mosattir.
Libertine,   } fâlit,
Profligate, } falétiey.
Licentious (Audacious), fâjir.
Loose, Free, mokallaγ [sic. B. Gaillard].
Sensual, nefsêniey, neziez.
BAD, BASE, DIRTY, SHAMEFUL.

LIE, τn (flat), israʃl, teserraʃl, inseτuʃl.
— on back, istelqi.
— on face, inbaτuʃl, ibτaʃl B.
— on side, ittcci (recline), inʒajus (loll, lounge).
— at full stretch, temaddad, ixτaʃl, texarraʃl (sic B.).
Fling oneself down, intariʃl.

LIGHT (lux), s. ʒau, ʒaiya, pl. 8, aʒwiya.

Day (of daylight), nehêr 2.
Full Daylight, ᴢoflâ, ᴢaflöu, ᴢaflwa. Lustre, nour 4.
Sunbeam, xoṡâṡ 8.
Noonday light, ṛazêln c.
MORNING. SUN.

LIKE, *adj.* ᴢabich, naẓuir.
Similar, moxêcil, motexêbih.
Homogeneous, mojânis.
Agreeable (to), mohêci.
Conformable, moṭâbiq.
Co-ordinate, moṭarâbíq, motesêwí.
Affiliated with, moxârio maṡ.
In Affinity with (Congenial?), moṡâxir.

LIGHT-MINDED, Light-headed, ṭâyix. Blundering, sêhi.
Capricious, flâlâtiey ṡ.
Careless, Negligent, têric.
Changeable, motclawwin.
Fickle, qallâb, moteqallib, quloub. Empty, Silly, raqiṡ.
Flighty, Giddy, ṭâyir.
Flippant, recieo el ṡaql, hefiq.
Frivolous, ṣubbieθ, motcseqqiṡ.
Forgetful, nêsi, nessê.
Heedless, motchêwin.
Inconstant, qaxiṡ.
Injudicious, aṭyar.
Inobservant, ṛiflī, moṛaffil.
Meddlesome, foᴅöuliey.
Oblivious, ᴀêhil.
Pert, Impertinent, sefleh.
Remiss, hêmil, mohmil.
Restless, motezeszis, zêlîl ?
Saucy, Wanton, baṭrân.
Shallow, reciec el ṡulm, ṡckief el ṡaql.

Shifty, flöuwal, flöwâliey.
Unsteady, moteqalqil.
Vacillating, mokalkil, motelaklik.
Volatile, moṡṭaṭnir, ṭayyariey.
FOOLISH. BAD.

LIMB, järifla 12.
Member, ṡoᴅou, *pl.* aṡᴅâ, *lit.* and *fig.* Joint, mafṣnl 11.
Leg, sêq 2, 9.
Foot, rijl, *pl.* arjol.

LITTLE, ṣaṭier 5; (in quantity) qaliel, yesier.
Small (in body), ᴅâmir ? (*slim*).
Short, qaṣuir.
— (of stature), cêbîl.
Dwarfed, moctebil.
Puny, mamṣöuz, ᴢâwi.
Tiny, diqq, diqqiey.
Minúte, ṣöṛaiyir.
Stunted, Pygmy, moqarqam.
Paltry, kasies. Petty, nezier.
Insignificant, flaqier.
Trifling, Slender, zehied.
Scanty, flarij, qaxif (*shabby*).
Concise, moujiz.
Abridged, moktaṣur.

LOCK, ṛâl 2.
— (Egypt, céloun 12 ʙ.)
Bolt (of lock), lisên el qofl ʙ.
Padlock, qofl 4, 5.
Key, miftéfl 11.
Wooden Lock, ᴢabba 10, miṛlâq (*fastening*).
Gate Bolt, darbâs ᴀʟ
Door Bolt, mizlêj (*a slider?*), *vulg.* mizlâq; Bag. mandal (*a dangler?*).

Drop Bolt, soqqâr-a.
Fastenings, ṛaluq; miṛláq.
Bar, daqr 3.
— (wooden), kaxaba 4.
— (iron), makl 4, qaḍuib 9.
 ṅadieda.
Chain, silsile 11, zenjier 11.
Staple, rezze, also ẋabba b. 10.

Loins, ẓalab, ẓölb 4; pl. ṅöqwi?
Trunk, badan 4.
Flank, soql, ẓöql x.
Waist, kaẓr, ṅaqou 4, ṅaqwa.
Middle, wast.
Side, jânib 12, janb 4.
Rib, ḍulṣ 3, 4; or pl. aḍloṣ.
False Rib, xarxouf 11 (kilf, Gol.)
Pit of Stomach, kâẓura; noqrat el musda.
Navel, sorra 10.
Lap, ṅöjr 3; also aṅjira x.
Abdomen, ẓafâq, me'na 2, 3.
 BELLY.

Look, cm (seem to be) bien, uzhir.
— at, onzōr ila'; iqxas al terallas sala'; urralus sala'.
— for, fottix. Seek.
— out for, orẓöd, toraẓẓad.
— out; Observe, cm teraqqab.
— out (or in) upon, röll sala'.
— down upon, axrif sala'.
— into, Inspect, ofsor, istecxif.
— sideways, Turn to Look at; iltefit ila', tewejjah ila'; ilṅaz.
Gaze, ṅaldiq (Descry).
Fix the eyes, amcun el nazar, sajjir (fanjir) el söyoun.
Examine,) nâzur ṅe, sala';
Inspect, } ḥarrir sala'.

Glance at, ormoq.
Look at one another, telâṅaz.
Leer, ṅawwiq bil tain b.
Peep, buẓẓ li, barbuẓ sala'.
— (take side glance at), tejessas.
Peep, Peer, röll.
Pry, ijtiss, istebẓur.
Reconnoitre, tefarras.
Revise, Review, tcẓaffaṅ ẓ.
Scan, lâṅuz. Study, râlis.
Scrutinize, daqqiq sala'.
Spy after, orqob, râqib.
Stare, Glare, ixkar ṅe.
Survey, istexrif, komm.
View, farzin, röll sala'.
Look out for with hope, te'émal bi.
I got a good Look out; istexraft (laṅazt) jaida".
I got a clear sight, ṅaddaqt jaida". Sex.

Love, os ṅübb, aṅubb, wodd.
— mutually, toṅâbab, tesâxaq.
Be in Love, uxxaq, tewammaq? (Beloved, maumouq.)
Be Enamoured, inxarif bi. (Draw into Love, xarrif.)
Like, vs ihwi, irḍa' bi.

Love, s. ṅübb, muṅabba.
Vehement Love, xoraf b.
Love to a Woman, suxq, miqa?
Affection, wadd, widâd, mawadda, towaddod.
Affections, asrâf.
Kindliness, tosarröf.
Amity, ẓadâqa.
Attachment, taqayyod.
Familiarity, istisués.
Friendship, kaléla.

ANGLO-ARABIC VOCABULARY. 91

Intimacy, 'olfa, indimâj.
Union, ittiflâd.

Mad, majnoun.
Cracked, ⎱ raql maxrour?
Crazy, ⎰ mastouh c.
Daft, moscuscll b.
Delirious, mostehêm.
Desperate, zêlil b. (Restless?).
Frantic, secrân.
Frenzied, mosersem.
Furious, bêyij.
Halfwitted, maltöux.
Harebrained, makwout b.
Fatuous, aflmaq.
Infatuate, meh wous, mohewwas.
Deluded, mafrour.
Silly, raqies.
Wandering (in mind), hêai, metlouh el raql.
Restless? zêlil (b. Ambulant).
Angry, Foolish, Lightminded.

Make, ra usmel, ijral.
— away with, anfid, eziell.
Exhaust, Spend.
— up, compose; reccib, 'ellif, wellif, raunif.
— up for, compensate for; cêfi, rawwiĂ-he.
Make out (with eye or mind), teflaqqaq, w'eccid. See.
Make for (rn), Aim towards; oqröd, flöjj, teflarra' li?
Make off (rn), Depart, Go; ibrad, zicfl, terazzel.
Create, ra cewwin : (theolog.) okloq, ofrör, ibra'.
Build, ibni. Construct, rammir.
Fashion, hendim.
Figure, hendis.

Form, uynar (also make).
Frame, röur, rabbur.
Invent, efldiê, Ikterur.
Mould, ojbol, rayyin.
Shape, rawwir.
Originate, aujid, anxi, ardir, bâdi bi, osboq fle. Contrive.

Maker, s. rânis.
Architect, musmûr, pl. -ieys.
Artificer, rânur, morranur.
Author, monxie.
Builder, bannâ.
Composer, mow'ellif, morannif.
Constructor (of ship), maddâd.
Creator, kâliq, bâri.
Engineer, mohendis.
Inventor, moujid.
Mechanist, ⎱ rannâr.
Mechanician, ⎰
Originator, mobdi, mocewwin.

Maltreat, ra behdil.
Aggrieve, esie sala'.
Attack, iftio. Baffle, aflbur?
Beat, oĂrob, uĂrub. Bite, röĂĂ.
Blame, loum. Cheat, [oxx.
Choke (strangle), farrus.
Compel, uĂturr. Confine, ofljor.
Crush, doxx. Daub, sokmir.
Deface, xawwih. Destroy, abied.
Defame, xannur. Devour, isterur.
Disable, rarrul.
Dishonour, ifĂafl.
Disparage, istekiff.
Disturb, aqliq. Efface, afni.
Encroach, tarâwal.
Enrage, afĂub. Expel, orrod.
Frighten, kawwif, akief.
Hurt, Ăörr. Pierce, iksiq.
Oppose, kâyum, rârul.

Prick, ɡozz, ɡizz.
Quarrel, ɛn tenâzeɛ.
Rage, ɛn hicj, θour.
Rob, oɛlob. *Scatter*, boθθ, baddid.
Spoil, inzeɛ. *Tire*, etɛub.

MANKIND, 'enâm.
Man (*homo*), inɛên, *pl.* nêɛ
 [*in higher style*, 'onêɛ].
— (*vir*) rajol 5 (*properly*, foot-soldier).
Woman, mar'a (*in modern prose*, imrâa), *pl.* niɛê, niɛwa, *vulg.* niɛwân. *Child*, welad 4.
Lad, Young Man, fete' 9.
Lass, fetêya.
Damsel, jâria 12.
Person, xaky 4, zelme *nu* Al.
Individual, naɛr 4, faried 4.
Man in years, rajol mosinn.
Old Man, rajol cebier el ɛinn, cebier el ɛömr, cebier.
Gray-haired man, xâyib.
Middle-aged man, cehl c.
Full-bearded man, xaik 3.
Elder men, Aldermen, maxâyik.
Man past middle age, ektiyûr (*mod.* Syria).
Young Man in full strength, xâbb 5, 7, 10; fete' 9.
People, Folk, chêli.
Population, chliyoun.
Souls of Population, neɛêm, enêsim.
Age (of one man), ɛömr.
Stature, qâma. *Family*, caila.
Offspring, ɑorrieya.
Nation, 'omma 10.
Wedlock, zewâj.
Manhood, marjalieya.

Manliness, marouwa.
Youthful Prime, xohonbieya.
Male, ʌecer 3. Female, 'onθa' 5.

MANNER, wejh 3, jihe 2.
Course (Behaviour, otc.), ɛiera 10.
Fashion, zeiy, ceam.
Form, ɛöura. *Measure*, qadr.
Guise, Wise, nehj, minhêj.
Likeness, Example, meθel.
Method, oɛloub 11.
Mien, hie'a, hieya.
Mode, naɛlöu, ceiɛieya.
Pattern (as of lace), ɢarz, ɢurâz.
Plan, Order, namaɢ 4, 5 [*drugget* with carpet-pattern].
Process, meɛlec, meɛboulieya.
Phase, ɢaur 4.
Rote,) ɛâyida,
Routine,) tɛɛawwod.
Rule, Law, Arrangement, neɛq.
Scheme, System, minwâl.
Standard, ɛuyâr. Style, ɛibr.
Tenor, mamarr, meɛicra?
Type, Character, ɣaiɡa.
Way, ɢarieqa 11, ɛebiel 10 (*path*). NATURE. SAMPLE.

MASON, fâɛul. Masonry, qabou.
Mason's Rule, muɢmâr, ziej c.
Plummet, faidam, xaqoul B.
Line, jadwal. Pulley, becera.
Trowel, mialaɛa, miɛyaɛa, miɛrârien B. miɛcija.
Minor's Pike, muɛwal.
Ladder, ɛellem 11 (staircase); muɛɛad c. mirqa' F.
Lever, makl 4, ɛatla c.
Wedge, ɛefien, σφήν.
Axis of Pulley, muɛwar c.

ANGLO-ARABIC VOCABULARY.

Mass, *s.* cotle 10. Bolus, qorya.
Block (of houses, etc.), jamc, jamm.
Clump (of turf, etc.), qovla 10.
Cluster (of dates, etc.), ximrâk.
Group, lomma. Lump, qory 4.
Bunch (of grapes, etc.), sanqoub 11.
Heap, coumo, coum 4.
Pile, mayraba, sarma, râbia.
Handful, Qöfna, molou el yed.
Pinch, comxa, cobxa, qobâa.
Sheaf, Piece, Quantity.

Materials, mawâdd.
Stone, Qajur 5. *Earth*, torâb.
Timber, kaxab 4.
Mineral, masdan 11.
Jewel, jauhera 11.
Cement, lezêq. Pitch, zift.
Bone, salm, ḷ, 5.
Shell, yadaf. Horn, qarn 3.
Ivory, sâj. *Wool*, yöuf.
Silk, Qaricr. Feathers, riex.
Cotton, qoto. Linen, cottên.
Hemp, qinnâb. *Hair*, xasr.
Leather, jild 3.

A Meal (Repast), 'ecla [but écila, a cancer].
Second Course, yömût ôêni.
Banquet, waliema 11.
Breakfast, farôur, terayyoq.
— cear el rieq, cear el yafrâ.
Midday meal, fadû.
Luncheon, taswieda?
Supper, saxâ.
Dessert, noqla, noql.
An Entertainment, kayûfa.
A Festivity, mê'doba [a *ball*, etc.]. Food.

Measure, *s.* qadr.
Scale, Dimensions, Quantity, miqdâr.
Amount, mablaf 11.
Quantity, cemmieya.
Size, Qajm y. b. Bulk, jirm.
Magnitude, sugm.
Length, röul. Breadth, sarâ.
Width, wassa, sesa. Space.
Depth, sömq. Heighth, sölou.
Stature, qâma.
A League, farsck, malqa b. 10,4.
A Mile, miel 4. An Ell, airâs.
A Foot, qadam 4.
An Inch, uybas 11 (*finger*).
A Span, xibr 4.
A Fathom, baus 4, bâs 2.

Meat, laQma, *nu.* 3.
Raw Meat, laQm naiy.
Fresh Meat, l. rari, l. furied.
Mutton, lân; l. fanem, al
Goat's Meat, musze'.
Game, Venison, l. yaid.
Beef, l. baqar. Veal, l. sujl.
Lamb, l. kârouf al l. rali Be.
Kid, l. jadie. Food.

Meat Dish [something *cooked*], rabiek, rubie b.
Broiled bits, cobba 5.
Cutlet, xarfla (*slice*).
Fricassee, qâourma.
Fried Meat, moqlouw.
Hash, qicma c. Roast, mâxwicy.
Mince, laQm mafroum.
Stew, moscbbec.
Ragout, yaknic.
Sausage, sclsicjou.
Round Sausage, manbâr.

Stuffing, } ḍaxou,
Forced Meat, } mocmour в.
Meat Pie, raqâq maflxouw.
Compost of Pigeons, mosbec el
flamâm. Pattics, scnbousaq.
Black Pudding, sojaq.

MEDDLE with, тн inflaxur fie,
oflxor flâl-cc fie (*sic* в);
qârix, uflexi fic.
Interfere, tedâkal fie.
Intermeddle, indaflux fie.
Interpose, тн odkol bain, te-
qârax (*be go-between*).
Intervene, tcwassat.
Introduce oneself into, lâbie?
Intrude, тн idmaq sala'.

INSERT.

MEDICINE, dawa, *pl.* adwiya.
Poison, scmm. Curative, xâfi.
A Compound, morecceba.
An Extract, mostckraj.
An Essence, mostcklay.
Application, } istuflxâr.
Adhibition, }
Emetic, moтrix, moqayyi.
Laxative, morakki, molayyin.
Purgative, naqicy, monaqqi.
Astringent, qâbuX.

MELT, тн aoub. — тa aewwib.
Thaw, тн siefl. — тa scyyifl.
Dissolve, тa flöll, ifack.
Fuse, Smelt, isbic, sebbic.
Mould, тayyin, ojbol, тabbic.
Model, qaulib, meθθil.
Cast, röbb.
Form, Fashion, тöuf.

MILK, *s.* ḍalieb.
Buttermilk, dau, dauf.

Curds, raub; ḍalieb râyib *or*
mojabban.
Cheese, jubon. Rennct, mayr.
Whey, maiy, mayl; feak el
ḍalicb, mâi el jubon.
Junket, lebon [*Egypt*, milk].
Cream, ceθic, ccθéyn.
Fresh Butter, zobd.
Clotted Cream, qaimâq, AL;
qaimâr.
Scalded Cream, bairâθ.
Custard, qaxтa. Syllabub, loba.
Skim Milk, makuiX x. [mâi el
ḍalieb?].

MILL, *s.* тâflōun-a, тaflflâna.
Miller, тaflflân.
Wind Mill, тaflōun hewâ.
Sail of Mill, jenâfl (8) тaflōun.
Mill Stone, rafla'.
Quern, Handmill, jârouxa,
muтflana.
Oil Mill, mucyaro.
Mortar, hê'oun, midaqq.
Pestle, midaqqa.
Horse Mill, madâr.

MINERAL, *s.* masdan 11.
Metal, a Minc, d°.
Quarry, maflјar 11 в.
masdan flajur c.
Diggings (of gypsum, etc.),
maqâlis.
Ore, masdan kâm (*raw*).
Precious Ore, tibr.
— in the soil, cinz 3.
Gold Dust, xaar.
Gold, аebeb. Silver, fuXXa.
Bronze, teuj. Iron, fladied.
Copper, neflâs aflmar, neflâs.

ANGLO-ARABIC VOCABULARY. 95

Brass, nefiâs ayfar; ṣöfr ʙǫ. tonbêc c.
Zinc, tonbêc? Lead, rayây.
Tin, tenec, ṣafiell.
Powter, qaydier ʌʟ; qaláï ʙǫ.
Copperas, zêj. Rust, ṣadâ.
Vitriol, zêj akẑar.
Verdigris, jinzêr, zinjâr.
Steel, ꜣecier; ṣölb ʙ. *vulg.* boulâd, foulâd.
Red Lead, selâqoun, zenjifra.
White Lead, isüedâj.
Orpiment, zernick (Arsenic).
Antimony, cofil, râsckor.
Yellow Ochre, eznicên ʙ.
Common Glass, zojêj; qozêz ʌʟ
Flint Glass, bellaur (*crystal*).

Mire, larôuk.   Clay, ruin 4.
Puddle, Ooze, lâya.
Sluab, rauba (*thick milk*).
Dirt, daran, lawaθ, lauθe.
Filth, qaꜣer, qâꜣourât.
Slime (of Egypt), ibliez.
Bog Earth, waflal 4.
Dung, zibl (*litter*).
Muck, Guano, kario.
Cow or Camel's Dung, jolla, baꜣr.
Manure, sebk, dimn? damâl?
Dunghill, sibâla, mezbala.
Refuse.

Miracle, *s.* morjize 2.
Marvel, râyiꜣa 12.
Portent, biele.
Monstrosity, sekra.
Prodigy, 'osjouba 11.
Sign (*divine*), ciya 2, êya.
Wonder, ꜣajieba 11.
A Very Astonishing thing, ꜣajab rojjâb; ꜣajab el ꜣajâyib.

Mistake, *s.* ꝑaloṛ, ꝑalaṛa.
Blunder, ꝑafia; flamrana, flamarieyn (ʙ. Anerie).
Delusion, ꝑorour, iꝑtirâr.
Error, Kalâl. Folly, ꝑabâwa.
Fault, Foible, hefwa.
Illusion, ꝑaiy, ꝑaiya.
Illusive Picture, teswiel.
Infatuation, flamâqa.
An Oversight, sehou.
A Slip, zelle.
Stupidity, belêbo, belâda.

Mix, *va* oklor; *vn* viii.
Mingle, *va* omzoj; *vp* viii.
Mess up, } kabbuy,
Mash up, } okboy.
Mix up, dawwif.
Muddle (*daub*), sekmur.
Adulterate, karbur.
Amalgamate, olflöm, elflum.
Disorder, lakbur. Dilute, xoub.
Jumble, cercib; zerwur?
Shuffle (cards), ꜣarqil?
Muddy (as cattle by trampling), okbor, ꜣaccir? Confuse.

Money, darâhim, ꝑoroux.
Cash, naqd 3.
Treasure, a Hoard, kaziena 11.
Earnest Money, ꜣaraboun, ꜣörboun, and *vulg.* racboun ʙ.
Small Money, folous; xoqaf ʌʟ mayâri, mayarieyât.
Sum, Amount, mablaꝑ 11.
Money Bag, cies el darâhim.
Treasury, kazêna, kazna, kaziena.
Money Market, souq el noqoud.
Money Lender, rajol mâliciey.

Money Changer, ṣarráf, ṣaira-fley.
Money in Advance, sclef.
Rate of Exchange, cembiou.
Ease of the Money Market, seɛa naqdieṣa.
DEBT, COIN, WEALTH, TRAFFIC.

MONTH, s. xehr, pl. axhor.
Current Month, xchr jâri.
Next Month, xehr qâdim.
Last Month, x. mûẕu or bâriſl.
Solar Months, axhor xamsicya.
March, adâr. April, niesên.
May, eiṣâr. June, ſloziernân.
July, temouz. August, âb.
September, ciloul.
October, tixrien el auwal.
November, tixrien el θêni.
December, cênoun cl auwal.
January, cênoun cl θêni.
February, xobâr.

MOON, qamar (m) 4.
Crescent Moon, hclâl 8.
Full Moon, badr.
Halo, hêla, tofâwa.
Eclipse, cosouf.
— of Moon, kosouf.
First day of New Moon, ṛorra c.

MORNING, ṣabûſl.
Dawn, ṣöbſl 4. Daybreak, fajr.
The Gloaming, cl sodſa.
Early Twilight, seber.
— ṛobxa, Bɛ.
Sunrise, ixrâq or xorouq or ṭölous cl xams.
Forenoon, ṣöbſlaiṣa.
To-morrow Morning, bocra, AL bûcir Bɛ.

Of Mornings and Afternoons, bil ṛodou wa el oṣâyil ɛ.

MOULD, s. torûb.
— of sepulture, θera'.
Grave, torba.
Soil, 'crẕ, pl. 'erâẕu.
Clod, dabxa, ṣôzoq ? madaro B. midâra. Green Sod, kiẕra.
Furrow, karṭ 3. Clay, ṭuin 4.
Dust, ṛubâr, ṛubra AL safâr, safra Bɛ.

MOUNTAIN, jebal 5.
Summit, asla'. Rock, ṣakra nu.
Declivity, ſladour.
Defile, maẕuiq. Dell, houwa.
Cavern, maṛâra. Vale, qâɛ.
Neck of Mountain, xinkâb?
Volcano, jebal nâr.
Mount, jobail. Hill, tell 3, 5.
Hillock, toleil.
Wold, Fell, Down, râbia 12; rabwa, pl. roba'.
Mound, Cliff, 'ecema, nu. pl. 2 or 'eoêm.
Hump (of earth), ſladab 5.
Knoll, Dune, ceθieb (8, 9, 10 ɛ.).
Eminence, cölwa.
Ridge, ṛârib 12.
Promontory, rê's 3.

MOUTH, fomm 4 ; in high style, fûh, pl. afwâh, vulg. tomm.
Lip, xaſah·5 ; vulg. xiffa, xafa, pl. xnſawât.
Palate, saqf cl fomm, saqf el ſlalq.
Corner of Mouth, xidq 4.
Muzzle (of beast), fanṭuise.
Tongue, lisên 8, or pl. clson.

Man's Chin (bearded), ᴀaqon 3.
Woman's Chin, ɛöqꜱe.
Jaw, fecc 4.
Chinbone, ɑaɒec 4.

MULBERRIES, tout.
Raspberries, } tout xauciey.
Blackberries, } tout el ɛöllieq.
Strawberries, tout 'erᴅuiy, tout Afranjicy.

Music, mousiqâ.
Bugle, bouq 4.
Drum, ᴛabl 3, 4 (Tambour).
Kettle-drum, ɑaqqâra.
Fife, ʏaffûra.
Pipe, mâʏöula, qaʏuiba 11.
Flute, xubbâba.
Double Flute, ᴢemmâra.
Flageolet, nâi. Lute, ɛöuᴅ 9.
Persian Harp, jonc.
Clarion, ɴaficr. Trumpet, ʏöur.
Hautboy, arꜰal. Reod, ꜰâba.
Shepherd's Pipe, xommârɴ.
Viol, } comanja,
Rebeck, } rubâba.
Wind Instrument, ᴢemr, mizmâr.
Musical Instrument, êlet el mousiqâ.

NAIL, s. mismâr 11 [ᴀʟ ʋᴜlg. bosmâr].
Spike, qâzouq (to fix in ground), ɴicco 10; ɛeiyour c.
Peg, ɛöʏfouɴ. Staple, rezze.
Screw, borma, birꜰa ʙg. bariema barieꜰa, ᴀʟ
Crank, Windlass, milwa'.
Hook (to hang things on), jencel, muɛlaq, collâba.

Ring, ɴalqa. Hoop, jolba.
Rim, ᴛâra.

NATION, 'omma 10.
A People, ᴛâyifa 12 (*Tribe*).
Folk, qaum 4, kalaq.
Race, ɴesl. Sect, meᴀheb.
Breed, ᴀorrieya 2, 11.
Established Sect, mille 10.
Local Population, 'ehl, *pl.* ehôli.
Household, 'ehl, *pl.* 'ehloun.
Family, ɛaila; êl.
Clan, Sept, ɛaxiera 11.
Horde, qabiela 11 (*Tribe*).
Tribe (as of Israel), sibᴛ 4.
People, Commons, el xaɛb.
The Vulgar, el ɛawâmm.

TROOP.

NATURE (order of the Universe), ᴛabieᴄa. Build, kalq.
Character, ʏuiꜰâ, xiema 10.
Complexion, ɛejieya 14.
Condition, State, ɴâla.
Conformation, tercieb.
Constitution, kolq 4.
Essence, ɛain, ᴀêt, jauher 11.
Genius, ɛariece. Mould, jibilla.
Vein of Genius, qaricɴa.
Material, mêhieya.
Quality, kaʏla 5; *oftener, pl.* kaʏâyil. Stamp, ᴛabɛ.
Structure, tecwien.
Substance, jirm.
Temperament, micꜱêj.
Trait, ʏufa 2.

NEAR to, qarieb min.
Pretty Near, qoraib. Nigh, dâni.
Next, } weliey,
Contiguous, } laʏuiq.

Conterminous, } mottókim
Bordering on, } mottásul.
Adjacent, } mojâwir,
Neighbouring, } motejâwir.
Adjoining, motelêziq.
Neighbouring countries, boldân ajniba.

NECK, *s.* raqba 5, sönq 4.
Cervix, breadth of shoulders; sâtiq 10; *also* sôtq ? 4.
Jugulum, naflr 3.
Gullet? bottom of throat, zenr.
Cervices, qifâ (also Nape).
Nape of Neck, nauqasa.
Clavicle, terqowa 11.
Shoulder, cetif 4.
Shoulder-blade, mancib.
Point of shoulder, rommânet el cetif.

NEEDFUL, lêzim, lozoumiey.
Urgent, Necessary, lörouriey.
Matter of Duty, wâjib.
Essential, aètiey, jauheriey.
Indispensable, lâ bodd minho.
Incumbent on, monbari, molzim.
Obligatory, mafroul, farluiy.
Fundamental, 'esêsiey.
Important, mohimm.
Radical, 'esliey
Requisite, moqtala'.
Compulsory, parbiey, iftirâbiey.

NET, *s.* xabace 5.
Snare, fakk 5.
Hunter's Net, xarace 4, 10 (*pl.* xoroc). Trap, musyada.
Springe, muslâya 11.
Mesh, Qubâla 11, nesieja 11.

Lasso, miehcqa, *pl.* mawêhiq; weheq 4 x. ribq x.
Slip-knot, xanicta (*sic*) B. (*classical*, onxoura).
Pitfall, makbâya.
Fishing Line, runnâra.
Fishing Hook, d⁰ B. bâlous c.

NICE (to the palate), raiyib.
Savoury, morrâsum, motaqaddi ? (flavoury).
Palatable, mosterûb.
Pleasant, fecieh. Choice, nafies.
Delicious, lesies.
Dainty (pleasant), mezih.
Fragrant, sarur.
Exquisite, zeciey (*pure*).
Luscious, röuyâb.
Nourishing, morai, marie'.
Voluptuous (enjoyment), monâsum.

NIMBLE, raxieq, raxiq.
Agile, Brisk, xamloul, neriq.
Alert, qaiyim, naxuir.
Frisky ? faQuij B. *sémillant.*
Frolicsome, marouQ.
Lively, moteyaqqus.
Swift, kañef (*light*).
— series (*quick*), reccâl, riccied.
Fleet, sesöum x. rayyâr.
QUICK.

NOISE, *s.* lajja; (of dancers) qasf.
Brawl (of waves), sajiej.
Echo, rada', yârio 12.
Clatter, } rauxa, joxxa.
Rattle, } rawêx, qarqasa.
Hooting, puura. Hubbub, jelabo.
Bellowing (of whale), royaQ.
— (of scale, etc.), valq, urtilâq.

Hum, Rumble, duwie.
Sound, Ωass; (of feet) dabace.
CRY, SCREAM, SOUND.

NUTS (generic?), jauz.
Walnuts, jauz. Almonds, lauz.
Nutmeg, jauz ʀaiyib.
Filberts, jillauz.
Hazelnuts, bondoq.
Pistachios, fistaq.
Pine-nuts, yanaubar.
Cocoanuts, argiel (sic), nargiel (sic), narjicl; ᴀʟ foufâl, jauz Hindi.
Betel-nuts, barr, ʀanboul, teneboul, jauz Hindi. FRUIT.

OBEY, ʋa ʀouɛ li, ʀûwiɛ; classical, ᴀʀuiɛ (which also means "cause to obey"), inqâd.
Bow, ʋɴ ʀâʀui, mâʀui (sic B.).
Bow the head, ʀâʀui râsec.
Bend, ʋɴ inΩani.
Cower, Crouch, Grovel, tewâƛas.
Cringe, temescen.
Cringe to, Ωâbi-oh.
Stoop, fig. teseffel.
Do Homage, imtoθil, temeθθel.
Behave Humbly, tekaxxas, iktexus.
Submit, ʋɴ iᴀsan, adsun.
Truckle, ᴀill, teᴀellel.
Yield, Do Reverence, ʋɴ ikƛas, tekaƛƛas, li. CROUCH.

OFFER, Proffer, Tender, ʋa osʀoƛ, asʀuƛ, qarrib.
Offer a price, imcis.
Bid (in auction), mêcis, zied sala', zêwid.
Outbid? moccis.

Proclaim an auction, Ωarrij.
Hand, ʋa nâwil.
Present, ʋa aΩƛur, aurid, qaddim, 'eddi. — also abdi (open, expose, display).
Promise, ʋa waɛad yaɛad.
— used (covenant).

OFFICERS (of army, navy, or police), el ƛabʀ, ƛabûyuʀ.
The Police, al ƛabûʀa, el darc.
A Policeman, ƛabaʀuiya.
The Guard, el xorra 10.
Their Commander, wâli el xorʀa.
One of them, xorʀaiy.
Commander-in-Chief, râis el jonoud, qâyid el jaix, sirsascer.
General, 'emier, jenerâl.
Colonel, 'emier elâi.
Quartermaster, moᴀscir c.
Captain, ra'ies lil firqa.
Leader, qâyid, moqaddam.
- Chief of Garrison, moΩâfuʒ.
Warden of the Marches, Ωâfuʒ el tokoum. GOVERNOR.

OFFSPRING, s. ᴀorrieya 11, 2.
Breed, Brood, nesl.
Issue (in pedigree), solêle.
Progeny, nojl.
Lineage, Race, Stock, 'eyl 3.
Posterity, kalaf. NATION.

ONIONS, s. bayal.
Garlic, θoum. Leek, oorrêθ.
Scallion, } ciboule,
Shalot, } bayl akƛar.
HERBS.

OPINION, s. râi, pl. ar'â; marieya ɪ. morté.

(1) Assurance, uṣtimād.
Confidence, uṣtiqād.
Conviction, icqān, teyaqqon, iṣtieqān. Belief, tardicq.
Trust, Faith, icmān.
(2) Caprice, zcnrara, ccif, soudā B.
Computation, ḥusēb, moḥāscba.
Conjecture, ḥads *presentiment*.
Doubt, xccc ; momārāya.
Estimate, taqdier, tcḥarros, qiyās. Fancy, kiyēl.
Fantasy, wehmieya.
Guess, ḥazr, maḥzcra.
Idea, Notion, rouya, *vision*.
Imagination, tayawwor.
Impression on the mind (spontaneous), hejs.
Prejudice, wehm.
Supposition, tckmien.
Surmise, seema *ru*. tckawwax.
Suspicion, tohma, xobhe.
Sentiment, ḥassicya.
Reflection, tefoccor.
Thought, ficra *ru*. 10.
(3) Axiom, qāsuda 12.
An Assumption, farā B. (?).
Postulate, taqdier (?), iktiyār B.
Condition, xarr 3.
Proposition, moqaddama.
Maxim, qānoun 12.
Topic, maḥdis.
Problem, mcsyala. PURPOSE.

OPPOSE (*i.e.* set *oneself* against), sārul.
Contest, kāyom.
Contravene, ḍādid.
Counteract, sānid fie, usnid fie, nāḥ F. Contradict, nāqul.

Conflict with, kālif, tesarral.
Disobey, ojfou sala', cāyu, asyu sala'; (*a parent*) cöqq.
Dispute, *en* teḥājaj. ARGUE.
Dissent, *en* texājar, iktelif.
Hinder, imnas, mānus.
Be Insurgent, qoum sala'.
Interfere with, zēḥum c.
Obstruct, sodd. Resist, qawim.
Rebel, tomarrad, tenamrad.
Retard, asuiq, souq, son.
Revolt, *en* iḥtin, tezarban B.
Secede from, xūqiq, okroj san, sala'. Thwart, sācis.
Withstand (firmly resist *blows pressure, wear* and *tear*), āayin, oxlob B.
QUARREL. STOP.

ORANGES (πορτογάλλος), bortoḳāl, bortoqān.
Sweet Orange, nārinj B₈.
Bitter Orange, tērinj B₈.
Citron, toronj, otrojja B.
Lemons, licmoun AL FRUIT.

Owl, bouma.
Eagle Owl, el boum el mostensir.
Horned Owl, nāhoum.
Screech Owl, qobaiya.
— mayyāya (*Horn* Owl?).
— el boum el nāru.
— el boum el nāsub.
Barn Owl, boum el xowan.
Night Raven? hēma 2.
Night Hawk? bouh.

OX (*gener.*) baqar.
Bull, θour 4, 9.
Ox, θeur mekroiy.
Cow, baqara 2, also *ru*. m.

Bullock, cujl ꝺ.
Calf, dᵒ·; sujjaul 11 ӿ.
Heifer, sujala 5, 10.
Buffalo, jâmous 12.
Horn, qarn 3.   Hide, jild 3.
Cloven Hoof, ʒulf 4.
Dewlap, zeucma.
Paunch, Stomach of Cow, cirӿ 3.
The Cud, el jirra.
Ruminant, mojtürr.
Udder, ɻurs 3.
Teat, ɲulma (*nipple*).

Pack, *va* sabbi; ausu; rezzim.
Amass, ɻömm.
Cram, Stuff, Pad, oɲӿou.
Barrel up, Put in skins, ʒarrif, aʒrif.
Crush Down, icbis, cebbis.
Encase, ɼallif bi.
Gird up, uɲzim, ɲazzim.
Heap, cewwim, cewwir.
— (in cocks), ceddis.
— (one on another), ccrdis.
Pile up, sarrim, nehhuɻ.
— (in rows), rabbiq.
Rope up, ɼörr.   Stow, rozz.
Squeeze down, saffis.
Set firm, waʒʒub.

Pain, *s.* 'clem.   Ache, wcjas.
Smart, meɻaɻ, maɻɻɻa.
Pang, ӿouɀa, ӿaiɀa.
Prick, Sting, Throb, naki.
Throe (of childbirth), makâɻ.

Painful, 'eliam.
Afflictive, mostaɻuim.
Calamitous, fajous.
Deplorable, mobecci.
Distressing, moɻajjir.

Doleful, cêriθ.
Embarrassing, bêliӿ.
Grievous, moujis. — momuɻɻ.
Malign, naɲus, naɲsiey.
Mournful (event), moɲzin.
Poignant, nókis, mowêciʒ.
Sorrowful (event), mocerrib.
Vexatious, moɼimm.
  Wretched.   Dreadful.
    Hurtful. .

Paper, *s.* waraqa *nu.* 4; qarrâs
  P. B. cêɼid ᴇɴ. cêɼit ᴀɴ.
Coarse Paper, waraq, kauӿif
  waraq el codӿ B.
Fine Paper, waraq janwiey B.
Parchment, Vollum, raqq.
Sheet of dᵒ·, rurs 3, 4 (*pa-limpsest*).
Ream? rizmat waraq.
Quire, joz; corrês 11; ceff
  waraq.   Roll, malaff.
Sheet, ralɲuiyat waraq.
Pasteboard, maqouwa 2.
Manuscript, karr ɀed.
Blotting Paper, waraq tenӿicf
  or noӿӿêf.
Portfolio, jozdân, dorja *nu.* muɲfaʒa.   Book.

Parliament, el majlis el asla'.
House of Lords, qâsat el arbâb.
— of Commons, qâsat el sömoum, majmus el ӿasb.
A Session, jilse. Consessors, jels.
Member, saɻöu 4, *pl.* asɻâ.
Delegate, weciel 6.
Representative, mofawwaɻ, moӿakkiy.
Majority, ccθerieya.
A Convoking, teltiem.

Convention, insuqâd.
Assembly, iltiyâm.
Dismissal, ilṛâ.
Leading men, sômda.
Legislation, ixtirâs.
Supplies, mieri.
Vote (of the House), tesried, taqrier.
Vote (of a Member), saut 4, ridâ, ṛûi B.
Bill, taqdiem. Act, xaricsa.
POLITICS.

PASTRY, makbouz, masjoun.
Paste of Pie, roqâq.
Cheesecake (Almond Cake?), baqlâwa.
Dough, sajicn. Tarts, fatuir.
Patties, scnbousaq.
Puff, cinésa, hewâ AL
PUDDING. SWEETS.

PAY, ca wefa yofi; aufi, 'cddi, qabbuś.
Compensate, sawwuś qalaibi.
Content, Satisfy, aqnus, arâu.
Defray, uſlmil el colfa, idfas, el masrouf.
Discharge, Acquit a debt, iqău dain.
Fulfil engagements, aufi tesahhodèL.
Indemnify, Reimburse, wêzin, qâbil B.
Recompense, Reward, cêfi.
Refund, Render, rodd, rujjis.
Repay, idfas, sôdd suwaśuⁿ.
Requite, jêzi, ijzoʻ F.
Retaliate, sâqib.

PEACE, s. völſl, sclâm.

Pacification, mosêlama, movâlaſla. Amity, 'olfa.
Amnesty, 'cmâu, safou sâmm.
Armistice, motêrace.
Disarmament, ſlaTT (or nezs) el silâſl.
Footing of Peace, nesq el 'cmn.
Herald, monâdi.
Neutrality (probably Neutrality imposed by treaties), ustizêl.
Neutral (Power), mostezil.
Parley, mocêlama.
Security, 'omniya.
Tranquillity, utmicnûn.
TREATY.

PEN, s. (for writing) qalam 4.
Reed of Pen, qasaba, yarâsa.
Quill Pen, qalam ricx, qasab ricx.
Brass Pen, qalam neſlâs.
Slate Pencil, qalam louſl.
Lead Pencil, qalam rasây.
Penknife, mous 4, mous el aqlâm, AL qalam-tirâx B₆. mibraʻ (el aqlâm) F.
Nib, sinn 4, sinna 10.
Pencase, dawâya AL. qalamdûn B₆. miqlama x.

PERHAPS, bolci, AL.
Belike, lasal, lasalla.
Haply, Mayhap, robba, robbama.
Perchance, Peradventure, sasc'.

PERPETUAL, samad, sermad.
Abiding, bâqi. Lasting, θêbit.
Ceaseless, } motewâsul,
Continuous, } motewassul.
Continual, modâwim.

Constant, ӡalîel.
Enduring, mostemirr.
Endless, ġair motenêhi, sermad.
Eternal, 'ezeliey.
Everlasting,ebadiey,mowebbad.
Immortal, kâlid.
Immutable, qaiyoum.
Permanent, dûyim.
Perennial, sermadiey,mokallad?
Standing, qâyim.
Uninterrupted, min ġairinquтâs.
INNATE. STEADY.

PICKLE, *va* icbis (*sic c. bis*; qu. *Press* meat?)
— (in salt), melliû.
— (in spices), tebbil, teubil, behhir.
— (in vinegar), kallil.
Season, itqil? bezzir, ûayyiq.
Embalm, ûannит.
Cure (meat), eâlij F. *vp* соulij.

PIECE, *s.* qυтса. Bit, cisra.
Fragment, fitêt 11.
Gobbet, moӡгa, kimma.
Handful, ûôfba.
Instalment, qiет 3.
Morsel, qimma (*tip*).
Mouthful, loqma 10, loqaima.
Part, jezou, *pl.* ajzê; basâ.
Portion, qism(a) 4.
Lot, Allotment, sehm 5.
Share, ûυууa 10.
Sample, mастаrа 11.
Scrap (of meat), ûôtte 10, 5.
— (of writing), nobӑe 10.
Shred, Sherd, xoqfa 10.
Shiver, ûuтma 10, ûoтâma.
Slice, xarûa. Strip, xiqqa 10.
Splinter, xaӡuiya 14.

Wedge (of rock), foхх 10, 3.
Orts, fawâӡul.
Scantlet, Scantling, zehd.

PIERCE, *va* ikziq, okrot (ear, needle).
Bore, obkox, ôθqob.
Dig (Drill) thro', onqob.
Penetrate, aûuic.
Punch? ikrim?
Stab, weeez yeciz.
Stick in, *vn* inxico fie, iгraz fie.
PRICK. DIG.

Pig, Hog, kinzier 11.
Sucking Pig, kinnauу 11.
Hedgehog, doldol 11.
Porcupine, qonfoa 11.
Snout, ûnтuise, zelтöum karröum 11.
Tip of Snout, bouӡ el ûnтuisc, 'ernebet el zelтöum.
ELEPHANT.

PIGEON, Dove, yemâma *nu.*
Young Pigeon, zeгloul 11.
Tame Pigeon, ûamâma *nu.* 11.
Rock Pigeon (Biset), terгal, darгal, dalam в.
Woodpigeon (Cushat, Ring Dove), fâkite 12.
Turtle Dove, qomriey 11.
Love Bird, Small Dove, xaгufien, soteitieya (*little lady*) AL.

PINCER, *s.* mêdic (*vulg.* mêxic?) collâba 11 AL (*grappling iron*).
Smith's Tongs, cemmâxa; celbetein AL.
Tongs (to pick up with), milqат.
Vice, Crank, laulab.
Scissors, miqaуу.

Shears, mijeaz, jelam 5.
Nippers, miqrât, miqráḍ.
Snuffers, mintâf.
Tweezers, mintêf.

Pipe, *s.* (for water), *large*, qanâya; *small*, mâyöula 12;
o. N. mêsoura; qayaba lil mâi.
Pipe (for smoking), xaTb 9,
xaTba 2 Bɛ. (properly, a rod);
xoboc 2 B. xoboq, B. But
AL ɣaliyoun 11; qaliyân o.
[prop. when the smoke passes
thro' water; but this at AL
is, nargiele].
Pipestick, ɛöud 9, qayaba,
dawâya.
Pipe, Tube, anboub 11.
Pipe for Music, qayuiba, mâyöula 12.
Flexible tube to smoking pipe,
narbieTa AL
Pipe-bowl, baudaqa 11.
Wire Cap, qabaɛ.
Mouthpiece, bizz 3 (*nipple*) AL
imâma Bɛ.
Tobacco, tobaɣ F. toton AL
Persian Tobacco, compounded
and moist, tenbeo AL

Pitch, *s.* (natural), zift.
Tur (extracted by fire), qaTrân.
Boat Pitch, cofr.
Bitumen, qâr, qier.
Asphalt of Judæa, flömar, qofr.
Naphtha, nafT.
Turpentine, termintien, zeit el
boTöm.

Place, *s.* mecên 8 and *pl.* of
pl. amêcin.

Place (house or street), mafiall 2.
Site, mauqaɛ. Seat, maqaɣɣ.
Centre, marces. Spot, mafiall 2.
Place of a thing, maTrafi AL
Place, Post, maqêm.
— Office, manyab.
— Function, waɜuifa 11.
— Area, sêfla 2, maidân 11.
SPACE.

Platter, *s.* ɣafifa 5.
Plate, siete, *pl.* siyèt AL
— sitieya (soteiya?) B.
Tabae' 11 De Bɣ.
Metal Plate, anjar 4.
Dish, yafin 3.
Bowl, Deep Dish, qaysa.
Metal Tray, Metal Saucer for
drink in travel, Tabɛi 11 B.
Tâse' AL ɛiniewa Aɛ.
Leather (?) Tray, sofra (*dining
table* AL).
Tray, Tabaq 8, Tabso' 11.
Round Metal Dish, masoun
(ma'oun?) Bɛ.
Tureen *or* Ladle (!), muTbâqieya F.

Play, *vn* ilsab.
Amuse, Divert, *oneself*, telèhe,
tefarraj, teceyyaf B.
Loaf (*pop.*), tesecces.
Sport (in field), teqayyaf.
Trifle, usbaθ. Dawdle, Laugh.

Pleasant (person), laTuif, fecieh.
— (facetious), moherrij.
— (place), moxrifi, moshir.
Agreeable (person), 'enieq,
mostelTuf; (event) morâui.
Amiable, mostefiabb.

Pleasing, mostezrif.
Delightful, behiej.
Delicious, rɑſied, leᴀieᴀ, monᴀrum.
Gladsome, } mofriſl,
Joyous, } moᴀirr, mobsuᴛ.

PLENTIFUL, wûfir, mowaffar; wâfi, wefley. Ample, jeziel.
Abundant, raſſâd, motemelli.
Copious, ſazier, ſafier?
Common, ʀamiem 10.
Exuberant, zêkir, ʀokariey; zekkâr, moktayub c.
Excessive, zêyid.
Luxuriant, warief, fêcih, ʀekwar; (hair) ʀeθieθ.
Many, Much, ceθier.
Numerous, ʀadied.
Profuse (tears), monsejim.
Redundant, fᴀyuʌ, fayyâʌ.
Teeming? morsᴛruᴛ (ɴ. abundant), meθmour.
Widespread, Frequent, xâyuʀ.

RICH.

PLOVER (bird), Dottrel, forfor ʀ.
Ruff, el morawwaq.
Hoopoo, hodhod, xobab, (Barb. ᴛair abarbiel).
Sand Piper, zemmâr el raml.
Avoset, nicêt. Curlew, courlie.
Lapwing, Peewit, Tirwit; ᴛaᴛawiet.

PLUMS, kauk. Cherries, ceraz.
Damsons, ajês, ajâr, anjâr Mardien.
Egg Plums, barqouq.
White Damsons, janârieo ᴀʟ
Black Cherry, waʀna ɴ.

Peaches, dorrâq, darâqin c.
Nectarines, toffâſl Farsieya.
Apricots, muxmux.
— with sweet kernel, muxmux lauziey.
— with bitter kernel, muxmux cilâbiey.

POEM, s. naxied, 'orjouze 11.
Ode, Lyric Poem, qaʀuida 11.
Sonnet, Love Song, ſazel.
Song, } ſinâ, ſanwa,
Ditty, } ſanieya 11.
Ballad, } ʀoʀniyo 11.
A Chant, tesbieſla 11.
Hymn (of praise), madieſla 11.
Psalm, mezmour 11.
Canticles, zobour ɴ. s.
Psalmody, tezmier, tertiel.
Dirge, marθiya 11.
Satirical Poem, 'ohjouwa 11.
Stanza, } morabbaʀ,
Strophe, } daur.
Distich, Couplet, bait 4.
Verse, Line, Hemistich, muʀrâc.
Rhyme, cêfiya.
Measure, miezên, mowêzens.
Rhythm and Assonance, ʀejc.
Metre, Prosody, ʀarouʌ.
Poetry, xuɴʀ 4. Poet, xâcur 6.
Versification, naᴢm.

POLITICS, axyê siyêsieya.
Ambassador, ʀefier, 6.
Constitution, tenguima.
Council, diewân.
Court, el daula.
Diploma, farmân.
Coin, mescouce.
Govern, oſlcom.
Government, el ſlôcouma.

ANGLO-ARABIC VOCABULARY.

Governor, wáli 8.
King, melic 3.
Kingdom, memloce 11.
Parliament, el majlis el asla'.
Rank, rotba 10. *Title*, laqab.
Revenue, maflvoul 2.
Treaty, mosâheda. *War*, flarb.

Poultry, forouk, dojâj, farâriej.
A Fowl, farrouj 11.
Cock, diec 3. Heu, dojâja, ny.
Chick, fark 3, 4, 5, 8, 9.
Pullet, farrouja.
Capon, diec makyuiy.
Henroost,   } konn 4 (qonn 4 f.)
Henhouse, } el dojâj.
Fresh Egg, baiẑa têzihe.
The White, el biyâẑ.
The Yolk, el yufâr.
Turkey, diec Hindi.
Hustard, flôbâra' 11.
Peacock, tâwous 12.
Guinea Hen, dojâja Gienieya f.
Ostrich, nacâma.
Cassowary, xabnam f.

Pour, ta röbb, oscob.
— (favours), afuiẑ calaihi.
Cast up (waves), dûfiq.
Empty out, farrif, cobb, adûq, daffiq.
Shed, arieq, isfic.
Slop? Spill? oscob, arieq.
Let Stream, csbil b. Flow.

Power, *s.* qodra, maqdara.
Ability, Strength, tâqa.
Authority, iqtidâr, cuzze.
Energy, flamâse, maronwa.
Force, xidda.
— of steam, zekm el bokâr f.

Might, cazama.
Momentum, dafca b.
Potency,   } qouwa,
Efficacy, } fiɛlieya.
Prowess? sorwa.
Robustness, tâqa, rayâna, jelâda, yalâba, metêna (*stoutness, solidity*).
Strength, qouwa. Sway, solta.
Vigour, râfiya. Talent.

Pray (to God), yalli.
Adjure, aqsim cala'.
Ask, Request, terajja'.
Ask pardon, istaɛfir.
Apologize for, câair, ucaor fie, usteair cala'.
Beg, isterji. Entreat, iltemis.
Beseech, tedakkal cala'.
Conjure, Protest, nâxid.
Deprecate? isteɛair.
Implore, ibtehil.
Intercede, texaffac.
Meditate, tewasant.
Plead for, nâtul can.
Petition, Sue, Solicit, temannâ.
Supplicate, taẑarrac.
Praise (God), oflmod.
Adore, sebbifl.
Bow down, osjod.
Worship, Serve, osbod.
Chant, Hymn, rettil.

Press (cloth), Calender, Mangle, idcec, bardik.
— (grapes), ocvor.
— (an enemy), izniq, lózz cala'.
— (in argument), lozz bi'en, flarrij calaihi.
— (as poverty), flöff.

Pinch, Nip (*lit.* or *fig.*), qarriṭ, ɛaluihi bi в.
Crush, ɛaffis (squeeze *down*).
Squeeze, cöyy, ɛayyuy.
Throng, Press in crowd, zêflum, cebbiɛ, ʟáɾiṭ, flöff.
Tighten, xodd, qannib, uflziq.
Wring, flazziq.
Insist, ɐn lijj fle, eliflḷ fle, eliflḷ ɛalaihi bi.
Urge, ɐa clfluf ila', clijj.
GRIPE. CONFINE. COMPEL. INCITE.

PRICK, ɐa ɾozz, ɾaẓɾiz, uflmiz.
Goad, onkos, inɾax bil xauc в.
Gore, xocc c.
Nudge, idciz. *Pierce*, ikziq.
Spur, ohmoz, hemmiz.
Stab, wecez yeciz.
Stick in, ɐa oɾroz (ixcak ?).
Sting (as bee), onkoz, oncoz.
— (as flea), oqrɑy, uɛqiy.
— (as serpent), ildaɾ, ilɛeɾ, uɛqiy. PIERCE.

PROFIT, s. fâyida 12.
Interest, d⁻ˡ or fâyuḋ(a).
Advantage, } manfiɛa,
Benefit, } intifâɛ.
Advantageousness, nafiɛa.
Avail, jadwa ғ.
Service, } tâyil, tâyila 12.
Use, } ifâda,
Utility, } istefâda.
DEBT. TRAFFIC.

PROFIT, ɐa afled, ajdi, ajdi nafɛaⁿ; ɛn istefiɛd.
Avail, ɐa ɛyuil, tâyil.

Advantage, } ɐa infaɛ,
Benefit, } naffuɛ.
ɐp or ɐn viii.
Conduce to, afdi ila'.
Promote, ʌqdim, 'ewwil ila'.
Tend to, 'oul ila'.

PROUD, ɛâti, ɾaᴛries.
Arbitrary, moteɛajrif.
Arrogant, moteɛaʒʒum, moleɾaᴛris ғ. x.
Assuming, motecebbir.
Boastful, jaffâk, jammâk, ʌou jakkʟ в.
Conceited, moktél.
Contemptuous, mozdori.
Defiant, rehdil.
Despotic, jabbâr.
Disdainful, Contrarious, monêcif.
Domineering, moteɛellit.
Haughty, moleɛâli.
High-handed, moleɛannif.
Imperious? qâbir.
Insolent, mohenjim.
Lofty, xâmik.
Elated, teyyibên ? motcfakkim.
Lordly, moteɛâʒum, moto'êmir.
Magisterial, flâciwicy.
Ostentatious, moteʒâhir.
Outrageous, mofteri.
Overbearing, Intolerant, motejabbir.
Overweening, ʌou ɛôjb.
Pompous, moᴛannib, ʌou ɴakwʌ.
Puffed up, nâflk.
Scornful, mofltaqir, moɛtaflqir.
Stately, ɾairân.
Swaggering, motebehrij, moleɾaᴛrif.

Tyrannical, mofartan B. mote-
fartun.
Vain, maɣrour, tâyir.
Vainglorious, fikkier, motefâkir.
CRUEL. HEADSTRONG. ROUGH.
UNJUST.

PRUDENT, raxied.
Attentive, montacif.
Careful, ſlaries, moſlteris.
Cautious, moſlteriz, ſlaair.
Circumspect, fârun.
Considerate, ra'wiey, mortéwi, moetorwi.
Contemplative, morâlus?
Decorous, moſltexim.
Demure, motewâqir?
Dignified, Solemn, waqour.
Discerning, baruir, motebaryur.
Discreet, labieb.
Discriminating, fâriz.
Firm, râmil.
Grave, ʌou hieba.
Guarded, moſltât.
Heedful, motaqayyid fie.
Intelligent, fchiem.
Inquiring, mostarlus.
Judicious, ſlaziem, ſlâxim.
Meditative, mote'emmil.
Mindful, wâru ɛala'.
Moderate, moqtarud.
Modest, mostaſlui, ſlaiyiey.
Observant, molteſt, râſlub iltifêt.
Penetrating, Profound, wâfil.
Quiet, Calm, sêcin.
Reserved, moſlábis.
Restrained, mortedus.
Reticent, rummiet.
Sage, Knowing, ɛârif.

Sagacious, ʌeciey.
Scrupulous, waries, wârus.
Secretive, cetoum, mictêm.
Sedate, hêdi el TABƐ.
Selfcontrolled, monſabit, mote-ſlabbis.
Serious, rezien, rêzin.
Sobered, râſlu, motɛcaqqil.
Sober, Staid, motewaqqir.
Taciturn, secout.
Thoughtful, ⎫ fecour,
Pensive, ⎬ fecier,
Wistful, ⎭ motefeccir.
Vigilant, ⎫ nebieh, montebih
Wideawake, ⎭ moteyaqquʒ.
Wary, moſlteair, moteſlaʌir.
Watchful, raɣuid, raɣoud, moteraɣyud.
Well-balanced, mensoun.
Well-bred, 'edoub.
Well-informed, morralus.
Wise, Sensible, ʌou ɛaql, ɛaqoul, ɛâqil.
CLEVER. EARNEST.
INDUSTRIOUS. JUST.

PUBLISH, va axhir.
Advertise, aɛlin.
Announce, baxxir, 'eʌʌin.
Blab, bouſ bi sirr.
Blurt out, faxx B. onθou? noθθ?
Diffuse, axies. Disclose, ecxif.
Disperse, boθθ. Display, abdi.
Disseminate, onθor, beʌʌir, baθθiθ, batriq.
Divulge, afxi. Edit, nory.
Noise abroad, qarqus.
Proclaim, jêhir bi, nâdi, 'eʌʌin.
Promulgate, eʌies.
Reveal (theol.) auſlu.

Set Forth, aʒhir.
Spread abroad, onxor.
SPEAK, INFORM, SAY.

PUDDING, falouae F. *vulg.* boudicna.
Rice Pudding, zerda.
Rice Milk, rozz bi flalieb, moflallaba.
Rice with Lentils, mokaꞩara.
Rice with butter, etc., rozz mofalfal ; pilau.
Boiled Wheat, bolaila.
Firmity, barḡal.
Omelette, sӧjjet baiꞩ.
Fritter,) zolâbisya,
Pancake,) sojien maqliey.
HERB. FOOD.

PULSE, mâx, qaruniey.
Scarlet Bean, fâwala AL
— (*faséole*) flönbal B.
French Bean, loubiya AL
Large Bean, foul AL
Lentils, ɛades.
Bean, bâqala B₆. Peas, jolbân.
Grey Peas, flōmmay.
Vetches, arâkis, qarfâl.
Bitter Vetch, circonna, cexana.
HERB. FOOD.

PUNISH, ɛa sâqib.
Chasten, ʼeddib. Correct, sazzir.
Chastise, qâvuy, iqtuyy.
Impose Penance, qaunin.
Requite, jêzi, ijzê.
Torment, ɛaꞩꞩib.

PURE (colour), nâyur.
Clear (sky), yâfi, yâflu.
Clean, naꞩuif ḅ waꞩuiy.
Pure, Mere, maflꞩ.

Chaste, ɛaflef. Genuine, zeci.
Cleanly, Blameless, naqi 8.
Innocent, barr 4, bari 8, 1.
Pure (in flavour or colour), ɛeci.
Pure (water), tâhir.
Limpid, qarâfi 8.
Pure, Uncorrupt, tâhir, masyöum.
Disinterested, kâluy.
JUST. RIGHT. SINCERE.
CLEAR. BRIGHT.

PURPOSE, s. qayd.
Secret dº, ɛawioya.
Aim, hedaf, r̄âya.
Design, moqyad 11.
Desire, morâd, marâm.
Contrivance, iktirâs, têjieda.
Enterprize, messa', maxrousa.
Intention, nieya.
Invention, ufldâӨ c. iejâd.
Object, ɣariꞩ (ɣaruꞩ B.) marloub.
Plan (*lit.*), resm.
Plot, cemien, cemna.
Project, ibtidâs.
Scheme, tedbier.
Determination, qaꞩâ.
Will, irâda. OPINION.

PUSH, ɛa odfor, idfas.
Push and Pull, tertus.
Push a boat, zeflfluf.
Drive on, odfox.
Hustle, yâdim, cebbis.
Jostle, naffuꞩ, izflam, ɛêflum.
Knock, doqq. BEAT.
Nudge, ideiz.
Precipitate (one into), qaflflum, warrir, hebbir.
Poke, Poke in, ɛoqq.

Propel, idfaε, maxxi.
Ram, docc. Thrust, ibheε.

A QUANTITY, majmaε.
A Great Quantity, ciθra.
An Assortment, nokba.
A Collection, jamε.
A Company, jamâεa.
A Group, lomma.
A Lot, jomla, jamm.
A Number, εudda.
A Selection, γüfwa.
A Set, ᴛaqm, εüdda.
Several, xette', baεΔ.
A Suit, râqim?
A String, ᴛörqa?
A Train, qaᴛᴛ, qitâr.

QUARREL with, xâqiq.
Bicker with, nêziε, jâdiε.
Combat, εâric, teεârec.
Contend, ɤâlib, teɤâlab.
Dispute with, mâri, jâdil.
Encounter, ᴄa oεroΔ(li).
Engage, ᴄa nâwix, mâriε.
Fight, ᴄa qâtil; as champion,
  tebârez. Face, ᴄa wâjih.
Jangle, ᴛn teεâyaᴛ, tenêzeε.
Jar (with), Be in Conflict, ibεel,
  tenâεor. Riot, texaɤab.
Match, ᴄa (prove oneself a
  match for), cêfiɴ.
Squabble, teɴârax, teΔârab.
Wrangle, lodd, ɴâniq.
STRIVE, OPPOSE, ARGUE, CAVIL.

QUARTER, s. (lit.) robs 2. — of
  heavens, ᴋâɴq 12. — of
  city, ɴâra, maɴalla, γâyih.
  — (camp), εaurâui B. ôrdi.

North, ximâl.
South, janoub, qibla.
East, xarq, maxriq.
West, ɤarb, maɤrib.
Quarter of Wind, mehebb.
N. Wind, semâwi Syr, hier.
S. Wind, qibliey, teiman.
E. Wind, xarqiey, γabâ.
N.W. Wind, xarax (Syr).
N.E. — barrâni (Syr).
S.W. — libx (λιψ).
S.E. — ɪalouc B.

QUICK, seriεs. Speedy, fârit F.
Expeditious, mosteiεir.
Hasty, εajil, εajoul, mosteεjil.
Headlong, motehewwir.
Rapid, wexiec. Rash, mojêzif.
Swift, εeεöum ᴋ. NIMBLE.

RAGE, ᴏɴ hiej, uɴnaq, θour εala'.
Be Angry, iɤΔab.
Boil up, four, taqalla'.
Chafe, ᴏɴ uɴma', teɴamma'.
Be Enraged, Wroth, iɤtêz, iεkaᴛ.
Be Exasperated, uɴtidd.
Flame out, jiex, xier, isteziet.
Fret, iktemir, inzeεuj.
Fume at, tewaɤwax εan.
Be Indignant, tckallaq.
Be Irritated, incêd (sic B.),
  uɴrad εala'.
Be Frantic, εoεur, teεcεar,
  isteεur, teεeεran.
Be Offended at, ixmir min.
Resent, ɤill εala'?
Rave (with fury), teεerεem.
  — (in delirium), ihɐi.
Be Vexed, inɤimm min,
  teεekkaᴛ.

ANGLO-ARABIC VOCABULARY. 111

Repine, inqahir, inflasir.
Go Mad as dog, iclab, isteclib.

RAIN, s. matar 4.
— (abundant), ɣaiθ F.
Rainbow, qaus Qozeḥ, qaus semâwi.
Heavy Shower, wabl, wâbil.
Burst of Rain, zikkat matar, matar zekûk (ɣabyu K.).
Lowering Sky, ɣubou F.
Deluge, taufân.
Water Spout, tinnien, fawwâra.
Hail, barad.   Sleet, ɣaqieɛ.
Small cold rain, nafnouf, nafnâf.
A Sprinkling, raxx 5.
A Dropping, qaṯṯ.
Slight Shower, taxx, sobla?
Scud of rain, qiṯqiṯ.
Fine Drizzle, tenkiel.

RAISE, ɛa anhuẊ, ɛalli, aqiem.
Erect, onɣob, ɛp vii.
Heave, Hoist, ɣaɛɛad, ɣalluɛ.
Mount, ɛa ɣaqqi (cause to step up). Lift, irfaɛ.
Take up, axiel bi.

RANK, s. rotba 10.
Class, marteba 11.
Grade, menzele ; ṯabaqa 2.
Station, muqâm.   State, xân.
Office, Post, manɣab.
Function, woẓuifa 11.
High Degree, ɛalâ, sölou.
Power, qodra, maqdara.
A Power, Potentate, daula, pl. dowal.
Authority, iqtidâr.
Sovereignty, ɛelṯana.
Empire, ɛolṯa.

Royalty, molce, mâlicieɣa.
Primacy, ɣadâra.
Supremacy, ɛalawieɣa ?
Ascendancy, xarâfa.
Headship, riɣâɛe.
Preeminence, qodamicɣa.
Superiority, faẊl, faẊuila, afẊalicɣa.
Leadership, taqaddom.
Predominance, istielâ.
Dominion, moxaika.
Reign, mulc.   Nobility, xaraf.
Independence, istiqlâl.
Dignity, icrâm, ictirâm.
Honour, cerum, cerâma.
Consideration, ustibâr.
Respectability, nûtirâm.
Eminence, niɣâfa.
POLITICS. TITLE. SPECIES.

RASH, adj. mojêzif.
Audacious, waqiḥ, waqicḥ.
Dashing, ɛou θêra, moθier, miqḍâm.   Foolhardy, fâjir B.
Hasty, ɛajoul.
Headlong, } motehejjim,
Precipitate, } motehewwir.
Headstrong, lefout, jamouḥ.
Impetuous, héɣij, ɣawwâl, ɛou barx.
Impulsive, kolqieɣ.
Rude, Abrupt, ɛatries, moteɛatris.
Reckless, majoun.
Vehement, xadied.
BRAVE. LIGHTMINDED. RUDE.

RAT, s. jorea 9.
Norway Rat, jaraɛun 11.
Water Rat, jorea el mâi.

112　　ANGLO-ARABIC VOCABULARY.

Beaver, seqlâbi, celb el mâi, badaster.
Otter, θeɛlab el mâi.
Mouse, fâra. Dormouse, zoɣba ꜰ.
Field Mouse, nâfiq? qidâd?
Jerboa, jarbous 11.
Marmot, joreᴀ jebalicy.
Shrewmouse, mexân ꜰ. fârat el semm.
Mole, kold(a) 9.

RED, *adj.* aſlmar.
Reddish, moſlmirr, aſlmarâni?
Deep Red, qâni, aſlmar qûni.
Vermilion, zenjifricy, cewâzicy (colour of red pots?).
Bay (horse), aſlmar.
Rosy, warad, wordicy.
Crimson, qirmizicy (*also* scarlet).
Scarlet, qaxar? ᴋ. motcɅarrij, qoklicy? Ba. κοκκινος.
Carmine, Ruby, lasliey.
Carnation,) jouricy,
Pink,　　) sönnabicy.
Livid Red, arbad ꜰ.
Fallow, axhel ʙ.
Ruddy, axqar.　Rusty, ayda'.
Itusset, axqârani.
Roan (Raspberry cream), ampar.
Sorrel, ayheb ᴋ.
Chocolate? aybaſl.
Fox-coloured, sinjâbiey.
Freckled, abrax, monaddar ʙ.
Dark Chesnut? adbes.
Light dᵃ· eclef, mour.　COLOURS.

REFUSE, *s.* (place of), meljâ.
Asylum, sayᴀᴀ, mostâyam.
Lair, mabwâ, marqad, marbaɅ, wajêr 10.
Place of Escape, maklay.

Haunt, mê'laf; marlêb, marâd.
Resort, masâd, maradd.
Resting-place, marûſl, mosterâſl.
Retreat, Retirement, kalwa.
Shelter (place of), mêwa', ᴀera'?
Station (for caravan), maſlaᴛᴛ, menzil.

REFUSE, *s.* nofûya, rajies.
Carrion, jiefa.
Chippings, noſlâte.
Clippings, qoyâya, qorâɅa.
Dregs, sacêr, ᴛaſll, noᴛâfa.
Dripping (of meat), rosâfa, raqrâq.
Dross, tilf (Waste).
Faeces, birâz.　Filings, borâda.
Fag-ends,) tewâli,
Remnants,) bawâqi.
Flue, hibricya, nosêlo? (*lint*).
Garbage, qixxa, qoxâx.
Grape skins, jozcina.
Grouts, θoſl, θeſil.
Grounds (of coffee), tonwa.
Impurities, cedarn, aqᴀêr.
Leavings, baqâya, daxâr ʙ.
Lees, sayuir, sôyâra (*also* jam).
Lees of oil, cozb(a), θoſl.
Malt, θoſl el xasuir.
Nailparings, tefûyif ᴋ.
Litter, zobâla.
Lumber, aɛbâ? θiqala, eθqâl.
Offal, seqaᴛ 4.　Riffraff, koxâra.
Offscouring, qomâma, komâma.
Orts, Remains, faɅla 2, faɅâyil, fawâɅul.　Residuum, ɼidra.
Rubbish, safx(a).
Rubble, radm.
Sawdust, noxâra.
Scrapings, ɼoceɛa.

ANGLO-ARABIC VOCABULARY. 113

Scraps, ſōtet, nobeA.
Sediment, resoub.
Slag, Scum of metals, toubâl 11.
Sweepings, conêse.
Trash, noſàwa (Tare and Tret).
PIECE.

RELIGIOUS (person), daiyin.
— (institution), dicniey.
Devout, sâbid.
Holy, moqaddas.
Pious, taqi, têqi.
Right Reverend, Venerable, mowaqqar.
Righteous, moqsiт.
Sanctimonious, moteqâdis.
Saintly, râhir, qadies.
Virtuous, vâliſi.

RELY upon, vs weθaq yeθiq bi, isteuθiq bi, itteθiq enna.
Cast oneself upon, terâma' sala', raff sala'.
Count upon, } teweccel sala',
Confide in, } ittecil sala'.
Depend on, } vâdiq sala'
Trust in, } (also ratify!); te'emman sala'.
Lean upon, istenid ila'.
Rest upon, ircen ila'.
Have Recourse to, waqas yaqas li, inbari bi r. ustemid sala'.
Resign oneself to (God), tewessel sala'. See Betake oneself.

REMEDY, s. sulâj 2, xafâ, pl. axfiya.
Bandage, ſumâda.
Outward application, melſlam.
Medicament, rubb.
Ointment, marhem 11.

Embrocation, naröul, morka'?
Poultice, labka.
Plaster (sticking), lezqa.
— (blistering), ſlarrâqa.
Splint, jabiera, râb.
MEDICINE.

REPEL, vs idfas, dâſls, ſlâmi-ho san, yadd-oh san.
Avert, Ward off, aſluid, isteſlris min, лewwid san, sawwiλ san.
Debar, oſljoz.
Drive back, rodd san.
— away, otrod, тarrid, тârid.
Fence off, } ſlawwil san,
Parry, } uvrif san.
Repress, Check, irdas.
Repulse, odfox. Rebuff, mokk.
Scare, naſflr. —(by shout), ozjor.
Snub (pop.), cexxir li.
BRIDLE. STOP. DIVERT.
EXPEL. PUSH. GUARD.

REPTILE, s, dabieb.
Snake, ſlanax. Dragon, tonnien.
Shellfish, yadaf 4.
Tortoise, soſllifa 11.
Crocodile, timsêſl.
Lizard, ſlurdaun, warn, warl 4.
— ſlaiyat xams. — λabb 5.
— wezer (stellio).
Crab, selsarân 11, zelsarân, serarân baſlriey.
Lobster, arbiyân. — cercend.
Frog, Toad, ſafdas 11, söqroq? Chameleon, barbakti, ſlörbâya; tếtê. BARB.

REST, s. râſla. Repose, hiena.
Comfort (of mind), selwa.
Ease, sohoula, yeaêra.

8

Ease and Comfort, raká.
Leisure, mchl, faláwa.
Quiet,   ) ramán, romániya,
Quietude,   } urmienán.
Quietness,) romániena.
Peace, selám(a).
Safety, 'emûn, 'omniya.
Security, yaun, ruyâna.
Serenity, rawâqa.
Stillness, socoun, socna.
Tranquillity, hodou.
Vacation, batála.

RETURN, ra irjas, rôud.
Recoil, irjas ila' wará, tcdâfas.
Recur (as fever), rájis, cáwid.
Relapse, intecia.
Resort to, intéb ila'.
Retrograde, teqahqar.
Reverse one's course, indâr.

REVENUE, Rent, mafiyôul 2.
Gross Profit, el fiâyul.
Net Profit, yâfi; motcflayyul x.
Raw Produce, flayalêt.
Receipts, Incomings, wúridét.
Land Rent, flômla.
Ground Rent, flacer el bait.
Income, ierâd; madkoul 11.
Outgoings, yarf.
Treasury, cl kazienat el jeliela.
Exchequer, el mieri, 'cmieriey.
Supply, miera, *pl.* miyar.
Public Money, mâl el miori.
Finance, el mâliya.
Tax, báj. Cessa, jawâla x.
Personal Tax (Poll Tax), jizya.
Excise? mieri.
Impost, rosouma 2; *pl.* rosoum.
Tribute, karáj (*sic*).
Duty, qânoun 12, fará(a) 10.

Fixed payment, masloum.
Customs, cawâyid.
Custom Duty, mecs 3, *vulg.* gomroc.
Road Toll, kafar.
Salary, jâmecieya 12.
Pay, Stipend, côloufa.

COMMERCE.

RICH, raniey 8; (of mind) jeziel.
Affluent, morrid.
In Easy Circumstances, mousir, moyessir, râfih, moteraffih.
Flourishing (place), câmir; (author, person) nâbir.
Moneyed, modarhem, *vulg.* morrax.
Opulent, motemawwil, motenassum.
Wealthy, sou 8erwa, mo8ri.
Well-provided, marzouq (marrous x.).

PLENTIFUL WEALTH.

RIGHT (thing to do), yawâb, yâyib.
Just (thing), sedied.
Rightful, motewajjib.
Accurate, yaqien.
Correct, moyafiflaf.
Genuine, flaqqâni, 'eyliey.
Accurate (person or thing), mazbout.
Exact, moflarrar, modaqqaq.
Strict, motexaddid.
Judicious (deed), masqoul.
Pure, kâluy, zeci.
Real, flaqicqiey.
Sound, scliem, yâr seliem AL
Sterling, dorri AL
True, yafluifl. LAWFUL.

River, *s.* nchr 4, or *pl.* anhor.
Brook, sêqiya 12.
Stream, majra' mâi.
Torrent, seil 3. Beck, joefâr.
Rill, judwal 11. Conduit, wanâ'.
Aqueduct, siqqâya 2.
Watercourse, qanâya 10,
   qanâ'a, *pl.* qanawât.
Cascade, } xallâl,
Waterfall, } darbecct el mâi B.
Rapids, janâdiel.
Cataract, karâra.
Current, jaryân, jiryat el mâi.
Main Stream, fojra.
Eddy, tecercor el mâi; xaima?
Whirlpool, } dordour,
Vortex, } dawwâr el mâi.
Deep Water (*gurges*), bâlour, naul.
Bed, } manher, mafjara,
Channel, } majra' (*sic*).
Bed of Torrent, Gill; mesiel, mesrub.
Bed of Brook, mesteqa'.
Mouth of River, mayabb, maklat. Ford, makâla.
Ferry, Crossing-place, mařbar, maqtař.

Road, *s.* darb 3.
Way, raricq 10.
— (*fig.*) raricqa 11.
Thoroughfare, majêz.
Highway, minhêj, darb soltâni.
High-road, xârif 12.
Route, nchj, yurât 10, seir.
Career, miayar, xaut s.
Course, siera. Path, sebiel 10.
Railroad, siccet el fladied, rarieq el fladied. Track, sicce 10.

Raised Footpath, mamxa'.
Terrace, carimet el torâb, *pl.* carim.
Bridge, Causcy, jisr 3. Street.
Rob, *va* (a person), ruyub, oslob.
Bare, carri. Denude, jarrid.
Depredate, yaɤɤim c.
Deprive, acdim, allrim.
Despoil, intezie. Fine, ɤarrim.
Extort, balluy B. ocbox min.
Maraud, ozou, tclayyay.
Poach, iɤtelis (iktelis).
Plunder, inheb.
Seize, ('e)koa (*take*).
Ravish, } iɤyub,
Snatch away, } iktuf.
Strip, xalliû al.
Tax, cellif-oh bi.
   Attack. Steal.

Rock, yakra *nu.* 3.
Shoal Rock, dabr 5.
Reef of Rock, silsilet rökour.
Crag, helba. Sand, raml 5.
Boulder, jalmoud 11.
Stone, flajar(a) 4, 5.
Pebble, flaywa, *pl.* flayâ.
Sediment, resoub.
Quicksand, ɤawwâr. Stone.

Roll, *va* up, loff.
— screw up, obrom.
— curl up, dog's car, sesbil.
— into a ball, cobb, cebbib, cebcib, cebtil, cesbil.
— in dust, caffir, marriɤ.
— the eyes, dawwir el söyoun.
— the ground, mandir.
— on, Trundlo, daûrij; va tedaûraj.

Trundle off, ʋa cerrit ʙ. (ʋa icret).
Roll, ʋa as ship, tebarcel, tedarcel.
— as horse, temarraɼ, temardaɼ, tedarcel.

Roof, s. (vaulted), saqf 3; (flat) satʜ 3; (sloping) jammâle
Bʀ. jamloun ʙ.
Ceiling, ʀawûn. Frieze, ifriez.
Cornice,) qnuʋara ʙ.
Vault,) calâwa c.
Niche with shelf, raff 3.

A Room, beit 3.
Apartment, öuʟa 2, 10.
Hall, Saloon, qâca.
Drawing Room, diewân.
— ʋâla (French?).
Chamber, flöjra.
Small dº. flöjaira.
Vaulted dº. qobba 5 (Alcove).
Dining R. flöjrat el mâida.
Upper Room, ɼorfa.
Bedroom, beit el naum; marqad ʀ. (cemetery).
Parlour) beit el qoɾöud,
Sitting R.) maqɕad.
Closet, very small R. makdac.
Underground Parlour, ɕcrzemieɣa ʙ. sirdâb 11 Bɢ.
Recess, mokbâɣa.
— for sleeping, maʟjac.
— arched, in court, iewân.
Dais of Hall, maflrâb 11.
Kitchen, marbak.
Loft, saqiefa. Dairy, lebâna.
Cellar, celâr, cerâr.
Buffet, kacna 10.
Wardrobe, karistân, jobbekâna.

Roots (edible), joʟour.
Carrots, jezer. Turnips, luft.
Parsnips, jezer abɣaʟ.
— Barb. jacda, sefrânia ʙ.
Rape Turnip, seljem ʙ.
Beet, silq. Radish, fijl.
Red Beet, banjar, ɾawandar.
Horseradish, fijl flârr.
Potato, baтâтa. Food.

Rough, adj. kaxin, aflrax.
Abrupt (in manner), molehwaj, motɕlehwij, nabr.
Awkward, xalix, xaloux.
Boorish, ɾajrieɣ (gipsy-like).
Clownish, fellâfluiy.
Clumsy, neɅiel? mostehjin ʀ.
Coarse, qabâ, kouxif.
Fierce, bêsil. Gawky, hibill ʟ.
Gritty, morammel.
Gross, lit. or fig. semij.
Harsh, Violent, motɕatrif.
Impetuous, motɕɕatria.
Passionate, kolqiey.
Ill-made, Rude, tuʋlaq ʙ.
Insolent, mohenjim.
Morose, nâxif (curt, dry).
Novice (unskilful?), baɾnous ɕ.
Queer, mosawwaj, mamɕouk, motebarrim?
Rough-handed, Rough-dealing, ɾaxoum ʀ. Violent, ɕanief.
Rugged, wacur, (style) xêzz ɪ.
Rude (lit. or fig.) ɾalieɕ; ɕymotɕcatria. Snarling, cexu.
Uncouth, akraq ʟ. molakbər.
Vulgar,) hemij,
Barbarous,) hemjieɣ.
Cruel. Rash. Unjust.
Proud. Ill-natured.

Rub, ʋa flöcc, (between fingers) ofroc.
Chafe by rubbing, ofroc, mezzik?
Curry (leather), odbor.
— (a horse), flōss (sic), ojbor (sic), temmir; qaxxiq AL
Soften (clay) by rubbing, Knead; idsec, louk.
Embrocate, uTli bi.
Rub in (an embrocation), omror.
Fret, ʋa illflas (lick); aflrid, flarrid.
Gall, caqqir, aflrix.
Peel, oqxor. Polish, ijli, oyqol.
Rasp? iqflaT (rake off, scratch).
Scrape, obrox P.
— off, Skim off, iqxaT, qaxxiT.
Scrub, imcec.
Shampoo, dallic, ceyyis.
Wipe, imsefl.
— (a wound), oqxor.
— (the face), ocroc. WASH.

Run, en ijri, orcoś (osdou P.).
— down, ʋa oqfox.
— at, iqflam, iqteflum.
— wildly, iflit.
— away, ihrab, firr.
— away from, oxrod.
Course, sier, teseyyar.
Gallop, Canter, irmafl.
Pursue, ʋa ocrox.
Race, sebiq, teracaś.
Rush, ihjim.
Keep pace with, maxi, jâri.
Sally from, ihjim min.
Scramble, sajrim?
Scamper, Amble, herwil.
Scour, Skim, qaxxiT.

Scud, tezeflaf.
— (as ship), injac.
Skate, tezellaq.
Trot, kabb, kojj; leclic AL imxi lenc.
— classic. arqil (Barb. hercil).
ATTACK. JUMP. CATCH.
HASTEN. WALK. WANDER.

A RUSH, s. (gener.) ṛâba, nu.
Bamboo, kaizorûn, kaizour.
Bulrush, firief, sosâda.
Cane, Reed, qayaba, pl. qoyōb.
Flag, dalbout, cesicfoun.
Marshweed, flōlfa (ulva).
Papyrus, bardie.
Reed for pens, yarâsa.
Rush for mats, ʾesel.
— qaxx el flōyōr.
Sedge? dies.

SADDLE, s. serj 3.
— (for travel), bardasa 11.
Padsaddle, fluls 3.
Packsaddle, scmar (sic B.).
Camel's S. xâfir 12.
— rafll 4, 5; riflâla 11, marflöul 11 (of leather).
— cour 4 (also clay oven).
— fladâja (woman's litter).
Housings, jildl, firâx.
Pummel, qarbeus 11 AL
Croup, sabeus, qarbeus warâol
Undercloth, rarrâfla.
Sweating Cloth, mirxafla AL
Over-cloth, diexêc AL
Haircloth, sebad.
Felt, lobbâd. Leather, jild 3.
Girth, fluzêm 10.
Surcingle, qolâns AL qoulâm c.

Martingale, aelibind AL.
Iron Stirrup, ricéb 10,
zencêwa AL.
Leather Stirrup, ɼarz?
Stirrup Leather, zekma 10?
— seir el ricéb.
Spur, mihmâz 11.

SAMPLE (of wheat), suina.
Example, moθel 8.
Exemplar, moθla, miθél.
Scantling (strip of cloth as pattern), mixq(a).
Specimen, mosтaro 11, xaxna'B.
Model, qâsuda 12, nemauaej S.A. (inmaudaj B.).
Pattern, qidwa, qodwa [object to imitate], timθél.
— (in writing), mexq c.
MANNER.

SAW, s. minxâr.
Sawdust, noxâra.
Plane, fûra (*mouse!*).
— randaj AI. Rasp, miflacce.
File, mibrad. Filings, borâda.
Chippings of metal, qoɣâɣa.
Shavings, noflâto.
Grater, Scraper, miqzaт.

SAY, raa Tell, qoul.
Affirm, *cceid, weccid.
Allege, uftijj. Assert, izsam.
Asseverate, auXufl.
Announce, anbi*.
Aver (specify), abriz.
Avow,   ) aqirr,
Confess,   ) usterif
Own,   ) qorr bi.
Declare, abien, baɼɼin.
Enunciate, ɣarriſl bi.

Express, afɣufl, ixrafl.
Mention, OACOF.
Narrate, irwi, qoɣɣ.
Proclaim, jèhir bi.
Pronounce, elfuʒ bi, onтöq bi.
Recite (verses), anxid.
Recount, Relate, uflci, Oaddiθ.
Repeat, cerrir, asnid.
Report, axies; (officially) qarrir.
ADVISE. DENOTE. EXPLAIN.
INFORM. PUBLISH.

SCATTER, *va* boθθ.
Break up, baddid, xatlit.
Crumble,) ɣa fott, fettit,
Moulder,) fetfit, farfit.
Disband, xattit, farrid.
Dispel, oтrod (EXPEL).
Disperse, bezzim, farriq.
Disseminate, beaair, bezzir.
Dissipate, xassuθ.
— (SPEND fast), badriq.
Distract, ixɼal san, xâɼil. DI-VERT.
Dispel, Dissipate (grief), afrij, farrij, ijli, iexif, cabib.

SCREAM, en) ɣarɣur,
Screech,   ) uɣkab.
Baa, ibza, marmis.
Bark, inbafl. Bleat, oθɼou.
Bellow, insar, *vulg.* surr.
— (as camel), тuiт.
Bray, inheq, nchhiq.
— ixheq (*sob*).
— xchniq (*hiccup*).
Caterwaul, nawwi. *Cry*, ɣuifl.
Growl, Moan,) ihdir, ohmor.
Grumble,   ) iz*er, barbir.
Grunt, qanbus, qabbus.

Hoot, ɾujj (as wind, wave,
   bulls, pigs).
Howl, waɾwuɾ. Low, kour.
Mew, mouʼ ꜰ.
Neigh, Whinny, ſlamſlum.
Purr, Hum, donn, dandin.
Roar (as lion), inhcm.
Skirl, Shriek, uyſlaL
Snarl, icxir, ohmor, jaɾɾur?
Snort, tenakkam.
Squeak, zeqziq. Squeal, uywi.
Trumpet (as elephant), hemhim.
Whine, odɾou. Whoop, uyliq.
Yell, zicr. Yelp, ɾawwi.
Cʀʏ. Cʀᴏᴡ. Sɪɴɢ. Sᴏᴜɴᴅ.

Sᴄʀᴇᴇɴ, ɪ. dorwa (ᴀorwa?).
Fire Screen, ſlâyil lil nâr, ʙ.
Partition, ſlujâb.
Curtain, kidr 3, ɾulg. bardâya.
Blind, sitêra, settêra 11.
Vallance, rafraf. Dorder, sijâf.

Sᴇᴀ, ɪ. baſlr 3, 5, yamm 9.
Open Sea,   } el ɾobba.
Trough of Sea? }
The Deep, el ɾömq, lojja 10.
Abyss, ɾamra (elɾarieq? but qu.)
Waters, the Tide, el miyâb.
Flow of Tide, madd.
Ebb of Tide, jozr.
Ocean, ɾommân c. el baſlr el
   moſluiʏ. Straits, zoqâq.
(English, etc.) Channel, kaliej.
Frith, bouɾâz 12.
Dead Sea, baſlr el Lauʏ.
Red S. b. el Qolzom (ancient
   city of Clysma, by the Red
   Sea x.), el b. el aſlmar.
Mediterranean S. baſlr el Roum,

el baſlr el abyaẋ (sic), el
   baſlr el jouwâni or ausʙʏ or
   motewassiʏ.
Indian Ocean, el baſlr el akbar;
   baſlr el Hind.
Caspian S. baſlr el Kazer.
Persian Gulf, bouɾâz el Fâris.
Black S. baſlr el Qirim, el baſlr
   el eswad.
Adriatic, baſlr el Bendaqieya.
Gulf of Venice, jaun el Benda-
   qieya.
Straits of Gibraltar, bouɾâz je-
   bal el ʏarieq; baſlr el zoqâq.
AtlanticOcean,baſlrelẋölmét,ʟ.

Sᴇᴀsᴏɴ, ʼewân, pl. êwina
   ibbân ꜰ. (favourable time x.).
Time, waqt 4. Epoch, ſluin 4.
Crisis, qoʏöus ʙ. Cycle, daurân.
Conjunction, Juncture, qirân.
Era? ɾaſld. Period, medâr, daur.
Spring, rabiec.
Summer, yaif.
Summer-time, yaifleya.
Autumn, karief. Winter, xitê.
Winter-time, xitewieya.
Four seasons, foyöul arbaɾ.
S. of year, sayl el sene.
S. of fair, of crop, of festival,
   mausim 11. Harvest, ſluyûd.
Seed-time, badâr (beʌér, bezêr).
Vintage, qaſr el ɾunab.
Solstice, inqilâb.
Equinox, ustidâl.
Autumnal Equinox, mihrijân c.
   Tɪᴍᴇ.

Sᴇᴇ, ʋa ɾulg. xouf, iqxas ʙ.
Behold, râʼ; I behold, araʼ.

Eye, va sâyin. Espy, fladdiq.
Desory, abyur (See Clearly, tebayyar). Discern, töyy.
Distinguish, mayyiz.
Discover,) icxif,
Detect,   ) ictexif sala'.
Notice, Perceive, ilflaz, lâfluz.
Get glimpse of, ilmafl, istelmifl.
Witness (See), xâbid.
Look. Learn.

Seek, va oqyöd (make for).
— fettix (look for).
— orlob (demand).
— terallab (go in quest of).
— teqayyad en — (aim, desire).
— iltemis (seek to get).
Chase, iqnuy, iqtenuy.
Examine, put to proof; imteflun. Explore, oncox.
Forage for, rond, inkabix bi.
Grope after, dasdis c.
Hunt, lit. yuid, uytêd.
Hunt after, teyayyad.
Inquire into, iflae, ifteflue.
Inquire after, iftaqid, tefaqqad.
Investigate, istaqyu.
Pry into, tejesses.
Pursue, tûrid, idrec.
Push hard after? ocrox b.
Rake up, onbox. Rifle, bakyuy.
Rummage, joua, vulg. dawwir.
Search, ifflay, tefafflay san.
Search after, ibflae san, bâflue sala', dasbis sala', flawwis al
Search into, tesammaq fie, tebafflar fie.
Search (a person), va jessis.
Track, iqtefi, tetebbas.
Follow.

Sentence of Law, s. qaلâ, flöcm xarsuiy.
Verdict, tuqrier qaلwiey.
Punishment, quyây.
Fine, jizê naqdicy.
Forfeit, jarâma, jariema.
Penalty, jezê, jizêya, mojêze?
Condemnation, flöcm sala', qaلâ sala'.
Acquittal, tebrier.
Pardon, rafou, maffara.
Justice, sadl, masdala.
Decision, flatm, fayl.
Damages, Xarar, maXarra sw.
Repayment of Damages, mojêze'? moocfa, teswiel el Xarar.
Costs, karj, tecêlief.
Compromise, terâلui, morâkaya.
Jail, Prison, sijn, flaba.
Gallows, maxnaqa. Law.

Set, va aqsud, ijsal.
Set up, Erect, onyob, aqiem.
Set down, Put down, flôtt.
Set even, Adjust, sewwi.
Set forth, Show, aghir.
Set, Plant, ofros, xettil.
Set, Stick in, kayyix.
Settle, reccin, aqirr.
Set off, Embellish,   ) flassin,
Invest with grandeur,) flufBl.
Appoint, sayyin.
Clap, Fit (one on another), rabbiq.
Implant, ofros. Fix, orcoz.
Lay, Cast, utrafl.
Place, waلas yaلas.
Post, Station, nayyub.
Set, on, Set about, Set to work

at; uTâq fle; istaqbil sala'.
Qoum wa—. Ustemid wa—
(with a second verb) Qoum
bi. [TAKE in hand].
Set, ʋn (as a blossom), tesaqqad.
Set in, ʋn (as winter), istoflcim.
Set off (on journey), ʋn teseffar.
Set out for, ʋn teweijjah ila',
ittejih ila'.
Set upon (make onset), ʋn iftic
bi. ATTACK.
Set fast, ʋa (jam tight), arʋik.
Set (another) to work, ʋa
messic-oh el xofl.
Set a dog at, ʋa arlïq celba° sala'.
Set forth, Set forward, Present,
against one, ʋn aurid sala'.

SEW, ʋa akier, kayyut.
Baste, xallil s.; qaxxut c(?).
Cobble, raqqis. Mend, ramrim.
Darn, Finedraw, irfa°.
Embroider, Tarriz, raqqim,
xajjir. Fell? (join), ilfiq.
Hem, coff. A Hem, cofafa.
Patch, irqas. Quilt? kayyix.
Seam, Sew, odroz. Stitch, orroz.
Whip, Overcast, serrij s.

SHAKE, ʋa hozz, qalqil.
Brandish, rojj. Dandle, zejzij.
Churn, Shake up, koll, imkal.
Jerk, Shake about, onfol.
Jog, Rock (a cradle), hezhiz.
Jolt, ʋa inkas.
Nod (the head), ʋa infax.
— ʋn (vacillate), tenaffax.
Pull and Push about, testis.
Toss, zojj. Toss about, heyyij.
Toss and Shake out, oncoθ.
Toss to and fro, Tawwifl.

Rock (a ship), barcil, darcil.
— ʋn tebarcel, tedarcel.
Vacillate, Be Shaky, teqalqal.
Vibrate, ʋa zelzil.
Wag, ʋa rajrij, arsux.
Wave, ʋa rajrij, tortir.
— anies? (the hand) rabrub li.
TREMBLE.

SHAMEFUL, faʒuis.
Shameless (deed), majouniey.
Disgraceful, } faluifl,
Dishonourable, } mofluf.
Flagitious, mojarras.
Hideous, qabiefl.
Foul, fallux. Gross, semij.
Ignoble, doun, wâru.
Ignominious, sofliey.
Indecorous, kârij.
Infamous, mebtouc.
Inglorious (Abject), Tariefl.
Loathsome, xanies.
Scandalous, mosuib.
Smutty, dâsur. BASE. LEWD.

SHARP, fladd. Intense, xadied.
Keen, rchief, morbif.
Piercing, mowêciz, kâriq.
Poignant, nâkis. Severe, vârim.
Trenchant, ʌerib, qâtus.
Vehement, flâmi.
Violent, sanief.

SHAWL, xâl(a) 2, 9,
also pl. farmâyix c.
Head Shawl, coufieya.
Kerchief, } mafirima 11.
Scarf, } mandiel 11, Tarfla.
Necktie, } robrat el sünq,
Cravat, } maflrimat el raqaba.

Sheaf, truss, ḏözma.
Faggot, jorze.
Shock (of wheat), cods 4.
Cock (of hay), sarama 10 (pile).
Stack, Mow, couma 4, 9 (heap).
Rick, sanbar c. [Anbar?].
Armful, bât b. ḏamar 4 b.
Handful or Armful, ḏöfna 10.
Bundle of grass, bât ḏaxiex.
FARM.

Sheep, ḻân, ḏanam;
 (more antique), xâ', maxâ'a.
Ram, cebx 5.
Ewe, ḏanama al. najsa bₓ.
Wether, karouf 9.
Lamb, kârouf 12 al. tali bₓ. *pl.*
 tölyân. ramies, qauzicy b.
— (*eccles.*), ḏamal.
Wild Sheep, mafloun.
Fleece, jizze 10. *Wool*, yöuf.

Ship, Vessel, marceb 11.
Gunship, seḏena midfaṣuiya.
Deck, saqicfa, ḻahr (ḻ) el
 marceb.
Berth, maqsad.
Cabin, tûrima, cêmara f.
Small Cabin, kazna.
Hammock, marjieḏa.
Mast, ṣâri; sêri b. 12, daqal bₓ.
Yard, râjis 12; scran.
Sail, qils 3, xirâs 2.
Anchor, mirsêya.
 — with 4 beaks, helb 3, 4.
Cable, qils 3, ḏaumana c.
Mooring rope, mirse, sebala.
Buoy, xamandara c.
Keel, konn el marceb.
Rudder, daffet el marceb.
Helm, el soccên s.

Prow, moqaddam, moqdim?
Poop, Stern, moukir, ceuθel.
Freight, xaḏn, xuḏna.
Cargo, wesqa.
Oar, mijaêf 11, *vulg.* miqdâf 11.
Boat-pole, midra' 11 (*but also*
 Paddle b.). FLEET.

SHINE, *vn* aḻui, *vulg. male* aḻwi.
Shine brilliant, xasxis.
Beam, tenawwar.
Blaze, wehej yehij.
Burn clear, *vn* baybuy.
Dawn, tebellaj.
Flame, telehheb.
Flame out, telaxza'.
Flare, uḻrim, uḻtarim.
Flash, to'ellaq, obroq.
Flicker, tewehhej.
Glance forth (as light), ilmaḏ.
Glare, isras? isras el nour b.
Gleam, telâlû. Glister, irhej.
Glitter, ilmas. Sparkle, laḏliḏ.
Glow, buyy; 'ijj, wijj.
Illumine, *vs* nawwir.
Kindle, *vs* ixsal, axsul.
 — *vn* inxasul, ixtesul.
Radiate, *vn* toxasxos.
Twinkle, ibziq, ibzif.

SHIRT, qamicy 9, 10.
Skirt, ḏàxiya 12.
Gore, banieqa c. 11.
Hem, ccfàfa b. Tuck, qarb.
Seam, Double Seam, lafq.
Frill, cexcex. Plait, tuiya.
Crease, ḏaḻn.
Striped Shirt? baxt 3.

SHOE, *s.* marcoub; (in older
 style) huaê, *pl.* aḻaiya.

Sandal, naɛla ʃu.
Heavy Shoe, zerboul 11.
Light Shoe, yörmâya 11.
European Shoe, tɛsouma 12.
Morocco Boot, mouze.
Moccasins, buskins without sole, most ʌL bolɼa 10 B.
Woman's Buskin, koff 4, 5 B.
Leather Socks, qalxicn.
Carpet Socks, tɛrliec.
Stocking, jauráb 11.
Outer Slippers, bâbouj.
Patten, qabqab ʌl.
Shoelatchet, xiɛc 3, xarêc.
Shoestring, bend 3.

Snow, ɛa arie (ɛulg. malè, arwi.)
Demonstrate, auʎuʃl.
Display, aʒhir, abdi (lay open).
— oneself, teʒahher.
Evidence, ɛa bayyin, abien.
Manifest, ajli, waʎah yaʎaʃl.
Point at, doll ɛala', li.
— wama' yami.
Reveal, Detray, icxif.
Presént, wajjih.

Shrub, s. xojaira.
Bush (thorny?), ɛöllieq.
Bay, ɼàr; (classical) daʃna.
Rose laurel, Rhododendron, dofla. Bramble, ɛausej.
Lotus, sidr(a), ʃlandaqouq.
Ivy, qiɛsous, ʃlabl el mesécien.
Ground Ivy, kamâ qiɛsous, χαμαι κισσος.
Privet, faqou, ʃûqiya.
Lentisc, ʎarou, cemcên.
Tamarisk, rarʃa, eθl.
Whortleberry, ês barriey.

Myrtle, ês.
Southernwood, qaiyöum.
Wormwood, afsentiem (absinthium) kiθraq mámiete, xieʃl?
Ricinus, kirwaɛ.
Broom, wezêl, retma B.
Spanish Broom, tranjebiel.
Camel's Thorn? ⎱ ɛalqa',
Gorse? ⎰ ɛalqâya.
Heather, kalnaj.
Thorny Burnet, netx belân.
Juniper, ɛarxar, abhel, concilên, sindarouɛ.
Acanthus, cencer, ɛcliek. Tree.

Shun, ɛa nâːr, jânib, ijtenib ɛan, tejannab ɛan.
Avoid, uʃlterix ɛan, isteʃlris min.
Keep aloof from, ɛn inʃar ɛan, ibtɛɛud ɛan.
Beware, uʃlɛer, uʃlteɛir, teʃlaɛɛer, ɛan, min.
Elope, iʃlet. Flee, ohrob.
Elude, omrof, ʃlâwil ɛan, inɛill min.
Escape, firr, inji (onjou), inʃlɛ, iklay.
Evade, inmeluy, temellaɛ ɛan; ɛulg. ofroc B.
Guard against, ɛn waɛu yousa' min; teterres, teʃlûmâ, ɛan.
Provide against, teʃlaɛɛeb min, todarrec, iddaric.
Slip. Swerve.

Sick, marieʎ, pl. marʎa'.
Ailing, ɛalieL Ill, dâ'yi.
Indisposed, moɛtell.
Weakly, Poorly, ɛayyân.
Sickly, ɛeqiem, misqûm.

Stricken (by a malady), wasnc, mausouo b. Afflicted, moyâb.
Invalid, maknouc. Infirm, sâjiz.
Disabled? saqut.
Bedridden, lézim el firâz, tariefl el firâz. Weak.
Silk, flarier.
Sarsenet, abruxiem.
Taffety, flabaru, darâya, randal b.
Brocade, diebâj, sondos, qomûx moqayyab.
A Cocoon, xornoqa 11.
Damask, moxajjar.
Flowered Brocade, cimkâ, cimk.
Gauze (unspun silk?), qazz.
Pile of Velvet, qa'ou.
Moire (b.), watered silk; cermesoud.
Plush (cloak?), qaruifa.
Satin, atlas. Silk thread, silc.
Sincere, rûdiq, radieq, barier.
Frank, Blunt, nabr b.
Disinterested, kâluy, mokluy, mokâluy. Candid, râfi.
Faithful, mômoun s. wefiey, nâyoufl (f. of *horse*).
Constant, wéôiq, rêsik, resiey.
Ingenuous, yamiemiey.
Open,) besier,
Simple,) sédij, sédifl?
Pure, rahir 4, râhir 1, naqi 6.
Racy, 'ayliey. [al
Straightforward, Sterling, dofri
True, rafluifl. Trusty, 'emien.
Trustworthy, raidaq, weôieq.
Truthful,) radouq k.
Veracious,) ruddieq.
Just. Right. Pure.

Sinew, Tendon, caqaba, nk.
Muscle, raKala, nk. 3.
Flesh, lafim 3.
Gristle, fakrouf; *vulg.* qarqonx (crackling).
Ligament, ribât 2.
Tendon of neck, ronob b.
Nerve, rayaba, nk. 2.

Sing, ranni. Carol, farrid.
Chant, Hymn, rettil.
Hum, donn, dandin.
Intone, Recite, lafiflun, oxdon.
Recite verses, anxid.
Sing Psalms, zemmir.
Sing Lullaby, hemhim.
Sing a Dirge, irôi.
Strike up (in music), uydafl.
Trill? tcrannam (tinkle?).
Twitter,) watt,
Chirp,) tewarwat.
Warble, nâri. Whistle, uyfir.
Crow, Cry, Sound, Scream.

Size, *s.* flajm. Body, jcsed 4.
Bulk, jism. Bulkiness, jesêma.
Enormity, cuzm. Mass, jirm.
Hugeness, Bigness, Kakâma.
Minuteness, diqqa.
Smallness, rufr, yofr b.
Volume, ôekan.

Skin, *s.* jild 3.
Cuticle, Epiderm, baxara.
Follicle, cimm 4.
Membrane, fixâ, jolsida.
Mucous dº, fixâ mokâruiy.
Midriff, flujâb.
Periosteum, Karies c.
Peritoneum, yufâq.

SKY, æther, jawou.
Atmosphere, nau (B. *sic*).
Climate, manâk (*rare word?*)
Weather, ʀaqs el donyâ, ɴâl el donyâ, (or simply) el donyâ.
Clear Sky, ɣaɴöu, ɣaɴwa.
Murky Sky, dojn, dojna.
Lowering Sky, ʀabou.
Cloud (*nubœ*), seɴâba, ᴨu. 10, 11.
Cloud (*nimbus*), ʀaim 3.
Dusk, qoᴛma, *vulg.* ʂötma, ʀutema.

SLAVE, *s.* ʂabd, *pl.* ʂabied.
Serf, Thrall, raqq.
Household Slave, qinn 4 (*verna*).
Handmaid, qâyina 2, 4.
Chattel (slave), mamlouc 11.
Captive, *ᴇsier 6.
Drudge, ʂaʂief, dâqiʂ, ceddâɴ.
Hireling, 'ejier. Menial, mêhin.
Servant, kâdim 6; kaddâm, kozmetoêr ᴀʟ

SLEEP, *vn* nâm, orqod, *ger.* naum, ʀaqâd.
— profoundly, iĥcir ; *ger.* hecr (coma). Slumber, inʂas.
Doze, iʀû, iʀfal (forget oneself).
Drowsiness, *ger.* noʂâs, nowâm, wasen.
A Nap, *ger.* ʀafya.
Dream, *vn* oɴlom.
A Dream, ɴölm 4.
A Dream or Vision, manâm.

SLIP, *vn* glide, be slippery; izlaq, zeɴliq.
Slip, *vn* (generally in moral sense) ezill.
Let Slip, *va* aflit, ealit ?

Slip off, *vn* izhal.
Slip in, *va* doss, ldɴax.
— *vn* indiss, indaɴux; izbaq B.
Slip out, away, off from, *vn* ;
Steal away; Slink, Sneak; siel, inʂaiɫɫ; inɣal, inzeh; aieɴ, islet, inselit; iɴet, inʀaliq; inmelis, inmeluɣ, temellaɣ.
Creep (glide, march), izɴaf.
Slide (in gen.), zcɴliq.
Slide in sport, tezellaq.

SMILE, *vn* ibaim ʀ.
Smirk? tcbâsem. *Laugh*, uẍɴac.
Snarl, Grin, ccxiʀ, cexxir li.
Scowl, tejehbem, iclaɴ, tecellaɴ.

SMITH, qain 3, 4.
Blacksmith, ɴaddâd.
Coppersmith, naɴɴâs.
Locksmith, ceffâl.
Goldsmith, hibraqiey, ʀâyiʀ, ɣayyâʀ.
Smith's Hammer, muʀʀaqa.
Tongs, cemmâxa, celbatein, ᴀʟ
Anvil, sindûn.
— maʀʀaba ɢ. (stone slab).
Tools, *edâwêt, ĉlĉt.
Kiln, qamien ɞ (*caminus*).
Clay Furnace, cour 4, 9.
Forge for Iron, tennour.
Iron, ɴadied. Steel, boulâd.
Copper, naɴâs (aɴmar).
Tin, tenec, ᴀʟ ɣaficɴ, ʀ.

SNAKE, *s.* ɴaɴax 4.
Serpent, ɴaiya.
Basilisk (Boa ? Dragon, ᴋ.), θoʂbân 11.
Viper, Adder, 'ifʂa 11.

Eel, enclies (εγχελυς).
Lamprey, muraina (μύραινα).

A Sob,   ) s. xchqa,
Hiccup,   ) xehieq.
A Sigh, 'éhe, te'éwoh.
— (of desire, x.) flasra.
Cough, vocâl, ceflfla.
Sneezing, sutâx.
Gasping, lehed, nehej.
Panting, lohej, leheθ (as dog lolling tongue).
Heaving of bosom, tenehhod.
Puffing, naffl, toneffos.
Asthma, nefθ. Breath, nefès 4.
A Breath, nesema.

SOLDIER, jondiey, *pl.* jonoud.
Land force, sascerieya barrieya.
Marines, sascerieya baflrieya.
Infantry Soldier, râjil, zelma, qarâb (B. *sic*). nafar 4.
Cavalry Soldier, kayyâl, fâris.
Fighting man, moqâtil.
Guard, rafar, kafar, flâris 7.
Soldier in garrison, flâfuz.
Sentinel, Sentry, waqqâf.
Patrol, el sases, el τauf.
Private Soldiera, anfâr.
Scout,   ) râyid el sascer,
Explorer,)   *pl.* rowwâd.

WAR.

SOUND, *en* (*in gen.* rinn, vawwit; (as musical instrument) doqq, izmar?
Bellow, sujj, sajsuj.
Boom, hidd. Click, τaqτuq.
Brawl (as water), sersur.
Clack (as mill), jasjis.
Clang, Clank, τunn.

Jingle, Tinkle, τanτun.
Clatter, τarτuq, θerθir.
Clash, Rustle,) koxx,
Clink, Chink,) kaxkix.
Crackle,   ) qarqis,
Rumble,   ) teqarqas.
Crackle (as suit in fire), tectic.
Crash (in exploding), τoqq.
Creak, Grate, zeyyiq, zeqziq.
Make a Din, masmis.
Echo, idwi, anbifl.
Gurgle, baqbiq, ralril.
Hiss, fiflfl. Hum, donn, dandin.
Hoot, uxkab (scream).
Jar, Grate, Screech, varvur.
Murmur, idri. Peal, insaq.
Make Noise, xujj.
Patter, Dash (Drop), kirr.
Purl, temarmur (Itipple).
Racket, Riot, rawwix, dawwix.
Rattle, valyul.
Ring, Twang, rinn.
Rustle, Whirr, oqroτ, tekaxkax.
Roar (as thunder), iqzuf.
Rumble, Mutter (as d⁰.), zemzim. Seethe, ratrit x.
Tick, Throb, irfiz.
Tinkle, Twang, terannam.
Whiffle, Huffle, fluff.
Whistle, uxfir. Whizz, qarquτ.
CRY. CROW. SCREAM. NOISE.

SOUND, epithets of;
Clear, bâyin, varieft.
Dull, Obscure, Faint, kâmil.
Distinct, jehier, jehour B. fâriz.
Loud, vâliq (Deep bass?).
Low, wâτu, kafi.
Harsh, yakih (deafening, x).
High, Shrill, sâli, rafiec.

ANGLO-ARABIC VOCABULARY. 127

Sweet, Shrill, rakiem.
Rough, ráſul, raſul, ayſal.
Hoarse, mabſouſ, abaſſ?

Soup, xauraba.
Broth, maraqa. Gravy, zoum.
Gruel, Porridge, cayuida.
Sauce, TARATOUR (sic F.).

SOURCE, maydar.
Fountain, yanbouc 11, manbac.
Spring of water, ain mûy.
Woll-head, ra's mûy.
Well, bi'r 4 (in gen.).
Pit, Artificial Well, jobb 10.

SPACE, el besiera.
Spaciousness, fosſla.
Open Space, faſâ.
Expanse, nodſla, mandaſl, mandouſla.
Room, Volume, } wosen,
Capacity, } sesn.
Area, sêſla, mesraſl, maidan 11.
Extent, made'. Length, röul.
Distance between, Interval, mabain, meséfa.
Short interval, kilal, fout?
fowait?
SIZE. MEASURE. PLACE.

SPADE (in gen.), muſlfar; qazma 10 B. (trowel?).
Spud, marr. Pick, miezeqo.
Pronged Spade, moyabbas B.
Mattock? TÜURiya.
Shovel, miqlab, misſláya Bg.
Axe, Pickaxe, fa's 3.
Hoe (to scrape off with), miqxaT, jârouf AL. B.
Dunghoe, zebbâl (dirt box).

Rake, mijrafa B. maxTB. (comb), mikdaxa?

SPARE, ra teſlâſaz fle, calo';
ſlâfuz cala'; uſltefiz bi, cala'.
Eke out, Economize, waffir.
Hoard, yammid (KEEP).
Husband, dabbir.
Be Parsimonious or Chary of, iqtir, teqatter cala'.
Reserve, abqi, kalli, afſul.
Save, tewaqqa' fle.
Stint yourself, qarmiT cala' nefsec.

SPARROW (or in gen. any small bird), söyfour 11.
Hedge Sparrow, s. el zerâyib.
Redbreast, el aſlmar el yadr.
Wren, nomnoma 11.
Wryneck, el motelaffit.
Wagtail, qaubas.
Cuckoo, coucou, waqouq, târawi, raiTawi.
Oriole, tenawwot.
Yellow Hammer, yöfariey(a).

SPEAK, cellim. Declaim, jêhir.
Address, cêlim, csmic.
Blab, noθθ, bouſl bi sirr.
Blurt out, faxx, onθou?
Bluster, tcsazran.
Deliver (a speech), telchhej bi.
Descant, tefawwah bi.
Discourse upon, teſladdaθ bi.
Exclaim, yuiſl, sayyur.
Harangue, oktob, kârub.
Intone? laſlſlun.
Mouths, maτmif.
Pour forth (as a sweet or divine voice), ihtif. Recito, oxdou.

Pronounce, telaffa͜g bi.
Rant, Inveigh, hêti.
Rehearse (verses), anxid.
Spout, Rave, ihai.
Storm against, flaxxic cala'.
Utter, intuq bi. Vent, naffis c.
Whisper, waswis (waxwix c.),
 tewaswas, tcbetbet.
BABBLE. CHAT. CRY. PUBLISH.
 SAY. STAMMER. TALK.

SPECIES, yunf 4.
Category, maqoula.
Class, marteba 11.
Description, wayf 4.
Genus, jins 4. Grade, tabaqa 5.
Head, bâb, pl. abwâb.
Kind, naus 4.
Order, nizâm ? naguim ?
 manzam ?
Quality, wayf 4, yufa 4.
Rank, rotba 10.
Sort, Shape, xecl 4.
Tribe, Clan, qabiel 10.
 NATURE. MANNER.

SPEND, ca (money), anfiq,
 (time) aqău.
Spend fast, badriq.
Dispose of, texarraf bi.
Dissipate, beasir, bezzir
 (SCATTER).
Expend, osrof (change).
— tecellef b. (charge oneself).
Exhaust, xaffit. Absorb, naxxif.
Lavish, ibail, xott bi.
Make away with, usmel bi, afni.
Misuse, behdil.
Put out (expend), akrij.
Squander, esrif fie.
Throw away, dahwir.

Trifle away, héwin.
Use up, anfid, naffid.
Waste, etlif, aăni.

SPICE (in gen.), fouh (sic).
A whiff of odour, funfla 2 (sic).
Spices in food, bahêrât.
Perfumery, ceturiey.
Cruet (raw condiment), qizfl,
 pl. teqâziefl.
Round Cloves, bahêr.
Cloves, qoronfol.
Cinnamon, qirfa, nariera B. dâr
 Juiniey.
Autour (B), bark resembling
 cinnamon, latr.
Ginger, zinjibiel.
Mace, bizbâze.
Coriander, cozbara.
Nutmeg, jauz taiyib, jauz el
 tuib, jauz bawa' B.
Seeds as spice, abzêr, abâzier.

A SPOT (in all senses) boqca 5.
Dot, noqta 10, 5.
A Point, a Stop (in punctua-
 tion), maflatt.
Speckle, nocte 5.
Speck, lecce ? o.
Stain, latka, rabca.

STABLE for horses, ekour.
Stall, Pen, Post-Station for new
 horses, marbat 11.
Manger, Trough, madwad.
Hayrack, maslaf.
Nosebag, mislaf, miklâya.
Greenfodder, qayuil, kâyuil.
Grass, flaxicx. Hay, θinn.
Lucerne, barsiem. Straw, tibn.
Barley, xacuir.

ANGLO-ARABIC VOCABULARY.   129

Bran, nakâl.
Horse Beans, foul.
Carrots, jezer.
Bin, sebad c. sebat b.
Grain sack, cadil 4.
Dung, zibl.
Refuse, rajiec.   FARM.

STAFF, minsê'ya.
Stick (*in gen.*), cóud 9.
Walking Stick, cayâ 10.
Club, nabbout, dabrec.
Crutch, cuccêze.
Crosier, Sceptre, voulajân.
Hooked Stick, qarqal.
Crook to throw, muûjan (boomerang?).
Shepherd's crook, coqqâfa.
Hockey (a game), jaucên, (traugan c).
Bludgeon, zaqla.
Cudgel, taqvuira (Truncheon).
Mace of iron, } qaXuib.
Bar of iron, }
Rod, Cane. Switch, miswaqa.
Shaft (to throw), jaried.
— of spear, senec.
Light Stick, cóyâya.
Perch, Pole, } xabier b.
Measuring Wand, }
Withe, Switch, xarba nu. 9.

STAMMER, *vn* } tamtum,
Stutter, } temtim.
— tehtih, teftif.
— lajlij, belrum.
Falter, irtijj, irtij ; irticc, nacnio (waver).
Hesitate, teraddad.
Lisp, θeŗθiŗ. — ilθeŗ, *vulg.* ildac.
Grumble, damdim.

Mumble, hesbis, jamjim.
Murmur, temarmar ; tedammar, damrim.
Mutter, barbir, zemzim.
BABBLE.   SOUND.

STAR (*étoile*), najma 3.
Heavenly body (*astre*), ceuceb 11.   Luminary, naiyir.
Meteor, 'eθer calawiey.
Constellation, yöura, nu.
Sign of Zodiac, borŗ 3.
Comet, najma moaennaba.
Planet, seyyâra, najma sêyira.
Mercury, cótârid.
Venus, zebera.   Mars, marriek.
Jupiter, moxteric.
Saturn, zöûal.   Earth, el 'erâ.

STEADY, *adj.* θêbit, moteweθθiq.
Constant, galiel.
Durable, moðâyin.
Established, mosteûcim, moûcem.
Fast, weθieq, wêθiq.
Firm, resiey.   Fixed, mortociz.
Rooted, Radical, 'cruil.
Settled, mosteqirr.
Stable, waruid. Steadfast, réaik.
Sure, 'ecied, auced.
Solid, jelied.   STOUT.
PERPETUAL.   SINCERE.   INNATE.

STEAL, *va* isriq.
Decamp with, ofroc bi.
Embezzle, iktelis.
Filch, oxmot.   Pilfer, ontox.
Poach (by night), iŗtelis.
Purloin, onxol, uûwi.
Swindle, sesbir cala'.

9

STEM, Bole of tree, s. jiac 3.
Trunk (Stump?), qarma 10;
 also pl. 11 qarámi (κοpμl?).
Log, ſlaraba, zend ſlarab b.
Stalk, sêq f. 2, 9 (leg).
Stock, 'eyl 3 (lit. or fig.), Lat.
 stirps.
Root, Radicle, εörε 3, xorε 3,
 xolε 3 b.
Root (fibrous, veiny), curq 3.
Root (globular? edible), jiar 3.

STINGY, bakiel. Chary, Kanien?
Avaricious, xaſluiſl.
Closefisted, jômid (or majmoud)
 el ceff.
Covetous, rûmic, ταmmάc.
Frugal, moqattir.
Grasping, mostecθir.
Illiberal, lc'iem. Mean, daniey.
Miserly, fáyin. Paltry, kaκies.
Niggardly, felſlas c.
Parsimonious, qazien b.
Penurious, qarut.
Pinching, jcsous.
Saving, Hoarding, moγammid.
Shabby, moteqaxxif.
Sordid, qaair.
Sparing of, mostcſlſiz.
Tenacious, moqorbut.
Thrifty, mowaffir. GREEDY.

STONE, ſlajara, nu. 4, 5, also pl.
 ſlujâra.
Alabaster? Basalt, rokâm.
Flint, yawwân. Gravel, ſlaxba.
Marble, marmar.
Paving Stone, belât, bellâr.
Pebble, ſlaywa, pl. ſlavâ.
Porphyry, ſlajar γömmaqiey o.

Quarry, maſljar? 11; maqlic 11;
 macdan (11) ſlajar.

STOP, ca anhi. Arrest, auqif.
Block up, irdim.
Bung, Dam, up; sodd.
Debar, oſljoz ean.
Detain, ſlöuz ean.
Forbid, Prohibit, aſlrim, ſlarrim.
Hinder,) imnac, mânic.
Impede,) couq ean, acuiq.
Retard,) cawwiq.
Hold back, osfos?
Hold in, Keep in, oābot, uſlbis.
Intercept, iqrac, kâzim.
Obstruct, ocroi bi, tecarraī.
Obviate,) dâric, tedâres,
Prevent,) iddaric min, tedarrec.
Repress, oſlγör, ep vii. okzol.
Restrain, irdas, warric.
Restrict,) ſlarrij cala', oqγör,
Limit,) aqγur, qaγγur.
Suppress, idſlas? ſlött, abrul.
 BRIDLE. CONFINE. OPPOSE.
 REPEL.

STOUT, rayuin. Hardy, moruiq.
Compact, mocteniz.
Dense, γölb; molezzcz.
Enduring, γabour, ſlummicl.
Hale, Vigorous, cafi θ.
Hard, jâfi f. waqioſl.
Hard and Dry (soil, wood),
 yebis, γald b.; valoud.
Harsh (as cotton), qûsiſl.
Massive, rayuy. Robust, belict.
Plump of barrel, ſalies.
Rude (and Big), ſaliez.
Solid, jelied, mecien.
Stark, qaab, qaisebân k.
Staunch against, rûbir cala'.

Stiff, jâff, yêbis. Stubborn, qâsi.
Strong, qâwi, mêcin ᴀʟ
Sturdy, casi, câsi (*sic*).
Substantial, metien.
Tough, xâsif, ceθief.
Thick, θakien, ceθief, ceθicθ, moteceθθib.

Sᴛʀᴇᴇᴛ, Place, maθalla 2, maθall, *pl.* maθâll.
Alley, Narrow Street, zoqâq θ.
Thoroughfare, majêz.
Opén Area, miedûn, maidân 11.
Cranny, Lane, fajj.
Square, carya 2, 4, 5.
Court, scha 2. Market, souq 4.
Meat Market, meslak.
Clothes Market, bâzâr.
Portico (on pillars), ostowâna.
A Turning of the Street, carafa lil zoqâq. Rᴏᴀᴅ.

Sᴛʀᴇᴛᴄʜ, ra modd, (with effort?) maʀʀu.
Broaden, } falʀuθ.
Widen, } farʀuθ.
Dilate, moʀʀ.
Distend, ifraθ (*sic*).
Enlarge, wessic, fessiθ.
Expand, obsoʀ, bassiʀ.
Flatten, baʀʀuʀ, ifcax.
Lengthen, ʀawwil.
Spread out, onxor, ofrox, basziq? (Prolate).
Strain (a rope), qannib, xodd.
Straddle, tcfellas, farxik.
Stride, ifxik (ifxiθ ᴢ).

Sᴛʀɪᴠᴇ, ca (see Wᴏʀᴋ).
Adventure, } jêzif bi, tejêser
Venture, on } cala', teradda'.

Attempt, tehejjam, θâwil
Endeavour, iscu, ijtehid.
Essay, imteθun.
Exert oneself, usteni.
Take pains, bâlic, jêhid.
Strive, tesâluj; imθan? tebârez (*as champion?*).
Strain (*the sinews*) qannib, rannib.
Stiffen oneself, injiff (*in rowing*).
Struggle, kâbiʀ, câfis? nâzic (as one mortally stricken), ihrij, tehêrâj, ikiabuʀ ʙ.; *gen.* agitate oneself, hêbir ʙ.
Tustle, mârir, temârar.
Work hard, câθr.
Wrestle, xâric, terârac, jâliʀ?
(Strive, quarrel; see Qᴜᴀʀʀᴇʟ). Dᴀʀᴇ.

Sᴛᴜᴍʙʟᴇ, on ucθer, tesaθwar.
Flounder, ittarjil, uʀʀarjil, texarjal, tefaxcel.
Reel, donk (*be giddy*).
Stagger, terannaθ (*with wine?*), ikʀal? iqθaz?
Topple, } tekalkal, teterter,
Totter, } tezolzel.
Waver, terajraj.
Trip (take false step), itcas, tesarqal. Sʟɪᴘ.

Sᴜɪᴛ of Law, } daswa',
Lawsuit, } daswâ.
Accusation (accusatory deposition), tohma. Apology, cüᴀʀ.
Allegation, borhên.
Appeal, morâfaca.
Charge, Complaint, xeowa.
Litigation, ladad.
Proof, iθbât. Plea, θöjja 10.

Pretext, tecallol.
Procedure, siera.
Prosecution, mohácema.
Oath, yemien, ſialif, qasem 4.
LAW.

SUMMIT, aɛla'.
Brow, Head, râ's.
Crest, *lit.* or *fig.* xouxa.
Crown (of hill), aima.
Peak, qimma 10.
Top, ᴀirwa, *pl.* ᴀora'.
Tip, nocte 10.
Ridge, ſârib 12.
— metn, metna 5, xinkâb 11.
Vertex, Apex, auj c.
Pinnacle, xorſa 10.
MOUNTAIN, DECLIVITY.

SUN, xams, *f.* 3.
Sunbeam, xoɛâɛ 8.
Noonday beam, ɽazêla c.
Full Daylight, ᴌohâ, ᴌaſlou, ᴌaſlwa.
Light, ᴌau, ᴌaiya, *pl.* aᴌwiya.
Lustre, nour 4.

SUPPLY, *va.*
(1) sufficio; become substitute for, ajxi ɛan, aɽui moɽna', ecâ, min.
(2) Afford (a thing), Minister, qaddim, aſᴌur, aurid, najjim, aſicd. Yield (fruit), aẑmir, jieb, aɽᴌil, ajdi.
(3) Supply (a person with), Stock him (with provisions), moun, mier bi; (for a journey), zewwid.
Stock (a shop), waᴌᴌub.
Furnish (a house), jebhiz.

Assist (a customer), esɛuf, sêɛuf, ezbun.
Provision, Purvey; mawwin-oh bi, zewwid.
Supply (an army), amidd, mâdid.
Ask Supplies, istemidd.
Accommodate (a person) with, yessir, hêwid, tesêhel mas-oh.
Take in Supplies, teſlawwaj, tezehheb.
Be well supplied with, tɛmawwan min.

SURROUND, aſluiᴛ bi, uſtêt bi.
Beset, terêcem ɛala'.
Encircle, ſlawwiᴛ, ſlâwiᴛ.
Encompass, cennif, ictenif ɛala'.
Environ (an enemy), uᴌrib ſlalieqatoh.
Enclose, } uſlwi.
Include, } uſtewi ɛala'.

SWEEP, *va* icnis; cennis ᴀʟ
— away, oxmoᴛ. Brush, qomm.
Flap away, noxx.
Shake, Jerk, onfoᴌ.
Whisk, izɛaf.
— away, coxx? cexcix.
Wipe, imseſl.

SWEETS, ſlôlawa, secêcir.
Sweetmeat, ſlalâwa.
Sugar, soccer.
Loaf Sugar, ablouj.
Sugarloaf, qâlib soccer.
Powdered Sugar, soccer hezz, soccer nâɛum.
Sugar-candy, qand, qandaⁱ nebât ʙ. soocer mocerrar c.
Barley-sugar, ᴛabarzed.

Sugar-plums, molabbas.
Honey, rasel. Liquorice, sous.
Treacle of raisins or figs, dibs.
Syrup, jalâb. (In Persian, rose-water.) Preserve, morabba'.
Fruit Jelly, robb.
Jam, } kabuiya,
Compost of Fruit, } cövâra.

SWERVE, en fluid can, inflarif san.
Deviate, nedal can, incacif min.
Flinch? zief, zour san.
Miss (as an arrow), Tuix.
Shrink, Slink from, ixmâzz.
Slope, Incline, miel.
Start, Shy from, ijâl min.
SHUN. SLIP.

TABLE, s. mâyida 12, meiz, Bq. tâwola AL
Dining Table, sofra, AL kowân 8, 10 F. (long), yomât B.
Toilet Table, bextekte' flariem.
Small Tray, misnada K.

TABLE UTENSILS, êlêt el mâyida.
Table Knife, siccicna 11.
Fork, forqatte c. forteico 2 AL
Blade of Knife, novla.
Handle, novûb.
Prong of Fork, sinn 4.
Spoon, milraqa 11.
Large Spoon, kâxoufa B.
Ladle, cefcier o. mirrafa B. F.
Fish Slice, mixrafl.
Table Cloth, melâya; kâm (or biez or bicâ or mendiel or mafraz) ol sofra.
Napkin, pexciera.

Doyley, mendiel, maflrima 11.
Corkscrew, boraima.
Funnel, qomc. Strainer, muyfa'.
Sugar-tongs, milqât el soccer.
Saltcellar, mimlafla.
Cruetstand, miqzefla 11.
Pepperbox, wucâ (or flâffet) el fulfol.
Rasp, muflacce.
Nutmeg-grater, miqxat.

TAKE, va imperat. koA ('ekaA, yêkoA).
— away, Remove (see EXPEL), xiel; eziefl.
— up, irfac, xiel; olqoT, iltaquT.
— in (house), uflwi, adkil.
— off (clothes), iklac.
— out, pull out; iqlac, focc.
— away (deprive of), acdim, ikTuf. ROB. CATCH.

TAKE in hand, 'ekaA bi, fie, te'ekkaA bi; urzim.
Begin, ibdi, abdi, ibtedi.
Commence, ixrac fie, tecâtâ.
Set about, urfiq en, inbari bi, weßer yeßer en, cala', tehejjam cala', tecazzem.
Take heart to, ustemid wa.
Undertake, qoum bi, bâxir fic.
— (boldly), tecarraâ li.

TALENT, firûse. Ability, 'ehlieyu.
Aptitude, isticdâd, liyâqa.
Adroitness, cuyâqa (B. sic).
Acuteness, flaacqa.
Art (high), fenn 3.
Capacity, utâqa.
Character, } Tabc,
Stamp, NATURE, } Tabieca.

Clearsightedness, basuira.
Cleverness, xaтâra.
Craft, Experience, marâna ʀ.
Force of mind, selieqa.
Genius, qariefla, aiera.
Information, istislâm.
Ingenuity, ciyâse.
Intellect, saql (Good Sense).
Intelligence, fehm.
Understanding, idrâc.
Insight, basr, basâra.
Knowledge, maʃrifa 11.
Learning, diráya.
Readiness, nebâhe.
Quickness, laqâna.
Sagacity, ʌecêwn.
Science, ʃulm.   Skill, mehêrs.
Superiority,   } barâsa.
Preeminence, }
Subtlety, ʌihn.
Temperament, mizêj.
Versatility, lebâqa, lauʌʌsuiya.
Wisdom, flucma (antiq.).

Talk, ʏn tecollam.
Accost, va aʃrnʃ.
Address, kûtub, cellim, cêlim;
  (confidentially) nâji, fâwuʃ;
  (familiarly) flâdiθ, flûci,
  flûwir, sêmir.
Commune, teʌêcer, tenâja'.
Confer, tedâwal, tekâbar.
Converso, } teqâwal, teflâddaθ,
Disconrse, } teflâce', teflâwar,
  tesêmar.

Tame, adj. dâjin, dajoun,
  moddâjin.
Compliant, moʀâwis, ʀuwâsuiy.
Docile, monqâd.

Domestic, beitiey, 'ehliey,
  jouwiey.
Familiar, 'enies, mênous,
  mostênis, mote'êlif.
Groveling, motewâʃus.
Gentle, mosêbil, damieθ.
Humble, kâxis.
Lowly, } wadies,
Meek, } motewâdis.
Obedient, ʀâyis, moʀuis.
Obsequious, tebies, moʌʀun.
Servile, waʀd, mowâʀid.
Submissive, miʌsûn, kâʃus,
  kaʃous. Towardly, mosêyir.
Tractable, molâyim.

Tame Animal, dâjin 12.
Horses, kail.   Oxen, baqar.
Ass, flumâr.   Camels, 'ibl.
Sheep, ʃân, xâ.   Goats, masz.
Dog, celb 5.   Cat, quʀʀ 10.
Deer, mehê.   Pig, kinzier 11.
Rabbit, fenec ʀ.   Elephant, ficl.
Ferret, suʀsc.   Pigeons, yamâm.
Poultry, faronj 11.
Ducks, baʀʀ.   Geese, wezz.

Tart, adj. yârim.
Acid, flamiez, flûwiz.
Acerb, flâʌiq (Biting).
Acrid, flurricf, cafus.
Ardent, bêsil.   Bitter, morr.
Crude, Harsb, ʀuʃʃ.
Pungent, xeʌicy.
Salt, mâliñ.   Sour, flâmuʃ.
Sour-sweet, meziz, mezouz,
  lafluu, melies ɴ.
Stinging, leʌʌês.

Tear, va mezziq.
Claw, va iklib, iktelib.

ANGLO-ARABIC VOCABULARY.   135

Crack, oxrot. Split, xiqq.
Grate, Rasp, oqſlöt, oqxot?
Rend, okroq; karbiq?
— with claws or nails, inhex, okmox. — in pieces, ifteris.
Scrape. obrox f. (sis).
Scratch (as cat), ikdix, ikrix, karmix.
Scratch, Scrawl, karbix; lakbit (boggle).
BREAK. PRICK. RUB. CRUSH.

TENT, kaima 5.
Tentpole, mismâq.
Tentpeg, qâzouq.
Tentropes, atnâb 10.
Awning, zölla 10, sorâdiq 2, janfâya (canvas).
Booth, fossât, fostât.
Curtain, kidr, flabâ f.
Canopy, Cope, somâya? mizalla.
Dome, qobba.
Tabernacle, Pavilion, watâq.

THIN, raqioq, ĺa'icl f.
Delicate, Fine, raqieq, nézic.
Frail, recicc, wêhi.
Gaunt, Haggard, ezell.
Lank (as greyhound), ĺamr.
Lanky (tall and slim), hcfhef, mohefhif. Slight, xokit.
Lean, ĺâwi, qatien?
Meagre, heziel, mehzoul.
Puny? momyous (sucked dry).
Scraggy, Skinny, ruee, raɵiee.
Shriveled, xêzib, xêsif.
Shrunk, cczz.
Slender, nafluif, nafluil, nafful.
Slim, ehyaf. Sparc, seflef, B.

THINK, vn iftecir.

Apprehend, ofldos.
Attend to, iltéfit cala'.
Believe, vaddiq.
Brood over, oĺmor sala'.
Conclude, istedill.
Conjecture, kammin.
Consider,   ) onzör cala'.
Contemplate,) tâlis cala'.
Discriminate, ifriz, afriz.
Deem, Judge, flassib.
Estimate, ustebir, qaddir, soum.
Fancy, tekayyal, akiel.
Guess, oflzor.
Imagine, tazawwar, wehem yehim. Infer, antij, istentij.
Meditate, to'emmel.
Opine, kammin, izcam (allege).
Plan, oqvöd, dabbir, va.
Ponder, râjifl, wêzin.
Reflect on, tefecocr fic.
Revolve, dâwil (or ijcal), fle bâl-ec.
Question inwardly, Debate, irtêi.
Scan, tefarras?
Scheme, tedabbar, vn.
Suppose, zönn.
Surmise, tewehhem.
Survey, farzin, komm.
Suspect, tekawwax; tefarros bi; (perceive) istexsur bi; (have an inkling) ihjis bi.
OPINION.

THREAD, Twine, kait 3, 9.
Thread, Wire, silc.
Braid? Tissue, flabco.
Bobbin? Lace, Tag, qaitâna.
Loop, kaiya, akya, sürwa.
Lutestring, Shoestring, bend 3.
Tape, Galloon, xarict 8.

Ribbon, riebân ᴀʟ Twist, ɼazl.
Distaff, miɼzel, rocce.
Spindle, miɼzel, mibram.
A Ball of Thread, râba, cobbâba, œbcoub, ccbtoula.
A Hank, sclâla, sclicle.
A Skein, xilla, ᴀirâs.

Throat, ɦalq 3, ɦölqoum.
Bottom of Throat, zewar ꜰ.
Jaw, ɦanec.
Gullet, naſlr 3 (*jugulum*).
Larynx, ɼulyama? 11, qaꝛabat el riɣa ʙ. Tonsil, lauzet el halq.
Weasand, ɦönjour, ɦanjara.
Windpipe, marie c.

Thunder 3, raɛd 3.
Clap of Th. qayf raɛd.
Thunder Storm, ꝛâɛuqa 12.
Thunder Bolt, ꝛaɛâqa.
Lightning, barq 3.
Earthquake, zelzele 11.
Shock of dᵒ rajɛa, kuʒʒa.

Till, ꝛa iſlaɦ ʙ, ſelliɦ ꜰ.
Plough, oſlroθ.
Ear (*antiq.*), oɦoj ᴋ.
Break up (ground), uɛziq.
Cultivate, okdom. Sow, ezraɛ.

Timber, kaxab 4.
Sawn Timber, cereɛto c.
Board, } tekt(e) ʙg.
Plank, } duff(a) ᴀʟ
Bedstead, Framework, tekt ᴀʟ
Woodwork, tekxieba.
Panel, Plank, lauɦ 4.
Beam, Boom (of ship), barrōum, 11. Rafter, xauɦuya 11.
Transverse, *s.* ɛâruʌ 12.
Pole, Stick (Staff), ɛöud 9.

Stake, Post, weted 4.
Lath, kaxaba 4.
Spar, fenda 3 ᴏɴ.
Splinter, xarte ʙ. xaꝛuiya 14.
— xauce (*thorn*). — xoqfa 10.
— ɦasece (*fish spine*).

Time (continuous), zeman 4, *vulg.* zemân 8.
Space of time, modda.
Limit of time, zarf 3.
Interval, borhe.
Crisis of time, ɦuin 4.
— ên; *vulg.* waqt 4.
Season, 'ewân 8.
Opportunity, ibbân.
Instant, laɦza, loɦaiza ꜰ.
Moment, borhe, boraihe ꜰ.
Age (lifetime), ɛümr.
— (old age), (millennium), dahr.
— (*seculum*), ɛöyr.
— (generation), jiel 4.
Era, Epoch, ɛahd. Period, medâr.
Cycle, daurân. Century, qarn 3.
Year, sena, *pl.* senien *or* senawêt; ɦaul 3, ɛâm, *pl.* aɛwâm.
Month, xehr 3, *or pl.* axhor.
Week, 'oɛbou𝑐 11, sobou𝑐 11 ʙg. jomɛa 10 ᴀʟ
Day, yaum, *pl.* eiyâm.
Hour, sêɛa 2.
Minute, Moment, daɋieqa 11.
Present Time, waqt ɦâʒur.
The Future, el mostaqbil, el moqâbil.
Approaching (time), qâdim, qâbil, moɋbil.
Past Time, el mâʒu, ɛêlif el zeman, *pl.* el ezminet el mâʒuya.
(Past) Eternity, 'eɛel, 'ezelieya.

(Future)Eternity,'cbad,'ebadieya. [But the distinction is not always preserved.] SEASON.
TIMID, rasuib. Timorous, wajil.
Afraid, käyif, fezrûn, hêyib.
Anxious, mehmoum, ɟâjir.
Apprehensive, rani, ɟâdis, hêdis.
Bashful, kajlân, kazyân.
Cowardly, jabbân.
Coy, mostencif, monêcif.
Dastardly, tenbal c. nadiel seqies B. (?).
Fearful, kayouf, kayicf, kawwâf (wakfân B.).
Pusillanimous, aerour, maqxoul, heyoub, motcheyyîb.
Shy, nafour, ʌou nofour, motenaffir.
Wild (Shy), xaroud, xaried, ʌou helas, jiffel (easily startled).

TIRE, ra etrub, sayyì, aryi.
Ennui, ezrul. Exhaust, xaffit.
Irk, abrim, zchhiq.
Jade, lawwix (Kasrawan).
Overwork, farhid B. elhid.
Wear out, kawwir.
Weary, amill.

TITLE (of book), sônwân.
— (epithet), nart.
— (political), laqab 4.
Rank, menzila.
A Personage, ʌêt, pl. ACwêt.
Distinguished Persons, ACwêt ceriemo.
The August Person, el ʌêt el homâyounieya.
His Majesty, jelâletoh.
His Highness, yûɟub el semou.

His Royal Highness, yâɟub el semou el moloucicy.
His Grandeur (High Mightiness), fikâmetoh, sagâmetoh.
His Excellency, yâɟub el sesâda.
His Lordship, doulatoh, siyâdetoh, yâɟub el daula.
His Honour, ɟaʌratoh.
His Worship, jenâboh.
His Grace (the Archbishop), ɟibratoh, his blessedness.
His Eminence (the Cardinal), niyâfatoh.
His Preeminence (the Grand Vizier), yadâratoh.
The Premiership, el yôdour.
His Excellency (the Chief Imam), yûɟub el fuɟnila.
His Pontifical Holiness, qudâsetoh el ɟubrawieya.
The Venerable, el mowaqqar.
The Right Honourable, el moraʒʒam.
Lords, arbâb, sêda.
A Lord, seiyid 4.
Lady of Title, seiyida.
A Noble, xarief 4, 6.
Aristocracy, aryân. POLITICS.

TOOTH, sinn 4.
Canine Tooth, nûb, pl. anyûb.
Foretooth, 6enicya 14.
Grinder, ɟurs 3, 4.
Molar Tooth, raflna c.
Front Teeth, el csnân el maqâdim B.

TOUCH, ra mosa.
— (attain), loqq B.; elimm bi.
Touch (the heart), ɟarric, ɟôce, ɟannin, raqqiq, xajji, ixcer.

Touch (at a port), elimm bi, irsi fie. — (be in contact with), ittaṣul bi, lâṣiq bi. — (as curves), mêsis, temêses.
Explore, joss. Feel, ḥusa.
Handle, olmos, lâmis.
Graze, hiff; odqor, indaqir B.
Grope, dasdis c. (?).
Reach, Lay hand on, istas B.

TRADESMAN, ᴀou ḥurfa, moḥtarif F.
Artisan, ṣanâyiṣuiy, seccêf.
Broker, dallâl, ṣumyâr, simsêr.
Dealer, moteacbbib.
Dealer in odds and ends, saqqât.
Maker, ṣâniṣ, ṣannâs.
Merchant, têjir 7.
Seller, Chandler, bayyâs.
SPECIAL TRADES,
ḥuraf koṣûṣuiṣa.
Baker, kabbâz, furrân, ṭâhi.
Barber, ḥallâq, ḥaffâf.
Brazier, Coppersmith, naḥḥâs.
Butcher, vulg. qaṣṣâb; also (antig. ?) jezzêr.
Butterman, semmân.
Capitalist, motcrasmil B.
Cheesemonger, jabbân.
Clerk, cêtib 7.
Confectioner, ḥalwâniey.
Cooper, barâmieliey.
Cotton-dresser, ḥallâj.
Cutler, secêcieniey.
Currier, ᶜeddâm.
Draughtsman, rassêm.
Driver, Drover, sewwâq, ḥâdi.
Druggist, ijzêi, ṣaidaliey, ṣaidalâni. Dyer, ṣabbâḡ.
Embroiderer, ṭarrâz.

Engraver, naqqâṣ.
Executioner, jallâd (scourger).
Farrier, baiṭâr.
Falconer, bâzdâr, pl. bâzdâriya.
Fishmonger, semmêc.
Fruiterer, fêcihêni.
Fuller, qayyâr. Furrier, farrâ c.
Gardener, bostênji AL baṣwân Bg. janâyiniey.
Glass dealer, zojâjiey.
— (superior), bellsurji.
Glazier, quzzêz.
Goldsmith, ṣayyâr, hibraqiey.
Goatmaster, marẓâz.
Grazier (Cowherd), baqqâr.
Greengrocer, baqqâl, knẓâriey.
Grocer (of candles), ẓammâs; (of dry fruit), zebbâb, temmâr; (of perfumes and tea), saṭṭâr.
Haberdasher, ḥabbêc.
Hairdresser, mozeyyin, zeyyân.
Ironmonger, seqṭuiy F.
Jailer, sejjân.
Jeweller, jauheriey.
Herbalist, saxxâb.
Land-surveyor, messêḥ.
Lapidary, ḥaccêc.
Limeburner, cellês, jayyâr B.
Locksmith,) ccffûl,
Tinman,   ) senceriey.
Mason, Miner, fâcul ê.
Matseller, ḥöṣöriey.
Mercer, kordajiey.
Miller, ṭaḥḥûn.
Muletcer, baṣṣâl, mocêri.
Oilman, zeyyêt. Potter, fakkâr.
Papermaker, Stationer, warrâq.
Seller of Pottery, fakouriey.
Cotton Printer, basmajiey? baṣṣâm? Printer, ṭabbâs.

ANGLO-ARABIC VOCABULARY. 139

Dealer in Rice, rezzêz.
Saddler, serrâj, jallâl.
Sculptor, faṉḉâr.
Seamstress, kayyâṭa.
Shepherd, râɛu, *pl.* roɛâya.
Shoemaker, varmâtiey, iɛcêf 13.
Smith, ḉaddâd, qain 3, 4.
Stonecutter, ḉojjâr.
Surgeon, jarrâṉ.
Swordcutler, soyoufiey.
Tanner, dabbâḉ. Tailor, kayyâṭ.
Turner, karrâṭ.
Upholsterer, najjâd.
Vintner, kammâr, nabbêa.
Washer, ɣaɛêl. Weaver, ḉayyêc.
Watchmaker, sɛâtiey.
Woollendraper, joukiey.
Writing-master, katṭâṭ.

Traffic, tijâra.
Custom, zoubena.
Customer, zeboun.
Buyer, xâri, xarrâ, moxteri,
    mobtês B. Purchase, xirâ.
Seller, bayyâɛ. Sale, bais.
Barter, moɛâwaɛa, modêcexa,
    mobâdala.
A Purchase, xarya, moxtera'.
Commerce, matjar.
A Trade or Craft, ṉurfa 10.
Active and Lucrative Trade,
    tijâra râyija rûbiḉa.
Exchange, qauɛ, moqâwaɛa.
Gain, ribḉ, mecɛeb, tccessob.
Loss, kisôra. Cost, teclief.
Deficiency, naqɣ. Value, qiema.
Intrinsic Value, qiema raṉuiḉa.
Prime Cost, 'eyl el qiema.
Price, θeman 4, 8. Rate, suɛr 4.
The mean rate, el suɛr el wasuṭ.

Good Price (adequate, that pays),
    θeman wâfi.
Low Price, θeman baka.
Very Low d⁰, abkas θeman.
Profit, fâyida 12, istifâda.
Interest, fâyiɛ 12.
High Profit ⎱ boɾâya x.
(or Interest), ⎰ boɾya F.
A Bonus, ɛulâwa, ziyâda.
Commission, moɛâmala.
Discount, ḉaɛm, isqâṭ.
Abatement, koɾöum (*sic*).
Deduction, taqɣuir, tejhiya.
A Bid, Offer, momêcese.
Auction, ḉurâj, mezêd.
Money Market, maidân, souq
    el noqoud.
Active Market, rawâj.
Dull Market, ceɛêd.
Rise of Price, tavâɛod.
Fall, tenêzol, nozoul, hobouṭ.
Depreciation, tedannie, soqouṭ
    el uɛtibâr.
Stockjobbing, morâbaḉa.
Investment of Money, maxɣulat
    (11) el darâhim.
Principal of Money, reɛmâl,
    yarmiya B. Bargain, xaṭṭ.
Annulling a Bargain, iqâla B.
An Estimate, moɛéwama.
Goods, ⎱ buɛâɛa 11,
Merchandize, ⎰ rizq 4.
Staple (chief article), el ɛômda.
Returns (of money), faiy'êt.
Demand, istimdâd, istiɛdâr.
Supply, taqdiem, madad.
Full Supply, cifâya, *pl.* cofûyâ.
A Glut, tedqier.
Consumption, naɛaq.
Average d⁰ el maqṭouɛ.

Importation, jelb, ijtilâb, istijlâb.
Exportation, korouj, irsêl ila'
el kârij. Imports, idkâlêt.
Import, dâkil, mostoflâar.
Cargo arriving, el wârid.
Cargo outgoing, el sâdir.
Exports, ikrâjêt, irsêlieyêt.
Contraction of Business, flayr el axfâl.
Financial Pressure, moâyaqa mâlieya.
Restriction, flajz, taqyuir.
Prohibition, taflriem, manc.
COMMERCE.

TRAFFIC, en têjir, ettejir.
Act as Broker, qârix, s. teqarrax K.
Bargain, istcalil, istedni.
Cancel a Contract, nqicl K. B.
Chaffer, texâlaj fil Ocman.
Faddle, terâqas.
Haggle, temêces.
Huckster, tesewwâm, qâlib B.
Job, xârib, râbifl. Barter, dâcix.
Exchange, sâwicl, bâdil qâwal.
Offer in Exchange, istebdil.
Bid, mêcis. Buy, ixteri, ibtês.
Peddle, tekassea.
Market, tesewwaq.
Retail, tescbbab.
Trade, tebaâns, istebâus.
Make Gains, tecensch.
ESTIMATE.

TRAY, misnada K.
Dinner Tray, sofra.
Metal Tea Tray, Tabsi 11.
Lady's Tray (bowl), qasra.
Needle, 'ibra 10.
Pin, dabbouse, nu.

Thimble, coxtebân.
Bodkin, mikrâz.
Surgeon's Bodkin, miel 4.
Scissars, mikasr 2.
Casket, kozcina 11.
Straw Tray, Tabaq? 5.

TREATY, mosâbeda.
Agreement, ittifâq.
Alliance of offence and defence, ittiflâd modâfasa wa hojoum.
Article, mâdda, pl. mawâdd; bend 3. Compact, râbira.
Bargain, xarr 3. Clause, fasl 3.
Coalition, sôyba. Debate, irtiyâ.
Compromise, taqârob, terâlu.
Conclusion, iktitêm.
Confederation, moflâlafa.
Conference, modâwala, moflâda-Oc. Consultation, moxâwara.
Convention, moxârara, taxârot.
Covenant, sahd, saqd.
Discussion, mokûbara, mobâfla-Oc. Intervention, modâkala.
Interview, mowâjahe, moflâxara, moqâbala (mutual confronting). League, micOâq.
Memorial, icrâd.
Memorializing, mosêcera.
Parley, mocêlema, moflâcêya.
INTERCOURSE. WAR. POLITICS.

TREE, xajara, nu. 4.
Shrub, xojaira, jeuba K.
Sapling, xijrieya; — transplanted, jariese, sesicle 11.
Plant, nabât 2; without stalk like melon, yaqruin. GOURD.
Drooping Plant (Blade), xetle 3.
Bush, söllieq.
Forest Tree, daufla, nu.

(Gall) Oak, bellouт.
Holm Oak, sindiyân.
Horse Chesnut, ɪâh bellouт.
Terebinth, boтm.
Acacia, ɪant, ɪenzelakt.
Acorn, bajm. Galls, ɛafs.
Alder, ɛlaura Roumieya.
Arbute, qaтlab, muɪmoɪ
  barriey. Cedar, 'erz.
Ash, daɪx boudâq.
Hiccory ? waɪiej. Decch, ɪên.
Beechnut, ɪaɪɪ el sowwâɛl.
Boxtree, baqa. Birch, bêtoula.
Brazil-wood, baqam c.
Cypress, ɛerwa, ɛerou.
Ebony-tree, ɛêj c.
Larch, ɪarbien.
Linden, zeizefoun.
Mahogany, cêbiliey.
Maple, ɪajar el eɛɪfendân.
Mastich, seraɪɪ. Mimosa, talɛɪ.
Pine, ɪanaubar. Poplar, ɛlaur.
Plane, dolb. Olive, zeitoun.
Spruce Fir, tennoub.
Wild Olive, 'otom.
Willow, ɪufɪâɛ. Withy ? kauɪ.
Osier ? ɛlaтab el ɛlunâ.
Bough. Shrub. Staff. Timber.

Tremble, ɪɪ irteɪud.
Oscillate, ʌebʌib, terajraj,
  tehezbez.
Palpitate, ikɛɪɪq, teʌebʌeb.
Quake, tezelzel.
Quiver, orjoɛ, irɪax, irteɪuɪ.
Shiver (with cold), teqaɛɪqaɛ.
Shudder (with horror), iqɪaɪuтт,
  vulg. tewehher.
Shy (as horse), ijɛɪil. Start, inɛɪir.
Throb, irɛɪɪɪ, irteɪuɪ ?

Totter, teteтter.
Vacillate, terudrad, tekalkal.
Vibrate, ɪɪ terajraj, irteɪuɪ.
Wave (with wind), tchebheb.
Waver (as army), terajraj;
  telaɛɪlaɛɪ.

Trinket, ɪanteɛɪa ?
Bauble, behraja. Tinsel, zokroɛ.
Coral with bella, ɪokɪieka.
Gauds and Gewgaws, ɛɪali wa
  ɛɪölel в. Plaything, loɪba.
Toy, dâɛɪa, ʀu. ɪabaɛɪc, ʀu.
Trifle, heleɛe, tentieɪ в. (bis).
Clasp.

Troop, s. jauq 4, jamhera.
— cetieba 11 (of elephants) ɪ.
Band, ɛöɪba 10. Crew, fauj 4.
Company, jamâɛa.
— (of soldiers), ɪiɪaima.
Drove, mawâɪi cattle, ɛɛecui в.
Crowd, ziɛɪlâɛu, zeɛɪm.
Flight of Birds, ɛɪlauma.
Flock, qaтuiɛ 4, 5, 9.
Gang, zomra. Herd, тaɪɪ 3 в.
Horde, Clan, qabiela 11.
Group, jomla, lomma.
Pack, 'ilb, 'olba.
Party, ɛɪuzba, ɛɪazb 4.
Shoal (of fishes), zeɛɪlm 4,
  ɪiɪaima. Tribe, qaum 4.
Swarm, Flock, sirb 4, sorba.
— of new bees, ɛɪenl, тarad naɛɪɪɪ
Rabble,   ⎫ riɛɪɛɪc, raɪâɛ,
Mob,   ⎬ aubûɪ, ɛöɛâɪa.
Retinue, cobcoba в.
Suite, tebaɛ. Army. Quantity.

Trowsers, Drawers, libâs 8.
Women's Silk Tr. ɪintiyân.

Light stuff Tr. rakxour.
Cloth Trowsers, sarwâl.

Try, vn. See Strive.
Try, va jarrib, ibteli, vp obtali.
Assay, sâyir. Test, rouz.
Experiment on, } imtellun.
Examine,
Prove, Put to Proof, iktebir.
Strain, qannib, rannib.
Tempt, iftin (also Rebel).

Tumour, warm.
— of gland, fâh.
Blotch, fuqfaqa, faqfâqa.
Boil, Abscess, dommela 11.
Bubo, rodda 10. Bunion, dofláa.
Blain, Pustule, flubna, nu. 3.
Blister, baqbieqa.
Callosity, qaxab, cenab.
Chilblain, qiyâs 2 b. doflâs,
 qimarlay. Corn, damân.
Eruption, raffla.
Erysipelas, flamou, flômra.
Freckles? södd x. lofłθe ? 2.
Mole, kâl. Pimple, xarie 8.
Red Pimple, lasl. Pustule, nifra.
Tuber, baθr 3, baθra 10.
Tubercle (moveable), silsa 2,10.
Ulcer, qarfla 3; (in mouth;
 Aphthee) flulâ, qolâ b.
Wart, flabbe, nu. esp. of Alep.
Whitlow, dâflöus 12 b. x.

Ugly, baxies, mostebxis.
Deformed, mamaouk.
Frightful, hêyil.
Hideous, qabiefl.
Loathsome, xanies.
Monstrous, Foul, fâflux.

Uncouth, mowaflflax.
Unwieldy, faliez.
 Shameful. Clumsy.

Undertake, va take in hand;
 qoum bi, tehejjam sala',
 ixras fla, urtemid li, sala';
 terâtâ bi b. bâxir fla; also
 qâwim bi.
— become responsible for, Engage to do; iltexim bi.
Guarantee, ocfol, teceffal bi.
Vouch for, osqod-he ilaihi.
— oqrod bi, teqarrad bi?
Warrant, uâman, telamman bi.
 Take in Hand. Intend. Set to.

Unjust, janif r.
Arbitrary, motexajrif, mote-
 sellat.
Despotic, } jabbâr,
Domineering, } motejabbir.
Extortionate, mobelluy, sasouf.
Grasping, bâri, pl. barâ.
High-handed, Rough-handed,
 raxoum r. Injurious, Xâyim.
Oppressive, zâlim.
Partial, Unfair, Xâlis.
Rapacious, râxub.
Tyrannical, motefarsun, jâyir.
Violent, sanief. Cruel. Proud.

Unpleasant, } cerieh,
Disagreeable, } mecrouh.
Accursed, } laruin,
Execrable, } melroun.
Detestable, maqiet.
Fulsome, zêhiq, zehic?
Hateful, barieš, mabrouš.
Odious, meakout.

ANGLO-ARABIC VOCABULARY.   143

Offensive, morieᴣ.
Provoking, maṛḋönb.

USEFUL, expedient; nâfiɛ.
Advantageous, tâyil ᴦ.
Conducive to, mofʰu, moˤewwil, ila'. Convenient, heniey.
Handy, Available, moyessir.
Helpful, Beneficial, mosâwin.
Profitable, mofled.
Serviceable, mosidd ᴦ. moṛni.
    Fɪᴛ.

USELESS, bâᴛul.
Frivolous (thing), hefiq.
Futile, Vain, behruj.
Null and Void, sâᴛul?
Worthless, helis.

UTENSIL, ᴣarf 8.
Bag, joråb. *Barrel*, barmiel 11.
Basket, qoffa 10.
Chamber Vessel, 'erᴅuiya, mostermela; mibwala (*urinal*); qaᴢaricyɑ (*vase*).
Cup, cê's 3.   *Kettle*, ṛallâya.
Jar, zier 4.   *Jug*, ˤibrieq 11.
Platter, yaʃifa 5.
Vessel, wuɛâ, *pl.* 8, auɛuyɑ.
— ˤěniya, *pl.* 12, ˤewâni.
Ware, maᴣrouf.   FURNITURE.

VALE, qâs.   Dale? webda.
Valley, wâdi 8, 9.
Plain, sehil(a).
Wide Plain, wesɛɛa, saᴛuiſla.
Expanse, tefessoU, imtidâd.
Lea (Spot), boqɛn 5.
Low Ground, Ground, ſlaᴅuiᴅ.
Lowest Slope, luſlf.
Foot of Mountain, saſlf, (*for* yaſlf?). Lowlands, esêfil.

VEIL, *s.* seter; ṛiᴛâ (*cover*), niqâb, ſlujâb (*screen*); for face alone, xasrieyɑ; for all but eyes and nose, kimâr; shroud for whole person,ˤizêr.
Nun's muffler, borqaɛ 11.
Bedouin's face-cover, liθêm.

VEIN, ɛurq 3. Veins, rawâyix ᴦ.
The two Veins of *temples*, ardaṛân. — of *throat*, nâſlurân.
Artery, ᴅârib 12, râfiz 12, xaryâu. Pulse, nabᴅ.
Jugular Vein, ɛurq el zeur.
Aorta, abber, auricᴛui ʙ.
Duct, nâqour.
Pore, mesêm 2; miesem 11; manfes 11.
Lacteals, majâri el ciemous.
Nerve, saᴢab(a).   Fibre, liafa.
Blood, dam", *pl.* dimâ.
Clot, jolᴛa 10.

VIE, ᴛɴ ſlâxir, sêɛu, fâᴅul?
Aspire, nâfis.   Race with, sêbiq.
Cope with, sêwi, bâri, wêzi, sâdil, xâbih; bâliṛ ᴦ.
Compete mutually, tesêwa', tesêma'.
Emulate, ṛâyir, ṛâlib?
Have Mania for, tehêfet.
Rival, ṛârim, ɛârnᴅ.
Strive together, tojâhad, teṛûlab, tesâraɛ. EQUAL.

WAGE, Wages (paid by the job), ˤejr, ˤojra; joɛl ᴦ.
Allowances, rawâtib, marâtib?
Earnings, mawâjib.
Fare, Hire, cirâ (*rent of lodging*).
Fee, Perquisite, resm 3.

Fee to a guide, dilála.
Mileage? Viaticum? karajieya.
Meed, wajieba.
Pay, súmla? sumâla?
Daily Pay, jiráya.
Monthly Pay, xohrieya.
Pocket Money, nafaqa.
Reward, Guerdon, θewâb.
Salary,) sŏloufa 11
Stipend,) jâminicya 12.
Remuneration, Requital, jizê.

WALK, ɛɴ imxi. Pace, tekarrâ.
Walk for exercise, temaxwar.
March, izflaf (*creep*).
March in file, osloo, tarâraq, taqâтaɾ. Parade, teseyyar.
Patrol, rawwif, tarawwaf.
— by night, sósa.
Proceed, sier. Step, terajjal.
Promenade, temaxxa'.
Souffle along (walk rapidly), ikxif (but ʙ. Trotter, ikxib).
Shuffle (walk scrapingly), tedabbec, tesarqal.
Stalk, ries? mice ʙ.
Step out, madd (ʙ. Trotter).
Stride, ifxik, faxxik, jallib (ʙ. *sic*). Stroll (see Wᴀɴᴅᴇʀ).
Strut, tebakter, tebardad, tebehraj.
Swagger, torarraf, terarras.
Toddle, Trip (as child), behwin.
Trip (walk lightly), tenaxxat.
Wade, koul. Waddle, tedâdâ?

Wᴀɴᴅᴇʀ, touh, tieh, rŏuʃl, ruifl.
Emigrate, hojj (*sic*).
Go to and fro, teraddad.
— (esp. as pilgrims), flõjj (*sic*) with acc. of place.

Gad about, roud (as gossip, or army-scout).
Jaunt, dour. Journey, tenaqqal.
Migrate, irflal, irteflul, teraflflal.
Penetrate into (a country), aurîl fle ʀ. Rove, oxrod, urâx.
Prowl, rascus. Ramble, sieb.
Range, ᴇɴ joul. — over, israfl.
Ravin, sôus. Roam, hiem.
Saunter, tebehnes, tebehres, tebaflbafl ʙ.
Scour (a country), flõum, flõus.
Skim (the seas), qaxxuт.
Stroll, tenezzeh, xomm el hewâ.
Tour, make tour; rŏuf, tefarraj.
Travel, Voyage, sêfir, siefl.
Traverse, ugean ғ. morr, sier fle.
Visit, zour.
— (in official progress), rawwif.
Wᴀʟᴋ. Rᴜɴ.

Wᴀɴᴛ, *s*. flâja, uflliyâj.
Anxiety, sôjra.
Deprivation, ursâm, Xaim.
Privations, moncidêt.
Destitution, kawar?
Distress, Xaiqa, Xuiqa; Xanc, Xônouc.
Drudgery (abject state), dauqasa. Indigence, iflês.
Misery, mescine, belâ.
Necessity (-tude), suwaz.
Need, sáze, *pl.* (things needed) marâwiz.
Pauperism, tayasloc.
Poverty, faqr.
Wretchedness, xaqâwa.
Wʀᴇᴛᴄʜᴇᴅ.

Wᴀʀ, *s*. flarb, *f.* 3.
Peace, sôlfl. *Treaty*, mosâheda.

ANGLO-ARABIC VOCABULARY. 145

Army, jaix.   *Officers*, el ẓabṭ.
Battle, qitêl.   *Camp*, moɛascer.
Soldier, jondiey.   *Arms*, silâḥ.
Gun, bondiqieya, micḥala.
Insurrection, qauma.
Raid, ɣâra. Hostility, moɛâdâya.
Enmity, mobâɣaẕa.
State of War, moḥâraba.
Intestine War, ḥarb jouwieya.
Casus belli, hieyat ḥarb.
An Expedition, tejrieda, ɣâziya.
An Enterprize (Crusade), jihêd.
Trysting-place, Rendezvous, meḥẕir, matmax.
Campaign, sefar 4, sefara; maɣze' 11; serḥat el sascer.
Siege?   } ḥuɣâr.
Blockade? } moḥâɣara?
Arming, tesliefl.
Victory,   } nesara, intiɣâr,
Triumph,   } istighâr, qâhira,
Conquest, } ẓafar, fauz, fetcḥ.

WARBLERS (birds), yawâdiḥ.
Blackbird, xoḥrour.
Bullfinch, daɣnâx.
Canary Bird, ḥôzêr, teranjiey.
Chaffinch, xarxour, dojj ʙ.
Goldfinch, denoura.
Humming-bird, zennân.
Lark, dâlous.
Tufted Lark, qônbara.
Linnet, Finch, zeqâqiya.
Barbary Finch, maqnien, bardour ʙ.
Nightingale, bolbol, ɛandalieb.
Thrush, dojj ᴀʟ sommona ʙ.

WARE (pottery, etc.), maẓrouf.
Wares, Goods, silɛa.
Small Wares, korda.

Stone Ware, Earthenware, fakkâr.
Crockery, ɛajama ᴀʟ cêxi ʙɢ.
Glazed Ware, teinaq ᴀʟ
China,   } faɣfour,
Porcelain, } ɣuini ᴀʟ txieni ʙɢ.
Fine Goods, emtiɛa ḥasena.
Cabinet Work, menjourât fâkira; baxtekte, maxtckte ғ.

WASH, ɛa iɣsil; oneself, tewaḏḏâ.
Bathe, ɛa (in hot bath), ḥammi.
Clean, naḏḏuf, ḳ; — out, inẕeḥ.
Foment, hebbil, cemmid.
Rinse, maḏmiḏ, oxrof ʙ.
Scour out, ɛa oḥqon.

WATCH, ᴠɴ be awake; isher, intebih, tenabbeh.
— ɛa onᴛor, teraqqab.
— over, râqib, teqayysd fie; waɛu yaɛa' ɛala'.   GUARD.
— against, istcḥris, teḥarras, uḥtɛair min. SHUN.
— for, lie in Wait for; orɣöd, terayyad.
Be on Watch by night, ɛöas.
Waylay, ɛa terawwaɣ, irbuḏ li, râbiḏ.
Lie in Ambush, cɛmin, tecemman, terâbaḏ, terabbas.
Wait, ᴠɴ uxtcbir, oɣbor, te'enna', istenna', tewaqqaf.
Wake, ᴠɴ istaiquẓ; hobb ғ. (*also* blow), *vulgo* fleq.
Wake up from wine, etc., ᴠɴ uɣḥa'.

WATER, mâ', *vulg.* mâi ʙɢ. mowaiy, mo'i ᴀʟ *pl.* miyâh, emwâh.

VOL. II.   10

Sea, baßr 3, 5. River, nchr 4.
Lake, boḥaira 11. Bay, joun.
Coast, xàtu 12. Bank, xatt 3.
Dike, sedd 3. Source, maydar.
A Sup of W. mowaiya aL
Fresh W. mâi saaib.
Sweet W. mâi ḥölou, mâi forût.
Running W. mâi jâri.
Stagnant W. mâi nâyim, mâi motewaqqif.
Mouldy W. mâi mosattan.
Salt W. mâi mâliḥ.
Brine, sebk.
Surface of W. wejh el mâi.

Waters, Tide, Surgo; miyâh.
Flowing Tide, madd (sêßḥ).
High Water-line, jorf 4.
Deep Water, bâlous.
Abyss, ḡamr(a) 2, 5, lojja 10.
Ebb, mâi herbân; jozr.
Wave, mauja 4. Surgo, teyyar.
Breaker? rámouz 12 (Psalm 42).
Spray, Surf, raxâx.
Ridge (of wave), ḡârib 12.
Crest (of wave), xouxa.
Foam, Froth, raḡwa, roima.

Weak, Lasuif. Weakly, naḥuif.
Brittle, ḥötâm c.
Crippled, mokabbal.
Consumptive, mealoul.
Defective, qâsur.
Delicate, raqieq, nězic, nâḥul.
Disabled, aaqut.
Drooping, faxil.
Effeminate,) kaniê,
Enervated,) mokanna0.
Faint,) Xâni, moXna',
Languid,) wâni, wanicy.

Feeble,) rakou ng. rakiey aL
Listless,) mosterki.
Flabby,) morehrut,
Flaccid,) moterehbil.
Flimsy, sekief. Frail, wêhi.
Friable, hexx. Helpless, kâmil.
Impotent, Infirm, ḡâjiz.
Invalid, calicl, mostell.
Palsied, maḥouj.
Puny, mamyöuy.
Rickety, ceaieḥ. Soft, laiyin.
Sick, marieX, pl. marXa'.
Sickly, seqiem. Blight, reciec.
Stunted, moqarqam.
Withered, aêbil, aeblân.
Thin. Sick. Defective.

Wealth, θerwa.
Affluence, raḡl.
Abundance, wofour, ḡozêra, seca.
Ease, rafâhe, rakâ.
Luxury, tenassöm.
Opulence, nacuim 6.
Exuberance, zekr, zokour.
Riches, ḡinâ. Substance, nacma.
Property, Stock, mâl, pl. amwâl.
A Possession, qonya, metêc 8.
Pelf, mowail. Estate, molo 4.
Money making, temawwol.
Inheritance, mieraê.
Landed Estate, caqâra, 'erX, pl. 'erâXu.
Wide Estates, raḥâyīb.
Rent (yearly revenue), madkoul 11.
Income, ierâd, dakl y.
Returns of money, faiy'et.
Surplus, culêwa.
Balance (of money), el bâqi, baqioya. Commerce. Money.

WEAVE, } ta ſlöuc, ſlayyic;
Wattle, } onsoj.
Braid, oɪfor, ɪaſſir.
Knit, Plait, ojdol.
Knot, osqod. Noose, wehhiq?
Net (Wattle), xabbic.

WEDLOCK, zowâj, izdiwâj.
Wedding, zieja, teckiel.
Union, iqtirân.
Wedding Feast, ɪörɪ, faraſl.
Bridegroom, caries, katin.
Bride, carous 11.
Bridal Pair, carsên, ziwâj.
Husband, zenj. Wife, zeuja.
Partner, Consort, qarien(a).
Father-in-law, ſlemou, ruhr.
Mother—, ſlamâya, ruhr.
Son—, ruhr. Brother—, silſ 4.
Daughter—, cenna, pl. canâyin.
Sister—, silſa.

WEEK, s. 'osbous 11, sobous
 11 Bɪ. also jomɪa (sic) 10 AL
Sunday, yaum el e'ſlad.
Monday, yaum el iθnain.
Tuesday, yaum el θelâθe.
Wednesday, yaum el arbaca.
Thursday, yaum el kamies.
Friday, el jomɪa (sic).
Saturday, el sebat (sabbath).

WEIGHT, wezn. 4, zeun.
A Weight (standard), seuja.
Hundredweight, qinrâr.
Pound, ratl 4, liebra.
Ounce, ouqieya (uncia), vulg.
 oqqa, pl. owaq.
Dram (⅛ oz.), dirhem 11.
Scruple (24 grains), qierâr.

A Grain, qamſla.
Grapestone, cerâm.

WET, adj. mabloul (wetted).
— with rain, mamrour.
Wet Day, yaum mârur.
Damp, nadi, nadyân.
Moist, rarub.
Soaked, moxarrab.

WET, va boll; vp vii. narwil?
Be Wetted, tenarwal.
Damp, Moisten, naddi, rarrub.
Soak, } inqac, xarrib,
Steep, } usrun.
Sop, isqi. Swamp, rawwiy.
 DIP. PLUNGE.

WHALE, ſlöut 9.
Great Whale, Rorqual, fâtous.
Spermaceti Whale, qirx.
Narwal, ceroedân el bâſlr.
Grampus, ecrambous r.
Swordfish, el semac el sêyiſ.
Whale of Jonah, noun(a).
Dolphin, dolfien.
Whalebone, caxm(ﻟﻰ) ladn r.
Spouting-hole, fouwehe.
Blubber, dohn.
Spermaceti, mokk?

WHIP, s. qamxe AL farqalla B.
 jiama r. corbâj c.
Scourge, } miqraca,
Switch, } miswaqa.
Lash, seur, pl. siyâr.
— plaited, jadiela.
Small Cord, marase.

WILD Animal, waſlx 3.
Wild Beast, sebox 5.

Antelope, ŗazêl. *Ape*, qird.
Cat tribe, sinnour.
Ferret, ɛurɛe. *Wolf*, ʌieb 5.
Bear, dobba. *Rat*, jorɴᴀ.
Deer, mehê.

Wɪɴᴅ, rieṇ, *f.* 4. Air, hewâ 8.
Puff of Wind, hobba.
Quarter of the Wind, mehebb.
Breath of Air, nesema.
Breeze, nesiem (yabâ).
Blast, nafṇa. Gust, zoɛzɛs 11.
Hard blowing, *s.* hobouba.
Tempest, ɛcubaɛa 11.
Gale of Monsoon, nau.
Gale, Storm, rieṇ ɛâyuɛa, *or simply* ɛâyuɛa 12.
Squall, telqieṇat rieṇ.
Thunderstorm, râɛuqa 12.
Hurricane, forrȫuna.
Tornado,) usyâr 11 ꜰ.
Cyclone,) niffa (*Barb.*).
For names of Winds, see Qᴜᴀʀᴛᴇʀ.

Wɪɴᴅow (small arched), râqa.
— (in roof), rauzen(a) ʙɢ. rauxen ʙ.
— (dormer), couwa, *pl.* ciwê.
European W. xabbêc 11.
Lattice, maxbace c.
— ɛariex, mokarram.
— tecɛuib, xaɛrieya.
Grating, qaɛay.
Shutter, ʌalafɛ 10 (daraɛa ᴀʟ).
Niche with window, rêzouna ʙⱼ.
Window-frame, borwâs.

Woʟꜰ, ʌieb(a) 5. Fox, θeɛlab 11.
Fox's Cub, θoɛailab ʙ. titfol?
Fox's Den, wajâr 10.

Jackal, wâwi, ibn âwi, jaqâl, forâniq.
Hyæna, ʌabaɛ *f.* 5 ; jaiɛar.

Woᴍᴀɴ, mar'a (*in modern prose*, imrâ'a). Women, nisê, nisswa ; *vulg.* niswân.
Women, The Sex, el nisê, el ṇariem ʀ.
Old Woman, ɛajouz 11.
Lady, Ḍôrma 10, kânum c.
Matron, kâtoun 12.
Young Woman, xâbba, *pl.* xawâbb.
Lass, ɛetiya. Female, 'onθe 5. Dᴀᴍsᴇʟ.

Woɴᴅᴇʀ, *v.* istaᵹrîb, istɛɛjib.
Admire, terajjab min.
Marvel, ro'iɛ yorâɛ.
Be Aghast, istehwil.
Gape (at), bohit, inbehit.
— after, oxkoy (Dᴇsɪʀᴇ).
(See also the passives of Aᴍᴀᴢᴇ, Cʜᴀʀᴍ.)

Woɴᴅᴇʀꜰᴜʟ, ɛajieb.
Wondrous, ɛâjib.
Amazing, râyiɛ.
Astonishing, badieɛ.
Astounding, modhix, kâriɛ.
Marvellous, Stupendous, ɛöjjâb.
Strange, ɣarieb, mosteᵹrab.

Wooʟ, ɛöuf. A Fleece, jizze 10.
Goat's Down, tefticc.
Camel's Hair, wabar.
Woollen Cloth, jouk ; milf *Bb*.
Flannel, jouk abyaḍ.
Mohair? Camlet, mokayyar.
Felt, lobâda, cexâya.

Sackcloth, miaíl (Kersey?
 Frieze ?).

Work, ʿn uɛmel.
Work hard, ɛâfir, kâbur.
Work zealously at, doub fie.
Be Busy at, ixtaɛil fie.
Drudge, imtehin, idqaɛ.
Fag, Plod, iodaíl. Slave, qârif.
Labour, codd. Serve, okdom.
Toil, itɛab, etɛub nefɛec, ɛâtil ɛ.

Worms, } hewâmm,
Vermin, } flaxarât.
Earthworms, karâruin, ɛalaq el jonaina.
Glowworm, uílbier.
Leech, ɛalaqa. Grubs, kixâx.
Snail, ílalezoun, meɛqala ɛ.
Small Worms, sous, doud.
Moth, ɛōθθe ɛu. 3, 10.
Caterpillar, } lafls 4.
Silkworm? } τōττör 11.
Maggot, ʿearouɛ 11.

Wretched, xaqiey 8.
Abject, τarieíl, dâɛir.
Abandoned, modaxxar.
Barren (year), jâroud.
Dejected, kâfis, kafɛên.
Depressed, waɛuiɛ.
Desolate, maɛqoud.
Despondent, ɛâjir.
Destitute, makɛoul 11.
Doleful, ɛâbis, ɛabouɛ.
Dreary, moɛeudan.
Evil, Sorry (case), bâyis.
Hapless, mancoud (mancouɛ) el ílaʒʒ. Helpless, kâmil.
Ill-fated, mencouɛ el fâl.
Ill-omened, max'oum.

Indigent, ɛaɛlouc 11.
Luckless, naílus, manílöus, qaliel el bakt.
Mean, Groveling, ɛeliel.
Melancholy, moɛeudan.
Miserable, necid.
Mournful, ílazien, maílzoun.
Painful, ʿaliem, mowellim.
Poor, faqier 6.
Sad, ceʿieb, mocteʿib.
Sorrowful, oerieb, mecroub.
Stript, motcjarrid.
Unfortunate, meɛcien 11.
Vexed, mortimm, xâjib.

Weak. Bare.

White, ɛɛ octob.
Compose, ʿellif, ɛannif.
Dictate to, amli ɛala'.
Indict, noɛɛ. Pen, ílarrir.

Yellow, *adj.* aɛfar.
— colour, *s.* ɛōfra.
Yellowish, moɛfirr.
Deep Yellow, fâqiɛ, aɛfar fâqiɛ.
Saffron, mozeɛfir.
Orange, borroqâniey.
Sallow, moɛafran.
Pale, mocemmad.
Buff, } ecwel,
Yellow Dun, } qoulah (Turk.),
Nankeen? } qalij x.

Zeal, Earnestness, ɛairɛ ilaʾ, himma, ibtimâm.
Attention, iltifêt, raddân el bâl, intibâh ɛala'.
Care, el qiyâm bi.
Concern, ictirâθ.
Devotion, Attachment, inhimêc, teqayyod, inɛucêf, moɛâoɛfa.

Diligence, uflinâ, nûtirâs.
Interest in, roṛba fie.

Zone, *s.* minṭaqa 11.
Frigid Zone, el m. el bârida.
Torrid Zone, el m. el râmiḳa,
— el moflriqa, mofiteriqa.
Temperate Zone,—ol moctedila.
Tropic, modâr.

Clime, qöṭr 4.
Cancor, el Seraṭân.
Capricorn, el Jadie.
Tract (of world), ṣöqṣ.
The two Tropics, el dâyiratein.
Arctic Circle, el dâyirat el
   ximâlieya.
Antarctic Circle, el dâyirat el
   janoubieya?

LIST OF SELECT WORDS IN THE VOCABULARY.

Abase	Armour	Belt, *s.*	a Building
Abate	Army	Bid	Bundle, *s.*
Abide	Arraign	Big	Burn
Abode, *s.*	Arrange	Bind	Business
Abound	Aspect	Bird	
Abstain	Ass	Bite, *va.*	Call, *va.*
Account	Assemble, *vn.*	Black, *adj.*	Calm, *va.*
Admit	Attack, *va.*	Blame	Camels
Adorn	Augur, *va.*	Blow, *vn.*	Camp
Adverse	Averse	Blue, *adj.*	Cap, *s.*
Advise	Awl	Boast	Captious
Age		Body	Car
Aggrieve	Babble, *vn.*	Boil, *vn.*	Caress, *va.*
Agree	Back, *s.*	Bone	Carpenter
Allow	Bad, *adj.*	Book	Carpet
Alone	Baffle, *va.*	Booty	Carry
Amaze	Bag, *s.*	Border, *s.*	Cast, *va.*
Ambassador	Bank, *s.*	Bough	Cat
Amuse	Banner	Box	Catch, *va.*
Anger	Bark, *s.*	Brave	Cause, *s.*
Angry	Barrel, *s.*	Bread	Cavern
Animal	Base, *adj.*	Break	Cavil
Antelope	Basket	Breast, *s.*	Cease, *vn.*
Antiquities	Bath	Breathe	Cellar
Ape	Battle	Bridle, *s.*	Cement, *s.*
Apples	Bay (of sea)	Bridle, *va.*	Cement, *va.*
Arch	Beat, *va.*	Bright	Certain
Argue	Beautiful	Bring	Chair, *s.*
Arise from	Bed	Broad	Champaign.
Arm, *s.*	Bee	Broom	Change, *v.*
Arms	Belly, *s.*	Brown	Change, *s.*

Charm, va.	Counterfeit, va	Delay, va.	Eagle
Chat, vn.	Court, s.	Delight, va.	Earnest, adj.
Cheap	Covenant, vn.	Deliver, va.	Earth
Cheat, va.	Crane	Demand, va.	At Ease
Cheek	Crime	Denote, va.	Efface
Child	Criminal, s.	Dense	Effort
Chisel, s.	Criticize	Deny	Element
Choke, v.	Crouch	Depart	Elephant
Choose, va.	Crow, s.	Desart, s.	Eloquent
Church	Crow, vn.	Desire, va.	Encroach
City	Cruel	Destroy, va.	Endure
Clasp, s.	Crush, va.	Devote	Enrage
Clear, adj.	Cry, vn.	Devour	Equal, va.
Clergy	Cup	Dig	Err
Clever	Curdle, vn.	Dike	Especial
Cloth	Curl, va.	Dip, va.	Especially
Coast, s.	Cushion, s.	Dirty, adj.	Establish
Coat, s.	Customary	Disable	Estimate, v.
Coffee	Cut, va.	Disaster	Evening
Coin, s.		Disease, s.	Excavation
Cold, s.		Dishonour	Exceed
Colours	Damsel	Disincline	Excellent
Comfort, va.	Dapple, va.	Disparage	Excessive
Commerce, s.	Dare, v.	Distraction	Excretion
Companion	Darkness	Disturb	Exercise, va.
Company, s.	Dates	Diver (bird)	Expel
Compare, v.	Daub, va.	Divide	Explain
Compel	Dawdle, vn.	Do	Extract
Conciliate	Day	Document	Eye
Condiment	Deal, v.	Dog	
Confine, va.	Dear	Door	Fall, vn.
Confuse	Debt	Doubtful	False
Conquer	Decay, v.	Draw	Family
Constitution	Decide, va.	Dreadful	Fanciful
Consult	Declivity	Dress, s.	Far
Contrive	Decoy, va.	Drink, va.	Farm, s.
Cook, va.	Deer	Drink, s.	Fat
Cookery	Defame	Duck, s.	Fear, va.
Cord, s.	Defective	Dull, adj.	Fear, s.
Council	Deform	Dwell	Ferret, s.

Fetter, s.
Field
Fill, va.
Fine, adj.
Finger, s.
Fire, s.
Fireirons
Fireplace
Fish
Fit, adj.
Fit, va.
it Fits, va.
Flag, vn.
Flat, adj.
Fleet, s.
Flour
Flow, vn.
Flower, s.
Fly, s.
Fly, vn.
Follow
Food
Foolish
Foot, s.
Forest
Forgive
Fortress
Fraud
Frequent, va.
Frighten
Fringe, s.
Frost, s.
Fruit
Fruit Tree
Fuel
Funeral
Furniture

Game Birds
Gather, va.

General, adj.
Generous
Get
Give
Go
Goats
Good, adj.
Goods
Gourd
Govern
Government
Governor
Gown
Grain
Grand
Grapes
Grass
Grave, s.
Gray, Grey
Grease, s.
Greedy
Green, adj.
Greens
Grief
Grieve, vn.
Gripe, va.
Groin
Grow
Guard, va.
Gun

Hair
Hammer
Hand, s.
Happen
Happy
Harbour, s.
Harness, s.
Hasten, vn.
Hate, va.

Head, s.
Headstrong
Heat, s.
Heaven
Help, va.
Herb
Hide, v.
High
Hold, v.
Honour, va.
Horse
Hot
House
Hurt, va.
Hurtful
Husbandry

Idle, adj.
Illnatured
Imitate
Improve, va.
Incite
Increase, va.
Industrious
Inform
Ink
Innate
Inquire
Insect
Insert
Insurrection
Intend
Intercourse
Invert

Jar, s.
Jewel
Jocose
Join
Joyful

Judge, s.
Jug
Jump
Just

Keep
Kettle
Kill
Kind, adj.
King
Kingdom
Kitchen
Knife

Lad
Lake
Lamp
Land
Laugh, vn.
Lavish, adj.
Law
Lawful
Lay
Lead, va.
Leaf
Learn
Leather
Leave, va.
Leg
Lewd
Lie, vn.
Light, s.
Like
Lightminded
Limb
Little
Lock, s.
Loins
Look, vn.
Love, va.
Love, s.

Mad
Make, v.
Maker
MALTREAT
Mankind
Manner
Mason
Mass, s.
Materials
a Meal
Measure, s.
Meat
Meat Dish
Meddle
Medicine
Melt
Milk
Mill
Mineral
Miracle
Mire
Mistake, s.
Mix
Money
Month
Moon
Morning
Mould, s.
Mountain
Mouth
Mulberries
Music

Nail
Nation
Nature
Near
Neck
Needful
Net, s.

Nice
Nimble
Noise, s.
Nuts

Obey
Offer, va.
Officers
Offspring
Onions
Opinion
Oppose
Oranges
Owl
Ox

Pack
Pain, s.
Painful
Paper
Parliament
Pastry
Pay, va.
Peace
Pen, s.
Perhaps
Perpetual
Pickle, va.
Piece, s.
Pierce
Pig
Pigeon
Pincers
Pipe, s.
Pitch, s.
Place, s.
Platter, s.
Play, v.
Pleasant
Plentiful

Plover
Plums
Poem
Politics
Poultry
Pour
Power
Pray
Press, va.
Prick, va.
Profit, s.
Profit, va.
Proud
Prudent
Publish
Pudding
Pulse(*legumes*)
Punish
Pure
Purpose, s.
Push, va.

Quantity
Quarrel, vn.
Quarter, s.
Quick

Rage, vn.
Rain, s.
Raise, va.
Rank, s.
Rash, adj.
Rat, s.
Red
Refuge
Refuse, s.
Religious
Rely
Remedy, s.
Repel

Reptile
Rest
Return, vn.
Revenue
Rich
Right, adj.
River
Road
Rob
Rock
Roll
Roof
a Room
Roots (edible)
Rough
Rub, va.
Run
Rush, s.

Saddle
Sample
Saw, s.
Say
Scatter
Scream, vn.
Screen, s.
Sea
Season, s.
See, va.
Seek, va.
Sentence, s.
Set, va.
Sew, va.
Shake, va.
Shameful
Sharp
Shawl
Sheaf
Sheep
Ship

Shine
Shirt
Shoe
Show, va.
Shrub
Shun
Sick
Silk
Sincere
Sinew
Sing
Size
Skin, s.
Sky
Slave, s.
Sleep, vn.
Slip, vn.
Smile, vn.
Smith, s.
Snake
Sob, s.
Soldier
Sound, vn.
Sound, s.
  epithets of
Soup
Source
Space
Spade
Spare, va.
Sparrow
Speak
Species
Spend
Spice, s.

Spot, s.
Stable, s.
Staff
Stammer
Star
Steady, adj.
Steal, va.
Stem, s.
Stingy
Stone, s.
Stop, va.
Stout
Street
Stretch, va.
Strive
Stumble
Suit (of law)
Summit
Sun
Supply, va.
Surround
Sweep
Sweets
Swerve

Table, s.
Take
Talent
Talk, vn.
Tame, adj.
Tame Animal
Tart, adj.
Tear, va.
Tent
Thin, adj.

Think
Thread, s.
Throat
Thunder
Till
Timber
Time
Timid
Tire, va.
Title
Tooth
Touch, va.
Tradesman
Traffic, s.
Traffic, vn.
Tray
Treaty
Tree
Tremble
Trinket
Troop, s.
Trowsers
Try, va.
Tumour

Ugly
Undertake
Unjust
Unpleasant
Useful
Useless
Utensil

Vale
Veil s.

Vein
Vie

Wages
Walk, vn.
Wander
Want
War, s.
Warblers
Ware (vessels)
Wash
Water
Waters
Weak
Wealth
Wedlock
Week
Weight
Wet, va.
Whale
Whip, s.
Wild Animals
Window
Wind, s.
Wolf
Woman
Wonder, vn.
Wool
Work, vn.
Worms
Wretched

Yellow

Zeal
Zone

CORRIGENDA IN THE VOCABULARY.

Page 1, col. 2, line 10 from bottom, *erase* temâda'.
 ,,   2, ,, 2, ,,   6 *for* ʒuif *read* aʒuif.
 ,,   6, ,, 2, ,, 10 from bottom, *read* Deliberate, irtêi. Demur to, irtêb bi.
 ,,   10, ,, 1, ,, 10 *read* Blade Bone, mancib 11.
 ,,   28, ,, 2, ,, 18 *for* sêyih *read* sêyiʃl.
 ,,   29, ,, 2, ,,   6 *read* Muslin.
 ,,   29, ,, 2, ,, 11 from bottom, *read* yâbonja.
 ,,   33, ,, 2, ,, 17 *for* Threat *read* Thread.
 ,,   40, ,, 2, ,,   7 probably ofzor must be corrected into جزر, *i.e.*, ofroz, or rather ifriz.
 ,,   41, ,, 1, ,,   8 *for* ᴛammiq *read* ᴛammis.
 ,,   45, ,, 2, ,,   3 *read* Incapacitate for.
 ,,   45, ,, 2, ,,   9 *for* akdil *read* akᴀil.
 ,,   52, ,, 2, ,,   9, 10 from bottom, *read* Worry, Bait, ʃlarrix, ʃlârix; herrix, hêrix.
 ,,   57, ,, 2, ,,   7 *for* indihêl *read* inᴀihêl.
 ,,   60, ,, 2, ,,   6 from bottom, *for* infid *read* inflᴀ.
 ,,   63, ,, 1, ,,   7 *for* tejbien *read* teᵽbien.
 ,,   63, ,, 1, ,,   6 from bottom, *erase* uʒᴛarib.
 ,,   70, ,, 2, ,, 19 *for* qarruʒ *read* qarruᴛ ʙ.
 ,,   76, ,, 1, ,, 18 I cannot verify ᴛawâla; elsewhere I have ᴛalâwa, stud.
 ,,   83, ,, 2, ,, 26 *for* Cruet, Bottle, *read* Cruet-bottle.
 ,,   96, ,, 1, ,,   7 from bottom, *for* seher *read* seʃlar.
 ,, 101, ,, 2, ,, 12 *read* waraq kauxif *without comma between*.
 ,, 112, ,, 1, ,, 17 *read* wardiey.
 ,, 112, ,, 1, ,, 24 *for* Livid *read* Lurid.

A SKELETON DICTIONARY

OF

MODERN ARABIC,

EXPLAINED IN ENGLISH.

EXPLANATION OF THE ARRANGEMENT OF WORDS.

A very slight acquaintance with Arabic may satisfy any one that the interpreter of Arab words must not arrange them by our alphabetical methods, but kindred words must be placed under their common *root*. The immediate difficulty to the learner is, to ascertain what root he must seek. For this, some small knowledge of grammar is needful. The same necessity is found in other tongues; with Greek the difficulty is often serious. In every case the duty of the lexicographer is, to exact a mere minimum of grammar from him who is to consult the Dictionary.

If the radical letters in Arabic were never auxiliary, and the auxiliary never radical, the root would be discovered mechanically by mere inspection. But, not only are the weak consonants, ʼ W Y, which degenerate into vowels, very often radical; also the strong consonants M, T, N, St, are in certain connections auxiliary; and in Syria D also. The latter have to be thrown away, the former have to be introduced, in order to arrive at the root; a process, in which even a native may err. Suppose that we reach the letters M N and believe both to be radical; for what root are we to look? It may be a Duplicate root, as Mann;

or Reduplicate, as Manman; or by the addition of a weak radical it may be one of *nine* other forms, 'MN, WMN, YMN; M'N, MWN, MYN; MN', MNW, MNY. Surely it is a serious disadvantage to have these *eleven* possible roots scattered in different parts of the Dictionary. Not only does it save much time to him who consults its pages to find them altogether, but it warns every learner *not to confound* one with another; which is of all advantages most precious. So far indeed this change of arrangement would be serviceable to an uneducated Arab as well as to foreigners. Thus, Xawal must be looked out under XL, and Zèwiya under simple Z.

But besides this, the Arabs have seven pairs of consonants, coarse and fine, which a European is apt to confound when he hears them from even a native; which also, in the Arabic imported into Turkish, Persian, and Indian languages, are for the most part systematically confounded. Here again to all these foreigners it is a very great convenience to find side by side in the Dictionary the coarse and fine h, the coarse and fine t, the coarse and fine s, and so on. This method is here followed, with one exception. The Arabic *Ain* is not here treated as a mere variety of the soft Hamze; because, as I judged, the number of roots brought together would be too great, and the perception of any alphabetical order would have been embarrassed. Thus, such words as 'eccid, saqqid, are *not* found side by side under the root CD or QD. Indeed, I am unwilling to seem to treat ع as a weak consonant, which it certainly is not in Arabic, soft as it becomes in Persian and Hindostani.

Once more, the modern Greek sounds of Θ Δ (the twofold Th of English) are incorrectly pronounced in Syria and in Africa, being popularly corrupted into T and D. I have therefore thought it best to coordinate them with T and D. Thus, Tion, Tuin, Θinn will be found in succession under TN. An inevitable inconvenience arises, since the half-learned think to be more accurate by sounding Θ and Δ as S and Z; which is just as though in speaking English one Frenchman were to correct another Frenchman's pronunciation of This, from Dis into Zis. Thus Δeciey and Zeciey are confounded, and a person who hears the sound Zeciey does not guess that Δeciey is intended.

A learner is soon aware that participles very generally begin with Ma, Mo, Mole, Mon, Most, and that those syllables must be struck off as auxiliary, before searching for a root. A noun expressing an instrument often begins with Mi, and a noun of place with Ma. The vii[th] verbal form begins with In, the xth with Ist, the vth and vi[th] with Te. Both initial and final T are often auxiliary; so too is T even *after* the 1st radical in the viii[th] form, as Ijtenab, Icteteb, of which the roots are JNB, CTB; nay, in Ittekas *each* t is auxiliary, and the root is 'KΔ, which must be looked for under KΔ. Final -an, -ân, -oun, -ain, -ein, -ien, -uin, are terminations ordinarily to be rejected; though in ên, awân, tien, ruin, the *n* is radical. In Maries we may consult either MRΣ or RΣ; and so in some other cases. Thus in Madâr we may equally well look to MDR or to DR. Ambiguities cannot be wholly evaded.

After prefixing a few words which have no strong consonant in the root, I arrange the alphabet *nearly* as in English; only *postponing C to keep company with* Q, and making Γ take the place of G. I begin with Σ in place of A.

Thus: Σ B D (Δ Δ̄) F Γ (G) H (Π) J K L M N Q (C) R S (Ϛ) T (Θ T) X Z (3).

When several roots have two strong consonants in common, I arrange all the possible forms as above denoted concerning MN. Or, supposing them to be XR, you find in order:

XRR, XRXR; 'XR, WXR, YXR; X'R, XWR, XYR; XR', XRW, XRY.

Or rather, as many of them as exist in the language. Besides such list of roots, we may find one more, XRX in its own place, making a 12th as in Xorx, fibre of a root. If the two strong radicals be the same letter, as TT in Tout, the word must be looked out at TT, treating the letters as separate.

In the verb of the first form the second vowel of the Present Tense is of peculiar importance. The *same* vowel is found in the Imperative mood, which on the whole best represents the root. Thus I write Oqtol, kill (thou), in preference to Qatel, he killed. In the verbs called Hollow, equally as in the Duplicate verb, the imperative (as pronounced by the moderns) is exactly the true root, as in English and often in Latin; thus, Coun, be (thou); though classical texts here shorten the vowel, as Con, be thou. Only when the root begins with W it seems requisite to give *two* tenses; and then I write down the *third person* of Past and Present, as Wajab yejib; Waqas yaqas. The organized passive has no imperative, but in it there is no grammatical ambiguity of vowels; hence the received method suffices. I write thus, under LD, "Wolid, was born." The ten forms of imperative for the triradical verb, from XRF are: i. Oxrof (Ixraf, Ixrif); ii. Xarrif; iii. Xârif; iv. Axrif; v. Texarraf; vi. Texâraf; vii. Inxarif; viii. Ixterif; ix. Ixriff; x. Istexrif. In the quadriradical the modern language rarely goes beyond two forms, as i. Zekrif; ii. Tezekraf. A third form takes auxiliary N *after the second* radical, as in Moſtranjim from Harjim, of which I have given barely a second instance.

A single root has often widely different senses. This sometimes is from the internal development of the language, as in English Drip and Droop; sometimes by accident, as in Drilling (a hole) and Drilling (soldiers); sometimes by foreign importation, as with Grave, *adj.* from Latin Gravis, while we have a native verb Grave (to dig or cut in). I use numerals (2) (3) ... heavy enough to catch the eye, in order to distinguish diverse senses under one root.

ARABO-ENGLISH DICTIONARY.

OBSERVE.—*Words printed in Small Capitals refer to the Second Part or Complement of this Dictionary.*

ROOTS DESTITUTE OF STRONG CONSONANTS.

'E, *interrogative particle*. Is it? *Latin* An, Num.
An, or. Eiwa, yes.
Ai, that is to say.
Ai? *m.* Aiya? *f. adj.* which? In Syria, Aina, d°. (quisnam).
Aya! Aiyaho! ho there!
Yâ, oh.
Ya—ya (Persian), either—or. Catafago gives it as modern Arabic.

آية Eya, *nu.* 2, sign, token. A verse of Korân or Bible.

اوى I'wi, *vn* take shelter.
iii. or iv. êwi, *va* shelter.
Iewâ, Mawieya, *ger.* a sheltering, harbouring.
v. Te'ewwa', *vn* = i. but commoner. Mo'êwi el çorabâ, hospitable B. [refuge.
Mê'wa' 11, place of shelter,
(2) Wâwi, Ibn âwi, Ibn 'ewa', jackal.

ايوان Iewân 2, *also pl.* ewâwien, (*Pers.*) arched recess in the court of a house. In Syria, *vulg.* Liewân.

ع (Ain).
عوى Sowâ, a yelping.
ii. Sawwi, *vn* yelp as jackal.
عى Sayy, *vn* hesitate, *lit.* and *fig.*
Sayyân, weary, languid.
Sayâ', weariness, languor.
Masyiey, tired out.
iv. Asuiy, *va* TIRE. Also *vn* Usâya, *s.* fatigue.
v. Tesayyâ, *vn* be tired out.

عب Söbb, *va* gulp down, swill B. *ger.* Sabb.
v. Tesabbab, *vn* guzzle, tipple.
(2) Sabb(a), breastpocket.

عب, x. Isteucub, *va* exhaust (a topic), finish it completely.

عيب Saib, *s.* a flaw, a cause of disgrace, a scandal.
Sayyâb, apt to utter base reproaches.
Masuib, faulty, scandalous.
Masyoub, reprehensible.
ii. Sayyib, *va* reproach, insult.
v. Tesayyab *vp.* be put to shame. BLAME.

عبء Asbû, *pl.* heavy goods.
(2) Osbou, *vn* be esteemed.

ΣBW
Lâ yasbou bihi, no esteem is set on it.

عبي Sabâ, camel's hair cloak.
Söbâya, jacket of the same. Also, European dresscoat, *commoner*, beala.
(2) ii. sabbi, *vs* pack close, cram, fill (pipe with tobacco). PACK. *Also*, arrange troops in masses.

عبد Sabd, SLAVE, vassal, devotee; *pl.* sabied *or* subâd.
Subdiey, slavish (work).
Subâda, devotion.
Söbouda, *commoner* Söboudieya, Masbad, temple. [slavery.
i. Osbod, *vs* serve, worship. *ger.* Sabad.
ii. Sabbid, *vs* enslave.
Mosabbad, subdued, tame; beaten (path).
v. Tesabbad, *vn* be devout.
x. Istasbid, *vs* reduce to slavery, reconcile to slavery.

عبق Usbaq, *vn* adhere, as odour. *ger.* sabaq, sabâqa.
ii. Sabbiq, *vs* perfume.

عبر Osbor, *vn* go across; cross (a river); *ger.* söbour.
Masbar, a ferry, a pass.
(2) ii. Sabbir *can*, EXPLAIN, comment on.
Subra, a lesson.
Sabâra, explanation, expression.
viii. Ustebar, *vs* esteem, ACCOUNT.
Ustibâr, consideration.

ΣD
Mostcbar, considerable.
x. Istesbir, *vs* draw instruction from, improve a subject.

عبس Usbis, *vn* look gloomy. *ger.* Söbous.
Sâbis, Sobous, sad faced.
ii. Sabbis (el wejh), make gloomy. By omitting el wejh, the verb becomes neuter; viz. Sabbis, *vn* frown, look gloomy.
v. Tesabbas, *vn* d°.

عبث Usbaθ bi, *vn* trifle, sport with, in. *ger.* Sabaθ, frivolity, nonsense.
Sabθe, *nu.* a frivolity.
Subbieθ, very frivolous.
El rabiesa sabaθet bi tezwieq el flaiwânêt el jouwieya; Nature has sported (amused herself) in painting domestic animals v.

عبيط Sabier, an idiot s. *See also* *ebida.

عد Södd, *vs* count. *ger.* Sadd, Sudâd.
Sudâd, enumeration c.
Sadad, a number, a *numero*.
Sudda, a number; several.
Sadied, numerous.
ii. Saddid, *vs* enumerate, specify.
iv. Asudd, *vs* equip, get (a thing) ready. Usdâd, equipment.
Södda, equipment, equipage, apparatus, tools.

ꭶD

Södd, freckles on the face.
Satied, prepared, ready.
El usdâdieya, the engineers.
v. Tesaddod, plurality.
Motesaddid, numerous.
viii. Ustidd, *va* Account.
x. Istesudd, *vp* of iv. *ger.* Istusdâd, preparation; hence, aptitude of mind, solertia = Liyâqa.

عَضَ Söꭶ, *va* bite. *ger.* Saꭥa.
Saꭥöuꭥ, Saꭥâꭥ, apt to bite.
عَضَد Saꭥad, *s.* arm.
Muꭥad, armlet.
iii. Sâꭥud, *va* support, uphold.
Mosâꭥud, *s.* supporter.

وَعَد Wasad yasad, *va* promise, threaten. *ger.* Wasd 3.
Wasda, *nu* a promise.
Mausöud, a thing promised.
Miesâd, trysting place, rendezvous.
iii. Wâsud, *va* appoint (a person) to meet in a place.
Mowâsada, mutual engagement to meet somewhere.
iv. Ausud (fie), make appointment; also *va* as iii.
v. Tewassad, *va* threaten (a person) bi, *with.*
vi. Tewâsad, agree on rendezvous mutually. [miss.
viii. Ittesud, *vn* accept a pro-

سَود Söud (*pl.* 9, Suidân), stick, pole, (lucifer) match; a tall palmstem; aloes; a lute, lyre.

ꭶWꭥ

Sawwâda, female luteplayer.
(2) Söud, *vn* recur, Return.
ger. Saud.
Söwâda, Sauda, *s.* return.
Sâda, *s.* custom 2. Also *pl.*
Sawâyid.   [mar.
Mâ sâd, not again. See Grammusâd, place of resort, haunt.
ii. Sawwid sala', *va* accustom to.
iii. Sâwid, *va* recur to, relapse into (a practice).
Mosâwid, assiduous.
Mosâwada, relapse (into a habit). Habituation.
iv. Asuid, *va* repeat, repay *r.*
Mosuid, experienced.
Usâda, repetition.
viii. Ustêd sala', bi, be used to.
Mostêd, habituated.
Ustiyâd, habitude.   [mary.
Ustiyâdiey, ordinary. Custox. Istesuid, *va* claim *encore*, ask (a singer) to repeat.
(2) v. Tesawwad, *va* lunch.
Teswieda, *s.* lunch.

عُوذ Söus *vn* take refuge (b'illâh, in God), *ger.* aus, masâsa, *commonest* suyâs.
Sawas, *s.* Refuge, asylum.
Söuse, Muswas 11, amulet.
ii. Sawwis, *va* drive to take refuge in God.
v. Tesawwas = i.
x. Istesuis, invoke deliverance.
ger. Istesâse.
[This root is popularly sounded Söuz, causing confusion.]

عِوَض Suwaꭥ 4, *s.* recompense; a substitute, a proxy.

SWƉ

Suwaɖaⁿ ꞅan, *prep.* instead of.
Ꞅawiɖ? (*vowels doubtful*) a substitute or proxy in voting.
ii. Ꞅawwuɖ, *va* recompense.
iii. Ꞅâwuɖ, *va* require (PAY), remunerate.
Moꞅâwaɖa, retaliation.

ـعِيد Ꞅuid 4, feast day, birthday.
Ꞅuidiey, *adj.* festive, festal.
Ꞅuidieya, *s.* festal present.
ii. Ꞅayyid, *v.* keep feast.
iii. Ꞅâyid, *va* compliment (a person) on a feast day.
Moꞅâyada, festive compliment.

عدو Oꞅdou, *vn* overrun (as disease, or as marauders). *Simply,* run F. B.
Ꞅôdou, running (of stag), F. X.
Lâ yaꞅdou ꞅehilaⁿ, it does not easily *pass, i.e.* happen F.
Ꞅadwa, contagion.
Ꞅadâ, encroachment, transgression. *adv.* besides.
Ma ꞅadâ, what goes beyond, *i.e.* Besides. [ꞅkiffer B.
Maꞅdieya, a ꞅkiff. Maꞅdâwi, Ꞅadou, *f.* Ꞅadouwa, invader, *i.e.* enemy. *pl.* aꞅdâ.
Ꞅadâwa, hostility.
Ꞅadawân, invasion.
Ꞅadâwiey, hostile, aggressive.
ii. Ꞅaddi ꞅan, *va* reflect (light) from. Also *vn* leave off B. Also Ꞅaddi min, *vp vn* be reflected from B. (*qu. cp* Ꞅôddi).
Teꞅdiya, hostility B.
v. Taꞅadda ꞅala', go beyond, pass, encroach upon, usurp, invade, harass. (This super-

sedes i.) *As a legal phrase*, Assault, AGGRIEVE.
vi. Teꞅâdâ, invade mutually.
Moꞅâdâya, mutual hostility.
viii. Uꞅtedi, be contagious.
Moꞅtedi, contagious.

عذب Ꞅaab, *adj.* sweet (water), sweet (sound).
Aꞅꞅeb, sweeter. [sweetness.
Oꞅaob, *vn* be sweet. *ger.* Ꞅöaouba, (2) ii. Ꞅaaaib, *va* torment, punish.
Ꞅuaêb, torment, punishment.

عدل Uꞅdal, *vn ger.* Ꞅadl, be balanced, even, just.
— ꞅan, tilt, swerve from. *ger.* ꞅôdoul.
Sâdil, JUST.
Sadâla, Ꞅadl, justice.
Sadiel, even-balanced, alike.
Maꞅdal, *s.* average? fair sum.
ii. Saddil, *va* rectify.
iii. Sâdil *va* cope with.
Moꞅâdil, equivalent, an equal match.
Moꞅâdala, equilibrium.
vi. Teꞅâdal, *vn* be on parity.
viii. Uꞅtedil, *vn* be moderated, tempered, symmetrical.
Karr el uꞅtidâl, the Equator.
x. Iꞅteꞅdil, ponder?
(2) Sadl, large sack for grain.
Sôdaila, satchel.

عذل Oꞅaol, *va ger.* Ꞅaal, censure, BLAME.
Ꞅaael, *s.* censure.
Ꞅaaoul, Ꞅaaaêl, censorious.
ii. Ꞅaaail, intensive of i.

ƧΔL

Teꜱʌêl, severe censure.
Moꜱʌʌʌel, highly censurable.
viii. Usteʌil, *vp* of ii.

عضل Ƨaδala, *nu* a muscle.
Ƨaδul, muscular, strong.
Ƨaδaliey, muscular, *i.e.* appertaining to the muscles.

عدم Uꜱdam, *vn* be nonexistent. *va* fail (a person). *ger.* Ƨödm, Ƨadam.
Ƨödm, nonexistence. [Used before a noun, to express our Un, In, Non; as, Ƨödm cefâya, *insufficiency*.]
Ƨadiem 5, destitute of. [So Ƨadiem el ḥarace, motion*less*.]
Ƨadamiey, *adj.* privative.
iv. Aꜱdim, *va* 1. deprive of, strip away (a thing). 2. fail (a person), escape him. 3. annihilate.
viii. Inꜱadim, *vp* be annihilated.

عدس ii. Ƨaddin, *va* work a mine x.
Maꜱdin 11, mine, mineral.
(2) Ƨadn, (garden of) Eden. Aden, a town of Arabia.

عدد Ƨaudaq, *pl.* Ƨödoq (10), hooked tool *c*.

عذر Ƨöʌr, Maꜱʌer, *s.* excuse.
ii. Ƨaʌʌir, *va* excuse (another), plead for.
iii. Ƨâʌir, *va* plead for, with vain excuses.
Moꜱâʌera, shuffling apology.
iv. Aꜱdir, *va* excuse, forgive.

ƧFY

v. Teꜱaʌʌer; viii. Usteʌir, excuse oneself, apologize.
Teꜱaʌʌer min, excuse oneself from, shuffle off, make difficulties against b. *Also* Teꜱaʌʌer ꜱala', be difficult to (a person) F.
(2) Ƨuʌér, the cheek near to the whisker.
(3) Ƨaʌrâ, a Virgin, especially in Theology.

عدس Ƨades, lentils.
Ƨadesieya, a dish of lentils.

عفّ Ƨuff san, *vn ger.* Ƨafaf, Abstain from (illicit pleasure).
Ƨuffa, chastity. Ƨafief, chaste.

عيف Ƨuif, Ƨâf, *vn* dislike food. *va* disrelish. *ger.* Ƨayâfa, Ƨayafân. Hate.
Ƨâyif, disdainful, coy.
Ƨayouf, fastidious (as to water or food).
Ƨayyifân, d° x.
Ƨuyâfa, fastidiousness, coyness.
(2) Teꜱayyaf, *vn* augur.
Ƨayâfa, augury.
Moteꜱayyif, *s.* augur x.

عفو Oꜱfou, (Uꜱfi ꜱan b.) *va* exempt from. *ger.* Ƨafou, forgiveness, absolution *c*.
ii. Ƨaffi, *va* efface x.
x. Isteꜱfi, ask pardon.

عفي Ƨafi, *adj.* hale, robust; *pl.* Aꜱfiya 8. Stout.
Ƨâfiya, good health.

SFY

iii. Moṣáfáya, convalescence.
vi. Teṣáfa', be convalescent.

عَفِن Ṣafin, Masfoun, putrid, rotten.
Ṣófouna, putridity, rottenness.
ii. Ṣaffin, va rot, make putrid.

عَفِق Uṣfiq, va snap up (as dog) B. CATCH.

عَفَر Ṣafar 4, dust x.
Ṣafár, Ṣafra, dust n̄ₐ. [θαι?]
iii. Ṣáfir bi, vn toil at (κονιεσ-
(2) Ṣufr, s. the red stag F.

عَفْرِ ب Ṣufrier, gigantic demon.
Moṣafrir, surly, fierce.

عَسْف Osfos, va hold back, clog, encumber? [B.
ii. Ṣaffis, va compress by weight
iii. Ṣáfis, try to trip up x. struggle against.
Moṣáfase, a (mutual) struggle.
vi. Teṣáfes, vn struggle together.

عَسْف Aṣfet, lefthanded, clumsy
Ṣuffiten, huge, gawky x. [x.
Maṣfout, sullen. B. Bourru.

عَفْص Ṣafṣ, gall nuts.
Ṣafuṣ, acrid.
Ṣófouṣa, acridity.
ii. Ṣaffuṣ, va dye with galls.
Moṣaffaṣ, stuff so dyed.

عَفَش Safax, s. rubbish lit. or fig.
Ṣófáxa, rubble.

عَسْن Ṣuhon, s. strong young animal (camel, horse) x. c.

ṢWJ

عَهد Ṣahd 3, a covenant, an agreement. Also, era, epoch F.
iii. Ṣáhid, va receive into treaty.
Moṣáheda, a treaty.
Ṣahied, client, liege. Also, contemporary x.
Ṣóhda, a document (of attestation), a charter? It may be rendered, "a trust." Thus: El maṣallét el moṣawwala li ṣóhdatec, the places transferred to thy trust [said by the Sultan to his vizier]. [x.
Ṣuhdán, a document of warrant?
vi. Teṣáhed, vn confederate.
(2) Uṣhed, vn be familiar F.
Maṣhoud, customary, familiar, el qaṭṭ el maṣhoud, the domestic cat F.
Maṣhed, a familiar haunt.

عَهْر Ṣábira, harlot c.

عَجّ Ṣajj, vn bellow (as wind, waves, bull, pig). ger. Ṣajicj.
Ṣajjáj, adj. bellowing, blowing hard. s. The Bellower, or Bittern (bird). [camel).
Ṣajcuj, vn bellow, rumble (as
(2) Ṣajj, vn grow windy? run into straw?
iv. Aṣjij, raise dust.
Ṣajája, nu. dust, smoke c.
(3) Ṣójja, an omelette. Hebrew.

عَوج Aṣwaj, adj. crooked.
ii. Ṣawwij, va make crooked.
Moṣawwaj, Moṣwaj, crooked.
Moṣuwwajaⁿ, askew, awry.
Uṣwijáj, obliquity B.

ʕAJ

عاج Ṣâj, ivory.
Ṣâjiey, made of ivory.

عجب Ṣajab, a wonder 4.
Ṣajieb, wonderful.
Ṣajjâb, marvellous.
Ṣajieba 11, a marvel.
ii. Ṣajjib, *va* astonish. [person].
iv. *va* please, gratify, satisfy (a
v. Teṣajjab *can*, wonder at,
admire. x. Isteṣjib min, d°·
(2) ṣajb, rumpbone of animal.

عجل ṣujl 3, 5, bullock, calf.
Ṣujla 5, *f.* heifer, calf.
(2) Ṣajal, Ṣajala *s.* haste.
Ṣâjil, *parte.* making haste.
Ṣajiel, *adj.* hasty, speedy.
Ṣâjilaⁿ, Bil ṣajal, quickly.
ii. Ṣajjil, *va* hasten.
v. Teṣajjal, *va* hasten.
x. Isteṣjil, *va* or *va* d°·

عجم Ṣajam, *s.* fruit stone.
(2) Ṣajm, Ṣöjm, root of the tail *r.*
(3) Ṣajam, barbarians; *esp.*
Persians. [ture.
Ṣajmâ 2, a brute, dumb crea-
Ṣajamiey, *adj.* Persian.
Ṣajamistên, Persia. (So at
Aleppo. *See* Fars.)
iv. Aṣjim, talk as a barbarian.

عجن Oṣjon, *va* knead.
Ṣajien, dough, paste.
Maṣâjien, confections, pastry.

عجن Oṣjoq, *va* pother?
Maṣjouq, over-busied.

ṢL

عجر Ṣajir, *adj.* unripe *s.*
Ṣöjra, unripeness.
(2) Ṣajour, cucumber with corrugated skin.
Moṣajjar, corrugated (horn) *r.*
ii. Ṣajjir, *va* corrugate.

عجرف Ṣajrafa, violence, caprice, arbitrary conduct, pedantry. PROUD. CRUEL.
Ṣajârief, caprices (of Fate).
ii. Teṣajraf, *vn* domineer.
Moteṣajrif, *adj.* arbitrary and
capricious (ruler).

عجرم Ṣajrim, *vn* move rudely
and quickly, scramble?

عجز Ṣâjiz, enfeebled.
Ṣajouz 10, 11, old woman.
Uṣjiz, *vn* be feeble, dwarfed.
Uṣjiz *can*, li, be too WEAK for.
ger. Ṣöjouz, Ṣajazên.
ii. Ṣajjiz, *va* enfeeble, DISABLE.
x. Isteṣjiz fla, regard (a person)
as too feeble for.
(2) Ṣajz, Ṣujz, Ṣöjz, *s.* 4, buttock, croup (of an animal).
See Ṣajb.
v. Teṣajjez, *va* ride behind (a
person) on the croup.

عل Ṣulla 2, 10, cause, pretext,
casualty, ailment.
Ṣaliel, ailing, sick; an invalid,
pl. Aṣulla? [for.
ii. Ṣallil, *va* occasion; account
v. Teṣallal, *vn* pretend, make
pretext.
Teṣalṣal, *vn* make excuse.

ƸL

Söllieya. See Sala'.
(2) Salla, Lasalla, mayhap, belike. PERHAPS.

عسول Söul, va tend the sick B. ger. Sōwoul, Suyâla x.
Saila, a family, esp. large.
Saul, domestic victuals.
iv. Asuil, va rear a (large) family. ger. Usâla.
(2) Sawiela, s. a howl, shriek.
ii. Sawwil, vn SCREAM.
iv. Aswil, d⁰·
Moswal (salaihi), lamented over.
(3) Miswal, miner's pike.
(4) Masōul, adj. castrated o. (but qu.) exhausted (patience) o.

على Sala', prep. upon, towards, against, over.
Saliey, adj. upper, high.
Asla', higher, highest.
Aslâ, highest part, acme.
Sōlâwa, upper part, top.
Söllieya, an attic B.
Sulwa', excessive.
Sulâwa, surplus.
Sulâwateⁿ, in addition, besides.
Salawiey, supernal, sublime; superior (being), celestial (phenomenon). [Osrou.
Oslou, va overlie, cover r. See
Oslou san, vn rise above, escape from. ger. Sōlou, height, high station.
Sâli, high, lofty, grand.
Salâ, dignity. Min salâ, from above.
Sâliya, s. culminating part, pl. 12, Sawâli, high qualities.

SLJ

Maslâya 11, a dignity.
ii. Salli, va raise, hoist up; san, from.
iv. Asli va d⁰· x.
v. Tesallâ, vn ascend by degrees.
vi. Tasîlâ, vn be exalted (as God).
Allâh Tasâlâ, God, may he be exalted! i.e. God most High.
Motesâli, exalted.
x. ger. Istislâ, emphasizing (of a syllable).
(2) vulg. Tesâl, f. Tesalie, come thou! Tesâl ila' heun, come hither! AL.

علبة Sölba 10, 5, wooden box, wooden pail.

علف Salaf, s. fodder.
Sallâf, seller of fodder.
Salief, fattened up.
Sallâfa, pl. foragers.
Maslaf, manger, rack. [lâya.
Muslaf, horse's nosebag — Mik-
Sōloufa, stipend, salary.
i. Oslof, va fodder, feed. ger. Salf.
Maslouf, fattened up.
iv. Aslif, same as i.
viii. Ustélif, vn feed, as horse at manger.

علج iii. sâlij, va treat, manage; cure (meat). vp. Söulij (meat) is cured r. ger. Sulâj, a remedy. Mosâlaja, medical treatment.
(2) vi. Tesâlaj, vn struggle, STRIVE B.

SLJ

viii. Uslelij, *va* toss about (as waves) x. [silver o.
(3) Salaja, tissue of gold or
(4) Sulj 4, a barbarian r.

سلم Sâlam 1, 11, world *theolog*.
Sâlamiey, mundane.
(2) Uslam, *va* know. *ger*. Sulm 3, knowledge, science.
Sulmiey, scientific.
Salam, 4, 5, ensign, flag.
Salâma 2, mark, token.
Sâlim, Saliem 6, 7, learned. El Sölamâ, the learned.
ii. Sallim, *va* (frequentative) teach. Mosallim, teacher, doctor.
Sallim sala', *va* set a mark upon.
iv. Aslim, *va* inform (a person).
v. Tesallam, *va* LEARN as pupil.
vi. Tesâlam, learn in company x.
x. Isteslim, *va* ask information, inquire.
Musloum, *adj*. well-known, notorious; *adv*. assuredly, no doubt, yes. *s*. (*pl*. 11) a fixed salary.

سلن salan, the PUBLISHING.
Salanieya, publication.
Salânieya, publicity.
Salânieyatⁿ, notoriously.
Söloun, the becoming public.
Sölwân, advertisement, title of a book.
iii. Sâlin, *va* notify (a person).
iv. Aslin, *va* advertise (a thing).

سلع Uslec, *va* champ, chew. *ger*. Salc. BITE.

SLQ

Salce, gabble, verbiage.
ii. Sallic, *va* gabble, mumble. BABBLE. STAMMER.
(2) Sulc, gum of pine, juniper, etc. c.

سلق Söllieq, any bush? a certain camel's thorn, thorny plant. Hence, Toutel Söllieq, mulberries of the bush, *i.e.* raspberries or blackberries.
Salqa', a plant of which brooms are made x.
Salaq, fodder for beasts.
ii. Salliq, *va* fodder (a horse). See Salaf. But x. says it is elliptical for *hanging* (a nose bag) on a horse.
(2) Uslaq min, bi, *va* be hung by, fastened to. *ger*. Salaq.
Muslaq, hook, lever. [fection.
Sulaq, Sölqa, attachment, af-
Sulâqa 11, Tesalloq, connexion, relation.
Salaqa, a leech. [delay.
ii. Salliq, *va* hang, suspend,
v. Tesallaq bi, *va* be related to, cling by, depend on.
Salqa, *s*. relay (of horses) B.
Salâqa, surgeon's sling to support the arm.
(3) Salouq, embryo c.
i. Uslaq, *va* conceive (as female), with Bi of the foetus.
Salaqat minnoh bi, she has conceived by him.
(4) Salqa 10, bastinado, a beating, blows with a stick B.
Uẕrib *or* Oxmor salqa, inflict the bastinado.

ṢLQ

(5) Maṣlaqa 11, *vulg.* a spoon; *corrupt for* Milɛaqa.

عَلقَم Ṣalqam, colocynth.

عم Ṣamm, Ṣammou 4, 8, father's brother.
Ṣamma 2, father's sister, *amita.*
Ṣamaumiey, belonging to father's brother ᴋ. [commonalty.
(2) Ṣamam, *pl.* Ṣawâmm, the Ṣamiem, Ṣâmm, General, common to all.
Ṣâmmiey, belonging to the community. A ṣamm, more general.
Ṣōmoum, generality, universality.
Ṣōmmiey, plebeian.
i. Ṣōmm, *ca* be common to (many), embrace in common, reach to all.
ii. Ṣammim, *ca* make common.
(3) Ṣamâma 5, 11, turban, *esp.* worn by learned men.
ii. Ṣammim, *va* dress (another) in such a turban.
v. Teɛammam, viii. Uɛtimm,
x. Isteɛumm, *vn* wear such a turban ᴋ.

عوم Ṣōum, *vn* float, swim.
Ṣawwâm, swimmer.
(2) Ṣâm, *pl.* aɛwâm, year.
Ṣōwaim, *dimin.* of Ṣâm.
Ṣâmiey, yearly, annual (plant).
ii. Ṣawwim, yield yearly crops.

عمى Ṣamâ, blindness.
Aɛma', *adj.* blind.

ṢMD

Ṣamie, the being blind o.
Ṣamawiey, purblind, silly.
ii. Ṣammi, *va* blind (a person).
Taɛmiya, mystery.
Moɛamma', enigmatic, apocryphal. *s.* an enigma. Doubtful.
vi. Teɛâma', *vn* feign blindness.
vii. Inɛami, *vp* be blinded.

عمد Oɛmod ɛala', *vn* set to work at, purpose. *ger.* Ṣamd.
Ṣamda, the being relied on; possession of confidence.
Ṣōmda, mainstay; staple in commerce; spokesman for an army, *parlementaire;* committee? representatives? trustees?
Ṣamad, Ṣamd, deliberate Purpose. Ṣamdaⁿ, purposely.
Ṣumâd, pillar, confidence.
Ṣamoud 8, prop, chief support.
Ṣamouda, a stand, small support ʙ.
Ṣâmouda 12, candlestick ʙ.
ii. Ṣammid, *va* prop up; *hence* (in Christian Eccles.) confirm; *also* baptize.
iv. Aɛmid, *va* prop up.
v. Teɛammad, vii. Inɛamid, *vp* be propped up.
viii. Uɛtemid ɛala', rest upon, Rely upon, trust in; *also,* make up one's mind to; resolve upon.
Moɛtemad fiehi, reliable, trustworthy. Moɛtemad, esp. of a book or writer; standard, classical ʙ.

SML

عمل Uᴄmal, *vɴɑ* work, act, be active, practise (an art), pretend. *ger.* Samal.
Samal 4, work. [artificial.
Samaliey, practical, effective,
Samalieya, the effecting, *ger.*
Sâmil 7, workman, artificer; *adj.* executive.
Sömla, *s.* what is earned, pay, salary. Sömla fuḍḍuiya, silver pay, *i.e.* silver currency.
Sömlat el qawâyim, banknote currency.
Samiel, a commissary.
Samoul, active, busy, efficient.
Sammâl, workman, *pl.* Sammâla.
iii. Sâmil mas, *vɴ* behave towards, treat, deal towards.
Mosâmala, behaviour, dealings of business, *sp.* commission, pay for agency.
Waraqa mocâmala, paper *used in transactions?* hence, a bill of exchange; and simply, Mosâmala, paper that is current, of whatever kind.
iv. Asmil, *va* cause to work.
v. Tesammal, *vɴ* go to work.
vi. Tesâmal, *or* have mutual dealings.
vii. Insamil, *vp* be made, done, transacted.
x. Istesmil, *va* employ (workmen or means). *Also,*
Samala, *s.* the Executive; the Service; officers.
Saml 4, a prefecture, a county.
Sumâla, a department, province, *lit.* and *fig.*

SMR

ii. Sammil, *va* make a prefect; but now Nazzub, Wajjih, are commoner.

عمر Sömmân, ocean c. *vulg.* Baḍr el Moḍuiṭ.

عمق Sömq, depth.
Samieq 11 (*vulg.* Tamieq), deep.
ii. Sammiq, *va* deepen.
v. Tesammaq fie, *vɴ* plunge into, study profoundly = Tebaḍḍar.

عمر Sömr, life, space of life, *Lat.* ætas.
Usmar, *vɴ* live, pass one's life. *ger.* Samr.
(2) Sömra 10, the visiting of holy places round Mecca x. c.
(3) Osmor, *va* (as German Bauen, unites the ideas of building and tilling) *sp.* cultivate.
Sâmir, (land) under cultivation, flourishing. (Complimentary epithet of any imperial establishment.) B. renders a "flourishing city" (Ville florissante) by, medienª macmoura *or* sâmira.
Samier, cultivated, populous.
Asmar, better peopled or cultivated.
Masmâr, inhabited country.
Sumâra, edifice; fleet.
Mismâr, architect x. c.
ii. Sammir, *va* colonize, people, fill (a land). *ger.* Tesmier, colonizing, peopling. [In Al-

SMR

giers, *vulg.* fill, load (a gun),
fill (the heavens) as do clouds].
iv. Aᴄmir ᴋ. Istecmir, *va* establish as cultivators.

عمى Aᴄmay, blear-eyed.
ii. ᴄammuy, *va* make to be blear-eyed.
Moᴄammay, blear-eyed.
Sömây, blearness of eye.
Samay, [Samax] ophthalmia.

عن Ṣan, *prep.* from, away from (*Latin* De, rather than Ab).

عن Sunân 8, 10, rein of Bʀɪᴅʟᴇ *met.* reins of government.
(2) Sönwân, frontispiece, title page of a book. See Sölwân.

عون Ṣaun 4, an aiding, aid, *pl.* aids, things helpful.
Sawân, an assistant c.
Sawien, auxiliary (band).
Sawâniey, sycophant ʙ. c.
Aᴄwan, more helpful.
Maᴄöun(a) = Ma'ouna, supplies, munitions.
[Maᴄöun (Ma'oun?), round metal dish ʙ₅.]
iii. Sâwin, *va* Hᴇʟᴘ.
Moᴄâwin, aider; adjutant (military title).
Moᴄâwana, succour.
iv. Aᴄuin, *va* aid (with Min or Sala', of the enemy). *ger.*
Uᴄâna, succour.
Moᴄuin, helpful, helper.   [ᴠ.
vi. Teᴄâwan, *vr* aid one another
viii. Uᴄtewin, d° ᴋ.   [ᴄâna.
x. Isteᴄuin, ask aid. *ger.* Iste-

SNY

Mostecân, one called to aid.
(2) Sâna, *pl.* Söun, *pubes* ʙ. ᴋ.
(3) Ṣaun, colossus ʙ.
Sauniey, colossal, gigantic.

عين Ṣain 3 *f.* an Eʏᴇ; *fig.* eye of needle, fountain. *Also,* essence of a thing, the same (thing). *Also, pl.* 4, *m.* person of distinction. El aᴄyân, the gentry.
El soltân bi ᴄainihi, the Sultan in himself.
Δou ᴄainain, a possessor of two eyes, *i.e.* any one not blind.
Söyaina, a little eye.
Sâyin, *part.* viewing with malignant eye c.
Sayân (*sic*), manifest c. [holes.
ii. Sayyin, *va* pierce with small
iii. Sâyin, *va* eye, see with the eye. *ger.* Suyân.
Moᴄayan, manifest.
Suyâna, the being a spy. [eye.
Moᴄâyana, a sight seen by the
Suina, a sample.
iv. Aᴄyin, *va* gaze at enviously. *Prov.* xvii. 9.
v. Moteᴄâyin, conspicuous.
(2) ii. Sayyin, *va* define, appoint.
v. Teᴄayyan, *op.* of ii.
Moteᴄayyin, definitive.
(3) ii. Sayyin, *va* rot as fruit ʙ. *bis. gw.* to become drilled with small holes?
[Sayyân, tired, is from Sayy.]

عني Uᴄni, *v.* mean, signify.
Maᴄna', the meaning.

SNY

Masniya, sense, substance.
Masnawiey, significant.
(2) Sanâ, *s.* trouble, effort.
Sanâ mosni, severe toil x.
Sanwate", by force o. [dence.
Sunâya, care, provision, provi-
Sâni, apprehensive, troubled.
ii. Sanni, *va* distress.
iii. Sâni, *va* take pains with.
iv. Asni = ii.
Mosni, *adj.* distressing.
v. Tesannâ, *vp* of ii. be worn out.
vi. Tesânâ, make rival Effort, strive hard.
viii. Usteni, *vn* take pains.
x. Istenis, d⁰·
Ustinâ, pains, great care.
Mosteni, *adj.* pains-taking.

ـــــــ Sunaba, *nu.* grape.
Sönnâb, jujube, tree and fruit o.
Sönnâbicy, of carnation colour c.
οἶνοψ ?

عنبر Sanbar, ambergris, a perfume. [Also Sabier, perfume of mixed spice x.]
Sanbariey, of ambergris.
Sanberieya, ratafia, or other fragrant liqueur al.
(2) In modern literature Sanbar seems to mean, 1 store, storeroom ; bread-room, larder of ship ; 2 rick of corn. Perhaps for the classical Anbar.

عند Sand, *prep.* near, at, with, along, in the opinion of. *Lat.* apud; *French,* chez.
(2) Sanied, obstinate, wilful.

SNQ

Osnod, *vn* be obstinate x. *ger.*
Sönoud, obstinacy.
iii. Sânid, *va* thwart, resist wilfully. *ger.* Sunâd, contumacy. [nate.
vi. Tesânad, be mutually obsti-

عندليب Sandalieb, nightingale (bird).

عنف Sönf, violence, harshness, animosity.
Sönfate", by rude violence.
Sanief, violent, fierce.
Sönfiey, rigorous (law, etc.).
Sönfawân, impetuosity (of youth), flower (of age).
ii. Sannif, *va* maltreat. Cruel.
iv. Asnif, *va* d⁰·
v. Tesannaf, *vn* do work rudely and ignorantly x.
viii. Ustenif, *va* take by storm x.

عنكب Sanceb(â), Sancebout 11, spider.

عنق Sanâq 3, kid o. x.
Sanâq el 'erâ, the badger, *called also,* Toffa.
(2) Sönq 4, neck.
ii. Sanniq, *va* catch by the neck, collar (a person).
iii. Sâniq, *va* embrace by the neck. *ger.* Sunâq.
iv. Asniq, *va* put a collar on (a Musnaqa, a (dog) collar. [dog].
vi. Tesânaq, *vn* clasp one another by the neck.
(3) Sanqâ, griffin, fabulous bird. Gripe.

ƵNQ

Ƶanqoud 11, bunch (of grapes).

Ƶanqil, *va* tangle, embarrass = Ƶarqil.

Ƶönʀöur 11, element.
Ƶönʀarieya, elementary body.
(2) Ƶanʀara, Pentecost B.

Ƶaqieq, ruby, garnet, cornelian. JEWEL.
(2) Ƶöqq, *va* disobey (parents). *ger.* Ƶöqouq. HEADSTRONG.
Ƶaqâq, disobedience.
Ƶaqaq 8, disobedient.
Ƶaqqâq, habitually so.

Waɾuc, Mauɾōuc, stricken (by a malady).

Ƶönq ɾan, *va* retard, impede from. STOP. *ger* Ƶauq. *Also*, delay.
Ƶâyiq, one who retards; *pl.* Ƶouwaq x.
Ƶâyiqa 12, an obstacle.
Ƶaiyiq, disposed to hinder.
ii. Ƶawwiq, *va* = i.
iv. Aɾwiq, *va* = i.
v. Teɾawwaq ɾan, *vn* be too late for, be hindered from.

(*modern word*) ɾâyiq, adroit B.
Ƶuyâqa, adroitness B. *Compare* Lâyiq, Liyâqa.
Xoɾl ɾuyâqa, a masterpiece of adroitness B.

ƵQD

Ƶöqâb 9, vulture; *also*, osprey? SEA-EAGLE.
(2) Ƶaqb 5, the heel.
Ƶaqaba, *nu.* tendon of the heel, tendon in general, sinew.
Ƶaqaba 5, heel (?) of a mountain; mountain-side.
(3) Ƶaqieb, a follower.
Ƶâqib 12, successor, one who comes later.
Ƶâqiba 12, a consequence.
Ƶöqb, Ƶöqba', final issue x.
Ƶaqib 4, issue, offspring. [lion.
Ƶöqba 10, d°. *Also*, an alternaiii. Ƶâqib, *va* FOLLOW, prosecute, requite. *ger.* Ƶuqâb, Ƶöqouba, retaliation, punishment.
vi. Teɾâqab, *vn* come alternately.
Moteɾâqib, in rotation, successive, alternate.

Oɾqod, *va* knot, clot; make a necklace of beads; form an arcade, joined as if by knotting and lacing; make a knot or compact; form organic union, as in a PARLIAMENT, convene; make knotty buds. [These senses spring from one idea, yet in the following it will be clearer to separate them.] *ger.* Ƶaqd.
(1) Ƶöqoud, knottiness c.
Ƶöqda, a knot, knop, knuckle; a hard bud; an articulation. *Also*, a compact.
Aɾqad, knotty, jointed.
ii. Ƶaqqid, *va* knot thoroughly, interlace. [entanglement.
Teɾqied, knottiness, obscurity,

ṢQD

Taṣqieda, ambiguity ʙ.
Moṣaqqad, full of knots, entangled, obscure.
iv. Aṣqid, ʋa make clotted, congeal.
Ṣaqied, clotted (as milk). *Also,* confederate.
viii. Uṣtaqid, ʋn clot, curdle.
(2) Ṣnqd, Ṣaqad, necklace.
Ṣnqd, Ṣuqâda, arcade ʙₐ.
Maṣqoud, vaulted. Beit ṣnqd, stone-vaulted room ʙ.
v. Teṣaqqad, be vaulted. *Also,* ʋp of Ṣaqqid, interlace.
(3) Ṣaqad, *s.* the setting of the (grape) blossom.
ii. Ṣaqqid, ʋa set in blossom.
v. Teṣaqqad, ʋn of preceding.
(4) Ṣaqad, Ṣôqda, a compact.
Ṣaqied, a confederate.
i. Oṣqod el rôlfi, make peace.
Ṣaqd el morâselêt, the keeping up of written correspondence.
iii. Ṣâqid, ʋa receive into league.
vi. Teṣâqad, ʋn confederate.
vii. Inṣaqid, ʋp be knotted, as a marriage COVENANT.
(5) Oṣqod, ʋa convene and organize (an assembly).
vii. Inṣaqid, ʋp of last. *Also* ʋp Ṣôqid, is the same.
(6) viii. Uṣtaqid bi, be firmly tied to, or persuaded of.
Uṣtiqâd, conviction, belief.
Ṣaqieda 11, article of the Creed. See ʻEccid.

عسل Oṣcof, ʋn be braided, tangled, matted (as, hair, foliage).

ṢQL

(2) Uṣcef ila', ʋn turn to, turn one's attention to.
ii. Ṣaccif, ʋa braid, tie up (hair); hamper, detain.
iii. Ṣaccif, ʋa attend closely to.
vii. Inṣacif, ʋp be hampered, hindered (from). *Also,* be detained, entangled, deeply engaged (in).
Monṣacif ṣala', ongaged upon, assiduous in ʋ.
Inṣucêf, Moṣâcefa, attention.
viii. Uṣtacif ṣala', ʋp be engaged upon.
[Monṣacif seems to be sometimes used (by error?) for Monṣaqif.]

عسف Aṣqaf, crooked.
Maṣqouf, Ṣaqouf, d°.
Uṣqif, ʋa crook. *Oftener,* ii. Ṣaqqif, ʋa crook.
Ṣôqqâfa, shepherd's crook, a clamp.
vii. Inṣaqif, ʋa be crooked.

عقل ,عقل ; Ṣucêl; *also* Ṣuqâl, Ṣôqla, a shackle. [*With* Ṣucêl, *compare* Xicêl.] FETTER.
Ṣôqla lil fomm, a gag.
Ṣâqoul, an embarrassment.
Ṣôqqâl, cramp in the leg ʙ.
Uṣqil, ʋa hobble (a horse).
ii. Ṣaqqil, ʋa d°.
vii. Inṣaqil, ʋp suffer cramp in the leg ʙ. ʋp to be blocked up, filled with entanglements?
Ṣâqoul 12, pathless.
Ṣôqoul, brushwood ʙ.
(2) Uṣqal, ʋn moderate oneself

ƧQL

B. [keep within one's own tether?] be possessed of good sense. *va* conceive (a thought).
Ƨaql 3, intellect.
Ƨaqil, Ƨâqil 6, 7, intelligent, sensible.
Ƨaqoul, full of good sense.
Ƨaqliey, intellectual (pursuit).
Maƨqoul, reasonable (thing), wisely devised. TALENT. PRUDENT.

عقم Ƨaqiem, effete.
Ƨöqm, barrenness (Ƨöqr).
iv. Aƨqim, *va* strike barren.

عكر Ƨacêr, lees (of oil, wine).
Ƨacir, full of lees or dregs.
ii. Ƨaccir, *va* besmear. [FUSE.
Moƨaccir, turbid. DIRTY. RE-

عقر Ƨöqr, barrenness.
Ƨâqir, barren. [back).
(2) Ƨaqqir, *va* gall (a horse's
Ƨaqier, galled (horse).
viii. Inƨaqir, *vp* (a horse) is galled.
Inƨuqâr, a gall, a sore place.
(3) Ƨaqâr, landed estate. Compare 'Ecr, ploughing, *Engl.* Acre, *Lat.* Ager, etc.

عكس Uscis, *va* reverse; travestie, burlesque.
Ƨacƨ, inversion, reverse.
Bil ƨacƨ, on the contrary, conversely.
Maƨcous, Moƨtecis, preposterous.
Ƨucƨ 3, elbow B.
Ƨucêƨ, anagram, *i.e.* line which

ƧWR

reads the same, when the letters are inverted.
iii. Ƨâciƨ, *va* be contrarious towards; thwart. [trariety.
vi. Teƨâceƨ, be mutually in convii. Inƨaciƨ, *vp* be reflected (as light).
Inƨucêƨ, reflection (of light).

عقض Uƨquƨ, *va* bite as a serpent, sting.
Ƨaqƨ, *s.* sting of insect (B. aiguillon, dard).

عكز Ƨöcêz(c), STAFF with iron ferule; crutch.
Oƨcoz, *also* v. Teƨaccez, *vn* lean on a stick or crutch.
(2) Ƨaciz, slimy?

عر Ƨurr, *vn* SCREAM (as ostrich K.). *Compare* Inƨar.
(2) Ƨurr, *va* DISHONOUR K. derogate from B.
Ƨarr, vice, malversation.

عرعر Sarƨar, the juniper.

عور Aƨwar, one-eyed.
Ƨawar, the being one-eyed.
Ƨöur, *vn* [Uƨwar?] be one-eyed.
Maƨöur, defective in body.
ii. Ƨawwir, *va* make one-eyed; deprive, injure, insult.
Ƨawâr, flaw, defect; damage to merchandize.
Ƨâr, a disgrace.
ii. Ƨayyir sala', *or* Ƨayƨirob bi, reproach; *for* Ƨawwir.
(2) iv. Aƨuir, *va* lend (an article,

ⳭWR

not money); with double accus. Aɛuirni ḟaliyoun, lend me a pipe ᴀʟ

عُمَر Ɛair 3, wild Ass; *esp.* zebra ᴘ.
(2) Ɛaira, Ɛuyâra, preposterous? ɴ. Postiche.
Xaɛr ɛairo, a peruke, wig ɴ.
(3) Ɛuyâr, standard of money; calibre, *lit.* and *fig.*
ii. Ɛayyir, *va* assay (money).
iii. Ɛâyir, *va* adjust to standard weight. *See also* ⳭWR *for* Ɛayyir, Aɛuir.

عرو Sörwa, handle of jug.
Ɛurwa, loop to a button.
(2) Oɛrou, *va* overspread, as *hair overspreads an animal.*
ʏ. Compare Oɛlou.
viii. Uɛteri, *va* supervene (with acc. of person). ʜᴀᴘᴘᴇɴ.
Uɛterâ-ni, (fear) came over me.
Moɛteri, suddenly coming over (one).

عرى Ɛâri, Ɛöriey, Ɛöryân, naked.
Ɛörie, the being naked.
Ɛörya, nakedness.
ii. Ɛarri, *va* strip naked.
Moɛarra', stript, bare.
v. Teɛarra', be naked.

عرب Ɛarab, Araba in gen.
Ɛarabân, independent Araba?
Ɛarabiey, *adj.* Arab, Arabic.
— *s.* a civilized Arab o.
Aɛrâb, Bedouins ᴋ.
Söroubieya, an Arabism.
ii. Ɛarrib, *va* translate into Arabic.

v. Teɛarrab, *vn* become an Arab.
(2) Ɛaraba, ɴᴜ. a car.
Ɛarabâna, d⁰ ᴀʟ ᴇx.
Ɛarabahji, driver of car.

عرد Ɛarbid, *vn* maraud.
Ɛarbada, marauding.
Ɛarbied, Moɛarbid, marauder.

عربن Ɛaraboun, a pledge.

عرق i. and ii. Teɛarbaq, *vn* catch one's foot (in); entangle oneself. *Compare* Orboc, ⲭarbic, ɛarqil.

عرش ii. Teɛarbax bi, *vn* cling to, = Teɛarbax, Teⲭarmax.

عرض Ɛarⲇ, *s.* breadth.
Ɛarieⲇ, *adj.* Bʀᴏᴀᴅ.
Ɛurⲇ, *s.* honour (morally).
Söⲇ, *s.* side, broadside. [ject.
Söⲇⲭa, *s.* butt, object of aim, ob-
Söⲇⲭuiy, awry, restive (camel).
Söⲇⲭuiya, indocility ɴ.
Ɛaraⲇ, Ɛarieⲇa, *s.* respectful address publicly presented.
Maɛrouⲇ, *s.* d⁰.
Ɛaraⲇ 4, accident; *rather,*
Ɛârᴜⲇ 12, accident, event.
Ɛaraⲇuiy, Ɛâruⲇuiy, accidental.
Ɛâruⲇa, crossbeam, crossbar.
i. Oɛroⲇ, *v.* occur, meet, encounter, come across, with acc. *or* li. *ger.* Ɛarⲇ. *Also,* *va* present.
Maɛruⲇ, place of meeting.
ii. Ɛarruⲇ, *va* present, expose, oppose (A. to B.)

SRZ

iii. Sârui, *va* keep abreast of, thwart, rival.
Mosâruż, a rival.
iv. Asruż, *va* make broad, spread out; *vn* with *san*, turn the side to, turn away from.
Mosruż, averse, abhorring.
v. Tesarraż, *vn with* li, be liable, exposed to, expose oneself to, rashly set to work at, venture upon. -fle, dodge *or* wind in a place, as the ground permits. (So, a mule on a mountain). [another.
vi. Tesâraż, come across one
viii. Usteruż, *vn* present oneself, come about, HAPPEN by ill-luck.
Usteruż san, digress from B.
Ustirâż, digression B. episode. But see Istirrâd. Perhaps Ustirâż san is properly *transition from*. [trarious.
Mosteruż, cross, transverse, con-
(2) Sarouż, prosody, metre.
(3) Saurâui, *s.* camp (*Turk.*) *c.* writes it Aurdie.

عردش Sardix, *va* gnaw.

عرف Sarf, *s.* scent, odour.
Sörf, *s.* Equity (distinct from Law).
Sörfley, belonging to Equity or arbitration. Hâcim Sörfley, an arbitrator.
i. Usrif, *va* know; recognize (politically). *ger.* Surfân. *Also*, Gnosticism.
Sarrâf, *s.* augur.

SRJ

Surâfa, art of the augur.
Sarief 6, Ædile, inspector of public buildings: monitor of a school, substitute for the master; captain's mate.
Sârif, *adj.* knowing, sagacious.
Sawârif, *s. pl.* sciences c. (des connaisances?).
Masrouf, a benefit.
Masrifa 11, knowledge, recognition, acquaintance.
ii. Sarrif, *va* notify, cause to know.
Tesrief, notification, inventory; *esp.* "tariff."
Mosarraf, limited by the definite article El. [defined.
v. Tesarraf, *vn* become known or
vi. Tesâraf, be mutually acquainted.
viii. Usterif bi, confess.
(2) Sörf, *s.* crest (of bird), mane (of horse).
Sörfa 4, crest of hill.
Masrafa, crest of horse's mane.
Asraf, maned, having a mane x.

عرج Asraj, lame.
Usraj, *vn* limp. *ger.* Sarj, Sarjân, lameness.
Masrij, ladder.
ii. Sarrij, *va* make lobsided.
iv. Asrij, *va* lame, cause to limp.
v. Tesarraj, *vn* be lobsided.
Tesarroj, proclivity x. [sun).
vii. Insarij, *vn* decline (as the Insurâj (sun's) declination.

عرجن Sarjoun 11, cluster of dates.

ⲤRM

عرم Ⲥarma, sandheap.
Ⲥarima, barrier, dike.
ii. Ⲥarrim, *va* pile up.

عرك Ⲥariece, natural genius. NATURE. TALENT. *For* Ⲥarieqa?
(2) Ⲥsroc, *va* rub (leather), wipe (the face); wear and tear. *ger.* Ⲥarc.
Masrouc, Mosarrec, rubbed and used.
(3) Masrac(e), arena of combat, place of tournament.
iii. Ⲥâric, *va* engage (another) in combat. [ment.
Mosârace, combating, tournavi. Tesârec, *vn* combat mutually.

عرق Ⲥurq 3, fibrous, veiny root.
Ⲥurqa, *ns.* of do A vein? Orignal fund of a fortune.
Ⲥarieq, racy, inbred, high bred. *See* Ⲥariece. [soil.
iv. Asriq, *vn* root itself in the
(2) Ⲥaraq, sweat; arrack, *i.e.* distilled spirit. *Also* Ⲥarqiey, arrack, brandy.
Ⲥaraqieya, sweat cap; *i.e.* cotton cap worn on the shaven skull, under the turban. [sweat.
Ⲥarqân, *adj.* sweating, in a
ii. Ⲥarriq, *va* cause to sweat; dilute x.

عرقب Ⲥarqib, *va* hough a horse.
Ⲥörqoub, tendon Achillis; hough of a horse B. narrow pass over a mountain c.

ⲤⲤⲤ

ii. Tesarqab, *vn* follow the windings.
عرقل i. Ⲥarqil, *va* tangle(thread).
ii. Tesarqal, *vn* be tangled; catch one's foot (in) = Tesarbaq.

عرقص Ⲥarqus el flâjeb, contract the eyebrow, frown B.

عرس Ⲥörs, wedding; 2, 4, wedding feast.
Ⲥaries, bridegroom 11, 10.
Ⲥarous(e) 11, bride.
Ⲥursên (dual), wedded pair.
Ⲥurse, Ibn ⲥurse (the white weasel), the FERRET.
ii. Ⲥarris, iv. Asris, take possession of one's bride. *ger.* Tesries. [groom.
v. Tesarras, *vn* play the bride-
Mosarria, *m.* a go-between, dishonest matchmaker, pander. (B. spells it Mosarruy.)

عرص Ⲥarsa 2, 4, 5, court, arena, palæstra c.

عرش Ⲥarx, 3, 4, any framework; *esp.* a throne.
Ⲥariex, lattice for a vine.
Ⲥariexa, *ns* an arbour; tangled brake B.
ii. Ⲥarrix, *v.* make trellis work, make an arbour.

عصص Ⲥöss, small of the back. B. Croupion.

588

عسّ Sôss, *vn* keep ward, patrol by night. *ger.* Sasca.
Sûsa, Sasséa, the night-watch, the night prowler.
Sases, the nightwatch c.
Saasus, *vn* prowl.

عوس Sôus, *vn* prowl by night; *also*, go the rounds by night. See Sôss.

عوص Sawwis̃, twisted, crabbed, abstruse, cross-tempered.
Aswas̃, more twisted, etc.
ii. Sawwus̃, *va* make abstruse, make obscure.
iii. Sâwus̃, *va* twist (another) in wrestling.
vii. Insawus̃, *vn* twist oneself (as a dog wagging his tail).
viii. Ustawus̃, be abstruse, obscure. Compare Γawuis̃, profound. [problem.
Ustiyâs̃, a puzzle, a difficult

عسى Sâsi, *adj.* tough, hard (meat, etc.).
(2) عسى Sase', perhaps, lest perhaps. (It is conjugated in old grammar like a Past Tense.)

عصا Sasâ, staff, stick.
Sŏsâya, *dimin.* a cane, switch.
iii. Sâsu, *va* bastinado.
viii. Ustasu, *vn* rest on staff.

عصى Sâsu, disobedient, mutinous, *pl.* Sŏsâyâ. Compare Sâsi.

582

iii. Sâsu, *va* disobey, mutiny against.
Mosâsâya, revolt, rebellion.
Sosyân, Masyuya, d⁰ *pl.* Masâsu 11.

عصب Sasab, tendons, nerves.
Sasaba, a ligament, band.
Sŏsba 10, a band, troop; the (German) *Bund*, league.
Sasba, Susâb, turban.
Susyâba, bandage, filet.
ii. Sassub, *va* bind the head, put a headband on (another).
iii. Sâsub, *va* form (others) into a band, enlist.
v. Tesassab, *vn* wear a headband. Go in clans or bands.
vi. Tesâsab, *vn* be banded together.
viii. Ustasub bi, *vn* restrict oneself to. *Also*, Ustasub = v.

عصيدة Sasuida, thick gruel, porridge.

عسوف Sasouf, hard master or mistress.
Sasief, a drudge.
Saséfa, drudgery.
ii. Sassif, *va* put to hard service, constrain to work; bustle (a house) about, *i.e.* clean it thoroughly в.
v. Tesassef, act arbitrarily, wantonly; put violent meaning on a word.
viii. Mostasif, constrained, affected (manner) в.
Sasf, *s.* constraint, *fig.* в.

SSF

عسف Usɣuf, *vn* whistle, bluster, blow hard.
iv. Aɣsuf, *vn* dº
Sâɣuf, blustering (wind); *fig.* obstreperous (as wild animal newly caught).
Söɣöufa, obstreperousness?
Sâɣufa 12, blast, fierce gale.
Saɣöuf, Saɣɣuif, *adj.* intensive of Sâɣuf.

عسفر Söɣfour 11, sparrow or other little bird.
Söɣfoura, peg (as of violin).
(2) Söɣfar, saffron in flower c.

عسج Sausej, bramble.

عسل Sasel, honey.
Massela, honeycomb.
ii. Sassil, *va* sweeten with honey, preserve in honey.

عسم Sâɣum, safe, chaste.
Suɣma, defence, chastity.
Masɣöum, defended, innocent.
Sâɣuma, virgin (city, fortress); *esp.* Medina; but *now*, any capital city, metropolis.
iv. Aɣsum, *va* protect.
v. Teɣaɣɣam, protect oneself.
vii. Inɣaɣum, dº c. x.
viii. Uɣtaɣum bi, seek refuge with; *mas*, adhere to (a party).
Mostáɣam, an asylum.
Mostaɣum mas, adhering to.
(2) Musɣam, the wrist.

عسكر Sasœr 11, army.

SƟӨ

Sasceriey, a private soldier.
Masascer, camp.
Mosascir, quarter master c.
i. Sascir, *vn* encamp.

عسر Sösra, *nu* a pinch? a difficulty.
Massera, dº· *ger.* Saser, the being difficult c.
Sasier, difficult.
ii. Sassir, *va* make difficult. [x.
iii. Sâsir, *va* treat hardly, pinch?
iv. Assir, *va* press (a debtor) hardly x. *pinch* (him).
v. Tesasser, *vn* be difficult.
Motesassir, difficult.

عسر Sayr, afternoon.
Söyr, age, century, *seculum*.
(2) Usɣâr, tornado F. X.
(3) Söɣâra, ɣaɣnira, juice squeezed out. [juice.
Musɣar(a), vessel to catch the
Masɣara, wine press.
Masɣöur, juice squeezed out.
Saɣɣâr, man who squeezes out the juice.
ii. Saɣɣur, *va* press (grapes, etc.)
vii. Insaɣur, *vp.* of ii.
viii. Uɣtaɣur, *va* same as ii.

[The root Saɣar, in this sense, seem to express the coarse and physical idea (squeeze), while Saser is its diminutive, (pinch) in metaphorical sense.]

عس Söөө, *va* eat as a moth.
Masөou, moth-eaten. [cloth.
Söөөe, *nu* 3, 10, moth, that eats

ΣYT

ܥܝܛ Ṣaiṭa, s. hue and cry.
Ṣuyâṭ, s. outcry.
ii. Ṣayyuṭ, vn CRY aloud.
v. Teṣayyaṭ, vn cry with joy or triumph x.

ܥܝܬ Ṣuiθ fie, vn pounce on, spring at (as tiger) r. JUMP. ATTACK.

ܥܬܪ Ṣatou, s. pride.
Ṣâti, PROUD, CRUEL; pl. Ṣôtiey.
v. Teṣattê, vn assume airs of pride.

ܥܛܪ Ṣarâ, a gift.
Ṣaruiya 14, dº
Ṣarrâ, munificent.
iv. Aṣrui, va GIVE (admits double accus.) [pursuit].
vi. Teṣârâ bi, give oneself to (a Maṣâṭâya, a dose (in medicine).

ܥܬܒ Ṣateba, threshold, royal court c.
(2) Oṣtob, va chide.
Ṣutêb, expostulation, reprimand.
iii. Ṣâtib, va expostulate with (a friend). [BLAME.
vi. Teṣâteb, chide mutually.

ܥܛܒ Ṣarab, destruction.
Maṣrab, place of great peril.
Uṣrab, vn rot, perish.
iv. Aṣrub, va ruin, rot, disintegrate. DESTROY.

ܥܬܕ Ṣatied, prepared.
Oṣtod, vn be ready.
ii. Ṣattid, va provide.

ΣTL

iv. Aṣtid, va make (a thing or person) ready. Compare viii. of Ṣôdd.

ܥܛܦ Uṣruf ṣala', vn bend towards. ger. Ṣarf.
Ṣôṭôuṣa, bending (of body). Hence in B. sehl el Ṣôṭôuṣa, laiyin el aṣrâf, flexible, supple.
Ṣarafa, a turning in the street.
Muṣṭaf, 11 binge (Proverbs).
[But in modern use this root oftener takes a moral sense.]
Ṣâruf, Ṣaṭôuf, compliant, affable.
Ṣâṭufa 12, gentle affection, sympathy. [scension.
Maṣṭôuṣa, compliance, condeii. Ṣâṭruf, va bend, turn, make favourable.
Maṣṭôuf, Moṣarraf, bent.
iii. Ṣâruf, va treat KINDLY, befriend. [pity c.
v. Teṣarrafṣala', condescend to,
vi. Teṣâruf, have mutual affection, sympathize.
vii. Inṣaruf, vp. be bent.
x. Isteṣruf, va CONCILIATE.

ܥܬܗ Maṣtouh, delirious c.

ܥܬܠ Ṣatela, crow-bar, iron lever, a hod B.
(2) Ṣâtil, vn toil B. (?).
iii. Ṣâtil, va cavil, wrangle (with?) B. Ergoter. Wrestle with B. (Mésurer). Flutter (Se tremousser) B.

ܥܛܠ Ṣâṭul, idle, vain.
ii. Ṣaṭṭul, va make idle, dis-

STL

able (an engine), dismantle (a fortress), make (a law) inoperative.
Satraltec, "I have made you idle (Je vous ai dérangé);" an apology for intrusion.
v. Tesattal, *vp.* of ii. [rative.
Mosattal, obsolete (law), inope-

ᶜᵃᵗᵐ Satm, Satema, *vulg.* Sutema, dusk of evening [common at Aleppo].
Sâtim, arriving by dusk. *See* x.
iv. Astim, *vn* be in the dusk. *Compare* Fatim and DARKNESS.

ᶜᵃᵗⁿ Otton, *vs* tan (leather). *ger.* Satn.
ii. Sattun, *vs* supersedes i.
vii. Insatun, *vp* be plunged into liquid tan.
Sutân, material for tanning.
Satuin, subjected to tanning.

ᶜᵃᵗᵗ ii. Saθθin, *vn* smoke x.
Saθen, Saθen (Sâθen?) 12, smoke.
Sôθnoun 11, long beard.
Sôθnoun bouz, icicle.

ᶜᵃᵗᵗ Sâtiq 12, back of neck, *Lat.* cervix, cervices.
(2) Satq, Sutêqa, emancipation.
Satieq 11, dismissed from service, *emeritus*; hence, old, worn out.
Mosattaq, antiquated, obsolete.
Sutêqa 11, an antiquated worthless thing.
iv. Astiq, *vs* emancipate.

STR

Mostaq, *pp.* emancipated.
vii. Insatiq, *vp.* of iv.

ᶜᵃᵗʳ Sutr, odour, fragrance.
Sâtur, odorous.
Sutrâr, perfumer.
Sutâra, perfumer's art.
Uttar, *vn* emit fragrance x.
v. Tesattar, *vn* perfume oneself.
x. Istestur, dᵃ.

ᶜᵃᵗʳ Usθer, *vn* stumble; sala', upon (*fig.*) *i.e.* find by accident.
Saθra, a trip, false step.
Saθour, apt to trip.
ii. Saθθir, *vs* trip up.
iv. Asθir, *vs* dᵃ. [in.
v. Tesaθθer fie, entangle oneself
Tesaθwar, *vn* stumble much.

ᶜᵃᵗʳ Satrif, *vn* be harsh, violent. See Sajrafa, Satris, Tatris.

ᶜᵃᵗʳ Satrase, a seizing by violence *s.* impetuosity *n.*
Satries, Motesatris, impetuous, rude.

ᶜᵃᵗʳ Ustus, *vn* sneeze, *ger.* Sats, Sutâs. Sâtöus, snuff.
ii. Sattus, *vs* cause to sneeze.

ᶜᵃᵗʳ Ustax, *vn* thirst.
Satxân, thirsty, *pl.* Sutâx(i).
Motesattux, eager, curious, inquisitive (in good sense).

ᶜᵃᵗʳ Söxx 5, 4, nest in a tree.
Söxx el forâb, mushroom.

ƧXX

ii. Ɛaxxix, make a nest.
viii. Uɛtixx provide oneself with a nest.

عيش Ɛuix, ʋn live, pass life.
Ɛaix, life, mode of life.
Ɛuixa, mode of life.
Maɛâx, living, livelihood.
Maɛuixa, 11, victual.
ii. Ɛayyix, ʋa feed, maintain.
v. Teɛayyax, ʋn get a (bare) living.

عشى Ɛaxwa, dusk of evening x.
Ɛaxâ, supper, pl. aɛxiya.
Ɛaxâ, evening; also, Ɛaxieya 2, evening. Ɛaxwiey, belonging to the evening.
ii. Ɛaxxi, ɛa give supper to. Also, dim, dazzle (the eye). See Гaxxi.
v. Teɛaxxa', ʋn take supper.

عشب Ɛöxb, green Grass, herbage.
Ɛaxâba, grassiness. [grass.
Ɛaxieb, Moɛxib, grassy, full of
ii. Ɛaxxib, or iv. Aɛxib, ɛ. produce herbs.

عشم Uɛxom, ʋa long for.
Ɛaxam, ɛ. hope with Desire, a coveting, craving.
ii. Ɛaxxim bi, ɛa excite hopes of.
v. Teɛaxxam, ʋn flatter oneself with hope в.

عشق Ɛuxq, ɛ. Love.
Ɛuxq Ilehiey, divine love c.
Ɛaxieq, a lover.

WƧƷ

Ɛâxiq, d°. 7, 12.
Ɛuxxieq, violently in love.
Uɛxaq, ʋa be in love with.
ii. Ɛaxxiq, iv. Aɛxiq, ɛa dovetail (in carpentry).
v. Teɛaxxaq, ʋn become amorous.
vi. Teɛâxaq, ʋn love mutually.

عشر Ɛuxra maɛ, familiarity with; an amour.
Ɛaxiera, kindred, clan?
Maɛxar, a group of associates.
Ɛaxier, an associate. [self.
iii. Ɛâxir, ʋa associate to oneMoɛâxara, familiarity. Society. (Intercourse.)
(2) Ɛöxr 4, a tenth part, tithe.
Ɛoxara, ten, f. Ɛaxar.
Ɛâxir, tenth. Ɛuxrien, twenty.
Ɛaxxâr, tithe collector.
Ɛöxour, a decimating.
Oɛxor, ʋa tithe. [lus x.)
Aɛxâriey, adj. decimal (calcu-

عز Ɛuzz(e), excellence, rarity.
Ɛaziez, precious, rare.
Aɛazz, more precious. Dear.
i. Ɛuzz, ʋn be rare. ger. Ɛuzze.
ii. Ɛazziez, ʋa glorify; endear.
Moɛazzez (political title), his Excellency?
iv. Aɛuzz, ʋa Honour, cherish.
v. Teɛazzez, ʋn become grand.
vii. Uɛtisz, d°
x. Isteɛuzz bi, prevail over x.

وعظ Waɛag yaɛuz, preach, exhort, warn. ger. Waɛg, Ɛuga.
Maɛuɛga 11, sermon.

ƐUZ

عوز Ɛöuz, *va* need B.
Ɛawaz (K.), Ɛauze, Ɛâze (B.), *s.* need. Ɛawiz, needy K.
iv. Aɛwiz, *va* need. [deratum.
Miɛwaze 11, thing needed, desi-
Ɛâyiz, needing; *also* Ɛâwiz B.
viii. Uɛtêz, *va or with* ila', need.
Uɛtiyêz, *s.* need.

عزى Ɛazê, *s.* condolence.
ii. Ɛazzi, *va* console, condole with.
Moɛazzi, comforter in sorrow.

عزب Ɛazeb 4, Ɛâzib 7, Aɛzeb 9, bachelor, unmarried man.
Ɛözouba, Ɛözoubieya, celibacy of man.
v. Teɛazzeb, *va* live in celibacy.

عزف Uɛzif, *va* play on stringed instrument P. K.

عزل Ɛazl, displacement, removal (from a post).
Ɛözla, retirement.
Maɛzoul, displaced, discarded.
ii. Ɛazzil, *va* discharge, depose, dislodge.
v. Teɛazzel, *Imper.* off with you!
viii. Uɛtezil, *vn* become *neutral* in wars by virtue of treaties (bo set aside?).
Moɛtezil, (necessarily) neutral.

عزم Uɛzim, *va* take in hand, undertake; *also,* invite. *ger.* Ɛazm.
Ɛaɛma, *nu* enterprise.
Maɛɛem, an enterprise K.

ƐZB

Ɛaziema 11, an enterprize; *also,* incantation c. [over B. a.
ii. Ɛazzim ɛala', make exorcism
v. Teɛazzem, begin work.
[Ḥazm expresses mere resolve, but Ɛazm actual work.]

عظم Ɛaʒm 5 (*pronounced* with ض) bone.

Ɛaʒmiey (ض), bony.
ii. Ɛaʒʒum, *va* ossify; harden (flesh); make callous B.
(2) Ɛuʒm, greatness, enormity, importance.
Ɛaʒama, pomp, immensity.
Ɛaʒâma, grandeur.
Ɛaʒuim 5, grand, direful, capital.
Ɛaʒâyim, *pl.* great events, great crimes.   [K.
Ɛözma, Uɛʒâma, woman's bustle
Moɛʒam, major part K.
Moɛʒama, important event c. K.
Aɛʒam, grander, mightier.
ii. Ɛaʒʒum, *va* magnify, glorify.
Moɛaʒʒam, Right Honourable?
Taɛʒuim, hyperbole, exaggera-
Taɛʒuimiey, hyperbolic. [tion.
ii. Ɛaʒʒum, *va* magnify, glorify.
v. Teɛaʒʒam, be magnificent.
vi. Teɛâʒam, be pompous.
x. Istaɛʒum, *va* esteem highly.

عزق Uɛziq, *va* break up (soil).
Miɛzeqa, pickaxe.

عزر ii. Ɛazzir, *va* correct, teach politeness.

عزرن ii. Teɛazran, *vn* bluster, make bravado B.

B.

ب Bi, Preposition of instrument or manner; in, with.

بى *'Ebi, v. ṣala', 'en, decline, refuse, disobey. ger. ibâ.
Ėbi, unwilling ᴘ.
'Ebya, disdain ᴇ.
'Ebiey, disdainful ᴇ.
Mèbiey, declined, shunned c. disagreeable.

بو *'Abou ('abie, 'abâ, 'ab), father, pl. 'abâ.
'Abawiey, paternal.
'Obouwa, paternity.
ii. 'Abbi, va call (one) father ᴇ.
Te'biya, ger of ii.

وبر Wabâ, plague, pest; pl. Aubâ.
Maubou, ravaged by pest.

'بو [entering, Heb.]
Mabwâ, nest, lair, a hare's form.
v. Tebawwâ, vns enter (the nest, as bird), ᴘ. come back home.

بوبو Boubou o.
Dowabbou ʙ. pupil of the eye.

بوع Bauṣ 4, Bâṣ 2, a fathom, full spread of the two arms.
Bouṣ, v. Tebawwaṣ, measure by spread of the arms, fathom?
vii. Inbâṣ, vp? be fathomed.
[ᴇ. makes it active, as i.]

بيع Bieṣ, va sell; ger. Baiṣ.
Bayyâṣ, seller, dealer.
Biyâṣa, goods for sale.

Mobâṣ, adj. on sale.
viii. Ibtêṣ, va buy.
Mobtêṣ, buyer.
iii. Bâyiṣ, va make contract with; conclude allegiance.
Mobâyaṣa, a promising of allegiance; hence, inauguration of a prince.

بعى Ibṣa', on baa as sheep.

بعو Baṣöu, a spectre ʙ.

بعد Baṣd, prep. after.
Baṣda", Baṣdo(h), afterwards.
Baṣd, Baṣdoh, still, even yet (vulg.)
Baṣdoma, after (conjunction).
Fie ma baṣd, in the future.
Boṣd, Boṣda, distance.
Baṣuid 6, distant; as interj avaunt! Abṣad, further.
Boṣaid, a little way off, aloof.
Boṣaid zemân, a short time hence.
Ibṣad ṣan, vn keep aloof, take oneself off from.
Lâ tebṣad ṣan, depart not from.
iv. Abṣud, va repel, drive off.
v. Tebaṣṣad ṣan, as i.
vi. Tebâṣad ṣan, shun mutually.

بعض Baṣḍ 4, a part, portion. Some. Others.
Baṣḍ li baṣḍ, one to another.
Baṣḍahom baṣḍ, one another.
Baṣḍ, one or other.
ii. Baṣṣuḍ, va part, divide, into lots for auction.
Tebṣniḍ, partition. [In gram-

BSA

mar, min (*from*) is the *prep.*
of Tebsuix.]
Mobassux, partitive?
v. Tebassax, *sp.* of ii. [sandfly.
(2) Basöuxa, *nu* gnat, midge,

بشج Ibsaj, *vs* rip up with knife.
See Fetq. [lence.
ii. Bassuj, *vs* tear open by vio-

بعل Basl 3, lord and master,
husband.
Basla, mistress. [band.
v. Tebassal, *vs* accept as hus-

بعق Ibsaq, *vn* burst as a cloud.
v. Tebassaq, vii. Inbasuq, burst
into torrent of words.
Inbisâq, fury of words, volu-
bility *v.* [(orator).
Monbasuq, voluble, gushing

بعر Basr, *s.* dung, especially
globular. [camel.
Basuir, *pl.* 11, Abâsur, male

بعص Basy, *ger.* writhing,
struggling x.
v. Tebassay, *vn* writhe.
Tebasyay, *vn* d°. See Irsay viii.
[x. has also Tebasray, palpitate,
as an amputated limb.]

بعث Ibsaθ, *vs* send, impel.
Bâsuθ, impulsive (force). *s.*
12, a motive, cause.
Bâsuθ 12, impulse, motion.
Basθa, Mabsaθ, mission x.
vii. Inbasuθ fie, *vp* or *vn* be
pressed, (hasten) upon (a
journey).

BYA

Inbusâθ, resurrection s.
[Bâsöuθ, Easter x.]

بزرق Basziq, *vs* spread out; *ger.*
Baszeqa, dispersion?
Mobassriq, elongated, prolate in
Geometry.

يب Yabâb, ruin, desolation,
emptiness.

بوب Bâb 9, *or pl.* Abwâb,
door, gate; *fig.* chapter of
book, subject, category.
Bâba 2, paragraph.
Bowaib, little door.
Bawwâb, porter of gate.
Biwâba, portal; office of porter x.

بد Bodd, *s.* escape.
Lâ bodd min, it cannot but be.
vulg. Min coll badd, of all *necessity.*
ii. Baddid, *vs* break up, disband.
iv. Abidd, *vs* distribute equally x.

بد ʼEbad, *s.* perpetuity.
ʼEbadaⁿ, ever, for ever.
ʼEbadiey, eternal.
ii. ʼEbbid, *vs* perpetuate, im-
mortalize.
(2) ʼêbida, a frightened animal
x. an idiot s.

بيد Baid, *s.* ruin x.
Died, *vn* go to ruin, perish.
ii. Bayyid, iv. Abied, *vs* destroy.
Ibâda, destruction, perdition.

بيض Baixa, *nu.* 2, 3, egg.
Baixuiy, oval.

BYA   BDN

Bayouḍ, oviparous, a good layer (of eggs).
Buiḍ, v. lay eggs B. [white.
(2) Abyaḍ, f. Baiḍá, pl. Buiḍ, Bayáḍ, s. Bayáḍa, whiteness.
ii. Bayyuḍ, va whiten.
Buiḍán, white men, opposed to Soudán, negroes.
Mobuiḍ, washerman of linen.

بدو Badou, Bedou, s. open country. Bádiya, d⁰ 12.
Mabdau, rural place.
Badawiey 11, nomad, Bedouin.
Badâwi, rural, rustic.
(2) Obdou, Ibda', va open, begin. Bádi, s. beginner.
iv. Abdi, va lay open, display.
viii. Ibtedi bi, en begin on.
Ibtidâ, Mobtedâ, s. beginning.
iii. Bádi, va take the lead of, esp. in aggression; act aggressively against.
Bedwa x. Mobâdâya, aggression.
Mobádi, he who does a thing first, i.e. before others, originator.
Mobdi, d⁰ x. See next.

بدع Badas, innovation.
Bidsa, novelty, heresy.
Badies, pl. Bods, ingenious, very clever, an original genius.
iv. Abdis, va invent.
Mobdis, inventor, innovator.
viii. Ibtedus, va d⁰
x. Istebdus, judge heretical.

بضع Baḍsa 2, 5, a piece x.
Buḍâsa 11, merchandize.

v. Teballas, x. Istebḍus, en traffic (in retail?).

بده Ibdeh, en arrive unexpected x. [guise B.
Bedieh, simple, without diṢala' bedieh, offhand, extempore.
Bediche, offhand thought.
Bediehiey, unexpected.
Bediehieyaⁿ, unexpectedly.
viii. Ibtedih, en speak extempore.

بدهنج Badahenj, airflue in a house.

بدل Bedal, prep. instead of.
Bedal 'en, d⁰ (with verb).
Bedalaⁿ, in exchange.
Bedáliya, price of a substitute, a vicarious tax, exempting for military service.
Ibdal, va exchange, change.
Bedala, a change.
Baddâl, chandler, dealer.
ii. Baddil, va exchange.
Tebdiel, permutation. [tion.
vi. Tebâdal, er change in rotax. Istebdil, propose exchange.

بذل Obḍol, va lavish, give freely. ger. Beḍl.
Béḍil, Beḍoul, adj. lavish.
(2) Biḍle, common coat, esp. European coat.

بدن Bedan 4, body, trunk of body.
Bediev, Bedaniey, Mobeddan, corpulent.

BDN

Bodn, Bedâna, corpulence.
Obdon, *vn* be corpulent x.

بَدِنْجَن Bâdinjân, *melongène*, a large purple cucumber.

بدق Baudaqa 11, pipe-bowl; crucible.
(2) Baidaq, a pawn in chess.

بدر Bedr 3, full moon.
(2) Biedar, grain in the barn; threshing floor.
El Bídâr, the crops of grain. See Bar, Bzr.
(3) iii. Bâdir, *va* outrun, anticipate, hasten to; *also vn* hasten. Be early at.
Mobâdara, vying in haste.
Bedriey, early.
Bodour, early arrival?
Bedarân, promptitude?
Bedâr bedâr, haste! haste! x.

بذر Bear, *s.* pip, seed. See Bzr.
ii. Beaair, *va fig.* disseminate.
[Obaor, *va* sow x. Beaier, prone to divulge.]
Mobeaair, Mobair, prodigal.

بدرق Badriq [or Beariq?], *va* dissipate, spend fast.

بفت Bafto, calico x. [not in B. or C.]

باغ Bâṛ, a garden Bṣ.
Baṛwân, gardener.

بغي Ibṛi ṣala', be ambitious for.
viii. Ibteṛi ṣala', d°.

BUH

Baṛiey, ambitious.
Biṛya, ambition B.
Boṛâya, high profit.
Δou boṛâya, one who makes exorbitant gain.
x. Isteḅṛi, *va* claim. [that.
(2) vii. Yanbaṛi 'en, it is suitable

بغض Obṛoδ, *va* hate. *ger.* Boṛδ.
Boṛδa, Baṛiδa, hatred.
Baṛieδ ila', hateful to.
vi. Tobâṛaδ, *vr* hate mutually.

بغل Baṛl 5, a mule.
Baṛla, *f.* d°·   Baṛṛâl, muleteer.

بغنس Baṛnous, *s.* novice B.

بغت Ibṛat, *vn* arrive suddenly x.
iii. Bâṛit, *va* catch by surprise x.
Baṛte, a sudden event. *Also, adj.*
Baṛtetea, suddenly. [sudden B.

بح Baḥḥ, *vn* be hoarse.
BoḥḤa, hoarseness.
ii. Baḥḥuḥ, *va* make hoarse.
iv. Abuḥḥ, d°·
vii. Inbuḥḥ, *vp* be made hoarse.

بحبح Baḥbuḥ, *va* give room, space, accommodate. See Bouḥ.
Baḥbaḥa, accommodation (in a Mobaḥbuḥ, roomy. [house).
Baḥbouḥ, merry (compare Inbisêr).
ii. Tebaḥbaḥ, *exspatior*, stroll for pleasure, be merry, chuckle B.

بح Bouḥ bi, *vn* lay open (a secret), divulge.

BUH

Bawûfla*, openly, publicly, etc.
iv. Abicfl, *va* lay open, *i.e.*
license, legalize.
Ibâfla, license, authorization;
also, challenge (to combat):
B. *under* Dúfi: perhaps rather
an *overture*, *i.e.* proposal.
x. Istibâfla, free leave c.

بهى Behê, *s.* gaiety, brilliancy.
Bêhi, splendid, elegant.
iii. Bêhi, *va* beautify, bedizen.
vi. Tebêhê, *vn* plume oneself.
Ebhê, more splendid.

بهج Behja, glee, delight.
Behij, Behiej, gleeful.
ii. Behhij, iv. Abhij, *va* gladden,
make festive.
Abhej, gayer, gayest.
v. Tebehhij, viii. Ibtehij, *vn* be
in festive delight.
Ibtibêj, public glee.

بهل Behele, imprecation x.
iii. Bêhil, *va* bind under con-
ditional imprecation; adjure.
Mobêhela, adjuration.
viii. Ibtehil, *va* implore, *either*
cala' against, *or* li, for.
iv. Abhil, *va* dazzle *morally*
(B. *sic*, under Eblouir). *See*
Abhir.
Ibhêl, ceremony of devoting x.

بهل Behloul, silly; a buffoon B.
Behlela, pasquinade, satirical
raillery B.

BIIR

بهلق Bafiliq. Mobafllaq, fixed,
(gaze, eye) B.

بهم Behiema 11, brute.
Abhem, unable to talk, barbarous, a foreigner.
Behiemiey, of the brute.
Behiemieya, brutality.
iv. Ebhim, *va* make obscure,
indistinct, unintelligible.
Mobhem, indistinct, obscure,
vague.
v. Tebehhem, be vague, indistinct, uncertain.
Ibhêm, ambiguity B.
(2) Ebhem 11, *or* Bêhim 12,
the thumb.

بهون Behwin, *vn* step irregularly
as a child, trip.

بهر Bêhir, brilliant, superfine,
superior.
Bêhira*, publicly.
iv. Abhir, *va* dazzle, *lit.* and *fig.*
vii. Inbchir, *vp* be dazzled.
Behier, Mabhour, out of breath
with effort.
(2) Behêr 2, spice.
ii. Behhir, *va* spice.
(3) Ebher, *s.* the aorta, great
artery of the heart.

بحر Bafir 5, 4, 3, sea.
Bafiriey, marine.
Bafiflâr (*pl.* -a), mariner.
Boflaira, 11, a lake.
v. Tebafllar, *fig.* plunge deep,
study profoundly.
Bâflôur, depth of the summer x.

BHR

Boḣrân 11, Baḣrâ d°? fit of fever, fainting fit; crisis of disease.
Bâḣöuriey, critical ʙ. x.

بهرج Behraj, futile, vain.
Behraja, a bauble, a brilliant but false notion ʙ.
Behrajân, tinsel ʙ.
ii. Tebehraj, *vn* assume tinsel, indulge conceit; swagger.

بهت ii. Behhit, *va* amaze. [*also* i. Ibhet, d°?] *vp* Bohit, be amazed.
vii. Inbehit, d°
(2) Bohtên, calumny ʙ. x.
Behhêt, calumniator x.
Ibhet, *va* dissemble?

بحث Ibḣaθ, x. Isteḃḣuθ, *va* delve, mine. *ger*. Baḣθ, *s*. research.
Mabḣaθ, field of research.
Γair mabḣouθ, inscrutable.
iii. Bâḣuθ, *va* discuss, make research.
Mobâḣaθa, discussion.

بهز Ibhez, *va* thrust.
Bêhiz, overweighty.

بوج Bâj, *s*. tax (*Pers*.)
ii. Bawwij, *vn* tack (as a ship).

بجق ii. Bajjiq, *vn*, maunder, twaddle.

بجل ii. Bajjil, *va* honour, respect.
Mobajjal, dignified and somewhat large of body.

BLL

بق Bokk, *va* squirt ʙ.
بقة Wabka, a rebuke.
ii. Wabbik, *va* rebuke.

بخل Ibkal bi, *vn* be stingy of. *ger*. Bokl, Bokoul.
Bakiel 6, Bâkil 7, stingy.
Bakkâl, very stingy x.

بخار Bokâr, steam.
Bakour 8, incense.
Mibkara 11, censer.
Ibkar, *vn* steam, reek.
ii. Bakkir, *va* steam, fumigate.
Bokâriey, of steam.
Marceba bokâriey, railway car.

بخس Ibkas, *va* cut down, lessen, deprive (with double accus.). *ger*. Baks, deprivation.
θeman baks, a wretchedly low price. [price.
Abkas θeman, the very lowest

بخش Bakxus, *v* rummage, ransack.

بخت Bakt, *s*. luck, good fortune. [luck.
Son' bakt, qillet el bakt, ill-Bakiet, Makbout, lucky.
(2) Bokt, two-humped camel x.

بخش Bakxiex, *vulg*. a small gratuity.
Bokx, ᴀʟ a hole right through (a board or vessel); a flaw.

بل Boll, *va* wet.
Belel, Billa, moisture x.

BLL

Beliel, moist (wind) x.
Mabloul, drenched.
ii. Bellil, *va* drench.
vii. Inbill, *vp* be be wetted.

بلبل Belbil, *vn* be in confusion.
Bilbâl, Delbele 11, confusion, Babel.
(2) Bolbol 11, nightingale.
(3) Belboula 11, tap to cask. See Lablouba.

بل˙ 'Ibl 4, camels.
'Iblicy, belonging to camels.
'Ebbâl, camelfeeder x.

وبل Wâbil, Wabl, a heavy shower.
Mauboul, heavily rained upon.
Wabâl, a nuisance, an infliction.
Wabiel, noxious, baneful.
(2) Toubâl 11, slag, dross of metals. See θofl.

بل Bel, nay but even.

بول Baul, urine.
Boul, *va* make water.
Diwâla, bladder.
Mibwul(a), chamber-pot.

بال Bâl, *s.* mind, memory.
Fie bâli, (it is) in my memory; I remember. Karar fie bâli, it flashed through my mind.
Dierbâlec(*vulg.* for Adierbâlec), turn thy mind *or* attention.

بلى iii. Bâli, *va* care for.
Mâ obâli, I do not care.

BLA

Mobâlâya, care, concern.
(2) Bâli, worn out.
Delâ, Bilwa, Delwa', Delieya 14, affliction.   [Obtoli.
viii. Ibtcli, *va* try, tempt. *vp* Ibtilâ, trial, tribulation.
(3) Bilâ, *prep. vulg.* for Digair, without.
(4) Beli, yea, verily Bg.

بلع Iblae, *va* swallow.
viii. Ibtclis, d°   [swallow.
ii. Bellis, iv. Ablis *vc.* cause to Bâlous, deep water, quicksand. [flashhook c. *sic.*]
Billousa, underground drain.

بلد Belad 5, canton, district.
Beladiey, of the canton.
Belda, town.
Bolaida, small town x.
Bilâd (*pl.* of Belad) a country, *pl.* 9 Boldân.
Ibn el belad, a native.
v. Tebellad, *vn* dwell in a new country.
Motebellid, immigrant.
(2) Belied, stupid, inert.
Belâda, stupidity.
(3) Boulâd, Foulâd, steel (from *Pers.* Poulâd x.
(4) Bolid (?) *s.* nautical plummet; βολίς. But see Boulies.
Oblod, *va* sound a depth of sea; Sabat, Acts Apost. xxvii. 28.

بلم Belxum, *vn* jabber, mumble = Belrum, Barrum, B. *bredouiller.*

BLΓ

بلغ Obloẹ, *vs* reach, attain; *vn* attain full age. Balaẹ-ni, it has reached me, *i.e.* I have heard.
Balaẹ bi, (an event) occurred to.
Bâliẹ, *adj.* of full age.
Boulouẹ, *s.* full age.
Ablaẹ, consummate.
Mablaẹ 11, an amount, sum (of money). [of i.
ii. Balliẹ, iv. Abliẹ, *v* causative
iii. Bâliẹ, *vs* exaggerate, do in excess. [bole.
Mobâlaẹa, exaggeration, hyperBelieẹ, eloquent.
Balâẹa, eloquence.
Sulm el balâẹa, rhetoric.

بلغم Balẹam, phlegm; *corrupt Greek.*

بلح Belaḥa, *ns* a date (fruit).

بلج Bolouj, *ger.* gleaming.
Belja, clear light of dawn.
Beliej, clear, evident.
v. Tebellaj, *vn* dawn.
Tebliej, *ger.* dawning. [proof.
viii. Ibtilûj, evidence, clear
(2) Boulouja, a stork.
(3) Ablouj, loafsugar.

بلم Iblam, *va* besot, imbrute [B. Abrutir].
ii. Bellim, *va* deform, disfigure x.
vii. Inbelim, *vp* be besotted.

بلن Bailoun, clay used for soap. *Gr.* βαλανος.
Bellâna, tirewoman B.

BLT

بلق Ablaq, piebald.

بلر Bellaur, crystal, finest glass.
Bellaura, any vessel of very fine glass.
Bellauriêy, crystalline.
Bellaurji, dealer in fine glass.

بلس Iblies 11, Satan.
(2) Boulies, *s.* nautical plummet for sounding. *Gr.* βολίς.

بلص Belṣa, extortion.
ii. Bellaṣ, *vs* oppress by extortion, tax heavily.
(2) Bouliṣa, written document, *esp.* bill of exchange. *Ital.* polizza.
(3) Bellâṣ 11, pitcher.

بلسم Belsim, *vs* embalm a dead body, from *Gr. Lat.* See also Belsên.

بلسن Belsên, balsam of Judæa.
Bolsona, *ns* lentil x.

بلط Bellâṭ 11, pavement.
ii. Bellut, *vs* pave.
Mobellut, paviour.
(2) Bellout, oak.
Xâh bellout, horsechesnut.
(3) Bolṭa 10, hatchet AL. B.
(4) Bôlṭa, a cruise at sea C.
Belluṭ, *vs* cruise.
(5) Bolṭuiy, turbot (fish).

بلطم Belṭum, *vn* stammer. [*But* Belṭim *in* E.] See Belẓum.

BLX

بَلْش Belxa, a plight, a being deeply involved в.
Oblox, *va* embarrass в.
Iblix bi, *va* fill (a person with extravagant love of [в. *Infatuer*].
iv. Ablix bi, *va* inoculate with (an opinion), involve in (a difficulty), entangle in (love).
vii. Inbelix bi, *vp* be involved, etc. in в.

بَلْشُون Belxoun, a heron; *vulg.* Doncola.

بُوم Boum, *s.* owl.

بُن Bonn, coffee beans.

بِّين ** Ibbân, season F. favourable crisis F.

بين – بون Bann, *s.* interval.
Bain, *prep.* between.
Ma bain, what is between. [Improperly used for simple Bain?]
Fie ma bain, in the interval.
Bien, *vn* be distinct (min, from).
Bân 'en, it is clear that.
Baiyin, clear, manifest.
Bayân, exposition; an exposition or *exposé*. An inventory.
ii. Bayyin, *va* distinguish, make clear, explain.
Mobayyan, manifest.
Tebyien, explanation.
iii. Bâyin, *va* contrast.
Mobien, distinctive.

BNF

vi. Tebâyan, *vr* separate themselves one from another.
Tebâyon, *s.* contrast.
Bainouna, hiatus x.

بنو Ibn, son, *pl.* 4, Abnâ. [But in the names of tribes, *pl.* Benoun, Benien.]
Bint 5 (*pl.* Binât, as if t were radical), daughter, girl, maiden.
Benawiey, filial.
Bonouwa, posterity. [son.
v. Tebannâ, *va* adopt as one's

بني Ibni, *va* build.
Binya, construction.
Binâ, *s.* building, *pl.* 8, Abniya, Mabâni.
[Binâ *ralaihi*, in pursuance of it.]
Mabniey, built.
Bannâ, builder, architect.
Bonyân, fabric, edifice, *also ger.*
iv. Abni, *va* cause to build.
Mobna', built c. (but *qu.*).

بند Bend, a ream of paper BL
Bend 3, article of a document, clause; a braid, a tie, a lace.

بندقي Bondiqieya 2, 11, musket.
Bandiq, *va* shoot down.
(2) Bondoqa *nu.* 11, filbert.
(3) Bandouq, *s.* bastard.
(4) Bandaqiey 13, Venetian ducat.

بندر Bandar 11, seaport town, emporium, mart.

بنفسج Benefsej, violets, *Pers.*

BNJ

بَنْج Banj, henbane.
(2) Bâbounâj, camomile.
(3) Yabounja, cowl.

بنك Benc 3, bank (in commerce).

بنى Banieqa, gore of a shirt c. (epaulet x.).

بنصر Binyur, third or ring finger.

بنط Bont (Fr. pont), deck of a ship B.; dock for ships B.

بنش Beniex, s. cloth pelisse; also, cavalcade (B. sic).

بق Baqqa, nu. sandfly.
(2) Baqbiq, vn gurgle. ger. Baqbaqa.
Baqbieqa, swelling from a bruise; a pustule B.

باق Bâqa, s. bundle (of herbs), nosegay.
Bâqat silâfl, a trophy.

بوق Bouq, bugle.

بكى Ibci, vn weep. ger. Bocô.
ii. Becci, or iv. Abci, va cause to weep.
x. Istebci, va draw tears from.

بقى Ibqa', vn abide, remain over.
Bâqi, enduring, permanent.
Abqa', more durable.

BQR

Baqâ, duration; immortality.
Baqieya 14, remainder, mercantile balance.
iv. Abqi, va reserve, preserve, spare.
vi. Tebâqâ, cn survive.
x. Istebqi, va anxiously reserve, preserve.
Mâ baqa', no longer.

بقع Boqca 5, a spot; a stain or a place, pl. Biqâs, grounds.
ii. Baqqic, va stain, spot.

بقل Baqla, nu. 3, potherb.
Baqqâl, greengrocer.
Mabqala, kitchen garden.
(2) Boqâl, Bouqâl, tankard.

بكم Abcem, Beciem, mute.
Becêma, dumbness.

بقم Baqam, logwood c.

بكر Bicr 4, maiden; firstborn.
Bêcira 12, maiden.
Becier, early, soon.
Becour, precocious x.
Becourieya, primogeniture.
Bicêra, virginity.
Bâcir Bg. Bocra al the early morning; to-morrow.
Bâciraⁿ, early to-morrow.
Obcor bi, vn be early at.
(2) Becra 2, 10, a pulley.
(3) Biecêr, or dual, Biecêrein, a pair of compasses; for Bircer.

بقر Baqar, kine; also a single ox B.
Baqara, nu a cow or ox.

BQR

Baqariey, of ox or cow. Laßm baqariey, beef. [cowherd.
Baqqâr, master of kine, grazier.

بكرج بقرج Becraj, Baqraj, coffee biggin.

بقس Boqa, boxtree.

بر Barr, land, terra firma. Darr 'evuil, continent. Darra" wa baßra", by land and sea.
Barriey, rustic, wild (animal, plant).
Barrieya, wild country.
Barrâ, *vulg.* out, out of.
Barrâni, *vulg.* outer, exterior.
(2) Birr, *vn* be simple-hearted, pious. Dirr, filial piety.
Barâra, simplicity of heart.
Bârr, Barier, simple, innocent.
ii. Barrir, *va* justify, acquit.
Tebrier, Ibrâr, justification, acquittal.
v. Tebarrar, *vp* of ii.
(3) Borr, the finest wheat; πυρος, *purus*?
(4) Bârour, dung Bg. (Bârouz? or Basrour?).

بربر Barbir, *vn* grumble as camel, mutter.
Barbar 11,13,barbarian, Berber.

ابر 'Ibra 10, 5, needle.
'Ebbâr, 'Ibriey, needleseller.

وبر Wabar 4, goats' or camels' hair; shag, down, nap, bloom on flower.

BRZ

بور Daur, fallow land.
Bawâr, absence of culture, wildness of land, waste.
ii. Bawwir, or iv. Abier, *va* make uncultivated, depopulate.

(بار) بير Bier, Bi'r, 4, *i.e. pl.*
Abyâr, natural well, spring; opposed to Jobb.

برى Ibra', *va* shape, cut, create.
Ibri, *va* cut, pare, shape (a pen).
Bâri, Creator; *lit.* shaper.
Barieya 14, creature x.
Mibra' el qalam, penknife.
Borâya, *pl.* Borâ, parings.
iii. Bâri, *va* take as shape or model; imitate.
Mobâri, competitor b.
(2) Bariey 5, free, exempt, healed, recovered.
Barâ'a', immunity, passport, franked letter.
ii. Barri, *va* exempt, acquit.
Tebriya, Barrâya, justification.
Ibrâ" min, *vn* recover from, be healed of b.
Borou, recovery from illness b.
iv. Ebri, *va* heal, recover b.
Ibrâ, release, writ of release.
v. Tebarrâ min, *vn* break with a person, get clear of him Bg.
(3) vii. Inbari bi, *vn* set about, go forwards with r.

برع Ibras, *vn* be superior.
Bûris, excelling, excellent.
Barâsa, superiority (in genius).
Motebarris, spontaneous.

BRȜ

برعم Barȝum, *s.* bud, burgeon B.

برد Bard, *s.* cold.
Barùd, *s.* hail.
Bârid, *adj.* cold; *fig.* frigid, tame, ungenial, monotonous.
Abrad, colder.
Bardân, sensible of cold.
Boroud, coldness of temperament, frigidity of style, want of sympathy. [ague.
Borouda, coolness, chill, fit of
Barâd, cold state (of meat).
Barrâd, vessel for cooling, a cooler.
Obrod, *vn* be cold.
ii. Barrid, *va* cool, chill.
iv. Abrid, d°
v. Tebarrad, *vn* refresh oneself.
viii. Ibterid, *vn* nearly as v. but *esp.* bathe in cold water.
(2) Borâda, filings.
Mibrad, carpenter's file.
Bâroud, gunpowder.
Barouda 12, a gun.
(3) Beried (*Lat.* Veredus), courier, post.
Kail el beried, posthorses.
Sâḥub el beried, postmaster. [But *vulg.* the word Bôsta (post) supplants Beried.]
(4) Bardiey, papyrus, Egyptian rush.
(5) Bardieya, Pardieya, curtain.

برذع Bardaȝa 11, mule's wooden packsaddle.
Bardaȝuiy, seller of such saddles.

BRH

برنح Bardik, *va* squeeze flat in a press.

برفر Birfier, πορφυρεος, purple, scarlet.

برغ Birɤa, *s.* screw B.
Barieɤa, d° AL
Barɤie, a vice, carpenter's tool K.

برغل Barɤul, firmity, fromenty; *i.e.* wheat broken and boiled. It is the staple dish of Syria.

برغث Barɤouθ 11, a flea.

برغش Barɤaxa, gnat, midge.

بره Borhe, a space of time, generally short.
Borsihe, a moment of time.

برح Ibraḥ, *vn* pass, cease, go forwards, make progress.
Lâ baraḥ, without cessation K.
Bâriḥ, (time) past. El leilet el bâriḥa, last night; *vulg.* simply, El bâriḥa, and corruptly, embâraḥ.
(2) Barḥâ', a fit of disease (which comes and goes?) B.
ii. Barriḥ bi, *va* afflict with (a fit).
v. Tebarraḥ, *vn* suffer a fit.
Tebâriḥ, fitful sufferings.

برهن Borhên 11, proof, demonstration; *also* the purple coot, a waterbird Bɢ.
Barhin, *va* demonstrate by argument.

BRJ

برج Borj 3, tower; sign of the Zodiac; nest of stork.
(2) v. Tebarraj, *vn* dress finely; display finery in dress.
Motebarrij, ostentatious of finery.

برخن Barkâna, luggage c.

برم Obrom, *va* coil, twist, screw.
Borma, a screw Bg. touchhole of a gun.
Baurama, breech of a gun B.
Bariema, gimlet, corkscrew AL
Mibram 11, spindle.
ii. Barrim, *va* screw hard.
iv. Abrim, *va lit.* splice rope? *fig.* torment, importune I.
Mobram, spliced; *fig.* surely fastened. [twisted.
v. Tebarram, *va* be crabbed, Motebarrim, *vn* morose.

برمل Barmiel 11, barrel.

برنجك Barenjic, crape.

برنس Bornos, Bornous, hooded cloak.
(2) Dirius, prince (Europ.).

برنط Barnaita, a European hat.
(2) Barnouтuiy, snuff, powder for the nose.

برنش Barnix, *vn* make grimaces.

برك Obroc, *vn* sit on one's heels and kneel, as a poor man in presence of a greater.

BRT

(2) iii. Bâric, *va* bless.
Barace, a blessing.
Mobârec, blessed. [pond.
(3) Biroe, Borce 10, a pool,
(4) Briec, a brig (ship).

برق Barq 3, lightning.
Barieqa, a flash of lightning I.
Barráq, flashing, brilliant.
Obroq, *vn* lighten, flash, glitter.
(2) Bauraq, borax.
(3) Barwaqa, daffodil.

برقع Barqis, *va* cover with a veil.

بركل Barcil, *va* rock (a ship or cradle).
ii. Tebarcel, *vn* rock, roll, as ship. *See* Darcel.
(2) Barcelain, Parcelain, a pair of compasses. *See* Biecêr.

برنش Barqix, *va* streak, variegate. *See* Arqax, Abrax.

برص Abray, leprous.
Ibray, *vn* be leprous.
Baray, leprosy I.

برسم Barsem, pleurisy = ôêt el janb.
Mobarsem, pleuritic (person).
Barsim, *vn* suffer pleurisy.
(2) Birsiem, clover L. B. hay F.

برت Bârout, gunpowder. (Bâroud.)

برطل Barrul, *va* bribe (a judge).
Barruil, *s.* bribe to a judge.
Barrala, Tebarröl, bribery.

BRT

برطم Barrum, *va* jabber в.

برطقل Borröqâl, Bortoqâl, Bortōqân, oranges; from *Gr.* πορτογάλλος, fruit of Portugal?

برطز Barruiz, crupper to a saddle в.

برش Abrax, speckled, freckled.
Barax, spots on a hide.
Borxa, white spot on the nails в.
ii. Barrix, *va* speckle.
ix. Ibrixx, *vn* be speckled.
(2) Obrox, *vn* fade by washing.
(3) Obrox, *va* scrape F.
(4) Darx 3, small jar в.
(5) Abraxieya, diocese; from *Gr.* παροικία?

برشم Barxim, *va* clench (a nail), spike (a cannon) в. rivet (in metal).

برشن Borxân 11, wafer; wafer of Eucharist.

برز Obroz, *vn* stick out, project; be prominent.
Bâriz, signal, eminent; projecting, in relievo.
ii. Barriz, iv. Abriz,*va* make prominent or signal; bring into full light; hatch (chickens).
iii. Bâriz, *va* challenge to single
Mobâriz, champion. [combat.
Barâz, field of battle? open plain к.

BSL

Birâz, *med. t.* secretion, excrement.
(2) 'Ebriez, pure gold.

بس Bes (in Syria), only; only just so much.

بص Bayya, a live coal.
Buyy, *vn* glow, gleam; — li, take a glimpse or sly glance at.
Baybuy, *vn* burn clear as coal; glitter tremulously; — xala', glance frequently at, get glimpse of.

يبس Yobs, Yobouse, dryness, drowth. [(egg).
Yabis, Yâbis, dry (wood), hard
Yabis, *vn* was dry; *present tense* Yaibis, is dry.

باس Bâs, *s.* evil, harm, mischief; bravery.
Mâ fiehi bâs, no harm in that.
Lâ bâs, not bad, not the worse.
Also, Lâ bâs fiehi, there is no bravery in him F.
Bâyis, *adj.* evil.

بوس Bous, *va* kiss.
Bouse, *nu.* a kiss.

بسل Bêsil, fierce, stern (man), monotonous (music), ardent (spirits).
Besiel, strong, fermented (liBesêla, fierceness. [quor).
Ibsel, *vn* jar with, be repugnant. *ger.* Bosoul.
v. Tebessel, *vn* be fierce, defiant.
iii. Bêsil, *va* attack sharply к.

BSL

بصل Baṣal, onion, bulb.

بسم Ibsim, vn smile p. *vulg.*
v. Tebessem, or viii. Ibtesim, d°.

بصم Obṣöm, va print (cloth, cotton). *ger.* Boṣm.
Boṣma, cotton print.
(2) Boṣm, s. interval o.

بسق Bosâq (Boṣâq o.), spittle. Boṣâq, d°.

بسر 12, Bêsour (*also*, Bâṣöur 12), piles, hæmorrhoids (a disease).

بصر Baṣar, *ger.* discernment.
Baṣuira 11, d°.
Baṣuir, *adj.* discerning.
Mabṣara, evidence, proof.
iv. Abṣur, va discern.

بستن Bostên 11, large or public garden; park; nursery garden. [dener.
Bostêniey, al. Bostênji Bg. gar-

بسط Basṭ, extension, expansion.
Besieṭ, simple, wide open.
Bisâṭ 10, carpet for room.
Besâṭ, Besieṭa, expanse k.
Besṭra, amplitude, simplicity k.
Obsoṭ, va expand; *fig.* delight, gratify. [ease.
iii. Bâsiṭ, va set a person at his
v. Tebassaṭ, vp be spread out.
vii. Inbasiṭ, vp be gratified; *a popular word.*

BTY

Inbisâṭ, s. ease and freedom, comfort, pleasure.
(2) Besṭâni, pedlar, hawker b.

بستق Bestouqa, water jar, urn b.

بت Bott, va sever, dissever, cut off.
(2) El bette, [a stroke] for Là .... bette, pas une *fois*, not at all.
(3) Bettieya 11, butt, hogshead. See بتى.

بث Boṯṯ, scatter.

بط Baṭṭ, a duck (*fem.* Baṭṭa) 3, drake.
(2) ii. Baṭṭuṭ, va flatten.
(3) Baṭâṭa, potato.

أبط 'Ibṭ 4, armpit. 'Ibṭuiy, belonging to the armpit.

بيت Beit 3, house; 4, a stanza.
Bieṭ, vn pass the night, sojourn.
Bâyit, *adj.* stale (bread, meat) Bg.

باط Bâṭ, bundle? an armful b.
(2) Bâṭ el sêq, calf of leg o.

بطو Boṭöu, slowness.
Baṭui', Bâṭu, slow.
iii. Bâṭu, va put off.
vi. Tebâṭa', vn dawdle (san).
(2) Bâṭuya 12, large wine jar.

بتى Bettieya 11, butt, hogshead. *Also*, Baṭṭuiya 11.

BTḤ

بطح Ibraḥ, *va* fell (tree), lay prostrate. [hole.
(2) Baṭuiḥ 11, morass B. water Abṭaḥ 5, d°. F.

بطخ Biṭuika, *nu.* melon.
Mabṭaka, melon bed.

بتل Betoul, virgin.
Betoula (*betula*), birch tree; called "the lady of the woods," by Coleridge.

بطل Bâṭul, vain, void, null.
iv. Abṭul, *va* make void, abolish, baffle. [pity! ᴀʟ
Bâṭul! que dommage! what a

بطم Boṭma, *nu.* turpentine oak.
(2) Obṭōm, *va* graft (a tree) B.

بطن Baṭn 3, belly.
Baṭun, large bellied, gluttonous.
Mibṭân, very gluttonous.
Bâṭun, *adj.* interior 12 (mystical), inner.
Buṭâna, lining of garment 11.
Mobâtun, intimate.

بطر Ibṭar, *vn* be wanton, saucy.
Baṭrân, wanton.
Baṭur, d°.
Baṭar, wantonness, petulance.
(2) Baiṭar, a farrier.
Baiṭara, farrier's art.
Baiṭur, *vn* act the farrier.

بطرخ Baṭârik, roe of fish.

BXQ

بطرك Baṭriyṛo, Baṭrieo, Baṭreo, Patriarch, *i.e.* chief pontiff of an Eastern church, *pl.* 15.
Baṭriciey, belonging to the Patriarch.
Baṭricieya, patriarchate.

بطرشن Baṭraxien, *s.* stole, sacred robe. *pl.* 11, Baṭârix.

بطش Baṭx, onset, rush, violence.
Ibṭux bi, fie, rush upon.
iii. Bâṭux, *va* seize violently.

بشش Baxoux, open-faced, merry.
Baxâxa, affability. [affable.
Baxbix, display joy ᴋ.

وبش Aubâx, rabble o.

بوش Boux, gloss of cloth B.
ii. Bawwix, *va* starch, calender, mangle, press (cloth), smooth by pressure.

باشا Bâxâ, Pasha, *pl.* Bâxâwét.

بشع Ibxaɛ, *vn* have bad breath.
Baxieɛ, hideous, disgusting.
Baxâɛa, offensiveness.

بشل Bexla, tiara?

بشم Baxam, surfeit, indigestion, disgust ᴋ.
vii. Inbexim, *vp* be surfeited, gorged B.

بشق Bâxiq 12, sparrow-hawk.
(2) vii. Inbixâq, procession (of

BXQ

the Holy Spirit) in Christian theology.

بشكر Bexcier, Poxciers, *n.* a doyley.

بشر Baxar, mankind, human nature.
Boxâr, low people x.
Baxariey, human.
Baxarieya, human nature.
(2) (Baxr) Bixâra, good news. Obxor, ii. Baxxir, announce good news, gladden by news. [x.
x. Istebxir, rejoice in good news
Baxier, bearer of good news.
Boxra', the gospel, good news.
(3) iii. Bâxir, *va* undertake (work), superintend.
Mobâxir, manager, superintendent.
Mobâxara, management.

بز Bezbouz 11, tap for a cask.

بوز Bâz, hawk 9, *or pl.* Bowaz.
(2) Bouz, ice (*modern*).
(3) Bouze, beer (*modern*).
(4) Bouz, muzzle, snout of beast. [pleasure n.
(5) Tebwiez, pouting, disii. Bawwiz, *vn* pout x.

بزغ Bozouſ, rising of star.
Ibziſ(Ibziq), *va* sparkle, twinkle.

بزل ii. Bezzil, *va* bore or tap (a cask of liquor). [x.
Bizêl, auger for boring the cask
Mibzela, colander with holes

ΔWY

bored for straining; strainer for liquor.

بزق Ibziq, *va* sputter, sparkle.
Bozêq, spittle. See Bosêq, Borâq.

بزر Bizra, pip *nw.*
Ibzir, *ger.* Bezr, *va* sow x.
(2) Bâzâr, bazaar.

D Δ Δ.

دا Dâ, *s.* malady.
Dâyi, sick.
Dawâ, *pl.* 8, Adwiya, medicine.
(2) Dawie, *s.* rumble (hum x.).
iv. Adwi, *vn* rumble, resound.
(3) Dawâya, *s.* tube, inkhorn.

دي Dieya, retaliation, *pl.* 2, fines.
(2) Dâya, *s.* nurse, midwife.

ذو Δou, Δie, Δê; *f.* Δêt; *pl. m.* Δewien, *f.* Δewêt. See Grammar. Δou may be rendered *possessed of;* Δou xaql, possessed of good sense.

ضو Δau, *pl.* 4, AΔwâ, light.
Δaiya, a light, *pl.* 8, AΔwiya.
OΔou, *va* light up, kindle.
iv. AΔui, *va* d°.
Δuyê, Δuwê, *s.* blaze, lustre.
Δawiey, MoΔui, lustrous.

ضوى Δawa', leanness.
Δâwi, meagre, emaciated.

AWY

Uǎwa', *vn* be meagre.
iv. Aǎwi, *va* emaciate, wear out.
Moǎwi, wearisome (distance, etc.).

ا Iǎe, Iǎe bi, behold !
Iǎeⁿ, Iǎen, therefore.
Iǎ, *conj.* when. Iǎe, *conj.* if.

أدى ii. Eddi, *va* present, pay. *Also modern* Woddi, *va* convey, present, hand over.

أيد ii. Eyyid, iv. Ewidd, *va* corroborate, establish.
v. Te'eyyad, *vp* be consolidated.
'Eid, *ger.* of i. establishment.
Moweyyad, consolidated.
Te'yied, (divine) support.

ودّ Wadd, *s.* affection.
Wodd, *s.* desire, [*Vulg.* Boddi for Bi woddi, (it is) in my desire, *i.e.* I wish, I want اـ]
Wodd, *va* love.
Wadâd, *s.* love, attachment.
Wadoud, affectionate.
Wadied, an attached friend.
Mawadda, affection.
Wadwid, *va* caress.

ودى Wâdi, valley ; *pl.* 8, Audiya.
(2) Weddi, *va* present. *See* Eddi *above.*

وضو Waǎuiy, clean and bright by ablution.
Waǎâya, cleanness.
Waǎöu, ablution.

WDS

ii. Waǎǎu, *va* perform ablution on another. [tion.
v. Tewaǎǎâ, *vn* undergo ablu-
vi. Motewâǎu, clean, spruce.

أذى Eǎê, Eǎêya, *ger.* damage, being harmed.
iii. iv. Eǎi, *va* damago, harm. Mouǎi, damaging, mischievous.
Ieǎê, Eǎieya, mischief.

يد Yed, *f.* hand, *pl.* Eyâdi.
Yediey, *adj.* of the hand, handy.
Yedawiey, of the hand, manual.
iv. Aidi, *va* consolidate. *See* Eyyid. *ger.* Iedâ, consolidation.

ضغ or ذغ Ǎaǎǎus, *va* shatter, demolish. [In x. Aeǎais, disperse, dilapidate.]

ودع Wadas Yadas, *va* leave as it is, leave at rest. *Imperative,* Das, let. Daǎui en, permit me to. Daǎna min el euz, let us have done with compliment b.
Daǎa, quietude.
Wadies, quiet, tranquil.
ii. Waddis, *va* as i.
iii. Wâdis, *va* bid farewell to; *ger.* Widâs, an adieu.
Maudous, consigned (goods).
Wadiesa, a deposit in trust c.
iv. Audie, *va* consign property, as, to a legal officer b.
v. Tewâdos, reconciliation.
x. Isteudis, *va* require (a person) to be consignee of property.
Mosteudas, consignee b.

WAS

وضع Waḍaɛ Yaḍaɛ, ʋa place, deposit, put down, enact; ger. Waḍɛ, Waḍaɛ, Waḍuiɛ, enactment.
Ḍaɛa, Woḍöuɛ, humility.
Mauḍuɛ, a place.
Mauḍöuɛ, object, subject, topic.
Waḍuiɛ 6, humbled, abased.
v. Tewâḍaɛ, ʋn act humbly, condescend.
Tewâḍoɛ, humility, modesty.
Waḍâɛa, Ittiḍâɛ, humiliation.
viii. Itteḍaɛ, ʋp be humilitated.

ضيع Ḍuiɛ, ʋn go astray, be lost. ger. Ḍayâɛ.
ii. Ḍayyiɛ, iv. Aḍuiɛ, ʋa send astray, throw away, waste.
(2) Ḍaiɛa 5, a farm, small country estate.

دعى Idɛu, ʋa call, summon, invite; call upon, invoke, pray.
Doɛâ, prayer, pl. 8, Adɛuya.
Daɛwâ, Daɛwa', lawsuit, call to prayer.
Dâɛuya 12, a (divine) call, a determination of spirit to a certain course.
Madɛöu, invited.
vii. Indaɛu, ʋn reply to an invitation r. [profess c.].
viii. Iddaɛu, ʋa claim, pretend, profess.
Moddaɛu, prosecutor, plaintiff.
Moddâɛâ ɛalaiha, the called upon, i.e. the defendant.

DSC

دعب Idɛab, ʋn sport (= Ilɛab).
Dâɛub, sportive.
Doɛâba, pleasantry.
iii. Dâɛub, ʋa sport with.
v. Tedâɛab, ʋr sport mutually.

ذعبل (with د in s.) Aeɛbil, ʋa rumple, curl, dog's-ear, disturb, derange.
Aeɛbala, illness, indisposition.

دعبس Daɛbis ɛala', ʋn hunt after s. (perhaps Daɛbis, make disturbance, turn things upside down?)

ضعف Oḍɛöf, ʋn be weak; ger. Ḍöɛf, weakness. Ḍaɛuif, weak.
ii. Ḍaɛɛuf, iv. Aḍɛuf, ʋa weaken.
x. Istaḍɛuf, ʋa regard as weak.
(2) Ḍuɛf 4, the double, so much again. After numeral, -fold.
Moḍâɛɛaf, folded in two x.
iii. Ḍâɛuf, ʋa double, give twice as much.
Moḍâɛaf, adj. double.
vi. Teḍâɛaf, ʋn grow twice as big, be doubled.

دعم Diɛâma 11, pillar.

ذعن iv. Eɛɛun, ʋa obey; ger. Iɛɛân, obedience, submission.
Moɛɛun, obedient.
Miɛɛân, very submissive.

دعك Idɛaɛ, ʋa rub, scour, roll, calendar (cloth), ger. Daɛɛ.

DSR

دعر Idɛar, vn smoulder ĸ.
Dâɛur, smutty, grimy.
v. Tedâɛar, vn be smutty.

ذعر Δaɛar, Δoɛr, s. dismay.
Δêɛur, Meʌɛöur, dismayed.
Moʌɛur, terrible.
Δeɛöur, coward, dastard.
iv. Eʌɛur, va dismay.
v. Teʌeɛɛar, vp be dismayed.

دعس Idɛas, va trample, ger. Daɛa.

دب (See Idbi).
Dibb, vn creep, ger. Dabb.
Dobba, a bear.
Dâbba, pl. Dawâbb, reptile, creeper, but popularly, a quadruped, esp. a packhorse.
(2) Dabba, a butter pot.
(3) ii. Dabbib, va sharpen, make pointed ʙ. Modabbab, adj. pointed, sharp.
Dabdouba, a sharp point.
(4) Dabdaba, noise of drum, of scuffling feet, of horse's feet. See Daqdaqa.

ضب Δabb, lizard.
(2) Δabba 10, an (iron) staple ʙ.

ذب Δobâba, ns a fly, pl. Δobbân.
(2) Δebʌib, vn oscillate.
ii. Teʌebʌeb, vn dᵒ.

ادب 'Edab 4, good breeding, refinement.

DBГ

ii. 'Eddib, va refine, educate; chastise, correct.
Té'dieb, chastisement.
Mo'eddib, preceptor.
'Edabieya, literature.
'Edieb 6, well bred, cultivated.
Mêdoba pl. 11, Ma'êdib, a festive entertainment.
v. Te'eddab, vn receive good education.
x. Istêdib, vn cultivate polite accomplishment.
Beit el 'edab, (delicate phrase for) privy, water closet.

دأب Doub fie, vn work zealously at; ger. Do'oub.
Dâb, pl. Adwob, condition, habit.
Dâ'ib, adj. zealous, spirited.

ذوب Δoub, vn melt.
ii. Δewwib, va melt.

ذيب Δieb 5, wolf.
Δiebat el kail, glanders (pulmonary disease of horse).
Δiyâba, dᵒ (diyâba, ʙ.)

دبى Idbi, vn crawl as worm. See also Dibb.

ضبع Δabɛ, f. hyena.

ذبح Iʌbaḥ, va slaughter, butcher, sacrifice.
Δebieḥa 11, victim.
Maʌbaḥ 11, altar.

دبغ Odboɣ, va tan.
Dibɣ, s. tannin.

DBΓ

Dabbâɣ, tanner.
Madbaɣa, tanyard.

دَبّج Diebâj, brocade; *fig.* a flowery, superfluous preface.

دبل Dobla, an abscess; *vulg.* Dommela 11.
Dibla 3, misfortune K. O.
Odbol, *va* manure (the soil) K.
Dobâl, *s.* manure K. *Compare* Zibl, Odmol.

ذبل *vn* Labal, *vn* wither, *ger.* Δoboul.
Δêbil, Δcblân, withered.
ii. Δebbil, *or* iv Eabil, *va* wither.

دبك Dabce, a bustle, fidget.
ii. Dabbic, *vn* fidget, scuffle.
Modabbic, fidgety, bustling.

دبق Dibq, birdlime, viscous matter.

دبر ii. Dabbir, *va* plan, scheme, regulate; *with acc. or* fie: (in physiology) elaborate B.
Modabbirat el bait, housewife.
v. Tedabbar, *vn* reflect, meditate.
Tedbier, management, economy.
(2) Dobr 4, back part, the posteriors. Ɛan dobr, behind; (after death K.) result, consequence K.
Modabbar, set free after a master's death K.
Dabr, shoalrook, *pl.* Adbor.
Dâbir, *adj.* astern.
(3) Dibr (5, 3), swarm of wasps.
Dabbour, a drone.

DF

(4) Dobâra, packthread.
(5) Dabourn, swelling from a bruise B.

دبر Oabor *or* ii Δebbir, *va* copy (a book).

دبرك Dabrec, club, heavy stick.

دبس Dibs, syrup, treacle.
Adbes, treacle-coloured, dirty red.
(2) Dabbous 11, a mace or baton.
Dabbouse, ʀu a pin.

ضبط Oȝbor, *va* hold in check, control; *also* confiscate; *ger.* Ӡabr. [or police.
Ӡâbuт 5, officer in army, navy, El Ӡabт, Ӡabâyuт, the *gens d'ormes.* [police.
Ӡabâтa, control, government,
Ӡabaтuiy, a police officer; *pl.* el Ӡabaтuiya, the police.
(2) Aӡbaт, skilful with both hands B.

دبش Dabxa, a clod.

ضد Ӡudd, *prep.* against.
iii. Ӡâdid, *va* thwart.

دود Doud, worms.

ذود ii. Δewwid, *va* repel, avert.

دف Daffa 3, one side of what has two flat sides; board, plank AL helm of ship.
(2) Daff, a drum.
Daffâɣ, drummer.

DWF

دوف Douf, *va* or ii. Dawwif, *va* mix up, mix (medicine).

ضيف Ẕaif 3, guest, lodger.
Ẕuyâfa, hospitality.
Maẕuifa, lodging, chamber.
Muẕyâf, very hospitable.
ii. Ẕayyif, or iv. Aẕuif, *va* entertain (a guest).
Moẕuif, host.
v. Teẕayyaf, *vn* be guest.
(2) iv. Aẕuif, *va* annex.
Moẕâf, annexed, adjunct.
Uẕâfa, adjunction.
vi. Taẕâyaf, be conjoined.

دفى ii. Daffi, *va* cherish by natural heat, warm.
Dafâ, *ger.* warming.
v. Tedaffâ, *vn vp* be kept warm (by clothing).

ضفى Ẕâfi, complete r.; ample, as a robe or hair x.
Oẕfou, *vn* be overbrimming x.
Ẕafwa, affluence, abundance x.

دفع Idfaɛ, *va* repel, propel; also repay.
Idfaɛ ɛan, defend.
iii. Dâfiɛ, *va* repel.
Dafɛa, a time, une fois.

ضفدع Ẕafdaɛa, *nu* frog.

دفل Dofla, rhododendron.

دفن Odfon, *va* bury. *ger.* Dafn.
Madfan(a) 11, burying ground.

ΔΓΤ

vii. Indafin, *vp* be buried.
(2) Dafna, δαφνη, the bay-tree; *vulgo* Γâr. *See* Dofla.

دفق Odfoq, *va* pour out, empty. *ger.* Dafq, flowing, gushing.
Dâfiq, *particip.* flowing.
ii. Daffiq, iv. Adfiq, *va* empty (a vessel) of liquid.
vii. Indafiq, *vp* be poured out, empty out.

ضفر Oẕfor, *va* braid the hair with silk. *ger.* Ẕafr.
Ẕafiera 11, a tress.
ii. Ẕaffir, *va* same as i.
vii. Inẕafir, *vp* be braided together.

دفتر Dafter 11, blank book, ledger; portfolio?
Dafter-dâr, finance minister.

دفش Odfox, *va* repulse (an army).
vii. Indafix, *vp* be repulsed.

دغدغ daɣdiɣ, *va* twitch, tickle, finger. *ger.* Daɣdaɣa.

داغ Dâɣ, *s.* a scar.

ضغو Oẕɣou, *vn* whine.

دغل Daɣla, *nu.* underwood.
Madɣal, a copse, jungle.

دغر Doɣri, true, upright, straight; sterling, genuine (in breed).

ضغط Ẕoɣṭa, constraint.

ΔΓΤ

Uδrat, va coop in, press close. ger. Δart.
vi. Taδárat, vp be jammed together in a crowd.
vii. Inδárat, vp of i.
Inδuŕat, tribulation s.

دغش Daŕxix, va dazzle (the eye) в. ger. Daŕxaxa. See Γaxxi, Γaτmix.

دج Difidán, a dwarf c.

ضم Δuñña, *nu* sunbeam.
Δuñň, radiance. See Δaña.

دجار Dáña, a toy.

دوج Dauña, *nu* tall tree.

دهى Dèhi, *adj.* cunning (δεινός).
Dchwa, sudden fright в. (δέος).
Déhiya, a terrible thing (δεινόν).
(2) Madhiey, afflicted, sick.

ضهى Δahiey, similar.
iii. Δâhi, va resemble.
vi. Taδâbé, vn correspond, or be mutually alike.

ضحى Δaña, full day.
Δaňuiy, sunny.
(2) Δaňuiya 14, a sacrifice.

دهب Iaheb, vn depart; ger.
Δihêb, departure.
Medheb, sect, school.
(2) Δcheb, gold. Δeheba, *nu.*
Δehebicy, golden.

ΔHN

fi. Λε ib, va gild.
Moδeł gilded.

دهب Dahebieya, Nile boat.

ضد viii. Uδrañud, va persecute s.

دحدر Dañdir, va roll down.
Compare Uñdar, Dañrij.

ذهل Iahil, va; Iahil ran, vn omit, neglect, be absent in mind.
Δêhil, preoccupied, absent; forgetful c. [rapture.
iv. Eahil, va preoccupy, en-
vii. Inahil, vp of iv.

دهليز Dehliez, lobby, corridor.
Dehliz tala', vn wait on in the lobby, dance attendance on.

دهم Odhom, va surprise, come on (a person) suddenly.
vii. Indahim, vp of i.
(2) Adhem, *adj.* greenish black, dark olive.
Dohma, s. this same colour.

دهن Dohn, *s.* grease, ghee.
Dohna, *nu* a coat of paint.
Dahin, oily. [in oils.
Odhon, va anoint, varnish, paint
Dibên, varnish, oil colour.
Madhonnêt, oil paintings, frescoes.

ذهن Δihn, *s.* acumen, keen intelligence.
Δehien, *adj.* acute.

DHN — ZJS

دهنج Dehnaj, emery B.

دكس Idhec, *va* crush by weight, squash, pound. CAUSH.

ضكت Uḏḥac, *vn* laugh; *ger.* Ḍaḥc.
Ḍuḥce, *nu* laughter.
Ḍaḥḥâc, great laugher.
iv. Aiḥuc, *va* cause to laugh.
Moḍḥuc, a jester.
Moḍḥucêt, pleasantries which move laughter.

دهقن Dohqân 13, landowner, *Pers.*

دهر Dahr 3, age, millennium.
Dahra", in perpetuity.
Dohriey, very aged, as a tree.

دهور Dahwir, *va* waste, throw away.
ii. Tedahwar, *vp* be thrown away, destroyed.

دحر Idḥar, *va* avert, repel, *religious t.*
Madḥara, reprobation.
vii. Indaḥur sanni! avaunt! begone! (O Satan!)

ضهر Ḍohr, Ḍahr, so pronounced, but spelt with ظ. See under Ẓahr.

دحرج Daḥrij, *va* roll along.
Modaḥraj, globular.
ii. Tedaḥraj, *vn* or *vp* of i.

دهس Odhos, *va* trample.
—Idsas B.

دحس Doḥâs, chilblain, bunnion B.
Dâḥöus 12, whitlow B. I.

دحص Idḥaṣ ṣala', *vn* glide over, alur over, suppress. *ger.* Doḥöuy.

دهش Idhex, *va* stun, amaze. *ger.* Dehxa, dismay.
iv. Adhix, *va* same as i.
vii. Indahix, *vp* be amazed.

دحش Idḥax, *vn* glide in; also *va* insinuate, slip in, palm off, pass off.
vii. Indaḥux, *vn* glide in.

دج Dojâja, *nu* hen; *vulg.* 'jâja.
(2) Dajâjiey, *adj.* pitch black C.
(3) Dajjij, *va* arm in armour, accoutre.
Modajjaj, armed cap-a-pie.
v. Tedajjaj, *vp* be thus armed.

ضج Ḍajja, *s.* noise.
Ḍujj, *vn* make noise. *ger.* Ḍajiej.
Ḍajouj, noisy.

دجى Dâjiya, obscurity C.
iii. Dâji, *va* dissemble.
Modâjâya, dissimulation.

ضج Ḍajs, *ger.* reclining C.
Maḏjac, sleeping place, *esp.* recess with a bed.
vii. Inḏajuc, *vn* lounge.

DJN

دجن Dojna, Dijna, gloom, murkiness. Adjan, gloomy. Midjân, murky.
(2) Dâjin, Dajoun, *adj.* tame.
ii. Dajjin, *vs* tame.
viii. Iddajin, be tamed or tame.

ضجر Ďajr, Ďojra, anxiety.
ii. Ďajjir, iv. Aďjir, *vs* distress.

دوخ Dauka, giddiness, sickness of stomach?
ii. Dawwik, *vs* make giddy, disgust, revolt.
[These senses are modern. The verb in x. is very different. So in P. *subdue.*]

دخل Odkol, *vs* enter.
Dakiel 6, refugee, client, proselyte.
iii. Dâkil, *vs* insinuate, slip in.
iv. Adkil, *vs* admit, receive (a fugitive). [vene.
vi. Tedâkal, *vn* interfere, inter-
Motedâkil, *partic.* entering or composing a large number, by being its *submultiple*, as 7 or 5 of 35.

ضخم Ďakam, Ďökm 2, big, huge.
Ďakiem, d° c.
Ďakâma, bigness.

دخن Dokân, *s.* smoke.
Idkan, *vn* smoke.
Madkana 11, chimney.
ii. Dakkin, *vs* smoke.
Modakkan, smoky c.

DWL

Adkan, *adj.* of smoke colour, dun.
(2) Dakn, millet c.

دخر Ďekiera 11, store.
Maďkar, storehouse.
viii. Iďďekir, *vs* select for keeping, store up; adopt (a son).
Ďekier, Moďďekar, adoptive son.

دل Doll, *vs* point, direct.
Daliel 9, 11, guide, proof.
Dalâla, guidance.
Dilâla, pay to a guide, brokerage.
Dallâl, crier.
ii. Dallil, *vs* fondle, pet.
x. Istedill, *vs* indicate.

دلدل Daldil, *vs* oscillate, swing.
ii. Tedaldal, d° only *vn.*
[For this, *also* Tedallal is used, and Tedandal. See Dalou and Dandil.]
(2) Doldol 11, hedgehog.

ضل Ďull, *vn* go astray [also *vs* miss. *s. ger.* Ďalal, Ďalâla, misconduct. [c.]
Ďâll, *partic.* gone astray (devious
Ďull, Ďulla, error.
Ďaloul, apt to go astray.
Ďulliel, in grievous error.
Oďloula, delusion, superstition, *pl.* 11, Aďâliel.
Maďalla, grave error of life.
iv. Aďull, *vs* lose; also, lead astray, seduce.

دول Daul, a turn. *Pers. see* Daur.
iii. Dâwil, *vs* turn over in the mind, revolve.

DWL

vi. Tedâwal, *vn* confer together.
(2) Daula, lordship, power, dynasty, *pl.* Dowal.
El Dowal el cibâr, the Great Powers, chief governments.
Daulatoh, his lordship (*title*).

ذيل Δeil 3, 4, lappet, flap, horsetail; *fig.* appendage, appendix.
v. Teλeyyal, *vn* sweep the ground with one's train.

دلو Dalou, *pl.* Dolâ, leathern bucket, for a well.
v. Tedallâ, *vn* dangle.

دلع Dalis, tasteless, insipid.
ii. Dallis, *vα* make insipid; spoil (a child).
(2) Odlos, *va* loll (the tongue).
vii. Indalis, *vn* loll, hang loose.

ضلع Χuls 3, side, rib.
Χâlis, onesided, partial, unfair.
Moχallis, overweighting one side, too heavy. [side.
ii. Χallis, *va* overweight one
(2) Χalies, plump-barrelled (horse).
Χalâsa, robustness (of horse) r.

دلب Dolb, plane tree.
(2) Daulâb, *Pers.* waterwheel; hence any machine, engine.

دلفن Dolfien 11, dolphin.

دلم Adlam, raven black. Compare the next.

'DM

ظلم Χalam, (so pronounced, but spelt with ظ. See under Σalm). *ger.* becoming dark.

دلك Dalc, *ger. lit.* rubbing of the body. Dalcᵃ, by rubbing in oil. [instruct.
Odloc, *va fig.* train, refine,
ii. Dallic, *va lit.* shampoo.

ذلق Δeliq, *adj.* well pointed; *fig.* sharp in repartee. [end x.
Δelq, Δeuliq, *s.* point, pointed
ii. Δelliq, iv. Ελiq, *va* sharpen (a knife) x.
Moλellaq, pointed (remark).

دلس ii. Dallis, *va* feign.
iii. Dâlis, *va* dᵒ overreach.
Dals, *ger.* cheating = Modâlase.

ذم Δomm, *va* blame. *ger.* Δemm.
Δemien, blameable.
Madmoum, much blamed.
Δimma, responsibility [in affirmation, Σala' Δimmeti, upon my *honour!* upon my conscience!].
Δimmiey, tributary, client under protection.

ضم Χömm, *va* amass, concentrate. [ment.
Χamiema 11, appendage, increvii. Inχumm, *vp* be annexed.

أدم 'Ediem 10, red leather, scented Russian leather, a large tanned skin.

'DM

'Eddâm, currier.
(2) 'Edamiey, *s.* a man; *adj.* civilized, cultivated.

دوم Doum, *vn* abide.
Dawâm, permanence.
Dáyim, permanent, lasting.
Dáyimaⁿ, always.
Daimouma, eternity s.
iii. Dâwim ɛala', continue at.
iv. Adiem, *va* perpetuate.
(2) Modâm, wine (in high style).
(3) Douwâma, a boy's top c.

ضيم Xaim; *ger.* oppression.
Xâyim, oppressive.
iv. Aʃuim, x. IsteXuim, *va* oppress, afflict.

دم Dam', blood.
Damawiey, bloody.
ii. Dammi, *va* wound v.
Dima', murders, carnage, *pl.* of Dam'.

دمع Damɛa 3, a tear.
Damiɛ, prone to weep.

ضمد Xumâd(a), a bandage.
ii. Xammid, *va* bandage.

دمغ Dimâɣ, brain.
Damɣa, a stamp, impress c.
Odmoɣ, *va* stamp, mark by stamp c.

دمج Dammij, *va* introduce.
iii. Dâmij, *va* assume intimacy with. [coalesce.
vi. Todâmaj, *vr* form intimacies;

DMQ

vii. Indamij, viii. Iddamij, *vp* or *vn* become dovetailed, united.

دمل Dommela 11, boil, abscess.
v. Tedammel, vii. Indamil, viii. Iddamil, *vn* form an abscess.
(2) Odmol, *va* manure? x.

دملج Domloj, Domlouj, armlet.
Modamlaj, round and smooth c. x.

دمن Damân, a corn on the foot.
ii. Dammin, *va* make callous, inure.
iv. Admin, *va* make familiar, practise continually. *ger.* Idmân, practice, application.
Modmin, *adj.* practising; devoted to. [callous.
v. Tedamman, *vn* become inured,
x. Istedmin, *va* as iv.

ضمن Uxman, *va* guarantee. *ger.* Xamn, becoming surety.
Xumn, *s.* interior (of a thing); *prep.* within.
Xâmin, bail, person responsible.
MaXmoun, comprized, contained. The contents.
ii. Xammin, *va* make responsible. Insert.
v. TeXamman, *vn* become responsible. *va* contain, comprize.

دمق Idmaq ɛala', *vn* intrude upon.
vii. Indamiq, (nearly same).
ii. Dammiq, *va* push in, intrude, obtrude.

DMR

دمر Damâr, desolation, ruin; a breakdown.
ii. Dammir, *va* demolish.

ضمر Ďamr, Ďâmir, lank (as greyhound), slim.
(2) MuĎmâr, hippodrome, circus, amphitheatre.
(3) Ďamier, spirit, heart, self, personality, personal pronoun.
OĎmor fic, iv. AĎmir calu', brood over (a thought).
UĎmâr, rumination, *fig.*

دمث Damieθ, gentle (animal).
Damâθo, gentleness.

دن Dann 5, a tun, vat.
(2) Donn, *en* humm.
Dandin, *vn* d°. purr as cat.

ضن Ďunn bi, *vn* grudge, give stingily.
Ďanien, stingily, *i.e.* scarcely.
B. *Guère.*

أذن 'Eĸen, *vulg.* Weĸen, the ear, *pl.* ěĸên; *fig.* handle of a jar.
ii. Eĸĸin, *va* (frequentative) cause to hear, *i.e.* proclaim, esp. from the mosque.
Mo'ĸĸin, crier from the mosque.
iv. or iii. êĸin, *va* inform (a person) of (*bi*) a thing.
v. Te'ĸĸen, *vn* be aware, be informed.
Iĸên, public call to prayer. *ger.* of iv.
Mêĸena, *pl.* 11, Mo'êĸin or

DYN

12, Mowêĸin, steeple of mosque, whence is the call to prayer; hence simply, a steeple, as of lighthouse.
(2) Iĸn, leave, permission, passport.
Eĸin, usher who gives leave to pass or enter.

دون Doun, *adv. prep.* below.
Doun 'en, (with verb) short of.
Doun, Bi doun, Min doun, *prep.* without; = Min ŋair, *vulg.* Bilâ.
Doun, *adj.* low; *fig.* base.
Dowain, somewhat low, a little way below.
iv. Adien, *va* lower, make base.
(2) Dicwân, *pl.* Dawâwien, from *Pers.* gener. a frame.
a. Sofa, esp. formed in masonry.
b. Council of State (*cf. Engl.* Board).
c. Register, Budget.
d. Album, ledger x.
e. Collection of select poetry x.
ii. Dawwin, *va* schedule, digest into a single corpus, coordinate and arrange, register.
v. Tedowwan, *vp* of d°
Diewâni, form of court MS. official handwriting; *also,* a certain small coin.

دين Dain 3, debt.
Dâyin, debtor x.
Madyoun, indebted, debtor.
ii. Dayyin, *va* lend (money).
Modayyin, lender, creditor.
v. Tedayyan min, *va* borrow from.

DYN

x. Istedien, *vs* ask a loan.
(2) Dicn 4, creed, faith.
Cals' dicni, upon my creed!
Daiyin, religious.
Diyâna, religion, religiousness, loyalty.
Dayyân, (God) the judge, retributor.
Adyan, more religious.
Dicnouna, s. last judgment c. s.

ضين iii. Xâyin, v endure, last, stand wear and tear в.

دنو Donouw, proximity.
Danâwa, d°. *fig.* affinity.
Odnou min, ila', li, *vn* come near, approach.
viii. Iddani, *vn* be imminent x.
x. Istedni, *vs* invite to come nearer, call to come.

دني Dani, Daniey, inferior, base.
Danâya, inferiority. [thing.
Danîcya 14, baseness, a base
Adna', lowest, smallest.
Wala adna' xai', not even the slightest thing.
(2) Donyâ' (*fem.* of Adna'), this *lower* (world), *pl.* Dona'.
vulg. weather, atmosphere.
Donyawiey, Donyâwi, worldly, secular.

ضني Xâni, *adj.* faint, pining.
UXna', *vn* be vitally weak.
Xonâya, emaciation, decline.
iv. AXni, *vs* debilitate, drain away vitality.

DC

MoXns', moribund.
viii. UXXani, *vn* pine away.

ذنب Δenab 4, tail, appendage.
Δinâb 11, gulley in mountain.
ii. Δennib, *vs* add as appendix.
(2) Δenb 3, fault, offence.
x. Istcadnib, *vs* tax with guilt.

دندل Dandil, *vs?* dangle.
Modandal? dangling в.
ii. Tedandal, *vn* dangle. See Dalou, Daldil.

دنم Dounanma, a fleet.

ضنك Xanc, tight, distressing x.
Xanâce, distress.
MaXnouc, afflicted (with illness).
iv. AXnic, *vs* afflict (the body).
UXrunêc, affliction.

دنر Dicnâr, a ducat, *pl.* Danânicr, as if from *sing.* Dinnâr. *Lat.* Denarius.

دنس Danis 4, foul, unclean.
Danâse, impurity.
ii. Dannis, *vs* pollute, profane.
v. Tedannas, *vn* or *vp* of ii.
Madânis, dirty places, *fig.* impure houses.

دكك Docc, *vs* ram (a gun).
Midecc, ramrod.
(2) Decce, *pl.* 10, Doceo, waist band to drawers.
(3) Docce 10, wooden bench.
(4) Deccct (10) ﬂarab, pile of firewood в.

DO

دكدك Daodic, *va* finger, tickle. See Dardir.

دق Doqq, *va* knock, strike, pound; also, *vn* knock, strike.
Midaqq, thumper, pestle.
Daqieqa 11, a moment, a minute.
Daqieq, *s.* fine flour.
Daqqâq, seller of d°
Diqq, *adj.* fine, pounded small.
Diqqa, minuteness, delicacy, minute accuracy.
Daqieq, *adj.* subtle, minute.
iii. Dâqiq, Dâqiq fie, *v* criticize minutely. [feet.
(2) Daqdaqa, sound of horses'

دوك Dauce, Douce, a brawl.
(2) Dawaic, two handled jug B.

ديك Diec 3, a cock (bird).

ضيق Ẍuiq, *vn* be narrow, be scanty; be hard pressed.
Ẍâq ṣadri, my breast is contracted, *i.e.* I suffer inward distress. *ger.* Ẍaiq, Ẍuiq, *s.* distress.
Ẍâyiq, Ẍaiyiq, narrow, distressing.
Ẍaiqa, Ẍuiqa, *ns?* affliction.
MaẌuiq 11, narrow place, defile. *fig.* embarrassment.
ii. Ẍayyiq, *va* make narrow, hem in, trammel.
iii. Ẍâyiq, *va* (with acc. of person), distress, roduce to strait; distress (a ship).
iv. AẌuiq, *va* same as ii.
v. TaẌayyaq, *vp* of ii.

ΔCB

vi. TaẌâyaq, *vp* of iii.
vii. InẌâq, *vp* be distressed (as a ship). MonẌâq, distressed.

ذكي Δeci, Δeciey, sagacious.
Δecê, Δecêwa, sagacity.
EΛce', more sagacious.
LΛce', LΛci, *vn* be subtle, acute Σ. See Zeci.

ذل Idqar, *vn* slave, grovel.
Dâqur, an abject drudge.
Dauqasa, drudgery, pauperism.
iv. Adqus, *va* grind into pauperism.

دكج Deccouja, small jar, gallipot.

دقل Daqal, mast of ship Bs.

دقمق Doqmâq, mallet Λl; nutcracker B.

دكن Doccên 13, shop.

ذقن Δaqon 4, bearded chin.
Δiqn, old man Σ.

دقر Odqor, *va* brush against, touch in passing B.
vii. Indaqir ṣΛla', d°· B.
(2) Daqqir, *va* glut (the market) as in Polit. Econ.

ذكر Δecer 3, male.
Moseccer, masculine.
(2) OΛcor, *va* remember.
Δicr, remembrance.
Δicra, mention.
TeΛcira, memorandum, official document, ticket.

ΔCR

ii. Δeccir, iv. Eacir, ea remind.
iii. Δécir, ea commemorate.
Tiacér, a remembrance, *i.e.* a small gift x.; commemoration (of a saint) b. Also iv. Eacir, commemorate with culogy x.
Moaceccra, great calamity x. (memorable event).
vi. Teaécer, remember one another.
viii. Iaaccir, ea call to mind.
x. Isteacir, ea try to remember.
(2) Δecier, s. steel.
ii. Δeccir, ea sharpen.
Eacer, *adj.* sharper x.

دكش iii. Dùcix, ea barter.

دكز Idciz, ea nudge.

درّ Dorra, nu pearl, *also*, parrot.

ذرّ Δerra, nu atom, corpuscle.
Δiráricy, corpuscular.
Δorricya 11, seed, issue, posterity, (royal) line.

ضرّ Xörr, ea hurt.
Xarar, s. damage, harm.
Xúrr, Moxurr, hurtful.
(2) Xaroura, Xároura, constraint, necessity.
viii. Uxturr, ea constrain.
Uxturár, constraint.
Xarouricy, necessary.
(3) Xaricr, blind c.
Xarára, blindness c.

دور Dour, ea go round. *ger.*
Daur, circuit, circle in logic.

ΔRY

Dawâr, vortex.
Dâr, house, *pl.* Diyâr.
Dawwâret bewâ, weathercock.
Daurân, circulation, cycle.
Daura fil celâm, circumlocution.
Dauricy, moving round, circular (letter ?) circulatory; *also* alternate b.; but *qu.*
Dair 6, abbey.
Dâyira, 11, circle.
Medâr, period.
Modâr, pivot, tropic.
ii. Dawwir, ea turn round, move round; wind up (a watch).
Modawwar, *adj.* round.
iii. Modâwara, revolution.
iv. Adicr, ea manage, inspect. [*vulg.* Dier, ea turn, apply; as if in i. Dier bâlec, pay attention.]
Modicr, manager, rector.
x. Mostedicr, circular.
Iatidára, circumference.

درى Idri, ea know.
Diráya, knowledge.
iii. Dâri, ea tend, attend to.
(2) Midra' 11, [horn x.] boatpole. But see Miara ?
(3) Daráya, taffety.

ذرى ii. Δcrri, ea winnow.
v. Toaerrâ, *ep* of d°.
Miara', winnowing fan, paddle, hay fork.
(2) Δcrâ, s. shelter, a shed, a carthouse; protection.
Darâ, shelter b. (Δerâ ?)
Dorwa (Δorwa ?), a fire screen b.

ΔRY

(3) Δora, a species of millet. [Dorra, pearl.]
(4) Δirwa, Δorwa, tip, summit.

ضرى Δâri, *adj.* (a hound) trained to hunting; (a beast) which lives by hunting.
ii. Δarri, *va* train to hunting or war.

درع Dirs 3, 4, body-armour.
Dorrâsa, corslet of warrior, corset of woman.

ذرع Δirâs, *pl.* Earos, cubit, ell (from elbow to point of middle finger); skein (of thread) B.
Δers, compass of the arms.
iii. Δêris, *va* sell by the ell.
(2) Δeries, sudden (death) P. X.

ضرع Δarâsa, suppliancy.
v. Taδarras ila', *vn* supplicate.
(2) iii. Δâris li, *vn* be like to [*cf.* Greek, εἴκω, be like and yield].
Moδârus, similar; *also*, aorist of verb X.
(3) Δaries, periosteum (skin on the bone) o.

درب Darb 3, road.
(2) Darrib, train, drill, ply.

ذرب Δerib, sharp, keen; *fig.* keen of mind.
Δerb, paring knife of the leather-cutter X. [Δerab, *s.* flux B. X. Δerb el barn,

DRJ

diarrhœa. Perhaps rather zerab.]
ii. Δerrib, *va* sharpen X.

ضرب Uδrib, *va* beat, strike. *ger.* Δarb.
Δarba, a blow. [upon.
Yaδrib ila' *or* min, it verges
Uδrib, *rather* ii. Δarrib, *va* multiply in arithmetic.
Maδroub, multiplicand.
Δarb, multiplication in arithmetic (*also*, of animals?).
Δarrâb marêcib, pirate.
iii. Δârib, *va* job for another in stocks and purchases, for a commission; sell by retail.
vi. Teδârab, *vn* squabble.
viii. Uδtarib, *vp* be agitated in mind.
Uδturâb, agitation, disquiet.

دربند Darbend, mountain passc.

درد Dard, *s.* torment, grief o.
Dardi, *s.* poison B.

دردش Dardis, *va* prate, rant; stammer B.

درهم Dirhem 11, drachma; *pl.* money.

درج Odroj fie, insert, intercalate.
Madrouj fie, contained in (a writing). [drawer?
Dorj, roll of paper, portfolio;
Daraja, *nu* step, degree, grade.
viii. Indarij, *vp* be contained in (a treaty).

ƘRJ

ضرج ii. Ẋarrij, *va* encrimson.

دركوش Darkoux 11, peephole. See Tarxaqa.

ضرم Ẋurâm, conflagration.
Ẋarama, *sa* blazing brand.
iv. Aẋrim, *va* kindle up.
viii. Uẋrarim, *vn* flame up.

دركت Idric, *va* follow, pursue.
Dâric, a pursuer.
Darc, the police в. x.
Darec, a step; *fig.* consequence (of an action), evil consequence.
Darace, descending step c. (*esp.* figurative and moral.)
Dariece, quarry, animal pursued.
iii. Dâric, *va* overtake.
iv. Adric, *va* seize mentally, apprehend. [gence.
Idrâc, apprehension, intelli-
v. Tedarrec, viii. Iddaric, *vn* obviate.
vi. Tedârec, *va* anticipate, take precautions, bespeak (of a tradesman). [Fetch ʀ.]
Tedâroc, reparation x.
x. Istedric, *va* try to recover or repair, try to retrace; restrict and modify (what has been said.)
Istidrâc (in grammar), restriction; as by the particles, Lêcin, *but*; Bel, *nay but*.

دركل Darcil, *va* rock (a ship or cradle).

DRZ

ii. Tedarcel, *vn* tumble in sport; rock, as a ship.

درق Dorrâq, peaches.
Darâqin, a white peach c. [в.
(2) Dauraq 11, two handled jug

درس Odros, *va* tread grain, thresh, plod as a student.
ger. Dars, Dirâs, threshing.
Dars, Dirâse, studying x.
Daras 3, course of study.
Dorse, an exercise.
Daries, threshed grain?
ii. Darris, *v* teach as Professor.
Modarris, professor at a college.
Madres, Madrase, college, public school.
Midres, manual, class book.
Modarras, an exercised scholar.
iii. Dâris, *va* learn in class with.
Modâris, fellow disciple.
vi. Tedâres, *vn* study together.
(2) vii. Indaris, *vp* be effaced; *qu.* trodden out. *See* Indaθir.

ضرس Ẋurs 3, molar tooth, grinder.
Uẋras, *vn* have one's teeth on edge.
ii. Ẋarris, *va* gnaw, champ with the grinders, set the teeth on edge.
Moẋarres, notched as with teeth; *dentelé* as cloths.

درش Darwiex 11, dervish.

درز Darz, *s.* seam, suture.
Odroz, *va* sew together.

DS

دسّ Doss, *vn* glide in, intrigue.
   ger. Dass. Bil dass, secretly B.
Dâsous 12, emissary, spy.
Dasies 10, d° intriguer.
Dasse, an intrigue.
vii. Indiss, *vn* same as i.

دسدس Dasdis, *vn* (glide in darkness), grope c.
Dasdase, secrecy B.
Bil dasdase, covertly.

دوس Dous, *va* trample down;
   ger. Daus, Diyâse. *See* Odhos.
Dause, a trampling.
Medâse, threshing floor.
Midwas, a flail x. [Odros.
vii. Indas, *vp* of i. Compare

ديس Dayyous, cuckold.

دسم Dasem, *s.* fat, grease.
Dasim, greasy.
Dosouma, greasiness.
Adsem, very greasy, oily x.
ii. Dassim, *va* grease, add fatness to a dish.

دست Dost 3, stewpot.   [x.
(2) Daste, *Pers.* bundle of paper
(3) Dasteja 11, *Pers.* packet x.
(4) Destour 11, authority (hence, in some connections, permission); a charter.

ذت Δét, *pl.* Δewât, self, essence, pith (*masc.*), personage. *See* Δou.

WFY

دثر Idθer, *vn* be obsolete, neglected, rusty; *ger.* Doθour.
Daθir, *partic.* growing obsolete.
Daθour, lazy x.
vii. Indaθir, *vp* be effaced x.

دش Doxx, *va* crush B.
Daxdix, d°.

دش Tedaxxâ, *vn* belch B.

دشم Doxmân, enemy (*Turk*).

دشر ii. Daxxir, *va* cast off, discard, abandon B.
Daxâr, leavings, refuse B.

دشكت Diexêc, *s.* overcloth to saddle AL.

F

ف Fa, then, next.
Fie, *prep.* in (locally), concerning, upon.
Fouwa, *s.* madder.

وفى Wafa' Yafi, *va* fulfil, pay (a debt). *ger.* Wafâ.
ii. Waffi, iv. Aufi, d°
Wâfi, *adj.* complete r. plentiful B.
Wafiey, entire, full.
v. Tewaffâ, *vn* pay the debt of nature; die, depart.
Wafâya, decease, demise.
iii. Wâfi ila', *vn* come over to, join (a party).
Wâfi, *va* exact, extort.

WFY

x. Isteufi, *va* exact payment in full. Mosteufi, entire F.
Isticfâ, *ger.* full treatment of a subject.

نعل Ifɛal, *va* act, do. *ger.* Faɛl.
Fiɛl, Faɛûla, a deed.
Fâɛul, workman, *esp.* miner.
Faɛɛâl, efficient (person).
Fiɛlicy, effectual (measure).

نعم Ifɛam, *va* fill full.

نعش Ifɛax, *va* flatten.

نذ Faʑʑ 4, single, unique F.
Foaĉae⁸, singly, one by one.
v. Tefeʑʑeʑ, *vn* remain isolated.
x. Isteflʑʑ, *va* claim for one's single self x.

نض Foʑʑ *va* break off, splinter off. *ger.* Faʑʑ.
Faʑuiʑ, broken to bits x.
Fuʑâʑ, splintered pieces.
vii. Infuʑʑ, *vp* be splintered.
(2) Fuʑʑa, silver.
Faʑʑuiy, made of silver.
ii. Faʑʑu, *va* plate with silver, bedeck with silver, adorn.

وفد Wafod Yafid, *vn* arrive. *ger.* Wafd.
Wofoud, arrival (of envoy?)
Wafiod 6, envoy.
iv. Aufid, *va* send as envoy.

نود Fawâd, *pl.* 8, Afyida, vitals, πραπίδες, *fig.* heart, mind.

FAII

نوض ii. Fawwuʑ, *va* entrust (a person) with.
Mofawwaʑ, a commissary.
vi. Tefûwaʑ, *vn* settle terms together.

نيد Fâyida 12, advantage, profit (in trade); *also*, interest of money. *But see* Fâyiʑa.
iv. Afiod, *va* profit; *fig.* instruct, inform.
Ifâda, giving of advantage.
Mofied, profitable, instructive.
x. Istefied, *va* gain profit.

نيض Fieʑ, *vn* overflow, redound. *ger.* Faiʑ.
Fâyiʑ, redundant. [money.
Fâyiʑa, surplus, interest of
Fâyyâʑ, profuse.
iv. Afieʑ, *va* flood, spill? *fig.* disclose a secret.
Moficʑ, lavish.
Ifâʑa, overflow.

ندي Fidâ, Fidya, *s.* ransom.
Fâdi, Redeemer.
Ifdi, *va* redeem.

نضا Faʑâ, open field.
Foʑöa, spaciousness.
iv. Afʑu ila', *vn* open the way to, conduce to.

نح Faʑâʑla, Faʑuiʑla, an outrage, contumely.
Faʑuiʑl, *adj.* outraged.
Foʑʑâʑl, Mofʑuʑl, outrageous (person).
ii. Faʑʑuʑl, *va* outrage.

FAL

فضل Offôl, *vn* remain as surplus; *ger.* Fadl, superfluity, superiority. *In argument*, Fadlan, much more then; Fadlan ᵹan en, much less.
Faḍala 2, remainder, surplus.
ii. Faḍḍul, *vs* leave as surplus.
Faḍoul, exuberant.
Fâḍul, Faḍuil, excellent.
Faḍuila, excellence, virtue, (his) Excellency.
Foḍöul, superfluity? [tinent.
Foḍöuliey, meddlesome, impertinent.
Foḍöuliëya, impertinence.
v. Tefaḍḍal, *vn* (*conventional phrase*) do the favour of; be so kind as to —

فدم Faidam, *s.* a mason, plumb-line B.

فدن Fadân, Faddân, a plough with yoke of oxen.

فيف Faifâ 11, extensive desert.

فقل Foufal, cocoanut.

نفش Fâfoux, chink, crevice B.

نغفور Faɣfour, china (ware); Emperor of China.

فح Faḥḥ, *vn* hiss. *ger.* Faḥḥîḥ, Fuḥâḥ.

فاخ Fâh, swelling of a gland.

فوح Fouḥ, *vn* be fragrant, *ger.* Fauḥ. Fâyiḥ, fragrant.

FHS

Fâyiḥa, fragrance.
iv. Afieḥ, *vs* diffuse odour.

فحوى Faḥwa', signification, argument; substance, general sense (of a document).

فهد Fahed, Fahd 3, the lynx.

فحج Faḥuij, frisky B. *sémillant*.

فحل Faḥl 3, 5, male. *s.* a stallion.

فهم Ifhem, *vs* understand.
Fehm, *s.* understanding.
Fehiem, intelligent.
ii. Fahhim, iv. Efhim, *vs* cause to understand; Efhim-ni, explain to me.
v. Tefehhem, *vs* understand gradually.
viii. Iftehim, same as i.
x. Istefhim, *vn* inquire.

فحم Faḥm, charcoal, coal.
Faḥma, *nu.*
Faḥuim, coal black.

فجر Ifḥar, *vs* notch B. excavate.
Faḥḥâr, sculptor.

فهرس Fihris, Fihrise 11, index to a book.

فحص Faḥṣ, inquisition.
Fâḥuṣ, inquisitor.
Ifḥaṣ, *vs* mine; search into. Compare μεταλλᾶν.

FΠΘ

فحست Ifhâθ, vn inquire, search.
viii. Ifteθuθ, dº

فحش Faθx, foulness, monstrosity.
Fâθux, foul, monstrous.
Faθθâx, dº
Faθxiya, an enormity.
Fâθuxa, an impure woman.

فج Fajj, a. unripe, lit. or fig.
Fojâja, unripeness.
(2) Fajj 5, a secret corner, cranny. Min coll¹ fajj el mediena, from every corner of the city. Coll° ʌie fajj samieq, all who come from deep corners s.
(3) Afajj, Mofâjj, bandy-legged (with toes turned out too much x.). See Faxxik.
Fajja, interval (of legs) x.

فجا Fajâ', Fajâ'a, happening unexpectedly. adj. sudden s.
Fojâ'a, a sudden surprize.
Fojâyiey, unforeseen, sudden.
iii. Fâji, va catch by surprise, catch in an act s.

فج Fauj 4, a troop, legion.
(2) Fauja, a stroke in swimming (modern?). See Afajj, Fajja.

فجل Fijl, Fijla, s radish.

فجر Fajr, dawn of day.
(2) Fojra, bed of a torrent, gill.

FWL

Mafjara 11, dº
(3) Fâjir, Fajour, audacious in bravery, audacious in wickedness. Reckless; a dare devil, foolhardy s. Also perverse s.
Fajara, a bouncing lie.
(4) ii. Fajjir or Fanjir el sōyoun, fix the eyes, stare (at).

فك Fakk 5, a snare.
(2) Fakfik, va flaunt? [vn show oneself off x.]

فخم Fakiem, mighty, grand.
Fikâma, high mightiness.
Faikamân, hetman (of a tribe), president (of a republic).

فخر Fakkâr, potter's clay (see Farfour).
Fakkâriey, seller of pots.
(2) Fakr, Fakar, splendour.
Fakâr, glory, éclat.
Fâkir, splendid. [tious.
Fikkier, vainglorious, ostentaFakrânieya, state of glory, beatitude.
ii. Fakkir sala', va glorify (one) above (another).
iii. Fâkir, va vie in glory with x.
v. Tefakkar, vn assume vainglorious airs.
vi. Tefâkar, vn mutually vie in glory x.
viii. Iftekir, vn pride oneself.
Iftikâr, ostentation.

فأل Fê'l, s. omen.

فول Foul, broad beans.

FLF

فلفل Filfil, Fulfol, pepper.
Falfil, *va* pepper.

فلو Falou, a foal.

فلع Falas, *ger.* splitting, cleaving.
Iflas *or* ii. Fallis, *va* split up.
Fils 3, a crack, chap.
(2) Fâlis, *adj.* contrary (wind) s.

فلق Fall 3, cleft in a rock, chap in the foot.
Iflall, *va* cleave (the soil).
Falâlla, agriculture.
Fellâll, a ploughman, peasant.
(3) Felâll, Falall, prosperity.
Moflill, prosperous.
iv. Aflill, be prosperous.
x. Isteflill, come off safe x.

فلس Fellss, niggardly c.

فلذ Filze, *nu* 4, piece (of metal).
Foulâs, Boulâs, *vulg.* Boulâd, steel (from Pers. poulâd x.).

فلج Fâlij, the palsy.
Mefiouj, paralyzed.
[(2) In x. also: Falj, victory, success. Falaj, interval, interstice. Follouja, ploughed land. But see the root Fill. c. has: Falj, *ger.* separating. Falaj, tears.]

فلن Folân, such or such a one.

فلك Felec, *s.* vault of heaven.
Falesiey, *adj.* celestial.

FLT

(2) Folo 10, statebarge, yacht.
Filouca, cutter, felucca.

فلتى Falaq 3, fissure; stocks, pillory c.
Iflaq, *va* split.
ii. Falliq, d° intensively.
v. Tefallaq, vii. Infeliq, *op* of i.

فلس Fils 2, scale of a fish; para (small coin).
Folous, *pl.* small money.
(2) Felas, indigence.
iv. Aflis, *en* (be stript, scaled?) be bankrupt.
Felâse, bankruptcy.
(3) Tefelles, *vn* straddle.

فلسف Filsefe (*Greek*), philosophy. Filsouf, philosopher.
Filsefiey, philosophic.

فلست Filistiey, Philistine.
Filistien, Palestine.

فلت Fâlit, *adj.* run away (horse), *said in praise*, a scamperer; *also* a libertine, a scamp. [lous.
Falétiey, libertine, unscrupu-
Falte 2, a slip, a word or deed that has slipped from one.
iv. Aflit, *va* let slip (an incautious word or deed).
vii. Infulit, *vn* slip out, drop from one; as a word ill-considered.

فلط Felrull, *va* broaden = Farrull.

FLT

فلطس Tafelṭas, *vn* be broad and flat.

فم Fomm 4, mouth.
Fommiey, Femmawiey, oral.

فن Fenn 3, art, high art.
ii. Fennin, *va* assort? classify? Motefennin, various in tone, chromatic (as music).

فني Ifni, *vn* pass away, vanish.
Fanâ, evanescence.
Fâni, vanishing, transitory.
iv. Afni, *va* annihilate.

فند Fanda 3, spar (of ship) ON.

فندل Fandil, *va* debauch B.
Findâl, debauchery, dissipation.
Mofandal, debauched.

فندق Fondoq (*Gr.*), hotel.
(2) Fondoq = Bondoq, filberts.

فنجن Finjân 11, coffee cup.

فنجر Fanjir, *va* expand and fix (the eyes). *See* Fajjir.

فنك Fenec 4, Egyptian rabbit.

فنس Fânous 12 (*Gr.*), lantern.

فنطس Finṭuise 11, snout.

فك Fecc 4, jaw, cheekbone.
(2) Focc, *va* undo, pull out.
ii. Feccic, *va intens.* detach.
vii. Inficc. *vp* of i.

FQ

Fecce, laxity? ease?
[B. renders *Commod*... rافla; fichi fecce...

وفق Wafaq Yafiq, *vn* fit in.
ii. Waffiq, *va* adapt, adjust.
iii. Wâfiq, *va* adapt oneself to (a person); suit (him).
iv. Aufiq, *va* same as ii.
v. Tewaffaq, *vn* succeed, prosper.
vi. Tewâfaq, *vr* match, suit one another, accord.
Motewâfiq, consistent.
viii. Ittefiq, *vn* coincide, happen, concur. [incidence.
Ittifâq, *s.* accident, chance, co-Wofq, *s.* opportunity.
Wafieq, *s.* counterpart, match.
Aufaq, more conformable.
Teufieq, (divine) adjustment, wise government.
Ṣala' wifâq, Teufieqa" li, in accordance with.
Tewaffoq, *s.* success.
Tewâfoq, *s.* accord. [(wind).
Mowâfiq, suitable, favourable
Mowâfaqa, congruity.

فوق Fauq, *prep.* above.
Fowaiq, *adv.* a little above.
Fauqâni, *adj.* upper.
Foug, *vn* exceed, surpass, excel.
Fâyiq, superior.
iv. Afieq, *vn* recover (health or sobriety) K.
Ifâqa, recovery B. F.

فيق (*modern*) Fieq, *vn* wake, get up.
ii. Fayyiq, iv. Afieq, *va* awaken.

F

فق Ifqa', Ifqac, va burst; a abscess; also va burst.
ii. Faqqus, Farqi, va burst.
vii. Infaqic, vp bo burst.
Faqsa, crack, crevice. [B. X.
Faqqâsa 11, bubble (on water)
(2) Foqâsa, barley water.

فكة Fecieh, pleasant (amœnus).
Focéhe, amenity.
Feciehe, pleasantry.
iii. Fêcih, va banter (a person).
vi. Tefêceb, vr be mutually jocose.
Ofcouhe 11, matter of pleasantry.
(2) Fêciho 12, table fruit.
Fêcihêni, fruiterer B.

فكل Ifcell, va tread down (a shoe) B.

فقة Fiqh, skill in sacred law.
Faqieh, doctor in theology.

فكر Ficr 4, Ficra 10, thought.
Fecour, Motefeccir, pensive.
Ifcir fie, va think upon.
v. Tefeccer, va meditate.
viii. Iftecir fie, dᵃ·
Ifticêr, reflection, reverie.

فقر Faqr, poverty.
Faqier 6, poor, *fakeer*.
Afqar, poorer.
iv. Afqir, va impoverish.
(2) Fiqra 10, vertebra.
Faqâra, nu. dᵃ·

FRS

نفق Ifqis, va burst, be hatched, fall in pieces, fall in a heap, die.
iv. Afqis, va hatch (an egg).
(2) Faqsên, out of humour B.
(3) Faqous, Faqqous, Syrian melon.

فر Firr, va flee. ger. Firâr, flight, escape.
iv. Afirr, va put to flight.•
vi. Tefârr, va disperse in flight.
Farrâr, a fugitive, a runaway.

وفر Wafar Yafir, va abound.
Wâfir, abundant.
Aufar, more abundant.
Wofour, abundance.
viii. Ittefir, va be numerous.
(2) Wafra, s. lock of hair r.

فور Four, va boil, bubble. ger. Faur. [bubbles.
Fawwâr, gushing up with
Fawwâra, *jet d'eau*, artificial fountain that throws up water.
(2) Fâra, nu. a mouse; a carpenter's plane.
Fowaiyar, little mouse.

فرو Forwa, a fur, furcloak.
Farrâ, a furrier.

فرع Fars 3, branch, top-branch; ramification.
Farsa 4, top of mountain c.
Farsuiy, derivative.
ii. Farrus, va ramify, derive, deduce.
Tefries, development.

FRS

v. Tefarraɛ, ʋn ʋp be ramified, wide-spread; be deduced, branch out.
x. Iɛtefruɛ, ʋa commence x.

فرعن Farɛaun, Pharaoh, tyrant.
Farɛana, craft, perfidy.
Tefarɛan, ʋn act the tyrant.

فرد Farad, single.
Fard furd, singly o.
Faried, singular, unique.
Farieda", singularly.
Fordân, unique.
Fardânieyn, singularity, unity.
Fârid, solitary.
Ofrod, ʋa unwind (silk from a ball) ɴ.
Ifrid, ʋa smooth a garment, take out creases, make it uni (as the French say).
ii. Farrid, ʋa set apart, separate, disband. Mofarrad, separated x.
iv. Afrid, ʋa single out.
Mofrid, simple, not compound; opposed to Morececb x.
Mofrad, singular (in grammar).
Mofrida 2, a simple (herb).
Mofridêt, simples, herbs.
Mofrâd 11, private domain of the prince.
v. Tefarrad, ʋn isolate oneself.
Tefarrod, isolation, singularity.
vii. Infarid, ʋp be isolated, sequestered.
Infirâd, isolation.
Infirâdaⁿ, especially. [tered.
Monfarid, single, alone, seques-
(2) Farieda 11, large pearl. (*Lat.* unio).

FRΓ

Farrâd, dealer in pea s.
(3) Farda, a bale; ʼ *Europ.*?
φόρτος. *See* Forɖa.

فرض Furɖ 5, *grr.* notching, a notch; sacred precept, code.
ii. Farriɖ, ʋa notch; mark out, enact a code.
Mafrouɖ, marked out, obligatory, prescribed.
Farɖa, impost, land tax (Egypt).
Farɖuiy, obligatory [nominal o.]
Faricɖa 11, divine precept.
iv. Afruɖ, ʋa proscribe by law.
viii. Ifteruɖ, ʋa receive one's appointed pay.
(2) Forɖa, *s.* port, harbour, *Europ.*?

فردس Fardaus, Paradise, *Pers.*

فرفر Firfier, purple.

فرفت Farfit, ʋa moulder; a variety of Fetfit. See Fott.

فرغ Ifraɣ min, ʋ leave off from, finish.
ii. Farriɣ, ʋa empty.
iv. Afriɣ, ʋa pour out, shed (blood), pour into a mould.
v. Tefarraɣ, ʋn be at leisure.
x. Iɛtefriɣ, ʋn reach to vomit.
Fâriɣ, Fâriɣ, empty, at leisure.
Farâɣ, Farâɣa, cessation, leisure.
Fariɣ, empty (land), void.
Firâɣ 8, large skin x.; large vessel ɴ.
Ifrâɣ, fount, foundry of metal.

FRH

فرح Ifrah, *vn* be lively, witty, spirited. [mettlesome.
Farih, Fârih, lively, witty,
Farâhe, Forouhe, liveliness, mettle.

فرح Ifrafl, *vn* rejoice; *ger.*
Farafl, gladness.
Faraflan, gladly.
Forfla, a gratuity.
Farifl, Farflûn, glad.
Mifrafl, very glad.
iv. Afrifl, *va* gladden.

فرحد Farhid, *va* overtask b. *vn* overwork oneself b.

فرج Farj 3, the fork of the body (in either sex). Bocthor gives Farj for *sex*. [At Aleppo the word was thought inadmissible in conversation.]
(2) Farrouj 11, domestic fowl.
Farrouja, young hen.
(3) Farij, *adj.* airy (place) b. at ease, free from care.
Farja, diversion, pleasant sight.
Forja, Forouj, Faraj, dissipation of cares, ease, relief of heart.
Forja, a curiosity, an interesting sight.
iv. Afrij min, *va* relieve (the heart) from.
v. Tefarraj, *vn* divert oneself, take one's ease, see pleasant sights.
[Farj, it seems, must mean divarication; hence, diversion.]

فرخ Fark 3, sucker, young bird.

FRQ

ii. Farrik, iv. Afrik, *va* sprout, have young.
Mofrika, hatching place.

فرم Ofrom, *va* hash, mince.
(2) Farmân 13, *Pers.* diploma of prince.

فرن Forn 4 (*Lat.* Furnus), oven for bread, or for hatching chickens.
Farrân, master of oven, baker.
Fârina, *s.* bakery x.

فرنك Franc, francs, French coin.

فرنسى Fransê, France.
Fransêwi, French.
[But Franji, Afranji, Frank, *i.e.* European.]

فرك Ofroc, *va* crumble between the fingers, grate.

فرق Ofroq, *va* part, separate, *ger.* Farq, separation, difference.
Fâriq, *adj.* distinguishing o.
Farieq 10, portion, quota part [*also*, Farieq, vice-admiral of Turks.]
Firqa 10, a band, troop.
Forqa, separation of friends?
Mafraq, parting of roads c.
ii. Farriq, *va* separate, distribute, disperse.
Tefriqa, absorption of mind (in things invisible).

FRQ

Tefrieq, division (of money), instalment, *pl.* 11.
Fâriq, *va* part with.
Firâq, departure, separation.
v. Tefarraq, vii. Infariq, or viii. Ifteriq, *vp* be parted. *san*, from (a place).

نرع Farqis, *va* burst (intensive?) See Faqqus.

نرس Faras 3, 9, a mare.
Foraise, a filly.
Fâris 9, 12, a horseman. [art. Forouse, horsemanship, groom's (2) Fâris, *Persis* proper. Forsi, a Persian, *pl.* Fors. Fârisiey, *adj.* Persian. Fârisieya, the Persian tongue. [But Fariesiey, Pharisee.]
(3) Firâse, talent, sagacity, skill in physiognomy.
v. Tefarres, *va* survey, reconnoitre. [*See* Ifriz.]
(4) Farics, *pl.* Farse', rent, or devoured by a wild beast.
Foriese, prey, killed game.
viii. Ifteris, *va* rend the prey, tear asunder, devour.

نرص Forsa 10, occasion, opportunity.
iv. Afros, *va* present an opportunity to x.
viii. Ifterus, *vn* seize an opportunity *v*.

نرسخ Farsek 11, *Pers.* parasang, league, 3 or 4 miles.

FRX

نرت Forâ¹, the Euphrates.
Mâ forât, sweet water B. K. *pl.* miyâh fortên.

نرط Ofrot, *va* surpass.
iii. Fârit, *va* overmatch.
Ifrât, excess.
Bil ifrât, in excess.
iv. Afrot fie, bi, be excessive in.
Afrat bil bocê, he wept much.
Mofrat, excessive.
v. Tefarrat, vi. Tefârat, *vn* surpass, exceed, excel.

نرطح Farrufl, Faltufl, *va* broaden, widen.

نرتق ii. Tefartaq, *vn* crash, break with noise.

نرش Farx 3, bed, carpet, mat.
Firâx 10, bed, mattress.
Farrâx, upholsterer.
Fariex, *fem.* lying in, brought to bed.
Ofrox, *va* spread out (carpet, bedding).
ii. Farrix, carpet (the soil), as do grasses and crops.
Mafroux, *stratus*, paved x.
Mafrouxêt, *pl.* carpets.
viii. Ifterix, *vp* of i.
(2) Farâxa, *nu* a butterfly.

نرشخ Farxik, *vn* spread the legs in sitting as a tailor, or in striding.
ii. Tefarxak, *vn* stride in walking, straddle. See Ifsell.

FRZ

فرز Ifriz, Ofroz, *va* or iv. Afriz, *va* discriminate, select.
Fâriz, discriminating, distinct, lucid. [ence.
Firze, a point of marked differ-
ii. Farriz cala', *v.* decide upon.
viii. Ifteriz, *vn* come to a decision, determine, resolve.
(2) Ifriez, *s.* the frieze in architecture, copings.

فرزن Farzin, *va* survey, reconnoitre, scan.
(2) Firzên, *Pers.* queen in game of chess.

نس Fiaflae 11, a bug.

فس Fozz 10, 3, mass, fragment, wedge (of rock).
Fozz, *va* detach, shiver off. *vn* suppurate, break up.
ii. Fazzuz, *va* shell (beans) B.
iv. Afuzz, *va* detach, shiver off.
vii. Infuzz, *vp* of i.
viii. Iftuzz, *va* same as iv.?

فاس Fê's 3 (*i.e. pl.* Fo'ous), pickaxe, axe.

نصع Afvac, lame in the foot.
Mafvöuc, lamed.

نسد Ifsed, *vn* be spoiled.
Fésid, vicious. [affection.
Fesêd, corruption, vice, dis-
ii. Fassid, iv. Afsid, *va* spoil, corrupt, spread disaffection.
Mafsoda 11, germ of corruption.

FSK

Mofsid, *adj.* depraving.
(2) Fésid, a chimera B.

نصد Ifsud, *v.* open a vein. *ger.* Fasd.
Fazzâd, a bleeder.
Mifsad, a lancet.
Fasuid, Mefvöud, *adj.* bled.
viii. Iftavud, *va* bleed (a patient).

فسح Ifscfl, *vn* be spacious; [stride in walking x.; see Farsik]. *ger.* Fesfl.
Fesiefl, spacious.
Fosfla, amplitude; latitude of action, liberty.
ii. Fassifl, *va* accommodate with space, give room and ease to.
iv. Afsifl, *va* d⁰
v. Tefessefl, *vn* expatiate, *i.e.* take a stroll; find elbow-room, be comfortable.
viii. Infesifl, *vp* be expanded or wide open.

نصح Ifvafl, *vn* be clear of speech, lucid.
Favuifl, lucid, clear of speech.
Afvafl, more lucid.
Favâfla, lucidity.
iv. Afvufl, *va* express clearly.
v. Tefavvafl, *vn* express oneself clearly, be a lucid speaker.
(2) Favfl, Pascha, passover *Hebr.* Easter.

نسخ Ifsek, *va* undo, dissolve, annul, dislocate. *ger.* Fesk.
Fesiek, broken up, roasted to a rag.

FSK

iv. Afsik, *va* forget x.
v. Tefcæsck, *va* break up, be dissolved.
vii. Infesik, *vp* of i.
Monfesik, dissolved, undone, annulled.
(2) Fasiek, *s.* herring.

فسل Ofsol, *va* wean (a child).
Fesicl, weaned child.
Fesicle 11, sapling transplanted.

فصل Ifsul, *va* separate, decide. *ger.* Fayl.
Fayl 3, division, section (of book), portion (of year).
Fâsul, decisive.
ii. Fassul, *va* cut up (as butcher), cut out (as tailor); detail.
Tefsuil 11, detail.
Bil tefsuil, Tefsuîla", in detail.
iii. Fâsul, *va* break up alliance with. [from.
vii. Infasul *san*, *vp* be separated
Mafsul 11, hinge, joint (of the body).
(2) Fasuil 9, interior wall of a city x. (*separating* wall ? curtain ?) barbican B. C.

فستن Efsentien, *s.* wormwood, αψίνθιον.

فسق Ifsiq, *va* be dissolute; *ger.* Fisq, libertinism.
Fesiq, Fêsiq, dissolute.
Fissicq, very profligate.

فسر Ofsor, *va* bring to light, clear up, explain. *ger.* Fesr.

FTW

ii. Fessir, *va* expound, paraphrase (the Koran).
Tefsier, exposition. [from.
x. Istefsir, *va* ask explanation

فستن Fistên, petticoat.

فسطاط Fostât 11, hair tent.

فستق Fistaq, pistachio nuts.
Fistaqicy, of bright green.

فت Fott, *va* crumble. *ger.* Fett.
Fitte 5, 10, crumb, small piece.
ii. Fettit, *va* intens. of i.
v. Tefettet, vii. Infitt, *vp* of i.
Fetfit, Farfit, *va* intensive of i. crumble, moulder.

فوت Fout, *vn* pass; *esp.* pass in, enter. Fât ila' sandob, he entered his house; also *va* pass by, omit, pass beyond, go past.
Faut 4, interstice, interval x.
Fowait, small interval x.
ii. Fawwit, *va* cause to pass, lead, conduct.
iii. Fâwit, *va* surpass, go beyond.
v. Tefawwat sala', *v.* surpass, excel (some one).
vi. Tefâwat, *vn* be mutually separated by an interval.
Tefâwot, interval, odds between two persons (defect x.).

فتو Fetwa', a religious decree or verdict.
Mofti, grand judge.
iv. Afti, *va* pronounce upon (a

FTW

religious question), enlighten a person upon (fle).
x. Iſteſti, *va* solicit a decision.
Iſtiflê, solemn consultation.
(2) Fete', *pl.* 9, Fityân, young man (a word of some honour).
Fetêya 2, young woman.
Feticy, adult (man or beast).
Afle', younger; having more of youthful (generous) qualities.
Fetê, adolescence.
Fotouwa, full age, youthful generosity.

نفح Iſteñ, *va* open. *ger.* Fetñ 3.
— conquer (a fortress).
— sala', reveal to, inspire.
Fêtiñ, Fettêñ, a conqueror.
Fetêña, conquest.
Fotouñ, d° c. inspiration.
Fêtiña, exordium, prologue.
Fatouñ, having open eyelids c.
Mifteñ 11, key. [roominess?
Moſteñuya, house room c. *i.e.*
vii. Infetiñ, *ep* of i.
viii. Iſtetiñ, *va fig.* open an affair, commence.
Iſtitâñ, inauguration.
x. Iſtiftiñ, *v.* seek to begin traffickings, open the market, make overtures.
Iſtiftâñ, overture.

نفخ Oftouka 11, bulb of a plant.

نتل Iſtil, *va* twist (rope). *ger.* Fetl.
q 11, a wick.
ol to twist rope.

FTR

نطم Ifrum, *va* wean (a child). *ger.* Farm c. Furâm x.
Faruim, weaned. *See* Fesiel.

نتن Iftin, *va* tempt, seduce, *esp.* to mutiny and revolt. *ger.* Fetn.
ii. Fettin, *va* d° intensive.
Fêtin, Fettên, tempter, stirrer of sedition, turbulent.
Fitna, seduction to mutiny, sedition.
viii. Iſtetin, *ep* of i.
Meftoun, mad with love c.

نطن Ofrön, *va* understand. *ger.* Farn [in high style?].
Ifran, *vn* be prudent. *ger.* Forôuna.
Fârun, Farun, Faruin, prudent.
Farâna, Forôuna, prudence.
ii. Farrun, *va* or iv. Afrun, *va* cause to understand, in-sense (a person), as the Irish say.

نتك Oftoc, *va or with* bi, attack unawares. *ger.* Fetc.
Fêtic, assailant, robber, daring in assault.
Eftec, rasher in assault.

نتق Oftoq, *va* rip up (sewing). *ger.* Fetq.

نتر Oftor, be lukewarm, *lit.* or *fig. ger.* Fotour, lukewarmness, languor.
Fêtir, tepid, languid.
Fetra, interval between two prophets; hence, interregnum.

FTR

iv. Aftir, *va* make languid, damp (another's) spirit.
(2) Féloura, an invoice c.

فطر Oftör, *va* knead, mould, create. *ger.* Fatr.
El Fâtur, the Creator.
Futr, creatures.
Futra, nature, mould, character.
Fatuir, dough.
Fatuira, a tart, a pie?
Faröurât, pastry.
Fatâturicy, a pastrycook.
(2) Forour, *s.* breakfast AL
iv. Aftur, *vn* breakfast. *ger.* Futâr, breaking of fast — Terayyoq Bz.

فتش ii. Fettix, *va* seek, hunt for (much used at Aleppo).

فش Faxx, *va* cause (air) to explode, smooth down (what is swollen), dissipate (grief).
ii. Faxxix, *va* dissipate (a tumour).

نيش Faixa, *nu* an ivory counter B.

فشى Fâxi, divulged, spreading (as rumour).   [Foxou.
Ofxou, *vn* be divulged. *ger.*
iv. Afxi, *va* divulge.
v. Tefexxâ, *vn* spread, as report or disease.

نشل Faxil 4, 10, lazy, languid, droop.   [Faxal.
Ifxal, *vn* droop, languish. *ger.*
Faxla, withered arm.

ΓWY

Afxal, crippled in the arm.
iv. Afxil, *va* wither.

فشق Faxaq, evil jollity x. See Fisq.

فوز Fouz bi, *vn* win, gain, succeed in. *ger.* Fauz, success.
Lem afouz bi aêlic, I did not succeed in it.
(2) Mafêze, *pl.* Mafâwiz, desert without water v. x. aleppo.

فزر Fizra, a rent, tear x.
Fozir, *vp* is burst, torn B.
iv. Afzir, *va* rend B.
v. Tefezzer, *vn* tear, yield, as an old garment (B. So Fendre, S'ouvrir.)

Γ

غى Γâya 2, end, purpose; extremeness, extremity. Also, *pl.* Γây.

وغى Waγa', *s.* tumult, clamour, as of army.

غوى Iγwi, *vn* go astray; *ger.* Γawa' o.
Γâwi, Γawioy, misled, astray.
Γaiy, Γayγân, d°
Γieγa 2, a caprice.
Γaiγa, error, wrong road.
Oγwiγa 11, Miγwâγa, entrap wild beasts.
ii. Γawwi, iv. Aγwi.
vii. Inγawi,

ΓB

غب Γibb, *prep.* after.
Γibbaⁿ, at intervals, seldom.
(2) Γobba, trough of the sea [open sea?].

غيب Γieb, *rn* be absent.
Γaib, absence, invisibility.
Γaiba, Γiyâb, absence.
Γayoub, Γaibiey, invisible.
Γaibouba, disappearance.
viii. Iɽtêb, *va* backbite s.
(2) Γâba, *nu* thicket, jungle.
Also, socket of candlestick.

غبو Oɽbou, *rn* be stupid.
Γabâwa, stupidity.
Γabi(ey), stupid, brutal.
v. Teɽâbâ, *ra* overlook, not see.
Γabou, lowering sky.
Moɽbi, heavy with rain.

غبن Oɽbon, Iɽbin, *ra* outwit;
ger. l'abn, Γaban.
ii. Γabbin, iv. Aɽbin, as i.
Γobn, fraud, trickery; *also,* displeasure B.
vii. Inɽabin mac, misunderstand one another, quarrel.
Monɽabin, displeased B.
(2) Maɽbin, the groin.

غبر Γabra, Γabara, Γobra, Γobâr, dust.
Oɽbor, *rn* be dusty; *ger.* Γobour.
Aɽbar, of the colour of dust, whity brown. [x.
) Γâbir, future (in grammar)

غ ، ، tan, tawny, dirty
اغبس ، ،

ΓYΔ

Iɽbes, *rn* be dusky, tawny.
ix. Iɽbiss, *rn* grow tawny.

غبط Iɽbuᴛ, *ra* count happy.
ger. Γabᴛ.
Maɽbouᴛ, happy, blessed.
Γibra, blessedness. Γibratoh, his blessed Reverence, title of Patriarch.
Maɽbaᴛa, rich (soil).
iv. Aɽbuᴛ, *va* bless, enrich (the soil) x.

غمش ii. Γabbix el sain, *ra* dazzle the eye B. *See* Γaᴛmix.
vii. Inɽabix, *vp* be dazzled.

غد Γodda 10, morbid node, bubo, hard tumour.
Γodadiey, nodular.

غضى Γaλδ 5, fresh B. c. full of sap and vigour (Γarieδ.).
Γaλâδa, Γoδüuλa, freshness.
Iɽaλδ, *rn* be fresh.

وغد Waɽd, servile.
iii. Wâɽid, *ra* imitate servilely.

غيد [Perhaps not in modern use at all.]
Γayad, suppleness.
Γâyid, flexible, buxom.
Aɽyad, more supple.
Γaidân, tender youth.
Γâda, flexible twig. So x.

غيض Γaiλa 5, a wood, holt.
Compare Γaiᴛ.
(2) غاض he disobliged c. (*sic.*)

ΓDW

غَدْوٍ Γad, Γadwa, Γadouwa, the morrow, the morning.
Γadaⁿ, on the morrow.
Γadû, pl. 8, Aγdiya, early meal, i.e. midday dinner.
Γâdi, matutinal x.
v. Teγaddâ, vn dine.

غِذَاء Γiθê, nourishment.
ii. Γassi, iv. Aγsi, va nourish.
Moγsi, nourishing (food).
v. Teγassê, vr nourish oneself.

غِضَ iv. Aγδu sala', vn close the eye against, avoid to see.

غَضَب Γaδab, rage, wrath.
Γaδabaⁿ, in rage.
Γaδub, Γaδbân, wrathful.
Γaδoub, passionate.
Iγδab, vn be wrathful, sala', li.
iii. Γâδub, va dº only with accus. of person x.
iv. Aγδub, va enrage.

غَضَن Γaδn 3, wrinkle. [face.
v. Teγaδδan, vn be wrinkled in

غَدَر Iγdir, vn remain behind. ger. Γadr.
Γidra, residuum. [run.
iv. Aγdir, vs leave behind, out-
(2) Oγdor, va abandon, leave in the lurch, betray. ger. Γadarân.
Γodra, perfidy.
Γaddâr, Γiddier, perfidious.
(3) Γadiar 10, 9, 8, pond.

ΓL

غَفَّ Γoff, va mod. t. overreach, catch in argument, captivate, ingratiate oneself with B.

غَفِي Iγfi, vn doze, be sleepy.
Γafya, a nap.

غَفَل Oγfol, va neglect. ger. Γofoul.
Γâfil, Γafoul, neglectful.
Γafla, a blunder.
Γafal, negligence.
v. Teγaffal, same as i.
vi. Teγâfal, pretend inobservance, ignore.

غَفَر Oγfor, va forgive. ger. Γofrân. viii. Iγtefir, dº.
Γafour, prone to forgive, indulgent.
Γafiera, indulgent temper x.
Maγfira, forgiveness.
(2) Γafur, protection, body guard = Kafur.
(3) Γafier, all, many c.

غَوْغ Γauγa, uproar, brawl, tumult (modern). See Γauxa, Joxxa.

غَلّ Γoll, Γalal, extreme thirst.
Γall, vn thirst for vengeance.
Γaliel, exhausted, worn out.
Γaliel, s. a yearning.
Γallân, Moγtill, Maγloul, thirsty.
(2) Γill, s. spite.
(3) Γalla 2, 4, crop of corn.
Γaliel, fertile (land) B. [crops
Moγall 2, Mosteγill 2, year
x. Isteγill, va gather the crop

ΓL

(4) Γoll 4, iron collar, fetter s.
Γoll, va fetter s.
Maγloul, fettered. [B.
(5) Γilála, tunic, pellicule, film

غل Waγul Yaγil fie, vn penetrate into.
iv. Anγil, va cause to penetrate, carry (water) in pipes. See Welij, Aulij.

غال Γâl 2, (European) fixed lock; opposed to Qofl, padlock.

غول Γoul 9, demon, fiend, cannibal.
Γâγil, invasive, suddenly bursting on one.
Γâγila 12, an outburst.
viii. Iγtêl, va carry off suddenly.
Iγtiyâl, sudden invasion and carrying away.

غلو Γolou, extravagance, exaggeration.
Γalâwa, dearness, high price.
Γâli, dear, high priced.
Aγlâ, dearer. [dear.
Γalû, dearth, scarcity, the being

غلى Iγli, vn boil, as water. ger.
Γalie ; also, nu Γalya.
Γalyân, Γaliey, adj. boiling.
Γaliyoun, pipe (properly, in which the smoke passes through water and makes it seem to boil).
In Aleppo any pipe for smoking is Γaliyoun.

ΓLB

غلب Iγlib sala', vn prevail over.
Γâliba", prevalently, generally.
Γâlib, prevalent ; comp. Aγlab.
Γalaba, pedantry s.
Γallâb, victorious.
Γolobba? victory.
iii. Γâlib, va struggle with.
v. Teγallab sala', prevail against, conquer (a city).

غلف Oγlof, va sheathe.
Γilâf, sheath, scabbard.
Γolfa, foreskin. [Γalaf.
Iγlaf, vn be uncircumcised. ger.

غلم Γolâm 8, 9, young man, guardsman.
Γolâmicγa, adult age.

غلن Γaliena, a calm (on the sea).
Gr. γαληνη.
ii. Γallin, vs calm.
v. Teγallan, vn grow calm.

غلق Γalaq 4, bolt, door bar.
Miγlaq, dº
Maγlouq, fastened (gate), concluded (bargain).
ii. Γalliq, va close an account finally. Taγlieq, ger. closing, clearing off.
Γalâq, clearance of accounts.
iv. Aγliq sala', fasten up.
vii. Inγuliq, vp be fastened.
x. Istaγliq, vn stipulate for a final clearance.

غلس viii. Iγtelis, vn poach by night, embezzle. But see Iktelis.

ΓLṢ

غَلَمَ Ġalvama, larynx?

غَلَطَ Iṣlaṭ, vn blunder, ger.
Ġalṭa, Maṣlaṭa.
Ġalaṭ, error, slip.
Ġolouṭa, Oṣlouṭa 11, solecism.
Miṣlaṭ, great blunderer.
ii. Ġallut, va make out to be a blunderer, i.e. disprove. ger.
Taṣliċт, disproof.
iii. Ġâluṭ, va divert (an enemy).
iv. Aṣluṭ, va mislead.

غَلَظَ Oṣloẓ, vn be rude, coarse, clumsy, gross; lit. or fig. with sala', of person.
Ġalicẓ 5, coarse, cumbrous.
Ġilẓ, thickness, coarseness, etc.
ii. Ġalliẓ, va make rude, etc.
iv. Aṣliẓ sala', act rudely or harshly towards.

غَم Ġamm, Ġomma, vexation.
Ġomma, Ġimâma, cloudy sky, N. C.
iv. Aṣimm, va choke, vex.
viii. Iṣṭimm, vp of iv.
Moṣtimm, Maṣmoum, vexed.
Moṣimm, vexatious.

غَم Ġaim 3, cloud.
ii. Ġayyim, iv. Aṣiem, vn become cloudy.
v. Teṣayyam, dᵃ
Moṣayyim, cloudy (sky).

غَمِي Ġama', ger. fainting c.
ii. Ġammi, va hoodwink ʙ.
See Ġaxya and Oṣxou.

ΓNY

غَمَد Oṣmod, va sheathe. ger.
Ġamad.
Ġimd 4, 3, sheath, pod, husk.

غَمَض Ġomḍ, ger. blinking of eyes. [wink.
ii. Ġammiḍ, va blink the eye,
viii. Iṣṭemuḍ, blink, close eyes in sleep.

غَمَن Ġaumana, cable c.

غَمَق Ġâmiq, adj. deep (in colour) B. But Ġamicq is vulgarly said for Ɂamicq, deep, in all senses.

غَمَر Oṣmor, va overwhelm, drown. ger. Ġamr 3, inundation.
Ġamra 2, 5, deep water, abyss.
vii. Inṣamir, vp. of i.
Ġomoura, a flood; fig. abundance.
viii. Iṣṭemir, va flood (a field).
Moṣtemar, flooded.

غَمَس Iṣmis, va dip.
vii. Inṣamis, vp of i.
viii. Iṣṭemis, vr dip oneself.
Ġammâse, diver (bird). See Iqmis.

غَمَز Iṣmiz, vn make sign by eye or hand.
vi. Teṣâmez, be in connivance.
Ġammêz, intriguer.
Ġomzêt, pl. twirlings (of gazelle's horns)? v.

غَنِي Ġani(ey), rich.
Ġins', riches, content.

ΓNY

x. Istefni san, be contented with.
(2) Γinâ, Γanwa, song.
Γannieya 11, do.
Ofniya 11, do.
ii. Γanni, va sing.
Moranni, singer.
Moranniya, f. songster.

غنج Γonj, Γináj, amorous airs.
Γanij, adj. ogling, ogler.
Ifnij, vn cast amorous glances.
v. Terannaj, do.

غنم Γanam 4, (booty), sheep.
Γanema, nu a sheep al.
Γaniema 11, booty.
Γonaima, a little sheep x.
Γânim, laden with spoil c.
Mafnam, gain won without effort.
viii. Iftenim, va carry off booty; hence simply, win.
Iftenam forva, he gained an opportunity.

غر Γorr, va delude. ger. Γarar,
Γorour, vanity, delusion.
Γarour, delusive.
Γorouriey, specious B.
Γarier 8, a dupe.
Γarrâr, swindler.
Γirra, inexperience.
Morirr, delusive.
(2) Γorra, topknot. See Törra.
(3) Γorr, first day of new moon.
(4) Afarr 9, adj. signal, brilliant, (horse) with white star on forehead.
(5) Γirâra 11, sack for grain.

ΓRB

(6) Γarrara, ger. gargling.
ii. Tefarrar, vn rattle in the throat, as in gargling.

وغر Wafar Yafir, vn chafe inwardly. ger. Wafr, animosity.
iv. Aufir, va incense, enrage.
x. Isteufir, vp bo incensed.

غور Γaur, depth; lit. or fig.
Γâr, pl. Afwâr, or 9, a cavity or hollow. [Γâr, laurel; vulg. bay tree.
Γour, vn sink (as a ship), sink (into the earth, as water).
Mafâra, Mofâra nu 11, cavern.
(2) Γâra, Ifûra, an incursion, inroad.
iv. Afier sala', make inroad on.

غير Γair, other (precedes its noun).
ii. Γayyir, va alter.
iii. Γâyir, va be different from.
Γiyâr, s. change, relay (of horses).
v. Tefayyar, vp of ii.
vi. Tefâyar, be heterogeneous.
(2) Γâr sala', be zealous for (pres. Yafâr). [jealous.
Γâyir, Γayour, Γairân, zealous,
Γaira, jealousy.
vi. Tefâyar, be mutually jealous. (See just above.)

غرو v. Tefarrâ, vp be cracked by creasing (as old sails).

غرب Γarb, the West.
Mafrib, sunset, West.
Γarbiey, western.

ƔRB

Ɣaricb 6, strange, a stranger.
Ɣarieba 11, a strange thing.
Ɣarâba, strangeness.
Oɣrob, *vn* set, as sun or star. *ger.* Ɣoroub.
v. Teɣarrab, *vn* go abroad.
x. Istaɣrib *va* wonder (at).
Mostaɣrab, strange, odd.
(2) Ɣorâb 9, raven, a rowing galley.
(3) Ɣârib 12, ridge, crest, of camel's back, of wave, etc.

غربل Ɣirbâl, large sieve of iron wire.
Ɣarbil, *va* sift (sand, etc.).

غرد ii. Ɣarrid, *vn* carol, warble.
Ɣirried, great warbler.
Oɣrouda 11, *ger.* warbling.

غرض Ɣaraƶ 4, end, scope, butt, purpose.
(2) Ɣarieƶ, fresh (meat) x.

غرف Oɣrof, *va* draw (water), pump up.
Miɣrafa, machine for hoisting water; a ladle.
Moɣraifa, small spoon x. (*vulg.* Milcaqa, Maclaqa).
viii. Iɣterif, same as i.
(2) Ɣorfa 10, upper chamber.

غرم Iɣram, *vn* be under obligation. *ger.* Ɣarm, obligation.
Ɣarim, bound over, attached, addicted (*Obsol.?*).
Ɣariem, opponent in law, *either* debtor *or* creditor; *also* rival.

ƔS

ii. Ɣarrim, *va* cost.
Ɣarâma, an obligation, fine, debt.
Maɣram 11, a debt.
iv. Aɣrim, *va* force to pay up.
Móɣram, indebted.
Moɣram bi, doating upon.
iv. ɛp Oɣrim bi, *devinctum esse*, doat upon.
iii. Ɣârim, *va* rival.
Moɣârim, a rival.
Moɣârama, rivalry.
v. Teɣarram, viii. Iɣterim, *vn* assume and acknowledge debt.

غرق Iɣraq, *vn* be drowned. *ger.* Ɣaraq.
iv. Aɣriq, *va* drown.
Ɣarieq 9, drowned person [*also* drowning water; deep sea].

غرس Oɣros, *va* plant. *ger.* Ɣars.
Ɣirs 5, sapling; a proselyte.
Ɣirâs, planting time.

غرش Ɣarx 3, piastre (*groat*).
Maɣrax, moneyed, rich. From *Germ.* grosch. See also Qarx.

غرز Iɣriz, *va* prick with needle; stick in, plant, implant.
Ɣorze, a stitch.
Ɣarieze, innato temper.
Ɣarieziey, implanted, innate.
v. Teɣarraz, *vn* penetrate, plunge deep.
(2) Ɣarz, leathern stirrup?

غص Ɣaƨƨ, *vn* bo choked.
Ɣoƨƨa, suffocating grief, affliction B. x.

ΓWS

غوص Ḡouṣ, *vn* plunge, dive; be in swamp. *ger.* Ḡauṣ, Ḡiyâṣ.
Ḡauṣ, state of swamp.
Ḡawwâṣ, diver (man *or* bird).
Ḡiyâṣa, pearl fishery.
Maḡâṣ, diving place.
Ḡawieṣ, profound (in science) B. (Not the same as Sawieṣ).
ii. Ḡawwuṣ, *va* swamp.

غصب Iḡṣub, *va* snatch violently. *ger.* Ḡaṣb, violence, constraint.
Iḡṣub ṣala', force (a person) to.
Ḡaṣbaⁿ, by force.
iii. Ḡâṣub, *va* rob (*with double accus.*). [off.
viii. Iḡtaṣub, *va* seize and carry

غسل Iḡsil, *va* wash, bathe. *ger.* Ḡasl, Ḡosl.
viii. Iḡtesil, *vp* or *vr* of i.
Ḡassêl, washerman.
Ḡasséla, washerwoman.
Ḡassoul, soap, etc. [ing.
Ḡosêla, refuse water after wash-
Ḡasiel, Maḡsoul, washed (linen).
Miḡsêl, washing pan.

غصن Ḡoṣn 3, 4, bough.
Ḡaṣna, small bough, twig.

غسق Ḡasaq, evening dusk.
Iḡsiq, *vn* be sombre x. *ger.* Ḡosouq, Ḡasqûn.
Ḡâsiq, time of evening dusk.

غط Ḡoṭṭ, *va* douse, duck.

ΓΤR

iii. Ḡâṭuṭ, v. Ṭeḡâṭṭ, plunge one another, etc. x.
Ḡaṭṭ, *ger.* of i.

غطط Ḡawwuṭ, *va* plunge (a weapon in.
iv. Aḡieṭ, *va* dᵒ (as *spade*).
Ḡouṭa, soft fertile valley, (*esp.* of Damascus).
Ḡauṭa, a single dip x.

غوث Ḡouθ, *va* succour. *ger.* Ḡiyâθ(e).
iv. Aḡieθ, dᵒ *ger.* Iḡîθe.
x. Iateḡieθ, ask succour of, appeal to, *va* or with *bi.* *ger.* Iatiḡâθe, appeal in law.

غطا Ḡuṭa, *pl.* 8, Aḡṭuya, covering.
Oḡṭou, *va* cover. *ger.* Ḡoṭou.
ii. Ḡaṭṭu, dᵒ *intens.* [of i.
v. Teḡaṭṭâ, viii. Iḡtaṭu, *vp. vr.*
Ḡuṭâya, coverture, underclothing, underpacking.
Ḡaṭuiy, covering (with darkness) c.

غطمش Ḡaṭmiš, *va* dazzle (the eye) B.

غطرس Ḡaṭrasa, arrogance.
Ḡaṭries, arrogant, defiant.
ii. Teḡaṭras, *vn* be arrogant.
Moteḡaṭris, arrogant F. x. (See Saṭrase).

غطرش Ḡaṭriš, *va* pretend not to see or feel. B. *Dissimuler.*
ii. Teḡaṭraš, affect blindness x.

ΓΤS ΓZL

خطس Iȝtus, ɛn dive.
Γotöus, ger. sinking (of a star), occultation, in Astronomy.
ii. Iɔttus, ʋa souse.
Γutûs, baptism ɪ.
Γattâs, diver (bird).
Miȝtas 11, plunging bath.

غوش Γauxa, Γawâx, clatter, rattle mod. t. See Joxxa, Γauȝa.

وغوش Tewaȝwax ɛan, ɛn make a fuss concerning.

غش Γoxx, ʋa cheat.
Γaxxâx, a great cheat.
Γixx, ger. of i. trickery.
iv. Aȝixx ɛan, fraudulently divert (a person) from; cause him to mistake.
viii. Iȝtixx, ʋp. be cheated.
x. Isteȝixx, ʋa regard as a cheat.
Γâxx, fraudulent (person).
Maȝxoux, adulterated x.

غشا Γixâ, pl. 8, Aȝxiya, membrane, envelope.
Γaxwa, veil.
Γixâwa, purblindness.
Γaxiey, stupefied, fainting.
Oȝxou, ʋa hoodwink? blindfold?
  gen. in figures. ʋp. Γoxi ɛalaihi, dimness fell on him; he swooned.
Γaxȝa, a fainting fit.
Maȝxicy ɛalaihi, partic. fainting.
ii. Iaxxi, ʋa dazzle (the eye).

iv. Aȝxi ʋa or with ɛala', cover over, envelop.
Moȝxa', covered up.

غشم Iȝxim, ʋn do work rudely.
  ger. Γaxom, clumsiness.
Γaxiem, unpractised, inexpert, unskilful, credulous.
Γaxmana, rusticity ʙ.
Γaxoum, arbitrary, capricious ɪ.
Γaxoumieya, inexpertness, inexperience ʙ.
v. Teȝaxxam, ʋn act arbitrarily ɪ. But the moderns seem to prefer Teȝaxmar, in this sense.

غشم Γaxmara (also Γaxmier ɪ.) violence, impetuosity, brutal recklessness.
Teȝaxmar ɛala', rush impetuously upon; play the tyrant, act capriciously.

غز Γozz, Γazȝiz, ʋa prick, sting.
غزو ʋn make inroad. ger. Γazèwa, Γazwân.   [war.
ii. Γazzi, iv. Aȝzi, ʋa send to the Γûzi, pl. 7, Γozze, warrior.
Γâziya, military expedition.
Γazewicy, military, warlike.
Maȝze' 11, theatre of war, campaign; pl. Maȝâzi, recitals of a campaign ɪ.

غزل Iȝzil, ʋa spin (thread). ger.
  Γazel. viii. do.
Γazl, (cotton) thread.   [ner.
Γazzèl, seller of thread, spinMiȝzel 11, spindle.
(2) Γazèl 9, fem. Γazèle, gazelle.

ΓZL

v. Teṃzzel, *vn* make love.
vi. Teṛâzel, d°· mutually.
Γazel (love-poetry x. an ode c.), a sonnet.
(3) Γazêla, noonday light c.

غزر Oṛzor, be abundant (as milk).
Γazier, plentiful *or* teeming with.
Miṛzêr, a good milker (as cow, camel).
iv. Aṛxir, *vs* increase, multiply.
Moṛzer, enriched (estate) x.

H. II.

اٰ Âh, ah! Eiyyohê, ho! See Grammar.

وحى Wehe' Yehi, *vn* droop, decay.
Wêhi, Wehiey, flabby, frail.

وحى Waḥui, revelation, inspiration. [inspire.
iv. Auḥu, *vs* warn by revelation,

وحى Ihwi, *vn* fall headlong, swoop, souse, as eagle.
Hêwiya, deep chasm, gulf.
Houwa, d°·
(2) Hewâ, *s.* air, *pl.* 8 Ehiya.
Hewâ'iey, airy, whimsical.
x. Istehwi, *vn* catch cold.
Istihwâ, a cold. [passion.
Hewa', *pl.* 4, Ehwâ, caprice,
Hewieya, *s.* fancy, desire.
Ihwi, *vs* like, fancy, be pleased with.

HB

حوى Uḥwi, *vs* contain, house. [*hence, pop.* steal.]
viii. Uḥtewi cala', *vs* contain.
(2) Moteḥawwi, convoluted as a serpent.

حى Hieya, mien, manner.
Hieyat Ḥarb, *casus belli.*
ii. Heyyi, *vs* make ready, prepare.
v. Teheyyâ, *vn* be ready.
Heyâ'a, the being ready.
(2) Hê! behold! compounds of this are, Hêḍe, this; Heḍêc, that (*iste* of Latin). See Grammar.

حى Ḥuyâ, *s.* shame.
Moḥayyâ, *s.* countenance (seat of shame). [modest.
x. Istaḥuiy, *vn* be abashed,
Mostaḥuiy, modest, well bred.
(2) Ḥaiy (Yeḥa'), *vn* live.
Ḥaiy, alive, *pl.* Aḥyâ.
Ḥaiya, Ḥaiwa, life; *also*, Ḥaiya, 2, a serpent.
Ḥaiwân 2, animal.
Ḥaiyâwiey, serpentine.
Ḥöwaiyan 2, animalcule.
ii. Ḥayyi, *vs* cause to live; salute with *Vivat!* hail as king, bless. [tion.
Teḥuiya, salutation, benedic-
iv. Aḥyi, *vs* reanimate.
(3) Ḥaiy, *pl.* Abyâ, town, parish.

حب Hobb, *vn* blow as wind.
ger. Hoboub.
Hobba, a gust, puff.
Heboub, blowing, boisterous.

HB

Mehebb, quarter of the wind.
Tehebheb, *vn* wave with wind.
(2) Hobb min, *vn* wake from r.

حبّ Habba, *nu* berry, grain, pimple, a grain-weight.
Hŏboub, grains, grain, corn.
Habab, a bubble.
(2) Hŏbb, *va* love.
ii. Habbib, *va* endear r.
iv. Ahubb, for i. love. [amity.
vi. Tehâbb, *vr* be in mutual
x. Istahubb, like, prefer.
Hŏbb, *s.* love. Mahabba, d°·
Höbbiey, friendly.
Höbbieya, friendliness.
Habieb, dear friend, darling.
Mahboub, beloved.
Mostehabb, amiable; a favourite; liked, preferred.
(3) Hŏbb 10, earthenware butt for filtering water B₂.

اهبا 'Ohba, munitions of war.
'Ehhib, *va* rig, accoutre, furnish.

وهب Weheb Yehib, *va* grant, *imperative*, Heb.
Wehhêb, generous.
Mauhiba 11, gift.
vi. Tewâheb, *vn* exchange gifts.
Hiba 2, a grant, gift.
viii. Ittehib, *va* receive a gift.
x. Istcuhib, *va* ask a gift.

هيب Hieb, Heb, *va* fear, respect.
Heiba, *s.* fear, respect; respectfulness, gravity.
Heiyib, Heyoub, timid.

HBN

iv. Ehieb, *va* awe.
v. Teheyyab, *vn* be awestruck.
Mohieb, awful.

هبو Ohbou, *vn* rise as dust x.
Hébi, powdery, dusty.
Hebwa, fine dust, powder.
Hebâ, *pl.* 4, Ehbâ, atoms seen in the sunbeam.

هبي Ihbi cala', *vn* hunger after; *ger.* Hebâ, craving.
Hebyân, famished, ravening n.

حبر Ohbou, *vn* stoop and crawl, *esp.* to hide oneself.
iii. Hâbi, *va* connive at, cringe to, favour unjustly. [sion.
Mohâbâya, connivance, collu-
(2) Habâ, *s.* curtain r.

هبذ Hebbadê, bravo! *fem.* -die.

هبل ii. Hebbil, *va* foment (a limb).
(2) Hibill, gawky x.
(3) Hebâla, a conceit n. flummery, *persiflage.*

حبل Habl 4, 5, a rope.
Hubâl, cordage.
Uhbil, *va* rope, cord.
Hubâla 11, mesh of a net.
Habbâl, ropemaker.
viii. Uhtobil, *va* catch in net.
(2) Uhbil, *vn* be pregnant. *ger.*
Habal, pregnancy.
Hâbil, Hŏbla', pregnant.

حبن Haban, *s.* dropsy.
Hubna, blain, pustule.

ПВС

حبك Ⲏаbce, tissue, braid.
UⲎbeo, va enlace.
ii. Ⲏabbic, va d⁰
Ⲏabbêc, lacemaker, haberdasher, *also* bookbinder в.

حبق Ⲏabaq, pennyroyal (plant).

حبر Hebr, s. lean of meat в. о.
(2) iii. Hébir, vn put oneself into agitation в.
(3) Hibrieya, fine dust of feathers or cotton; flue, scurf. See Ⲏabara.

حبر Ⲏubr, ink.
MuⲎbar, inkglass, inkstand.
(2) Ⲏubr, (from the word *Hebrew* or *Subri* ?) high Rabbi; Pontiff, Pope.
Ⲏubriey, pontifical.
(3) UⲎbar, vn glitter and rejoice in beauty. *ger.* Ⲏöbour, gaiety of heart. Ⲏâbir, blithe.
iv. AⲎbur, va make (the fields, etc.) gay; make blithe.
UⲎbier, glowworm ₁.
MoⲎabbar, brilliant, elegant (style).
(4) Ⲏabara, taffety, silk cloth.
Ⲏöbâra, flue of silk?
(5) Ⲏöbâra 11, bustard.

حبرج Ⲏubraqiey, goldsmith.

حبس UⲎbis, va confine, hold, detain. *ger.* Ⲏabs. [ment.
Ⲏabs, confinement, imprisonMaⲎbes, prison.

ПД

Ⲏöbes, self-control.
Ⲏabies 6, one under religious restrictions, devotee.
MoⲎâbis, abstinent.
v. TeⲎabbes, vr control oneself.
viii. UⲎtebis, vp of i.

حبط Uhbut, vn rush down, fall with violence. *ger.* Hobout.
ii. Hebbut, va depress violently.

حبط UⲎbat san, vn fall away from, abandon, fail (him).
iv. AⲎbut, va disappoint? baffle?

حبش Ⲏabax 9, Abyssinian.
Ⲏabaxa, Abyssinia.

حد Ⲏadd 3, a limit.
MoⲎâdda, d⁰.
ii. Ⲏaddid, va limit.
MaⲎdoud, limited, finite.
Гair maⲎdoud, infinite.
Ⲏadda, TeⲎdied, limitation в.
(2) Ⲏudd, vn be sharp.
Ⲏâdd, sharp, fierce.
iv. AⲎudd, va sharpen.
Ⲏudda, sharpness.
viii. UⲎtidd, vp be exasperated.
x. IsteⲎudd, vn put oneself into rage.
(3) Ⲏudâd, mourning weeds.
(4) Ⲏadied, iron.
Ⲏadieda, nw an iron, a piece of iron, iron tool.
Ⲏaddâd, blacksmith.

حض Ⲏall sala', va incite against. See Ⲏaθθ, Ⲏarriδ.
(2) Ⲏaδuiδ, floor, ground, bottom.

HD

هدّ Hodd, *va* pull down, demolish. *ger.* Hedd, Hodoud. [See Hedm.]
(2) Hidd, *vn* boom, sound.
ii. Heddid, *va* threaten.
v. Tebedded, d°.
(3) Hodhod, the hoopoo (bird).

هذّ Hoṣṣ fie *or* bi, *vn* meditate upon; Psalms i. ii. *ger.* Heṣiṣṣ bi.

وهد Wehda, dale, lowland.

حد — وحد ' Waḥḥud, one, a certain one.
'Eḥad, *f.* Uḥda', one, any.
ii. Eḥḥud, *va* unite.
viii. Itteḥud, *vp* of ii.
Ṣala' Ḥuda, separately.
Waḥd, singly, *with pron.* as, Waḥdi, I alone; Waḥdec, thou alone, etc.
Waḥda, singleness.
Eḥad, *pl.* ones.
'Eḥadieya, unity.
Waḥuid, unique.
Auḥad, unique, incomparable.
Waḥdân, the being solitary?
Waḥdânieya, solitariness; unity.
ii. Waḥḥud, *va* worship one
v. Tewaḥḥad *or* [God.
x. Isteḥud, isolate oneself.
Tewaḥḥöd, isolation.

حوض Ḥauḍ, *pl.* 5 Ḥuyâḍ, basin, pool, pelvis of human body.

هوذ Hewâda, sweetness of temper.

HDY

iii. Hêwid, *va* conciliate, accommodate, meet by an accommodating price.
Mohêwid, *adj.* accommodating, reasonable (trader *or* price).
Mohewwad, gentle (voice, sound)
Motchewwid, a proselyte.

حيد Ḥuid, *vn* deviate.
Ḥaida, deviation.
iii. Ḥâyid, *va* avoid (a person), by deviating to right or left.
Ḥuyâd, Moḥâyada, evasion, shunning, dodging.
Ḥayâd! beware! x.
vi. Teḥâyad, *vn* dodge.
iv. Aḥuid, *va* divert from, cause to deviate.
Maḥuid, place of deviating, turn of road or river.

حيض Ḥaiḍ, a woman's monthly illness.
Ḥâyiḍ, (a woman) at this crisis.

هيض Hieḍa, cholera.

حدى Ḥâdi, *s.* camel driver.
(2) Ḥudâya, kite (bird).
(3) Ḥada', from 'Eḥad.

هدو Hodou, *s.* repose.
Hêdi, *adj.* tranquil.
Ihda', *vn* be tranquil.
ii. Heddi, iv. Ehdi, *va* calm, tranquillize.

هدى Ihdi, *va or* iv.
Ehdi, *va* guide; present a gift.
Hêdi, *s.* guide (in religion), spiritual director.

HDY

Hidâya, guidance.
Hedieya 14, gift, *cadeau*.

هذى Ohᴧou, Ihᴧi, ᴠᴀ ravo, spout.
Héᴧi, delirious.
Heᴧê, delirium.
(2) Hêᴧe, this (See Grammar),
Houᴧe! Lo!

هذى Iluᴧê, in face of.
iii. Πâᴧi, ᴠᴀ front.
Moflâᴧi, opposite.
vi. Teflâᴧê, ᴠᴀ follow, imitate, [ape.
Moteflâᴧi, imitative.
(2) Iluᴧê, *pl.* 8, Afldiya, shoe, sandal? buskin?

هذب Hodba, ᴠᴇ eyelash; hair of eyebrow.
Hoddâb, fringe; *pl.* of Hêdib.

هذب ii. Heᴧᴧib, ᴠᴀ prune (style), chasten, correct.

هضب ii. Heflba 5, isolated crag.

حدب Afldab, hump-backed.
Iladaba, hump, convexity.
Ufldab, ᴠᴀ be convex.
ii. Iladdib, ᴠᴀ hump up.
Mofladdab, convex.

هدف Hidfa 10, butt for marksmen.
Hedaf, aim, purpose.

حذف . Uflᴧif, ᴠᴀ fling, fling away (a letter); -bi, fling at.
Ilᴧᴧf, elision (of a letter).

IIDQ

هدج Heudaj 11, camel-panniers for women travelling.
Iludâja, Iludâᴋa, camel's saddle.

هدم Ihdim, ᴠᴀ pull down, demolish. *ger.* Hedm.
vii. Inhedim, *vp* of i.
Inhidâm, demolition, ruin.

هضم Ihᴧum, ᴠᴀ digest (food). *ger.* Heᴧm.
vii. Inheᴧum, *vp* of i.
Heᴧnm, Heᴧóum, Heᴧẑâm, aiding digestion.

هدن iii. Hêdin, *v.* make truce.
Hodna, Hodâna, state of truce.
Hodoun, quietude x.
Mohêdana, truce.

حضن Iluᴧn 3, 4, bosom.
Oflᴧön, ᴠᴀ sit on eggs, carry in the bosom or lap.
vi. Teflâᴧan, ᴏʀ embrace mutually.
viii. Uñtaᴧun, ᴠᴀ carry (a child) in the bosom; brood over (morally).

حذق حدق Ilâᴧiq, sharp-sighted, acute.
Iladaqa, pupil (ball?) of eye.
Iladâqa, Ilaᴧêqa, sharpness of sight.
ii. Iladdiq, ᴠᴀ see distinctly from afar. [another.
vi. Teflâdaq, ᴏʀ gaze at one
(2) Iladieqa 11, walled garden, orchard.
iv. Afldiq, ᴠᴀ wall in, fence in.

HDR

حدر Ihdir, *vn* moan (as pigeon), growl (as lion or camel). *ger.* Hedier.

حذر Ihair, *vn* twaddle, tattle. *ger.* Heaer, Heaêr. Heaaêr, twattler, gossip.

— Oḍdor, *vn* slope down (as ground), descend (as a stream). *ger.* Ḥôdour.
Ḥadour, a slope, a steep.
vii. Inḥadir, *vn* go down hill, descend as water.
(2) Ḥaddâr, a pedlar B.

حذر — Uḥaer min, *vn* beware of. *ger.* Ḥuar.
Ibn Ḥuar, prudent man.
Ḥuara² min, by way of precaution against.
Maḥaoura, precaution.
ii. Ḥaaair, iv. Aḥair, *vs* warn (another).
v. Teḥaaaer, or viii. Uḥteair, *vn* use precaution.

حضر — Uḥḍur, *vn* be present. *ger.* Ḥôḍour.
Ḥaḍra, presence (as a title of compliment; Ḥaḍratec, your presence, your honour, etc.).
Ḥâḍur, present, ready.
ii. Ḥaḍḍur, *vs* make ready.
iv. Aḥḍur, *vs* present, bring before (another).
Moḥḍur, usher, beadle.
iii. Ḥâḍur, *vs* present oneself side by side with (another).

HF

Moḥâḍara, company, conversation K.
(2) Ḥaḍâr, rheumatism B.

حدس Ihdas, *vn* be disquieted. *ger.* Hedas, disquiet.
Hêdis, disquieted.

حدس — Oḥdos, *v.* conjecture, opine; *also* apprehend, fear B. *ger.* Ḥads, presentiment, conjecture.
Ḥadaiey, conjectural, resting on mere opinion.
Ḥudâs, aim, scope.
Maḥdis, topic K.

حدث — Oḥdoθ, *vn* arise, happen as something new. *ger.* Ḥôdouθ, occurrence, apparition.
Ḥâdiθe, recent event; *pl.* 12, Ḥawâdiθe, news.
Ḥadiθe, new, recent.
Ḥadâθe, novelty.
ii. Ḥaddiθe, *vs* tell (news). Oḥdouθe, narrative K.
iii. Ḥâdiθ, *vs* inform of news K.
iv. Aḥdiθ, *vs* originate, invent, Moḥdiθ, originator. [cause.
v. Teḥaddaθ, *vn* talk, chat.
Moteḥaddiθ, modern F.

هف Hiff, *vn* whistle as the wind. *ger.* Heḥef.
(2) Hiff, *vs* graze (the skin), touch lightly.
Heffâf, light, nimble. *Compare* Kiff.
Haſhéf, Mohefhif, lank.

ḤF

حف Ḥuff, *ger.* Ḥaḣef, *vn* rustle; bluster as wind. *See* Hiff.
(2) Ḣöff, *va* press, pinch (as a throng, or as poverty).
ii. Ḣaffif, *va* intens. of i.
Ḣaffân, retinue x.
Maḣfouf, Moḣtiff, thronged (*stipatus*) as by a retinue.
(3) Ḣâffa, *s.* margin (of river), border, edge (of table or chair); *vulg.* Ḣâfiya.
(4) Ḣaffâf, barber b.
(5) Kobz ḣâff, dry bread b.

حيف Ḥéyif, Heifân, exhausted (by thirst, etc.). [belly.
Heif, slimness, emptiness of Ehyaf, empty bellied, as an exhausted horse. See Hefhef under Hiff.

حيف Ḣaif, alas!
v. Teḣayyaf, *vn* lament.

حفو Hefawa 2, fault, slip.
(2) Teheffâ, *vn* fan oneself Bg.

حفى Ḣâfi, *adj.* barefoot.
Ḣafâ, barefootedness.
viii. Uḣtefi, *vn* go barefoot.
(2) Ḣâfiya 11, brink. See Ḣâffa.

حفيد Ḣafid, grandson.

حفل ii. Ḣaffil, *va* set off, invest with grandeur.
viii. Uḣtefil, *va* go out in mass

ḤJ

to welcome (a great man); frequent his levy.
Uḣtifâl, solemn assembling.
Maḣfil, assembly, place of d°.

حفن Ḣöfna 10, handful.

حفر Ḣâfir 12, a hoof.
(2) Oḣfor, *va* dig. *ger.* Ḣafr.
Ḣöfra, ditch, trench.
Ḣafiera, pit as for gravel.
Ḣaffâr, digger.
Muḣfar, instrument for digging.

حفت vi. Teḣêfet, *vn* be flighty? *ger.* Teḣêfot, mania, passion.

حفظ Oḣföz, *va* keep, retain. *ger.* Ḣafz, memory.
Ḣâfuza 'ehlieya, national guard.
iii. Ḣâfuz, *va* guard, be guardian to. [son.
Moḣâfaza, Moḣâfuzöun, garri-
iii. Ḣâfuz sala', viii. Uḣtefuz sala'; spare, use sparingly, be chary of. *Also,* Ḣâfuz sala', abide by, *i.e. fig.* adhere to.

حج Hojj, *vn* emigrate b. *See* Hejira. *ger.* Hêjja.
Hêjij, an emigrant.

حج Ḣöjj, *vn* go on pilgrimage, make for. *ger.* Ḣöjj, pilgrimage.
Ḣajja, *ns* a single pilgrimage.
Ḣâjj 7, 12, pilgrim; *vulg.* Ḣâji.
Maḣjouj, frequented by pilgrims.
Maḣajja, road of the pilgrims.
(2) Ḣöjja 10, argument, attes-

tation, document; clause (of a written contract)?
iii. Ḥâjij, va debate, refute.
vi. Teḥâjaj, vn debate, discuss.
viii. Uḥtijj, va plead, allege.
Muḥjâj, disputatious.

حبج Wehej Yehij, vn blaze.
Wehhêj, blazing (fire, diamond).
v. Tewehhej, vn flicker.

حجر Heuj, s. ingenuousness, frankness B. [or Hewaj?]

حجة Ḥâja 2, necessity; affair (sufficiency, AL). [clothes.
Ḥawâyij, pl. baggage, goods,
iv. Aḥwij, va necessitate.
viii. Uḥtêj ila', vn be in need of.
Uḥtiyâj, s. need.
Uḥtiyûja 2, a thing needed, desideratum?

حيج Hicj, vn swell, as the sea, or as passion. ger. Heijân.
Hêyij, Heyyâj, swollen, raging.
ii. Heyyij, va excite to passion.

حجو Ohjou, Ihji, va taunt. ger. Hejou, Hejâ.
Hêji, satirical.
Ohjouwa 11, a satire.
ii. Hejji, va satirize.
vi. Tehêjâ, er do. mutually.
Mahjouw, satirized.
(2) Hijâ, ger. spelling.
Tehejjio, do.
v. Tehejjâ, v. spell.

حجس Ihjas, vn slumber, be at rest. ger. Hojous.

Hejsa, s. alum', light sleep; partial sleep.

حجب Uḥjub, va veil, hide; also exclude. [riff.
Hujâb, veil, curtain; the mid-
Ḥâjib 12, chamberlain, eyebrow.

حجفر Teḥajḥür, volvulus; (a wretched disease).

حجل Uḥjil, vn hop as bird.
Ḥajal(a), partridge; pl. Ḥajla'.
iv. Aḥjal, va cause to hop; i.e. tie a beast's forefoot.
Teḥanjal, vn dance a jig.
(2) Ḥajiel, having three feet white x.
Moḥajjal, white-footed r.

حجم Ihjim sala', vn rush upon. ger. Hojoum, come on suddenly, as storm.
Hejma, s. outburst, sally.
v. Tehejjam sala', vn attack, set about. [hasty.
Motehejjim, venturesome, over-

حجم Oḥjom, va or viii. Uḥtejim, cup with cupping glass. ger. Ḥujâma.

حجن Hejien 10, dromedary B. (properly, a mongrel).
Heijân, pl. -a, courier mounted on a dromedary.
x. Istehjin, vn be mongrel, i.e. degenerate.
Mostehjin, degenerate r.
Istihjân, degeneracy.

I N-

Hajna, Hojou. ݣ d⁻ ?
i. Ohjon, *vn* be mongrel x.

جمر Ohjor, *va* quit, leave. *ger.*
Hijrân.
Hojira, migration.
v. Tehejjar, *vn* travel x.

حجر Hajar 5, stone; *also, pl.*
Hujâra.
Hajariey, *adj.* of stone.
Hajjâr, stonecutter.
Muñjar, Motoñajjir, stony.
Mañjar 11, stonequarry B.
(2) Oñjor, *va* fence round, confine, forbid; *ger.* Hujrân, prohibition.
Hujâr, *s.* tether.
Mañjar 11, orbit of eye F.
Höjra 10, 2, chamber, walled enclosure, a close. [ber.
Höjriey, belonging to the cham-
Höjaira, small chamber.
(3) Höjr 3, the lap B.
Añjira, the lap x.

حجر Hejrar, greyhound.

حجس Ihjis bi, *vn* feel inwardly, spontaneously. *ger.* Hejs.

حجز Oñjoz, *va* pen up, debar; restrict (trade). *ger.* Hajz.
Hâjiz 12, a fender; a mole; a seawall. Hâjiz el nâr, the firefender. [x. gives only
Hajaze as *pl.*] [ment.
Mañjouz? Mañjize? compart-

هل Hel? particle of interrogation.

HL.

(2) Hilêl 8, (*pl.* Ehilla) new moon. [month.
Ihlêl, commencement of lunar
(3) v. Tchellel, *vn* be jubilant.
Tehliel, Heleliena, acclamation.

حل Höll, *va* loosen; in the widest sense of *solvo,* λύω; solve, pay, allow, analyse; *also* loosen (the bridle), halt, alight. Especially,
1. Höll, *va ger.* Hall; loosen, untie, solve, absolve.
Hall, *ger.* solution of a difficulty.
Halla, absolution of the public B.
Hallicy, absolutory B.
2. Höll, *va ger.* Höloul; pay. *vn* be solvent. [missible.
3. Hull, *vn ger.* Hull; be per-
Halâl, lawful deed or state.
4. Hull, *vn ger.* Höloul; alight, arrive as time, arrive.
Hull cala', *vn* alight or devolve upon.
ii. Hallil, *vn* analyse, as chemist; permit, authorize (a deed).
iv. Añull, *va* cause to alight upon, *i.e.* impose a burden.
Moñall li, subject to (an inconvenience) B.
viii. Uñtill, *vn* alight, arrive.
x. Isteñull, *va* regard as lawful.
Mañall, *pl.* Mañâll, place of halting; place, house, office; stage, station; room, houseroom. [of town.
Mañalla 2, place, street, quarter
Mañloul, a solution (in chemistry).

ΠL

Moβallal, frequented (place) x.
(2) Πalla 10, boiler (of steamer).
(3) Πölla 10, vestment, robe.

اهل Ehl 2, household; folks.
It enters many phrases, as:
'Ehl el qavf, sportsmen. Also, for the local public, is used the *pl*. Ehéli, households. 'Oheil, little folk, poor people. 'Ehoul,'Ehiel, Méhoul, populous.
vi. Te'êhel; *or* intermarry.
viii. Ittehil, *vn* become a family man; marry.
(2) 'Ehl, *adj*. (*Latin* affinis?) apt, adapted for.
'Ehlieya, affinity, aptitude.
ii. 'Ehhil, *va* capacitate.
x. Istêhil, *va* approve as apt.

وهل Wehla, a glance?
Fie 'awwal wehla, at first sight.

وحل Waβal 4, bog, bog-earth.
Waβul, boggy.
Mauβul, a boggy place.
Mauβöul, swampy, swamped.

هول Houl, *va* frighten. *ger*.
Heul. [fear.
Heul, *s*. fright, terror, object of
Héyil, frightful.
Hiela, a portent.
ii. Hewwil, *va* frighten.
x. Istehwil, *vn vp* be aghast B.
(2) Héla 2, a halo, *Gr*. ἅλω.
(3) Hiyoul, *in metaphysics*, matter, *Gr*. ὕλη.
Hiyouliey, *adj*. material.

ΠWL

حول Πóul, *vn* come about; come round as a period; change for the worse, fade.
v. Teβawwal, *vn* come about (as an event), come round (as a feast), change one's place.
Πâl, *pl*. Aβwâl, state, circumstance, present time. Self, *ipse*. Πâlec, thyself. El liséu βâl, the very spokesman.
Ceif βâlec? how is thy state? *i.e.* how is your health?
El βâl, the actual case.
Lil βâl, instantly.
Πâla", at present, presently.
Πâliey, *adj*. present, instant, actual.
Πâla 2, state, condition, phase.
Πâlâtiey, *adj*. changeable, fickle B. See ii.
Πaul, Πaula, shiftiness.
Πaul 3 (*pl*. Πöwoul), period of a
Πawâli, *pl*. environs. [year.
Πawâla, transference, conveyance of property; a banker's cheque; a document of conveyance.
ii. Πawwil, *va* change round; shift, convert; *especially* transfer (property or money) by a document or by a cheque; divert (money) from its rightful channel; embezzle.
Teβwiel, transference, etc.
iv. Aβuil, *va* transfer, convert (in widest sense). *vp* Oβuil, be transferred. [below).
x. Isteβuil, be converted (see
Πnyâl, face of a building.

ḤWL

Min ḥuyâl, in face of, in consideration of.
Ḥâyil lil nâr, firescreen B.
iii. Ḥâwil, va circumvent, overreach; garble, twist; also, bring round, i.e. seek, attempt.
Ḥöwwal, Ḥöwâliey, shifty, tricky. [Ḥawâl? Ḥöwwâl, crafty.]
vi. Teḥâwal, en double as a hare.
Moḥâwala, garbling; corrupted, it seems, into Maḥâla, trick, subterfuge. Lâ maḥâla, without trickery. [trick, wile.
(2) Ḥuila, pl. 10, Ḥuyâl, a Ḥayyâl, swindler.
Aḥyal, more sly.
iii. Ḥâyil, va wheedle.
Ḥuyâl, cajolery.
Moḥâyala, stratagem.
vi. Teḥâyal, en be tricky, shifty.
viii. Uḥtêl, en invent tricks.
Moḥtêl, tricky.
Uḥtiyâl, slyness, trickery.
(3) Aḥwal, adj. squinting.
Uḥwal, en squint.
ix. Uḥwill, en d°·
Muḥwâl, very crooked, absurd; corrupted, it seems, into Moḥâl, absurd.
x. Isteḥuil, en be crooked, absurd. ger. Isteḥâla, absurdity, impossibility.
Mosteḥuil, absurd, impossible.

حيل Hiel, or iv. Ehiel, va cast (earth upon), spread (corn on a floor).
vii. Inhêl, ep of iv.

ḤLB

حلا Ḥalâ', ulcers in the mouth B. a rash on the skin B. pimples on the lips x.

حلو Ḥölou, sweet, f. Ḥölwa 2.
Aḥla', sweeter.
Ḥalâwa, sweetness, sweetmeat.
Ḥölwân, honorary gift, college prize.
Ḥalwâni, confectioner.
ii. Ḥalli, va sweeten.
Moḥalla', sweetened.
iii. Ḥâli, va court (a woman).
vi. Teḥâla' cala', make oneself amiable to.
x. Isteḥli, va approve of.

حلى Uḥli, va embellish, decorate.
Ḥulya, pl. Ḥōla', embellishment (of a woman, or of a sword).

حلس Ihlas, en be uneasy. ger. Halas, uneasiness.
Δou helas, timid, shy (animal).
Holous, pusillanimous x.

حلب Holba, nu. a bristle.
(2) Hilba, anchor with four beaks.

حلب Ḥalieb, milk.
Oḥlob, va milk (a cow).
x. Isteḥlib, va d°·
Ḥaloub, milch (camel). [pail.
Ḥâloub 12, Muḥlab 11, milk-
Moḥallaba, ricemilk.
(2) Ḥalba, a stud (of horses).
(3) Ḥâlib 12, the groin B.
(4) Ḥaleb, Aleppo.
Ḥalebiey, Aleppine.

ḤLF

حلف Uḥlif, *vn* swear. *ger.* Ḥalf.
Ḥalief, confederate, ally or conspirator.
Oḥloufa, oath x. [swear.
ii. Ḥallif, iv. Aḥlif, *va* cause to
iii. Ḥâlif, *va* join into common oath.
vi. Teḥâlaf *vn* swear in common.
x. Istoḥlif, *va* claim that one swear, demand an oath of.
(2) Ḥölfa, kind of reed or water plant (*ulva?*).

حلج Oḥloj, *va* clean (cotton).
Ḥaliej, cleaned (cotton).
Ḥallâj, cleaner, carder.
Ḥilâja, trade of carding.
Muḥlâj, carding tool.

حلم Helâm, gelatine, jelly.
Helâmiey, gelatinous.
(2) Helomma! come hither!

حلم Ḥölm 4, a dream.
Oḥlom, *or* viii. Uḥtelim, *vn* dream.
Ḥâlim, dreamer.
(2) Ḥulm, mildness, forbearance.
Ḥaliem, mild, clement.
ii. Ḥallim, *va* make mild (soothe?)
v. Teḥallam, *vn* behave with gentleness and forbearance.
vi. Toḥâlam, *vn* affect gentleness, mildness x.
(3) Ḥulma, Ḥalama, *nu* nipple.

هلن Haliyoun, asparagus.

ḤLZ

هلك Ihlec, *vn* perish.
Helôc, ruin, perdition.
Mahloc 11, precipice; *esp.* morally.
iv. Ehlic, *va* destroy, ruin.
vi. Tebélic sala', *vn* (*Lat.* deperire), be brainsick for.

حلك Ḥölec, *s.* blackness.
Ḥâlic, *adj.* intense black.
Ḥâlic el ġorâb, raven black.
Esmar Ḥâlic, dark brown.
Eswad Ḥâlic, jet black.

حلق Ḥalqa 2, 10, ring, hoop, circle of company. [curb ال
Ḥalq el fecc, a horse's ring-
Ḥalieqa, ring fence.
Moḥallaq, annulated.
v. Teḥallaq, *vn* form a circle in sitting, soar in circles.
(2) Ḥalq 3, Ḥölqoum 11, throat.
Ḥalq 3, edge of a tool.
Uḥliq, *va* shave (the *throat*).
Ḥallâq, barber.
Ḥalâqa, trade of barber.
Muḥlaq, razor x.; *vulg.* Mous Ḥalâqa, knife for shaving.
Ḥalqiey, guttural.
Ḥalqieya, guttural letter.

هلس Helis, worthless.
Helese, a trifle.
Hellous, cobweb s.
viii. Mohtelis, imbecile.

حلس Ḥuls 3, padsaddle.

هلز Helezoun 11, snail.

HM

هم Homm bi, *vn* meditate on, be about to (do).
Hemm bi xorous, it was about to be begun *r*.
Hemm, Himma 10, earnest purpose, care, anxious effort.
ذو همة Dou himma, earnest, energetic.
Homâm (in high style?) energetic, heroic.
Mohimm, important. [ance.
Mohimmêt, things of importance.
Ehemm, more important.
Ehemmieya, greatest importance.
iv. Ehimm, *va* make anxious.
viii. Ihtimm bi, li, *vn* be anxious, zealous, exert oneself in mind and body for.
Ihtimâm, solicitude.
(2) Hêmma, creeping thing; *pl.* 12, Hewâmm, reptiles.
(3) Hom, *pron.* them; Homâ, them two.
(4) Hemhim, *vn* whoop, drone, sing lullaby.

هم Hömma' 2, fever.
Hömâm, hot fit of fever.
Hammâm 2, hot bath.
Hammâmicy, bath-man.
ii. Hammim, *va* heat the water for the bath.
x. Isteḥumm, *vn* take hot bath.

هم Wehm, *s.* notion, whim.
Wehmiey, fanciful, conjectural.
Wehmieya, hypothesis, chimaera.
Wehem Yehim, *vn* fancy.
Mauhoum, fancied, uncertain.

ПMY

ii. Wehhim, *va* cause to fancy, instil a notion, infuse suspicion.
v. Tewehhem, *vp* of ii.; also *vn* nearly as i. *or* suspect.
viii. Ittehim bi, *va* suspect (a person) of.
Mottchim, *s.* imputer, accuser.
Tohma, suspicion, slander, accusation.

هام Hêma, *nu* 2, head, crown, pate (old word).

حوم Höum, *vn* rest on the wing, hover, flit round and round, roam.

هم Hiem, *vn* stray, rove; generally *fig.* rave, doat with love.
Hiem bi, be enthusiastic for.
Hêyim, enthusiastic. [siasm.
ii. Heyyim, *va* fill with enthuHoyâm bi, enthusiasm for.
x. Istehiem, *va* make frantic with love.
Mostehêm, thus frantic.

همى Uḥmi san, *va* avert (danger) from.
Humâya, protection (by a prince), safe conduct.
iii. Hâmi, *va* protect (a person).
vi. Teḥâmâ san, *vn* beware of.
viii. Uḥtemi teḥt, *vn* shelter oneself under. *Also*,
Uḥtemi min, abstain from *s.*
Uḥtimâ, abstinence.
Moḥtemi, abstinent, sober.
(2) Uḥma', *vn* become hot *s.*

ḤMY

be full of natural heat; *fig.* chafe, be angry.
Ḥâmi, full of natural heat B. warm, ardent. Ḥâmi fie, vehement in.
Ḥömouwa, warmth of feeling.
Ḥamieya, ardour, earnestness.
Ḥömou, crysipelas. See (3).
ii. Ḥammi, *va* heat (water, an oven), bathe or foment in hot water; *fig.* foment, animate. See Ḥammim.
iv. Aḥmi, *va* heat up. Also *vn* glow in the fire s.
(3) Ḥamou, father-in-law.
Ḥamâya, mother-in-law.
(4) Ḥamâwa, deep mire (*in the Psalms*).

حمد Ohmod, *vn* die out (as fire).
Homoud, extinction.
Hemda, apoplexy.
iv. Ehmid, *va* quench (fire); *fig.* quench, quell.

حمد Oḥmod, *va* praise (God). *ger.* Ḥamd, praise.
Ḥamoud, Ḥamied, praiseworthy.
Aḥmad, more praiseworthy.
Maḥmoud, Moḥammed, much praised.
Ḥamâd leho! bravo to him!
Ḥammâd, great praiser.
iv. Aḥmid, *va* approve?
v. Teḥammad, *vn* deserve praise, cala', with (a person), bi, for (a thing) x.

حمض Oḥmoḍ, *vn* become sour.
Ḥâmuḍ, sour.

ḤML

Ḥömouḍa, sourness.
iv. Aḥmuḍ, *va* make sour.
Ḥömmâḍ, Ḥömmaiḍ, sorrel (herb).

حمج Hemej, the vulgar, the populace.
Hemij, Hemejiey, vulgar, brutal, barbaric, barbarous B. F.

حمل Homoul, *ger.* downpouring (of rain).
ii. Ḥemmil, *va* pour down rain (said of the heaven).
Hêmil, *adj.* straying loose; *fig.* abandoned.
iv. Ehmil, *va* leave to itself, neglect. Mohmil, negligent.
Mohmal, obsolete (word).
Ihmêl, negligence.
v. Tehêmal can, be neglectful of.
Tehêmol, neglectfulness.

حمل Uḥmil, *va* carry, bear (fruit); *fig.* impel. *ger.* Ḥaml.
Ḥamla, a cavalry charge.
Ḥuml 4, a load; *fig.* impost, Ḥumla, land-rent. [tax.
Ḥammâl, porter.
Ḥömla, transport.
Ḥömoula, porterage.
Ḥumâla 11, Ḥammâla, sash or belt supporting a sword.
Ḥamiela, amulet, often carried around the neck.
Ḥamoul, Moteḥammil, patient, much-enduring.
Ḥâmil, carrying, *i.e.* pregnant.
Moḥmil, pannier; bier; *uterus* of woman.

ḤML ḤMZ

iv. Aḥmil, va load (a beast).
ii. Ḥammil, va impel, incite (horse or man).
v. Teḥammal, x. Isteḥmil, vn be forbearing, patient.
vii. Inḥamil cala', vp be impelled, incited to or against.
viii. Uḥtemil, va admit, permit. Lâ yoḥtemal, it is incredible. Moḥtemal, admissible (possible or probable).
Uḥtimâl, admissibility.
(2) Ḥamal, Ram of the Zodiac, Lamb of Christian theology; Host, or Catholic wafer.
(3) Ḥoml (*vowel uncertain*) 3, carpet B. (woman's camel litter x.).

Hemmin cala', vn care for, watch over B.
(2) Homâyoun, august, royal. Homâyouni, belonging to royalty, imperial.

v. Tehemmec, vn persist.
vii. Inhemic bi, vp be devoted or addicted to.
Monhemic, debauched B.

Aḥmaq, fatuous, a dolt. Ḥamâqa, doltishness, infatuation.
Uḥmaq, vn be fatuous. [tion.
vi. Teḥâmaq, vn affect stupidity.
Ḥamqiey, stupid.

Ohmor, vn show the teeth, snarl as dog (B. under Dents); growl. *ger.* Hemr.

Aḥmar, red.
Aḥmar qâni, deep red.   [las.
Ḥömra, s. red, redness, erysipe-
Aḥmarâni, reddish?
ix. Uḥmirr, vn grow red.
Moḥmirr, growing red, reddish?
(2) Ḥumâr, ass, *pl.* Ḥamier.
Ḥammâr, muleteer.   [man.
Ḥummier, "great ass," stupid
Ḥamaricya, Ḥamrana, stupidity.
Yaḥmour, Numidian antelope F.
(3) Ḥömar, bitumen of Judœa.

Ḥamies, energetic.
Ḥamâse, energy, enthusiasm.
Ḥamâs, enthusiasm B.
Teḥâmase, emulation.
iv. Aḥmis, va animate.
viii. Uḥtemis, vp or vn be animated, energetic.

ii. Ḥammus, va toast, roast (coffee).
Moḥammas, s. toast AL.
Maḥmas, coffee roaster x.

Hêmix, margin of book.

Ohmoz, ii. Hemmiz, va spur. Hemezêt, instigations.
Mihmêz 11, spur; factotum B.
Mihmeze, a goad.
(2) Homze, a grammatical mark (').

Uḥmiz, va prick (the tongue), impress (the mind).
Ḥâmiz, Ḥamies, *piquant;* tart, acid; lively, impressive. See Ḥâmuḍ.
Ḥamâze, tartness, liveliness.

HN

هنّ Honna, *fem.* they, them.

(2) Hinn, Henhin, *vn* cry out with joy and tenderness.
Hennouna, Henhouna, compliments chanted in honour of those who aid in a wedding n.

حنّ Hunn ila', *vn* feel tenderness to; *Gr.* στέργω. *ger.* Hanien.
Hunn, compassion.
Hanna, tender affection.
Hannicya, commiseration.
Hanân, compassion (of God).
Hanuên, (God) the compassionate.
Hanonn, affectionate, tender.
v. Tehannen sala', *vn* be deeply moved for.
vi. Tehânan sala', yearn for.
x. Istehunn, d°· x.

وهن Wehen Yehin, *vn* be feeble, faint. Wêhin, feeble.
Wohn, feebleness.

هون Houn, *vn* be slight, worthless. [security.
Hewân, Mehêna, neglect, obiii. Hêwin, *vs* slight (a person); use (a tool) unfairly.
iv. Ehien, *vs* slight (a person).
Ihêna, *s.* slight, disdain.
Mohien, disdainful.
Mohên, slighted.
x. Istehien, *vs* underrate, disparage, slight.
Heiyin, *adj.* slight (task), easy.
Hiena, ease, comfort. Bi hie-

HNY

natec, at thy convenience. *So* sala' heun-ec c.
Ehwan, easier.

(2) Hêwân, Hé'oun, a mortar for pounding in. *Also*, a mortar, piece of artillery; *pl.* Hewâwien.

حين Huin, season, moment, crisis, occasion; *pl.* 4, Ahyân.
Huinama, at the moment when.
Ahyâna⁰, at times, occasionally.
Lil Huin, instantly.
Huina⁰, once upon a time.
Huina, hour or moment of the day.
Huin, *vn* arrive, as a crisis.
Hân el Huin, the crisis is arrived.
ii. Hayyin, *vs* fix a season.
Mohayyan, one whose hour (of death) is come n.

حنو Ohnon, Uhni, *vs* curve, arch. *ger.* Hanou.
Harab el Hunâ, osiers?
Hunâya, curvature; arch of doorway.
Hanieya, a curve.
Ahna', Monhani, curved.
vii. Inhani, *vp* be curved.

هني Heniey, digestible.
Henieya⁰ marieya⁰ ! (may your food be to you) digestible and nourishing !
Ihna', *vs* nourish (as food).
ii. Henni bi, *vs* compliment, congratulate for.
Tehniya 11, congratulation.

ΠNY

v. Tehenná bi, ⲧⲛ find oneself better for (food).
Motchenni, at one's ease, comfortable.
(2) Henâ, Honâ (*vulg.* in Syria, Heun, Hôn, Hôni), here.
Honêc, there (*istic* of Latin).
Honâlic, yonder (*illic*).
Hêniⲁe! look there! lo! (*Gr. ἠνιδε!*)

حنبل Πönbal, bean (fasóole) Β.

هند Hind, India.
Hindiey, Indian.
Honoud, Indians.

هندب Hindiba, endive.

هنذ Hêniⲁe, look there! behold!

هندم Hendim, *va* adjust symmetrically; plane (timber).
Hindâm, symmetry.

حندقوق Πandaqouq, lotus.

هندس Hindese, geometry.
Hindesiey, geometrical.
Mohendis, geometer, engineer.

هندز Hindázo, an ell Β.
Hindezo, Hindeziey, Mohendiz, perhaps have z or s indifferently.

حنف Πanâfi, orthodox.
(2) Πanafieya, a stopcock Β.

هنجم Henjim bi, *v* flout, insult Β.
Mohenjim, insolent.

ΠC

حجم Teñanjal, *va* dance a jig.
See Uñjil, hop.

حنجد Πönjond, phial Κ. [But v. has Πönjour.]

حنجر Πönjour 11, Πanjara 11, the windpipe.

حنك Πanec 4, underjaw, chinbone, jaw of animal.
viii. Uñtenic, *va* bridle (a horse) Κ.

حنق Uñnaq, *va* be wroth. *ger.* Πanaq, wrath.
iii. Πâniq, *va* chide angrily.
iv. Añniq, *va* incénse.
vi. Teñânaq, *vr* wrangle together wrathfully.

حنت Πânout 12, a tavern, wineshop, booth.

حنط Πουτα 10, wheat.
(2) Πunâra, art of embalming.
ii. Πannut, *va* embalm.
Πunât, *pl.* spices for embalming.

حنث Uñnaθ, *vn* perjure oneself. *ger.* Πunθ, perjury.
Πâniθ, perjured.
iv. Añniθ, *va* excite to perjury.

حنش Πanax 4, a serpent.
Mañnoux, bitten by a serpent.

حنظل Πangal, colocynth Β.

هت Heqhiq, *vn* trudge.

حكك Πöcc, *va* rub, scrape, scratch; harrow (the feel-

ПС

ings); polish (jewels); assay (metal) в.
Пöcêce, scrapings.
Паccêc, polisher of jewels.
Moflacce, friction.
Miflacce, a rasp.
iii. Пâcic, *va* tickle, cajole x.

حتى Пaqq 3, one's right, what is one's due; right, truth; a matter. *vulg.* belonging to.
Пaqieq, true.
Пaqieqa, truth.
Пaqieqat^{en}, in truth.
Пaqieqiey, real.
Пaqqûni, genuine.
ii. Пaqqiq, *va* ascertain, verify.
Moflaqqaq, ascertained, sure.
Teflqieq, verification.
v. Teflaqqaq, *vp* of ii.
vi. Teflâqaq, *vn* debate a right together.
x. Isteflaqq, *va* deserve; *also* judge to be right, approve.
Mosteflaqq, *adj.* due.
(2) Пöqqa, pomatum box.

وحتى Waheq 4, lasso, running noose.
Miеheqa, *pl.* Mawêhiq, d°-

حوك or حيك Пouc, *va* and ii. Пayyic, *va* weave. Пâyic, weaver.
Пuyâce, texture, weaver's art.
(2) iv. Afluic, *va* penetrate.

حول ii. Пawwiq, *va* leer at в.

حيك see Пöuc.

ПСМ

حين ii. Пayyiq, *va* season (meat).

حكى Ufici, *va* relate, recount.
Пucêya 2, narrative, tale.
iii. Пâci, *va* resemble (N.B.).
vi. Teflâcê, *vn* chat? confer.

حقد Пuqd, *s.* spite, grudge.
Пaqieda 11, d°-
Пaqoud, spiteful.
Uflqid sala', *vn* feel spite against.
iv. Aflqid, *va* excite to hatred.
v. Teflaqqad, *vn* nearly as i.
viii. Ufltaqid, *vn* grudge itself, *i.e.* be deficient x.

هيكل Haicel, temple and altar, *esp.* of Jerusalem.
(2) Ihcel, be agitated?
Yehcil hemmoh, he is disquieted; lâ tchcil hemm, be not disquieted в.
v. Tehêcel, *se battre* x.

حقل Пaql 3, cultivated or enclosed field.

هكم ii. Heccim, *va* sneer at.
v. Teheccom, *s.* sarcasm.
Teheccomiey, sarcastic.

حكم Oflcom sala', *vr* pass sentence on; be judge and governor over. Пâcim, governor, possessed of executive and judicial power.
Пöcm 4, ordinance, authority, post of command.
Пöconma, (the) Government.

ПСМ

Пасiem, *s.* a sage, wise man, doctor, physicist.
Пöcmicy, sententious.
Пucma, wisdom, philosophy.
Maſlcema, judgment hall; tribunal. [diction.
v. Teſlaccem, *vn* exercise juris-
Teſlaccom, sententiousness.
Moteſlaccim bain, arbiter between.
Moteſlaccim, *adj.* sententious.
(2) Пucema, martingale x. (in Aleppo, selibind).
iv. Aſlcim, *va* harness, bridle.
(3) ii. Пaccim, *or* iv. Aſlcim, *va* establish.
Пaccim (in physiology), *va* elaborate (juices of the body).
x. Isteſlcim, *vn* be solid, consolidated; set in, as winter.
Mosteſlcim, fixed, situated, as a mountain or region.

Oſlqon, *va* rince, scour out.
Пöqna (in medicine), lavement, clyster.
viii. Uſltaqin, *vn* take a clyster.

Ihcir, *vn* fall into deep slumber. *ger.* Hecr, deep sleep, coma (*medical t.*).

Пacer, Пacoura, enclosure between walls в.
Пacer, floor-rent, ground-rent of house.
Oſlcor, *or* viii. Uſltecir, heap (corn) on the floor, store up (corn).

WHR

Oſlqor, *va* despise, scorn.
viii. Uſltaqir, *or* x. Isteſlqir, same as i.
Пaqier, contemptible, insignificant, minúte.
Пaqâra, insignificance.
Teſlqier, contempt.

Hirr, *f.* Hirra, cat c. *obsolete?*

Пarr, *s.* heat (in philosophy).
Пarr, Пarâra, heat (of sun, or of water).
Пarûra, heat (of the body), inflammation.
Пurr, *va* heat, make hot в.
Пârr, hot (water, tears, sun).
Пarrân, burning (skin of man).
Aſlarr, hotter.
x. Isteſlurr, *vn* grow hot.
(2) Пarier 11, silk.
Пarieriey, silk merchant.
(3) Пörr 4, free, freeborn.
El aſlrâr, men of honour в.
Пörriey, belonging to freedom.
Пörrieya, freedom.
Пörra, noble character.
Ibn Пörra, man of honour.
(4) ii. Пarrir *va* adjust; *sap. with* cala', point (a cannon) at; *fig.* pass strictures on, censure.
(5) ii. Пarrir, *va* write with one's own hand. [в.
(6) Пariera, pap, infant's food

Wehra, horror (modern word).
v. Tewehher, *vn* shudder.

HWR

هور Hour, *vn* be dilapidated.
Hêyir, Heyyâr, ruinous (wall).
Hewâra, dilapidation, ruin.
ii. Hewwir, *va* dilapidate.
v. Tehewwar, *vn* fall in ruin;
fig. be precipitate.
Tehewwor, precipitation.

حور iii. Hâwir, *va* address by speech.
Moḣâwara, dialogue.
vi. Teḣâwar, *vn* converse, talk together.
(2) Aḣwar, black-eyed.
Ḣöuriya, (black-eyed) nymph, nymph of Paradise c.; *pl.* Ḣöur el ṣain.
(3) Ḣaur, poplar B. C.
(4) Ḣaur, red leather.
(5) Ḣaura, chalk B. Ḣawwâr, chalk AL
(6) Ḣâra, quarter (of city).
(7) Ḣawâriey 1, Christian apostle.

حير Ḣaira, stupor, perplexity.
Ḣâyir, Ḣairân, stupefied.
ii. Ḣayyir, *or* iv. Aḣuir, *va* stupefy, perplex.
v. Teḣayyar *or* viii. Uḣtêr, be stupefied, perplexed.

هري Horio, garner, *pl.* Ehrâ.
(2) iv. Ehri, *va* rot (cloth, etc.).
viii. Ihteri, *vp* be rotted (as clothes), be boiled to rags.
Mehriey, infected (person) B.

حري Aḣra', preferable.
Cem aḣra'! how much rather!

HRD

Ḣariey bi, worthy of s.
Bil ḣara' 'en, it is right that;
Hou ḣara' 'on, he ought to x.
v. Teḣarrâ li, *vn* have preference for.
Toharrie li, preference for.

هرع Ihras, *vn* hurry. *ger.*
Heras, Horâs, hurrying, hurry.
Mohras, hurried and trembling.
iv. Ehris, *va* hurry, alarm.

هرب Ihrab, *vn* flee, run away. *ger.* Herbân.
Herieba, Horoub, desertion of a soldier.
Hirâb, flight. [to flight.
ii. Herrib, *or* iv. Ehrib, *va* put

حرب Ḣarb 3, war, *f.* (but also *m.* x.).
Ḣöraib, little war x.
Muḣrâb, very warlike, *pl.* Muḣraba.
Ḣarba 5, javelin, bayonet.
ii. Ḣarrib *or* iv. Aḣrib, *va* excite to war.
iii. Ḣârib, *va* make war upon.
Moḣârib, warrior. [tually.
v. Teḣârab, *vn* make war mu-
(2) Ḣurbâ, *f.* Ḣurbâya 11, chameleon.
(3) Maḣrâb 11, chancel of mosque or church; sanctuary; dais or raised floor of hall.

حرد Uḣrad, *vn* fret. *ger.* Ḣarad, irritation.
ii. Ḣarrid, *va* fret, irritate.

ḤRD

Ḥardân, irritated.
(2) Ḥurdaun, Lybian lizard.

حرض ii. Ḥarruḍ, *va* excite, stimulate.

هرف Ihraf bi, *vn* vaunt of, puff off.

حرف Ḥurfa 10, a trade, art, craft. Ḥurâfa, dexterity B.
Ḥarief, fellowcraftsman.
vi. Teḥâraf ṣala', practise craft against.
viii. Uḥterif *vn* follow a trade.
Moḥterif, craftsman.
(2) Ḥarf, corner, tip, end; *pl.* Ḥörouf, letter of alphabet.
(3) Uḥrif *or* ii. Ḥarrif, change, derange, impair, misinterpret.
vii. Inḥarif, *vp* of preceding.
Inḥurâf, derangement.
Monḥarif, oblique, aslant.
(4) Ḥörf, watercress.
Ḥarâfa, piquancy.
Ḥurrief, pungent of taste.

هرج Ihrij *or* vi. Teḥêraj, *vn* struggle, as an animal when stabbed B.
Herj, a fray? See Hirâx.
(2) ii. Herrij, *vn* play the buffoon, mock.

حرج Ḥarij, narrow, scanty (garment).
ii. Ḥarrij, *va* make narrow, trammel; ṣala', restrict.
— calaihi bi'en, urge him to.

ḤRN

(2) Ḥarâj, an auction.
ii. Ḥarrij, proclaim an auction.

حرجم iii. *partic.* Moḥranjim, thronging, flocking r.

هرول Herwil, *vn* hurry, scamper, amble AL. *See* Hercil.

هرم Heram 5, pyramid (of Egypt).
(2) Herim, aged, decrepit.
Heram, decrepitude.

حرم Uḥrim, *or* ii. Ḥarrim, *va* forbid.
Ḥarâm, a thing forbidden; illicit or sacred.
Ḥarâmiey, rascally, a rascal, a robber.
Ḥörma, a lady, *pl.* Ḥariem.
El Ḥariem, the female sex.
Also, Ḥörma, respectability, as Uḥtirâm.
Ḥariem, toilet-table.
Maḥrima 11, toilet, kerchief.
Ḥurâm, woollen wrapper, blanket.
v. Teḥarram, *va* act recklessly, lawlessly; play the robber.
Teḥarrom, robbery.
viii. Uḥterim, *vp vn* be revered, be venerable.
Uḥtirâm, the being venerated, respectability.

حرن Oḥron, *vn* be refractory, restive. *ger.* Ḥurân.
Ḥaroun, restive, jibbing (horse).

ḤRC

حرك Ḥaric, stirring, alert.
Ḥurêc, motion.
Ḥarace, movement; vowel point.
Muḥrec, fire-rake, poker.
ii. Ḥarric, *va* move, stir (gently or violently).
v. Teḥarrec, *vp* or *vn* of dᵒ
(2) Ḥâric, Ḥaurec, withers of a horse.

حرق Oḥroq, *va* burn. *ger.* Ḥarq.
viii. Uḥteriq, *vp* be burned.
Ḥôrâqa, fuel.
Ḥarieqa, conflagration.
Ḥarrâq, incendiary *a.*
Ḥarrâqa, fireship, blistering plaster.

حرقف Ḥarqafa, the hip B.

هركل Hercil, *vn* trot (*Barb.*) for classical Arqil.

حركش Ḥarcix, *va* ransack.

هرس Ohros, *va* crush, smash B. *ger.* Hers, contusion.
(2) Mibres 11, howitzer, a kind of cannon.

حرس Uḥris, *va* defend.
x. Isteḥris sala', keep guard over.
Ḥares, the guard *or* guards.
Ḥâris 7, guardsman, guardian.
Ḥaresiey, guardsman.
Ḥurâse, defence, protection.
v. Teḥarres min, *vn* be on one's guard against, beware of.
(2) Ḥarsên (B. *sic*), measles.

ḤRX

حرص Oḥros sala', *vn* be eager for. *ger.* Ḥurs, avidity, eagerness.
Ḥarcis, eager, careful.
ii. Ḥarrus, *va* cause to covet; excite to eagerness.
viii. Uḥterus, *va* covet.

حرث Oḥroθ, *va* till (the ground). *ger.* Ḥarθ, Ḥurâθe, tillage.
Ḥâriθ, Ḥarrâθ, cultivator.
Muḥraθ, plough.

حرش Ihrix, *vn* be cruel, as fortune. Herix, cruel (event).
ii. Herrix, *or* iii. Hêrix, *va* bait (a bull, a bear), exasperate. *ger.* Hirâx, noise of fighting, squabbling.
vi. Tehêrax, *vp* be baited, fight.

حرش Aḥrax, Ḥariex, rough (skin).
Ḥôrxa, Ḥarâxa, roughness.
ii. Ḥarrix, *or* iii. Ḥârix, *va* exasperate, worry.
iv. Aḥrix, *va* blister (the skin) K.
vi. Teḥârax, *vr* exasperate one another, as dogs fighting.
viii. Uḥterix bi, provoke to combat.
Moḥterix, irritated.
Ḥarxiey, *fig.* bitter, sharp.
(2) Ḥurx 4, 3, forest, wood; *more classical* Ḥurj.

حرشف Ḥarxafa, scale of fish.
Ḥarxouf, artichoke Bg. (*Ital.* carciofi).

ḤRZ

حرز Ḥuraz 4, amulet.
Ḥariez, valuable, cherished; pl. 11, Ḥaráyiz, things choice.
iv. Aḥriz, vs cherish, guard, earn. Coll⁰ xai' yoḥriz θeman, everything earns value, has its value. Lâ toḥriz xai', it is worth nothing.
Moḥarraz, much prized.
viii. Uḥteriz ean or min, vn guard oneself against, abstain from. See Ḥrs.

حس Ḥass, vs feel, perceive, ger. Ḥass. Ḥasse, a sensation.
Ḥásse, pl. Ḥawáss, a sense.
Ḥassieya, sentiment.
ii. Ḥassis, vs handle, feel, try b.
(2) Ḥöss, vs curry (a horse) b.
Muḥass, currycomb x.
(3) Ḥasḥus, vn grope, fumble (b. tátonner).
(4) Ḥasḥus, vn jabber (b. baragouiner).

حص Ḥussa 10, share, portion.
ii. Ḥassas, vs divide into shares.
iii. Ḥasus, vs assign shares (or his share) to.
vi. Teḥásas, vn accept shares.

حوس Hewas, foolish passion.
ii. Hewwis, vs infatuate.
Mehwous, Mohewwas, infatuated. [with.
vii. Inhewis bi, be infatuated

حوس Ḥōus, vn go to and fro, scour (a country).

ḤSD

ii. Ḥawwis (corruptly Ḥawwix al.), hunt after, search for.
Teḥwies, promenade (Algiers).

حصو Ḥaswa, pebble; pl. Ḥaṣâ; also, gravel the disease.
iv. Aḥsu, vs compute (by pebbles). Lâ yoḥsâ, incalculable.

حصى Ḥasáya, embroidered belt.

حسب Oḥsob, vs reckon. ger. Ḥasb. Bi ḥasb, eala' ḥasb, according to.
Ḥusba 10, a computation.
Ḥuseb, Maḥsoub, bill, account.
ii. Ḥassib, vs account, deem.
v. Teḥasseb min, vn take precautions against. [account.
viii. Uḥtesib, vn draw up an Moḥtesib, clerk of the market.

حسب Ḥasaba, measles.
Maḥṣoub, ill of the measles.

حسد Oḥsod, vs envy. ger. Ḥased, envy.
Ḥasoud, envious.
Maḥsoud, envied.

حصد Oḥṣöd, vs harvest, crop, reap, etc.
viii. Uḥtasud, vs d⁰
Ḥasuida, ger. harvesting.
Ḥaṣád, harvest, crop.
Ḥaṣáda, harvest time x.
Ḥáṣud 12, Ḥaṣṣád, reaper, mower, etc.

ḤṢL

حصل Uḥṣul, *vn* happen, accrue; alight (upon), arise (from). El Ḥâṣul, the result, the produce. Maḥṣul 11, return, profit. Maḥṣûlât, crops, produce. Ḥaṣuila 2, net produce x.
ii. Ḥaṣṣul, *va* yield, produce, acquire. Taḥṣuil, acquisition.
v. Teḥaṣṣal, *vn* result, accrue. Moteḥaṣṣal, what accrues.
x. Isteḥṣul, *va* get, procure.
(2) Ḥauṣala, crop of bird.

حصم Oḥṣom, *va* cut away; generally *fig.* cut the knot of a question; deduct discount. *ger.* Ḥasm, *s.* discount, defalcation.
Ḥösêm, *s.* sword-edge x.

حسن Ḥasen, handsome. Aḥsen, better. Ḥösn, beauty. Ḥösein, pretty. Ḥasenêt, liberal actions. Maḥâsin, good qualities, good deeds, beauties.
Oḥson, *vn* be handsome.
ii. Ḥassin, *va* embellish.
iv. Aḥsin, *va* be rightful; do (a thing) well. Aḥsin fie, *vn* succeed in. (Mâ oḥsin, I do not succeed, *i.e.* I am not able, لا) Aḥsin li, do good service to, benefit.
Moḥsin, beneficent. Muḥsên, bounteous.
Uḥsên, the doing service.
x. Isteḥsin, *va* approve of, recommend; take in good part.

ḤṢR

حصن Ḥuṣn, *s.* fortress. Ḥöṣn, chastity x. Ḥaṣuin, fortified.
ii. Ḥaṣṣun, *va* fortify.
v. Teḥaṣṣan, *vp* be fortified, be chaste. [chaste.
iv. Aḥṣun, *va* keep safe, keep
vii. Inḥaṣun fie, *vp* be ensconced in. [horse.
(2) Ḥuṣân 8 (*also vulg.* 2) a

حسك Ḥasece, *ns* the spine. Ḥasec, fishbones, brushwood.

حسر Uḥser, *vn* stop short from fatigue. Uḥser can (of the eyes), fail to see, (as, when dazzled). *ger.* Ḥösour.
iv. Aḥsir (el ṭarf), *va* bedim (the eye).
(2) Ḥasra, a sigh.
ii. Ḥassir, *va* cause to sigh, displease, discontent.
Maḥsour min *or* sala', displeased at, sullen, sad.
v. Teḥasser, *vn* sigh.
vii. Inḥasir, *vn* repine.

حصر Oḥṣör (*see* Oḥzör), *va* coop up, hem in, restrict. *ger.* Ḥaṣr. [anguish.
Ḥaṣar, Ḥöṣra, tightness of heart,
iii. Ḥâṣur, *va* besiege. Moḥâṣara, a siege.
Ḥuṣâr, enclosure, palisaded ground; pen, pound; paddock.
vii. Inḥaṣur, *vp* be cooped up, distressed (by siege, *or* in heart).

ПЅR

Inꭡayur ſie, *vn* ensconce oneself in (for protection).
(2) Пayuira, *nu* 10 (*also* 11 ?), a mat of rushes.
Пöyöriey, matmaker or seller.

حصرم Пuyrim, verjuice, grape vinegar.

هات Hêt, *f.* Hêti, *pl.* Hêtou; (bring)hither. *More vulgarly* Jieb, Jiebi, Jiebou.

حتى Hatte', until, so that, in order that, = lecei.
(2) Пötte 10, 5, scrap, shred.
Пatꭡut, *va* slice up.

حط Пӧтт, *va* put, put down; suppress a practice. *vn* alight as a bird.
Maꭡaтт, resting place, stop in grammar.
Maꭡaтта, store place, depôt.
iii. Пáтuт, *va* encamp.
iv. Aꭡuтт, *va* depose, bring lower, degrade, depress.
vii. Inꭡuтт, *vp* of iv.
Inꭡuтât, the being lowered in estimation or power.

حث Пaөө, *va* incite. *ger.* Пaөө. [centive.
Maꭡaөөa, an incitement, in-
x. Isteꭡuөө, *va* same as i.

حوت Пöut 9, large fish.

حوط Пâyuт 5 (*vulg.* Пaiт 9), wall. [surround.
iv. Aꭡuiт, *va* fence around,

ПТМ

Moꭡuiт, *partic.* encircling.
Пöwâта, a safe, a larder.
ii. Пawwuт sala', hoard up, engross (corn, goods, etc.), в.
Пawwâт, engrosser, forestaller.
iii. Пâwuт, *va* surround or attend on, as *guard*; throng, beset.
viii. Uꭡtât, *vr* gird oneself around, be cautious.
Uꭡtiyât, caution.

حتى iii. Hêti sala', declaim against.

حطب Пaтab 4, firewood.
Пaтnib, covered with coppices.
Пaттâb, cutter or seller of firewood.
Пaтӧuba, a faggot of firewood.

حتف Ihtif, *vn* coo, moan, discourse sweetly and fluently.

حتف Пatf 3, natural death.

حتل Ohtol, *va* pour down (fine rain); also *vn* stream as rain.
Hêtil, streaming, as tears.

حتم Uꭡtim sala', *vn* pronounce upon, as judge. *ger.* Пatm, decree, ultimatum.
Пâtim, deciding, decisive.
Maꭡtoum, decided, definitive.
Пatmiey, imperative.

حطم Uꭡtrum, *or* ii. Пaттrum, split to shivers.
Пӧтâm, brittle.

ПТМ

Ηυrma 10, a shiver, splinter.
Πόrâma, a mass of splinters.

هتك Ihtic, va rudely unveil as by tearing, rend open; dishonour (a woman); unveil (faults) κ. ger. Hetc.
viii. Ihtetic, vp of i.

هتر Hitr 4, bravado, foolish boast.
v. Tehêter sala' or χ. Istehtir sala', dare, defy (any one); utter bravado against.

هش Soccer hexx, *powdered sugar* B. [*for* Hexim?]
(2) Hexxa, a cooler for water or wine B.

حش Πaxiex 11, grass, herb.
Πöxx, va cut grass for a horse.

وحش Waflx 3, wild animal.
Waflxiey, wild, savage; beastial, brutal.
Waflxana, savagery c.
Mauflöux, inhabited by savages.
ii. Waflflux, va reduce to savagery.
Mowaflflax, uncouth.
v. Tewaflflax, vn run wild, as beasts or planta.
Tewaflflöx, savage state.
x. Isteuflux, vp of ii. be given up to savagery.
Mosteuflux, (country) abandoned to wild nature.

هوش Heuxa, uproar.

НХМ

حوش Πöux, va detain, retain;
— nafseo min, abstain from.
Πaux, reserve, self-restraint B.
Ηuixa, reserve, modesty κ.
Πöuxa, forfeit for a wager B.
(2) Πöuxa 5, a cow Bg.
(3) Πaux, court of house, house with court AL

حشو Oflxou, va stuff, cram.
viii. Uflteri, vp be stuffed. ger.
Ηaxou, stuffing, padding.
Ηaxieya, padded vest or bed; *pl.* Πaxâ. (*See* the next).
Maflxouw, Maflxiey, stuffed.
ii. Πaxxi fie, va foist in, interpolate.
(2) Aflxâ, bowels.
Ηuxwa, *sing.* any viscus κ.
(3) Ηaxâ, thyme.

حشى Ηâxiya 12, skirt (of garment), clients (of great man), margin (of book).
ii. Ηaxxi, va put a border upon.
Moflaxxa', (book) written on margin.
(2) Ηâxâ! far be it! Except.

حشد Oflxod, va bring (an army) together.
ii. Πaxxid, d°.
viii. Uflterid, vp vn be gathered, as an army.
Ηâxid (Moflterid), ready c.

هشم Ihxim *or* ii. Hexxim, va squash, crack up (what is hollow and brittle).

ḤXM

حشم Ḥuxma, modesty.
Ḥaxam(a), band of respectful attendants. Ḥaxamwakadam, courtiers and servants.
viii. Uḥtexim, respect. [bred. Moḥtexim, respectful, well-
حشك ii. Ḥaxxic ṣala', vn storm against, pour invective on.
حشر Oḥxor, va press eagerly upon s. push in, foist in s.
vii. Inḥaxir, vn push oneself in, intrude s. to push oneself (into an assembly) s.
iii. Ḥâxir, va vie with. Moḥâxara, competition.
Ḥaxâra, rabble.
Ḥaxarât, pl. vermin.

حز Hozz, va shake. ger. Ḥizzo, a shaking.
ii. Hezziz, va do intens.
v. Tebezzez, and viii. Ihtizz, vp be shaken, vn shake.
Mahezze, commotion.
Hezhiz, va rock. ger. Hazheze.

حز Ḥözz, va notch.
Ḥazze, nu a notch.
(2) Ḥazêz, scurf of the head.

حظ Ḥaẓẓ, vn be happy, lucky. ger. Ḥaẓẓ, luck, fortune (good or bad).
Ḥaẓẓuiy, Maḥẓöuẓ, fortunate.

حوز Ḥöuz, va possess, enjoy.
Ḥauz, box containing sacred gear v.

HZM

Ḥauze, a possession, dominion.
(2) vii. Inḥâz, vn decamp, retire; ran, from.

حز Ihzi, va mock at, deride.
Hozzê, a mocker.
Hezwiey, ironical.
x. Istehzi, same as i.
Istihzê', mockery.

حظي Uḥẓa' bi, vn be victorious in; win, obtain. ger. Ḥaẓöu, success, advantage.
Ḥuẓwa, esteem, honour.
Ḥaẓuiy, successful, fortunate.
[See Ḥaẓẓuiy under Ḥaẓẓ.]

حزب Huzb 4, Ḥuzba, a party, faction, section.
ii. Ḥazzib, va divide into sections x. digest into portions.
iii. Ḥâzib, va take (others) as partizans.
v. Teḥazzeb, vn unite in troops, confederate. Compare Tesayyab.

حزل Hezil, Heziel, pl. Hezla', slight, flimsy, lean, spare.
Hozêl, leanness.
Mehzoul, slim, spare.
(2) Hezil, jocose.
Hezl, Hozêla, jocosity, fun.
iii. Hêzil, va banter.

حزم ii. Hezzim, va rout (an army); break in pieces.
viii. Inhexim, vp be routed, broken. [defeat.
Haziema, Inhizêm, rout, total

ḤZM

حزم Uḥzim, *va* gird, girth.
Ḥuzêm 10, a girth. [shcaf.
Ḥözma, bale, bundle, truss,
Muḥzem, bath-apron.
ii. Ḥazzim, *or* iv. Aḥzim, *va* belt, girth, nearly as i.
viii. Uḥtezim, *ep* of i.
(2) Ḥazm, Ḥazêma, resolution, prudence, firmness.
Ḥaziem, Ḥâzim, prudent, firm.

حزن Ḥözn 4, grief.
Ḥazin, Ḥazien, sorrowful.
iv. Aḥzin, *va* grieve.
v. Toḥazzen, viii. Uḥtezin, *vn* grieve; *vp* be grieved.

حزق Uḥziq, *va* tighten.
ii. Ḥazziq, d^a *intens.* wring.
Ḥözouq, *pl.* tightenings v.
(2) Ḥazqa, Ḥazouqa, a hiccup v.

حزر Ibzir, ii. Hezzir, *va* deride.

حزر Oḥzor *or* ii. Ḥazzir, *va* guess, estimate v. *ger.* Ḥazr.
(2) Ḥözêr, canary-bird.
(3) Ḥazierân, month of July.

حظر Oḥgör, *va* pound or park (animals) x. *See* Oḥyör.
Muḥgöur, parked, pounded.
Ḥaguira 11, a park or pound.
viii. Uḥtagur, make a park x.

J.

جأ Ewijj, *vn* I blaze. *pret.*
'Ejj, Wejj, it blazed.

JƐD

'Ejja, *vulg.* Wejja, a blaze.
'Ejouj, Wejouj, *adj.* blazing.

جي Jie, *vn* come. Jie bi, come with, *i.e.* come by, get.
Jâyi, *partic.* coming.
Majie, arrival.
v. Tejâwa' ila', *vn* frequent, repair to (often).

جو Jawou, *s.* sky.
(2) Jouwa(t), within, *adv. prep.*
Jouwâni, interior, domestic.
(Both words modern.)

جع Wejas 4, pain.
iv. Aujus, *va* pain. Youjus-ni, it pains me.
Wejies, Moujus, painful.
v. Tewejjas, *vn* suffer pain.

جوع Jous, *s.* hunger, famine.
Jous, *vn* hunger, be hungry.
Jausân, hungry; *f.* Jausa', *pl.* Jiyâs.
ii. Jawwus, iv. Ajwus, *va* famish.

جعب Jasba 5, quiver.
Jassâb, quivermaker.

جعد Josda 5, a curl of hair.
Jasd, curling hair.
ii. Jassud, *va* curl the hair.
(2) Jasd, scum, dregs of the people x.
Josdiey, Josaidiey, ragamuffin v.

جعدب Josdaba, bubble of water c.

JƐF

جَعْفَر Jaɛfar, *s.* beck, torrent.

جَعَل Ijɛal, *ʋa* set, make.
Joɛl, *s.* wage agreed upon, set-price r.
iii. Jâɛul, *ʋa* manage, tamper with, bribe.
vi. Tejâɛal, *ʋn* agree on a price.
vii. Injaɛul, *ʋp* of i. viii. Ijteɛul, *ʋr* of i. become such or such x.
(2) Joɛal 8, dung-beetle.

جَعْلَك Jaɛlic, *ʋa* rumple, crumple.

جَعْمَص Jaɛmaʋ, a lubber s.

جَعَر Jaɛr 3, dung of birds or carnivora x.
Jaɛâr, hyæna x.
ii. Jaɛɛur, *ʋa* snarl?
Majɛar (in anatomy), the anus. Less coarse are kâtim and maqɛada.

جَبّ Jobb 5, a well built with brick or stone, a cistern.
(2) Jobb, *ʋa* geld, castrate.
(3) Jobba 10, a robe.
Jobba-kâna, a wardrobe.

وَجَب Wejab Yejib, *ʋn* be obligatory.
Wojoub, fitness, propriety.
Wâjib, *adj.* seemly, due, incumbent (ɛala'). *s.* 2, a duty.
Wajieba, *s.* meed, guerdon.
Mawâjib, *pl.* earnings.

JBL

Maujoub, rendered necessary, made incumbent.
ii. Wejjib, iv. Aujib, *ʋa* make obligatory, require, occasion.
Moujib, *partic.* occasioning. *s.* 2, a motive, reason.
x. Isteujib, *ʋa* deserve.

جَوب Jawâb 8, reply.
iii. Jâwib, *ʋa* answer (a person).
iv. Ajieb, *ʋa* say Yes to, agree to, approve of.
Mojâb, approved, accepted.
Iejâb, Ijâba, approval.
x. Istejwib, *ʋa* as iv.

جَيب Jaiba 3, a pocket.
(2) Jicb, *ʋn* (*modern verb*) bring; *for* Jie bi.

جبى Ijbi, *ʋa* collect revenue x. *ger.* Jibâya.
Jâbi, tax collector o.
Majbâ, tax, tribute x.
viii. Ijtɛbi, *ʋa* select.
Mojteba', *adj.* elect.

جَبهَ Jebah 5, Jebha 2, forehead. *Commoner* Jebien.
(2) Jebah, iron armour c. (vizor?).

جَبَل Jebal 5, mountain.
Jobail, small mountain.
Jebaliey, belonging to mountains.
Mijbâl, big as a mountain.
(2) Ojbol, *ʋa* mould, create.
Jibilla, natural quality.
Jibilliey, innate.

JBN

جبن Ojbon, *vn* be cowardly.
Jabân, cowardly.
Jabbân, great coward.
Jabâna, cowardice.
(2) Jebien, *s*. forehead.
(3) Jubona, *nu* a cheese.
iv. Ajbin, *va* curdle.
v. Tejabban, *vn* d⁰.

جبر Jabr, *s*. force, constraint.
Jabbâr, oppressor.
Joboura, Jabrout, violence, pride.
Ojbor, and iv. Ajbir, *va* force, constrain, domineer.
v. Tejabbar, *vn* play the autocrat.
(2) Ojbor, *va* consolidate, set (a bone).
ii. Jabbir, d⁰ x.
vii. Injabir, *vp* of ii.
Jâbir, a surgeon.
Jibâra 11, a splint.
El jabr, algebra.
Jabriey, algebraic B.

جبس جبس Jibs, Jibsien, Jifyuin, gypsum, plaster (corrupted into Juyy at Bagdad).

جد Jidd, *s.* seriousness. Bi jidd, in earnest.
Jidda⁰, earnestly, very.
Jidd, *vn* make effort, be earnest, be serious.
Jidd fil seir, make forced march.
(2) Jadd 3, grandsire.
Jadda, grandmother.
(3) Jadied, *adj.* new.
Jadda, Jaddiya, newness.
ii. Jaddid, *va* renew.
Mostejadd, *adj.* novel.

JAع

وجد Wejad Yejid, *va* find. *ger.* Wijdân, finding. *Also passive ger.* Wojoud, the being found, *i.e.* existence.
Maujoud, found, existing ; *pl.* Maujoudât, things existing ; assets.
Wojid, Youjad, *vp* was found.
iv. Aujid, *va* bring into existence, create.
Iejâd, *ger.* creation, invention.
Têjieda, a device.
(2) Wejd, ecstacy of love, ardour.
(3) vi. Tewâjad, *vn* pick up, as drooping crops ; grow stronger.

جود Joud, *vn* be excellent.
Joud, Jouda, Jâda, excellence.
Jaiyid, excellent.
Jaiyida⁰, Jaida⁰, excellently.
Jawwâd, bounteous.
(2) Jawâd, a steed ; *pl.* Jiyâd.

جدو Ojdou, *oftener* iv. Ajdi, *va* give, add, yield; *esp.* in the phrase, ajdi nafca⁰, yield advantage.
Mojdi, of much avail.
Jidâ, avail, utility.

جدي Jadie 9, a kid.

جدع iii. Jâdis, *vn* bicker with. *See* Jâdil.

جذع Jaes 3, stem of young tree.
Jaaes 9, 5, Ajaes, young man,

JDC

brave man. Yâ jadee! my brave young fellow!
Jodouea, youth.

جدب Jadb, dearth.
Mojdib, *partic.* bringing dearth.
Ajâdib, *pl.* defects of character.
(2) Jadba, an empty silly person.

جذب Ijaib, *va* draw, attract.
Jadba 2, attraction.
iii. Jâaib, *va* pull against.
vi. Tejâaeb, *vr* pull mutually.

جذف Ijaif, *va* row; Mijaêf 11, an oar. *vulg.* Qaddif, Miqdâf.

جدل Ojdol, *va* knit, plait.
Jadiel 10, 11, braid (of hair).
(2) iii. Jâdil, *va* scold, chide.
vi. Tejâdal, *vr* wrangle.
Mijdâl, very quarrelsome.
Jidâliey, controversial.
Jaddâl, wrangler. Bâbâ jaddâl, false Pope B.
(3) Jadwal 11, column of a book; geometrical diagram; schedule; a level (surveyor's instrument); a rill, small stream. [dule.
Mojadwal, tabulated in a sche-

جذم Jodêm, elephantiasis.
Ajdem, Majdoum, afflicted with this disease.

جدر Ojdor bi, *vn* be worthy of.
Jadier bi, worthy of.
Ajdar, more worthy. El ajdar

JFL

lec, ennec ..., the best thing for you, is, to ...
(2) Jidâr 10, a wall.
(3) Jodariey, small pox.
Majdour, marked with d°

جذر 3, root, esculent root; root, as in Algebra. *See* Jizer, carrots.

جفّ Jaff, Jiff, *vn* become dry and stiff, as the hide of a beast.
ii. Jaffif, *va* dry, stiffen: (cover with scaly armour K.).
vii. Injiff, *vn* stiffen oneself, as in rowing hard.

جوف Jauf 4, inner cavity, belly. Ajwaf, concave.
ii. Jawwif, *va* hollow.
Tejwief, ventricle (of heart) B.

جيف Jiefa 10, 4, carrion, carcase.

جفو Ojfou sala', *va* be obstinate against, disobey.
Jâfi, hard, *lit.* or *fig.* impenitent, untamed.
Jafâ, insubordination v. hardship o.
Jifâwa, cruelty.
Jafwa, *nu* an injustice, injury.

جفّ Jaffâk, boastful K.
See Jakk, Jamk.

جفل Ijfâl, *vn* start, as a shy horse. *ger.* Jofoul.
Jafoul, skittish.

JFL

Jiffiel, easily startled.
Jáfil, d⁰· fleeting (as a cloud), floating (as hair).

جفن Jufn 3, 4, eyelid.

جفس Jifsuin (γυψον), gypsum. Also, Jibs, Jibsien.

جفت Joft (sic c.), a pair, couple; bag, sack (of wheat)?

وجه Wejh 3, face, side.
Jihe 2, side, region.
[Jâh, Jâhe, dignity. *Pers.*]
Wejieh, good looking, specious?
Wajâhe, consideration, credit which one enjoys x.
Mowajhen, disingenuous c. (specious?).
Tojâh, *prep.* face to face with.
ii. Wajjih, *va* turn the face (of another towards), direct, address; presént, display: presént (to office): presént (a badge of honour).
Teujieh, a presentation.
iii. Wâjih, *va* confront.
Mowâjehe, personal meeting (of princes).
v. Tewajjah ila', *vn* turn one's face towards, set out for.
vi. Tewâjah, *vr* meet one another, face to face.
viii. Ittejih, *vn* present itself, as a thought.

جهى ii. Jchhi, *va* deduct beforehand B.
Tejhiya, deduction.

JHR

جهد Jehd, effort.
Jehd jehied, extreme effort.
viii. Ijtchid, *vn* make effort.
Mejhoud, *s.* endeavour.
Ijtihêd, diligence.
Mojtehid, diligent.
iii. Jêhid, *vn* make crusade.
Jihêd, crusade, sacred war.
Jihêdiey, military (*Egypt.*).
iv. Ajhid, *va* instigate, impel.

جحد Ijhad, *va* deny, abjure, recant. *ger.* Jahd, Joñoud.

جحش Jehila 12, colt, foal. *fig.* a brat.
Jehus, a shapeless abortion.
iv. Ajhus, *va* give birth to such.

جهل Jêhil 6, foolish, ignorant.
Jehoul, d⁰· Jehêla, folly.
Majhoul, unknown, obscure.
iii. Jêhil, *va* misapprehend, misappreciate.
v. Tejehhel, *vn* affect ignorance.
x. Istejhil, *va* ignore, treat as silly.

جهم Ijhem, *va* scowl at.
v. Tejehhem li, d⁰·
Jehim, *adj.* scowling.
Jihêma, Johouma, *ger.* of i.

جحيم Jaḥnim, fierce fire, hell-fire. *Oftener,* Jehennam.

جهر Jehr, clearness of pronunciation.
Jehir, manifest, public.
Jihêr, Jehra, Johoura, publicity.

JHR

Jehiraⁿ, Johrateⁿ, publicly.
Jehier, clearvoiced, loud.
Mijbêr, very loud of voice.
(2) Ajher, *adj.* having a cast in the eye.
Ijher, *vp* be dazzled.
ii. Jehhir (el bayar), dazzle or embarrass (the sight) B.
v. Tejehher, *vp* of ii. B.
(3) Johra, yellow dye Bg. GN.
(4) جوهر Jauher 11, essence, Jauheriey, essential. [jewel.

جحر Johr 4, hole, den, of beast.
Jâflur, hiding in its den.
iv. Ajflur, *va* drive to its den.
v. Tejafflur, viii. Injaflur, *vn* betake itself to its den.
viii. Ijteflur, *vn* make or choose a den for itself.

جرم Jehrima, a bravado.
ii. Tejehram, *vn* make bravado.

جحش Jaflx 5, donkey; meaner word than Humâr, ass, and in constant use.
Johaix, little donkey.

جهز Jihéz, *s.* apparel, rigging.
ii. Jehhiz, *va* rig, furnish, equip.

جحظ Jûfluz, protuberant as eye of hare F.

جوج Jaujifl, *va* swing (a person) in a swing.
ii. Tejaujafl, *vn* swing oneself.
Jaujeflûna, a swing c. *See* Marjiefla.

WJL

جك Jakk, *vn* vaunt, play a brilliant part B.
Jâkk, egotist B.
Jikka, boasting, display, egotism.
Δou jikka, gaudy B. See the classical Jafk, Jamk.

جوخ Jouk, woollen cloth.

جل Jall, *adj.* glorious (God).
Jall, *s.* the noblest part. *See* Jaliel, majestic. [Jomm.
Ajlal, more majestic.
Jalêla, majesty.
iv. Ajlil, *va* glorify.
Iejâl, glorification. [of.
vi. Tejâlel san, *vn* be disdainful
(2) Jilâl, *pl.* housings, women's saddle.
Jallâl, maker of such saddles.
ii. Jellil, *va* cover (*properly*, a horse's back).
v. Tejellel, *vp* be covered.
(3) Jolel, Joljol (=Jinjal) 11, cymbals, camel's bells.

اجل 'Ejl, sake. Li 'ejl, on account of.
Êjal, Êjala 4, epoch fixed in advance, fate.
Moweijal, (payment) due on a fixed day.
(2) From *Gr.* ἀγέλη, herd; Te'ejjal, *vn* flock together, as wild animals.

وجل Wejel Youjal, *v.* fear.
Wejal, *s.* fear. Wejil, timid.

JWL

جول Joul, *vn* go round, range, jaunt. *ger.* Jaulân.
Jawwûl, ranger.
Majâl, range, area, sphere of action. Fie majâli, within my range, *i.e.* in my power.
iii. Jâwil, *vs* take an enemy in flank.
(2) Jiel 4, a generation.
(3) Jawâl, bag c.
(4) Jawâls, tax (impôt B.).

جلى Ijli, *vn* appear unveiled. *ger.* Jelâ. v. Tejellâ, d°·
Jilwa, brilliant apparition.
Jelioy, clear, shining.
Ajla', brighter.
Jelieya", expressly.
ii. Jelli, *vs* reveal, manifest.
Tejellis, the Epiphany.

جلب Ojlob, bring in, import; bring on (evil consequences). *ger.* Jelb.
Jalab 4, the slave trade.
vii. Injalib, *vp* be carried as merchandize.
viii. Ijtelib, *vs* import for sale.
x. Istejlib, *vs* give order for importing (goods), send for.
(2) Jallib, *vn* stride B.
(3) Jolbân, peas, pease.
(4) Jelba (Jilba?), a hoop B.
(5) Jolaba, a hubbub, noise of a flock of seals F.
(6) Jolba, strip of plaster.

جلد Jild 3, skin, hide, leather.
Joloudisy, leatherseller.
Ojlod, *vs* flog with leather strap.

JM

Jellâd, public scourger, executioner.
ii. Jellid, *vs* bind a book in leather.
Mojellad, bound (book).
(2) Jelied, *s.* frost.
Jelied, *adj.* solid, hard.
Jelâda, solidity, hardness.
ii. Jellid, *vs* freeze.
v. Tejellad, *vr* be frozen, freeze.
iii. Jêlid, *vs fig.* turn the cold shoulder to (a person).

جلف Jilfa, a clot B.

جلس Ijlis, *vn* sit. *ger.* Jolous (sitting, accession *to throne*).
Jilse, a session (of Parliament).
Jelies 6, consessor, courtier-guest.
Jeliese, maid of honour.
Majlis, political assembly, great or small; a Cabinet, a Parliament, a Committee, a Board, a Meeting; *also*, company in the drawing-room. [side.
iii. Jêlis, *vs* take to sit by one
vi. Tejêles, *vn* sit side by side.
iv. Ajlis, *vs* seat, cause to sit.

جلط Jolta, a clot B.

جلوز Jilwâs, petty constable.

جم Jamm 5, *adj.* plentiful.
Jomm 3, full measure, the greater part. [number.
Jamma", in mass, in great
(2) Jomma, comb of cock, tuft, mass of hair, mass.
(3) Jomjoma 11, skull.

JM

(4) Jamjim, *vn* mumble.
Jamjama, inward speaking, speaking to oneself, "reticence" (a figure of Rhetoric), "thing purposely omitted in the discourse" B.

اجم 'Ejma, *pl.* 10, 'Ojam, jungle, damp forest.

جام Jâm 2, *or pl.* Ajwâm, chalice, drinking cup.
Jâm el flujâma, cupping glass.

جمع Ijmas, *va* gather, assemble. *ger.* Jams, a troop, the plural.
Jamâsa, company, society, a company, an association.
Jimâs, union (of man and Jemies, all. [woman).
Jamsuiya 11, a committee.
Jâmis 12, high mosque, Mussulman cathedral.
Jomsa, Friday; *also at Aleppo*, the week. [meeting.
Majmis, place of meeting; a
ii. Jammis, *va* compile.
viii. Ijtemis, *vn* or *vp* of i. assemble, be assembled.

جمد Ojmod, *vn* grow thick, freeze. *ger.* Jomoud, the being frozen; *fig.* stiffness, obstinacy.
Jomoudiey, glacial.
Jâmid, lifeless, motionless.
Jâmid el ceff, close-fisted.
Majmoud el ceff, d° [stiffen.
ii. Jammid, *va* thicken, freeze,
vii. Injamid, *vp* of ii.

JML

جمح Ijmafl, *vn* run away, as horse with his rider. *ger.* Jomoufl.
Jâmifl, skittish.
Jamoufl, restive, obstinate.

جمهر Jamhera, a troop.
Jomhour, the public, the Commons, a republic. [can.
Jomhouriey, popular, republi-

جمك Ijmak, *vn* be vainglorious. *ger.* Jamk.
Jammâk, vainglorious.
iii. Jâmik, *va* defy; challenge to a contest of glory.

جمل Ojmol, *vn* be beautiful. *ger.* Jemâl, beauty, handsome conduct.
Jemiel, beautiful; *also s.* handsome conduct.
Ajmel, more beautiful. [lish.
ii. Jemmil, *va* beautify, embel-
v. Tejemmel, *vn* behave handsomely. *Compare* Cêmil.
(2) Jomla 10, totality, sum; a group, a lot, several.
Jomlat**, Biljomla, in summary, in short.
Mojmala, sum total.
iv. Ajmil, *va* summarize.
Ijmâl, summary. *Compare*
(3) Jemal 5, camel. [Xemal.
Jemmâl, camel driver.
Jomâla, herd of camels K.
Jimâl, ridge (as of camel's back?), ridge of roof? Hâyut jamloun, gable B.?
Jammâla, sloping roof B.

JMK

جمكت Jàmicieya 12, salary.

جمر Jomra 10, hot coal.
Mijmara 11, brazier, censer.
ii. Jammir, va roast (chestnuts).
iv. Ajmir, va fumigate with censer. [tion.
viii. Ijtemir, vn make fumiga-

جمس Jâmous 12, buffalo.

جمز Jommaiz, pl. Jommaize', wild fig, sycamore.

جن Jinn, pl. genii, demons.
Jinniey, a genie.
Jinnieya, a fairy.
Jonoun, madness.
Majnoun, possessed, mad.
vi. Tejânn, vn be possessed by a demon k. [Paradise.
(2) Janna 2, 5, garden, esp. of Jonaina 11, (private) garden.
Janâyiniey, gardener.
(3) Jonna 10, armour.
Mijanna, buckler, escutcheon.
(4) Janien 6, embryo.
(5) Tejaun, occasion, crisis.

وجن Wejna 2, 4, Ojna, cheek, cheekbone, Lat. and Gr.
(2) Wajin Yejin, va beat (linen) with a bat in washing.
Miejana, pl. 11, Mawâjin, a bat, thumper, rammer.

جون Joun, Jouna, bay, cove; (hollow in the line of coast).
Jawien, adj. deep.
ii. Jawwin, va deepen. Also,

JNB

plunge (a person) deeply into; implicate, involve him (in loss or danger) B.
v. Tejawwan, vp be plunged or involved (in trouble).
[Jouwâni, interior; fromJouwa.]
(2) Jân-bâz, horse jockey, horse courser, horse dealer c.

جنى Ijni, va cull, gather (fruit).
Jeniey, freshpicked k.
v. Tejennâ eala', vn carp at (compare Latin carpo), cavil, slander. [oneself.
viii. Ijteni, va cull (fruit) for
(2) Ijni, vn be culpable.
Jâni, culpable.
Jinâya, an offence.

جنب Janb 3, side; prep. at side of. △êt el janb, pleurisy.
Jânib 12, side. Also, a (large) quantity ox.
Jonâb, pleurisy k.
Jenâb, a title of respect; Jenâbec, "your Excellency;" applied to the Sultan or to private persons.
Ijnab, vn incline to one side?
Ajnab 4 (pl. Ajânib c.), one who is on the frontier, a stranger. [ries.
Bilâd ajniba, neighbour countAjnabiey, belonging to the stranger. Also s. a stranger.
Majnab, frontier district.
iii. Jânib, va shun. Yet Jânib el barr, keep along the side of the land, i.e. stick by the coast.

JNB

v. Tejennab can, viii. Ijtenib can, *vn* keep aloof from.
vi. Tejânab, *vn* keep aloof from (mutually ?).
(2) Janoub, the South.
Janoubiey, Southern.
(3) Jenbalâticy, factions (*Ober-leitner*).

جند ‍ Jond, troops, soldiers.
Jondicy, a soldier. [In Egypt, a trooper, horse-soldier]
ii. Jennid, *va* levy troops.
Tejnied, a levy, conscription.

جندل ‍ Jandâl 11, a rapid of a river.

جنف ‍ Ijnif, *and* v. Tejannaf, *vn* be eccentric and harshly strange, estrange oneself.
Janâf, estrangement.
iv. Ajnif fie, *vn* behave strangely to (one's kinsfolk), estrange oneself from them.
Janif, unjust *v*.

جنح ‍ Janâll 8, wing, flank.
Ijnall, v. Tejennall, viii. Ijtenill, lean to one side ? sidle ?
Mojannall, flanked by something on each side.
(2) Janâll, elecampane *c*.

جنجل ‍ Jinjal, Jenjiel 11, ball, gong. *See* Jolel, Joljol.

جنك ‍ Jonc, *s*. fray, riot B*s*.
(2) Jonc, Persian harp.

WJQ

جنق ‍ Minjanieq, engine, *esp*. engine of war; *pl*. Majâniq x.

جنكل ‍ Jancêl, *pop*. Jangêl, a hook ?

جنس ‍ Jins 3, 4, genus (from Gr. and *Lat*.), sex.
Jenies, congener.
Jinsiey, generic; sexual B.
Jinsieya*, generically.
Jinsieya, community of origin x.
iii. Jânis, *va* claim as of a common genus.
Mojânese, homogeneity.
Mojânis, Motejânis, *homogeneous*. [genus.
vi. Tejânes, *vn* be of the same
v. Motejennis, of many kinds, *heterogeneous*.

جنز ‍ Joniz, *vp* he was placed on the bier.
Majnouz, corpse on the bier.
Jinâze 11, bier, or hearse, carrying a dead body.
ii. Janniz, *va* lay on the bier.

جنزر ‍ Janzir, *vn* effloresce (in chemistry) B.
Janzera, efflorescence.
(2) Jenzier 11, *vulgo* for Zenjier, a chain.

جقى ‍ Jiqqa, *s*. a plume.
(2) Joqqa, *s*. gut B.

وجق ‍ Wojaq 2, hearth, fireplace, *Turk*.

JWQ

جوق Jauq 4, troop, crowd.

جقم Jaqim, opinionated, wilful B.

جكر Jicéra, ger. pestering, importuning.
iii. Jécir, va pester, teaze.
iv. Ajcir, va offer (merchandize) with importunity x.; tout.

جر Jarra 5, ewer, jug with pointed bottom.
Ojorra, brick B. [Jarr.
(2) Jorr, va pull, tug. ger.
Jirra, traction; the cud of ruminants.
Jirrieya, bird's stomach.
Jorra, a rut.
Jarâr, a truck B.
Jârour, pivot of the door's hinge.
vii. Injirr, vp be drawn; vn Injirr ila' warâ, drop behind.
viii. Ijtirr, vn chew the cud.
(3) Jarr, the ablative in grammar B.

أجر 'Ejr 4, wage, hire.
'Ojra, dᵃ [man.
'Ejier, hireling, hired workiii. Êjir, va engage by wages; hire.
viii. Ittejir, vn work for wages. (See Têjir.)
x. Istêjir, va hire, as iii.

وجر Wajâr 10, den (of fox); cavern, grotto?

JRY

جور Jour sala', vn be unjust to.
ger. Jaur, injustice, violence (vulgo Zeur).
Jâyir, violent, unjust, highhanded. El qouwat el jâyira, military force ON.
(2) Jâr 9, neighbour (client x. — Gr. πελάτης).
Jawâr, va neighbourhood (clientship x.).
iii. Jâwir, va neighbour upon. Mojâwara, neighbourhood.
iv. Ajier, va protect a client, patronize F.
Ijâra, patronage F.
x. Istejier, va ask for protection.
(3) Mâjour, bowl of red earth, flowerpot, kneading trough.
Jauriey, adj. of carnation colour.
(4) Joura, a dell B.
Jowâr, cavern in a mountain x.

جير Jier, lime.
Mojayyar, daubed with lime.
(2) Jair, assuredly x.
(3) Ajier iv. See Jour.

جرو Jarou, pl. Ajrâ, a cub; a bantling.

جرى Jariey, bold.
Ajrâ', bolder (root JR').
viii. Ijteri, vn be bold.
(2) Jâriya 12, a damsel, sup. a handsome female slave; a maid of honour.
(3) Jirâya, a day's wage.
Jariey, a journeyman, a day labourer.

JRY

(4) Ijri, *va* run (as water, or as horse), to have course, take effect, as a decree.
Majra' 11, river bed, stream.
iv. Ajri, *va* to execute, enforce a decree.
Ijrâ, *ger.* giving effect, enforcement of a law or edict.
v. Tejarrâ, *va frequentative*, make inroads.

جرع Ijraε, *va oftener* v. Tejarraε, quaff, gulp down (medicine); *fig.* of drinking the cup of misery.
ii. Jarriε, *va* cause to gulp down (medicine).
Jorεa, a sup, a gulp.
Joraiεa, a small sup x.

جرب Jarab, the mange.
Ajrab, Jarbân, mangy.
(2) Jarrib, *va* put to proof, test.
Tejriba, trial, experiment.
Mojarrab, tried and proved.
(3) Jorâb 9, bag, pouch (of pelican).
Jaurâba, *nu.* stocking.

جرد Jaried 11, rod, shaft; *esp.* javelin of horseman.
ii. Jarrid, *va* exercise a horse.
Tejrieda, a military expedition.
(2) Jarâd, flying locusts, from (3)?
(3) Ajrad, bare, bald.
Jorda, Jarad, a barren year.
Jâroud, barren.   [land).
ii. Jarrid, *va* strip, desolate (a Majarrad, *participle* bared, laid

JRM

bare; *adv.* barely, simply, merely.
Tejarrod, Jorda, nakedness.

جرذ Jorεa 9, rat.
Jaraεun 11, large rat.

جرف Ojrof, *va* rake, sweep, off.
Jirfa, edge or ribbon of sand swept up by wind or water.
Jorf 4, outmost edge of a river at highest water Bg. x. alluvium B.
Jârouf 12 AL *more classical* Mijrafa 11, shovel or hoe to rake up dung.

جرح Ijraḥ, *va* wound. *vp* Jorifl. *ger.* Jarfl.
Jorfla, a wound. Jirâfla, d° nu.
Jarâfl, a being wounded x.
Jarâyifluiy, surgeon.
Jârifla 12, carnivorous beast.
ii. Jarrifl, *va intens.* of i.

جرهم Jarhêm, keen, active, diligent c.

جرخ Jark, a wheel B. See Cerk.

جرم Jirm 4, mass (as of moon); (heavenly) body.
Jirmân, mass, volume, bulk x.
Δou jirm, corporeal; r. massy?
Majroum, massive.
(2) Ojrom, *va* fine for an offence.
ii. Jarrim, d°· c.
Jariema, a fine. See Γarâma.
Lâ jaram, no error! assuredly.

JRN

جرن Jorn, barnfloor.

جركش Mojarcex (Mozercex), embroidered.

جرس Jaras 4, bell.
ii. Jarris, *va* lead (a criminal) through the streets before punishment (with bell ringing?) x.   Brand with public disgrace B.

جرسم Jirsĉm, pleurisy.

جرش Ojrox, *va* grind in a handmill.
Jârouxa, *s.* handmill.
Jariex, crushed (wheat, etc.), roughly ground.
Joraxa, groats, grits (of grain).

جرز Jorze, truss of hay, sheaf, faggot.

جس Joss, *va* feel, explore; feel (the pulse).
ii. Jessis, *va* search (a person).
v. Tejesses, *va* pry into, spy out.
Jesies, a spy x.
Jêsous 12, d°· B. x.
Tejessos, espionage.

جص Juvv, see Jibs.

جوس Jous, *va* rummage.

جسع Jesous, stingy.
Josous, stinginess.
Ijsos, *vn* be stingy.

JYX

جسد Jesed 4, body (*esp.* of animals). [bodily.
Jesedicy, Jesedâni, corporeal,
Tejcssod, incarnation.

جسم Jism 4, bulk, substance, matter; solid body.
Jesiem, bulky, huge (city); huge (sin).
Ajscm, greater in volume.
Mojessem, solid (in geometry).
Josmâni, material; opposed to Roußâni, spiritual.
Jesêma, bulkiness.

جسر Jesour, bold, venturesome.
Jesêra, hardihood.
v. Tejesser, *vn* be bold.
— sala', venture upon.

جث Joθθe 10, carcase.
Joθθ, *va* disinter (a body)? [pull up a tree from the soil x.]

جثو Ojθou, Ijθi, *vn* roost as a bird. [before x.
iii. Jêθi sala', sit face to face

جثم Ijθim, *vn* lie on the breast, roost.
Jeθoum, inert, fixed to his place.
Joθêm, incubus, nightmare.
Majθim, place of roosting.

جوش Jâwoux (Txâoux), sarjeant, beadle? *Turk.*

جيش Jiex, *vn* bubble up?
Jaix 3, army, host.
v. Tejayyax, *vn* form themselves into military organization.

JYX

Jâx, *s.* high spirit.
Joxxa, confused noise, hubbub x. For this the moderns seem to say, Γauxa, Γauρa. *Also,* Taxxa.

جز *ca* shear (sheep). *ger.* Jezz.
viii. Ijtizz, *ca* cull, gather in crop x.
Jizêz, *s.* shearing (time?).
Jezieze, wool of a recent shearing x.
Jezouze, flock newly sheared x.
Mijezz, shears.

جزّ, Wejez Yejiz, *vn* be short, succinct (in speech).
iv. Aujiz,ra abridge,do promptly.
Wejiez, succinct (narrative).
Icjêz, brevity, succinctness.
Bil iejêz, summarily.
Moujiz, an abridgment x.
Miejêz, habitually laconic x.

جزو Jouz, *vn* pass, (used morally, for) be permitted.
Jâyiz, allowed.
iv. Ajiez, *ca* allow, approve.
ii. Jawwiz, *ca* let pass (light coin); wink at (deficiency), tolerate (religion).
v. Tejawwaz, hurry over (prayer), do perfunctorily x.
Motejawwiz, perfunctory.
Jawêz, passport.
Ijêze, permission. [phor.
Majêz (passage, *i.e. fig.*), meta-
Majêze, a passage, thoroughfare.
Mojâwiz, transitive (verb).
Mojâwaze, allegory.

JZF

vi. Tejâwaz, *vn* pass the bound, transgress, be exorbitant.
Motejâwiz, exorbitant.
viii. Ijtêz, *ca* traverse, penetrate, or *vn with* fle, travel to remote places.
Ijtiyêz, distant expedition, *esp.* by sea.
(2) Jauze, *nu.* a walnut.

جزء Joz' 4, *pl.* ajzê', part, section, part (of book).
ii. Jezzi, *ca* divide, partition.
Joz'icy, partial, special x. *vulg.* Jozwiey.
Jozdân, portfolio.

جزو Jozou, ingredient; *pl.* Ajzê в.
Ijzi, *ca* recompense; commoner in iii. Jêzi.
iv. Ajzi, *ca* satisfy, content.
Jizê, requital (good or evil). In grammar the *apodosis* or *response* following a condition x.
Mojêzêya, d°.
Jizya, poll-tax.

جزع Ijzec, *vn* be disquieted.
Jezec, inquietude, fear.
iv. Ajzic, *ca* agitate, disquiet.
Mojzic, alarming.

جزف Jizêf, *s.* a purchase in the lump x. *Hence*, inconsiderate word or act.
iii. Jêzif, act rashly.
Mojêzefa, rashness в.
Majâzief, sales in the lump?

JZL

جزل Ojzol, *vn* be rich (mentally). *ger.* Jezéla.
Jezial 5, ample, rich of mind.
Ajzal, more copious, more richly endowed.

جزم Ijzim, *va* cut off, retrench. *ger.* Jezm, a grammatical mark, syncopation, syncope.
Mijzem, a section x. [ly.
viii. Ijtezim, *va* calculate rough-
(2) Jezma, *nu.* boot (*Turk.*).

جزن Jozeina, grape skins.

جزر Ijzir, *va* massacre (enemies).
Jezzêr, butcher, tyrant.
iv. Ajzir, *va* cause to slay, give order to slay.
(2) Jozr, ebb tide.
Ijzir, *vn* ebb, as the tide.
(3) Jazer, Jizer, *vulg.* carrots.
Jezera, *nu.* *See* Jíar.

K.

اخو Ak, Akou, brother; *dual* akwân; *pl.* ikwa, âkâ, ikwân.
Okt, *pl.* Akawêt, sister.
iii. Aki, *va* fraternize with.
vi. Te'âkâ, *in pl.* cultivate fraternity.
Akawiey, fraternal.
Oktiey, sisterly. [hood.
Akwiya o. Mowâkâya, brother-

خاو Ka'ou, pile of velvet.

KBR

خوى Kâwi, desolate.
(2) Kawie, manners, temper, turn of mind.

خى Kaiya, a loop, tag, *pl.* Akyâ.

خب Kabb, *vn* trot (as horse).
Kabab, *s.* trotting.

خيب Kieb, *vn* be baffled; min, fail of.
ii. Kayyib, iv. Akieb, *va* BAFFLE.
Kaiba, disappointment.

خى ii. Kabbi, *va* hoard, secrete.
HIDE. KEEP. [stored.
v. Tekabbâ, lurk, lie hid, be
viii. Iktebi, be hidden.
Moktebi, hidden.
Makbâ, storeroom.
Kâbiya 12, great wine jar.
Kabâyâ, secrets.

خبل Kabal, *ger.* mutilation; paralysis of one side of body.
Kabâl, defect, flaw.
Koboul, mutilated parts, stumps of the legs.
Kabla, bewilderment.
ii. Kabbil, craze, bewilder *va.*
v. Tekabbal, *vp* falter from bewilderment.
viii. Iktebil, suffer paralysis?
Akbal, defective (in mind) x.

خبر Kabar 4, *s.* news.
Kabier, *adj.* experienced.
Kibra, experiment.
Makbar, place of trial.
iv. Akbir, *va* inform, acquaint

KBR

vi. Tekâbar, *vn* confer together. Mokâbara, conference. [trial.
viii. Iktebir, *va* test, find by Moktebir, expert.
Makbara, certified knowledge.
(2) Kobyar, roe of fish c.

خبص Okboy, *va* mess, mix up.
ii. Kabbuy, *va* jumble, muddle.
Kabieya, fruit jam.

خبط Okbot, *va* trample, paw (defile water by trampling).
iii. Kâbut, *va* struggle against.
viii. Iktebut, *vn* struggle.
vi. Tekâbat, d° *mutually*.
Iktibât, a struggling.

خبز Kobz, *s.* bread. Kobza, *nu.*
Kabbâz, baker.
Ikbiz, *va* bake.
ii. Kabbiz, d°.
Kibâze, art *or* office of baking.
Makbaze 11, bakehouse.
(2) Kabieze 11, marsh mallows.

خبث Kobθ, Kabâθe, malice.
pl. Kabâyiθ, iniquities.
Kabieθ, malicious. BAD.
v. Tekabbaθ, *vn* act maliciously.
x. Istekbiθ, *va* reprobate, vituperate. BLAME.

خد Kadd 3, cheek.
Mikadda 11, pillow.
Kodaidieya, small pillow.
(2) Kadd 3, a furrow.
Kodd, *va* furrow.
ii. Kaddid, *va* d°.

KΛS

خض Koλλ, *va* churn, agitate, terrify. *See* Omkoλ, churn.
Kuλλa, a panic.
vii. Inkuλλ, *vp* be agitated.
Motekaλkuλ, violently moved.

اخذ ’Ekaa, he took. Koa, take thou. Begin.
iii. Ekia, Wêkia, *va* reprove (*corripio*).
viii. Ittekia, *va* assume, adopt.

خطو Wakd, *s.* stride of the ostrich γ.

خوذ Kouʌe 10, helmet.
(2) ii. Kawwiʌ, *va* bewilder.
vii. Inkawiʌ, *vp* of d°.

خوض Kouʌ, *vn* wade, step into, ford. *ger.* Kauʌ.
Makâʌe, a ford.
[Makâʌ, birthpain, from Omkoʌ.]
iii. Kâwuʌ, *va* stem, encounter.

خدع Ikdas, *va* beguile, betray.
ger. Kodsa, Kadiesa, fraud.
Makdas, storeroom, closet.
vii. Inkadis, *vp* be beguiled.

خضع Iklas li, *va* submit to, be humble to, do homage to, *ger.* Koλöus, the being *submitted* physically; [as, Lâ xai‘ yasʌou san koʌöus li nagarihi, nothing escapes *being submitted* to his gaze.]
ii. Kaλλus, or iv. Akλus, *va*

KẔC

cause to do homage, humiliate, subjugate.
v. Tekaẕẕac, cʀ humble oneself, do homage.
viii. Iktaẕoc, dᵒ· or ʀp of ii.
Káẕuc, Kaẕöuc, submissive.

خَضَــ ii. Kaẕẕub, ca stain (with blood) B.

خَذَل Ikʌil, ca fail (a person), disappoint c. [benumb B.]. ger. Kʌal. Also Ikʌel, cʀ fail, break down, be helpless. ger. Kiʌlân. [less.
Káʌil, helpless, nerveless, friendMakʌoul, destitute, pl. 11, forlorn.
Makâʌiel, low people, rabble c.
ii. Kaʌʌil, ca abandon, disappoint, leave in the lurch.
iv. Akʌil, ca dᵒ·? or disconcert, paralyse.
vii. Inkaʌil, cp be disabled. [B. gives to this verb in i. and vii. the sense of *Benumb*. Is this possibly a confusion of it with Ikdar?

خَدَمَ Okdom, serve, till. ger. Kidma, Kadâma, service.
Kadam, suite of servants.
Kâdim 7, Kaddâm, servant.
[Koʌmetcêr, servant.]
Makdoum, one waited upon; a gentleman ʀ.
v. Istekdim, ca employ (another) to labour; — fie, use (a tool).

خَدَر Ikdar, cʀ be benumbed, torpid.

WKF

Kâdir, torpid, inert.
Kadar, ger. numbness.
Kodrat el leil, dead of night.
ii. Kaddir or iv. Akdir, ca benumb.
Mokaddir, narcotic.
(2) Kidr 3, veil, curtain.
ii. Kaddir, ca hide (*esp.* a girl) behind curtains. But Kaddir (in modern use) seems to mean *store up*, or rather *cure raisins*.

خَضِر Akẕar, adj. green.
Koẕra, s. green, greenness.
Kiẕra, nu. green sod.
Kaẕar, verdure. [tables.
Kiẕâr, Kaẕarawêt, green vegeMokẕara, verdant place.
ix. Ikẕurr, cʀ grow green.
Mokẕurr, greenish, verdant.

خَدَش Ikdix, ca scratch. See Okmox, Karbix.

خَفّ Kiff, cʀ grow light, abate. ger. Kiffa, lightness, swiftness. Kiffateⁿ, superficially.
Kafief, adj. light, swift.
ii. Kaffif, ca lighten, assuage, dilute.
[Tekfiefat el râs, night cap B.]
iv. Akiff, ca lighten.
v. Motekaffif, lightly clothed B.
x. Istekiff, ca make light of, undervalue.

وَخَفَ, Wakaf Yakif, ca fear B.
Wakfân, timid. [Modern: a *vulgarism*? See Kâf.]

KWF

خُوْف Kâf min, *vn* fear from.
Kift, I feared. *ger.* Kauf,
Makâfa, fear.
Makouf, dreadful; Makoufât,
dangers.
Kayouf, Kawief, Kawwâf, timid.
ii. Kawwif, iv. Akief, *va* frighten.

خِيف Kaif, *s.* steep slope of
mountain; cliff?

خَفِي Yakfa', Yakfû, *vp* it is
hidden (*vn* latet). *ger.* Kafâ.
Kofya, concealment.
Kafiey, clandestine.
Kafieya 14, a secret.
ii. Kaffi, *va* hide, conceal.
Tekfiya, concealment.
iv. Akfi, *va* hide.
viii. Iktefi, *vp* be hidden.

خَفَض Ikfuḍ, *va* lower a number, lessen (an amount), reduce, deject, depress.
ii. Kaffuḍ, *va* lessen (an officer's)
authority, derogate from.
Mokaffuḍ, derogatory.
vii. Inkafuḍ, *vp* of ii.
Inkifâḍ, derogation.

خَفَق Ikfiq, *vn* palpitate; flutter (in the air).
Kâfiq 12, point of the compass.
(2) Kâfaqi, mortar of lime and
sand s.

خَفَر Ikfir, *va* watch, guard.
Kafar, road guard; road toll.
Kafier, protector c.

KL

خَفَس Ikfis, *vn* fall in (as ceiling); *fig.* be dejected.
iv. Akfis, *va* overthrow, lay
prostrate.
Mokfis, *adj.* laying prostrate,
epithet of *wine.*

خُفَّاش Koffâx, bat (animal),
= Koxxâf.

خَجّ Kojj, *vn* trot s.

خُوْج Kawâja 2 (Kauja Bg.),
merchant, European gentleman.

خَجَل Ikjal, *vn* blush. *ger.* Kajl.
ii. Kajjil, iv. Akjil, *va* abash.
Kijâla, bashfulness.
Kajlân, abashed.
Kajoul, bashful.

خُوْخ Kauka, *nu.* peach, plum.
(2) Kauka, wicket in gate.
Kaukat el bararicya, embrasure
of a battery.

خُكَم Kakam, Jewish priest c.

خَلّ Kall, vinegar.
ii. Kallil, *va* pickle in vinegar.
Mokallal, pickles.
Kallâl, seller of vinegar and
pickles.
(2) Kalal, *s.* disorder.
Kilâl, *s.* interval, interstice.
ii. Kallil, *va* pick the teeth s.
iv. Akill, *va* impair, derange.
viii. Iktill, *vp* be impaired, be
emaciated.

KL

Iktilâl, derangement.
(3) Tekalkal, *vn* be unsteady (as a tooth), be disjointed.
Mokalkil, vacillating.
(4) Koll, *s.* intimacy.
Kaliel, intimate friend; gallánt to a woman; *pl.* 9, kollân.
Kalâla, close friendship.
iii. Kâlil, *va* befriend.
(5) Kolâl, dates boiled and dried B₆.

خول Kâl, *s.* mother's brother; *pl.* akwâl.
Kâla, *s.* mother's sister.
(2) Kâl, *s.* a mole in the face.
Kowail, *dimin.*
(3) ii. Kawwil, *va* endue; vouchsafe, bestow.
(4) Kawâliey, *s.* quit-rent B.

خيل Yakiel, (a coat) fits.
iv. Akiel, *va* fancy, imagine. *vp* Yokâl, it seems.
ii. Kayyil, *va* imagine. *vp* Koyyil, it is imagined, it seems.
Kayâl, phantom, shadow.
Kayâliey, fantastic.
Mokayyala, fantasy.
v. Tekayyal, *vn* surmise.
(2) Kail, horses; *pl.* koyoul.
Kayâla, cavalry.
Kayyâl, horseman.

خلى Kâli, *adj.* void, free, empty.
Oklou, *vn* be free, void (*min.* can).
ii. Kalli, *va* leave; *vulg.* let.
v. Tekallâ can, quit.
viii. Ikteli, be in privacy.
Kalwa, retirement, privacy.

KLF

Mokteli, retired, private.
Kalâ', empty country, solitude.
Kalâ, *prep.* except.
Kaliey min, free from.
Kalâwa, isolation.

خلى Kalâ (*nw.* Kalâya), χιλος, green fodder.
Miklâ, sickle to cut green fodder.
Maklâya, horse's nose-bag, to hold fodder.

خلع Iklas, *va* take off (clothes), take out, remove, depose.
vii. Inkalis, *vp* be dislocated.
viii. Iktelis, *va* pull out; repudiate.
Kolâs, palsy.
Kilsa, robe of honour 10.
Kalies, dissolute.
Kalâsa, libertinism B. (amiable *abandon* B.).

خلب Iklib, *va* claw.
viii. Iktelib, d°
Miklâb 11, claw, talon.

خلد Kolda 3, a mole.
(2) Kold, Koloud, perpetuity.
Kalied, Mokallad, perpetual.
Oklod, *vn* be perpetual.
ii. Kallid, *va* perpetuate.
Mokallad, perennial?

خلف Kalf, *prep.* behind, backward.
Aklaf, lopsided?
Kâlif 12, backward, disobedient.
Iklif, *va* succeed, follow.
Kaliefa 11 (*or pl.* kolâfâ), succession, successor, Caliph.

KLF

Kalâfa, Caliphate.
Kiláfiey, successive.
ii. Kallif, *va* bequeath, leave behind.
Mokallafa, heritage, bequest.
iii. Kâlif, *va* resist, thwart.
Kiláf, *s.* opposition, thwarting. *adv.* contrary to.
Mokâlafa, contentiousness.
Mokâlif, contentious.
iv. Aklif, *va.* substitute, cause to succeed another; disconcert.
v. Tekallaf, *vp* of ii. *en* remain behind; be backward.
viii. Iktelif, to be diverse.
Moktelif, diverse, various.
Irtilâf, diversity.

خلف Kalfit, *va* caulk, careen (a ship).

خلج Kaliej 9, channel, gulf.

(2) Kalajân, commotion o.
(3) Iktiláj F. 192, outgrowth? development? (of upper lip), abstraction?
viii. Iktelij, *en* F. retire, abscond, go apart, move separately.

خلج Kalnaj, heath, heather.

خلق Okloq, *va* create. *ger.*
Kalq, *s.* creating, make, build.
Kalaq, the world, folk.
Kolq, quality, temper, nature.
El kâliq, the Creator.
Kâliqicy, creative F.
Maklouqa 2, a creature.
Kolqa, fiction o.
Kalieq li, worthy, fit for.

KMK

Kalieqa 11, creation, creatures, a creature.
Kolqiey, innate, impetuous.
viii. Ikteliq, *va* invent, fabricate. Rom. i. 30.

خلس Iktelis viii. seize and carry away. *Compare* Iftelis.

خلص Iklas, *vn* min; escape from, cease from.
Kâlus, pure, sincere.
Moklus, frank.
Kolous, sincerity.
Mokallas, loose, dissolute B.
Koláṣa, essence, summary (of news).
ii. Kallus, *va* deliver.
Mokallus, Saviour.
x. Isteklus, deliver.
Mosteklas, refined essence.

خلط Oklot, *va* mix.
ii. Kallut, *va* combine. [fused.
viii. Iktelut, *vp* be mixed, confused.
Kalt, mixture, confusion.
Iktilât, Mokâlata, intercourse, relations.

خم Komm, *va* survey, [conserve fruits?].
(2) Komm, Kimm, *va* guttle, gormandize B.
Kimma, a gobbet of meat.
(3) Kimm, *vn* spoil (as meat) B. E. *See* Wakam.

خمكم Kamkim, *vn* speak through the nose o. K.
See Konna, Kankin.

WKM

وخم Wakam Yakim, *vn* be indigestible.
viii. Ittekim, d°.
v. Tewakkam, be unwholesome (as meat, or as a climate).
Wakim, Wakiem, Wakoum, insalubrious.
Wakûma, insalubrity.

خام Kâm, *adj.* raw (as ore).
Persian: *s.* raw cotton, calico.

خيم Kaima 10, a tent, or *pl.* kiyâm.
ii. Kayyim, *or* iv. Akiem, *va* pitch a tent.
Kayyâm, tented, nomade (tribe).
Mokayyam, encampment, camp.

خمد Okmod, *vn* abate (as fire).
iv. Akmid, *va* allay.
Kâmid, torpid? quiet, dead.
Komoud, an abating.

خمل Ikmal, *vn* be nerveless B. be dull, as sound.
Kâmil, helpless, nerveless B. C.
iv. Akmil, *va* enervate B.
Komoul, being helpless.
(2) Mikmal, velvet.
Mikmalicy, velvety.

خمن Kammin ii. *v.* conjecture, opinion.
Tekmiena*, by conjecture.

خمر Kamr, wine, strong drink.
Kammâr, vintner.
Makmour, Mokammir, tipsy.
Kamâra, wine tavern.
Kamiera, leaven.

KAN

ii. Kammir, *va* ferment; *fig.* leaven (enter and modify) human life.
viii. Iktemir, *vp.* of ii.
(2) Kimâr, woman's face-veil.
iii. Kâmir, *va* veil oneself from (a person), elude him.
vi. Tekâmar sala', collude (with another) against.
v. Tekammar, *vn* wear a veil, put on a veil.

خمس Kamse, *f.* Kams, five.
Kâmis, fifth.
Koms 4, a fifth part.
Kamsoun (-ien), fifty, fiftieth.
Youm el Kamies, Thursday.
Mokammes, a pentagon.

خمش Okmox, *va* scratch, rend, gash. See Karmix, Karbix, Ikdix.
Komâxa, laceration, wounding.

خن Kinn, Konn, dark corner?
Konn el wirie, the groin.
Konn, sty? kennel, hovel B. henhouse?
Konn el merceb, keel of ship B. (hull of ship K.) See Qonn 5.
(2) Konna, nasal sound, snuffling.
Kanien, snuffling laughter K.
Kankin, *vn* snuffle. See Kamkim.
(3) Konân, Kanab, glanders in a horse K.

خان Kân 2, caravansery.
(2) Kân 2, king, prince (of Tartars).

KWN

خون Koun, v. betray.
Kiyâna, treachery. [ous.
x. Istekwin, suspect as treacher-

خندق Kandaq 11, moat.

خندس Kandis, vn be confounded (Etre capot B.).

خنفر Kanfir, vn snore B. See Karkir.

خنفس Konfous 11, Konfose 11, beetle.

خاجر Kanjar 11, dagger (cimetar x.). ARMA.

خنم Kânam, s. lady (sic) o.

خنق Oknoq, va strangle.
Konâq, s. quinsy.
Kanâq, s. the throat.
vii. Inkaniq, vp be strangled.
(2) Kânaqâ'a 12, convent, hospice o. x. from Pers.

خنصر Kinṣur 11, little finger c.
(2) Kanṣar, cruet-bottle B.

خنس Iknis, vr skulk, lurk.
ii. Kannis, va cause to d°. x.
Konous, ger. of i.

خنث ii. Kanniθ, vs emasculate, enervate.
Konθe' 5, 11, hermaphrodite.
Mokannoθ, effeminate.

خنزر Kinzier 11, hog.

VOL. II.

KWR

خقن Kâqân 12, emperor (Tartar).

خر Kirr, vn dash, splash (as water); leak, drop violently.
ger. Karier (noise of water).
Karrâra 2, cataract, Psalm xlii. cascade.
Karrâr, adj. splashing, dashing.
(2) Karkir (Karrir, Prov.), vn snore. See Kanfir.

الخر 'Ekar, other, f. 'Okra', pl. 'Okar.
'Êkir, last, f. êkira.
'Êkir, pl. ewâkir, s. end.
'Êkira", finally. 'Ekariey, final.
'Okrawiey, belonging to the other world.
'Ekâri, s. pl. others.
El êkira, the future life.
ii 'Ekkir, vs retard, hinder.
Mo'wekkar, placed at the end x.
Moukir, stern, hinder part.
iii. Êkir, va place at the end x.
Mote'wekkir, modern, recent.
(2) Ekour, horse's stable (Pers. x.).

خور Kour, vn bellow. ger. Kowâr. SCREAM. SOUND.
(2) Kouri, a parson (curé?).
(3) Kaur 4, gulf, chasm x.
(4) Kawwir, va enfeeble, exhaust.
Kawar, exhaustion, prostration.
(5) Kâr Ꞩuiniey, zinc B.

19

KYR

خير Kair, *s.* good. *adj.* good.
Kaira 2, a good thing.
Kaiyir, benign.
Kairieya, a piece of good luck.
Akyar, Kair, better, best.
Kiera, the chosen one, the *élite* or choice.
ii. Kayyir, *va* count good, propose (ةَيِّخ.)
Mokayyir, volunteer (soldier).
viii. Iktêr, *va* choose, elect.
Iktiyâr, choice, selection.
(2) Kiyâr, *s.* cucumber (*Pers.*).
(3) Ektiyâr, hale old man AL.
(4) Mokayyar, mohair, camlet.

اخرا Kirâ', dung (esp. of birds?) guano.

خوري Kouriey, *s.* parson; from *French* curé?

خرع Ikras, *va* astound B.
Yakras, romantic (country) B.
vii. Inkaris, be entranced.
(2) viii. Ikteris, *va* invent.
Iktirâs, invention.

خرب Ikrib, *va* pillage, ruin, ravage.
ii. Karrib, d° *intens.*
Ikrab, *vn* ruin oneself B.
Karâb(a), *s.* ruin.
Karbân, *adj.* ruinous (building).
Mokrib, Mokarrib, *adj.* desolating. [tree.
vii. Inkarib, *vp* be rotten, as a
(2) Karroub, Karnoub, locust-fruit.

KRJ

خربق Karbaq, hellobore.

خربط Karbut, *va* adulterate, vitiate. CONFUSE. COUNTERFEIT.

خربش Karbix, *va* scratch, scrawl.

خرد Korda, *pl.* -awêt, small wares, hosiery (*Pers.*).
Kordajiey, mercer.

خردل Kordal, mustard.

خردق Kardaq, small shot.

خرف Karouf 9, Kârouf 12, lamb, young mutton.
(2) Kariof, autumn.
Kariefley, autumnal.
(3) Korâfa 2, *s.* fable.
Karaf, *s.* dotage.
ii. Karrif, *vn* twattle.

خرج Okroj, *vn* go out. *ger.* Korouj.
Karáj, issue, outgoing; — 9, tax, revenue (!).
Korj, saddlebags (*pl.* Kiraja x.).
ii. Karrij, *va* distil (spirits).
Kârij, *adj.* external, *prep.* outside of.
Kârija*, externally.
Kawârij, *pl.* externals.
Kârijiey, *adj.* appertaining to the exterior (of a country).
Makraj, place of outgoing, outlet c.; also *medio.* faeces, excrement.

KRJ

iv. Akrij, *va* expel, bring out; pay (tribute).
Ikrâjêt, exports.
x. Istekrij, *va* elicit, extract.
Istikrâj, result (of calculation).
(2) ii. Karrij, *va* educate to a profession.
v. Tekarraj, *vp* of ii.
Kirricj, well educated in a profession x.
NB. The second sense of Karrij, as related to Akrij, is illustrated by Latin Edŭco and Edūco.

خرم Ikrim, *va* bore the nostrils; split, burst (a shoe) B. *ger.*
Karm, piercing (of beads).
ii. Karrim, *va* drill? groove? pierce throughout.
Tekriema, latticework.
Mokarram, lattice; pierced, open work.
vii. Inkirâm el saql, derangement of the intellect.
viii. Iktcrim, *va* cut off, destroy.

خرمش Karmix, *va* (nearly as Karbix), claw, scratch with claws.

خرنب Karnoub 11 = Karroub, locust fruit; carob-bean; St. John's bread.

خرق Okroq, *va* rend.
ii. Karriq, d^a *intens.*
Karq 3, rent, fissure.
Kirqa 10, a rag.
v. Tekarraq, be rent; *vp* of ii.

KRZ

Kâriq, penetrating (mind).
(2) Karaq, Korq, stupor x.
iv. Akriq, *va* stupefy, stun.
Kâriq, *adj. vulg.* stunning, *i.e.* prime, first-rate.

خرس Akras, *adj.* dumb, *pl.* Kors or Korsên.
Karas, dumbness.
Ikras, *vn* be mute (Imperative, hush! B.). [astound.
iv. Akris, *va* strike dumb,
viii. be struck dumb, aghast.
(2) Koristên 11, wardrobe, *Pers.*
(3) Kars 3, wine jar of earthenware x.
Karsêni, mortar of crushed pots.

خرت Okrot, *va* drill (an eye in a needle), (the ear for a ring).
Kort, needle's eye B.

خرط Okrot, *va* shave off in turning; strip off leaves.
Kirâta, art of turning.
Karrât, a turner.
(2) Kârra, Kârita, map, chart (*Latin*); also Egyptian?
(3) Okrot, *vn* romance.
Karra, balderdash x.
(4) Karruit, rhinoceros.

خرطم Korrōum 11, proboscis, snout (of pig), (of tiger).

خرطش Karrux, *va* erase B.

خرز Okros, Ikriz, *va* perforate B.
Mikrêz, an awl.

KRZ

Karaz, beads, vertebræ.
Karréz, a cobbler x.
Kiráze, cobbler's art.
Karaziey, dealer in beads and glass toys.

خَسّ Kass, vn Kiss, become petty, fall off.
Kasíes, adj. mean, sordid.
Kissa, Kasêse, Kasíese, mean-
Akass, more ignoble. [ness.
Kases, insignificance.
(2) Kass, lettuce.

خَسّ Koss, va endow (a person) bi, with (a thing). vn belong to, concern.
viii. Yaktuss bi him, it appertains to them. [lent.
Kâss, chief, particular, excel-
El kâssa, principal men.
El kawûss, pl. private possessions of the prince.
Maksöus, special.
Kâssuiya, pl. Kasâyus (as if from Kosöus), property, peculiarity. [business.
Kosöus, special, peculiar; s. a
Kosöusaⁿ, particularly.
Kâssuten, principally.
Kosöusuiy, especial.
Moktuss, appropriated (to).

خَسّ Kies, vn disappear, lie hid, bury itself.

خَسّ Iksui, va castrate. ger.
Kuvá.
Kuvu, s. f. testicle; dual Kosyatén, pl. Kova'.
Kasuiy θ, eunuch.

KSR

خَسّ Kusb, s. fertility.
iv. Aksub, vn be fertile.
Kasub, Moksub, Kasuib, fertile.
Aksab, more or most fertile.

خَسّ Iksif, vn fall in (as ceiling), subside (as crust of the earth), be eclipsed (as the moon). [But Icsif, eclipse the sun].
Kosouf, eclipse (of the moon).
Kesf, diminution (of dignity).

خَسّ Kayla 5, quality, nature, pl. Kasâyil, qualities, human characters.

خَسّ Kasm 3, Kasuim 6, litigant, adversary, rival.
Kosöuma, lawsuit, dispute.
iii. Kâsum, sue at law.
Motekasum, disputations.
(2) Oksöm, va deduct as discount B. C.
Kasm, discount. Better perhaps Oßsom, Ilasm.

خَسّ Ikser, vn be loser (esp. in trade), suffer defeat. ger.
Kosrán.
Kasr, delinquency.
Kosr, Kisêra, loss, damage.
Kâsir, adj. astray; delinquent; morally lost.
ii. Kassir, va cause to lose; deteriorate (morally), desecrate.
Kisêra, a wronging (of others); injustice.

خَسّ Kasr 3, the waist, the narrow part of the body.

K3R

Káyura 12, trunk of the body, from collar bone to hip.
Mokayyar, narrow in the waist, arched in the foot.
viii. Iktayur, *va* contract, abridge.
Ikturâr, abridgment (of a book).

خـت Okt, sister. See under *Ak*.

خـت Katt 3, line, stripe.
ii. Kattut, *va* stripe, flute.
Kattât, elegant writer.

خـيـط Kait 9, thread, twine.
ii. Kayyut, *va* sew with thread.
Kayyât, tailor.
Kiyâta, needlework.
Kaita, a thread, a needleful.
Mikyat, instrument for sewing; bodkin, mesh, needle.

خـطـو Katwa 2, a pace.
Kotwa, *pl.* Kota', d°
v. Tekattâ, *va* pace.

خـطـى Ikta', or more usually, iv. Aktu, *va* sin, miss the mark. *ger.* Kitâ, Kitâ'ya, sinning.
Katuiya, sin, *pl.* 14, Katâyâ.
Kâtu, sinner, *pl.* 6, Kota'a.

خـطـب Kâtub, orator, haranguer.
iii. Katub, *va* address (in harangue), make addresses to (a lady).
Kotba, an address; a preface, prologue; proposal of marriage.
Kutâb, an address.
Mokâtaba, discourse.

KTM

Kutb 4, suitor. [marriage.
Kotb, Kutba, lady asked in
Kattâb, matchmaker.
Katuib, preacher.
Maktöuba li, betrothed to x.
El Mokâtab, the 2nd person (in Grammar).

خـطـف Iktuf, or viii. Iktetuf, snatch away, carry off.
Kâtuf, plunderer, rapacious; *pl.* Kawâtuf, rapacious (beasts).
Kattâf, d°· esp. a shark.
Kottâf 11, a grappling iron; a harpoon; *also*, a swallow (bird); *pl. clutches* of a beast.
(2) Katuifa 11, a crumpet.

خـتـل Iktil, *vn* lurk.
iii. Kâtil, *va* entrap.
v. Tekattel, lie in wait.
Katel, lurking place of a hare.
Kâtil, *partic.* lurking, deceiving.
vi. Tekâtel, lie in wait to deceive *mutually*.
Mokâtela, mutual deceit.

خـتـل Iktal, *vn* maunder, drivel.
Katul, palsied.
ii. Kattul, *va* paralyse.

خـتـم Oktom, Iktim, *va* seal with a ring; *fig.* conclude. *ger.* Katm.
ii. Kattim, *va* seal carefully x.
Kitêm, *s.* close, end.
viii. Iktetim, *va* finish.
Iktitêm, end, completion.
Kâtim 12, seal-ring; also in anatomy, the anus (*i.e.* the ring-muscle).

KTM

Kâtima, conclusion, epilogue.
Katm 4, impress of a seal.
v. Tokattem can, *vn* seal oneself up concerning, *i.e.* be carefully silent about.

خَتْن Okton, *va* circumcise. *ger.* Katn, Kotna.
Kitêna, circumcision, profession or art of circumcising.
Aktên, circumcision-feasts *c.*
Kitên, the holding of such a feast.
Katn, Koton, retrenchment *x.*
viii. Iktetin, *vn* submit to circumcision.
(2) Katen, *s.* γαμβρὸς, a man allied through marriage. (Father-in-law, Son-in-law, Brother-in-law, etc.)
Katna, *fem.* of preceding.
Kotouna, alliance through intermarriage.
Kâtin, bridegroom *c.* (but in B. it is Katen).
Kâtoun, a lady *c.* (*Pers.?*).
iii. Kâtin, *va* take into affinity.

خَتْر Oktör, *vn* flap, strike, flash; especially in the phrase, Katar fio bâli, it flashed through my mind.
Katr, sudden thought *x.*
Katra, an instant of time *x.*
(2) Katar 4, danger; a risk, a stake in a game or race.
Katur, Katuir, dangerous, grave, critical (affair).
Moktur, dangerous (person).
ii. Katrur? viii. Iktatur, *va*

KXY

beat backwards and forwards; bandy (in a game, as with shuttlecock).
iii. Kâtur bi, run risks with, expose to hazard.
Mokâtara, the taking of risk, *i.e.* insurance (term of commerce).
(3) Kâtur 12, liking, will, pleasure, inclination.
(4) Kâtur 7, guest, lodger B.

خَثْر Ikθar, *vn* grow thick as milk.
ii. Kaθθir, *va* make thick.

خَثْرَج Kaθraq, wormwood.

خَشّ Koxx, *vs* insert, tuck in *r.*
Kaxx, enter B₀.
(2) Koxx, *vn* chink, clink.
iv. Akixx, *va* d°. *transitive.*
Tekaxkax, *vn* clash, rustle.
(3) Kaxkâx, a poppy.

خَوْش v. Tekawwax, be suspicious, suspect B.

خَشّ Kaix, sackcloth (B. Treillis), hollandcloth (coarse and open).
(2) ii. Kayyix, *va* fix in, stick in, anything sharp B. cobble B. stitch, quilt?

خَشَى Ixxi, *va* fear, apprehend. v. d°. [hension.
Kaxya, Kixyân, *s.* alarm, approii. Kaxxi, *va* intimidate.
Kâxi, Kaxyân, timid.
Akxa', more formidable *x.*

KXS · L

خشع Ikxas? v. Tekaxxas, viii. Iktexus, humiliate oneself, behave humbly.
Koxous, humility.
Kâxus, humble, meek.
iv. Akxus, *va* humiliate.
ii. Kaxxus, d°·

خشب Kaxab, timber.
Kaxaba, *nu.* piece of wood.
ii. Kaxxib, *va* plank over, floor.
Tekxieba, flooring.
(2) Ikxib, *vn* (B. Trotter), *pop. t.?* stump about? But see Ikxif.

خشف Kauxif, coarse (paper) B.
Kaxf, inferiority in quality.
(2) Koxâf, sherbet of raisins B.K.
(3) Ikxif, *vn* scuffle along, walk rapidly K. *ger.* Kafxân.
(4) Koxxâf, a bat (animal) = Koffâx.

خشخر Koxkâr, bread, coarse bran.

خشن Kaxin, *adj.* rough.
Koxouna, roughness.
Okxon, *vn* be rough, *lit.* or *fig.*
ii. Kaxxin, *va* roughen, ruffle, exasperate.
iii. Kâxin, *va* deal roughly with.

خوز iii. Kâwiz, v. Tekâwez sala', collude with.
Mokâwaze, collusion.

خزي Kezê, the being affronted.
Kizya, an affront.
iv. Akxi, *va* affront.

خزعبل Kazesbila 2, a romance.

خزف Kazef, pottery.
Kazefley, *adj.* of pottery.

خزق Ikxiq, *va* pierce.
Kâzouq 12, stake for impaling a man with.
Kauziq, *va* impale. *ger.* Kauzeqa.

خزل Kezl (in prosody) syncope.
Okzol *van*, *va* restrict from, repress (B. Comprimer).

خزم Okzom, *va* curb, restrain.
Kizêma, camel's nose-ring.
ii. Kazzim, *va* ring a camel's nose.

خزن Okzon, *va* store up.
Kazna, Kaziena, treasury.
Kizêna, repository.
Kâzin, treasurer.
Kazendâr, Chancellor of Exchequer, High Treasurer.
Makzen 11, warehouse, storehouse.
ii. Kazzin, *va* engross (goods), buy up and withhold from sale.

خزر Kaizorân, *pl.* 11. Kayêzir, bamboo.

L.

ل Lâ, not, no. Le! verily.
Li, Le, *prep.* to, for, because of.
Lau, if it were so that—.

L

Laulâ, if it were not that; but Li'ella, Liyalla, lest. [for.

لؤ Loulou, a pearl.
Telâlâ, *vn* glitter, gleam. *ger.* Telâlou *r.*

أول A'lou, *vn* be deficient, fail *r.*
Ali, insufficient, too weak *k.* *pl.* Awâli.

ألى Eli, *vn* swear *r.*

أول Ya'oul ila', arrives at; *fig.* amounts to, results in.
El, has resulted.
ii. Awwil, *va* interpret, *esp.* in malicious sense. [Oula'.
(2) Auwal, Awwal, first; *fem.* Auwal, *s.* first point, commencement.
El auwaloun(-ien), the ancients.
Awâyil, first days (*also*, engines).
Auwaliey, primary, pristine.
Auwalieya, priority.
iv. Iyâla, leadership, government.
Ayâla, a province. *See* Wilâya.
(3) Êla 2, tool, weapon; instrument, musical instrument; *also* engine (of steamboat, etc.); *pl.* Awâyil.
Elêliey, *adj.* organic; *s.* musician.

ولى Wêli, governor of a province.
Wilâya, province, government.

WLS

Waliey, Maula', lord, master.
ii. Welli, *va* invest as governor; empower.
v. Tewellâ, *vn* hold government as prefect.
Tewellie, prefecture.
1. Isteuli cala', *vn* become master over.
(2) Weli Yeli, *va* touch, be contiguous to. *ger.* Welâ, contiguity.
Weliey, contiguous.
Aula', nearer *k.*
(3) ii. Welli, *vn* turn aside, turn back [*antiquated use?*].
(4) Weli, simple, easy to deceive [*sic* B.].
Mawâl, romance, poem, *pl.* Mowâliyât B.

لوى Ilwi, *va* bend. *ger.* Lawâ, winding (of river).
ii. Lawwi, d^o *intens.* twist.
Liwâ, *pl.* 8, Elwiya, and Elwiyât, a flag; a military district. [rope.
Laiya, *pl.* Liwa', a turn of the
v. Telawwâ, *vn* twist, evade.
Telanlau, *vn* dodge, zigzag.
viii. Iltewi, *vp* be bent.
Iltiwâ, a twist, a sprain.
Moltewi, crooked, twisted.

لع Lazlâz, cowardly c.

ولع Wolous, burning desire.
ii. Wellis, *va* kindle (a fire).
v. Tewellas bi, *vn fig.* devote oneself to.

LWS

لوع Lausa, difficulty, dilemma c. [agitation, preoccupation by love x.]

لعب Ilsab, vn sport, play. ger.
Losba, a toy. [Lasb.
Losbicy, sportive.
Malsab, a play, a playhouse.
iii. Lâsub, va outwit, trick, divert (in war). [fant.
(2) Ilsab, vn slobber, as an in-Losâb, foam at the mouth, slobbering.

لعل Lasl, a ruby, Pers.
(2) Lasalla, Lasall, adv. belike, haply.

لعن Ilsan, va curse.
Lasna, a curse.
Lasuin, Melsöun, accursed.

لعق Ilsaq, va lick c. x. [But in b. Ilflas, Ilsefl.] ger.
Losqa. [spoon.
Milsaqa 11 (vulg. Maslaqa), a

لب Lobb, s. Lobba, nu. core, heart, pulp; crumb of bread (Hob. heart); infant's pap.
Labieb, fig. discreet, prudent.
(2) Labbaic! (with pronoun -ic), here I am for thy service!
Labbi, vn answer "labbaic" to the call of a master.
Telbiya, ger. answering to a master's call.
(3) Lablouba 11, tap to a cask.
See Laulab.

LBN

ألب 'Ilb, 'Olba, a herd, pack (of jackals).
v. Te'ellab, vn congregate, form a pack.

لوب Loubiya, French beans al
(2) Loba, syllabub.

لبد Olbod, vn stop and remain fixed; (se poster b.) inhere.
Lébid, adj. immanent (God).
ii. Labbid, va await fixedly, lie in ambush for b.
(2) Lobâd, felt, grey frieze.

لبخ Labka, a poultice c.

لبن Leban, curdled milk, junket al sweet fresh milk, Egypt.
Leban Miryam, Leban saara', milk-white porcelain.
Lebâna, dairy.
Lebân, s. milk-drinking, sucking the teat. Akou-h bil lebân, his foster-brother?
Milbana, great spoon x.
Melboun, Lebien, (horse) nourished on milk. [milk.
iv. Elbin, vn have milk, give
Molbin, Leboun, giving milk.
x. Istelbin, va draw milk x.
(2) Libn, brick clay, brick (esp. baked in the sun n.).
Libna, nu. a square brick.
Labbân, brickmaker.
ii. Labbin, va make bricks.
Milban, mould for bricks.
(3) Lobnân, Mount Lebanon.

LBC

لبك Olboc, *va* (modern word, *see* Orboc) engage, entangle, preoccupy. *ger*. Labec, mental preoccupation, distraction.
ii. Labbic, *va* same as Olboc.
viii. Iltebic, *vp* be engaged, preoccupied, busied. Iltibéc, distraction, preoccupa- [tion. (2) Labbai-c. See Labbi.

لبق Ilbaq, *vna* fit, suit; be fitting, becoming. *ger*. Labq, elegance of manners.
Labiq, intelligent, clever.
Lebâqa, intelligence.
ii. Labbiq, *va* attemper (steel).

لبس Ilbis, *vn vp* be clothed.
Libs 3, garment.
Lebâs, *esp*. drawers, trousers.
Milbes 11, costume.
iv. Elbis, *va* clothe.
ii. Labbis, *va fig*. cloak, mask, sophisticate.
viii. Iltebis, *vp* of ii.
Labs, Lobse, ambiguity.

لبط Ilbat, *vn* stamp with the feet, paw the ground.

لبث Ilbaθ, *vn* linger. *ger*. Labθ, Lebâθe.
Lébiθ, dilatory.

لد Lodd, *vn* wrangle, cavil. *ger*. Ladad, warm dispute.
Ladoud, quarrelsome, litigious.

لذ Lass, *vn* be delicious. *ger*. Lisss, deliciousness.

LDN

Lesies, delicious.
Elcss, more delicious.
viii. Iltiss, *or* x. Istcliss, *va* find (a thing) delicious.

ولد Walad Yelid, *va* breed, engender; *vp* Wolid, was born.
Welad 4 (*pl*. Aulâd), child, son, young (of animal).
Wélid, *f*. Wélida, parent.
Wélidicy, parental.
Wilâda, birth, parturition.
Welound, fruitful (parent).
Maulid, nativity (*esp*. of Mohammed x.).
Miclâd, nativity (*esp*. of Jesus), Christmas.
ii. Wellid, *va* deliver (a female) in birth.
Mowellida, midwife.
Mowellad, of mixed breed.
v. Tewellad, *vp* be born = Wolid.
Tewellod, birth. [Manxâ.
Motewellid, birthplace v. —

لدى Lada', Ladon, *prep*. at the side of, near, before (a great man).
Min ladon, on the part of.

لأن Melâs, asylum.

لذع Lausecuiy, piquant, sharp (*See* Oldoς, Ilscs), clever, full of talent.

لذغ Oldoς, *va* sting as serpent.
Mildâς, sarcastic.

لدن Ladn, supple, pliant.
Lodouna, suppleness.

LDN

Oldon, *vn* be supple?
(2) Ladon, *prep. See* Lada'.

لَفّ Loff, *va* wrap up, roll up. *ger.* Loffa, coil of turban, winding of road.
Lafiefa, a scroll.
Lifâfa, wrapper, envelope, bandage. Milaff, coverlet.
viii. Iltiff, *vp* be wrapt, etc.
Moltiff, wrapt, coiled.
(2) Loffân, sour-sweet (aigredoux B.).
Loffaf, acidulated x.

ألف 'Elf 4, a thousand.
(2) 'Elif, first letter of Alphabet.
(3) 'Olfa, familiarity.
'Elouf, familiar, intimate.
Elif 7, 'Elief 11, companion, comrade. [place.
Mêlaf 11, a haunt, familiar
ii. 'Ellif, *va* assemble and make familiar; compose and organize (an army); compose (a treatise).
Mo'ellif, Mowellif, composer. [For 'Ellif, B. has also Wellif, for, match, join (two persons); *also for* Debauch.]
iii. Êlif, *va* frequent (a place).
v. Te'ellaf, *va* frequent the company of x.
viii. Ittelif, *vn* be familiar.

ليف Lief, fibres (of palm tree).

لفع Ilfar, *va* lash (with whip).

لفح Ilfaḥ, *va* gulp down, swallow eagerly. *See* Ilhif.

LFW

لفق Olfoq, *va* sew together.
ii. Laffiq, *va lit.* as i.; *fig.* trump up, invent a fiction; trim, make neat?

لفت Lift, turnips.
(2) Ilfit, *va lit.* turn aside; divert (a stream).
Lefout, stiffnecked; *fig.* headstrong.
Lafte, a turning oneself, demeanor (towards). Ḥôsn el lafte, kindness of demeanor.
Lâft ran, turned away from, indisposed to?
viii. Iltefît, *vn* turn the head aside, to listen or attend.
Iltifêt, attention.
Moltefit, *s.* a profile B.
Moteleffit, wry-neck (*bird*).

لفظ Olfoz, *vn* pronounce. *ger.* Lafz, pronunciation, mode of pronouncing.
Lafza, *nu.* of d°
Lafzuiy, oral.
v. Telaffaz, *vn* pronounce.

ولغ Welar Yelir, *va* lap, as a dog.

لغو Olrou, *vn* talk. *ger.* Larou, chattering.
Lora, language, popular dialect.
Lorwiey, linguistic.
(2) iv. Elri, *va* omit, skip over (a word); dismiss (a Parliament). *ger.* Ilrâ.
(3) Larwa', *adj.* mean o.; *pl.* Lirâ x.

LIT

لقط Ilɾaṭ, *vn* chatter, as bird.
ger. Laɾṭ.

لغز Loɾz 4, enigma; *pl.* Elɾâz,
maze, labyrinth.
iv. Elɾiz fie, *vn* speak enigmatically concerning.

ج Liññ ɛala', *vn* stickle for.
iv. Eliññ, *va* urge, press, insist.

الا Ilêh, *s.* god; *pl.* Elihe. El
ilêh, the God. Allâñ (with
broad *a*) for El ilêh, God.
Ilêhi, my God.
Ilahe 2, goddess.
Ilehiey, divine.
Ilehieyêt, things divine.
Lehout, divine nature.
Lehoutiey, theologian.

ولى Weleh Yelih, *vn* be panic-stricken. [astound.
ii. Wellih, *va* scare away.
v. Tewelleh, *vn* same as i.
viii. Ittilêh, *s.* panic.

لوح Louñ, *vn* shine out, appear
clearly, be evident.
Lâñ ileiya, it is clear to me.
Telwieñ, metonymy x.
(2) Lauña, *nu.* 4, plank, pane,
pannel, slab.

لهو Olhou, *vn* sport. *ger.* Lehou.
Δου lehou, sportive.
Olhieya, amusement, pastime.
Milhe' 11, musical instrument,
toy.
iii. Léhi ɛan, *va* divert from.

LHF

iv. Elhi, *va* amuse.
Molhi, *adj.* amusing.
Telhiya, diversion, drawing off
of the mind.

لهى Lehêya, *pl.* Lehe', uvula
of throat B.
(2) Lahiey, Polish.
Lehistên, Poland.

لحى Luñya, *pl.* Luña', beard.
Luñawiey, appertaining to the
Luñyâniey, bearded x. [beard.
Molteñuiy, bearded.
(2) Luñâ, rind of a tree.

لهب Ilhed, *vn* flame.
Lebba 10, a flame.
Lehib, *adj.* flaming.
Lebieb, *s.* flaming heat.
iv. Elhib, *va* kindle; *fig.* inflame.
viii. Iltehib, *vp* be inflamed.
Iltihêb, inflammation.

لهد Ilhed, *va* overtire. *ger.*
Lebd (oppression x.)
Lahid, oppressive o.
Lebied, overladen.
iv. Elhid, *va* overload (a beast),
oppress.

لحد Lañd 3, catacomb, ancient
tomb, sarcophagus.
(2)ii. Lâñud, act the hypocrite o.
iv. Elñud, *vn* be heretical, pagan,
impious a.o.

لهف Ilhif, *va or* iv. Elhif,
hanker for, crave.
Melhouf, famished.

LHF

Molhif, craving, gluttonous.
Lêhif, *adj.* yearning c.
v. Telehhef ɛala', yearn after.

لِحَف Luḷâf 10, a coverlet.
iv. Elḷuf, *va* wrap in a coverlet.
v. Telaḷḷaf, *vn* wrap oneself in d°.
viii. Ilteḷuf, *vn* same as v.
(2) *Also* iv. Elḷuf ɛals', *vn* urge, press on, importune.

لج Lehja, tongue, speech.
v. Telehhej, *vn* give tongue, pour forth words.
(2) Ilhej, *vn* loll the tongue, pant.
Lehij, panting, passionately eager x.

لجج Lehwij, *va* roast imperfectly x. *fig.* do crudely, rudely, dash off hastily. *ger.* Lehwaja.
Molehwij, a coarse, blunt dealer, a dabbler.
ii. Telehwaj, *vn* be crude, be abrupt in dealing B.

لج Loḷj 4, corner, retreat.
Melḷaj 11, asylum? an expedient.

لحم Lehoum, Milhêm, gluttonous.
v. Telehhem, *or* viii. Iltehim, *va* swallow down. *See* Olqom.
iv. Elhim, *fig. va in theology*, inspire.
Ilhêm, divine inspiration.

LḤS

لحم Laḷm 3, flesh, fleshmeat.
Laḷma, *nu* bit of meat, a bait.
Laḷnim, fleshy.
(2) Loḷma 10, the woof.
(3) Olḷöm, *va* amalgamate.
iii. Lâḷum, *va* unite (a family) to oneself by marriage.
iv. Elḷum, *va* weld, solder, consolidate as i.
viii. Ilteḷum, *vn* be inherent, immanent.

لحن Ilḷan, *vna* lisp, talk imperfectly. *ger.* Laḷn 4, lisping, chant, melody.
Leḷâna, incorrect accent.
ii. Laḷḷun, *va* chant, warble.
(2) Loḷana B₂. (*Greek*), green vegetables.

لحق Ilḷaq bi, *vn* cling to, overtake. *ger.* Loḷôuq. [on.
Lâḷuqaⁿ, continuously, on and Lawâḷuq, *pl.* appurtenances c.
iv. Elḷuq, *va* unite, annex (politically).
vi. Telâḷaq, *vn* come up in succession.
viii. Ilteḷuq bi, *vp* be added to, be numbered among.

لحوق Lehwiq fle, *vn* parade, make show or pretence, do with display, but with no zeal. *ger.* Lehwaqa.
ii. Telehwaq fle, d°

لحس Ilḷas, *va* lick B. *fig.* fret.
See Ilseḷ.

LHT

لَهوت Lehout, divinity. *See* 'Iléh.

لَهث Ilheθ, *vn* gasp. *ger.* Lehθ. Lehθên, *adj.* gasping.

لَحظ Ilflaz ila', glance at.
Laflza 4, a glance.
Lufläz, outer corner of the eye.
iii. Lâfluz, *va* notice, watch.

لج Lojja 10, deep water, depth, abyss, *lit. or fig.*
ii. Lajjij, *vn* reach deep water.
(2) Lijj fie, *vn* be urgent for.
iii. Lâjij, *va* press (a person) in argument.
Lejouj, disputatious.
Lejâja, urgency, insistency.

لج Welij Yelij, *vn* enter, penetrate. *ger.* Wolouj.
ii. Wellij, *va fig.* cause to enter or embark (in a duty or service), occupy (a person), commission (him).
Mowellaj bi, occupied upon.
iv. Aulij fie, *va* insert into.
v. Towellaj fie, *vn* enter into, embark in (an enterprize).
Lija, entry into work, enterprize. *fig.* as v.
viii. Ittelij, *lit.* nearly as i. or

لجى Ilji ila', *vn* have recourse to.
Meljâ, place of refuge.
iv. Elji, *va* drive into refuge, force, impel to.
viii. Ilteji, *vn* take refuge.

LM

لجد Lojoud, medallions?

لجم Lijâm 8, bridle for horse.
iv. Eljim, *va* bridle.
viii. Iltejim, *vp* of iv.

لح ii. Telaklak, *vn* vacillate, move up and down, bob.

لوخ v. Telawwak, viii. Iltêk, *vn* ferment, as fruit or dough.

لكبر Lakbur, *va* disorder.
Lakbəra, a jumble.
Molakbar, disordered (health), deranged (machine), uncouth (form).

لكم Olkom, *va* slap in the face; *fig.* disconcert, put out of countenance B. *Also* encumber B.

لخص ii. Lakkuy, *va* make abstract or extract; select (a passage).

ليل Leila, *nu.* night; *pl.* 11 Leyâli.
Leiliey, nocturnal.

للب Laulab 11, a turning peg, a tap to a cask, a crank, a vice.
Lablouba 11, tap to a cask.

لم Lomm, *va* amass.
Lomma, a group.
Limma 10, sidelock of hair.
Molamlam, collected into one c.

LM

(2) iv. Elimm bi, *vn* touch at (a port), attain to.
(3) Lemma, *conj.* when.
Lem, not (with pres. gives past sense).

ألم 'Elem 4, pain, bodily or mental. *ger.* of 'Elim Yelem min, *vn* smart from.
ii. 'Ellim, *va* pain. Eliem, Mowellim, painful.
v. Tewellum, *vn* suffer pain.
El 'elâm, the Passion (of Jesus).
'Elim, smarting x.

ولم Weliema 11, solemn banquet.
iv. Aulim, *va* give a banquet.

ألم Liem, *s.* accord, agreement x.
iii. Lâ'im, Lâyim, *va* conciliate; agree with; suit. [sons.]
Lâ'im bain, reconcile (two persons).
Molâ'im, Molâyim, agreeing well, suitable.
vi. Telâ'am, *vn* become reconciled, return into amity.
viii. Iltêm, *vn lit.* coalesce, as wounded flesh. *fig.* meet anew, as an assembly.
Iltiyâm, coalescing (of a wound).
Motelâ'im, patched up anew, reconciled.
x. Isteliem, *va* convene (an assembly).
(2) Le'iem, mean, stingy.

لوم Loum, *va* blame. *ger.* Malâm, Malâma.
ii. Lawwim, *va* blame much.
vi. Telâwam, *vn* recriminate.

LYN

Malâma, reproach; *pl.* 11 Malâyim.
Lawwâm, censorious.

لمع Ilmaε, *vn* shine.
Lamεa, a view, an *exposé.*
viii. Iltemiε, *vn* shine.

لمذ Telmieε 11, disciple; from *Heb.*

لمح Ilmaḥ, *vn* peep, look slyly.
Lamḥ, ocular evidence x.
Lamḥa, *nu.* a glance.
ii. Lammiḥ, *va* indicate, point at.

لمن Liemoun, lemon.
Liemounâda, lemonade.

لمس Olmos, *va* touch.
ii. Lammis, *va* handle much.
iii. Lâmis, *va* handle.
viii. Iltemis, *vn* beg, coax (by stroking?). *va* seek for.
Iltimâs, entreaty, coaxing.
(2) Elmâs, diamond; for *Gr.* ἀδάμας.

لون Laun 4, colour.
ii. Lawwin, *va* colour.
v. Telawwan, *vp* be coloured; *vn* be many coloured, be changeable.
Molawwan, coloured.
Motelawwin, of many colours.

لين Lien, *vn* be soft.
Laiyin, soft. Liyâna, softness.
ii. Layyin, *va* soften.
iii. Lâyin, *va fig.* conciliate.

LNC

لَنْكْ Lenc. *ger.* trotting.
Imxi lenc, go at a trot ʟ.

لَكّ Lecc 3, a hundred thousand.
(2) Locc, red sealing wax.
Lecce, a stain c.
Melconc, stained c.
(3) Leclic, *vn* trot. *ger.* Lec-
lece, a trot. *See* Lenc.

لَقَى Loqq, *vs* touch, attain ʙ.
(2) Laqlaq, *s.* a stork.
Laqliq, *vn* rattle in the throat.
vs swallow up, devour (another's good things). *ger.*
Laqlaqa.

لَوَقَ ii. Lawwiq, *vns* twist the
mouth, make grimaces. Tel-
wieq, grimace. Fomm mo-
lawwaq, a twisted mouth,
i.e. grimace.
v. Telawwaq, and vi. Teláyaq,
(*sic* ʙ.) make grimace.
Telaulaq d°· ʙ.

لِيَقَ Yelieq, it befits.
Lâq candi 'ennu —, it has
seemed good with me that—
i.e. I approve that—.
Lâyiq, decorous.
Liyâqa, decorum.

لَقَى Olqou, *vs* twist the mouth,
cause paralysis. (*See* Lawwiq.)
Laqwa, paralysis of the mouth.

لَقِى Ilqi, *vs* meet (commoner
in v.).

LQN

Tilqâ, *s.* meeting, occurrence ;
adv. in front.
iv. Elqi, *vs* cast (to earth,
cast (ashore).
v. Telaqqâ, *vs* meet.
vi. Telâqâ, *vr* meet one another.

لَقَسَ Loces, *adj.* sloven, sluttish.
Locesa, *f.* a slut. [porise.
v. Teleccec, *vn* dawdle; tem-

لَقَبَ Laqab, Liqb 4, title,
epithet. [name.
ii. Laqqib, *vs* entitle, give sur-

لَقَفَ Ilqaf, *vs* snap up.
v. Telaqqaf or viii. Iltaqif, d°·

لَقَحَ ii. Laqqiḥ, *vs* fecundate (a
plant or female animal).
Telqioflat riefl, squall of wind ʙ.

لَكَمَ Olcom, *vn* spar with fists.
vs break a line of battle ʙ.
Lecma, *ns.* blow of fist.
vi. Telêccm, *vr* box together.

لَقَمَ Olqom, *vs* gobble up; en-
gulf.
Loqma 10, gobbet, mouthful.
iv. Elqim, *vs* cause to swallow x.
viii. Iltaqim, *vs* swallow a
mouthful.

لَكَنَ Lecna, a jabbering (ʙ. *bre-
douillement*).

لَقِنَ Laqin, quick of intelligence. [gence.
Laqâna, quickness of intelli-

LQN

لقّن . Laqqin, *va* instruct, prompt, suggest.

لقط Olqoṭ or ii. Laqquṭ, *va* pick up, glean.
viii. Iltaquṭ, d°.
Loqaṭa, a Godsend x.
Laqieṭ 6, a foundling.
Loqâṭa, gleanings.
Laqqâṭ, Milqâṭ, pincers to pick up with.

لصّ Luṣṣ 3, robber, bandit.
Laṣaṣ, Luṣûṣ, brigandage.
v. Telaṣṣaṣ, *vn* maraud, play the robber.

لسّ Welis Yelis, *va* deceive x.
ger. Wels, double dealing.
iii. Wâlis, *va* deceive by equivocation.
Mowâlase, equivocation.
vi. Tewâles, *or* be in collusion.

ليس ii. Layyis, *va* plaster (a wall) B. O.

لسع Ilsaɛ, *va* bite as scorpion or serpent; sting. *ger.* Lass, Leasa, *ns.*
Lesiɛa, Melsouɛ, stung.
iv. Elsiɛ bain, *vn* sow enmity between.

لسن Ilsaɛn, *va* lick B. *See* Illaas.

لسن Lisân θ, tongue.
Lesin (*pl.* Losn x.), fluent of speech.

LTK

لصق Ilṣaq bi, *vn* adhere to.
ger. Loṣöuq.
Lâṣuq bi, in contact with.
Laṣniq, *adj.* neighbouring o.
iii. Lâṣuq, *va* adhere to.
Molâṣuq, contiguous.
iv. Elṣuq, *va* stick, glue, attach.
viii. Iltaṣuq bi, *vn* as i.

لط Loṭṭ, *va* compromise, damage (a person or cause) B. *affligo?*
iii. Luṭâṭ, dashing of waves (= Luṭâm, Telâṭöm?) [*qu.* Lâṭuṭ = Lâṭam?].

لت Lett, *s.* verbosity B.

لتث Teleθleθ, *vn* waver.

لوث Lawaθ, *s.* dirt.
ii. Lawwiθ, *va* daub, defile; run (a ship) aground s.

ليت Ya lait! oh that!

لطف Loṭf, Laṭâfa, gentleness.
Laṭnif, gentle, mild.
Laṭuifa 11, a pleasantry, a witticism.
iii. Lâṭuf, *va* treat kindly.
vi. Telâṭaf li, *vn* behave kindly
x. Isteltuf, *va* conciliate. [to.

لطّ Ilṭaṭ, *va* pat, slap gently.
Laṭḍa, a pat.

لطخ Ilṭak, *va* beamear, bespatter.
ger. Laṭk.
Laṭöuk, dirt, mire.
v. Telaṭṭak, *vp* be bespattered.

LTM

لطم Olᴛom, *va* slap. *ger.* Laᴛm,
  Laᴛma, *nu.* a slap.
vi. Telâᴛam, *vr* slap one another
  (at random), dash as waves.

لثم Olθom, *va* kiss, press the mouth.
  Liθêm, veil round the mouth, worn by Bedouins against the heat of the sand.

لطس Olᴛös, *va* slap.

لطش Olᴛöx, *va* slap, lash, pummel (в. *bourrer*).
  Laᴛxa, *nu.* a slap, blow; *fig.* a folly, mania в.
  Malᴛöux, maniacal в.
ii. Laᴛᴛux, *va* smack (a whip) в.

لشي Lâxa, carcase c.
iii. Lâxi, *va* annihilate (*modern from* Lâ xai', no thing).
v. Telâxâ, *vp* be annihilated.

لز Lozz, *va* press together; press, urge.
  Lozz ɾala', *vn* press upon.
  Lezouz, compact, shrunk up.
viii. Iltizz, *vp* be compressed.

لظى Laza', fierce blaze, hell-fire.
ii. Laʒʒu, *va* kindle a hell.
v. Telaʒʒâ, *vn* flame out furiously.

لوز Leuze *nu.* almond, gland, tonsil of throat.
  El leusetain, the two tonsils.

LZQ

لزب Ilzib, *vn* be compact.
  Lêzib, firm, solid.

لزج Lozij, sticky and soft, gummy.
  Lezouje, liquid gum.
v. Telezzej, *vn* be gummy.

لزم Ilzem, *va* hold fast, exact?
  vn be of importance.
  Ilzem el firâx, keep one's bed.
  Ilzem el darb, keep the road.
  Milzema, *s.* mangle to press linen.
iii. Lêzim, *va* adhere to, keep to.
  Lêzim, *adj.* necessary. (In modern use, Lêzim is Lat. Opus for Oportet. It takes suffix *pron.* as, Lêzim-ni, is necessary for me; *or,* I need.)
iv. Elzim, *va* compel; *also,* convict s.
viii. Ilterim, *vp* be compelled; *va* engage oneself, undertake; apply oneself.
x. Istelzim, *va* exact.

لزق Ilzeq bi, *vn* adhere to. *ger.* Lozouq.
  Lozouq, sticky.
  Lezqa, sticking plaster.
  Lizêq, glue, cement.
  Lezieq, inseparable companion.
iv. Elziq, *va* stick (two things) together.
v. Motalêziq, mutually adhering, contiguous.
viii. Ilteziq, *vp* be stuck together; *vn* adhere. See Ilvaq.

M

اَمْ Am (Em), or, (in an alternative, where *whether* has preceded or is understood), as, *Whether* early *or* late.
(2) Amma, Emma, but.
(3) 'Omm, *pl.* 'Ommehêt, 'Omma 10, nation. [mother.
'Ommiey, *adj.* maternal; *s.* a simpleton.
'Omaima, little mother; *dimin.* of affection. [ɪ.
'Omouma, 'Ommieya, maternity
(4) 'Emâm, *prep.* in presence of.
'Imâm, chief (priest); *pl.* Eyimma.
'Imâma, office of chief priest.

يَمّ Yamm 3, sea (*antiqu.*).
(2) v. Teyammam, *vn* rub oneself for legal ablution with sand or cinders.
(3) Yemâma, *nu.* pigeon, dove.

مَا Mâ, not (*sep.* in modern use).
Mâ, that which, what (*relative*).
Mâ? Mâee? what? (*interrog.*)

مَىّ Mâ', *vulg.* Mâi, water; *pl.* Miyâh, Amwâh.
Mowaiy, *dimin.* of d°· ᴀʟ
Mowaiya, *nu.* a sup of water, a little water.

مَوّ Mou', *vn* mew as a cat. *ger.* Mowâ ᴠ. *See* Nawwi.

مائة Mieya, a hundred; *spelt* Mâya.

MD

مَع Mas, *prep.* with.
Masaⁿ, *adv.* together.

مِعى Musa', *pl.* 4, Amsâ, bowel.

مَعِدة Musda 10, stomach.

مَعُون Mâsôun 12, metal platter (utensil, perhaps from sôun). *Also* Ma'oun.
Masuin, a rhombus or lozenge shape ʙ.
(2) ii. Massun, or iv. Amsun el nazar, fix the eyes (upon).

مَسَح Imsac, *va* scrub ʙ. (rub by dragging on the ground ɪ.).

مَعز Masz, goats *collect.*
Masze, *nu.* a goat.
Maszêya, she-goat.
Mâsuz 12, *f.* Mâsuze, a goat.
Mosaiz, a kid ɪ.
Massâz, goatmaster ᴠ.

مَدّ Modd, *va* stretch. *ger.* Madd.
Madd 4, flood of tide; a bushel.
Madda, extension, extent.
Modda, space of time.
Mâdda, *pl.* 12 Mawâdd, [continual enlargement ɪ.]; an article or paragraph; a subject, topic; matter, *opposed to* form.
Midda, *medic. t.* matter, pus.
[Midâd, ink ʙ. ɪ. *rare*?]
Madied 10, extensive.
Modda madieda, a long period.
viii. Imtidd, *vp* be extended.

MD

ii. Maddid, *vs* lengthen by stretching x.
(2) Madad, *s.* succour, supply.
iv. Amdid, *vs* supply (an army).
x. Istemidd, *vs* ask supplies.

مضّ Maḍḍ, *vn* smart. *ger.* Ma-ḍaḍ, Maḍâḍa.
iv. Amuḍḍ, *vs* cause to smart.
Momuḍḍ, *adj.* poignant, stinging.
(2) Maḍmuḍ, *vs* rince the mouth.

مذ Miḍ, Moḍ, Minḍ, Monḍ, since, ever since; *for* Monḍê.

مدى Mada', limit, full extent.
Fie mada' rômri, within the space of my life. Qadr mada' el baṣar, so far as the eye can
Imdi, *vs* extend. [reach.
v. Temâdâ, *vn* drag on, linger; dawdle, be tedious.

مضى Imḍu, *vn* pass (as time, as life), pass, penetrate (as a sharp weapon); pass, as an Act or Treaty.
Amḍa', sharper, *antiqu. ?*
El Mâḍu, the past, past tense.
iv. Amḍu, *vs* pass (an Act of State), sign and seal, execute. *See* Ajri.
Imḍâ, passing, execution, *i.e.* signature of a public Act, or important document.

مضغ Omḍoǧ, *vs* chew, champ.

مدن Medicna 10, 11, city.
Medaniey, *adj.* civil; civic. *s.* citizen.

MHD

Medianiey, living in a city, as the stork.
ii. Meddin, *vs* civilize.
v. Temeddan, *vn* live in civilization.
Temeddon, civilized life.

مدر Madar, clay.
Madara, a clod of clay.
Omdor, *vs* besmear with mud.
ii. Maddir, *vs* pave (a floor) with clay x.
Mamdara, clayfield x.

مذر Imḏir, *vn* be addled.
iv. Amḏir, *vs* addle.

مغب Maǧyib, *vs* pretend not to observe or feel b. *dissimuler.* *From* Ɣieb?

مغر Amǧar, roan, colour of raspberry cream.
Maǧra, ruddle, red earth b.

مغص Maǧṣ, *s.* colic.

موه ii. Mawwih, *vs* embellish, varnish (a tale).

مهى Mâhiya, quality. *From* Má hiya, what is it?

محو Omḥöu, Imḥâ, *vs* efface. *ger.* Maḥöu.
viii. Imteḥu, *vp* be effaced.
Imtiḥâ, effacement.

مهد Mehed 3, cradle, child's bed. [ground x.
(2) Mohd, Mihêd 4, level

MHD

ii. Mehhid, *va* level, make even.
v. Temehhed, *vp* be made level.
Motemehhid, Momehhid, *adj.* level.

مَحْض Maḥḍ, *adj.* mere, pure; *adv.* merely.

مُهْجَة Mohja, heart's blood, life-blood.

مَهْل Mehl, leisure. Mehla⁹, at leisure.
Mohla, an adjournment, respite.
iv. Amhil, *va* give respite, adjourn.
v. Temehhel, *vn* take things easily, act quietly.
Motemêhil, longsuffering s.
x. Istemhil, *va* ask (a person) for respite, for delay.

مَحْل Maḥul, barren x.
Momḥul, barren s.

مهن Imhen, *vn* be a menial.
ger. Mehn.
Mehna, Mihna, diligent service.
Mehêna, drudgery, plodding.
Mêhin(a), domestic servant, *m.f.*
viii. Imtehin, *va* take as a menial.

محن Imḥan, *vn* strive, put oneself to proof.
Maḥun, *adj.* plodding, hardworking. *See* Mêhin.
Muḥna 10, trial, distress.
viii. Imteḥun, *va* put to proof, tempt s.

MJD

Imtiḥân, temptation (of Jesus, s.), examination (as of pupils).

محكمة iii. Mâḥuc, *va* summon before a judge, indict?
vi. Temâḥac, *vn* be litigious?

محق Imḥaq, *va* efface, annihilate, consume.

مهر Mêhir, skilful (*solers*).
Mehêra, skill (of physician, of statesman).
iii. Mêhir, *va* vie with in skill x.
v. Temehher, *vn* be skilful, able.
Temehhor, ability, versatility.
(2) Mehr 3, dowry.
Mehiera, Memhoura, (girl) with large dowry.
iv. Amhir, *va* bestow dowry on.
(3) Mohr 5, a colt.
Mohra 2, 10, a filly.

محور Mahyur, *vn* romance s.
Mahyaya, *s.* romance, rhodomontade s.

محص ii. Maḥḥuṣ, *va* dash (a work) off rapidly.

محش Imḥax, *va* scorch black, char x.

مج Mojj, *va* repulse, rebuff (a person) s. (*jeter dehors* x.)

مجد Mejd, *s.* glory.
Mejied, glorious.
Amjad, more glorious.
ii. Mejjid, *va* glorify.
iii. Mêjid, *va* boast of x.

MJD

iv. Amjid, *va* eulogize.
vi. Temêjad, *vr* vaunt mutually.

مجن Mâjin, Majoun, reckless, unscrupulous.
Majâna, recklessness.
Majouniey, shameless (deed).
Majján, gratuitous.
Majjânaⁿ, *adv. gratis.*
(2) Mijann, a buckler; generally, a coat of arms, in heraldry.

مجر Majar, a ducat c.
(2) Mâjour 12, bowl or flower pot of red earthenware.

مخ Mokk 5, marrow.
Makiek, full of marrow.

مخض Omkoḍ, *va* churn.
(2) Makâḍ, travail of childbirth.

مخل Makl 4, iron lever.

مخن Miekâna, a tavern.
Miekânji, tavern-keeper.

مخر Imkar, *vn* cleave the waves (as boat or swimmer), set sail s.

مخاط Mokât (*medic. t.*) mucus.
Mokâtuiy, *adj.* mucous.
Omkor, Omkot enf-ec, blow the nose.
v. Temakkat, blow one's nose.
viii. Imtekur, dᵒ x.

ML

مل Mill, *vn* faint, be tired. *ger.* Melel, Melêle, weariness,
iv. Amill, *va* tire. [ennui.
(2) Mille 10, religious sect.
v. Temellel, *vn* enter a sect x.
(3) Melle, *s.* [Braise x. Crucible to hold food when placed under hot ashes.]
Kobz melle, bread baked in the ashes.
Meliel, baked in the ashes.

أمل 'Emel 4, hope, looking out for. ['Eml.
'Emel Yemol, *va* hope for. *ger.*
Mêmoul, thing hoped for.
Mêmal, object of trust x.
ii. Emmil, *va* hope, expect.
v. Te'emmel, *vn* meditate.

ميل Miel, *vn* slant, deviate, incline (towards). *ger.* Mail, slope, inclination, propensity.
Mâyil, slanting; Mâyil ila', inclined to, verging to.
Amyal, more inclined.
ii. Mayyil, *va* cause to slope.
iv. Amiel, *va fig.* incline (a person), dispose him, persuade him.
(2) Mial 4, a mile.

ملا Imlâ, *vn* be full.
Milâ, what fills.
Milâ ceff, a handful.
Memlou*, filled.
Mel'ên, *vulg.* Meliên, full.
ii. Melli, *va* fill.
viii. Imteli, *vp* be filled.
Imtilâ, flood state (of river)?

MLW

لم iv. Amli cala', *va* dictate (a letter) to.
ii. Melli, d⁰ в.
Imlâ, dictation. Imlâ, *pl.* Amâli, memorandum dictated.

ملح Milfl, *s.* salt.
Omlofl, *vn* be salt.
Mâlifl, *adj.* salt.
ii. Mellifl, *va* salt, make salt.
Melouſla, salt pickle, brine.
Mimlafla, saltcellar.
Memlafla, Mellâfla, saltmine.
Mellâfl, mariner.
Mellâfluiy, nautical.
Milâfla, Mellâfluiya, science of of navigation.
(2) Meliefl, *adj.* fair, elegant; *vulg.* good (thing or person).
Melâfla, beauty, elegance.
Molfla 10, masterpiece, good saying, witticism в.
x. Istemlifl, *va* deem handsome.

ملخ Melka, a sprain of the sinews, torsion. [wrench.
iii. Mêlik, *va* sprain, severely
(2) Melouka, garden mallows.

ملك Melic 3, king.
Melice, Meliece, queen.
Melcout, royalty, *in theology?*
Mileo, Mâlicieya, royalty.
Melciey, Molouciey, royal.
Moleic, petty king.
Milc 4, reign, dominion.
Molc, domain, ownership.
Molciey, *adj.* (land) held as freehold. [N.B. I cannot get any fixed convictions as to the vowel in Milc and Molc.]
[Melê'o 13, angel.]
Memleoe 11, kingdom, realm.
Mâlicêna, hereditary fief, held by crown grant.
Mâlic, master, owner.
Memlouc 11, slave.
Imlic, *va* possess.
ii. Mellic *or* iv. Emlic, *va* put (another) in possession of.
v. Temelleo, *vn* become master, act the king.

ملق ii. Melliq, *va* (*Lat.* mulceo), make smooth к. soothe, flatter в.
iii. Mâliq, *va* flatter, soothe c.
v. Temallaq li, vi. Temâlaq li, act the flatterer to.
vii. Inmeliq, *vn* be smooth.

ملس ملش Amles, Amlay, *adj.* smooth, hairless? (*glaber*).
Omloa, *vn* be smooth.
Melêse, smoothness.
[Melies, *adj.* sour-sweet в.]
ii. Mellis, *va* make smooth (*compare* μαλασσω, μαλακος).
viii. Imtelis, Imteluy, *vn* glide away, escape.

MN

موم Moum, smallpox? x.
(2) Moumiya *pl.* 11, Mowâmi, mummy.

من Mán, who? Mun, whoso. Min, from.
(2) Minn, *vn* act kindly. Mann

MN

ɛalaiy⁴ bi xai'i⁴, he has acted kindly *to* me *in* a thing. *ger*.
Menn, favour. [gation.
Minna, a favour, *esp.* an obli-
Memnoun, obliged; grateful.
Memnounieya, gratitude.
viii. Imtinân, *s.* favour, grace.

اٴمن 'Eman ɛala', *vn* rely upon; but *vp* 'Omin ɛala', be entrusted with. *ger*. 'Emn, security, loyalty.
'Emien, trusty, faithful.
'Emana, 'Emâna, faithfulness.
'Emân, safe conduct, amnesty, quarter in battle.
'Omniya, safety.
iv. Emin, *va* protect.
Iemân, religious faith.
Moumin, true believer.
v. Te'emman ɛala', *vn* confide in.
viii. Ittemin, *va* trust (any one), *also* Ittemin ɛala', *vp* be entrusted with? [perhaps rather in old passive, Outomin ɛala', he has been entrusted with.]
x. Istémin, *va* account faithful x.
Istémin ilo', *vn* seek refuge with.
Istémin ɛala', *va* entrust (a (a person) with s.

يمن Yeman, right hand, right side c.
Yoman, Yomna, success x.
Yemien, *adj.* on the right hand. *s.* right hand, right side; an oath.
Yomna', *pl.* Yomnayêt, right hand [in high style?]

MNK

Yomnâi, my right hand s.
Maimana, right side or hand.
Maimoun, fortunate.
(2) Maimoun 11, a baboon.

مون Moun bi, *va* stock with (provisions), victual, feed.
Mouna, Maunâ, Ma'ouna, provisions, store of food.
v. Temawwan min, *vn* be provisioned with, take in stores of.
(2) Ma'oun, platter, dish. *See* Maɛöun.

مينا Miena *s.* harbour; *pl.* Main n.
(2) Mienâ, *s.* enamel c. x.

منى v. Temennâ, *va* desire, re-
Temeunnie, a petition. [quest.
(2) Manie, sperm.
Manwiey, spermatic.

منع Imnaɛ, *va* hinder. *ger.* Manɛ.
Manɛa, inaccessibility.
Manieɛ, inaccessible.
Mânɛ 12, a hindrance, obstacle.
viii. Imtenie min, *vn* abstain from.

منح Imnaḥ, *va* bestow.
Minḥa 10, a gift.
Mannâḥ, generous.

منجنيق Minjanieq, machine.

منخ Menâk, climate. *Oberleitner*. He refers it to the root Nouk.

MNT

مِنْطَقة Minṭaqa 11, belt, zone.
ii. Temanṭuq, *vn* wear a belt.
Motemanṭuq, girded s.

مَكّوك Meccouc, weaver's shuttle.

مَاق Mâq, Mouq, *s.* inner corner of the eye.

مُقِل Moqil? opinionated, obstinate (B. *têtu*, مُقَل also B. *obstiné*, مُقَل).
Moql? obstinacy (B. *obstination*, مُقَل).
[Omqol, *va* stare at x.]

مَقَت Omqot, *va* detest. *ger.* Maqt, detestation.
Maqiet, detestable.
iv. Amqit, *va* render odious.
(2) vii. Inmaqit, *vn* become sullen, frown B.

مَكِن Mécin, strong AL.
Mecien, solid. Mecêna, solidity. *See* Metien, Metêna.
Mecna, mercantile credit.
ii. Meccin, *va* strengthen.
iv. Emcin, *vn* be able, possible.
Imcên, ability, possibility.
Momcin, possible. With *accus.* Yomcin-oh, it is possible *for* him.
v. Temeccen, *vn* grow powerful, assume power.
x. Istomcin min, *vn* make oneself master of (a thing), become capable for, able for.

MR

(2) Mecên 6, *pl.* Emcina; *pl.* of *pl.* 11 Amâcin; place.
Mecên, *prep.* instead of.
Mecêniey, local *r.*

مَكَر Omcor, *va* defraud. *ger.* Mecr, fraud; *pl.* Mewâcir, trickeries.
Meccêr, swindler.

مَكْرَجات Mecourjat^m, in the lump, wholesale (en bloc B.).

مَكْس Mecs, customhouse duty.
Mêcis, collector of duties.
iii. Mêcis, *v.* bid at an auction.
Momêcese, a bidding, chaffering.
vi. Temêces, *vr* bid against one another, haggle, chaffer.

مَكَث Omcoθ, *vn* sojourn, tarry, wait. *ger.* Mecθ.

مَرّ Morr, *vn* pass. *ger.* Marr.
Morour, passage, *act* of passing.
Mamarr, passage, *place* of passing.
Marra 5, 4, a turn, time. [ing.
Marratein, twice.
Mirâra^n, at times, sometimes.
x. Istemirr, *vn* persevere.
Istimrâr, persistence.
(2) Morr, *adj.* bitter; *s.* myrrh.
Mirra, bile, gall.
Marâra, bitterness, gallbladder.
Mamrour, bilious.
(3) iii. Mârir, *va* tustle with.
vi. Temârar, *vr* tustle mutually.
(4) Marmar, *s.* marble.
Marmir, *va* make tremulous?

MR

Temarmar, *vn* ripple and glister; be tremulous; *also* murmur, purl *s*. See Marmit.

مر اً 'Emr 3, affair.

'Emr *or* Êmira, a command; *pl.* 12, Awâmír.
Mor, *imper.* command thou.
Yêmor, he commands.
'Emier 6, prince.
'Emiera, princess.
'Emieriey, princely; *vulgo* Mieriey, in the phrase Mâl mieriey, royal finance.
'Emâra, signet, sign, index.
'Imâra, government, rule.
Mâmour, commissary.
Mâmourieya, commission(ers).
iii. Êmir, *va* consult.
vi. Te'êmar, Tewêmar, *vn* deliberate.

مور Mour, light chesnut coloured.
(2) Mâr, Christian saint.

مرأ Mar'a, a woman. In modern literature, Imrâ'a, a woman.
Marouwa, manliness.
(2) Mar'iey, nutritive (food).

مرى Marieya, *s.* doubt.
iii. Mâri, *va* call in question.
viii. Imteri fie, *vn* doubt of.

مرد Omrod, *vn* be rebellious.
ger. Moroud, rebellious spirit.
Mârid, rebellious.
v. Temarrad, *vn* rebel.

MRN

مرض Imrâḍ, *vn* be sick. *ger.*
Marḍ 4, disease.
Marieḍ, sick, *pl.* Marḍa'.
Mimrâḍ, a complete invalid.
v. Temarraḍ, *vn* fall sick.
vi. Temêraḍ, *vn* play the invalid.
viii. Imtiraḍ, debility from disease.

مرغ Omroġ, *va* anoint, rub-in (an embrocation). *See* Omrok.
(2) Imraġ, *vn* wriggle away from, elude.
ii. Marriġ, *va* cause (one's horse) to roll.
v. Temarraġ, *vn* roll (as horse).

مرح Imraḥ, *vn* frolic.
Marḥ, Maraflân, frolic, frolicsomeness.
Marouḥ, frolicsome.
Mimrâḥ, very frolicsome.

مرج Marj 3, meadow.
(2) Marjân, coral.

مرخ Omrok, *va* rub in; anoint.

مرم Marmit, Marmur, *va* derange, rumple, ruffle *s*.
Marmate, disarrangement, ruffling.

مرن Omron, *vn fig.* be callous; be a veteran, be experienced.
Marâna, craftiness (*calliditas*).
Mârin (*callidus*) 12, experienced, clever.
ii. Marrin, *va* habituate, inure.

MRN

v. Temarran, *vn* become habituated.
(2) Mairoun, Confirmation, a Catholic sacrament b.

مرق Omroq, *vn* go astray; *fig.* from religious truth; *va* elude b. See Imraɛ.
Morouq, *ger.* a missing of the truth, heresy.
Mâriq 7, heretic, heretical.
(2) Maraqa, broth of meat, meat soup, gravy.

مرس Marase, *ns.* 4, cord.
(2) iii. Mâris, *va* exercise, practise (an art or profession).
(3) Maristôn, *vulg.* hospital b.

مرزبان Marzobân, *pl.* 13, Marâziba, Persian satrap.

مس Mass, *va* touch. *ger.* Mess.
iii. Mâsis, *va* touch (in geometry), osculate.

مص Moss, *va* sip, sup.

امس Ems, yesterday.

موس Mous 4, surgeon's clasp-knife, razor.

ميس Meis, *s.* tinsel.
Mies, *vn* stalk? b. *rather* swagger. *See* Behraj.

ميص Maiɛ, rennet.

مسا Mesê, evening.

MSR

مسد ii. Messid, *va* stroke with the hand c.

مسح Imseḥ, *va* wipe. *ger.* Mesḥ(a). [*Hebr.*)
Mesieḥ, Messiah, anointed (from Mesieḥuiy, *adj.* Christian.
Mesieḥuiyoun, Christians.
(2) Miaḥ, coarse cloth, frieze? sackcloth?
(3) Mossêḥ, land surveyor.
Mesêḥa, geometry. *See* Sieḥ.

مسخ Imsek, *va* pervert, caricature, metamorphose. *ger.* Misk.

مسل Mêsoula 12, a tube ox. See also Mâɛoura, Mâɛoul.

مسل Imɛul, *va* filter b.
Mâɛoul, pipe, fife, tube.
(2) Maɛl, whey.

مسك Omsoc, *va* seize, hold.
Mosce 2, 10, handle.
Mêsic, Messêc, tenacious, stingy.
Mesêc, Imsêc, avarice.
Mêsic, a pincer.
v. Tomcessec bi, *vn* cling to; *fig.* stickle for (a doctrine).
Temessoc, bond, bill due.
(2) Misc, musk.
ii. Mossic, *va* perfume with musk.

مصر Maɛr, Egypt, Cairo.
Muɛr 4, any great city.
Amɛâr josiema, huge cities.
Muɛriey, Egyptian.
Muɛrieya 2, 11, a para, the smallest Turkish coin.

MƷR

(2) Màẏöura 12, tube, barrel of gun. Màẏöurat el ḋayyêc, weaver's shuttle.

موسا Moeʀ, women's mocassins al.

متى Mette? when? when. Ei mette? *vulg.* Emta, when?

مد Moʀʀ, *vɑ* dilate.

موت Mout, *vn* die.
Maut, Maute, death.
Momêt, death, decease.
Maiyit, dead; *pl.* Maute'.
iv. Amiet, *vɑ* (*lit.* kill), *fig.* mortify (the passions).

حمى؟ or بمى؟ iv. Amuiʀ, *vɑ* uncover ʀ.

مطو ii. Maʀʀu, *vɑ* stretch with effort.
iv. Amʀu, *vɑ* cause (another) to ride, mount (him).
v. Temaʀʀâ, *vn* stretch oneself in yawning.
viii. Amtaʀu, *vn* mount; go on horseback.

متع Metêc, possession; *pl.* 8, Emtisa, articles, goods.
v. Tematteс bi, *or* x. Istemtic bi, enjoy (possessions).
ii. Mettic bi, *vɑ* cause to enjoy (possessions); said chiefly of God.

مثل Miӫl, likeness; *adv.* like.
Meӫel 4, *adj.* similar; *s.* a simile, parable.

MXY

Moӫla, a pattern, an example, a warning.
Moӫliey, exemplary.
Miӫêl, a model.
Omӫoula 11, example as in grammar x.
Timӫêl 11, image, effigy.
ii. Meӫӫil, *vɑ* liken, compare; make example of, chastise.
(2) Moӫoul, respectful attitude before a great man, state of being presented, admittance.
ii. Meӫӫil, *vɑ* present (a person) at court.
v. Temeӫӫel, *or* viii. Imtcӫil, *vn* do obeisance before a king.

متن Metn, *s.* substance; text of an author.
Metien, substantial.
Metêna, solidity.
ii. Mettin, *vɑ* make solid.
(2) Metn, Metna 5, ridge of back or of hill.

مثن Meӫêna, bladder.

مطر Maʀar 4, rain.
Mâʀur, rainy (day).
Omʀör, *vn* rain.
iv. Amʀur, *vɑ* cause to rain.
Maʀara, skin for (rain) water.
Momʀur, rainy (sky, cloud).
x. Istemʀur, *vɑ* entreat for rain.
Mostemʀur, needing rain.

ماش Mâx, pulse, legumes.

مشى Imxi, *vn* march, walk, advance. *ger.* Maxie.
Imxi maxwa', play the part of ʙ.

MXY

Maxie, procedure at law.
Maxwa, procedure?
Mixya, gait. Mâxi, s. foot-soldier x. (= Râjil).
Mâxiya, quadruped; pl. 12.
Mawâxi, cattle.
Mamxa', place of walking, walk, raised footpath, gallery.
ii. Maxxi, or iv. Amxi, va cause to go forward; propel; promote, advance.
iii. Mâxi, va keep pace with r.
v. Tcmaxxâ, on promenade.

مشق Omxoq, va draw out (wool, cotton, silk) into threads; wind off b.
Maxq, pattern in writing c.
Mixqa, sample of cloth x.
ii. Maxxiq, va card (wool b.).

مشور Maxwâr, s. course, voyage, price of travelling, fare b. adv. (in High Syria b.) much, greatly.
ii. Temaxwar, on walk for exercise, Kayat.

مشط Moxt 4, 5, a comb.
Maxxûta, tirewoman.
Mixâta, occupation of dᵒ
ii. Maxxut, va comb.
viii. Imtexut, on vp comb oneself, be combed.

مز Mozz, va suck, sup (any thing sweet). Mezzo, a sip.
Mozz, acidulated taste x.
Mezêzc, dᵒ b.
Mezouz, acidulated.
v. Temezzez, va sup, sip (wine).

MZJ

موز Mouze, morocco boot. [Mauzej x.]
(2) Mouze, nu. banana.
Mawwâz, seller of bananas.

ميز ii. Mayyiz, va distinguish, discern. ger. Temyiez.
Momayyiz, discerning.
iii. Mâyiz, va contradistinguish, contrast.
v. Temayyez, vp of ii. or on distinguish oneself, fig.
vi. Temâyez, or be mutually in contrast.
vii. Inmêz, vp of ii. (x.).
viii. Imtêz, vp be distinguished, lit, or fig.
Imtiyêz, distinction; excellence.
Momtêz, a distinguished (man).

مزي Mezicy, distinguished, superior x. [cellence.
Mezieya 14, high quality, exii. Mezzi, va praise highly x.

مزح Imzeñ, on sport. ger. Mezñ.
iii. Mêziñ, va sport with, barter.
vi. Tcmêzeñ, or banter one another.
Mozêñ, Mozêña, a bantering x.

مزج Omzoj, va mingle.
Mizêj 8, mixture, temperament, constitution (of body).
viii. Imtezij, vp be mingled.
Imtizêj, commixture, admixture, intercourse.
Momtezij, sociable.

MZK

مزخ ii. Mezzik, *vs* chafe by rubbing n. *Frictionner*.

مزر Mézour, kingfisher.

N.

ن En, that (*ut*). Enna, that (*quod*).
In, if. Inna, surely. Innama, surely, only.
Na, us. Ain? where?
Nâna, grandmother c.

أن Enn, he groaned. Yawinn, he groans. *ger.* Enien, moaning.
'Enan, questdove, moaner x.

أني v. Te'enna', *vn* linger, loiter.
x. Istêni, *vulg.* Iatenni, *vs* await (a person's leisure).
(2) Eniya, vessel, vase; *pl.* 12, Ewâni.

أون Ên, time, moment; chiefly in the phrase, El'ên, this moment, now. Ên bi êni°, season by season. Êniey, El'êniey, now present (time).
Ewân, *pl.* 6, Êwina, season.
Êwina, *adv.* sometimes.
Ewânaisi°, at that time.
(2) Iewân, *pl.* Ewâwien *or pl.* 2; arched recess in court of house.

NSL

ونا Wanâ', conduit.

وني Wâni, Waniey, languid.
Winâ, Wana', languor.
vi. Tewânâ fie, *vn* dawdle over.

نوى Nau, *s.* monsoon, gale r.
(2) ii. Nawwi, *vn* mew as a cat. *See* Mou'.
(3) Niwâ', Niwâya, kernel.
(4) Inwi, *vs* intend. *ger.* Nawa'.
Nieya, intention.
Nâwi, *partic.* intending.
Nâwi yamrör, it is *going* to rain r.

نسنس Nasnas, Nasnâs, mint (herb).

ينع Yânis, *adj.* ripe.
Yonous, ripeness.

نوع Naus 4, sort, species.
ii. Nawwus, *vs* diversify in species. [species.
v. Tenawwas, *vn* be various in Nausa°, after a fashion, somehow.

نسى Insu, *vs* forebode (death).
Mausa' 11, news of death.

نعب Insab, *vn* crow.
Nassâb, croaker, crow x.

نعج Nasja 2, 5, ewe.

نعل Nasl 5, horseshoe, sole of shoe, sandal. Nasla, *nu.*

NSL

ii. Nassul, iv. Ansul, *va* shoe (beast or man).
v. Tenassal, *vp vn* be shod.

نَسَم Nasm, Nusma, pleasure.
Nasam, *interj.* yes. [goods.
Nasma, *s.* wellbeing, substance,
Nâsum, soft, velvety, fine (as powder).
Nasuim 6, Nasuima, enjoyment, luxury, opulence. [fine.
ii. Nassum, *va* comminute, make
iv. Ansum, *va* bestow favours on.
Monsum, benefactor, bounteous.
Ansam bi! bravo for!
v. Tenassam, *vn* enjoy delicacies.
(2) Nasâma, *nu.* 11, ostrich.

نعق Insaq, *vn* caw; peal.

نعر Insar, ii. Nassur, *vn* bellow. *ger.* Nasuir.
(2) Nasöura 12, hydraulic wheel B.

نعس Insas, *vn* be drowsy. *ger.* Nosâs.
Nâsus, Nassên, drowsy.
Sain nâsuse, languishing eye B.

نعت Nast 3, epithet, adjective.
Insat, *va* mark with epithets.

نعش Nasx, bier to carry the dead.
(2) iv. Ansux, *va* inspirit, revive; recover (a horse) after tripping c.
viii. Intesux, *vn* revive.

ونسب ii. Wannib, *va* reprimand.

NBS

نيب Nâb, *pl.* Anyâb, fang.

نوب Noub, *va* devolve upon (men) in turn; as *a duty* or *power*.
Noub san, *va* be agent for.
Nauba, *pl.* Nowab, turn, time.
Nâyib, *pl.* 7, Nowwâb, a substitute, a viceroy. [Hence *Engl.* Nabob.]
Nâyiba 12, vicissitude.
viii. Intêb, *va* resort to at times, frequent. [B.
(2) Nauba, musical time? music
Naubatiey, musician B.
Naubatieya, company of musicians.
(3) Nouba, *Nubia, Nubians.*
Noubiey, *Nubian.*

نبي Nebie 8, prophet.
Nebieya, prophetess.
Nibâ, Nibâwa, prophecy.
Nobouwa, mission of prophet.
Monebbâ, gifted with prophecy.
v. Tenebbâ, *vn* act the prophet.
Nebawiey, prophetical.
Nebawieyaⁿ, prophetically.
(2) iv. Anbi, *va* warn, inform.
Inbâ, information, news.
x. Istenbi, *va* inquire of.

نبع Inbac, *vn* gush up. *ger.* Nabs, Nobous.
Yanbons 11, spring, source.
Manbas 11, d^o
iv. Anbis, *va* cause to gush up, spout up, throw up.
v. Tenabbas, *vn* trickle K.

NBD

نَبّ Nabboud, s. club f. See Nabbout.

نَبِذ Nebiaa 8, date wine, toddy; vulg. any wine.
Nabbêa, wine merchant.
(2) Onboa bi, va throw away; cast out (an infant) f.a. vp. Nobia bi s.
Nabae, Nobae 10, a scrap, a short paragraph o.n.

نَبَض Inbuḍ, vn pulsate as artery. ger. Nabḍ, Nabaḍân, pulsation.
Nabḍa, nu. throb of pulse.
Nabaḍ, the pulse.

نَبِه Nebieh, wide awake, adroit.
Montebih, dº
Nebâhe, adroitness.
ii. Nebbih, va warn, arouse.
v. Tenebbah, vn wake up.
viii. Intebih, vn be aware, be attentive.

نَبَح Inbaḥ, vn bark as a dog, echo. ger. Nibâḥ.
Nabbûḥ, great barker.

نَبِل Nabiel, excellent, skilful c.
(2) Tenbâl, dastardly c.
(3) Nabla, nu. arrow.
Nabbâl, arrow-maker.
Nibâla, art of arrow-making.

نَبَر Nibar 4, Anbâr 2, 11, garner, granary. Also, Anbâr 11, larder, storeroom of ship? also, deck or story, as when we say, A ship of three decks B.

NB

Minbar 11, platform, pulpit, reading desk.
(2) Manbâr, meat sausage B.
(3) Nabr, Nabir, sharp and sudden x.; abrupt, unpleasantly frank, emphatic, expressive B.
Nabbâr, expressive (phrase), well-pointed, pungent.
Nabra, emphasis.
ii. Nabbir, va emphasize?

نَبَت Onbot, vn sprout, grow. ger. Nabt.
Nabât 2, a plant.
Soccer nabât, stick sugar, i.s. barley-sugar.
Nabâtiey, botanist. [tables c.
Nabâtieya, vegetation, vegeNabbout 11, staff, club B. (But Nabboud f. Nabbout x.)
Nabicte 11, bough x.
ii. Nabbit or iv. Anbit, va cause to grow, cultivate.
Manbat, place of growth. Thus Monbat el aenab, root of the tail f.

نَبَط Inbuṭ, vn gush up. ger. Nabṭ, Noböut.
ii. Nabbuṭ, va cause to gush up; i.s. 'get (water) by digging.
x. Istenbuṭ, va dig for (water), find (water), discover.
Istinbâṭ, discovery, a discovery.
(2) Nabaṭuiy, Nabathean.

نَبَش Onbox, va rake up; lit. and fig. dig up (treasure or dead bodies). ger. Nabx.

NBX   NÅL

ii. Nabbix, d^o
Onboux 11, stump torn up.
(2) Ôn-bâxi, serjeant (*Turk.*).

نذ Nad, aloes.

نذ Naania, *va* teaze c.

ندى Nodâ, dew; *pl.* Andiya.
Nadâwa, moistness, moisture.
Nadiey, moist, *active*.
Nadyân, moist, *passive*.
ii. Naddi, *va* moisten.
(2) iii. Nâdi, *va* call, summon.
(*vulg.* Indah, call.)
Nidâ, *ger.* a cry, the voice; the vocative in *gram.*
iii. Nâdi bil flarb, declare or proclaim war. *ger.* Monadâya.
vi. Tenâdâ, *tr* call mutually.
viii. Intedi, *vp* bo convoked.

ندب Ondob *va* speak funeral oration over. *ger.* Nadb.
Nadba, funeral oration.
Naddâba, hired female mourner.
(2) Nadib, Mindaba', *adj.* enterprizing, active B. X.

نضب Inñub, *vn* flow back, run off as water. *ger.* Noñöub.

نضد Inñud, *va* or ii. Nañud, lay (mats) one over the other, lay in successive beds, stratify B.   [pets X.
Nañad 5, heap of mats or car-
Monañad, laid in strata.
Nañuida(mattress X.), a stratum.

نذف Ondof, *va* or ii. Naddif B. clean (cotton) with a bow. *ger.* Nadf, Tendief.
Mindaf, the bow.
Naddâf, he who uses the bow.
Nadâfa, art of using the bow.
Nadief, *adj.* (cotton) thus cleaned and separated.

نظف Nañuif (*vulg.* so sounded; spelt with ج), *adj.* clean.
See Naguif.

ندى Indah, *va* call; *sic vulg.* for the classical Nâdi iii.
(Indah el welad, call the boy F.)

ندح Indafl, *va* expand X.
Nodfla, expanse.
Mandafl, Mandoufla, d^o.

نضح Inñufl, *vn* ooze F. X. *va* splash?

نضج Inñaj, *vn* be ripe.
Nâñuj, *adj.* ripe.
iv. Anñuj, *va* ripen, mature, elaborate.

نضح Inñak, *va* sprinkle X.
viii. Intañuk, *vn* spirt, splash.
Nañka, a splashing?

ندل Naudil, *vn* be pendulous.
See Dalou, Dandil.

نفل iii. Nâñul *can, vn* be advocate for, defend in law.

NDM

نَدِم Indam ṣala', vn repent of.
ger. Nadûma, repentance.
iv. Andim, va cause to repent.
v. Tenaddam, vn same as i.
(2) Nadiem 6, messmate.
iii. Nâdim, va take as messmate.
v. Tenâdam, vn prattle.

نَدِر Nâdir, adj. rare.
Nâdira, s. 12, a rarity, oddity.
(2) Andar 11, threshing-floor, heap of unthreshed grain.
(3) Monaddar, freckled в.

نَضِر Onḍor, vn be fresh coloured and bright. ger. Noḍöur, brilliancy of verdure.
Naḍuir, Naḍur, fresh coloured, bright coloured.
Naḍra, flourishing aspect.
ii. Naḍḍur, or iv. Anḍur, va make fresh and brilliant of colour.

نَذِر Onḍor, va vow, devote.
ger. Naạr, a vow. Naạier, a consecrated person, Nazarite.
(2) Inạer bi, vn be aware of (danger) beforehand.
iv. Anḍir, va warn (of danger).
Monạir, a warner, a prophet.
Noạra', beware! beware!

نَفّ Nafnif, vn drizzle. ger. Nifnâf.

أَنف 'Enf 4, nose, promontory.
iii. Ênif Yênif, vn disdain.
'Enafa, s. disdain.

NFẒ

'Enouf, disdainful.
(2) 'Enifa", Ênifa", adv. a little while ago, or above.

نَوف Nauf, ger. abutting, projecting. [than.
Anwaf min, in excess of, more
ii. Nawwif, also Nayyif, va exceed, surpass (a number).
Niyâfa, prominence; fig. Eminence (of Cardinal).
iv. Anief ṣala', vn project over. fig. exceed.

نَفي Infi, va banish, repel; deny, reject.
Nofâwa, Nofûya, s. réfuse.
Tenfiya, banishment.
iii. Nâfi, va counteract f.

نَفع Infaṣ, va profit, bring advantage. ger. Nafṣ, advantage.
Nafous, Naffâs, useful (person).
Nafieṣa, utility.
Manfaṣa 11, gain, fruit.
ii. Naffiṣ, va intens. of i.
viii. Intefiṣ, vn get profit; bi, avail oneself of.

نَفد Infid, Infad, vn be spent and gone. ger. Nefâd.
ii. Naffid or iv. Anfid, va use up, exhaust.

نَفذ Infẓ min, vn escape from, ooze from.
Infẓ fie, vn sink deep into; pervade. ger. Nofouẓ, influence.
Nâfẓ, adj. partic. penetrating, pervading.

NFḎ

Náfiḏe 12, pore, passage opening to daylight.
iv. Anfiḏ, va achieve, execute (an order).
Nafieḏ, executed, accomplished (order) x.
Nafouḏ, Naffâḏ, efficient to accomplish x.
Manfiḏ 11, passage, tunnel.

نفض Onfoḏ, va shake, beat (coat or tree). ger. Nafḏ.
Nafaḏ, Nofḏa, shock (as of fever).
Nofaḏa, fruit which falls from a tree when shaken, windfalls.
ii. Naffuḏ, va intens. of i.
(2) Also, ii. Naffuḏ (B.), and iv. Anfuḏ (K.), va exhaust (provisions), perhaps for Nafíd, Anfíd.
(3) Naffaḏa, pipetray (into which one shakes the ashes out of the pipe ?).

نفخ Infah, vn blow (fragrantly).
Naffha, (fragrant) puff of air.

نفخ Onfoh, va puff up.
Infak, vn puff, blow. ger. Nafk, inflation, pride.
Nofka, swelling of belly.
Minfak, bellows.
viii. Intefik, vp be swollen, be puffed out.

نفل Nafl, Náfila 12, a free gift, gratuity, work of supererogation.

NFS

نفق Infaq, vn sell well B. be spent.
Nafâq, consumption of goods.
Nafaqa 2, pocket money.
Minfâq, adj. lavish.
iv. Anfiq, va expend.
Infâq, expenditure.
x. Istenfiq, as iv. x.
(2) iii. Nâfiq, vn act the hypocrite. ger. Nifâq, hypocrisy.
Monâfiq, hypocrite, irreligious.

نفر Infar, vn spirt, start up, leap. Infar min, be shy of. ger. Nofour, shyness.
Nâfir (Nafour x.), shy.
ii. Naffir min, va cause to shun, estrange from.
iii. Nâfir, va be discrepant from, be unsociable to.
v. Tenaffir, vn be habitually shy.
vi. Tenâfar, er be mutually shy or averse.
(2) Nafar 4, a separate (person), an individual, a person.

نفس Nefs 3, or pl. Anfos, self.
Nefes, breath.
Nefsêni, selfish.
Nefsênieya, selfishness.
Nofiset, fem. pass. was delivered of a child x.
Nefesê, delivery in childbirth x.
Nifês, dº· x.
ii. Neffis, va vent c. (?) soothe, console x.
v. Teneffes, vn breathe.
x. Istenfis, draw in breath, inspire ?

NFS

(2) iii. Nêfis cala', *va* aspire to. Monéfase, aspiration.
vi. Tenêfes fie, *va* delight oneself in, find (it) choice.
Nefies, *adj.* choice, valuable; *pl.* Nefâyis, things choice, dainties.
Nefêse, choiceness.

نفط Nefṭ, naphtha.
(2) Nifṭa, a pustule.

نفش Onfoθ, *va* breathe hard (on one's fingers), puff.
Nefθ, Nafθe, hard breath, asthma.

نفش Onfox, *va* fray (a tissue), dishevel (hair).
vii. Innafix, *vp* be dishevelled.

نغى Naɣya, vague noise, rumour x.
iii. Nâɣi, *va* warble.

نغل Inɣal, *va* itch.

نغم Naɣma, tune, melody.
ii. Naɣɣim, *va* tune (musical strings).

نغمش Naɣmix, *va* tickle. *ger.* Naɣmaxa, tickling, sense of tickling.

نغص v. Tenaɣɣuy, *va* toss oneself about, be much troubled; — li, take offence at ɣ.

نفش Inɣax, *va* nod the head, make sign (of sympathy),

NḤW

hint (to a horse with the spur B.).
Naɣaxa, *ger.* a bowing; tender attentions.
iii. Nâɣix, *va* coax.
v. Tenaɣɣax, *va* vacillate.

نوه Nouhe, a meal c.
(2) ii. Nawwih bi, extol, recommend ɣ.

نوح Nouḥ, *va* bemoan. *ger.*
Nauḥ. *va* moan. *ger.* Niyâḥa.
Nauḥa, *nu.* a lamentation.
Nawwâḥ, moaning pigeon x.
Nawwâḥa, hired female mourner
Nâyiḥ, *pl.* 7, Nowwâḥ, mourner.
v. Tenawwaḥ, *vp* be wailed over in death?
Motenawwiḥ, *less regular* Motenayyiḥ, deceased.

نهى Nibêya, end, terminus.
iv. Anhi, *va* end, terminate.
viii. Intehi, *vp* be ended.
Intibê, *ger.* the being ended.
Montehê, end, termination.

نحو Naḥōu, *prep.* on the side of, towards. *adv.* about (in number or quantity). *s.* relation; grammar, syntax.
Naḥwiey, grammatical, grammarian.
Nâḥuya 12, side, district.
ii. Naḥḥu, *va* set aside, remove to the side; bend aside.
iv. Anḥu, *va* flank (an enemy).

NHW

v. Tenaḥḥâ, *vn* remain apart, turn aside; — ṡan, avoid F.
viii. Intaḥu ila', ṡala', *vn* direct oneself towards, upon.

نهب Inheb(*mil. t.*), *va* plunder, sack. *ger.* Nehb.
Nehba, booty.
viii. Intehib, *va* as i.
Intihêb, rapine.

نحب Inḥub, *vn* shriek, wail.

نهد Nebd 3, breast, bosom.
Monehheda, full-breasted (girl).
v. Tenehhed, *vn* heave the bosom.

نهض Inhaḍ, *vn* stand up.
iv. Anhuḍ, *va* arouse, cause to stand up; expel from one's abode. *Gr.* αναστατον ποιειν.

نحف Inḥaf, *vn* be lean.
Naḥuif, meagre, frail.
Naḥâfa, leanness.
ii. Naḥḥuf, or iv. Anḥuf, *va* emaciate.

نهج Inhej, *vn* pant, gasp. *ger.* Nehej.
(2) Nehj, highway; *fig.* way.
Minhej, d° route.
viii. Intehij, *vn* travel by the highway; pursue a regular course.

نهل Manhel, drinking pond.
iv. Anhil, *va* water (a horse).

NHR

نحل Naḥla, *nu.* bee.
(2) Naḥuil, slim, slender.
Noḥöul, slightness, frailness.
iv. Anḥul, *va* attenuate.
viii. Inteḥul, *va* be attenuated. [*also*, make false claim to authorship E. claim F.]

نهم Inhem, *vn* ravin, be ravenous. *ger.* Nehem.
Nehêma, craving hunger.
Nehiem, Nehim, ravenous.
Menhoum, d°.

نهم (*also* نحم) Inḥum (Inhim), roar (as lion), trumpet (as elephant). *ger.* Naḥma (Nehma) *nu.*

نهق Inhaq, *vn* bray as ass. *ger.* Nehieq.
ii. Nehhiq, *vn* same as i.

نهر Neher 4, or *pl.* Anhor, river.
Manher, bed of river.
(2) Nehêr 2, daylight, a day, opposed to night. [on.
(3) Inher ṡala', *vn* pass censure

نحر Inḥar, *va* stab, spur; cut throat (of ox, etc.). *ger.* Naḥr, immolation.
Naḥuir, butchered.
Nâḥura 12, jugular vein.
Monḥöur, *jugulum*? [bles.
Manḥar, slaughter place, shamviii. Inteḥur, *vn* cut one's own throat.
(2) Nuḥrier, ingenious B.

NHS

نحس Naḥâs, s. copper, brass.
Naḥâsiey, adj. of copper.
Naḥḥâs, coppersmith.
Noḥâse, copper utensil.
(2) Naḥs, evil star.
Naḥus, Naḥuis, disastrous.
Menḥöus, unlucky (person).

نحت Inḥut, va chip off, chop off, hew by chipping.
Noḥâte, stone chippings.
Naḥḥât, hewer of stone.
Minḥat, stone chisel.

نهش Inhex, va rend with claws.

نجو Najwa' 11, a secret.
Najiey 8, confidant of a secret.
iii. Nâji, va address in private.
vi. Tenâjâ, vn commune together, be closeted together.

نجي Inji, vn (also Onjou, antiq.) escape. ger. Najâ.
Najâya, deliverance, salvation.
ii. Najji or iv. Anji, va deliver, rescue.

نجع Injaᶜ, vn scud before the wind.

نجب Najieb, noble of race.
Najâba, nobility, good birth.
viii. Intejib, va select, elect; but vulg. Intakib.

نجد Najid, Nâjid, adj. enterprizing.
Najâda, enterprise, spirit.

NJR

Najda, an aid, reinforcement.
Najd 3, 5, upholstery.
Najjâd, upholsterer, undertaker.
x. Istenjid, va request for aid.

نجف Najfa, hanging lamp, chandelier.

نجح Injaḥ, vn be prosperous, succeed. ger. Najâḥ.
Nâjiḥ, prosperous.
iv. Anjiḥ, va execute successfully, achieve.
v. Tenajjaḥ, vn be successful.

نجل Najl, progeny, son (high word). Compare Neal.
vi. Tenâjal, va have progeny.
(2) Anjal, large-eyed r.
(3) Minjal 11, a sickle.
(4) Enjiel, evangile, the gospel.

نجم Onjom, vn rise as a star; appear, arise, accrue.
Najm 3, a star.
ii. Najjim, va yield, afford.
Monajjim, Najjâm, astrologer, astronomer.
Manjam, origin x.

نجن Injâna, cruise, pitcher. Compare vulg. Finjân, very small coffee cup.

نجر Najjâr, a carpenter.
Nijâra, carpentry.
Onjor, act the carpenter.
ii. Najjir, hew, cut, etc.
(2) Tenjara (Tanjara) 11, stewpot.

NJS

نَجِس Najis, foul, dirty.
Najáse, filthiness, impurity.
ii. Najjis, *va* defile.
Anjes, dirtier; worse AL.

نَجَس Najàsa, *nu.* a pear.

نَجَش Onjox, *va* chase, pursue x. *vn* hasten.
Najáxa, quickness o.

نَجَز Injez, *vn* be ready, complete. *ger.* Najz, Najze, Najêz, accomplishment.
Nâjiz, ready-made, complete.
Najiez, d°
ii. Najjiz, iv. Anjiz, *va* accomplish, effect.

نَكّ Nakk, long strip of matting.
(2) Nokk, *vn* kneel as a camel B.
Tenaknak, d°.

نَخْو Nakwa, high spirit, pride.
ii. Nakki, *va* inspirit, stir up pride and spirit.

نُخَع Nokâs, spinal marrow.
Mankas, highest vertebra of spine.

نَخَب Nokba 10, a selection, select number.
viii. Intákib, *va* select, elect.

نَخَل Onkol, *va* sift.
Nokâla, bran.   [aleet.
Tenkiel, fine rain, continuous
vii. Innakil, *vn* drizzle.
Minkal, a fine sieve.

NM

نَخِر Inkir, *vn* snort.   [kir.
Mankar 11, nostril. See Kar-
Nikwâr 13, snorting, high-
mettled.
(2) Onkor, *va* drill as worm.
Nâkir, carious o.; porous to wind x.

نَخَس Onkos, *va* goad, prick; also Onkoz, Onqos?
Naksis, *va* pick in pieces by criticism.

نَخَز Onkoz, *va* sting as bee, prick, twinge. So Oncoz.
Nakza, a prick, a twinge.

نِيل Niel, indigo.
(2) Nâl, *va* attain (*nilt*). *ger.* Nail, advantage.
iv. Aniel, *va* support F. *rather* cause to attain.

نَوَل Nawâl, Manâl, gift x.
iii. Nâwil, *va* hand over, present.
vi. Tenâwal, *va* accept with hand.   [river.
(2) Naul, deep water, bed of
Niwâl, cordage made of reeds.
(3) Naul, a loom.
Minwal, a loom, machinery; *fig.* mechanism, method, routine.
(4) Nauloun, ναῦλον, ship fare, payment for voyage.

نَمّ Nimm sala', tattle against.
Namiema, secret slander.
Nammâm, tattler, slanderer, intriguer.

NM

(2) Nammim, *va* streak, embellish κ. tattoo?
(3) Namâm, spearmint.

أنم Enâm, énâm, mankind.

نوم Naum, sleep.
Nowâm, a dozing.
Menâm, a dream.
Nâm, *vn* (nomt) sleep.
ii. Nawwim, lull, deaden (pain).

نمو Onmou, *vn* grow. Iumi, d°
Nomou, growth. Namâ, d°
Namâya, Namieya, vegetation κ.
Manma', place of (a tree's) growth κ.

نمذج Namausej, pattern, example s.

نمل Namla, *nu*. an ant.

نمق ii. Nammiq, *va* embellish; compose (a book) with rhetorical beauty.

نمر Nimr, Namir 3, leopard, tiger. [gate.
ii. Nammir, *va* bespeckle, varie-

نمس Nims, ichneumon.
(2) Nâmous, reputation, law (theolog. νόμος).
(3) Nâmouse 12, gnat.
iii. Nâmis, *va* blab to...
Nammâs, tattler.

نمط Namat 5, (drugget printed in a pattern κ.) *fig.* pattern.

NCB

نمش Onmox, *va* pick and choose, clean? choose.
(2) Namax, red spots B.
Monammax, freckled?

نق Niqq, Niquiq, *vn* croak, chick, as frog, hen.
Naqnâq, frog κ.
(2) Naqq, *adj.* froward B. *Reveche.*

ناق Nâqa, she-camel.

نكي Necêya, *ger.* teazing B.
ii. Necci, or iv. Anci, *va* teaze, exasperate, provoke to combat.

نقي Naqi, clean, pure.
Noqâwa, what is choice, the best part, the cream, flower.
Naqâya, *s.* a choice.
ii. Naqqi, *va* cleanse, purify; *also*, select, choose B.
Tenqiya, a picking out of the best, *triage* B.
v. Tenaqqâ, *vp* of ii.?
viii. Intaqi, *va* choose κ.

نقع Inqas, *va* steep, soak, dilute. *ger.* Naqs.
Noqâsa, water in which something has been steeped κ.
ii. Naqqis, *va intens.* of i.
Naqâsa 11, a swamp.
Manqasa, Mostenqis mâi, pool of water.
(2) Nauqasa, nape of neck.

نكب Oncob, *va* pervert, overthrow. *ger.* Necb, Necba *nu*.

NCB

Necieba 11, reverse, calamity.
(2) Mancib 11, junction of arm and shoulder в. blade-bone or shoulder of horse; *fig.* wing of army.

نَقَب Onqob, *va* bore, tap; break through wall; sap, breach (*mil. t.*). *ger.* Naqb, burglary.
Noqba, opening to daylight.
Naqqâb, sapper.
Manqab, thoroughfare.
(2) Niqâb, a veil.
(3) Naqieb, a chief, a prefect.

نَكَد Necid, atrabilious в. stingy, scanty (supply), pinched, ill-supplied (life).
ii. Neccid εala', *vn* deal severely with.
iii. Nêcid, *va* stint, maltreat.

نَقَد Naqd 3, coin.

نَقَض Onqoḍ, *va* unravel, annul, countermand.
iii. Nâquḍ, *va* contradict.

نَقَذ Onqoạ min, *va* deliver from в.
iv. Anqiạ, d°· o.

نَكَف Nêcif, coy x.
Incef εan, *vn* be shy of, disinclined to.
x. Istencif, *vn* be disdainful; min, decline, reject (a thing).
Monêcif, Mostencif, coy, hard to please, contrarious в.
Monêcefa, perversity of temper в.

NCB

نَقَف Noqfa 10, a fillip of the finger в.

نَكَح Nicêḥ, marriage, conjugal union.

نَقَه (نَكَه) Inqah min, *vn* get well from. *ger.* Noqouh (Nocouh). [health.
iv. Anqih (Ancîh), *va* restore to
viii. Intaqih min, *vp* be restored from (an illness).

نَقَح ii. Naqqiḥ, *va* prune (style), polish.

نَكَل Nicl 4, bond, fetter, manacle.

نَقَل Onqol, *va* transfer, transport, translate. *ger.* Naql.
Naqlaⁿ, by transference, at second hand. [dessert.
Noql, second course, a remove,
Naqâla, vehicle, cart.
Naqiel, interloper? (stranger x.).
v. Tenaqqal, *vn* remove oneself, travel.
vi. Tenâqal, *vn* pass, circulate (as reports).
viii. Intaqil, d°· remove, migrate, depart (in death).

نَقَم Naqim, avenger.
Naqma, Intiqâm, vengeance.
viii. Intaqim, *va* revenge.
Montaqim, vindictive.

نَكَر Oncor, Incer, *va* deny.
ii. Neccir, *va* alter, transform, disguise.

NCR

iv. Ancir, *vs* object to.
x. Istencir, d°.
Moncer, Mostencer, objectionable; mathematically deniable.

نَقَر Onqor, *vs* peck, bill. *ger.* Naqr; *fig.* sarcasm.
Noqra 10, cavity, small hole.
Noqrat el musda, pit of stomach.
iii. Nâqir, *vs* carp at.
Minqâr 11, bird's bill, chisel.
(2) Naqâra, kettledrum *c.*
Nâqour, clarion x.

نَكَس Nêcis, humiliated *c.*
Nocse, a relapse.
Mencous, overthrown.
ii. Neccis, *vs* (upset, overturn x.); *fig.* repulse, discountenance b.
viii. Intecis, *vp* be overthrown.

نَقَس Onqos, *vs* revile, banter x.
Niqâse, sarcasm, irony x.
ii. Naqqis, *vs* nickname x.
(*But see* Naksis, under Onkos.)

نَقَص Onqos, *vs* be deficient. *ger.* Naqs, Noqsân, deficiency.
Nâqus, Naqies, deficient.
Noqâsa, a deficit.
Naqiesa, defect, disadvantage.
Manqous, defective.
ii. Naqqus, or iv. Anqus, *vs* lessen (in quantity).

نَكَت Nocte 5, a speck, spot, point. Noctisy, satirical.
Neccêt, satirist.
ii. Neccit, *vs* satirise.

NWR

نَكَث Oncos, *vs* untie, undo. *fig.* break (a covenant).

نَقَط Noqra 10, a drop, a spot, a point (in writing).
ii. Naqqut, *vns* drip, distil.
(2) Naqt 4, a pun b.

نَكَش Oncox, *vs* pick and clean; explore; clear out a well.
Mincêx, spud or hoe x.

نَقَش Onqox, *vs* engrave, chase, emblazon, embroider.
Naqqâx, emblazoner, etc.
Niqâxa, embroidery, painting, sculpture.
Minqâx 11, sculptor's chisel.
ii. Naqqix, *vs* same as i.
(2) iii. Nâqix, *vn* cavil, wrangle s. *See* Naksis.
(3) Naqwix, *vs* variegate, mottle, dapple.

نَكَز Oncoz, *vs* sting as bee = Onkos.

نُور Nâr 9, fire.
Nour, light, brilliancy.
Nawir, Naiyir, luminous, bright.
Nâriey, *lit.* or *fig.* fiery.
Anwar, brighter.
Naura, *ns.* blossom.
ii. Nawwir, iv. Anier, *vs* enlighten, illumine; *lit.* or *fig.* Monier, Monawwir, luminous, refulgent. [minaret).
Menâra, lighthouse (*hence Engl.* x. Istenier, *vn* be refulgent.
Istinâra, refulgence.

NS

نِس Nisnês, dwarf, satyr, monkey; perhaps from root أَنس.

نَس Noᵴᵴ, ᵴa dictate (a letter), edit (a book).
Noᵴᵴ ɛala', ᵴn indicate, denote, make signal. ger. Naᵴᵴ, style, text (?) of book.
Manyöuᵴ ɛalaihi, made signal, extolled.

أَنس 'Ens, familiarity x.
'Ins, mankind.
'Ons, social life.
'Enies, 'Enous, familiar.
Insên, human being. Nês, man.
Insêniey, human.
Insênieyᵴ, humanity.
Nisê, Niswa, Niswân, women.
Nêsout, human nature.
Mênous, tame.
ii. 'Ennis, ᵴa tame.
iii. Enis, ᵴa be familiar with.
Mowênis, intimate.
Mowênese, intimacy.
v. Te'ennes, ᵴn become tame.
viii. Ittonis, ᵴn enter social life.
x. ger. Istienês, social life.

نَس Inse', ᵴa forget. ger. Nesou, Neswa, ᵴu. forgetfulness.
Nesiey, Nessê, Nosyân, forgetful ʀ. x. Nessêi ʙ. dᵃ.
Bil nesiya, gratis.
iii. Nêsi, ᵴa forget x.
iv. Ensi, ᵴa cause to forget.
Nisyân, forgetfulness ʙ. x.
viii. Intesi, ᵴp be forgotten?
Intisê, oblivion, disuse.

NSD

Montesi, obsolete?
(2) Insi, ᵴn correspond as two columns of a ledger.
Insiey, right and left, in parallel columns.

نَصي Nâᵴuya 12, forelock, as of a horse, long hair.
viii. Intaᵴu, ᵴn be long in front, as hair x. be long as a mountain ridge x.
Intiᵴâ, long ridge of mountain.
(2) Naᵴuiy, kind of thistly plant.

نَسب Onsob, ᵴa ascribe, attribute, recount pedigree x.
Neseb, lineage.
Neseba, proportion.
Nisba, relationship.
Nesieb, of same stock, related.
Anseb, more nearly related.
iii. Nêsib, ᵴa befit.
Monêsib, suitable.
Monêseba, analogy. [ship to.
v. Tenesseb ila', claim relation-
vi. Tenêseb, ᵴr mutually correspond.
Motenêsib, adequate.
viii. Intesib, ᵴn belong.
Intisêb, pertinence, relation.

نَصب Onᵴob, ᵴa set up, erect. ger. Naᵴb.
Naᵴuib, lot, lottery ʙ.
Yânaᵴuib 11, lottery oɴ.
Nuᵴâb 10, handle of knife.
Manᵴab, post, office.
Minᵴab, brasier ʙ. trivet x.
ii. Naᵴᵴub, ᵴa appoint to office.
نَصد ii. Naᵴᵴud, ᵴa enchase ʙ.

NSF

نسف Onsof, winnow, fan; ventilato c. gormandize B.
Insif, vn blow in gusts, fan.
Nosêfa, chaff.
Minsef, winnowing shovel, fan. *Lat.* vannus.
Nessêf, gluttonous B.

نصف Nuṣf 4, half.
iv. Ansuf, va divide equitably.
viii. Intasuf, vn behave moderately, be half spent, as day or night.
(2) Onṣöf, va serve (any one) as a domestic F. K.

نسغ Inṣaḡ, va water and enrich the soil K.; manure B. *fig.* instruct, admonish.
Nasuiḡa, admonition.
Nasöuḡ, faithful (F. of the horse).

نسج Onsoj, va weave. *ger.* Nesj.
Nessêj, weaver.
Nisêja, weaver's art.
Nesiej, woven.
Nesieja 11, web, tissue.
Mensej, weaver's shop.

نسخ Insek, va transcribe; *also* abrogate.
Noska, copy of a book.

نسل Nesl, progeny.
ii. Nessil, va cause to breed.
iv. Ansil, va engender.
vi. Tenêsel, vn breed, multiply consecutively. [tion.
Tenôsol, *ger.* breeding, genera-

NSR

Motenêsil, generative.
(2) Insil, va unravel, fray out, make lint. Nosôla, lint.

نصل Nâṣul, dim, faint (colour).
(2) Noṣla, blade of knife.
(3) Tenaṣwel, vn be drenched?

نسم Nesiem 5, a breeze.
Nesma 4, a puff of air, a soul (in counting population).
Anêsim, souls, mankind K.

نسك Nêsic, devotee.
Tenessoc, bigotry.
Motenessic, bigoted.
Monseo 11, a ceremonial.

نسق Onsoq, va arrange. *ger.* Nesq, order, series.
ii. Nessiq, va enumerate in order, co-ordinate.
v. Tenessaq, vp of ii.
vi. Tenêsaq, vn be mutually co-ordinate.
Motenêsiq, *adj.* co-ordinate.
viii. Intesiq, vp be specially arranged.

نسر Nesr 3, eagle.
Nesriey, aquiline.
(2) Nesior, the lean of meat (B. maigre).

نصر Onṣör, va aid.
Nâṣur, auxiliary.
Naṣr, Intiṣâr, victory.
viii. Intaṣur, vn be victorious.
x. Istenṣur, va call to aid.
(2) Naṣrâni, a Nazarene, *i.e.* a Christian; *pl.* 11, Naṣâri.

NSR

ii. Naʃʃur, ʋa christen, i.e. baptize.

نصت Inʃut, ʋn listen in silence. Noste, silence ĸ.
v. Tenaʃʃat sala', ʋn overhear.

نط Noṭṭ, ʋn jump; san, fig. digress from. ger. Naṭṭ.
Naṭṭât, jumper.
v. Tenaṭṭaṭ, ʋn skip, frisk.
Naṭnuṭ, ʋn caper.

أنت Ent, Ente, m. thou; Enti, f. thou.

أنثى Onθe', pl. 5, Inâθ, female. Mowennaθ, feminine.

نوط Nouṭ bi, ʋn depend upon, turn upon, rest upon ʙ.
Manouṭ bi, dependent upon.
Mauqouf wa manouṭ bi, it wholly depends upon.

نتف Intif, ʋa pull out (hairs, wool, feathers). ii. dº *intens*.
Mintêf, tweezers.
viii. Intetif, ʋp be plucked out.

نطف Inṭuf, ʋn drip (as a candle).

نطح Inṭaḥ, ʋn butt with the horn.
iii. Nâṭuḥ, ʋa dº.
vi. Tenâṭaḥ, er butt mutually.

نتج Netouj, parturient.
Nitêj, parturition. [result.
Netieja 11, brood, próduce,

NTR

iv. Antij, ʋa prodúce, propagate, infer.
Ontij Yontej, ʋp of dº.
x. Istentij, ʋa desire to infer.

نطل Naṭöul, Naṭuil, embrocation ʙ.

نتن Netêna, stench.
ii. Nettin, ʋa infect.
iv. Antin, be fetid.
Montin, stinking.

نطق Inṭuq, speak reasonably, utter.
Norq, human speech.
Nâṭuq, having the faculty of Manṭuq, logic. [speech.
Manṭuqiey, logical.
Minṭuiq, eloquent ĸ.
Naṭuq, fluent.
x. Istenṭuq, ʋa examine (a person) in court, force him to give evidence.
Istinṭâq, cross-examination.
(2) Minṭaqa, belt, zone. *See* Moṭq.

نتش Onθoq, vomit. [c. spells it نطق three times at least; ʙ. نتش. It seems to be the classical انثع.] Also, reject?
Moneθθiq, an emetic c.

نتر Netr, drawing the bow c. ʙʜ.

نظر Onṭör, watch (a garden, etc. ĸ.).

NTR

Nâtôur 12, watchman.
Celb nâtôur, watchdog.
Nattâr, scarecrow.

نشر Onθor, va disperse, shed, circulate (money).
v. Tenaθθer, vi. Tenâθer, be dispersed.
viii. Inteθir, d°.
Neθr, prose x. (*opposed to* naẓm).

نشش Ontox, Intix, grip, pull out (thorns with pincers); pilfer.
Mintêx, pincers.
Nottêx, *pl.* pilferers x.
(2) Tentiex, a trifle (B. *bis*).

نشش Noxx, whisk away (flies) = Coxx B.
Minaxxa, flyflap.
(2) Noxx? absorb (ink) Eg. ii. Naxxix d°.
Tenxiex, absorption.
Waraq tenxiex, blotting paper. See Naxxif.
(3) Tenaxnax min, vn recover (from) disease B.

نوش iii. Nâwix, va engage hand to hand.
Monâwaxa, close combat.
viii. Intêx, va seize for rescue; rescue.

نشأ Onxou, Inxi, vn arise.
Noxou, origin, rise.
Manxâ, place of origin, native country.
iv. Anxi, compose, construct; rear (a child), raise (a flag).

NXL

Nâxiya, rise, commencement.
El naxâ, the rising generation x.
Inxâ, composition, origination; literary composition; letter writing.
Inxâyiey, epistolary.
Monxie, composer.
Monxâwa, flag, token, symptom.
viii. Intexi, be reared.
(2) Nexâ', starch.
ii. Naxxi, va starch.

نشب Noxxâba, *nu.* arrow.
ii. Naxxib, va shoot, squirt, *fig,* into. v. Tenaxxab fie, bi, vn stick fast in.
Inxab fîl bafîr, va launch c.

نشد iii. Nâxid, va adjure.
iv. Anxid, va declaim (verses).
x. Istenxid, ask to recite.
Onxouda 11, poem often recited x. [until stale.
Motenâxid, *decantatus* x. recited

نشف Inxaf, be dried, fade. *ger.* Noxouf.
ii. Naxxif, va dry up, wither.
Nâxif, dry; *fig.* curt, morose.
Noxoufieya, incivility.
Minxafa, towel.

نشڤ Inxafî, vn rot (as wood) B.
iv. Anxifî, va spoil (meat) B.
Nâxifî, Monxafî, rotten.

نشل Onxol, carry away, remove (steal B.).
Minxâl, fork for taking meat out of soup x.

NXN

نيشن Niexân, token, mark, badge; sight on gun.
Naixin cala', level (a gun) at.

نشك Onxoc, bestrew.

نشق Naxaq, s. perfume.
Inxaq, va sniff, snuff in.
v. Tenaxxaq, vn take snuff.
Nâxouq, snuff.

نشر Onxor, va expand, spread, shed. Naxr, ger. disseminate.
viii. Intexir, vp.
Nâxir, editor. [loma.
Manxour, letters patent, dip-
Intixâr, dispersion, dissemination.
(2) Minxâr, a saw.
ii. Naxxir, va saw.
Noxâra, sawdust.

نشط Naxut, Naxuit, sprightly.
Naxât, alacrity.
ii. Naxxut, va encourage.
(2) Onxouta, a running knot r.
but in B. Xouta and Xanieta.
ii. Naxxut, va noose?

نز Nizz, vn exude B.

نزع Inzes, strip, spoil, deface.
Nezs, a stripping off.
iii. Nêzis, va scold at.
vi. Tenêzes, vr wrangle together. [torn up.
viii. Intesis, vp be spoiled; be
x. Istensis, va try to tear up.

نزف Inzif, vn bleed. ger. Nezf, depletion. Anxif, va bale

N3M

out, drain off (water). See Anzifl.

نظف Nazuif (pron. Naðuif), clean.
Nazâfa, cleanliness.
ii. Nazzuf, cleanse.
Nazâyiñey, cleaned up, spruce.

نزه Nozhe, delightsomeness (of a country).
ii. Nezzih san, exempt from o.x.
v. Tenezzeh, vn disport oneself.
Nezih, delightful (country).

نزح Inzell, va clear away, remove. [Nezzih.
ii. Nazzill san, free from. See
iv. Anzifl, va drain off, pump off.
Nêzifl, Montezifl, remote.

نزل Inzil, vn dismount, go down.
ger. Nozoul.
Menzil, alighting place, lodge, lodging, dwelling.
Neziel 6, guest.
Nozoul, descent (in pedigree).
Menzila, descent, rank.
ii. Nezzil, va rank, rate.
vi. Tenêzel, vn condescend;
— san, abdicate.

نظل Nazaliey, fastidious B.

نظم Ingam, va string pearls, versify.
Nazm, versification.
ii. Nazzum, arrange, organize.
Nizâm, chain, series, order; organization.

N

Menzöum, ner in good order.
Intizâm, good order.

نزك Nêzic, delicate, slight.
Nezêce, elegance, delicacy; politeness.

نز Nezeq, *mobility*, susceptibility; ease of being set in motion or stopped.
Neziq, agile.
Nezqa, dash (in a soldier).
Inziq, *vn* move easily? be susceptible.

نظر Onzōr, *va* look, look at.
iii. Nâzur *cala*, survey.
viii. Intazur. x. Istenzur, *va* expect.
Nazar, Nazra, *nu.* a look, glance.
Nazaraⁿ ila', in regard to, by reason of.
Nâzur, inspector (as a military title), major B.
Nazzâra, eyeglass.
Nozöur, vigilant, quick sighted.
Nûzuir 6, similar.
Nazuir el simt, (point) "corresponding to the *simt*" or zenith; *i.e.* the *nadir*, as we corruptly sound it.
Manzar, aspect, view, prospect.
Manzara, place of view 11.
Monâzur, mutually alike x.

C. Q.

قاو Qa'ou, touchwood; pile of velvet.

WQY

كو Couwa, *pl.* ciwâ, dormer-window.

كوى Iowi, *va* cauterize.
Ciey, a branding.
Cieyar, scar, place cauterized.
Micwâya, instrument for branding.
Micwa', laundress's iron.

قوى Qawi, *f.* qawieya, strong.
Qouwa 2, strength, force.
Iqwa, *vn* be strong.
ii. Qawwi, *va* strengthen.
iii. Qûwi, *va* try one's strength against B.
Moqawwa', pasteboard. [B.
v. Teqâwâ mac, wrestle together.

قى Qie', v. Teqayyâ, *vn* vomit.
x. Istoqie', desire to vomit.
Qoyâ, *s.* vomiting.
Moqawwi, causing to vomit.

كى Cei, li coi, in order that.
Ce, as.

وكى Tecêya, cushion.
viii. Itteci, *vn* lean (upon).
Mottocê, couch.

وقى Waqa, Yaqi, *va* keep, protect (*asservo*).
Wiqâya, conservation.
[Teuqa, a clamp B.]
viii. Ittaqi, save oneself; *esp.* be pious. See Taqi.
v. Tewaqqa', use precaution, guard oneself.

WQY

(2) ٮ, oqieya, Ouqieya 11, *vulg.* Oqqa, ounce. *Lat.* uncia; *pl.* Owaq.

ياق Yâqa, collar of a dress.

وقع Waqas Yaqas, *vn* fall. *ger.* Woqous, a falling, occurrence.
Wâqis fis, situated in.
Manqis, a site.
Wâqisa, *pl.* Waqâyis, adventure.
Waqiesa 11, case, condition.
Waqsa 2, combat.
Manqasa 2, event. [fields.
Mawâqis, *pl.* events, battle
(2) ii. Waqqis, *va* register, add the king's signature to, add public seal.
Touqies, royal signature.
(3) ii. Waqqis, *va* fill with false expectations?
v. Tewaqqas, *va* expect.

كوع Cous, anklebone κ. See Cesb. [elbow B.
ii. Cowwis, *vn* lean on one's

قاع Qâs, *s.* low ground, opposed to hill; beach, opposed to sea; landed estate s.
(2) Qâsa, hall of audience; chief drawing-room.

كعب Cesb, *s.* anklebone, dib, dic.
(2) Tecsuib, lattice, trellis B.

كعبل Cesbil, *va* mould into a ball. *See* Cobb, Cebtil.

قعد Oqsöd, وقعد *ger.* Qosöud.
Qasda, a sitting, session.
Qâsuda 12, a base, rule, axiom, fundamental principle.
Qasuid, a colleague.
Maqsad, seat, cushion; the seat (of the body); berth.
Maqsada, sitting room; *also,* in anatomy, the anus.
iii. Qâsud, *va* sit by the side of.
iv. Aqsud, *va* seat, cause to sit.
v. Teqassad san, desist from. Teyassad bi, vouch for.
vi. Teqâsad, *vn* be in garrison, stay at home; san, neglect. Moteqâsud, sedentary.

كعك Ceso, cake.
Cesce, a ring cake, biscuit.
(2) Moceswes, frizzled (hair) c.

قعر Qasr, *s.* interior bottom (of a vessel, a well, or the sea).
(2) Maqsara, socket of a bone.

كب Cobb, *va* overturn, spill. *ger.* Cebb.
Cobba, *s.* an overthrow.
vii. Incibb, *vp* be thrown on one's face. *See* Ceroib.
(2) Cobb, *va* wind thread into a ball.
Cobba 5, ball (of thread or of meat); *pl.* Cibâb, balls or collops of broiled meat.
ii. Cobbib, Cobcib, *va* make into a ball. See Cesbil, Cebtil.
Cobbâba, Cebooub, ball of thread.
v. Tecobbab, *vn* wind oneself

CB

into a ball, as does the hedgehog or sloth.
(3) Cebâba, round spice.
(4) Cobcoba, retinue B. *also*, Cobcoub(a), crowd K.

قب Qobba 10, dome, vault, arched chamber, alcove.
(2) Qobb, *vn* stand up (as hair).
(3) Qabqâb, clogs, high pattens.

وكب Weceb Yecib, *vn* move slowly, as in solemn procession. *ger.* Wecb, ceremoniousness.
Maucib, procession of state.
iii. Wêcib, *va* escort in state.

كآب Cê'ba, sadness.
Cê'ib, sad.

كبو Cêbi, livid, dull.
Cebâwa, lividity. [dull.
iv. Ecbi, *va* tarnish, sully, make
(2) Icbi, *vn* nod the head from sleepiness B.
Cobou, prostration.
viii. Ictebi, *vn* prostrate oneself.
Ictebi ṣala', be prone to.
Ictibâ, proneness.
(3) Cibâya, carpet B.
(4) Cobbâya, rug.

مقبو Oqbou, *va* curve, hunch up, vault.
Maqbiey, curved, aquiline (nose).
[B. has مقني perhaps by misprint.]
Qabou, masonry.

QBⅡ

Qabouwa, arcade.
(2) Qabâ, *adj.* coarse o.
(3) Qabâ, *s.* large gown with sleeves, *De Braine*, Alg.

نبع Iqbas, *va* pull out (a tooth. *Also* Iqlas, *sic* B.). See Icball. [cap.
(2) Qabas, Qabasa, Qabousa,
(3) Qaubas, wagtail (small bird).

كبد Cibd 3, 4, the liver.
Cobâd, liver disease K.
(2) Cebbâd, citron K. [ship).
(3) iii. Cêbid, *va* endure (hard-
(4) Cebboud, Cebbout, jacket, cape, cowl?

قبض Iqbuḍ, *va* clutch, seize, hold fast, get (money) in hand, receive (money).
Qobḍa, handful.
Qabḍa, a handle.
Maqbaḍ 11, handle K.
ii. Qabbuḍ, *va* cause to hold, pay.
vii. Inqabuḍ, *vp* be contracted, constipated.

كبح Icball, *va* pull (a horse) sharply up. [See Icmaṇ K.]
v. Tecebball, *vn* be at a nonplus.

قبح Oqboḥ, *vn* be hideous. *ger.* Qabḥ.
Qabieḥ, hideous, foul in crime.
Qabâḥa, foulness of crime.
Qabieḥa 11, a villainy.
Maqâbiḥ, things villainous.
ii. Qabbiḥ, *va* make hideous.
iii. Qâbiḥ, *va* treat vilely.
iv. Aqbiḥ, *va* do a hideous deed.

QBῙ

x. Istaqbiḷ, *va* regard as hideous, abhor.

كبل Cêbil, short of stature.
Moctebil, dwarfed, stunted.
(2) Cêbáliey, mahogany B.

قبل Qabl, *prep.* before.
Qablaⁿ, *adv.* before, previously.
Min qibal, in face of, on the part of.
Qibla, side fronting us; *esp.* the direction to Mecca,—the South.
Qibâla, side fronting us.
Qiblieya, pocket compass.
[Qiblace 2, dial.]
Oqbol, *va* receive, accept.
Qâbil, approaching (time); capable (of).
Qâbilieya, capacity, ability.
Qâbila 12, midwife.
[Qabiel, sort. Qabiela 11, horde, species].
ii. Qabbil, *va* welcome, kiss.
Qobla, kiss of welcome.
iii. Qâbil, *va* confront, collate.
Moqâbala, collation (of MSS.).
iv. Aqbil, *va* welcome. *vn* advance, arrive.
Iqbâl, advancement, success.
vi. Teqâbal, *rr* meet face to face.
x. Istaqbil, *va* go to welcome. *vn with* li, await. *vn (absolute)* be future. Istiqbâl, the future.
Istiqbâliey, *adj.* future s.
Mostaqbil li, *partic.* waiting for.
Mostaqbil, *adj.* future.

CBS

قبن Qabbân, [large pair of scales c.] A steelyard x.
Roumâna qabbâni, a steelyard B.

كبر Ocbor, *vn* be large, grow large.
Cibr, Cibra, greatness (of crime).
Cibr, Cobr, pomp, pride.
Cebier, great, old, *for*, cebier el sömr, great of age.
Ecbar, greatest, eldest.
Cibrieya, grandeur.
iii. Cêbir, *va* seek superiority over in argument; wrangle against, for victory's sake.
Mocêbir, disputatious.
Mocêbara, disputatiousness.
iv. Ecbar, *va* exalt.
v. Tecebbar, *vn* play the grandee.
Motecebbir, arrogant, grandiose.
(2) Cobbâr, capers.
Cebarieya, pickled capers.

قبر Qabr 3, grave, tomb.
Oqbor, *va* bury.
Maqbara 11, graveyard.

قنبر Qonbara', a bomb.
(2) Qonbora 11, tuft on a lark's head; the tufted lark.
Qonboriey, tufted on the head.

قبرس Qobros, Cyprus; copper.

كبس Icbis, *va* throw oneself upon or into; invade, usurp; occupy by force.
Cebse, invasion.
Micbês, piston (of an engine).
Mecbous, stuffed (as a cushion).

CBS

Cêbous, incubus, nightmare.
Cebies, overfilled? Sâm cebies or sene cebiese, leapyear.
ii. Cebbis, *vs* press, shampoo x.
v. Tecebbes, be crammed full, as a well stopped up.

نسب Iqbis, *vs* beg fire, beg a light from another x.
viii. Iqtebis, *vs* light one's lamp from another; *fig.* borrow his learning, *quote* from another B.

كبت Cebbout, Cebboud, jacket.

قبط Qobr, Copts.
Qobruiy, Coptic.

كبتل Cebtil, *vs* form into a ball.
Cebtoula, a ball of thread. See Cesbil and Cobb.

كبش Cebx 5, a ram.
(2) Ocbox, Icbix, *vs* pinch with finger and thumb.
— min, extort from.
Cobxa, a pinch, a small mass.
iv. Ecbix, *vs* same as i. See Ocmox, Cerbix.

كد Codd, *vn* work hard, drudge.
ger. Cedd, hard work.
Bil cedd, scarcely B. *See* Ceid.

قد Qad, *with past tense*, already; *with future*, probably.
(2) Qadd, *s.* stature, shape, cut; *also* quantity. *Vulg.* Eix qadd? Qadd eix? how much?
(3) Qaddid, *vs* dry (meat, raisins) in the sun.

CWD

Qadied, Moqaddad, (meat) dried in the sun.

أكد 'Ecied, *adj.* certain, sure (news).
ii. 'Eccid, Weccid, *vs* make certain, assure, confirm.
Têcied, corroboration.
v. Te'ecced, Tewecced, *vp* be certified.

وقد Waqad Yaqid, flame up.
ger. Woqoud.
Waqda, burning heat.
Waqied, Waqoud, anything very combustible, material for kindling; or gener. fuel.
Mieqâd, material for kindling.
Mauqid, Mosteuqid, fireplace.
iv. Auqid, *vs* kindle.
v. Tewaqqad, viii. Ittaqid, x. Isteuqid, *vn* all nearly as i.

كيد كأد كود, three ancient roots, are liable to confusion.

(1) كأد Ceid, *s.* pain, pains.
Bil Ceid, with difficulty, hardly.
Compare Bil Cedd, Bil Ceud.
iv. Ecied, *vs* irritate B.
Icêda, disobedience of a naughty child B.
vii. Incêd, *vp* be irritated; *vn* be disobedient, as a naughty child B. Compare Neccid.

(2) كود Cêd, *vn* fall short but little. Hence, adverbially, Cêd, almost. Cêdou yotcmâssou, they almost touch one another.

CWD

Lâ yecêd, scarcely.
Bil Ceud (Algiers Mercury), almost. See above, Bil ceid.
(3) كيد Cied, *va* deceive. *ger.*
Ceid, deception. Also, *vn* Cied li, lay snares for.
Macieda, trickery.
iii. Cêyid, *va* circumvent.

قود Qoud, *va* lead.
Qâyid, *pl.* Qouwad, Qowad; leader, general, admiral.
Qawwâd, seducer, pander.
Qiyâda, seduction.
Maqoud, led by halter.
Miqwad 11, halter.
vii. Inqâd, *vn* be docile (easily led).
Inqiyâd, docility.
Monqâd, docile.
viii. Iqtêd, *vp* be led.

قوض Qauḍ, *s.* exchange.
Qauḍaⁿ, in exchange.
iii. Qâwuḍ, *va* exchange.
Moqâwaḍa, *s.* exchange.

قيد Qaid 3, 4, a fetter.
Bi qaid el ḥayâᵗ, in the *space of life* B. [book.
ii. Qayyid, *va* fetter; enter in a Taqyicd, annotation.
v. Taqayyad, *vn* be attached or attentive.
Taqayyod, attention; (the being *ricsted* on?).

قدو Qidwa, Qodwa, model, pattern (in praise).

CΔB

viii. Iqtedi bi, imitate.
Iqtidâ, imitation. [x.
(2) Iqdi, *vn* be of fine flavour
ii. Qaddi, *va* flavour B.
Moqaddi, flavoury, savoury.

قضى Iqḍu, *va* decide, judge, prescribe.
Qâḍu, *pl.* Qoḍâ'a, magistrate.
Qâḍu el qoḍâ'a, chief Justice.
Qaḍâ, *pl.* 8, Aqḍuya, sentence at law, doom; local circle of jurisdiction.
Qaḍuiya 14, an affair.
iii. Qâḍu, *va* call before a judge.
vi. Taqâḍâ, *va* make claim at law F. [end.
vii. Inqaḍu, *vp* be accomplished,
viii. Iqtaḍu, *va* necessitate, exact, require.
Iqtiḍâ, exigence.
Moqtaḍa', a thing required, a necessity, necessary.
Bi moqtaḍa', by necessity of, by virtue of.

قذى Qaḍê, Qaḍéya, a mote in the eye.

كذب Icḍib, *vn* speak falsely, lie.
Cêḍib, false. Ciḍb, a lie. Ciḍba, dᵃ
Ceḍoub, mendacious, given to lying.
Ecḍeb, more false.
ii. Ceḍḍib, *va* give the lie to; flatly contradict.
iii. Cêḍib, *va* deceive by a lie.
iv. Ecḍib, *va* detect as a liar c.
vi. Tecêḍeb, *vr* lie mutually.

CAB

x. Istecaib, *va* accuse of falsehood.
Mecaeba 11, piece of falsehood.

قَذوب Qaẑuib 10, mace, sceptre; iron rail on road.

قذف Iqaif [compare Iṉaif], *va* pelt, fling; slander, cast (into prison) s. *ger.* Qaaf, aspersion.
Miqaêf 11, an oar [corrupt for Mijaêf. So Qammir, for Jammir.]
ii. Qaddif, *va* row, *vulg.* for Ijaif.

كدّ Icdaṉ, *vn* toil, plod.
Ceddaṉ, laborious (ant).

قدح Qadaṉ 4, goblet.
Qidâṉa, art of making goblets x.
(2) Iqdaṉ, *va* strike light by flint and steel (or by two pieces of wood x.). *ger.* Qadṉ.
Qadṉa, *nu.* a single striking.
Qaddâṉa, *nu.* steel for striking light B. (*not* flint).
Miqdâṉ 11, Miqdaṉa 11, tinderbox or other machine for striking light. Lucifer-box.

قدم Qidm, *s.* yore.
Qidma°, of yore.
Qidma, antiquity x. [B.
Qadâma, Qadicmieya, antiquity
Qadiem, ancient (*also*, old F.).
Aqdam, more ancient.
El Aqdam, *eccles.* the Dean.
Qodm, front line x.
Qodâma, vanguard x.

QDM

Qodamieya, preëminence.
Qaddâm, Moqaddam, chieftain.
Qiddiem, chiefest, supereminent.
Qoddâm, the front, *prep.* in front of.
Qoddâmiey, *adj.* front, in front.
Qaidâm, projecting x.
Qoddâmieya, *s.* forepart B.
Miqdâm, very forward (in battle).
[Qadam 4, foot, footstep; instep of the foot.]
Iqdam, *vn* approach, arrive. *ger.* Qodoum.
Qâdim, *partic.* approaching.
ii. Qaddim, *va* set foremost, set over as chief; bring to, presént, afford, supply. Also, *vulg. vn* Qaddim, *for* Teqaddam B. [leader.
Moqaddam, one who is in front;
Moqaddama, proposition, preface, advanced guard.
Taqdiem, presentation, bill in Parliament, supply (in political economy).
iv. Aqdim, *va* send to the front, promote (in office).
Iqdâm, promptitude, dash (in a soldier) x.
Moqdam, *adj.* in front; *pl.* Maqâdim 11 B. [ship.
Moqdim (Maqdam ?), prow of
v. Teqaddam, *vn* be foremost, precede.
Teqaddom, primacy.
Moteqaddim, antecedent, foregoing, preceding, foremost. *s.* forerunner, premise of a syllogism.

QDM

Moteqaddima", previously.
vi. Teqâdam, *vn* be very ancient.
Moteqâdim, primitive, antique.
x. Istaqdim, *va* count ancient.
Mostaqdim, antiquated.
(2) Qaidoum 11, hatchet with hammer at the back.

كدن Cidna, *s.* acre (n. *arpent*).
(2) Ceddin, *va* harness (horse) to car.

كدر Oedor, *vn* grow dim or turbid. *ger.* Cedar, Codour.
Cedir, turbid.
Cedara, dregs, sediment.
Codra, Codoura, turbidity.
Cedar, Codoum, mental disturbance.
ii. Ceddir, *va* make turbid, confuse, discolour.

قدر Iqdir, *vn* be able, powerful.
Qâdir, powerful, able.
Qodra, power, potency.
Qadar, divine will, fiat? *Also* Qadar, Qadr, Qadd, quantity. Qadar, measure, *i.e.* aim of bow or gun.
Miqdàr, quantity.
Maqdara, ability, means, material of power.
ii. Qaddir, *va* estimate, measure distance in aiming; decree (as God); assign probable meaning.
Taqdier, *s.* predestination; probable meaning of a sentence, virtual sense. [ing].
Taqdiern", virtually (as to mean-

CDX

El maqâdier, the Destinies.
iv. Aqdir, *va* empower, enable.
viii. Iqtedir, *vn* hold power.
Iqtidâr, power, authority.
(2) Qidr 3, Qidra, copper saucepan, stewpot.
Qodair, small d°.

قذر Oqaor, *vn* be dirty.
Qaaer 4, dirt, impurity.
Qaair, dirty, sordid.
Qaaair, *va* make dirty.
x. Istaqair, *va* account dirty, loathe.

كدس Cods 4, heap of grain, shock of corn.
Coddâse, *nu.* d°.
ii. Ceddis, *va* heap up (corn in sheaves), put (hay) in cocks.

قدس Qods, Jerusalem; sanctity.
Qodâs, the eucharist.
Qaddous, Qoddous, thrice holy (God).
Qadies, Christian saint.
Qadâse, holiness.
Qoddâs, liturgy.
Oqdos, *vn* be holy. [crate.
ii. Qaddia, *va* sanctify, consev. Teqaddas, *vp* of d°.
Maqdas, holy place.
Maqdasiey, Moqaddasiey, belonging to Jerusalem.
Moqâdis, *pl.* -e, pilgrim to Jerusalem.

كدش Iodix, *va* scrape off (skin), scratch off, scrub.
Codiex, a roadster, a common

CDX

horse; a gelding; *pl.* Ecêdiex, *qu.* a scrub?
Waraq el codx, grey *coarse* paper B. [Codx, scrubbiness?]

كَفّ Coff *can, vn* abstain from, cease, desist.
(2) Ceff 3, palm, hollow of hand. [palm.
v. Teceffaf, *vn* hold out the open x. Isteciff, *vn* ask alms.
(3) Coff, *va* hem (in sewing). Cefâfa, a hem.
(4) Cêffa*t*, all, almost all, of all sorts. Cêffat el ñôboub, all sorts of grain.

قَفّ Qoffa 10, round basket, round boat, coracle.
(2) Teqafqaf, *vn* shiver with cold.

وَكَفّ Wecef Yecif, *vn* leak (as the ceiling).
(2) Wicêf, pannier? [mule's saddle x.]

وَقَفّ Waqaf Yaqif, *vn* stand up, stop, halt; sala', understand, turn or depend upon.
Waqfa, *nu.* pause; quiescence of a letter.
Woqouf, *ger.* standing up; sala', understanding.
ii. Waqqif, iv. Auqif, *va* cause to stand, bring to a halt. But *vulg.* ii. Waqqif is *vn* same as i. or intensive of i.
(2) Waqf 3, 4, pious legacy.
iv. Auqif, *va* bequeath to pious uses.

CFY

كَرْف Coufi, Cufic (letters).
(2) Coufieya, a reel to wind on B. C.
ii. Cewwif, *va* wind (thread).
(3) Coufieya, shawl for the head.

قَوْف Qouf, *va* divine the interior by exterior marks. *ger.* Qauf, palmistry.
Qâyif, physiognomist.
Qiyâfa, semblance c.
Aqwaf, more sagacious (in physiognomy) x.

كَيْف Ceif? how? Ceif, *vulg. s.* liking, taste, fancy.
Teceyyaf, *vn* amuse oneself B. tipple, tope B.
Ceifieya, quality.

قَيْف ii. Qayyif, *va* track out, follow step by step, traverse x.
viii. Iqtêf, *va* follow closely x. But see Iqtefi.

كَفى Icfi, *vn* be enough.
Cêfi, sufficient.
Cifâya, a sufficiency.
Cofya, *pl.* Cofa', sufficient aliment, bare necessaries.
ii. Ceffi, *va* satisfy, suffice (a person). But *vulg.* ii. is used for i. as Yoceffi for Yoceffeni, it satisfies me.
iii. Cêfi, *va* recompense.
Mocêfi, equivalent.
Mocêfèya, retribution.
iv. Ecfi, *va* keep, support, feed.

CFY

viii. Ictefi, *vp* be satisfied, contented.
Moctefi, satisfied.

قِفَى Qifâ, *s.* back part, nape of neck.
Oqfou, *va* follow close x.
ii. Qaffi, *va* send in close pursuit x.
Qâfiya 12, rhyme.
iv. Aqfi, *va* postfix?
Iqfâ, a postfixing?
viii. Iqtefi, *va* track out B. See Iqtef, under Qief.

كَفّ Icfafi, *va* look full in face.
Cifâfla", openly, undisguisedly.
Cefiefi, a match, equal.
iii. Cêfifi, *va* prove oneself a match for, be ready for combat?
Mocêfafla, contentiousness B.

كفل Ocfol, *va* give bail, become surety. Have care of (a child).
Cefiel, he who becomes surety.
Cifêla, security, caution.
iv. Ecfil, *va* make (one) to be answerable.
v. Teceffel, *vn* become answerable.
ii. Ceffil, *va* confide the care of a child to (another).
(2) Cefel 4, 3, rump (of a horse).

قفل Qofl 4, a padlock.
Qaffâl, locksmith.
ii. Qaffil, iv. Aqfil, *va* (*also* Aqfil cala') look up.

QH

vii. Inqafil, *vp* be locked up.
v. Teqaffel, viii. Iqtefil, d°.
(2) Qâfila 12, caravan or company of travellers.

كفن Cefan, *s.* winding sheet.

كفر Ocfor bi, *vn* disbelieve in God, be impious.
Céfir, impious.
Cefra, ingratitude.
Cefr, *ger.* unbelief, impiety.
iii. Céfir, *va* defraud, disown a debt; with double acc. x.
(4) Ceffâra, expiation x. penance B.
(2) Cefr 3, market-town.
(3) Céfour, camphor.

قفر Qafr 5, Qafra 2, a desart.
Aqfar, *adj.* desart, barren.
iv. Aqfir, *vp* be desart, desolate.
Moqfir, desolate. [late.
Miqfâr, very desolate.

قفص Qafaṣ 4 [Qafnṣ c.], crate, lattice, cage. [as lattice.
viii. Iqtefuṣ, *vp* be interlaced

قفطن Qaftên, dressrobe.

قفش Oqfoṣ, *va* catch in running, clutch B. *ger.* Qafṣ (quickness, vivacity x.)

قفز Iqfiz, *vn* leap.
Qafze, a leap.

قه Qahqih, *va* laugh violently.
Qahqaha, a rude laugh, *cachinnus.*

WQḤ

وقح Waqaḥ Yaqiḥ, *vn* be hard (as a hoof); be impudent, hardened.
Waqieḥ, hard, impudent.
Wiqâḥa, hardness, impudence.
Waqâḥa, Qiḥa, hardness.
v. Tewaqqaḥ ʿala', be insolent to.
x. Isteuqiḥ, *vn* be hard (as hoof) ɪ.

قوح Qouḥ, *vn* suppurate.
Qaiḥ, matter, *pus*.
v. Teqawwaḥ, *vn* same as i.

قهو Qahwa, coffee.

قحوان Aqḥawân, camomile.

قحب Qaḥba, a prostitute.
Qaḥbana, prostitution.
ii. Qaḥḥub, *va* prostitute?

كهف Cehf 3, cavern, grotto.

قحف Qiḥf 4, cranium.

كهل Cehl 7, fullgrown (plant) ɪ.; of mature age, from 30 to 50.
(2) Cêhil, lazy (= Cêsil) s. c.
(3) Cêhil 12, crest of horse's neck.

كحل Coḥl, eye-salve, eye-paint.
Micḥal, instrument by which it is applied.
(2) Ceḥail, Ceḥulân, horse of noble breed ɢʟ. ʙ.

قحل Qaḥul, parched (land).
Qaḥḥoula, driness (of soil).

QHR

كهم Ichem, *vn* be blunt, blunted, *lit.* or *fig.* x.
Cehêm, blunt (sword), dull (intellect) ɪ.
Cchiem, torpid and worn out ɪ. [Perhaps this family is quite obsolete.]

قحم Iqḥam fie, *vn* rush precipitately on. Less common than v. or viii. [peril.
Qoḥma, *su.* rash enterprize,
Miqḥâm, foolhardy.
ii. Qaḥḥum fie, *va* precipitate (a person) into, *fig.*
v. Taqaḥḥam, *vn* be rash, venture rashly.
viii. Iqteḥam, *va* run (down) sheep. *vn* same as i.
Iqtiḥâm, precipitation.

كهن Cêhin 7, a priest; also *pl.* Cehena.
Cehnout, priesthood.
Cihêna, priesthood, divination ɪ.
Ichen, *vn* or v. Tecehhen, practise divination ɪ.

قهقر Qahqir, *or* ii. Taqahqar, *vn* retreat (as army).
Qahqarı, Taqahqor, *s.* retreat.

قهر Qahr, *s.* constraint.
Qohra, superior force, violence.
Qahrᵃ, Qohrateᵃ, by force.
Qâhir, victorious, imperious, peevish ʙ.
Qahrᵃ ʿanni, in spite of me ɪ.
Qahhêr, irresistible (God).
Qâhira, Cairo, victorious (city).

QHR

Iqher, *vn* domineer. *vs* tease? *B. iii.* Qâhir, treat violently.
vii. Inqahir, *vp* be irritated or peevish, repine *B.*
Qahermân, warden of palace or college.
Qahermâna, duenna, court-lady, and in bad sense, courtezan.

كهرب Cehrobâ, Cehrobân, amber.
Cehrobâ'iey, electric(telegraph).

كهرت Ceḣrit, *vn* roll over, tumble. *See* Cerrit.

قحط Iqḣat, *vn* be deficient in rain (as the year). *ger.* Qaḣṭ, drowth, dearth.
Qâḣuṭ, dear, distressing (time).
(2) Oqḣöt, *va* rake off, graze, scratch. *See* Iqxat.
Qaḣṭa, a grazing.
Miqḣaṭ 11, a rasp?

كوخ Couk 4, a reed hut, raised in the field.

قحل Qokliey? scarlet B*g.* κοκκινος.

كل Cill, *vn* be dull, blunt, enfeeble. *ger.* Coll, lassitude.
Celâl, Celâla, lassitude.
Celiel, weary, languid.
(2) Coll, *s.* all. Cellâ [entirely *K.;*] *not* at all (in answer to a question, as in French, *Du tout*).
Colliey, total, universally.

CL

Collieya, totality. Collieyat^m, Bi collieya, entirely.
Collân, Collâ-homâ, Collei-homâ, both, both of the two.
(3) Colla, Golla, a ball, bullet.
(4) *ii.* Cellil, *va* crown with a chaplet, marry.
Tecliel, ceremony of wedding.
Icliel 11, 8, chaplet, diadem.

قل Qill, *vn* be small in quantity.
Qilla 10, paucity.
Qaliel 11, 1, few, not much.
Qaliela^a, rarely.
Aqall, fewer, less in quantity.
Qalal, deficiency.
Qalâyil, few people *K.*
ii. Qallil, *iv.* Aqill, *va* lessen, make fewer.
iii. Qâlil-oh li, *va* stint him of.
x. Isteqill, *va* underrate.
(2) *Also x.* Isteqill, *vn* be an independent sovereign.
Istiqlâl, independence.
Mosteqill, independent; plenipotentiary.
(3) Qolla 10, 5, earthenware jar, ewer.
(4) Qalqil, *va* agitate, shake.
ii. Teqalqal, *vn* vacillate.
Qalqala, Qilqâl, agitation.
Moteqalqil, unsteady.
[Also Qalqil for Ġalġil, *vn* gurgle. *See* Ṡalṙul.]

أكل Col, *va* eat thou.
'Ecel, he ate. *ger.* 'Ecl.
'Ocl, victuals *K.*
Ocla, mouthful *K.*
'Ecil, *partic.* eating.

CL

'Ecila, a cancer.
'Ecla, a meal.
'Eccêl, Ecoul, voracious.
Mêcoulêt, victuals.
ii. 'Eccil, va cause to eat.
v. Te'eccel, vn feel oneself eaten up; itch x.

وكل Weciel 6, deputy, proxy (viceroy, agent, attorney).
Wicêla, agency.
ii. Weccil, va depute; bi, to.
Mowecoel, one deputed.
iii. Wêcil, va trust in x.
v. Teweccel sala', vn rely upon (God). [trust.
vi. Tewêcel, vr have mutual
viii. Ittecil calaihi fie, vn rely upon him in.

وثل Waqil, skilful to walk on edges, on ridges, as a goat.
Auqal, more skilful, etc.
v. Tewaqqal, vn balance oneself on the edge of a precipice, climb easily F.

كول Ecwel, yellow dun, buff B.

قول Qoul, va toll, say; vp Qiel, it is said.
Qâyil, partic. saying.
Qaul, utterance, speech.
Qaul el nês, public rumour.
Aqâwiel, (vain) words.
Qawwâl, talkative.
Miqwâl, great haranguer.
ii. Qawwil, va make (a person) say; represent that he has said.

CLY

iii. Qâwil, va address, talk to.
vi. Taqâwal, vn converse.
Qiel wa qâl, all sorts of talk.
Maqâl, talk, rumour.
Maqâla, a paragraph x.
Maqoula, subject of debate.
Moqawwal, often said x.
Motaqâwil, conversible.
(iv. Aqiel, va annul a bargain. See Qiel.)

كيل Ciel, va measure (grain).
ger. Ceil. [mug AL.)
Ceil, Ceila, a dry measure (a Ceyyâl, measurer of grain.
ii. Ceyyil, va same as i. B.

قيل Qâyila, noontide?
Qailoula, midday sleep B.
Taqyiel, d°. B.
v. Taqayyel, vn sleep at midday, take siesta.
(2) v. Taqayyel, va resemble.
(3) iv. Aqiel, va annul, retract (a bargain) B. X.
Iqâla, annulment, retractation.

قلا Oqlou, Iqli, va fry.
Maqlouw, Maqliey, fried.
Miqlâya, frying pan.
v. Taqallâ, vn boil up.
(2) Qaliyoun, pipe for smoking (also Γaliyoun AL.)
(3) Qillicya 11, cell of monk.
(4) Qolâ, ulcers in mouth B. See Πulâ.
(5) Qilwat el Zahr, the chine B.
(6) Qalâi, pewter Bg.

كلى Celâ, grass, pasturage; χιλός.

CLY

Celiey, grassy c. [rage.
iv. Ecli, *vn* abound with pastu-
x. Istecli, d°. x.
(2) Colwa 11, kidney.
Colya, d°. [tiara?
(3) Colâya, a peculiar cap, a

تلع Iqlar, *va* pull out. See
Iklar. [stable x.
Qalis, loose in the saddle, un-
Qalâyis! extirpations (?) *i.e.*
no quarter to the enemy.
Maqlis, quarry of lime, gravel,
etc.
ii. Qallis, *va intens.* of i.
v. Taqallas, *vn* be unrooted.
(2) Qalsa 5, isolated rock,
citadel, castle.
(3) Qils 3, sail of a ship.
iv. Aqlis, *vn* set sail.
Moqallas, in full sail.

كلب Celba 5, dog.
Celba, bitch.
Celb el mâi, beaver c.
Celab, hydrophobia B.
Celbân, Mecloub, mad as a dog.
Iclib, *vn* be mad, as dog.
x. Isteclib, *vn* be furious.
(2) Colûba c. Collâba B. pincers,
hook as support, grappling
iron. [tongs.
Celbatein, pincers at smith's
Collâb, meat-hook.

تلب Qalb 3, heart, pith of tree.
false money B. *adj.* spurious c.
Qalbicy, hearty, cordial.
Qolaibét, broccoli B. (sprouts?
small hearts?)

CLF

(2) Iqlib, *va* reverse. *ger.* Qalb,
inversion, permutation.
Miqlab, hammer of firelock, hoe?
ii. Qallib, *va intens.* of i. turn
up and down; revolutionize.
Taqlieba, inversion.
iii. Qâlib, *va* handle, manage,
knead? sell by retail.
Qâlab 12, a mould (for melted
metal), a model.
Qaloub, Qallâb, shifty, treacherous.
v. Taqallab, *vn* be fickle.
Motaqallib, fickle (climate).
Taqallob, vicissitude, revolution.
vii. Inqalib, *vp* be reversed,
overturned.
Inqilâb, reversal, total change.

تلبق Qalbaq, cap of hair.

تلد Qilâda 11, necklace.
ii. Qallid, *va* invest with a necklace; entrust with a public
office.
(2) Qallid, *va* ape, imitate.
Taqlied, imitation, mimicry
(*qu.* corrupt for Qarrid, Taq-
ried?).
(3) Iqlied 11 (from *Pers.* Also,
Gr. κλειδ), key of a country,
stronghold.

كلف Colfa, *s.* trouble, burden,
pains.
Celouf, troublesome x.
ii. Cellif, *va* trouble (a person),
burden, lay a burdensome
task upon (some one), cost
(a person).

CLF

Cellaf-oh 'en, he charged him to —, laid on him the task to —.
v. Tecellaf, *en* take trouble; *ep* ɛala', be imposed (as tax), be charged (as cost).
Motecellif, elaborate, gorgeous, far-fetched (phrase).
(2) Eclaf, light chesnut (in colour), [russet, tawny ᴋ.]

قلفط Qalfaṭ, *va* caulk (a ship). *ger.* Qalfaṭa.
Qalfâṭ 13, a caulker ʙ.

قلح Colâh, cowl of dervish, Tartar cap o.

كلح Iclaĥ, *vn* also, v. Tecellaĥ, be sombre of face, scowl.
Colouĥ el wejh, severity of countenance ʙ.
Cêliĥ, *adj.* scowling, darkfaced; dingy, (colour) faded by the sun, livid ʙ. [dingy.
ii. Celliĥ, *va* make sombre or

قلح Qoulah, yellow dun, buff; *Turk.* ʙ. [In ᴋ. it is Qalij.] *See* Ecwel.

قلس Qalĥas, *adj.* fatuous ʙ.

كلم Cilma 2, Celima, a word.
Celâm, speech, oration, language.
Celiem, person addressed ᴋ.
Celmâni, loquacious.
ii. Cellim, *va* speak (words).
iii. Cêlim, *va* address (a person).
Mocêlim, speaker.

QLN

Mocêlama, conversation.
v. Tecellem, *vn* talk.
Tecellom, *s.* discourse.
Metecellim, speaker. (In grammar, the first person.)
vi. Motecêlim, conversible.

قلم Qalam 4, (*Greek*) pen for writing; *fig.* office, writing place.
Miqlama, pencase; for which *vulg.* Qalamdân. ·
(2) From καλαμος (reed), come also:
Qalam 4, a stripe on cloth.'
ii. Qallim, *va* stripe (cloth); beat (a person) with a cane; *also* cut (rods) from a tree.
(3) Iqliem 11 (κλίμα), region.
(4) Qolmiya, apartment containing sacred vessels ʙ.
Qollamiey, churchwarden, sacristan ʙ.

قلن Qaulân, *s.* surcingle of horse, outer girth.

قلمن Qalamoun, chameleon.

قلندر Qalandar, a calendar, or wandering monk.

قلنج Qoulinj ᴋ. colio, *Pers. vulg.* Qaulanj ?

قلنس Qalansowa, high pointed cap, mitre o.
Moqalnas, capped (as a mountain with snow).

CLC

كَلَك Calec, raft supported by inflated skins, used on the Tigris.

قَلَق Iqlaq, *vn* be in agitation, in disquiet. *ger.* Qalaq.
Qaliq, *adj.* in disquiet. *See* Qalqil.

كَلَر Celâr, cellar, pantry; *Lat.* corrupted into Cerâr.

كِلس Cils, *s.* lime.
Cilsiey, *adj.* of lime.
(2) Cielous, *Gr.* χυλος, chyle.
(3) Celiese, *Gr.* εκκλησία, church.

قَلَص Iqlus, *vn* shrink (as a garment). *ger.* Qolous.
ii. Qallus, *va* shrink (cloth).
v. Taqallas, *vn* supersedes i.

قَلش Qalxien (Qaltxien AL.), mocassins, leather boots without soles, to wear on the carpet; generally of bright yellow or red untanned leather.

قَلزم Qolzom, the city Clysma (*Gr.*); hence Baḣr el Qolzom, the Red Sea.

كَم Cem? how much?
Ce-ma, as.
Cemmiey? in what quantity?
Cemmieya, quantity.
(2) Cimm 5, bud, follicle.
ii. Cemmim, *vn* bud, blossom.
(3) Comm 4, sleeve.

QWM

قَم Qomm, *va* brush, sweep.
Qomâma, sweepings.
Miqamma, brush, broom E.
(2) Qomma, morsel, mouthful.
(3) Qimma, tip, top, peak of a mountain.
(4) Qomqom, vessel shaped like a cucumber; glass retort.
(5) Taqamqam sala', *vn* grumble at? become disaffected with? [*or* frequentative of Qoum? *arise* against?]

أكَم 'Ecema 5, mound, bank; *also* 'Ecêm, *sing.* mound.

قوم Qoum, arise, get up, stand up. Qoum bi, go to work at, begin on, undertake. Qoum sala', rise against.
Qiyâm bi, *ger.* undertaking.
[Qaum 4, people, folk.]
Qauma, an insurrection.
Qâma, stature; a fathom.
Qiyâma, resurrection.
Qâyim, *adj.* upright, standing (order, committee), permanent, recovered (from illness).
Qâyima, right angle; — 12, note, banknote; inventory, catalogue.
Qaima, Qiema 10, value.
[Qiema, bash o.]
Qaiyoum, immutable.
Qiyâm, stay, continuance.
Qiyâm, permanence o. but *gw.* perpendicularity B.
[Qaiyim, adroit B.
Qaiyâma, adroitness.]

QWM

Qawiem, established.
Aqwam, more rightful.
Qawwâm, (*vulg.* Syr.) instantly.
Maqâm, place where one stands, place, post.
Maqâma, musical tone; *séance*.
ii. Qawwim, *va* set upright, correct; value, rate.
Taqwiem, *s.* digest (of days, feasts, countries), a calendar, a map. Estimation, correct arrangement.
Moqawwim, constitutive, constituent.
iii. Qâwim ʿala', *vn* be insurgent; or *va* resist. [lent.
Moqâwim, insurgent, equivaiv. Aqiem, *va* set up, raise from the dead. *vn* stay.
Oqiem, *vp* be constituted.
Iqâma, *act.* establishing; *neut.* staying, sojourning, continuance.
Moqâm, second course, dessert.
Moqâma, place of sojourning.
v. Taqawwam, *vn* set oneself upright, be corrected.
vi. Taqâwam, *vn* rise, one against another.
x. Istaqiem, *vn* be straight, upright; *vulg.* stay, sojourn, superseding iv. in this sense. Yet *vulg.* Istaqâm Ḋâloh, his health is re-established.
Istiqâma, soundness, uprightness, loyalty, recovery (from illness).
Mostaqiem, straight (line), upright, *lit.* and *fig.*; right, well-established.

CMK

Qâimaqâm, for Qâyim maqâm, lieutenant, substitute in office.

ڪَمَا Cemâ, *collect.* mushrooms; Cemâya, *nu.*; *pl.* Ecmou.
Cemmâ, seller of mushrooms.

ڪِمِيا Ciemioya, chemistry, alchemy; from *Gr.* χύμα, χυμός.
(2) Ceima, Li ceima, from Cei ma, in order that.

قَمَسَ Iqmas, *va* curb, tame, subdue. *ger.* Qams.
iv. *ger.* Iqmâs, self-control c.
vii. Inqamis, *vp* of i.
(2) Qimas, funnel.

ڪَمَدَ Cemed, Comouda, paleness.
Comoudieya, paleness r.
[Comoudiey, pale?]
(2) *ger.* Cimâd, fomentation.
ii. Cemmid, *va* foment B. K.
Cimâda, linen or bandage to foment a limb with.

ڪَمِهَ Icmeh, *vn* be blind from birth.
Ecmeh, blind from birth. *ger.* Cemeh, blindness from birth.

قَمْحَ Qamḥ, wheat.
Qamḥa, *nu.* grain of wheat, a grain weight.
Qammâḥ, corn-chandler.

ڪَمَاجَ Cemâja, pollen, fine bran?

ڪَمْكَ Cimkâ, damask silk.

CML

كمل Ocmól, *vn* be perfect.
Cemel, the total x.
Cemâl, perfection, totality.
Cemâlieya, perfection c.
Cêmil, pérfect.
Ecmel, more perfect.
Micmâl, consummate.
ii. Cemmil, *va* perféct.
iv. Ecmil, *va* d°.; *also*, take the total, add up.
Mocemmel, perfected, complete.
Tecmiel, *ger.* completing.
v. Tecemmel, *vp* be perfected.

نمل Qamla, *nn.* louse.

كمن Icman li, *vn* lie in ambush for. *ger.* Comoun.
Cemna 5, ambuscade, secret plot.
Cemien, d°.
ii. Cemmin li, iv. Ecmin li, *va* set (another) in ambush for.
v. Tecemman, and viii. Ictemin, *vn* same as i.
Moctemin, latent (grief, etc.) x.
vi. Tecêman, *vn* conspire.
Tecêmon, conspiracy.
Mocêmin, conspirator.
(2) Cemmoun, cummin (herb).
Cemmoun flôlou, anise.
(3) Cemân (*mod. Syr.*), again, yet more (as *Fr.* encore).

نمن Qamien 8, a kiln. *Gr.* and *Lat.*
Qamien jier, lime kiln.

كمنجة Comanja, Cemanza, violin.

VOL. II.

QMT

كمر Cemar (*Pers.* Cemâr, band), leathern belt with pouch for money. [coals B.
(2) Micmara, extinguisher for
(3) Mecmour, stewed meat B.

نمر Qamar 4, the moon.
Qomair, little moon.
Aqmar, bright as the moon x.
Moqmir, (night) which affords moonshine.
(2) Qimâr, a game of chance.
iii. Qâmir, *va* trick (a person) at play; stake at a game of chance.
Moqâmara, *ger.* gambling.
v. Taqammar, vi. Taqâmar, *vn* gamble.
(3) Qomariey, *f.* —ya, turtle-dove 11, 10.
(4) Qammir, *va* toast; *mod.* corrupt for Jammir.

كمس Ciemous (*Gr.* χυμός), chyme.

نمس Iqmis, *vn* dip, plunge, dive. See Ipmis.
iv. Aqmis, *va* causative of i.
ii. Qammis, *va* toss (as waves toss a ship). But x. has y for s.
Qammûs = Γammâs, diver (bird)

نمسى Qamiey 9, also 8, shirt, tunic. *Ital.* camisia.
v. Taqammay, *vn* wear a tunic.

نمش Oqmor, *va* grasp, extort B. (See Iqbuš).

853

23

QMT

(2) Bandage hands and feet x.
Qimât, swaddling band.
Qamt, *ger.* swaddling.
ii. Qammut, *va* swaddle, swathe.

تمطلس Qamarlas, chilblain в.
χίμετλον.

كمثر Comaθra', pears, pear c.

كمش Ocmox, *va and* iv. Ecmix, pinch between thumb and finger в.
Comxa, a pinch (as of snuff). See Ocbox.
x. writes it Oqmox.
(2) Icmex, *vn* nestle, lie snug.

كن Conn, *va* cover, screen; hide, cherish.
Cinn 4, 5, 8, Conna 2, caves.
viii. Ictinn, or x. Istecinn, *vn* hide (for safety?). [17.
Mecnoun, hidden s. in Rev. ii.
(2) Cenna, *pl.* Cenâyin, daughter-in-law, (sister-in-law x.)
(3) Cênoun, brazier, fire-box.

قن Qonn 4, henhouse r. (= Konn).
(2) Qânoun 12, rule, customary tax (*Gr.* κανών), penance.
Moqannin, author, institutor.
Qaunin, *va* impose penance on.
(3) Qaniena 11, Qinniena, thin glass bottle aī.

وكن Wocna, *ns.* bird's nest, or hole in a rock. See Wecr.

QNY

يقن Yaqin, he knew surely; *pres.* Yaiqan, he knows surely. *ger.* Yaqan, Yaqien, certainty.
Lina yaqien, to us it is a certainty, *i.e.* we know surely.
Yaqiena°, certainly.
Yaqieniey, certain, infallible (truth).
iv. Aiqin bi, *v.* make sure of, fully believe in.
Yaqin, Mouqin, fully convinced in mind.
Ieqân, certitude.
v. Tayaqqan bi, same as iv.
viii. Ittaqin bi, *vn* be perfect in.
Hence a new root Taqin.

كون Coun, *vn* be. Cên, he was, it was. Yecoun, it will be. *ger.* Ceun, being.
Cêyin, *partic.* existing. *s.* a being, entity.
ii. Cewwin, *va* create.

قون Qonna, a medal в. c.

قين Qain 3, 4, smith r.
(2) Qâyina 2, 4, handmaid.

كني Cinâya, hint, allusion, metaphor. Cinâya ran, a sort of; something like.

قنو قني Iqni, Oqnou, *va* get, acquire.
Qonwa, an acquisition c.
Qonyân, acquired wealth c.
viii. Iqtoni, *va* possess, hold.
[This root perhaps belongs to high style and religion.]

QNY

(2) Qâni, *in the union* Aḥmar qâni, deep red.
(3) Qanâya 8, tunnel, subterraneous (?) watercourse.

كنع Icnas, *vn* shrink as a garment.
Cenies, shrunken, withered (limb) x.   [ered x.
Ecnas, person with limb withii. Cennis, *vn* cause (a garment) to shrink.
v. Tecennas, be shrunken.

قنع Iqnas, *vn* be contented.
Iqnas san, be content without; forgo. *ger*. Qonous.
Qanous, Qanus, contented.
Qanâsa, contentment.
iv. Aqnis, *vs* content, satisfy.
v. Taqannas, *vs* cultivate contentment.

كنب Cenab, a callosity B.

قنب Qinnab, hemp.
ii. Qannib, *va* tie tight, tighten, strain.

قنبع Qanbis, *vn* grunt as pig.

قنبر Qonbar, Qonbara', a bomb used in war.
(2) Qonbara, tuft on the head. (Δou qonbara, tufted.) Also Qonbara, the lark; the *tufted* lark?
Qonbour, having a hump B.

كند Icnid, *va* be ungrateful to. *ger*. Conoud.

QNS

Cenoud, Cennâd, ungrateful (person), barren (soil).

قند Qanda, sм. sugarcandy.
Soccer qanda, d° B.
Qannâdiey, confectioner м.

قنديل Qandiel 11 (from *Lat.* candela), a lamp, table-lamp.
Qandaleft (?), *pl.* -tiya, sacristan, churchwarden в.

كنف Cenf 4, side, flap, wing.
ii. Cennif sala', *v.* spread wing over, encompass (for protection).
viii. Ictenif sala', same as ii.
Cenief, place of concealment, *latrina*, privy.

كنه Conh, *s.* essence, in metaphysics.

قنم Aqnoum 11, in Christian theology, a person of the Trinity.

قنق Qanâq 2, Guildhall?

كنر Cenâr, *s.* border c.
Cinâra, long strip of linen k.
Cienâr, selvage B.

كنس ii. Cennis, *va* sweep.
Conêse, sweepings.
Cennês, sweeper.
Micnese, broom.
(2) Cenies 11, church; *vulg.* for Celiess, ἐκκλησία.

قنص Qany, *ger*. hunting.
Qânus, Qannâs, hunter.

QNS

Qanieʿa, game, venison.
v. Taqannaʿ, *vn* be a hunter, hunt habitually. [after.
viii. Iqtenuʿ, *vns* hunt, hunt

قنصل Qonʿöl 11, consul, in modern politics.
Qonʿöliey, consular.
Qonʿöläte, consulate.

قنط Iqnaт, *vn* despair. *ger.* Qonouт.

قنطر Qanтaтa 11 (from *Fr.* cintre, *Ital.* cintura, *Lat.* cinctura), arch. *Hence also for* bridge.
Qaɴтur, *va* build arch-wise.
ii. Taqaɴтar, *vn* curvet, prance as a horse.
(2) Qinтâr (*Fr.* quintal), hundred weight.

قنش ii. Qannix el éʌên, prick up the ears. See Qarrin.

كنز Cinz 3, treasure, *esp.* in the soil; treasure, *fig.* [в.
(2) viii. Ictaniz, *vn* be compact

كوك Couce, morsel or flock of cotton or wool, flue в.

قوق Qouq, *vn* caw as rook.
Qâq 9, crow *generically.*
(2) Qâouq 12, cylindrical mitre, stuffed cap.

وقوق Waqouq, *s.* cuckoo (bird).

قيق Qâyiq 12, wherry.
Qâyiqтxi, boatman.

QR

ككب Couceb 11, star, heavenly body.

قم Qâqoum, *s.* ermine.

كر Corr, *vn* come round into one's own steps. *ger.* Corr.
Cerra, *ns.* single act of returning, *une fois* x. = Marra.
Corra, sphere, globe. See Cora under كرا.
ii. Cerrir, *va* repeat, reiterate. Tecrier, repetition.
Mocerrar, (medicine) of double strength.
Cercir, *va* turn (a mill) round and round; repeat, as Cerrir. *ger.* Cercera.
ii. Tecercar, *vn* spin round.
Tecercor el mâi, *s.* eddy.
(2) *Also,* Cercir, tickle в.
(3) Cerâr (for Celâr), cellar, pantry.

قر Qorr, *vn* abide, persist.
Qorr bi, persist in (a statement).
Qarâr, stability, fixedness; basis, bottom в. settling, settlement; *fig.* constancy.
El qârra, the continent.
Maqarr, fixed place, seat (of empire, etc.).
ii. Qarrir, *va* state, declare.
Taqrier, statement.
iv. Aqirr, *va* avow, confirm (a person) in office. [oneself.
x. Istaqirr, *vr* fix, establish
Mostaqarr = Maqarr.
(2) Qâroura, antique vase.

WCR

وكر Weora, *ms.* 3, nest of bird, *esp.* in a rock. See Woon.

وقر Waqour, grave in deportment.
Waqâr, Waqâra, gravity.
ii. Waqqir, *va* revere.
Mowaqqar, reverend, venerable.

كور Cour, clay furnace.
(2) Coura, country (*Gr.* χώρα).
(3) Cowâra 11, beehive.

قور ii. Qawwir, *va* cut a circle out of cloth, scollop.
Qowâra, scollop, cut out.

قير Qier, *s.* tar.
Qayyâr, seller of tar.
ii. Qayyir, *va* besmear with tar.

كرا or كرو Cora, Cor'a, ball, sphere, globe (of earth). See Corra.
Corawiey, spherical.
(2) Cerâwieya, herb skirret [caraway?].

كرى Cirâ, *ger.* and Cirwa, hire, hiring, price of hire.
Cèr, trade, profession.
Cèrawân, caravan, company of travellers.
iii. Cèri, *va* let on hire, let out.
Mocèri, one who lets out (*esp.* beasts of burden); muleteer, camel driver.
viii. Icteri, *va* accept on rent or hire?
(2) Icra', *vn* be drowsy. *ger.* Cara', drowsiness.

QRB

(3) Cerawân (*Gr.* κεραορνις), tragopan, horned pheasant.

قرأ Iqra', *va* read. *ger.* Qirâya, reading.
Qâri, reader.
Qor'ân, scripture, Koran.
Qarrâya, reading-desk.
iv. Aqri, *va* cause to read.

قرى Qarya, village; *pl.* qora' or 14, Qarâyâ.

قرع Qorta, lot, chance.
iii. Qâris, *v.* play a game of chance or of shooting x.
iv. Aqrus bain, *vn* cast lots between.
viii. Iqteris fie, same as iv.
vi. Taqâras, *vn* play game of chance together.
Qâris, one who plays x.
(2) Iqras, *va* strike, rap.
Miqrasa, whip, cudgel.
(3) Qars, gourd (bald head).
Aqras, bald of head, mangy.

كرب Cerb 3, *ger.* grieving.
Cerab, Corba, Corâba, sorrow.
iv. Ecrib, *va* grieve, afflict.
Mocrib, grievous, afflictive.
viii. Icterib, *vn* sorrow.
(2) Cerb, *s.* hiccup b.

قرب Iqrib min, *vn* approach to. *ger.* Qirâba, approach.
Qorb, nearness.
San qorb, from a short distance.
Qorba, neighbourhood.
Qarieb 4, near; 6, akin.

QRB

San qarieb, presently, soon.
Aqrab, nearer.
Qarâba, relationship by blood.
Aqârib, near kinsfolk.
Qarâb, nearness of time x.
Bi qarâb, soon, early.
ii. Qarrib, *va* bring near, tender, offer; approximate (in arithmetic).
Qorbân, offering, oblation; the eucharistic sacrifice.
Taqrieb, approximation.
[*Vulg.* Qarrib ii. is used for i. or viii.]
v. Teqarrab, *vn and* viii. Iqterib min, same as i.
iii. Qârib, *va* be akin to.
vi. Taqârab, *vr* approach mutually.
(2) Qirba 2, large water-skin.
Qirâb 2, case, sheath.
Qarrâba, large two-handed jar, amphora for wine.
Qârib 12, a ship's boat; *mod. Gr.* καράβι.
Qarâb, infantry soldier B. *pl.* Qarâba.

قربس Qurabous, pummel of the saddle.

قربع Qarbis, *va* quaff in long draught.

قربن Qarbâna B. Qarabiena c. a carbine.

قربط Qarbara, tenacity B. See Qarmut.
Qarbut, *va* hold fast?

CRD

كربش Cerbix, *va* gripe, pinch hard; — bi, cling to. See Ocbox.
ii. Tecerbax bi, *vn* cling to. See Tecermax, Tekarmax, Tesarbax, Tecebbax.

كرد Courd 4, 5, a Courd.
Courdistên, country of Courds.
(2) Cerdân, a necklace c.

قرد Qird 3, ape.
Qirda 10, she ape.
ii. Qarrid, *va* ape? See Qallid.
(2) Qorâda, tick of sheep.

قرض Iqruś, *va* nip off, pare, cut close, nibble (young shoots), clip (coin), cut off (an army).
Qorâśa, clippings as of gold.
Miqrâś, nippers.
[B. seems to prefer Qrr in this sense.]
vii. Inqaruś, *vp* be nipt off, extinct as a family.
(2) Iqruś, *va* lend money on interest. *ger.* Qarś, a loan; *esp.* public loan.
Maqruś, lent on interest.
Qâruś, *va* accommodate with a loan of money.
iv. Aqruś, *va* lend, same as i.
Moqruś, lender.
viii. Iqteruś min, *va* borrow money, contract a loan from.
x. Istaqruś min, *va* ask a loan from.

كردن Cerdoun, cowl of monk.

CRD

كردس Cerdis, *va* form into bands, heap one on another.
Cerdous(e) 11, band, squadron.
ii. Tecerdas, *vp* be banded, be formed into regiments.

تردس Qaraidies, a shrimp c.

قردش Qardix, *va* card (wool) with a comb.

كرف Icrif, *va* smell at B.

قرف Iqrif sala', *vn* accuse.
viii. Iqterif, *vp* be accused, be open to imputations.
(2) iii. Qârif, *vn* drudge, toil.
iv. Aqrif, *va* disgust.
(3) Qirfa, cinnamon.
Qorâfa, inner rind of tree x.
Qirrâf, d°.?

كرنس ii. Tecerfes, *vn* lurk in shortened posture. See Qarfur.
(2) Cerafa, celery, parsley.

قرفص Qarfur, Qarfix, *vn* squat on the heels B.

كره Icreh, *va* dislike. *ger*. Cerh. Commoner is,
x. Istecrih, *va* dislike.
Cerieh, Mecrouh, unpleasant.
Mecêrih, things unpleasant, annoyances.
Mecrouhe? unpleasantness.
Cerêhe, Cerêhiya, aversion.
ii. Cerrih, *va* disgust, revolt.
iv. Ecrih, *va* force (a person)

QRM

against his will, sala', to (a thing).

قرح Qarfl 3, ulcer.
Qaroufl, Maqroufl, ulcerous.
Qirriefl, covered with ulcers.
iv. Aqrifl, *v*. cause ulcers.
v. Taqarrafl, *vn* suffer ulcers.
(2) Qarâfl 8, pure limpid water.
Qariefla, native genius.
viii. Iqterifl, *va* improvise (a discourse). [genius.
Iqtirafl, gush or flow of native

كرخ Cerk, *s*. an engine.
Cerkâna 11, workshop, factory. Compare Jark, wheel.

كرم Ceriem, generous, noble.
Ecram, nobler, more generous.
Cerâma, generosity, honour.
Micrâm, very generous.
Mecêrim, generous deeds.
ii. Cerrim, *va* honour.
iv. Ecrim, d°(count honourable).
Mocerram, honoured.
Icrâm, *ger*. paying of honour.
iii. Cêrim, *va* emulate in generosity.
v. Tecerram, *vn* act nobly.
vi. Tecêram ean, *vn* be too noble for; scorn (an evil deed).
x. Istecrim, *va* account noble.
(2) Cerma, *nu*. 3, a vine.
Cerrâm, vine-dresser, gardener.

قرم Iqram, *v*. hanker after (flesh), burn with desire. *ger*. Qaram, craving.
Qârim, Moqterim, voracious.

QRM

Iqtirama, prize in war B.
(2) Qarma 10, 11 (*Gr.* κορμί), stump of tree. [roots.
ii. Qarrim, *va* tear up by the
v. Taqarram, *vp* be torn up.
(3) Qâourma, ragout, tender stewed meat (*Turk*).

قرمد Qarmied 11, tile (from *Gr.* κεραμίδ).

قرمط Qarmut, *va* contract, write in small hand; *cala'*, pinch, stint. [*x*.
Qarmata, small style of writing

كرمش Cermix, *va* wrinkle.
ii. Tecermax, *vp* of i.
Cermexa, a wrinkle.

قرمز Qirmiz, (kermes) cochineal.
Qirmiziey, scarlet c.

كرن Cerawân. See كرى, Cirâ.

قرن Qarn 3, horn, tip, corner, century.
Qorma, outer corner.
Iqrin, *va* couple.
Qarien(a) 11, fellow, mate.
Aqrân, *pl.* fellows, equals.
ii. Qarrin el êâên, *va* prick up the ears. See Qannix.
iii. Qârin, *va* associate to oneself.
Qirân, conjunction (of planets), crisis of time.
viii. Iqterin, *vp* be coupled.
Iqtirân, union of two.

CRS

كرنب Coronba, *as* cabbage.
Qarnabiet, cauliflower.

ترنفل Qaranfol, cloves, clove gillyflower.

كرنكت Cernec, battlement B.

قرنص Qarnus, *va* train (men) to war.
Qarnasa, discipline of war.

كركت Coro, fur pelisse *Turk*.
(2) Corciey 11, crane.

قرق Oqroq, *vn* cluck as hen,
Qorqa, *s.* brood of chickens hatched at one time B.

قرقع Qarqis, *vn* rumble, crackle, *va* bruit abroad.
Qarqasa, *ger.* rumbling; clang, report, rumour.
ii. Taqarqas, same as i.

كركب Cercib, *va* overturn.
Cerceba, *ger.* upsetting, confusion, a rumpus, a heap.
ii. Tecerceb, *vn* to tumble. *Compare* Cobb.

كركدن Cercedân, rhinoceros.
Also Cerceend, d°

ترقل Qarqal 11, a crook B.

كركم Corcom, saffron.

كرس Ceres = Cerez, cherries.

CRS

(2) Corsi 11, a chair, seat, *lit.* or *fig.*
ii. Cerris, *va* chair, enthrone, consecrate (a bishop).
(3) Corrâse, *nu.* quire of paper.
Corrâs, blank book, copybook.
(4) Cerosto, sawn timber.
(5) Cêrouse, Cêrouya (*Fr.* carrosse), coach.

قرص Oqros, *va* pinch, *lit.* and *fig.* (See Qrr, Qrâ), knap, nip, sting.
Qariey, Qorrâiy, stinging nettle.
Qorrâs, camomile.
(2) Qorsa, *nu.* 4, round mass (of dough), round cake, bun, roll. Bolus, large pill.
ii. Qarrus, *va* form into round masses.
Moqarras, round *n.*

قرنش Qarqoux, *s.* crackling. *vulg.* gristle.

قرقط Qarqut, *vn* whizz, rustle, crackle.

كرت Icret, *vn* roll, advance by rolling oneself. [away.
ii. Cerrit, *va* roll off, trundle

قرط Qort 3, 4, earring. See Okrot.
ii. Qarrut, *va* put earrings on (another).
v. Taqarrat, *vn* wear earrings.
(2) Qarit, *adj.* close cutting, penurious.
Miqrât, nippers.

QRX

ii. Qarrut, *va* pare, cut (nails or hoof) close; cut to the quick, exact severely *n.*; snuff (a candle).
Qirruit, shred, scrap *x.*
Qierât, weight of four grains, carat.
(3) Oqrot, *vn* rustle, whirr. See Qarqut.

كرث Ocroθ, *va* or iv. Ecriθ, *va* distress. [ing.
Cêriθ, Cerieθ, mournful, afflictviii. Icteriθ bi, *vp* be concerned
Ictirêθ, concern, regret. [at.

قرث Qorrêθ, leeks.

قرطل Qarrâl, pannier.

قرطم Qarrum, *va* cut close, crop (hair); dock, lop.

كرتك Cortêcieya, frock coat.

قرطس Qarrâs 11, sheet of paper, military cartouche.

كرش Cirx 3, paunch; stomach of ruminants.
(2) Ocrox, Icrix, *va* chase closely *n.*
x. has li. Cerrix, *va* wrinkle. But *vulg.* Cermix supersedes it.

قرش iii. Qârix or v. Taqarrax, *vn* act as broker *n.*
[Qarx 3, piastre, seems to be a corruption of Γarx.] [*v.*
(2) Qarx, the spermaceti whale

CRZ

كرز Cerez, cherries.

(2) Ikriz (*Gr. κηρύσσω*), preach (the gospel). *ger.* Cerez.
Cèriz, preacher.

قس Qasies 9, 8, priest, *sup.* Christian. But *pl.* 3 B.
Qosousieya, priesthood B.

قص Qosy, *va* clip with scissors. *Also* (2), narrate (a tale), cala', to (a person).
Qosâya, clippings.
Quyya, a narrative.
Aqâsuiy, annals, chronicles.
Miqayy, scissors.
(3) iii. Qâyuy, *va* retaliate upon, punish.
Quyây, retaliation, punishment.
(4) Qayy 3, Qayuiy, breast bone.

وكس Weces Yecis, *va* lessen, detract from; *fig.* disparage.
Weca, detraction.
ii. Weccis, iv. Aucis, *va* detract from, blame.

قوس Qaus, *pl.* Qisiey, *also* 4 ? a bow, an arch.
Qaus Qozeh, rainbow, bow of *the angel* Qozeh.
Qowais, little bow K.
Aqwes, arched.
Motaqawwis, Mostaqwis, arched (eyebrow) K.
ii. Qawwis, *va* arch, bend. *Also,* shoot with bow; shoot with gun. [Modern writers often spell the last Qawwuy.]

QSY

v. Taqawwas, *vp* be arched, bent; armed with a bow.

كيس Cies 4, purse, bag; the sum of 100,000 piastres.
(2) Ceiyis, refined, intelligent.
Ecyes, more refined, etc.
Ciyâse, intelligence.
Cowaiyis, pretty, elegant AL
Ecwes, prettier.

قيس Qies bi, *va* measure with.
Miqyâs el zeman, chronometer.
ii. Qayyis, *va* aim with gun AS.
iii. Qâyis, *va* measure, compare.
Qiyâs 8, measure, comparison, rule, analogy.
Qiyâsiey, regular.
Moqâyes, commensurate.
(2) Qiyâs 2, a chilblain B.
(3) Qiyâs, chintz for sofa-cover or curtains.
(4) Qiyâse 11, a lighter, a barge.

كسو Ocsou, *vn* attire oneself. *ger.* Cisê.
Cisê, *s.* vesture, *pl.* 8, Ecsiya.
Ciswa, Coswa 11, vestment.
Ecse', better clad K.
ii. Cessi, iv. Ecsi, *va* clothe.
v. Tecossê, *vp* be clad.
viii. Ictesi, *va* wear (a garment). *vp* be clad.

قسى Qâsi, rigid; generally *fig.* harsh, cruel.
[Qisiey, bows, *pl.* from Qaus.]
Qasêwa, rigour.
iii. Qâsi, *va* endure (hardship).

QSW

نصى نصو Oqṣöu, Iqṣa', *vn* be remote. *ger.* Qoṣöu, Qoṣâ.
Qoṣöu, remoteness.
Qârn, Moqṣa', remote.
Aqṣa', remotest.

نصع Qaṣaa, bowl, large saucer, tray in form of bowl, *esp.* for ladies' work.

كسب Icsib, *va* gain. *ger.* Cisb.
Mecseba, *nu.* 11, gain.
Cesseb, Cosoub, (man) devoted to gain. [earning.
v. Tecesseb, *vn* give oneself to Motecessib, careful, thriving.
viii. Ictesib, *va* gain for oneself. (This supersedes i.)

نصب Qaṣaba, *nu.* 5, cane, reed, tube, quill; a rood or pole to measure land (6½ ells long x.). *Also*, a country town.
Qaṣuiba, musical pipe.
Maqṣab, a cane brake.
Miqṣâb, *adj.* very reedy.
(2) Qaṣṣâb, *vulg.* butcher.
Iqṣub, *va* cut joints apart x.
(3) Qaṣab, gauze of gold or silver.

كسد Ocsod, *vn* be in little demand. *ger.* Cesêd, Cosoud, slackness of sale.
Cêsid, that sells slowly.
Ecsed, flat (market).

نصد Oqṣöd, *va* make for (a place); *also vn* with li, ila';

CSD

also aim, purpose, with 'en before verb.
Qâṣud 7, courier o.
Qaṣd, intention.
Qaṣda ͪ, on purpose.
Maqṣad 11, a design.
Qaṣâd, face to face with.
ii. Qaṣṣud, *va* make for (a place).
v. Taqaṣṣad 'en, *vn* purpose to (do, etc.).
(2) viii. Iqtaṣud fle, *vn* be moderate in, be frugal.
Iqtuṣâd, moderation.
(3) Qaṣuid, staff o. baton x.
(4) Qaṣuida, *nu.* 11, poem.

قصدر Qaṣdier, pewter [tin o.].

كسف Icsif, *va* eclipse (the sun). [But Ikaif, be eclipsed, as moon.]
Cisfa, an affront, slight B. disparagement.
Cosouf, eclipse of sun.
Cêsif, Cesief, in eclipse, sombre.
Cesêfa, dimness.
viii. Ictesif, *vp* be eclipsed.

نصف Iqṣuf, *vn* roar as thunder, dance heavily and noisily, sport rudely.
Qaṣf, *s.* sport, field sport.
'Ehl el qaṣf, sportsmen F.
v. Taqaṣṣaf, *vn* riot, indulge in noisy jollity, or in field sport.

كسل Icseﬂ, *va* lop (trees). *ger.* Cesêﬂa, lopping.
Cesseﬂ, lopper.

CSḤ

Cesieḷḷ, maimed, crippled, rickety
Ceaḷḷ, lameness.
Coséḷḷ, the rickets.

قسم Qâsiḷḷ, stiff, harsh to the touch (as a towel); stiff, cold, severe in manner.
Qaséḷḷa, stiffness, *lit.* and *fig.*

كسل Icail, *vn* be idle.
Cesoul, Cesêêl, idler.
Cealân, idle, *f.* -a, *pl.* 11, Cesêli. Cesêle, idleness.
vi. Tecêsel, *vn* dawdle.

قسم Iqsim, *va* divide (*vp.* Qosim). *ger.* Qasm.
Qism 4, a portion.
Qisma, portion, lot, destiny.
ii. Qassim, *va intens.* of i. distribute, allot. v. *vp* of ii.
vii. Inqasim, *vp* be divided.
iii. Qâsim, *va* dole out to, with *accus.* of person. viii. Iqtesim bain, *va* divide among.
(2) Qasm 4, an oath.
iv. Aqsim bi, *vn* swear by.
Aqsim sala', *vn* adjure, conjure (a person) x.
x. Istaqsim, *va* adjure, claim an oath from.
vi. Taqâsim, *vr* enter into common oath.

قسم Iqsum, *va* break to pieces, wreck (as *wind* wrecks). *ger.* Qasm.
Qusma, *nu.* fragment x.
v. Taqassam; vii. Inqasum, *vp.* of i.
(2) Qaivoum, southernwood.

QSR

قسقن Qosqoun, crupper to a saddle B.

كسكرى Cescêri 11, trivet, tripod B.

كسر Icsir, *va* break. *ger.* Cesr 3, a fraction.
Cesra, Cesora, fracture, rupture, defeat.
Ciarâ, *nu.* morsel.
Cosour or Cosourêt, fractions in arithmetic.
ii. Cessir, *va* break in pieces.
vii. Inccsir, *vp* be broken.

قصر Iqsur, *vn* be short, deficient; *can,* fall short of. *ger.* Qasr.
Qasar, Qosra, deficiency, insufficiency.
Qosôur, shortcoming, failure, incompetence, delinquency.
Qasuir, short.
Qasâra, shortness.
ii. Qassur, *va* shorten.
iv. Aqsur min, *va* interrupt from, cut short from, limit, restrict.
vii. Inqasur, *vn* be confined indoors.
viii. Iqtasur sala', *vr* restrict oneself to.
(2) Qasr 3, fortified palace.
Qaisar, Kaisar, emperor.
(3) Oqsör, *va* to cleanse, or full cloth.
Qassâr, a fuller.
Qusâra, art of the fuller.
(4) Qausara, cornice.
Moqausar, corniced.

QST

قِسط Qiṣr 3, portion, instalment, a railway *call* for one's share of payment.
ii. Qassut, *va* apportion fairly. Taqsier, *ger.* 11, an instalment. (Arbas taqâsier, four instalments).
viii. Iqtesut, *va* get one's share.

كِسْت Costebân, thimble.

كَتَكْ Costeo, clog of horse. Cestic, *va* clog, hobble (him).

كَت Cetcit, *va* giggle. *ger.* Cetcete.

قَت Qott, *va* cut across, nib (a pen). Qat, (not) at all.
(2) Qutt 5, cat; *f.* Qutta.
(3) Qutqut, drizzling rain.

وَقْت Waqt 4, time, moment. Mieqât, fixed time.
Mieqâtieya, periodical book, magazine (in literary sense).
ii. Waqqit, *va* fix a time.

يَقْت Yâqout 12, precious stone; *esp.* hyacinth, ruby, garnet (from *Gr.* ὑάκινθ).

قُوت Qout, Qoute 4, food, aliment.
Qout, *va* feed.
iv. Aqiet, *va* feed x.
v. Taqawwet bi; *also* viii. Iqtet bi, *va* live upon *or* by.
x. Istaqiet, *va* entreat for subsistence.

CTB

قَطا Qatâ, bird not unlike a pigeon.

كَتْع Ectes, (man) crippled in the arm.
Mectousa, crippled (hand).

قَطْع Iqtas, *va* cut, snap (a rope), interrupt, decide, go, make a breach (in friendship). *ger.* Qats.
Qatuiса, a rupture (of friendship).
Qutsa, bit, piece. Iqtâsa, fief.
Qâtus, sharp, severe, decisive.
Qâtus (7) el tarieq, highwayman, brigand.
Qotöus, a crisis.
Qatöus, critical.
ii. Qattus, *va* cut in pieces.
Moqâtasa, district, county.
vii. Inqatus, *vp* of i.
Inqitâs, interruption, intermission, breach of continuity.
viii. Iqtatus, *va* retain a fraction.
(2) Qatuis 4, small flock.

كَتَب Octob, *va* write; (Cotib *vp.*) *ger.* Cetb.
Citêba, writing.
Cêtib 7, scribe.
Citba, a copying of a MS.
Citêb 10, a book.
Cotobiey, bookseller.
Cottêb 11, primary school.
Cetieba, an edict, a writ; *also*, a squadron (of horse), a troop (of elephants).
Mecteb 11, writing place, counting house, school.

CTB

Mecteba, writing desk r.
Mectoub 11, epistle, letter.
iii. Cêtib, *va* address by letter.
Mocêtib, correspondent (by letter).
Mocêteba, correspondence.
ii. Cettib, *va* cause to write, teach to write; *also*, form a squadron of horse.
iv. Ectib, *va* cause to write, dictate (a letter).
v. Tecetteb, *vn* be formed into squadron.
viii. Ictetib, *va* write under dictation, register.

كَثَبَ Ocθob, *va* amass.
vii. Inceθib, *vp* be amassed (*compare* Ceθief).
Ceθieb 10, 9, 8, dune of sand, knoll of earth.
Ceθieba, mass? squadron? [See Cetieba.]

نَتَبَ Qatb 4, protuberance of back or belly B.   [B.
Abou qatb, humpbacked, humpy

قُطْب Qorb, iron axis of a mill; axis; pole; polestar.
Qorba, *su.* axis of mill.
(2) Qatb, *s.* tuck in a garment.
ii. Qarrub, *vn* contract the brow, frown.
Moqarrab, frowning.
(3) Qârubateⁿ, totally, all.

قَتَد Qatêd, *s.* the bush tragacanth or camel's thorn.

كَتِف Cetif 4, shoulder.

QTL

ii. Cettif, *va* pinion the arms behind (a man).

كَثَف Ocθof, *vn* be thick.
Ceθief, thick (trees, mist, cloud, body).
Ceθêfa, thickness, clumsiness.
ii. Ceθθif, *va* thicken.
vi. Tecêθef, *vn* grow thick, as liquids.

قَطَف Oqτof, *va* cull (fruit), gather in the vintage; snuff (a candle).
Qaτf 3, crop of fruit.
Qoτâfa, clippings, snuff (of candle) B.
Qaτâf, vintage x.
Qaττâf, vintager.
Maqτâf, fruit basket, pottle.
(2) Qaτnifa, coarse plush, shag; shaggy covering, fringed coverlet.

كَتْخُون Cetkouda, vicar, lieutenant.

كَتَل Cotle, a mass, lump.

كَثَل Ceuθel, poop, stern s.

قَتَل Oqtol, *va* kill (*vp* Qotil).
Qatl, homicide, beheading.
Qâtoul, *ger.* dᵃ?
Qitla, mode of staying.
Qatiel, slain person, *pl.* Qatle'.
Qâtil, slayer.
Qattêl, great slaughterer.
Maqtel, slaughter.
Maqtela, a carnage.
iii. Qâtil, *va* fight with.

QTL

Qitêl, Moqâtela, severe fighting.
iv. Aqtil, *vs* cause to kill, have (a person) put to death.

كتم Octom, *vs* conceal.
Câtim el sirr, secretary.
Cetonm, reserved, secret (man).
Mictêm, very secretive.
vii. Incetim, *vp* be concealed.

تنم Qâtim, *adj.* reddish black, sombre. Compare ᴌutm.
Qotma, *s.* (this same colour).

قطم Qaᴛum, close, near (B. *Rasibus*).

كتن Cettên x. Cottên c. linen; κιθών, χίτων, *also* Hebr.

قتن Qatien, starved, lean?

قطن Oqᴛön, *vn* reside. *ger.* Qoᴛöun.
Qâᴛun 7, resident.
Qaᴛuin 10, inmate of a house.
(2) Qoᴛn, cotton. Qoᴛna, *su.*
(3) Qoᴛnieya, Qaᴛâni, pulse, leguminous crops.
(4) Yaqᴛuina, *su.* gourd, melon, cucumber, etc.

كتر Cetiera, gum of tragacanth c. See Qatêd.

كثر Ocθor, *vn* be numerous, be frequent, happen often.
Ceθier 2, numerous.
Ceθieraⁿ, too much, often.
Ceθieraⁿ mâ, it is often that.

CX

Ecθer, more numerous.
Ecθeriey, of frequent usage x.
Ecθerieya, majority (in voting).
Ecθerieyaⁿ, generally x.
Micθêr, excessive (in words), redundant.
ii. Ceθθir, *vs* increase, multiply.
iv. Ecθir, *vs* do in excess.
Moceθθir, plural (in grammar).
Mocθir, rich x. [animals.
vi. Tecêθer, *vn* multiply as
x. Istecθir, *vn* be covetous.
(2) Ceuθer, nectar; a river in Paradise.
Ceθiera, resin of cedar x.

قتر Iqtir, *vn* be sparing. *ger.* Qatr, parsimony. [stint.
ii. Qattir, iv. Aqtir, *vs* grudge, Moqattir, frugal.
v. Taqatter, *vn* same as i.

قطر Oqᴛör, *vn* drip, drop. *ger.* Qaᴛr.
Qoᴛra, a drop, driblet.
Qaᴛrân, pitch.
x. Istaqᴛur, *vs* distil (spirits).
iv. Aqᴛur *vs* cause to drip.
(2) Qoᴛr 4, region of heaven, diameter of circle.
(3) Quᴛâr 10, file, chain (of camels). Quᴛâraⁿ, in file.
ii. Qaᴛᴛur, *vs* bring side by side, set abreast.
vi. Taqâᴛar, *vn* go in file.

كش Cixx, *vn* shrink as a garment B. [In x. Cᴌᴇs.]
(2) Coxx, Cexcix, *vs* whisk away (flies) B.

CX

(3) Cexcex, trimming of a gown; a frill.

نش Qaxx, stubble.
Qaxx el baĦr, seaweed.
ii. Qaxxix, *va* form straw, become ripe, as wheat.
Miqaxxa, brush of palm leaves.

نوش Qoux, *adj.* small in person, short (man) v. x.

نيش Qâyix, a thong.

نشع Iqxas, look! see! al
(2) Qaxic, inconstant x.

نشعم Qaxsam, king vulture v.

نشعر Qoxasriera, Iqxusrâr, shivering, shuddering of the skin. [shudder.
Iqxasurr, *vn* shiver with horror,

نشب Qaxab, a callosity b.
Moqaxxab, callous.
ii. Qaxxib, *va* make callous.

كشف Icxif, *va* uncover, reveal, detect, descry.
iii. Cêxif, *va* acquaint.
vii. Incexif, *vp* be revealed.
Incixâf, detection.
viii. Ictexif cala', *vn* become aware of, detect.

نشف Qaxif, squalid.
Motaqaxxif, shabby.

كشمش Cixmix, sultana grapes.

QZ

قشمر Qaxmara, a farce, low comedy.
Qaxmariey, farcical.
ii. Taqaxmar, *vn* play farce.

كشر Cexir, snarling, morose.
Icxir, *vn* show the teeth, grin, snarl. *ger.* Cexr, Cixra.

قشر Qaxr 3, Qixra, *nu.* bark, peel, scale.
Aqxar, bare, stripped.
Oqxor, *va* peel, strip of skin, wipe a wound.
ii. Qaxxir, dº shell (beans).
Moqaxxar, cleansed (barley).
(2) Aqxar, excellent, perfect?
(3) Qaxar, crimson x.

قشط Iqxat, *also* ii. Qaxxut, *va* scrape off, skim off. ii. *fig.* skim or scour (the seas). Baste (in sewing) c.
Miqxat, hoe or rake.

كز Cizz, *vn* dry up, contract x.
Cezz, dry; *fig.* dry in style.
iv. Ecizz sala', *vn* clench (the teeth) b.

نز Qazz, gauze? unspun silk.
(2) Qoxêx, glass.
Qoxêziey, of glass.
Qaxxêx, glazier.
(3) Qozz min, *vn* leap away from; *fig.* shun. In fig. sense, rather v. Tcqazzez min, abhor.
Tqazqaz min, dº

WCZ

وكز .'ecas Yeciz, *va* stab.
Mowêciz, poignant (grief).

كوز Couz 9, milk jug.
Ecwêz, pitcher K.
Cewêziey, vermilion B. (colour of red pots?)

قوز Qauziey, a lamb B.

قيظ Qiez, *en* be burning hot (weather).
Qaiz 3, 4, midsummer.
Qaizuiy, of midsummer.
Maqâz, Maqiez, summer encampment or dwelling.
v. Taqayyaz, *en* pass the summer (in a place). [K.
Moqayyaz, summer provisions

كزبر Cozbora, *nu.* coriander.

قزدير Qazdier *or* Qazdier, pewter.

قزل Qazll, Qizll 4, cruets, raw seeds for seasoning.
Teqâziell, condiment.
Iqzell, *va* season (broth, meat).
ii. Qazzill, d⁰ and *fig.* season (a discourse).
Miqzell, cruetstand.
(2) Qozell, angel of the clouds.
Qaus Qozell, rainbow.

كظم Iczum, *va* check, controul, stifle (passion). *ger.* Cozöum. See Okzom.

قزم Qazma 10, spade B.

VOL. II.

RWY

قزن Qazên 10, cauldron.
(2) Qazien, parsimonious B.

R.

رأى Râi, opinion, *pl.* Arâ.
Râ, he beheld. Ara', Ara', I behold.
Rouya, a vision, idea.
Ro'ouya, vision, power of sight.
iv. Arie [*vulg.* Arwi], *va* show.
iii. Râyi, *v.* make semblance.
Riyâ, hypocrisy.
Morâyi, hypocrite.
viii. Irtêyi, *en* consider, debate inwardly.
Mortê, considerato (opinion).
Rawiey, Mortewi, Mosterwi (w for '), considerate (person).
Rawieya, consideration, thought.
(2) Rayâ 2, flag, standard.

ورا Warâ, *prep.* behind, beyond.
v. Tewarrâ, *en* abscond.
(2) Riya 2, a lung.
Marie, windpipe c. (also feeding, nourishing). [teuch.
(3) Toura, Teura, the Punta-
(4) Touriya, allegory B.

ورور Warwar, the bee-eater (bird).

روى Irwi, *va* quench (thirst) c.
ii. Rawwi, *va* drench, saturate.
Morie? nourishing (drink).

24

RWY

viii. Irtewi, *vp* be satiated (with blood).
(2) Irwi, *va* (*modern*) narrate.
Râwi 7, narrator.
Riwâya, a narrative.

ع‍ Rasâs, the rabble.
(2) Rasris, *va* recruit. *ger.* Rasrasa, refreshment.
ii. Terasras, *vn* thrive, recover strength.
Moterasris, (boy) growing up.

ورع Waras, reverential fear.
Waris, Waries, scrupulous.
Risa, scrupulosity x.
v. Tewarras min, *vn* scrupulously abstain from.

يرع Yarâsa, reed from which pens are made.

رع‍ Rous, *va* surprize and astonish r. Also in *vp* Ries, be surprized, *either* painfully, be aghast, *or* admire.
iv. Aries, *va* amaze, terrify.
Mories, terrible.
viii. Irtâs, *vp* be aghast.

رعي Irsu, *va* feed (cattle).
Râsu, shepherd, grazier. [14.
Rasuiya, a subject (of a prince)
iii. Râsu, *va* tend, respect, observe; accommodate (by cheap sale) B.
Risâya, respect, observance.
Morâsâya, d°.

RSX

viii. Irtesu, *vn* graze. Hence a new root Rets.
(2) Irsa', *vn* itch B.

رعب Irsab, *va* fear.
Rasba, fear, timidity.
Rasuib, timid.

رعبل Rasbala 11, a tatter.
Rasbil, *va* tear to rags.

رعد Irsad, *vn* thunder.
Rasd 3, thunder.
Rassâd, that thunders much.
Rasâda, a thundering.
Rosda, a quaking.
viii. Irtesud, *vn* quake, tremble c.

رعف Rasf, flow of blood c.
Irsaf, *vn* bleed (as the nose), drip.
Rosâf, same as Rasf c.
Rosâfa, dripping of meat.
x. Istarsuf, *va* cause grease to drip.

رعن Arsan, silly, weak, garrulous c.

رعص Irsas, *va* frisk, swarm.
iv. Arsus, *va* vibrate.
viii. Irtesus, *vn* throb, wriggle? vibrate.

رعش Irsax, *vn* tremble. *ger.* Rasx.
Rasax, tremor. Rasxa, d°.
iv. Arsux, *va* flurry.
viii. Irtesux, *vn* quake.

RSX

Rasux, *adj.* in tremor.
Raccâx, d° *intens.*

رب Rabb 4, lord ; Lord God.
Rabba, mistress x.
Ribâba, dominion x.
Rabbâni, belonging to a lord x.
a Rabbi x. [reignty x.
Robonbieya, lordship, sove-
v. Terabba, *vn* play the lord.
Robbân, commodore of a squadron? Gol. navarcha (ship-
  master, pilota. Acts xxvi.11).
Terabban, *vn* be admirable of a
  fleet x.
(2) Robba, immense number x.
Robba, Robbama, very often.
  (*mod.*) probably, generally,
  perhaps.
(3) Robb 5, 3, fruit jelly, *Pers.*
(4) Ribba, clover, lucerne.
(5) Ribâba, covenant, quiver c.
(6) Rabâba, *ns.* violin.

ارب 'Erib, *adj.* active, clever,
  assiduous x.
Ma'êraba, necessary matter.
Ma'rab, *pl.* 11, Ma'êrib, an
  occasion.

ورب Warib, oblique ; *fig.* degenerate.
i. Warib Yourab, *vn* degenerate,
  decline. *ger.* Warb.
Teuricb, obliquity.
ii. Warrib, *va* insinuate indirectly, as by parable.
iii. Wârib, *va* deal indirectly
  with, intrigue against, overreach.

RBW

روب Roub, *vn* be thick as milk,
  curdled.
Rouba, Rauba, thick mud,
  slush, clotted milk, etc.
Râyib, Raubân, torpid (as with
  blood stagnant).
ii. Rawwib, *va* thicken (a fluid).
v. Terawwab, *vn* nearly — i.
Mirwab, cream vessel.
Râyib, clotted (milk, etc.).

ريب Raib, Rieba, strife,
  doubt.
Râyib, Rayyâb, (thing) causing
  doubt or suspicion x.
iv. Arieb, *va* inspire doubt.
viii. Irtêb bi, be in doubt of,
  demur to.
Irtiyâb, doubt, suspicion.
Mortêb, suspected x.
Δou rieba, inspiring doubt,
  justly suspected.

ربو Rabwa, highland ; *pl.* roba'.
  Also, Râbiya 12, d° wold x.
Rabâwa, eminence.
Râbiya, pile of stones as token.
Robou, augmentation x.
ii. Rabbi, *va* bring up, rear,
  nurture to manhood.
Morabbi, foster-father.
Terbiya, education, rearing.
Marba', place of rearing.
Marbie, educated, reared.
iii. Ribâ, usury = Ribâll.
Râbi, usurer c.
iv. Arbi, *va* increase (one's
  capital) by usury x.
Morbi? usurer x.

RDW

Morûbi, usurer ʙ.
(2) Morabba', preserved (fruit)
 = Morabbab. See Robb.
Arbiyûn, lobster.

رُبَا Marbâ', ladder ᴋ.

ربع Arbasa, four; *fem.* Arbas.
Robe 4, a quarter.
Râbis, fourth.
Robâsuiy, quadriliteral (verb).
Δou el arbas, quadruped.
Arbasâ, Wednesday.
Arbasoun (-suin), forty, fortieth.
Marbous, doubled in four.
Morubbas, square.
ii. Rabbis, *va* arrange into square, do four times. [square ᴋ.
v. Terabies, *vn* sit with legs
(2) Rabies, spring season.
Rabsuiy, vernal.
Marûbies, spring rains ᴋ.
iii. Râbus, engage for the spring ᴋ.
iv. Arbus, *vn* enter the spring season (as the year, the sun).
(3) Rabsa 5, a party, faction. (In Egypt) the cabinet ᴋ.
(4) Yarbous 11, jerboa, small kangaroo of Africa.

ربد Arbad, *adj.* lurid red.
Robda, *s.* dº.
v. Terabbad, *vn* become lurid red, as the sky, put on a louring aspect, as the countenance.

ربض Irbuḍ, *vn* lie on the bosom, as a quadruped.

RBT

iv. Arbuḍ, *va* put to rest, lull (pain). [ᴋ.
Marbuḍ 11, enclosure for sheep

ربح Ribḥ, *s.* gain, profit. *ger.*
Rabḥ. See Râbi.
Irbaḥ, *va* gain.
iii. Râbiḥ, play the stockjobber, make gains. [ness.
Morâbaḥa, large gain, gainful-

ربك Orboc, *va* entangle, mix.
ger. Rabc. viii. Irtebic, *vp.*
Irtibês, confusion. See Olboc.

ربس Orbos, [deposit sediment ʙ. *But see* Orsob.]
Raubas, *va* refine (metal) ʙ.
v. Terabbas bi, *vn* lie in wait for v.
Moterabbas, watcher of the market, a jobber.

ربط Orboṭ, *va* tie, bind. *ger.* Rabṭ.
Rabṭa, a bale, a tie.
Ribâṭ 10, a tie, bond, band.
Rabieṭ, *adj. fig.* high strung, intense.
Ribâṭ (*pl.* Arboṭ?), *fig.* a pledge, affiance.
Robâṭniya, a conspiracy, a cabal.
Rabieṭ, (a beast) tied up.
Marbuṭ, stall *or* place where a beast is tied.
Mirbaṭa a fastening, a knot.
iii. Râbuṭ, *va* tie oneself to, *i.e. fig.* attend to, watch. [For this also is said *vulgo* Irbuṭ li. Sic ʙ.]

RBT

Morâbuṭ, assiduous ᴋ.
vi. Tarâbaṭ, ᵥᵣ complot, conspire, league.

رد Rodd, ᵥₐ send back; give back, repay, requite; drive back, repel.
Ridda, apostacy ᴋ.
ii. Raddid, ᵥₐ repel.
iii. Râdid, ᵥₐ make retort to.
v. Teraddad, ᵥₙ go backwards and forwards; *fig.* waver. *Also* as ᵥₐ frequent (a place).
vi. Terâdd, renounce (an engagement), recant ᴋ.
viii. Irtidd, ᵥₙ turn back, apostatize.
Irtidâd, apostacy.
Mortidd, apostate.

رض Roḍḍ, ᵥₐ bruise, break into pieces. [ᴋ.ᴄ.
Miraḍḍa, crusher, mallet, flail
Raḍraḍ, ᵥₐ batter to pieces.
Raḍraḍ, rough gravel or broken flint ᴋ.

أرض 'Erḍ, the Earth, land; *pl.* 'Erâḍu, lands, wide estates.
'Erḍuiy, earthly.

ورد Warda, *nu.* 2, a rose.
Wardiey (Warid?), rosy.
ii. Warrid, ᵥₐ rouge (the cheeks).
Mowarrad, rouged.
v. Tewarrad, ᵥₚ of ii.
Tewarrod, rose-colour ᴋ.
(2) Warad Yarid, ᵥₙ arrive. *ger.* Woroud, arrival.
Wârid, (merchandize) arriving.

RWḌ

Wârid wa ṣâdir, imports and exports.
iv. Aurid, ᵥₐ bring in, convey; present; adduce, quote.
Ierâd, income.
vi. Tewârad, ᵥₙ concur ᴋ.
Tewârod, concurrence.
(3) Aurdi (ôrdi), camp c. But ʙ. writes Ḷaurḍu. It is Turkish. *See* Aurṭo, legion.

رود Rond, ᵥₙ go to and fro, as the scout of an army; gad about, as a gossip; glide about. Roud fle, frequent (a place).
Rond, gliding movement ᴋ.
Rowaid, *dimin.* gentle continuous movement. Rowaidⁿ, gently! gently!
x. Isteried, frequent (a place)?
Merâd, Mosterûd, haunt, customary place of resort.
(2) iv. Aried, ᵥₐ will, wish.
Mâ oried, Lâ oried, I do not choose, I will not.
Irâda, will (of God, of the king).
Morâd, thing wished for; sense of a word.
iii. Râwid-oh ᶜalu' xai', ᵥₐ make demands of him concerning something.
(3) Mirwad 11, earring ʙₑ.

روض Rauḍa, flowery prairie, flower garden; *pl.* Riyâḍ.
(2) Rouḍ, ᵥₐ train (a colt). *ger.* Rauḍ.
ii. Rawwuḍ, dᵒ intensive.
Morouḍ, trained.

RWḌ

Riyâḍa, exercise, training; (asceticism?) exact science; mathematics.
Riyâḍuiy, ascetic.
Riyâḍuiya, asceticism.
vi. Terâwaḍ, *vn* exercise oneself in rivalry.
viii. Irtâḍ, *vp* of i. be trained. Also *vn* live ascetically.
x. Isteruiḍ, *vp* be exercised and formed (said of the mind) x.

رذى Radi, *f.* Radieya, 8, bad, Ardâ, worse. [evil.
Radâwa, badness.
iv. Ardi, *va* make bad, spoil, ruin x.
(2) Ridâ 8, a mantle.
ii. Raddi, *va* mantle, clothe in a mantle.
v. Teraddâ, *vn* wear a mantle.

رضى Irḍa' sala', san, *vn* consent to; — fie, bi, be pleased with. *ger.* Riḍâ, consent, satisfaction. Ṣan riḍâhi, with his good pleasure.
Ruḍwa, consent.
iv. Arḍu, *va* please, satisfy.
Irḍa, Terḍuya, satisfying (another). [compromise.
vi. Teraḍâ, *vr* please mutually;

رذى iv. Arai, *va* harass, wear out s.

ردع Irdas, *va* repress, check. *ger.* Rads.
viii. Irtedus san, *vp* of i. *also vn* abstain from.

RḌL

رضع Irḍas, *va* suck (the breast).
Raḍus, a suckling.
Raḍuis, foster brother.
Marḍas 11, mother's breast x.
iv. Arḍus, *va* suckle.
Morḍus, wet nurse.

ردب 'Irdab 11, quarter of wheat.

رضب Raḍâb, water in the mouth, drop that exudes b.

ردف Ridf 4, croup of horse, buttocks of woman.
Radaf, appendix (of book), conveyance (of an action).
Râdif, coming after, coming in succession.
Radief, troops in reserve.
ii. Raddif, *va* subjoin.
iii. Râdif, *va* be substitute for.
iv. Ardif, *va* cause to ride behind, place later?
Mordif, posterior to x.
vi. Terâdaf, *vn* follow in series.
viii. Irtedif, *va* ride behind (another). [horse.
Mortedif, hindrider on one

ردخ Ordok [*also*, Orḍök x.] smash, crack (nuts). *ger.* Radk.

رذل Raḍiel 6, base, vile.
Arḍel, baser.
Raḍiela 11, vice, baseness.
Roḍêla, refuse (of the people).
ii. Reḍḍil, prostitute, vilify.
iv. Arḍil, *va* deprave.

RAL

vi. Terâaal, *en* grovel.
x. Istirail, *va* account base.

رْدم Irdim, *va* block up (with rubbish).
Radm, rubbish, ruinous masses of a wall, barrier x.
Ridâm, *adj.* unworthy r. (rubbishy?)

رْدن Rodn 4, cuff to a sleeve.
ii. Raddin, *va* add cuffs to (a sleeve).

رف Raff 3, shelf in a niche AL Bg. flock of birds B. c. (of cattle x.)
Rafrif, *en* flap the wings, spread the wings (over eggs, or over little ones).
Rafraf, skirt or vallance, hanging portion of drapery x.

ورف Warief, wide spreading, luxuriant.
ii. Warrif, iv. Aurif, *vn* spread wide (as a shadow, or as the branches of a tree).
Worouf, luxuriance.

رأف Ra'ouf, Râ'if, benevolent.
Râ'fa, benevolence.
Raufa, d° x.
Râ'f, be benevolent.
iii. Râwif, *va* treat kindly.
v. vi. Terâ*af *ɛala*, yearn over, compassionate.

رِيف Rief, *s.* cultivated border of land (on river side, or suburban), the inhabited and cultivated country (*Lat.* rus, opposed to *el badou*, the open wilderness).
Riefiey, inhabiting the *rief* x.
Raiyif, productive x. [*rief.*
v. Terayyaf, pay visit to the

رفأ Rifâ', peace, tranquility x. [superseded in modern style by Rifâhe?]
(2) Irfa', *radarn. ger.* Rafâ' B. x.
Rafya, a darning B.
Raffâ', a darner.
[Irfâ' bain, make peace between (those who have quarrelled) x.]

رفع Irfaɛ, *va* lift up, raise (eyes, voice, shoulders, a weight), exalt (a person). *ger.* Hafɛ.
Marfaɛ, platform.
iii. Râfiɛ, *va* summon by appeal before a judge.
Rafɛa, elevation, high rank.
v. Teraffaɛ, *en* exalt oneself; ɛala', overtop, tower above.
vi. Terâfaɛ, *er* summon one another mutually before a judge.
viii. Irtefiɛ, *ep* of i. [nence.
Irtifâɛ, elevation, height, eminence.
Rafieɛ, superior in rank or quality, superfine.
Rafâɛa, the being high (in price or rank), elevation of pitch.
Arfaɛ, more elevated.
Marfaɛ, raised stage, platform x.
Roffɛa, quilting of a woman's dress at the hips c. x. the wearing of a bustle.

RFꜤ

رنس Orfoá, ʋa renounce, abdicate. ger. Rafá.
Râfuá 12, a renegade, dissenter, dissident, sectary.
Râfuáuiy, sectarian.
Rafuiá, adj. cast away x.
Marfouá, dᵒ· x.

رفه Irfah, ʋa live at ease.
Râfih, Rafieh, Rafhên, living in ease and comfort.
Rafâhe, ease and comfort.
ii. Raffih, ʋa afford to (another) ease and plenty; treat indulgently; compose, quiet x.
iv. Arfih, dᵒ· x.
v. Teraffah, x. Isterfih, live indulgently.
Morufiah, tranquil, prosperous.

رفل Orfol, ʋa flaunt, display oneself. [at ease.
Râfil, partic. flaunting, strolling

رفق Rifq, benignity.
Rafieq 6, comrade.
Rifqa (Rofaqa), fellow travellers.
Rifâq, Rifâqa, sociability.
Morâfiq, Rifâqicy, sociable.
iii. Râfiq, ʋa escort.
v. Teraffaq bi, make oneself comrade with.
vi. Terâfaq, or live as comrades.
(2) Mirfaq 11, elbow.
viii. Irtefiq, ʋa rest on one's elbow, be well supported.
x. Isterfiq, ʋa ask support from.
Temarfaq, take for one's elbow cushion or support x.

RFB

رفس Orfos, Orfos, ʋa kick (as horse). ger. Rafs.
Rafse (x.), Rofse (c.), a kick.
v. Teraffes, ʋa be overfed, pampered.

رفش Rofs, wooden paddle, dung shovel x.
Mirfax, winnowing shovel B.

رفز Irfiz, throb (as artery), tick (as a watch).
Râfiz, artery.

رغ Raɼɼa (?), water melon Bₙ.

روغ Roup, ʋa dodge, sneak.
iii. Râwiɼ, deal craftily with; try to trip up; circumvent B.
v. Terawwaɼ, ʋa roll, wallow in the dust x.
vi. Terâwaɼ, wrestle together;
— bi, cheat (a person) B.
Rawwâɼ, prone to sidelong ways x.; a sneak.
Rawâɼ, crooked dealing x.
Riwâɼa, Riyâɼa, wrestling-ground x.
Rowaiɼa, trick, roguery x.

رغو Roɼwa, Raɼâwa, froth.
ii. Raɼɼi, iv. Arɼi, ʋa foam, froth.
(2) Irɼi, ʋa squall, scream, laugh as hyæna, bellow x.

رغب Orɼob, ʋa (Irɼab with fle, ila') desire [with min or ʋan, be disinclined to x.].
Roɼba bi, a desire for.

RGB

Rorba, avidity.
Rarbât, things desired.
Raṛieb 5, desirous.
ii. Raṛṛib, ɛa cause to desire, entice.
Marṛoub, desired, desirable.
Marâṛib, things desired.
Arrab, more covetous c.

رغد Raṛd, affluence.
Arrad, more commodious c.
Raṛied, opulent.
Raṛṛâd, abundant, existing in profuse quantities.
Irṛad, ɛn live in affluence.
(2) Raṛieda, farina (arrowroot) boiled in milk x.

رغف Raṛief 8, unleavened flat cake, round or oblong, baked on the hearth; a scone.

رغم Raṛm, outrage, despite; cala' raṛmihi, to his displeasure, in despite of him.
Marṛama, repugnance.
Râṛim, under humiliating constraint.

روح Rûḥ, wine x. qu. spirit?
(2) Râḥa, nu. palm of the hand; 2, handful. Râḥât el ḍcheb, handfuls of gold ox.
(3) Rouḥ 3, spirit, soul, vital principle, (ardent) spirit (of brandy).
Rouḥâni, spiritual, incorporeal, spirituous.
Rouḥânieya, spirituality.
Rieḥâniey, explosive? (powder).

RḤB

(4) Rieḥ, fem. 3, wind.
Rieḥa, dᵒ.
ii. Rawwiḥ, ɛa air, fan.
Mirwaḥa 11, a fan.
Marieḥ, well-aired, airy.
Marouḥ, windy.
Arwaḥ, more airy.
Râyiḥa 2, scent, also 12.
(5) Râḥa, s. rest.
iv. Arieḥ, ɛa cause (a beast) to rest. Marâḥ, resting-place, burial-place.
viii. Irtoḥ, ɛn rest oneself.
x. Isterieḥ, (mod.) dᵒ Isterâḥa, respite, taking breath, rest.
(θ) Rouḥ, (mod.) ɛn go. ger. Rawâḥ, for Seir or Δiheb.
Râyiḥ, going.

رحى Raḥa', Raḥâ, a handmill, millstone; pl. Arḥuya.
Irḥu, v. turn a handmill x.

رهب Réhib 9, monk.
Rehbân, dᵒ 11.
v. Terehheb, ɛn become a monk.
Robbânieya, monkery.
(2) Irbeb, ɛa fear.
Rehba, s. fear.
iv. Arhib, ɛa alarm.
Marheba 11, a terror.
ii. Rehbib, ɛa intimidate.
Terhieb, menace.

رحب Raḥb 4, wide, spacious.
Raḥuib, dᵒ. pl. 11, Raḥâyib, wide estates.
Raḥâba, spaciousness.
Irḥab, ɛn be spacious. ger. Roḥb, Raḥb.

RḤB

Marḥub, *va* welcome.
Marḥabá beo! welcome!
ii. Raḥḥub, iv. Arḥub, *va* enlarge.
Raḥba, area, *esp.* large.

رهدل ii. Terehdal ɛala', *vn* act the bully towards.

رهج Irhej, *vn* glitter, glimmer. SHINE.
Rehj ayfar, orpiment.

رهل Rebil, *adj.* flaccid, relaxed in muscle.
Irhel, *vn* be flaccid.
v. Terehhel, *va* d⁰.
Moterehhil, lazy (bird) r.

رحل Irḥal, *vn* migrate, travel (*san*, from). *ger.* Raḥl.
Râḥul 7, traveller.
Râḥula 12, camel, *monture.*
Riḥâla 11 (*also* Raḥl), camel's saddle.
Riḥla, art of camel saddler x.
Roḥla 10, route, journey.
Raḥuil, migration, departure.
Raḥoul, useful for carrying a rider x.

رهم Marḥam 11, medical plaister, cataplasm.

رحم Raḥm 4, the womb.
Raḥma, *s.* mercy.
Irḥam ɛala', *vn* have mercy upon.
Raḥuim, Raḥöum, Raḥmân, merciful (God).
Arḥam, more merciful.

RWJ

Marḥama, mercy (of God).
Marḥöum, on whom God has had mercy, *i.e.* deceased.
ii. Raḥḥum, *va* express pity for.
v. Teraḥḥam, *vn* as i.

رهن Irhen, *va* pawn, pledge. *ger.* Rehn 5, a stake.
Rehien 6, hostage.
Rehiena 11, thing mortgaged.
Marhoun, given in pledge.
ii. Rehhin, *v.* bet, wager.
iii. Rêhin, *va* d⁰ with accus. of the other party.
iv. Arhin, *va* stake (a thing), same as i.?
vi. Terêhen, *vr* enter into pledges mutually.
viii. Irtehin, *va* accept a pledge.
Mortehin, mortgagee, holder of thing pledged (*but also in* x. responsible).
x. Isterhin, *va* demand a pledge.

رحق Raḥuiq, Roḥiq, the best wine c. x.

رهرب Morehrut, flaccid (b. *ter*).

رج Rojj, Rajrij, *va* agitate. *ger.* Rajj.
viii. Irtijj, *ep* of i.
Irtijâj, vibration. [army.
ii. Terajraj, *vn* waver as an

روج Rouj, *vn* move rapidly as a wave; go off quickly (in the market).
Râyij, *adj.* current (money); (goods) selling quickly.

RWJ

Rawâj, quick sale.
ii. Rawwij, *va* make current, pass (money), quicken (salu).

رجو Orjou, Irjâ, *va* hope.
Rajâ, *s.* hope.
v. Terojjâ, *va* entreat.
viii. Irteji, *va* hope x.
x. Isterji, *va* entreat.
(2) Arjâ', *pl.* tracts, districts r.

رجع Irjas, *vn* return. *ger.* Rojouɛ.
Rajs, *ger.* repeating, restoring c.
Rajsa, return, resurrection.
Rajies, *s.* refuse, dung; *also*, cud of ruminants=Jirra.
Morjas 11, return x.
ii. Rajjis, *va* cause to return, send back. Refund. Remand. Repel. Repeat. Echo.
iii. Râjis, *vna* recur (as fever), recur to, revise.
Morajjas, poem with a refrain to the stanzas.
Morâjasa, recurrence.
Terjies, repetition, the refrain or chorus of a song.
x. Isterjis, *va* reclaim, resume, recover. *Also vn* desire to return (to God), *i.e.* pronounce the religious formula, "From Thee I came, to Thee I return."
(2) Râjis 12, yard of a mast.

رجف Irjaf, *vn* quake. *ger.* Rojouf.
Rajfa, shock of earthquake.
Rajjâf, trembling all over.

RJM

iv. Arjif, *va* cause to tremble; agitate (a people) by alarms.
Irjâf, seditious agitation; *esp.* in *pl.* 11, Arâjief.

رجح Irjaḥ, *vn* tilt. *ger.* Rojouḥ, preponderance, odds. *Also ger.* Rajḥ.
Orjouḥa 11, a swing x.
Marjieḥa, a hammock [=Jaujeḥâna c.]
Marjiḥ, *va* swing in a swing.
ii. Rajjiḥ, *va* cause to preponderate. Bias. Prefer.
iii. Râjiḥ, *va* ponder.

رجل Rijl, *s.* foot; *pl.* Arjol.
Râjil 6, foot soldier x. In *Egypt.* râgil), a man.
Rajol 5, man (*Lat.* vir). *Syria.*
Rojail (Rowaijil x.) mannikin.
Rojailiey, mannish (woman).
Rajjâl 11, manly person.
Rajoulieya, manliness.
Marjalieya, manhood.
iv. Arjil, *va* cause to go on foot.
v. Terajjal, *vn* set foot on ground; dismount; land.
(2) viii. Irtejil, compose or recite verse *impromptu.*

رجم Orjom, *va* pelt with stones. Mark a grave by casting stones. *ger.* Rajm.
Rojma 10, Rajam 5, tumulus of stones.
Rajiem, stoned, execrable x.
Marâjim, stones hurled, *i.e.* invectives. [stones.
viii. Irtejim, *vp* be heaped, as

RJM

(2) Terjomân, *s.* interpreter 13, from Jewish *Targum*.
Terjim, *va* translate.
Terjima, translation.
Moterjim, translator.

رجز Rija, Rijz, *s.* impurity, idolatry.
(2) Rajez, *s.* a peculiar metre or stanza of six couplets x.

رخ Rakk, *adj.* flabby o.
viii. Irtikk, *vn* be flabby.
(2) Rokk, *s.* fabulous bird, roc; condor?

أرخ ii. 'Errik, iv. 'E'rik, *va* date, set a date on.
'Orka, fixed epoch x.
Tériek 12, date; chronicle.
Mote'warrik, chronicler.
Mo'warrak, dated....

رخ Riek, *vn* be flabby x.

رخو رخى Rakâ, Rakwa, Rakâwa, looseness.
Irka', *vn* be loose.
iv. Arki, *va* loosen.
Rakou (Bg.), Rakiey (Al.), loose.
Rakioy, relaxed, at ease x.
Arka', looser.
viii. Irteki, *vp* of iv.
x. Isterki, d⁻
Irtikâ, Istirkâ, relaxation, flabbiness. Mosterki, feeble.

رخل Yorkal ileibi, interesting.

RWL

رخم Rakiem, shrill and sweet of voice r. opposed to yakib.
Rokouma, sweetness of voice r.
Irkam, *vn* be soft of voice.
ii. Rakkim, *va* soften (sounds).
(2) iv. Arkim ɛala', *vn* sit on (eggs) r.
(3) Rokâm, alabaster, black basalt.

رخص Itaky, abundance.
Itoky, cheapness.
Rakiey, cheap.
iv. Arkiy, *va* cheaper.
viii. Irtekuy, *va* buy cheaply.
x. Isterkuy, *va* depreciate.
(2) Raky, tender (meat), gentle (treatment), supple.
ii. Rakkiy, *va* indulge.
v. Terakkay, *vn* deal gently, be accommodating, fie xai'.
Rokya, indulgence.
i. Orkoy (Rakoy), *vn* be tender, delicate.
iii. Râkiy, *va* coddle; compromise, concede.
Morâkaya, a compromise.
vi. Terâkay, indulge oneself, coddle oneself.

رخت Rakt, trappings of a horse, splendid harness.
ii. Rakkit, *va* caparison.

ورل Waral 4, large African lizard x.

رول Bowâl, Raiwâl, Riyâlo, foam from horse's mouth.
Abou riyâla, foaming (horse).

RWL

ii. Rayyil, *v.* foam (as horse) B.
Rawwil, d°. x.
(2) Riyâle 2, Spanish dollar AL.
  ship of admiral x.

رم Rimm, *vn* be rotten (as bone).
Ramicm 5, carious, rotten.
Rimma, *nu.* 10, dry bone.
(2) Rammim, Ramrim, *va* refit,
  repair, patch up.
x. Istcrimm, *vn* need repair.

ورم Warim Yarim, *vn* swell.
Waram, *s.* 4, a swelling.
Warmân, swollen.
ii. Warrim, *va* swell.
Mowarram, swollen.

روم Roum, *va* desire. *ger.* Roum.
Marâm, thing desired.
ii. Rawwim, *va* cause to desire.

ريم Raima, *s.* froth, foam.
ii. Rayyim, *v.* froth.
Rowâm, *s.* foam x. *See* Rowâl.
(2) Riem, Ri'm, *pl.* Ar'âm,
  white gazelle x. fallow deer
  v. *dorcas* ?

رمى Irmi, *va* cast, throw,
  shoot [pelt, hit]. *ger.* Rimya,
  Rimâya.
iii. Râmi, *va* pelt.
vi. Terâmâ, *vn* throw themselves
  together in heaps.
Râmi, *pl.* Româya, shooter,
  darter.
Marmiey, *part. p.* shot.
Marma' 11, butt to shoot at x.
Mirma' 11, projectile x.

RML

رمد Ramâd, *s.* ashes.
Armad, *adj.* ashcoloured.
ii. Rammid, *va* bake in the
  ashes.
(2) Ramad, rot in cattle c. x.
  ophthalmia?

رمض Ramiđ, *adj.* torrid.
Irmuđ, *va* roast on hot stones.
  ger. Ramđ x.
iv. Armiđ, *va* parch, scorch, as
  does the sun.
v. Terammađ, *vn* be overpowered
  with the sun's heat.
viii. Irtemuđ, *vp. fig.* be con-
  sumed by inward fire x.
Armađ, scorched by the sun x.

رمح Irmaħ, *vn* gallop (as horse).
  ger. Ramħ.
Ramħa, a gallop.
ii. Rammiħ, *va* cause to gallop.
vi. Terâmaħ, gallop in squadron
  for review.
(2) Romħ 5. spear.
Râmiħ, a spearman.
Rammâħ, maker of spears.
Rimâħa, art of spearmaking.
Romaiħ, small javelin. *Also,*
Irmaħ, *va* pierce with a lance,
  spur x.

رمل Raml 5, sand. Ramla, a
  sandy strip.
(2) Ermel, widower; Ermele,
  widow; *pl.* Erâmil. (Ermele, implies *poverty* and
  desolation x.)
v. Terammal, be bereaved.

RMN

رمس Rommâna, *nu.* pomegranate; *also*, a steelyard.
Roumâna qabbâni (*sic*), a steelyard B.

رمق Irmaq, *v.* glance at. *ger.* Romouq, Rimâq.

رمش Ramxa, a glance, twinkle of the eye, a moment.

رمز Irmiz, *vn* nod, wink, make sign.
Ramz 3, gesticulation, signal. Enigma.

رن Rinn, *vn* sound, tinkle.
Ranna, *s.* sound.
Ranien, *s.* twanging.

رنب 'Arnab 11, a hare.
(2) Arniba, tip (of nose or tail) v. *also* the groin B. But see Arnima.

رنح ii. Ranniñ, *va* make dizzy.
v. Terannoñ, *vn* stagger (as with wine) x.
Ranñ, dizziness x.

رنق Raunaq, *s.* lustre, brilliancy, *lit.* or *fig.* x. c.

رنم Arnima, the groin B. perhaps corrupt for Arbina.

رنش Ternixân, blue cornflower B.

WRC

ركك Rceiec, thin, slender, flimsy, frail.
Recc, *vn* be thin, feeble.
x. Isteriec, *va* account flimsy, slight.
(2) Rocce, distaff.
ii. Rccoic, *vn* stammer, as a drunken man.
(3) viii. Irticn, *vn* tremble, hesitate, be in doubt, falter.
(4) Recoê, echo B. x.

رق Riqqa, delicacy, *lit.* and *fig.*
Raqieq, delicate, subtle.
Raqâyiq, subtleties c.
Riqq, *vn* be delicate, fine.
ii. Raqqiq, *va* comminute, pulverize.
iv. Ariqq, *va* make delicate.
v. Teraqqaq li, *vn* be compassionate to.
(2) Raqq, parchment, vellum.
Roqâqa, *nu.* 5, thin cake, parliament? piecrust.
Raqqâq, tartmaker.
(3) Riqq, thraldom.
iv. Ariqq, *va* enthrall.
Riqqieya, enthralment.
Raqq 5, a thrall.

ورق Waraqa, *nu.* 4, a leaf, a note, a lamina.
Waraq, paper.
Warrâq, paper maker, stationer.
Aurâq, scrip.
Wirâqa, art of paper-making x.
Warieq, full of leaves x.

ورك Waric 4, hip of the body.

YRC

يرك Eriece, *ns.* 11, sofa of the new bride, throne.

روك Rouc, *s.* a commune?
Mâl el rouc, communal property B.
Rouciey, communal B.

روق Rouq, *vn* be serene, limpid.
ii. Rawwiq, *va* clear, clarify; strain a liquid.
Râyiq, limpid.
Rawâq, serenity.
(2) Ruwâq 8, Rowâqa, porch, covered balcony. [B.
(3) Râq 2, a layer B. bedclothes

ريق Rieq, *s.* saliva in the mouth.
Icser el rieq, *v.* breakfast B₅.
Sato' el rieq, while fasting.
v. Terayyaq, *vn* breakfast B₅.
Terayyoq, *s.* breakfast.

رقو Terqowa 11, clavicle of the neck.

ركي Irqa', *vn* step up, mount x.
Marqa', Mirqâya, ladder, scala.
ii. Raqqi, *va* cause to mount.
Terqiya, promotion.
v. Teraqqâ, *vn* mount up.
Teraqqi, augmentation, growth, progress.
viii. Irteqi, d°.
Retaqa, *nn.* degree of dignity x.
Irtiqâ, ascent, advancement.
(2) Irqâ', *va* enchant B. X.
Râqi 12, enchanter.

RCB

Râqiya, enchantress.
Roqya, *pl.* roqa', enchantment.
Avllâb el roqa', sorcerers.
Raqiey, enchanting, fascinating.

ركع Irces, *vn* bow the head, fall prostrate or on the knees.
ger. Rocouc.
Récis 7, bowing in supplication.
Recra 2, an inclination of the body in prayer.

رقع Irqas, *va* mend, patch.
ii. Raqqus, *va* patch all over, cobble.
vi. Terâqas, *vn* faddle.
Roqsa 5, piece of cloth, scrap, a rag, bit of paper, a note or piece of writing paper.
Moraqqas, patchwork.
x. Isterqus, *vn* need repairs.
(2) Raqies, fatuous B.
Roqsa, fatuity B.
iv. Arqus, display fatuity x.

ركب Irceb, *va* ride, mount (a beast), embark, make voyage.
ger. rocoub.
Récib 7, rider, voyager.
Recceb, d°.
Recb, cavalcade.
Ricéb 10, stirrup, cavalcade.
Ricba, mode of riding x. o.
Recoub(a) 11, beast for riding.
Ricébiey, officer who holds the king's stirrup.
Marceb 11, ship. [coach.
Marceba 2, omnibus, public
(2) Rocba 2, the knee.

RCB

(3) ii. Reccib, *va* cause to mount; *also*, compose, compound; frame, construct (the skeleton of a beast), compound (the ingredients of a potion); set up (a picture on its frame), graft (a tree).
Morecceb, composed, composite.
Motcreccib, agglomerate K.
v. Terecceb min, consist of.
(4) viii. Irtecib bi, *v.* perpetrate (an evil deed).

رقب Orqob, *va* watch.
Roqoub, watching, observation.
Râqib, observer, rival.
Raqieb 6, guardian, watcher, rival.
Riqba, circumspection K.
iii. Râqib, watch for. [vation.
Morâqaba, (astronomical) obser-
Marqab(a), watch tower 11.
v. Teraqqab, *va* watch habitually; wait.
viii. Irtaqib, *vn* lie in wait ?
(2) Raqba, *nu.* the neck 2.

ركض Orcoḍ (pronounced Orguḍ, with English g, at Aleppo), *vn* run. *ger.* Racḍ.
Recceḍ, Riccieḍ, swift B.
Racḍa, an impulse K.

رقد Orqod, *vn* sleep. *ger.* Roqoud (Raqd, Roqd c.).
Roqâd, sleep.
Marqad 11, dormitory F. but *mod.* cemetery. [*fig.*
iv. Arqid, *va* lull to rest, *lit.* and
Morqid, soporific.

RQS

رقل iv. Arqil, *vn* trot F.
Irqâl, a trot F.
But in Barbary, Hercil, trot; in Syria, Herwil, scamper.

رقم Orqom, *va* inscribe, engrave, embroider, ceil.
Raqm 3, a character, letter.
Raqiem, inscribed slab.
Arqam, striped black and white.
Mirqam, bodkin for embroidering.
Marqoum, striped, rayed; denoted, marked out, prescribed ?
(2) Raqma, verdant savannah.

ركم Orcom, *va* heap up.
vi. Terécem, viii. Irtecim, *vp.* be accumulated, agglomerated.

ركن Ircen ila', *vn* lean, rest upon. *ger.* Rocoun.
Rocouna, firmness, constancy.
Rocn 4, pillar; *fig. pl.* the grandees are *pillars* of the state.
Recien, staid, grave K.
Moreccen, supported, propt up.
Rocein, small pillar K.
Mircen, stone washtub.
ii. Reccin, *va* settle, appease, set in its place, compose.

ركس Ircis, *va* reverse, intervert, overturn F.
viii. Lrtecis, *vp.*

رقس Orqoṣ, *vn* dance. *ger.* Raqs.
Raqṣa, a dance.

RQ3

v. Teraqqay, *vn* dance up and down.
ii. Raqquy, iv. Arquy, *va* cause to dance. [gun.
Raqqây, dancer, trigger of a

رقط Arqaṭ, spotted with black on white, or white on black [or black on *yellow*, as the leopard?].
Araqruyoun, a bur.

رقش Arqax, spotted; perhaps identical with Arqaṭ.
ii. Raqqix, *va* embellish. Compare Barqix and Abrax.

ركز Orcoz, *va* fix, fix in, set firm F. *ger*. Recz B. *also*, deposit sediment B.
Ricze, a pause B.
Mercez 11, centre of circle; site; place. [metal.
(2) Reciez, vein of precious

رص Royy, *va* arrange in rows; (dishes on the table, stones in building, boxes on a raft), pile up.
Rayya, a row, pile. [sonry.
Marÿouy, fitted close, as in ma-
Raÿuy, massive.
vi. Teràyy, be tightly pressed together.
(2) Raÿây, lead.
Raÿâya, a leaden bullet.
Raÿÿây, seller of lead.
Moraÿyar, covered with lead.

رصرص Rayruy, *va* chill, cool B.

RSD

رأس Râ's, head, point; *pl*. Arwos; *fig*. chief, *pl*. Ro'ous.
Râyis, Raiyis, Ra'ies, captain, *pl*. 6, Ito'wosê.
Raiyise, mistress.
Riyâse, headship.
Rieyies, supreme, chief captain.
Rawwês, main, principal.
Morawwas, pointed B. F. jagged?
ii. Rayyis, *va* make chief x.
Râ'seⁿ, *adv.* by the head, *i.e.* on equal terms with others.

رسو Orsou, *vn* be an anchor; be fast. *ger*. Rosou.
Rêsi, at anchor, fixed.
Resiey, fixed, constant.
iv. Arsi, *va* moor, anchor, fix steadily.
Morse', brought to moorings.
Marse' 11, mooring grounds, road, harbour.
Mirsêya, anchor.
Mirse' 11, mooring rope.

رسع Iryas, *va* bruise (grain) between two stones.
ii. Rayyuy, adjust, build (a nest), incrust with jewels, inlay. See Royy x.
Moraÿyas, bejewelled.

رسب Orsob, *vn* fall as sediment. *ger*. Rosoub. v. Teressab, d°.
Resoub, dregs, sediment.
Resoubiey, sedimentary.

رصد Orṣod, *va* lie in wait for. *ger*. Rayd. *Also*, Orṣöd, *va*

RSD

expunge, cancel. *sie* B. *bis*.
Biffer, Rayer.
Rasad, astronomical observation.
Râyud, Rayuid 7, lier in wait.
Rayöud, watchful.
Rasad, *coll.* 4, men in ambush.
Marsad 11, (place of) ambush.
v. Terayyad, *en* same as i.
Rayyâd, Rayadiey, police who watch against smugglers? (*douanier* K.) coastguard, preventive service, patrol.

رصف Irsuf, *va* range stones together, make a pavement. *ger.* Rayaf.
Rasf, paved path, pavement.
Rasf, Rayuif, a quay B.
Miryâfa, paviour's thumper.
ii. Rayyuf, *va* range, arrange.
vi. Terâyaf, *en* form in line of battle K. Comp. Rayy and Joff.
(2) Raysa, kneepan B.

رصك Irsek, *en* stick fast, be wedged tight, be firm. *ger.* Rosouk.
Rêsik, firm; firm (in the faith), well-grounded (in science), rooted and grounded.
Arsek, firmer rooted.
iv. Arsik, *va* ground, root, establish, jam tight.
v. Teressek, *vn* take deep root.

رسغ Rosy 4, fetlock of horse, wrist of man.

رسل Resoul 6, envoy, apostle, messenger.

RT

Risêla 11, mission, legation, a dispatch, an epistle.
iv. Arsil, *va* dispatch an envoy.
Irsêl, dispatch, sending.
iii. Rêsil, *va* (with fie, bi, sala', of the thing) be in *epistolary* correspondence with a person.
Morêsil, a correspondent.
Morêscla, correspondence.
vi. Terêsel, *pl.* be in mutual epistolary correspondence.
Irsêlieyét, exports.

رسم Orsom, *va* sketch, draw, map out, trace. *ger.* Resm.
Mirsem 11, a pencil.
Resm 3, sketch, trace, method.
Reemiey, official.
Rosoum, ordinances, taxes.
Marsoum 11, edict of prince.
Marsoumêt, appointments, *i.e.*, salary of an officer.
viii. Irtesim, receive a public order K.

رسن Resen 4, *or pl.* Arson, a halter. [Resn.
Orson, *va* halter (a horse). *ger.*
Marsen 11, horse's nose where the halter rests K.
(2) Torsêna, arsenal, from root Tors, shield.

رصن Rayuin, stout, staunch (as a ship), solid (as a man's intellect).
iv. Arsun, *va* make stout, strengthen.

رطب Moratrut, abundant B.

Rθ

رث Riθθ, *vn* wear out (as clothes).
iv. Ariθθ, *va* wear (clothes) out.
Riθθc 5, 10, trumpery, old upholstery. Rabble.
Roθicθ, worn out, threadbare.
Roθéθc, threadbareness.
Râθθ, shabbily dressed.

ارت Aurte, legion B. See Aurdie.

ورث Wariθ, Yariθ, *vn*, *va* inherit from; with accus. of thing. *ger.* Wirθ, Wiriθc, Irθ. Wâriθ, heir.
Mauraθ, Micrâθ, inheritance, thing inherited. *pl.* Mawâriθ.
ii. Warriθ, iv. Auriθ, *va* make Mouriθ, testator. [an heir.

ورط ii. Warriт, *va* precipitate.
v. Tewarraт, *vp* of d°· or *vn*.
x. Isтeuruт, *vn* leap down a precipice.
Warra, precipice, deep gulf, pit.
Mauriт, precipice.

رثى Irθi, *va* mourn, sing a dirge. *ger.* Reθie.
Roθê, dirge, elegy x.
Reθθêya, hired female mourner.
Marθiya 11, elegy, funeral discourse.

رتع Irтes, *vn* browse, graze. *ger.* Reтs. *Comp.* Irsu viii.
Reтs 3, prairie, rich grazing land. Marтes 11, d°·

RTL

ii. Retlis, iv. Artus, *va* pasture (cattle).
Retsa, living in clover x.
Mortes, one who lives in clover.

رتب Rétib, regular, unchanging, continual; *s.* fixed salary, *pl.* 12.
Rotba 10, grade, rank, ordinance, liturgy.
ii. Rettib, *va* institute, classify, arrange, sort, assort.
Marteba 11, rank, class.
(2) Marteba, sofa-mattress.

رطب Irrub, *vn* be fresh and moist.
Raтb, fresh, tender.
Roтüb, *pl.* juicy plants.
Roтab 5, fresh date.
ii. Raттub, *va* moisten, etc.
Morrub, abounding in juicy plants.
Roтöuba, juiciness, freshness.

رتج Ortoj, choke up, block up. *ger.* Retejân.
Martonj, (road) blocked up.
iv. Artij, d°· In passive, impersonally with sala'; Ortij salaihi, obstruction arose against him.
Mortej, impassable x.
iv. Artij salaihi, disable him, disqualify him, exclude him.
viii. Irtetij, *vp* of i. *pass.* Ortotij salaihi, he is disqualified.

رتل ii. Rettil, *va* chant (sacred words), sing in mosque or

RTL

church; chirp, as the cricket and insects.

رطل Ratl, Rotl 4, a pound of weight.

رطن Orton, vn jabber. ger. Ratâna.

رتق Ortoq, va consolidate (by welding, as a blacksmith). *fig.* repair, restore. ger. Rotq κ.
viii. Irtetiq, vp of i.
Retq and Fetq are opposites.

رش Roxx, va sprinkle. ger. Raxx. [garden).
ii. Raxxix, d° *intens.* water (a
v. Teraxxax, vp of d°
Roxx 5, slight shower.

ورش Warxa, s. workshop B.

ريش Riexa, nu. a feather 5.
ii. Rayyix, va feather (an arrow).
Raiyix, adj. Morayyax, well-feathered.

رشا Roxâ', a fawn, pl. arxâ'.

رشو Orxou, va bribe. ger. Raxou.
Raxwa, a bribe; pl. Roxa'.
Raxou, bribery.
iii. Râxi, va win over (by bribes).
viii. Irtexi, vn receive bribes.
x. Isterxi, require bribes.
Mortexi, Mosterxi, venal.

رشد Roxd, Raxâd, rectitude.
Roxd, prudence, years of discretion, orthodoxy.

RZ

Raxied, prudent.
iv. Arxid, va guide wisely.
x. Isterxid, seek wise guidance.
Râxid, orthodox. [riage κ.
Roxda, Rixda, legitimate marriage.
Marxad 11, the right path.
Morxid, spiritual guide, director.
(2) Raxâd, cress.
Raxâd el barr, horse-radish κ. (= fijl flârr).

رشف Irxif, Orxof, va sup, sip, quaff B.
v. Teraxxaf, drink in sips.

رشح Irxaf, vn ooze, sweat. ger. Raxfi, trickling.
Mirxafia, sweating cloth of horse, undercloth.
v. Teraxxafi, vn exude; drip, as the nose.
Roxfi, dripping at the nose AL
(2) ii. Raxxifi li, va educate for.

رشن Arxien, measure of four spans Bg. a yard.

رشق Orxoq, va fling (κ.)
iv. shoot.
Râxiq, slinger, archer.
iii. Rûxiq, va pelt.
(2) Raxicq 10, slim, nimble.
Raxâqa, nimbleness, litheness of movement.

رز Rezzo, nu. an iron staple, a loop.
(2) Rezze, a rap c. κ.
(3) Rozz, rice.
Arozz, d° r.
Marezze, rice ground.

RWZ

روز Rouz, *va* try, put to proof B.

ريز Raize, cambric Bg.

رزأ Rozeʼ, damage; *pl.* Rezêyâ, misfortunes c.
Reziya, bad fortune v.

رزع Irzeɛ, *va pop. t.* drub, pommel B. See Irvaɛ, bruise, crush.

رزم Rizma 10, a package.
Rozma, "une grosso," twelve dozen B.
Orzom, make a package, pack together. *ger.* Rezm x.
ii. Rezzim, dº·

رزن Orzon, *va* poise in the hand to try the weight x.
Rezien, Rêzin, grave in manner, serious. Rezêna, gravity.
v. Terezzen, behave with gravity.
(2) Ranzena 11, Rezouna, window with niche or recess.

رزق Rizq, goods, victual.
Orzoq, *va* bestow the necessaries of life (as God); vouchsafe, give in grace.
Rêziq, a father who feeds.
El Rozzêq, God.
Rizqa 2, daily food, supplies.
viii. Irteziq, *vn* cater for oneself.
x. Isterziq, *vn* ask or seek a livelihood.

SWY

س. ﺱ.

سوﺀ Souʼ, *s.* evil; *pl.* 4, Eswâ. Before another noun, it looks like an *adj.* as Sou bakt, badness of luck, *i.e.* bad luck.
Siey, *adj.* evil.
Eswâ, worse v.
Mesêya, an evil deed, offence.
Lâ sieya ma, especially. [Perhaps = Lâ bâs, no harm, no evil; *for*, Not the worse if. Compare the Gr. formula, Not least, for, Especially.]
iv. Esie, *va* do amiss, illtreat.
Isêya, bad conduct, illtreatment.
(2) Senʼa 2, *pubes;* poil des parties genitales B.

سوى Sewâ, *adv. vulgo,* side by side, alike, together. Often repeated, Sewâ sewâ, side by side, just alike. *Also* Siwâ, Siwaʼ, (in more classical style) beside, except.
Sewley, *adj.* even, level, straight.
Ɛalaʼ sewâyaʼ, in the direction of.
ii. Sewwi, *va* adjust, arrange. [This verb is widely used at Aleppo, *for* settle, manage, do (anything)]. [worth.
iii. Sêwi, *va* be equal to, be Yosêwi dirhemaⁿ, it is worth a drachma.
Mosêwâya, equivalence; equability (as of style?).
Mosêwi, equable, tempered; equivalent to.

SWY

iv. Eswi, *va* level, flatten, make unimportant.
v. Tesewwâ, *vp* of ii.
vi. Tesêwâ, *vr* be mutually equal.
Motesêwi, equal, each to each; parallel.
Tesêwic, equality (as of citizens?), parallelism. [But rather, Motewêzi, parallel.]
viii. Istowi, *vp* be equalized, moderated, tempered; be cooked *or* ripe.
Mostewi, cooked (meat), ripe (fruit) AL
Istiwâ, equality, equalization.
Katt el istiwâ, the Equator.

صوى Uswi, *va* squeal, as a brute B.
Sōwwa, *s.* echo B.

اس 'Es, myrtle.
(2) 'Eses, foundations.
Esês, *pl.* 10, Osos, the basis.
ii. 'Essis, Wessis, *va* found, establish.

وس Weswia, *va* whisper, suggest. *ger.* Weswesc 11.
Weswâs, suggester (of evil), Satan, a tempter.

وسى Wesiya, common property? a commune?
'Erḍ el wesiya, the village common; rabies el wesiya, common pasturage B. *Communes.*
(2) iii. Wêsi, *va* console (a person).
Mowêsêya, consolation.

SSY

وصى Wasuiya 14, a commandment (of God), a man's last will and testament.
ii. Wassu lcho bi, bequeath to him; instruct an ambassador.
Wasuiy 8, trustee, executor.
Mowassu, testator.
Mowassa' lcho, legatee.
Tesusuiya, instruction (to an ambassador).

رسح Wesis Yeses, *va* be wide.
viii. Ittesis, dº (commoner).
Sesa, Wossa, width, capacity of volume; opulence.
Wêsis, Wesies, wide.
Ittisês, extent, width.
Mottesis, extended, extensive.
ii. Wessis *or* iv. Ausis, *va* make wide, enlarge.
Mouses, opulent.
v. Tewesaes, *vn* have plenty of elbow room, be at ease.

ساع Sêsa 2, hour; a watch or clock; any short time.
Sowaisa, a little moment.
Sesâtiey, watchmaker.

سيع Sisês, mortar of mud and straw. [mortar.
ii. Seyyis, *va* daub with such

سعى Issa' fie, li, *vn* drive at, ply at, exert oneself on. *ger.* Sesui, effort, course, enterprize; a drove (of cattle) B.
Sêsu, courier; *pl.* Sosâya.
Mesa' 11, an effort.

ṢʿB

صعب Ṣaʿb, difficult, painful.
Yaṣʿab, it is hard, painful.
— ṣalaiyⁿ, it pains my feelings.
Ṣoṣöuba, difficulty.
Mayâṣub, difficulties.

سعد Isʿad, vn be fortunate.
ger. Seʿd 3; also Seʿâda,
Soʿöuda, good fortune.
Seʿuid, fortunate.
Esʿad, more fortunate.
iii. Sêʿud, va assist; reinforce.
Moṣêʿada, reinforcement.
iv. Esʿud, va prosper, make
fortunate (said of God).
(2) Sêʿud 12, the forearm.
Sêʿuda 12, duct in the body.

صعد Uṣʿad, vn go up, mount.
ger. Ṣoʿöud. [Egypt.
Ṣaʿuid, the highland, esp. of
Min yöʿd, from above.
Ṣöʿdaⁿ, upwards; henceforth.
Ṣaʿöud, acclivity, steepest part
of an ascent.
ii. Ṣaṣʿud, va (in chemistry)
sublimate.
Moyaṣʿad, sublimated.
iv. Aṣʿud, va send up, carry
up, help up.
v. Teyaṣʿad, vn ascend as vapour, evaporate. Rise from
the bosom, as a sigh. Rise,
as prices.

صعف Soʿaf 3, furniture of a
bride, upholstery.
Seʿafa, a supply, aid, succour ɒ.
iii. Sêʿuf, va supply (a person)
with a thing.

SB

Seʿâfa, subvention, supply.
iv. Esʿuf, va dᵒ F. also, aid,
succour (a person) ɒ.

صعف Teyaṣʿafl, vn limp, hobble.

سعل Isʿal, vn cough. ger. Soʿâl,
Soʿla, s. cough.

صعلك Ṣaʿlouc 11, indigent.
Ṣaʿlic, va impoverish.
ii. Tayaṣʿlec, vp be impoverished.
Tayaṣʿloc, impoverishment, indigence.

صعق Iṣʿaq, va strike (as lightning) x.
Ṣâʿuqa 12, thunderstorm.

سعر Sisr 4, price, rate of prices.
(2) Soʿâr, fury.
Seʿrân, furious; pl. Seʿra'.
Isʿar, va stir up (the fire);
enrage, infuriate.
Misʿar, a poker.
Seʿrin, va infuriate.

سعوط Seʿöuṭ, Ṣaʿöuṭ, s. snuff
(a medical appliance).

سعتر Seʿter (Ṣaʿter), the herb
savory.

سب Sobb, va revile, insult by
words. ger. Sebb.
Sobba, s. insult, railing.
iii. Sêbb, va scold, revile.
Moṣêbib, reviler.
vi. Teṣêbb, pl. scold mutually.
Osbouba, matter of quarrel x.

SB

Sebbâba, *index*-finger, first-finger. [tive.
(2) Sebab 4, a cause, a substan-
Bi sebab, because of.
ii. Sebbib, *va* cause, occasion.
Sebabiey, belonging to the cause
   x. an adjective x.
v. Tesebbab, *vn* sell by retail.
Motesebbib, a retailer, a small dealer. [Zebab].
(3) Sebieb, horse hair (*comp.*
Sebieba, *nu.*
Tesebeeb, *vn* curl, as hair; be curly, crisp.

سبّ Söbb, *va* pour out (water), melt (tallow or metal); *vn* empty itself (as a river).
v. Tasâbb, *vn* d°·
vii. Insubb, *op* of i.
Sabab 4, *ger.* of i. the streaming down of water.
Söbba, a small quantity of water poured out.
Masabb, mouth of a river.

سوب Sawâb, rectitude, success; the right side, merit.
Saiyib, Sayoub, right to the mark x. Sâyib, d°· c.
Soub sala', *vn* go right to the mark x. impinge upon.
ii. Sawwib ila', *va* direct toward.
x. Istaswib, *va* approve as right.
iv. Asuib, *va* alight upon, as an arrow; hit (the mark); strike (as calamity strikes).
Mosâb, stricken (by calamity).
Mosuiba 11, a calamity.
Saub, direction (of an arrow),

SBS

sido (of a mountain), quarter (of heavens or wind).

سيب Sieb, *vn* go at random; as an animal at large.
Sêyib, going without guide; sacred (animal) at large; emancipated slave; *morally* uncontrouled, an abandoned person.
Sêṣibaⁿ, *adv.* wildly.
ii. Seyyib, *va* set at large; abandon (a person) to his own devices.

سبي Isbi, *va* make prisoner, carry captive, win the heart of.
viii. Istebi, d°·
Sebiey, *pl.* Sebâyâ, a captive.
(2) Siebâ, *s.* tripod, trivet c.

سبي Sabi 9, a boy.
Sabieya, girl, *pl.* Sabâyâ (but *pop.* Bint 5).
Sobaiya, little boys x.
Sabwa, childishness.
Sabwiey, childish?
Sabâ, boyhood.
Osbou, *vn* be childish x.; ila', wanton after on. νεάζω.
vi. Tasâbâ, behave as a child.
x. Istasbi, count, treat, as a child.
(2) Sabâ, east wind, a breeze? (poetically as a *pleasant* wind?
b. translates Zephyr by rieß Sabâ, so c.), wind of Saba?

سبع Sebs, *f.*; Sebsa, *m.* seven.
Sêbis, seventh.

SBS

Sebsöun (-uin), seventy, seventieth.
'Osbous 11, week (pl. Esêbies).
Sobous 11, week ʙₛ.(pl.sebâyis).
Sobs 4, a seventh part.
(2) Sebos 5, f. Sebosa, fierce beast.
Mesbasa, land of fierce beasts.
Mesbous, infested by dᵃ˙

ﺻﺒﻊ 'Usbas 11, finger.
Maybous, pointed at with the finger (in admiration).
(2) Movabbas, pronged spade ʙ. gridiron ʙ.

ﺳﺒﺪ Sebad, haircloth.
(2) Sebada, Sepada, a basket.
Sebad, Sebât, bin for corn.

ﺳﺒﻎ Sêbiɣ, profuse (gift, rain, tail).
ii. Sebbiɣ, iv. Esbiɣ, va lavish.
vii. Insebiɣ, vp be lavished.

ﺻﺒﻎ Osboɣ, va dye, tint; dip. ger. Sabɣ, Sûbâɣ.
Subɣ, 4, immersion; baptism.
Subɣa, a baptism, a religion ᴋ.
Sabbâɣ, a dyer. Subâɣa, s. dye.
Subɣiey, seller of dyes ᴋ.

ﺳﺒﺢ Isbaḥ, vn swim (be prolix ᴋ.). ger. Sebâḥa.
Sebbâḥ, good swimmer.
iii. Sêbiḥ, vie with in swimming ᴋ.
iv. Asbiḥ, cause to swim.
(2) ii. Sebbiḥ, adore.
Sobḥân, s. or ger. adoration.

SBQ

(Sobḥân Allâḥ! praise be to God!) [praise.
Sobḥa 10, an ejaculation of Sobohât, praises (i.e. excellencies) of God ᴋ.
Sebbouḥ, Sobbouḥ, adorable ᴋ.

ﺻﺒﺢ Söbḥ 4, dawn of day.
Sabâḥ, morning.
Söbḥuiy, of the morning (matutinus).
Sabieḥ, fair, handsome.
Sabâḥa, beauty.
iv. Asbiḥ, vn dawn.
(2) Musbâḥ 11, lamp (gener.).
viii. Ustabiḥ, vn use a lamp.
(3) Aybaḥ, adj. reddish black.
Sobḥa, dº· s.

ﺳﺒﻴﻞ Sebiel 10, path, lit. or fig.
Ibn el sebiel, traveller.
(2) Sebil, adj. long streaming (hair) ᴋ.
Sobla, a shower.
iv. Esbil, va let (the hair) stream, dishevel ʙ.; pour down (tears, rain) ᴋ.
Sebcla 5, mustache?
Esbel, having long mustaches.

ﺳﺒﻦ Sabiena, apprenticeship, novitiate ʙ.
(2) Sâboun, soap.
Masâbin, soap works ᴏɴ. 9.

ﺳﺒﻚ Isbic, va smelt, fuse.
ii. Sebbic, dᵃ˙
Sebiece 11, ingot of metal.

ﺳﺒﻖ Osboq, va precede. ger. Sebq.

SBQ

Sêbiq, preceding; in front.
Sêbiqaⁿ, formerly.
Sebaq, stake, deposit made before a race x.
Sebq, previously ox.
Sêbiqicya, priority.
Mcsbouqicya, posteriority.
Sewâbiq, prior events. [race.
iii. Sêbiq, *va* vie with in the
Mosêbaqa, a race of speed.
vi. Tesêbaq, *pl.* race together.
viii. Istebiq, outstrip, arrive before.

ــبر Osbor, *va* probe (a wound).
ger. Sebr (viii. d⁰. x.).
Misbar 11, Misbâr 11, a surgeon's probe.

ــبر Oxbor, *vn* wait patiently
(*vulg.* wait). *ger.* Sabr, patience.
Oxbor sala', endure under.
ii. Sabbir, *va* cause to be patient (said of God).
iii. Sâbir, *va* endure (a person) patiently. [suffering.
iv. Axbir, *va* harden against
v. Tasabbar, *vn* put on patience.
viii. Uxtabir, *vn* persevere.
Sabier, Sabour, Sabbâr, enduring, very patient.
(2) Sâboura, ballast; from Lat. saburra.
(3) Sabr, prickly pear.
Söbbaira, d⁰.

ــبت Sebt, *s.* sabbath, Saturday; *pl.* Esbot, or 3.
Osbot, *vn* rest, sleep, observe the sabbath.

SWD

iv. Esbit, *va* make drowsy.
Mosbit, soporific.
(2) Sebat, bin for corn (Sebad).
(3) Sebte, a (long) space of time, Fs. x. Lâ yoxuiboom xai* *el sebte*, nothing shall *ever* befall you.

ــبط Sibṭ 4, a tribe of Israel.

ــد Sodd, *va* bung up, block up.
ger. Sedd.
Sodd 4, barrier, obstacle.
Sidâda, *ns.* bung, cork.
Mesedd, place of a barrier.
vii. Insidd, *ep* of i.
(2) Sedied, just (thing).
Sedâd, rectitudo x.
ii. Seddid, direct aright, correct.
(3) Sodda, a gate, threshold; *esp.* said of the *king's* gate; soddat el melic, "*the Porte*"
x.c. (not in B.).

ــد Södd san, *va* repel one from, set one against. *ger.* Södoud.
v. Tasaddad li, *vn* meet face to face, confront.
Sadad, turn, crisis?
Sala' xadad, on the business of.
El riefi, elleti ana fie xadadhe, the wind about which *I am speaking.*

ــد Wisêd 10, 11, pillow, bolster. [fort?
ii. Wessid, *va* bolster up, com-
v. Tewessed, *vn* pillow oneself, take one's ease.

ــود Eswad, black.

SWD

Seud, *s.* melancholy.
Soudân, *coll.* negroes.
Soudâni, *adj.* negro.
ix. Iswidd, become black.
Sewâd, blackness.
Seudin, make gloomy.
Scudâwi, Moscudan, melancholy.
Osayyid, Osewwid, blackish.
ii. Sewwid, *va* blacken.
Soudâya, black bottle.

صود Jônda, refreshments offered to a guest ; *esp.* coffee and pipes ʌɪ.

سيد Sciyid, lord, *pl.* Sêda.
Sciyida, lady.
Soyaid, little lord.
[Soudâ, caprice n.]
Siyâda, lordship.
Sêdât, Esyâd, lords of manors.
Sêdâtiey, seigniorial.

سيد Said, *s.* hunting, chase, game.
Suid, *va* catch in hunting.
Sayyâd, hunter, fisher.
Musyad(a) 11, hunter's tackle.
v. Tasayyad, follow the chase.
viii. Usvâd, same as i.

سدى Seda', yarn ; the warp. (Loßma, woof).
Sedâya, d°·
iv. Esdi, weave, yarn.
(2) Sodaⁿ, wantonly, recklessly.

صدى Sadû 4, an echo. (Sada', dᵃ·)
iv. Asdi, *v.* echo.
(2) Sadâ', *s.* rust.
Usda', *vn* rust, be rusty.

SDM

Sadiey, rusty.
Asdâ', of rust-colour, rusty-red.
(3) v. Tasaddu' li, venture upon.

صدع Usdas, *va* split x. *pass.*
Sôdis, suffer headache.
ii. Saddis el rê's, split the head.
Sôdâs, headache.
Masdous, suffering headache.

سدب Sedâb, rue (a herb).

صدف Sadafa, *nu.* 4, shell-fish, mother of pearl.
(2) Sôdfa, coincidence, accidental meeting ; *favourable* accident ʙ.
iii. Sâdif, *va* meet, fall in with.
vi. Tasâdaf, *vn* meet.
Sawâdif, coincidences ?

صدغ Asdaṛân, *dual.* the two veins of the temples.

سدح Sêdih, *Pers.* simple ; see Sêdij, blank (book) c.

سدج Sêdij, simple, unadorned, natural.

سدل Esdal, streaming, dangling x.
iv. Esdil, *va* let (the hair) stream.
vii. Insedil, *vn* trail, stream, as a robe.
(2) Sedala, sofa [*Latin* sedile?].

سدم Osdom, *va* knock, dash together. *ger.* Sadm.
Sadma, a blow, hard knock.

ṢDM

vi. Taṣâdam, strike mutually.
vii. Inṣadim, *op* be knocked. Ḥajaret ol inṣudâm, stone of stumbling s.
viii. Uṣtedim, *on* knock against.

صدق Ṣadq, truth.
Ṣudq, truthfulness, sincerity.
Ṣadaqa, (legal) alms.
Ṣâdiq, genuine.
Ṣadieq, truthful.
Ṣuddieq, very truthful.
Ṣadâqa, friendship.
ii. Ṣaddiq, believe (a statement).
iii. Ṣâdiq, *va* befriend, make a friend of.
vi. Taṣâdaq, be mutually loyal, live in friendship.
Ṣadâq, gift of betrothal to a bride's parents ɪ.

سدر Sidr, the lotus 3.

صدر Oṣdor, *on* issue, come out, emanate. [port.
Ṣâdir, outgoing (produce), ex-
iv. Aṣdir, *va* emit, originate, export? send forth (a decree).
Maṣdar 11, source, gerund of verb.
(2) Ṣadr 3, the front (what stands *out*?), the chief, president. Ṣadr el qaum, the chief of the commune. Ṣadr el daula, chief of the government.
Also, Ṣadr, front, *i.e.* the breast (of man), seat of emotion.
Ṣadrieya, waistcoat.
Ṣôdour, premiership.
Ṣadâra, dᵒ

WṢF

Ṣadârat-oh, the Grand Vizier.
v. Tâṣaddar, *on* hold primacy.

سدس Sods 4, sixth part.
Sêdis, sixth.
Moseddes, hexagonal.
Sitt(e), six; appears to be a corruption of a word which must have been Sidse, *f.* Sids.

صفـ Sofouf, powder, dust c. *esp.* medicinal powder.
Sofficya, ashes? (*Al.* Ṣöuficya.)
(2) Seficf, *adj.* spare, meagre ʙ.
Sefâfa, spareness of body ʙ.

صفـ Ṣöff, *va* range (troops). *ger.* Saff 3, row, rank.
Ṣöffa 10, stone bench, sofa.
Maṣaff, ranks of battle, army in its ranks.
ii. Ṣaffif, same as i.
vi. Taṣâff, *on* range themselves mutually face to face.
viii. Uṣticff, *op* or *on* of i.

صفصاف Ṣufṣâf, willow tree.

اسف 'Esef, *s.* regret, sorrow.
i. 'Esif, Yesef, *vn* grieve.
iv. 'Esif, *va* vex, harass.
v. Te'essef, same as i.
'Esief, 'Esouf, easily grieved, susceptible.
'Esefe, distress of mind.

وصف Waṣaf, Yaṣuf, *va* describe, praise; *also*, prescribe, as physician. *ger.* Waṣf 4, Ṣufa 2. These gerunds, like the word *Description* with us,

WJF

are vulgarly used to mean Kind, Quality.
Mauyöuf, praised.

سوف Souf, *va* spoil.
(2) Moséfa, distance.
(3) Seuf, hereafter. (Used with Aorist, to express Future.)
(4) Sewwicf, a beggar B.
v. Tesewwaf, *vn* act the beggar B.

صوف Jöuf 4, wool. Jöufa, *nu.*
Jawif, Aywaf, well fleeced, floecy
Jawwâf, wool merchant. [x.
Jöufâni, woolly x.
ii. Jawwif, *v.* become woolly, *i.e.* mouldy.
(2) Jöufi, a Soufi, σόφος, Oriental philosopher.
v. Tayawwaf, *vn* assume the mystic, following the Soufis x.

سيف Seif 3, sword.
Seyyâf, swordsman.
i. Sief, *va* wound with sword x.
v. Tesoyyaf, *vp* be slain with sword x.
viii. *vn* fight together.
Soyoufiey, sword cutler. [F.x.
(2) Sief 4, coast, bank of river

صيف Jaif 4, summer.
Jaificy, *adj.* of summer.
Jaifieya, *s.* summer time.
Mayuif, *s.* summer villa.
v. Tayayyaf (or viii. Uytef x.), pass the summer (somewhere).

صفو Oyfou, *vn* be clear, be serene, be pure of heart. *ger.* Jafou.

SFII

Jafou nieya, purity of intention.
Jafâ, purity, (*gener.*) sincerity.
ii. Jaffi, iv. Ayfi, *va* clear, clarify, filter.
Jâfi, limpid, serene.
Jaficy 8, pure, select.
Jafwa, the choicest part (of anything) x.
Ayfa', purer.
Jafieya, select portion of spoil x.
Muyfâya 11, a filter.
Moyâffa', filtered.
vi. Tayâfi, live in mutual sincerity of friendship x.
viii. Uyyafi, *va* select, elect (as God).
Moyyafa', elected, elect.
x. Istayfi, *va* choose the best portion, take the cream of a thing x.

صفع (Isfoc) Uyfac, *va* beat, slap, smack, *esp.* on back of head, or nape of neck.

صفد Isfed, *vn* breed, as animals; mount, sala' the female. *ger.* Sifâd F.

صفه Iafoh, be rash, pert.
Sefioh, port, silly 6, 5.
Sefoh, Scfého, pertness, silliness, rashness, rudeness.

صفل Isfull, *vn* flow as water. *ger.* Sofoufl, Safoflân.
[Seffèfl, shedder of blood x. See Seffôc.]
(2) Sefll 3, foot of mountain x. c. *qu.* for Jaffl, the *flat*?

SFḤ

سفح Safḥ 5, flat side, flank.
2. Pardoning.
Safḥ, Suffḥ, flat of a sword, flat of the blade.
Safḥa 2, flat side; page 10.
Suffaḥ, a slate, flat tablet 11.
Saḥoḥa, nu. broad flat face of a thing; thin lamina.
v. Tasaffaḥ, va peruse F. examine, review (a book) F.
Tasaffoh 2, a review.
ii. Saffḥ, va flatten.
Usfaḥ, v. clap the flat of the hands together K. See Usfaq.
(2) Usfaḥ li, v. grant pardon; san, remit, exempt from.
Usfaḥ san, va excuse from.
Safouḥ, gracious to remit (punishment, payment, service). Compare Ismaḥ, Semouḥ.

سفل Esfel, pl. Esêfil, low (opposed to high) gener.
Sifl, Sofl, low estate.
Esêfil, lowlands, low people.
Sêfil 7, low; Sefiol, Sefil, d° Sefiol, low, base.
Sefâla, lowness.
Sêfila, bottom of a thing, its low part.
Min sêfil ila', under s.
Sofliey, Soflâni, ignoble, mean, inferior.
Osfol, vn be low K.
ii. Seffil, va make lower, abase.
v. Teseffal, vn lower oneself.

سفن Safen (σφήν), a wedge.
Sefîna 10, 11, a ship.

SFR

Seffân, naval architect K. but, ship owner (ναύκληρος) s.
Sifâna, art of shipbuilding K.

سفنج Isfonja, nu. a sponge.

سفك Isfic, va shed (blood, tears), pour forth (a torrent of words). ger. Scfc.
Seffîc dimâ, shedder of blood.
Sefouc, profuse in shedding K. profuse (in false words), pro-
Misfêc, great talker. [lix.
vii. Insifêc, efflux.

سفق Isfaq, va slam (the door), smack (the cheek).
Usfaq, flap (the wings), clap (the hands), slap.
[See Isfas, Usfas, Usfaḥ.]
Safqa, a loud slap, smack.

سفر Sefara, nu. 4, a voyage, journey.
iii. Sêfir, vn travel, voyage.
Sefriey, traveller? s. has Sefriey el howâ, aeronaut.
Misfar, a good traveller (strong against hardship) K.
Mosêfir, traveller.
(2) Sifr 4, tome, codex. A cipher.
Sêfir, recorder (recording angel); pl. sefara K.
Seffêr, bookseller, bookbinder K.
(3) Sefior, envoy, nuncio, parlementaire; mediator of war 6. Hence (modern) Ambassador.

SFR 　　　　　ЗП

Sifâra, embassy, legation; members of a legation; post or functions of ambassador.
ii. Seffir, *va* send an envoy.
v. Teseffar, go forth as envoy.
(4) Sofra 10, table cloth, *esp.* of leather, used as a tray on the ground. Hence (mod.) a dining table; "board," "a board," *fig.* Thus, to sit "at a person's *board*," is, *and* el sofra. [fara.
(5) Sefiera, emery в. *See* Sen-

ڝفر Uyfir, *vn* whistle, hiss. *ger.* Зafler, *also*, Зöfar c. к.
Зâfler, whistling (bird); *esp.* a small bird so called.
Зuffarid, nightingale x.
Зaffûra, a whistle (fife, etc.).
(2) Ayfar, yellow.
Зöfr, yellow copper, brass.
Зöfra, *s.* yellow colour, yellowness; yolk of egg.
Зafrâ, bile, gall.
Зöfâr, biliousness? (disease).
Зaffâr, worker in yellow copper.
Зöffûrîoyn, yellowhammer? (a bird). [yellow.
ii. Зaffir, *va* make yellow, paint
ix. Uyfirr, *vn* become yellow.
Зöfâra, *nu.* plant faded and yellow x.
(3) Зafler, sapphire.

ڝفتج Softeja 11, bill of exchange.
Seftij, accept and pay a bill of exchange. *ger.* Sefteja x.

ڝوغ Souʕ, *vn* go down (the throat) easily, as food and drink; be digestible; pass, bo admissible. *ger.* Sowâʕ. Also Souʕ, *va* bolt down (food) в. x.
ii. Sewwiʕ, *or* iv. Esiсʕ, *va* carry easily down the throat; digest; *lit.* and *fig.* let pass easily, allow.
Seiyiʕ, gliding down easily x.

ڝوغ Зöuʕ, *va* mould, fuse into form; work in gold and silver; *fig.* forge, coin. *ger.* Зauʕ.
v. Tayawwaʕ, viii. Uyταʕ, *op* of i.
Зieʕa, type, fashion, frame, stamp. [smith в. x.
Зâyiʕ 7, artist in metal, gold-
Зayyâʕ, goldsmith в.
Зawwâʕ, coiner, forger x.
Зuyâʕa, art of working in precious metal.

ڝغر Suʕr, littleness, small size, infantine age.
Зuʕr, affront towards x.
Зöʕr, meanness c.
Зaʕier, little 5, *gener.*
Зaʕâra, smallness; insignificance x. Ayʕar, smaller.
Зöʕaiyir, Зöʕaiyier, very little.
Зöʕrân, *f.* Зöʕrâna, a little child.
Tayaʕran, *vn* romp в.
ii. Зaʕʕir, lessen, bo little.
x. Istayʕir, disparage.

ڝحح Заnn, Зunn? *vn* be right, sound; authentic, true;

ЗП

healthy; *vulg.* Mâ yaяuЛЛ, it will not do, it is not the right thing.
ii. ЗаЛЛuЛ, *va* rectify, correct.
ЗuЛЛa, health, soundness.
ЗаЛuiЛ 5, correct, authentic.
iv. AяuЛЛ, *va* make healthy.
MoяuЛЛ, salubrious.

ـح Sіeл, *vn* melt and flow; glide away. *ger.* Sciл, SoiЛân.
ii. Seyyiл, iv. Esieл, *va* cause to flow, melt; let drop (the tail) x.
(2) Sieл, *vn* travel. *ger.* So-youл, SсiЛân.
Seyyâл, a great traveller.
Siyâла, distant travel. [tion.
Meseлa, dimension, mensura-
Sела 2, area, court, district.
(3) Sеyiл 7, devotee x. в.

ـح Зuiл, *vn* cry out, aloud. *ger.* Зuyâл, ЗaiЛân.
Зöyâл, bellowing of a whale.
Sâyiла, a wailing.
Заiла, cry of vengeance from heaven x.
Sâyiл, public crier.
Зayyâл—Boötes x.

ـه Oshou, *va* overlook, neglect, forget. *ger.* Sehou.
Sehwa, an oversight. *pl.* 5, Sihê.
Sehwaⁿ, inadvertently.
Sêhi, Sêhwân, inadvertent.
iii. Sêhi, *va* ignore (a person).

ـص OяЛöи, Uяла, *vn* be clear, serene, sober. *ger.* Залöu.

ЗПF

UяЛâ min, *vn* recover from (wine), wake from (delusion).
ЗаЛöu, *s.* clearness of sky.
ЗâЛu, *adj.* serene (sky), sobered, disenchanted.

ـب iv. Eshib, *vn* be prolix, diffuse. Ishêb, prolixity.
Moshib, prolix.

ـب Iлlab, *va* train, trail, draw, drag; draw (breath), suck in (smoke), *ger.* Seлb. *Also vn* druggle, trail.
Siлâba, a train, *esp.* of clouds.
vii. Inseлub, *tp* of i.

ـب Ayheb, *adj.* sorrel (colour) x.

ـص Залub 4, 9, companion, friend, fellow, a second person of two; master (of servants); possessor, used for лон.
Зöhba, company; *esp.* as a prep.
Зöhbat, in company with.
iii. Залub, *va* accompany, escort.
MoяâЛaba, companionship.
viii. Uятaлub, *vn* live as companion.   [company.
x. Istayлub, *va* take in one's

ـف Залfa 2, platter, large round wooden dish.
Залuifa 11, broad sheet, *esp.* newspaper.
Залпâf, bookseller в.
Muyлaf 11, tome, volume; *esp.* the Koran x.
iv. Aялuf, *va* make into a volume, bind a book x.

SUF

Compare Uṣfaṅ, Sifr.
(2) ii. Saṅṅuf, *vn* commit an error in reading or writing.

ڛڡ Ishej, *vn* puff as wind.
Sebouj, *adj.* blowing hard.

ڛڪ Isṅaj, *va* excoriate; *fig.* harrow up.

ڛهل Oshol, *vn* be level, easy.
Sohoula, ease, easiness.
Sehel, *s.* 3, a level; *adj.* level.
Sehla, a plain.
Sehil, easy.
Schliey, belonging to a plain.
iv. Eshil, *va* ease (*esp.* the bowels).
Moshil, aperient.
iii. Séhil, *va* comply with.
Moschil, compliant.
v. Teschhel, *vn* become easy.
vi. Tesêhel, *vn* be conciliating.
Tesêhol, conciliation.

ڛحل Séṅul 12, shore.
ii. Seṅṅul, *va* drive on to shore, bring to shore.

ڛڪل Saṅul, Aṣṅal, Sûṅul, harsh, rough (voice).
Uṣṅal, *va* shriek, scream. *See* Ṣlq, Ṣlyl.

ڛهم Sehm 5, an arrow, a lot for divining (*Lat.* sors); a lot or share in a mercantile company.
iii. Séhim, *va* admit as shareholder and partner, join to yourself as coadjutor.
Moschim, a shareholder.

VOL. II.

SUR

iv. Eshim bain, draw lots between. [gether.
vi. Teschem, *vn* draw lots to-
viii. Istchim, *vn* receive shares in a company.

ڛحن Seṅana, external form, aspect.

ڛحن Oṣṅôn, *va* pound by heavy blows B. Al. (x. Iṣṅan, d°.)
(2) Saṅn 3, bowl, dish; interior court of house.
Mayṅana, soup-plate?

ڛحق Isṅaq, *va* rub to powder, crush; wear to rags. *ger.* Seṅq.
Seṅṅâq, one who pounds B.
vii. Inseṅuq, *vp* of L. *fig. with Christians*, be contrite.
Insiṅâq, contrition.

ڛهر Isher, *vn* lie awake at night. *ger.* Seher. [ness.
Sohêr, wakefulness, sleeples-
Sohrân, sleepless.
Schhêr, wakeful, apt to lose sleep, a bad sleeper.
iv. Eshir, *va* keep (another) awake.
v. Tesehher, *vn* become sleepless.

ڛحر Suṅr, enchantment.
Séṅur, *f.* Séṅura, magician.
Seṅṅâr, enchanter.
Mesṅôur, enchanted.
ii. Seṅṅur, *va* enchant, fascinate.
(2) Seṅar, dawn of day.
(3) Seṅṅâra 11, strong money box B.

26

JHR

جهر Juhr, m. 4, 6, connected by marriage; esp. son-in-law, father-in-law, brother-in-law.
Juhra 2, fem. of the preceding.
iii. Jâhir, va take (another) into marriage alliance.
vi. Tayâbor, vn make intermarriages.

جهريج Jahriej 11, cistern to a house.

جسر Aṣfar, adj. brown russet, colour of withered plants x.
Jaṣlar, Jôṣra, subst. brown russet.
Jaṣrâ 11, the open desert, parched (brown) country.

جص Sojj, va plaster with mud.
Misejja, wooden trowel.

جع Jajj, vn clank x.

جهز ii. Sewwij, va embroider; B. Broder.

جسيج Siyâj, a (thorn) hedge.
ii. Soyyij, va hedge.

جسجى Sejioya 14, nature, temperament.

جسع Sejr 4, assonance, rhyme in prose.
Esêjier, assonances.
Mosejjar, composed with assonances.
ii. Sejjir, va thus to compose.
Isjar, d°· x.

SJS

سجد Osjod, li; fall prostrate in adoration; worship. ger. Sojoud.
Sojjâda, prayer-carpet.
Sejjâd, worshipper.
Mosjad 11, mosque.
Sejda, nu. a prostration.

سجف Sejf, 3, 4, curtain x.
Sijâf, border, vallance.
ii. Sejjif, ra enshroud, enmantle.

سجل Sijill 2, diploma, public document (Lat. sigillum).
Sijjiel, inscription x.
ii. Sejjil, ra register, enrol a judge's decree.

سجم Isjim, vn flow as tears. ger. Sojoum, Sijâm x.
iv. Esjim, va shed (tears).
vii. Insejim, vn flow profusely.
Monsejim, profuse (tears).
Séjim, Sejoum, d°· x.

سجن Sijn 3, prison.
Osjon, va imprison.
Sejjân, jailer.
Sejien, prisoner.
Mesjoun, d°·

سجق Sojq, sausage B.

سجر Osjor, va heat an oven. ger. Sojr.
Sejour, fuel for oven x.
Misjer, d°· x.

سجس Sojes, turbulence r.
Sejis, Sojies, turbid.

SJS

ii. Sejjis, *va* stir up, make turbid, make turbulent.
Mosejjis, turbulent, troubler (of the public peace).

سخ Wesik, dirty, filthy.
Wesek, dirtiness.
Weaek 4, dirt.
Weack, Yeusik, *vn* be dirty.
ii. Wessik, iv. Ausik, *va* make dirty.
v. Tewessek, *vr* dirty oneself.
viii. Ittesik, *vp* be dirtied.

سخ Siok, an iron spit, a foil for fencing.

سخ Iskâ, *vn* be generous. *ger.* Sekâ, Sokouwa ɪ.
Sekiey, generous in gifts.
Sekâ, Sekâwa, generosity.
v. Tesekkâ, play the generous man.

سخب Uvkab, *vn* scream, vociferate.
Sakab, a hubbub, tumult; harshness of voice.
Sakib, dissonant, screaming.
Sakkâb, d⁰ intens.
Uvrnkâb, brawl (of waves) ɪ.

سخف Oskof, *vn* be flimsy. *ger.* Sekâfa, flimsiness.
Sakief, flimsy.
Iskâf, emptiness of head.
Sokf, Sokfa, d⁰ ɪ.

سخن Iskin, *vn* be hot (as water).
Sokn, *fem.* Sokna, hot, *vulg.*
Sokouna, heat.

SL

ii. Sekkin, iv. Eskin, *va* heat.
Mosekkan, Moskan, heated ɪ.
Miskana l l, a heater, cauldron ɪ.
(2) Moskin, humourist (c. *sic bis*). See Eskar.

سخر Sekr, forced labour, task work. Sokra, a ship, horse, etc., pressed into service.
ii. Sekkir, *va* force to labour (for a prince, etc.) without pay; subdue.
v. Tesekkar, *vp* of ii.
(2) Eskar min bi, *vn* jeer at, deride.
Temeskar sala', d⁰
Sekara, pleasantry ɪ.
Meskara, a pleasantry; one who plays masquerade.

سخر Sakra, *nu.* 3, a rock.
Sakr, *coll.* rock.
Moykir, rocky ɪ.

سختيـ Sektiyân, Morocco leather.

سخط Sokt, Sekut, Sokta, indignation.
Iskut, be angry. v. d⁰
iv. Eskut, *va* exasperate.
(2) Sekta, an abnormal monster в. o. *Compare* Soqt.
(3) Meskout, marmoset в.

سل Sill, *s.* pulmonary consumption. [tion ɪ.
iv. Esill, *va* afflict with consumption.
Mesloul, suffering consumption.
(2) Selle 5, flexible basket.

SL

Miselle, *pl.* Miséll, packing-needle, knitting-needle?
Solcila, small basket.
(3) Solélc, issue, in speaking of a pedigree.
Seliel, dº son.
Seliele, dº daughter.
(4) Soll, *va* draw (a sword)? ʀ.
viii. Istill, *va* draw *one's* sword; take out *one's* arrow.
v. Tesellel, vii. Insill, *vn* withdraw oneself gently, slip away ʙ.
(5) Soll, *vn* be tight strung (ʙ. *va* bander, *vn* être tendu).

سلسل Silsile 11, chain, wavy zigzag (of lightning) ʀ.
Selsil, *va* weave into a chain.
Silsilet el Xahr, backbone.

صل Sull, Salyul, *vn* rattle.
Salicl, *ger.* rattling, gurgling.
(2) Salyâl, potter's earth ʀ. clay mixed with sand c.

أصل 'Eyl 3, root, origin, principle. [mental.
'Eyuil, of true race, fundaBarr el 'Eyuil, the continent.
'Eyliey, radical.
x. Istéyul, extirpate.
(2) 'Eyuila 11, afternoon ʀ.

وصل Wûyal, Yayul, *va* join. *ger.* Sulo 2, union, bond of union. *vn* arrive. *ger.* Woyôul.
ii. Wayyul, *va* join.
iv. Auyul, *va* cause to arrive, convey.

SYL

viii. Ittayul, to be continuous, be joined continuously, ila' or bi.
Wayal, Wayla, junction.
Woyla, bond ʀ.
Wuyâl, union, *esp.* of lovers.
Ittiyâl, contiguity, contact.
Mottayul, contiguous.
Manyöula, relative pronoun.
Motowâyul, (road) communicating with.

سأل Is'el, *v.* ask. *ger.* Sêle.
Sowâl, a question.
Mesyala, Mes'âla, a problem.
Sewoul, beggar ʀ.
v. Teseyyal, play the beggar ʀ.
iii. Séyil, ask a person for a thing, with accus. of person.

سول ii. Sewwil, *va* delude by brilliant visions.
Teswiel, delusion.

صول Söul, *vn* leap, spring, sala'. *ger.* Saul, Sawalân.
Saula, a sudden spring, ᴘ. impetuosity.
Sawwâl, impetuous.
(2) Mâyöula 12 (Mâyöura, Mésoula), a pipe, a fife.

سيل Siel, *vn* stream. *ger.* Seilân. Siel bi, carry off (as a torrent). Soyil bihi, he was swept away by a torrent ʀ.
ii. Seyyil, iv. Esicl, *va* cause to stream.
Seil 3, a torrent.
Mesiel 11, bed of torrent.

SYL

Seyyâl, (cloud) pouring forth a torrent ĸ.
(2) Siyâla, breast pocket в.

سلو Selwa, Solwa, consolation, amusement.
ii. Selli, ʋa solace, amuse.
v. Tesellê, be comforted.
(2) Selwa', Selwa, the king quail.

صلو Salawa 2, a prayer to God. Salâ(y)a, dᵃ⁻
ii. Salli, v. pray; ɛala', bless.
(2) viii. Uyrali, ɛn present oneself (at the fire) F.
(3) Musláya 11, springe to catch birds.

سلع Silɛa 10, upholstery; wares for sale. 2, 10, movable gland, tubercle, bubo ? a sore place ?
iv. Eslus, have sore places.

اسلع Aylaɛ, adj. bald.
Salaɛ, baldness.
Sölɛa, bald part.

سلب Oslob, ʋa pillage, plunder.
ger. Selb.
Seleb 4, booty, spoil.
Sellâb, plunderer.
(2) 'Oɛloub 11 (route), method, routine ? form.
(3) Seleba, mooring rope в.

تسلب Teselbat, v. sponge upon, squeeze money out of в.

سلب Sölb, hard, dense.
Salâba, hardness, density.

SLF

Oslob, ɛn be hard, to endure, last, wear well. [opinion.
v. Tayallob el râi, obstinacy of
(2) Salieb 10, 9, cross, gibbet.
ii. Sallib, ɛa crucify.
Mayloub, crucified.
Moɛallab, (cloth) marked with a cross ĸ.

سلد Sald, Suld, hard, solid c.
[from Latin?] See Sölb.
Apparently not in use.

سلف Oslof, ɛa smooth down, vix. either as with trowel or with harrow.
Solfa, a harrowed field ĸ.
Mislafa, a harrow, a trowel.
(2) Silf 4, sister's husband.
Silfa, husband's brother's wife.
Osloufa, connection by marriage as sister or brother ĸ.
vi. Tesêlef, ɛn be thus connected.
x. Isteslif, ɛa marry one's brother's widow ĸ.
(3) Selef 4, predecessor, advance of money without interest.
Selefaⁿ, beforehand c. previously oɴ. El dafɛ selefaⁿ, the payment (must be) in advance oɴ.
Sêlif 7, adj. preceding. Min sêlif el dahr, from time long past.
Sêlifa 12, a precedent oɴ.
Sollâf, belonging to the past. Qaum sollâf, people of past time. [guard.
Solâf el ɛaɛcer, the advanced
Solâfa, first juice of the vintage;

SLF

fig. socèra' bi solâfot el waθbêt, intoxicated by *the firstfruits* of the combats, *i.e.* by first successes on.
ii. Sollif, *va* advance (money).
iv. Ealif, *va* dᵒ pay in advance; *also*, promise; say beforehand; *also*, to have said already.
Islâf, *ger.* paying in advance.
v. Tesollaf, *va* receive (money) in advance.

ܠ Silṉ 5, weapon ᴋ. *vulg.* only *pl.* Silâṉ, arms, and *pl.* of *pl.* Esliṉa 8.
Mcslaṉa, full accoutrement.
ii. Solliṉ, *va* arm (another).
v. Tesollaṉ, *vn* take arms.

ܠ Söln, *s.* good order, peace.
Uylaṉ, *vn* be in good order, be at peace. *ger.* Söloun.
Salâṉ, good order.
Sâliṉ, *adj.* honest, virtuous, in good state.
ii. Salliṉ, iv. Ayliṉ, *va* correct, improve, establish aright.
iii. Sâlib, *va* reconcile.
v. Tayallaṉ, *vp* be improved.
vi. Tayâlaṉ, *vp* be mutually reconciled. [arranged.
vii. Inyaliṉ, *vp* of ii. be well
viii. Uyraliṉ, *vn* be in due grammatical concord or propriety.
Uyrulâṉ, concord, good idiom.
Uyrulâṉuiy, idiomatic.
Mayraliṉ, dᵒ c.

ܠܚܦ Solṉafa 11, tortoise.

SLC

ܠ Saulajân, crooked stick for playing hockey.

ܠ Oslok, *va* flay, skin, peel. *ger.* Selk.
Silk, serpent's skin ᴋ.
Moslak, shambles ᴋ.
vii. Insclik, *vp* be stript off.

ܠ Islam, *vn* be sound and safe. *ger.* Sclâm, Sclâma, safety.
Sclicm, safe and sound.
Ealom, safer, more entire ᴋ.
ii. Sollim, *va* salute (say Sclâm caloic); consign in safety, resign, surrender.
Sclama, *nu.* deposit of money.
iii. Sôlim, *va* pacify.
v. Tosellam, *va* receive a thing consigned; receive a deputed office.
Motesollim, lieutenant governor.
vi. Tesôlam, *vr* make peace together.
Islâm, Mussulman religion.
Moslem, Mussulman.
(2) Sollem 11, a ladder.

ܠ Soilân, treacle of dates ʙₑ.

ܠ Silco, *nu.* thread, wire; wire of telegraph.
Selc, *ger.* threading, inserting c.
ii. Sollic, *va* wind thread on to a reel; disentangle, extricate; clear (a road, a space) ʙ.
(2) Osloc, *vn* go in file, proceed; *fig.* behave. *ger.* Solouc.

SLC

Solouo, behaviour, conduct; (ascetic) rule of life.
Meslec ll, course of life; course of water-pipes.
iv. Eslic, *va* cause to proceed, pass (one thing into another) x. guide as chief of a spiritual order x.

سلق Silq, (white) beet-root.
(2) Osloq, *va* stew (meat), boil (eggs or herbs) c.
Meslouq, meat out of soup.
Meslouqa, a decoction.
(3) Sclicqa ll, character, genius, stamp. [hound.
(4) Solûquiy, Solouqi, grey-
(5) Tesellaq, *vn* climb walls B.

صلق Uyliq, *vn* whoop, boom. *ger.* Ṣalq.
Ṣalqa, *nu.* loud cry, bellowing.
Ṣâliq, *adj.* loud mouthed (orator).
Ṣallâq, Muylâq, d° *intensive.*
viii. Uytaliq, *vn* as i.
Uytulâq, loud tumult.

سلسبيل Selsebiel, milk or wine x. (sillabub? nectar?) name of a fountain in Paradise.

سلسج Selsiej, Selsiejou, sausage AL.

سلت Ialet, *vn* glide, drop (out of the pocket) B.
vii. Inselit min, *vn* d°. B.

سلط Solṭa, Selṭana, power, empire.

WSM

Solṭân ll, sultan.
Solṭâniey, imperial.
ii. Selliṭ sala', *va* cause to rule over.
v. Tesellaṭ, *vn* be lord.
ii. Teselṭan, *vn* become sultan x.

سم Semm, *s.* poison.
Somm, *va* poison.
ii. Semmim, d°
Sêmm, poisonous.
Mesmoum, poisoned.
Semoum, poisonous wind.
Mosimm, (day) of this wind.
(2) Somm kiyâṭ, eye of a needle B. c.; orifice (of ear) c.
Mesêmma, *nu.* 2, orifice (as of nose). See Mesêm under Soum.

سميم Ṣamiem, the core of a thing; min yamiem el qalb, from the bottom of the heart.
Ṣamiemiey, cordial, sincere.
ii. *va* Ṣammim nefsec, steel oneself, resolve firmly B.
Moyammam, firm, resolute (man); determined (action).
(2) Ayamm, *pl.* Ṣömm, deaf.
iv. Ayumm, *va* deafen.
vi. Tayâmm, *vn* become deaf, affect deafness.
Ṣamam, obstruction, deafness x.
Ṣamâm, d°. c.

اسم 'Iam, *pl.* Esêmi, name. See Semi.

وسم Wesem, Yesim, *va* mark (sheep), brand. *ger.* Wesm.

WSM

Sima, Wesm 3, mark from hot iron. Wisma dᵃ c.
viii. Ittesim, *vp* be branded.
Motewessim, distinguished (honourably).
Wesiem, comely.
Wesêm, a badge of honour.
Wesêma, comeliness.
Siemû, features.
Mausoum 11, marked, distinguished. Mausoum bi, entitled.

سوم Soum, *va* rate, value, expose for sale at a definite price. *ger.* Scum.
iii. Sêwim, *va* estimate.
v. Tesewwam, *vn* traffic, deal.
vi. Tesêwam, be a valuer.
viii. Istewim, *vn* ask the price of a thing.
Souma, market price x.
Sowâm, valuation x.
(2) Mesêm 2, a pore b. See Semm. [turbid f.
(3) Soum, *va* trouble, make

صوم Jöum, *vn* keep Mohammedan fast. viii. Uxram dᵃ· x.
Jaum, *s.* fasting, fast.

سمى Semâ, heaven, *pl.* Semawât.
Semâwiey, heavenly, sky-blue (N.E. wind, Ag. x. but N. wind, Syr. b.).
Sêmi, Semiey, lofty (*fig.*).
Semâwa, loftiness.
Somâya, cope? canopy?
Osmou, be lofty x.; rise aloft. *ger.* Somou.

SMS

Somon, Highness (in political titles); yâßub el somou el Lôrd Jôn Rousel, his Highness Lord John Russell.
iv. Esmi, raise aloft x.
vi. Tesêmâ, aspire to eminence.
Somâ, celebrity x.
(2) Ism, *s.* name, *pl.* Esmâ, Esêmi. See Wesem.
ii. Semmi, *va* name, entitle.
v. Tesemmâ, be named.
Somawicy, belonging to a name (?).
Ismiey, belonging to a noun.
Mosemma', named, called.

سمى Jamayân, impetuosity f.
iv. Aymi, *va* strike (a bird or a deer) dead.
vii. Inyami sala', *vn* swoop upon, come suddenly upon.

سمع Ismas, *va* hear, obey. *ger.* Sems.
iv. Esmis, cause to hear.
v. Tesemmas, viii. Istemis, *vn* listen.
Sims, Somsa, reputation.
Δou sims, renowned.
Somous, quick of hearing x.
Semmâs, fond of hearing x.
Semâsaª, loudly enough to be heard, on purpose to be heard x.
Semâs(a), hearsay?
Semâsuiy, traditional.
Mismas 11, the ear x.

سمع Jaumas(a) 11, hermitage, small convent.

SMD

سمد Semied, finest white wheaten flour; B. oswego, arrowroot.

سمد Samad, perpetual o. See Sermad.
Uʏmad sala', or Iamad sala', persevere in.

سمغ Samor, s. 3, gum.
Samara, nu. dº·
ii. Sammir, va gum, stick.
iv. Esmir, produce gum x.

سمح Ismaḥ, v. with li, pardon. ger. Somouḥ.
iii. Sêmiḥ, treat kindly, with forbearance.
Sêmiḥ, Semouḥ, forbearing.
Semaḥa, indulgence, forbearance. [tually.
vi. Tesêmaḥ, vr concede mu-
Mosêmaḥa, compromise.

سمحد Semhid, va level. See Mehhid. The initial S seems to be causative.

سمج Semij, coarse, gross, rank, lit. or fig. ugly (thing), foul (word, deed), rancid (milk).
Semaja, grossness.
Ismaj, vn be gross, rank.
ii. Semmij, va defile.
x. Istesmij, va judge to be foul.

سمل Oʏmol, vn stand firm b. ger. Sömoul, firmness.

سمن Semna, nu. grease, esp. salt butter.

SMR

Semien, adj. fat.
Esmen, fatter.
Semmân, butterman.
ii. Semmin, va fatten, smear with butter.
Mosmin, fattening.
Simen, fatness c. [thrush b.
(2) Sommons, Sommûno, quail:
(3) Esmanjouni, hyacinth (precious stone).

سمك Semace, nu. 4, fish.
Somaice, little fish.
Semmêc, fishmonger.
Semmêce, fish market.
(2) Semice, thick.
Some, thickness.
(3) Mismêc 11, tentpole.
Scumec 11, a vinepole.

سمر Esmer, adj. brown.
Somra s. brown, brownness.
Sommour, the brown sable c.
Somair, brunet.
Mosmirr, embrowned.
Osmarâni, dº swarthy?
ix. Ismirr, vn grow brown.
(2) Semer, s. evening gossip.
Sêmir 7, gossiper, taletellar.
Simmier, devoted to such talk K. C.
iii. Sêmir, chat, gossip.
Mosêmara, story-telling.
(3) ii. Semmir, va nail.
v. Tesemmar, be nailed.
Mismâr 11, a nail (vulg. Bosmâr AL.).
Mesmir, va nail.
Temesmar, vp be nailed.
Mesmour, nailed x.

SMS

سمسر Simsér 13, a broker, intermediate agent, go-between.
Semsera, brokerage (payment or action).
Semsir, *va* be a broker.
(2) Simsim, the grain sesame.

سمت Semt 3, direction x.
El semt, azimuth.
Semt el râ'a, zenith.
Ismit, *va* tend towards, aim at x.

سمط Osmot, *va* scald B. *ger.* Semt. Semier, scalded.
(2) ii. Semmir, *va* arrange (a stanza of a certain kind).
Simât 10, long range of dishes, long dining table, a *course* of dishes.

سمت Oymot, *va* be silent. *ger.* Samt, Sumout.
Sâmit, silent.
Sömte, Samt, silence c.
Sömte, Sümât, a sop or cake which silences x.
Samout, Summiet, taciturn.

سن Sinn, *s.* 4, tooth. Age.
Mosinn, aged, *pl.* mesênn.
Sinna, nib of pen.
Sonn, *va* sharpen.
Also, ii. Sennin, sharpen x.
Misenn, a hone.
Mesnoun, sharpened, sharp.
Sinân 8, iron of a javelin x.
(2) Sonna 10, usage, tradition.
viii. Istinn, establish a usage?
x. Istesinn, follow a usage or tradition?

SNS

وسن Wesin, drowsy c.
Wesen, drowsiness c.
x. Isteusin, be drowsy?

صون Soun, *va* guard, protect. *ger.* Saun.
Suyâna, protection [chastity x.].
Mayân, a safe [wardrobe x.].
Miywân, bowcase x.
(2) Sawwân, flint, granite.
Sawwâniey, flinty.

سني Senâ, elevation, grandeur.
Seniey, grand, noble, magnificent.
ii. Senni, *va* ennoble x.
x. Istesni, account noble x.
(2) Seno, *pl.* senowât, year; *also pl.* senien. [with x.
iii. Sêni, *va* contract for a year
(3) Senâya 12, great waterwheel x.
Mesnou, Mesniey, watered by a great wheel x.
Osnou, *va* water (a plain) by a wheel x. *ger.* Senou, Senâwa. [Not in B. See Nâsoura.]
(4) Sonounou, house swallow, martin.

صنع Oynas, *va* make, fabricate, contrive. *ger.* Sans.
Sânis 7, artizan, artificer.
Sunâsa, artifice, art.
Sansa, artificialness, art.
Sons, dealing, behaviour x.
Saniex, Saniesa, work. [art x.
Maynasa 11, a construction of
ii. Sannis, *va* arrange carefully.

SNS

v. Taɣannas, *vn* prepare oneself, use artifice.
viii. Uɣtanus, *vn* deal affectedly. Uɣtunâs, Taɣannos, affectation. Jönuiy, Moɣannas, Junâsuiy, Uɣtunûsuiy, Maɣnous, artificial.

سنبذج Senbâdij, emery s. *See* Senfora.

سنبل Sonbola 11, spiked ear of corn. Lavender.

سنبك Senboc, elder tree.

سنبر Janauber, pine tree, pine nuts (*pinions*).

سند Osnod, ila', *vn* lean against. *ger.* Sonoud.
ii. Sennid, *va* prop up.
iii. Sènid, *va* support, aid, adduce authority for.
vi. Tesênad, viii. Istenid ila', rest upon.
Scnad, a prop, a vine trellice.
iv. Esnid, *va* cause to rest upon.
Misnad, cushion for the back; emblem of royalty, or of a Pashâlic.
Senada, *nu.* 4, voucher, written document, warrant, acknowledgment of a debt.
Isnâd, quoting an authority in proof 11 x.
Sendân, anvil.
(2) Sindiɣân, holm oak.

سند Janâdied, heroes, heroic troops o*n*. *sing.* Jundied, hero.

SNR

سندل Jandal 11, a wherry, large open boat.
(2) Jandaliey? armchair s.

سندق Jandouq 11, trunk, chest.

سندرس Sindarous, gum of the sandarakh, or *red juniper* c.

سنف Junf 4, species, sort.
ii. Jannif, *va* classify, arrange; compose (a book).
Moɣannif, composer, author.
Taɣnief 2, 11, a composition, a literary work.

سنفر Senfara, emery s. *also* Seflera. *See* Senbâdij.

سنح Isnaḥ, *vn* come into view, present itself, as game to the hunter, or as an idea to a writer; occur.

سنج Senja, steelyard; standard metal weight.
(2) Sinj, Janj 3, cymbal s.

سنجق Sinjaq 11, flag, military district.

سنجاب Sinjâb, grey squirrel; fur of d°.

سنم Janam, idolatrous image, *esp.* of metal.
ii. Jannim, *va* make such images to worship.

سنر Isnar, *vn* be froward, self-willed. *ger.* Senar.

SNR

Sinnaur 11, cat (generically).
(2) Sinnâra, fishhook x. b.

سَنطَر Senṭair, *s.* a chime as of bells.
ii. Tesenṭar, *vn* chime.

سَكّ Sicce, die for coining money 10; mint.
Mescouce, a medal, or coin.
(2) Sicce 10, iron peg.
(3) Sicce 5, ploughshare.
(4) Sicce 10, track. Siccet el Dadied, railway c.

صَكّ Sacc 3, 10, deed or scrip promising to pay b.; document, authentic parchment; a deed cn. Act (of Congress or Parliament).
Saccêc, notary, keeper of rolls x.

يَسَق Yeseq, sequestration.
Usmal yeseq, sequestrate b.
But see Yezziq, Yezzic.

سَوك Souc, *va* pick (the teeth).
ii. Sewwic, *va* d°

سَوق Souq, *va* drive (horses).
Séyiq, Sewwâq, driver (*vulg.* Souq! Souq! drive on! push on! go forward!).
vi. Tesêwaq, *vn* push one another on, as beasts in a herd.
iv. Eswiq, *va* make (another) to drive; give beasts to a drover in charge.
vii. Istaq, *rp* of i.
(2) Sêq (*pl.* 9. Sicqân), leg, stalk of plant, stem.

SCB

Eséqa, stirrup leather x.
Sowwâq, Eswaq, longlegged x.
(3) Souq 4, market for food.
Meswâq, dealing in the market, a bargain b.
Souqa, market people, common people x.
Souqiey, common, vulgar (word); a common man, market man.
Souqicya, dealers in the market, chandlers.
v. Tesewwaq, be a chandler; deal by retail.

سَقى Isqi, *va* water, irrigate.
Seqie, Soqyâ.
Seqqâ' 1, *f.* Seqqâya, water-carrier.
Mesqiey, Mesqawicy, irrigated.
Sêqiya 12, brook which waters the fields.
Siqqâya 2, aqueduct.
Mesqâyu, reservoir, tank.

سَكَع Tesecces, *vn* trifle, faddle, flirt. See Loqes, Telecces.

سَقَع Seqies, dastardly b.

صَقَع Sôqs, tract of country. [*Or* Soqs x.]
(2) Saqies, frost?
Suqsa, hailstone?
Masqous, frosted over x.
Sâqisa, hailstorm? (*Comp.* Sâsuqa, thunderstorm).
iv. Asqis, *va* cover with hoarfrost x.

سَكَب Oscôb, *va* pour out. *ger.* seeb.

SCB

Sêcib mûi, *aquarius* in the zodiac.
Socoub, *ger. pass.* the being poured out, flowing ᴋ.
Secoub, Secieb, *adj.* running (water) ᴋ.
vii. Inæcib, *cp* be poured out.

ڛڡٮ Saqaba, the vicinity; neighbouring people.

ڛڡٮ Seccêf, Escêf 13, bootmaker ꜰ. Sicêfa, bootmaking.
iv. Escif, *rn* work at such trade.

ڛڡٮ Saqf 3, arched roof.
Osqof, *ra* roof.
ii. Saqqif, d°·; deck (a ship).
Saqicfa 11, ship's deck; roofing, as slate.
Mosaqqaf, covered with arched roof; roofed.
Saqicfa 11, surgeon's boat or splint to protect a wounded arm.
(2) Esqof 13, bishop. [bishop.
Osqoficya, episcopate, rank of

ڛڡٮ ii. Seccij, *va* prop up.
Moseccej, bolstered up, made up, *i.e.* inferior (wares). [Kasrawân ʙ.]
Secêja, inferior article ʙ.

ڛڡٮ Escele, stairs, landing place. [*Lat.* scala?] *also* seaport ʙ.

ڛڡٮ Sqâla, stocks for ship c.
(2) Mesqala, snail ʙ.

SCR

ڛڡٮ Osqol, *va* polish (metal), iron (linen), make (a horse) glossy. *ger.* Saql.
Saqqâl, polisher. [swords ᴋ.
Saiqal 11, 13, sharpener of Musqal, material for polishing with (as, emery powder).
Suqâl, *s.* polishing, grooming of a horse; *also*, his polished flank ᴋ.
Sôql, Sôqla, the flank ᴋ.

ڛڡٮ Isqam, *vn* be weakly. *ger.* Seqam.
Saqiem 5, weakly, invalid.
Soqm 4, ailment.
Saqâma, weakliness.
Misqâm, quite out of health, a confirmed invalid.

ڛڡٮ Oscon, *vn* be at rest; be still, *ger.* Socoun: dwell, *ger.* Socouna. *Also va* inhabit. *ger.* Soena. [peaceable.
Sêcin 7, inhabitant; *also*, quiet, Socoun, repose, tranquillity.
Secina, stillness, *opposed to* movement.
Mescen, dwelling place.
Soccên, anchor s.
(2) Sicciena 11, table knife.
Siccienicy, Socêcieniey, cutler.
(3) Mescion 2, 11, humble, poorly provided, wretched.
Moscena, pauperism.
Temescen, *vn* cringe, truckle.

ڛڡٮ Secir, Socrân, drunken (*fem.* Secra', Secrâna, *pl.* Secra' ʟ.) *pl.* Secêra'.

SCR

Socr, Secra, drunkenness.
Socriey, Siccier, Miscier, drunk-
 Iscer, *vn* bo drunkcn. [ard B.
iv. Escir, *va* intoxicate.
Moscir, intoxicating.
Sccer, strong drink; whatever
 intoxicates x.
Secra, Sccera, stupor. [death.
Secerât el maut, the stupors of
(2) Soccer, sugar; *pl.* Secêcir,
 sweets.
Soocera, *nu.* of d⁰.
Socceriey, sugary.
Soccerji, confectioner.
(3) Sicr, dike, mound for con-
 fining water x. c. (not B.)
Secer, *ger.* damming up c.
ii. Seccir, *va* shut (a door) AL
Moseccer, shut, closed.

ـــــــــــــــــــــ

سقر Saqar, *s.* hellfire c.

صقر Saqr 3, a falcon.
Sŏqaira, kestrel.

ـــــــــــــــــــــ

سكت Oscot, *vn* be silent. *ger.*
 Socout, silence.
Sécit, silent.
Sccout, Sicciet, taciturn.
ii. Seccit, iv. Escit, *va* silence
 (a person).
Secte, apoplexy.
Socte, a lozenge, etc., which
 keeps a child silent x.
Sêcoute, taciturnity x.

ـــــــــــــــــــــ

سقط Isqat, *vn* fall (recido);
 as fœtus from the mother;
 esp. as in miscarriage. *ger.*
Soqout, stumbling, fall.

SR

Soqt, an abortion.
Saqat, refuse, rubbish, worthless
 furniture.
Saqqât, seller of old trash.
Saqat, merchandize spoilt or
 spoiling c. anything stunted
 or marred. (See Sckta).
Saqta, a trip, false step, fall;
 damage of goods; error 5.
Sâqit, Saqiet, a fallen young
 (man) x.
[Saqiota, fallen woman x.]
Siqât, small wares (= kordâ ?).
Saqtuiy, ironmonger v.
Soqât, windfalls, fallen fruit x.
ii. Seqqut, *va* inlay (steel with
 silver) B.
iv. Esqut, *va* cause abortion.
Mesqat, place of falling; Mes-
 qat el râs, native soil.

ـــــــــــــــــــــ

سر Sirr 4, a secret.
Sirra", secretly.
Cêtib el sirr, Cêtib el esrâr,
 secretary.
Walad el sirr, bastard.
Miserra, whispering tube x.
Sirricy, *adj.* secret, clandestine,
 confidential.
Sorrieya 11, concubine.
Seriera 11, a secret.
Seriericy, privy councillor.
iii. Sêrir, *va* entrust with a
 secret.
(2) Sorr, *va* to make glad; *vn*
 to bo glad.
iv. Esirr, *va* gladden.
vii. Inairr, *vp* be gladdened.
Sorour, *s.* joy. *ger.* of i.
Sêrr, glad. Mesrour, d⁰.

SR

Meserra, joyfulness.
(3) Serier 8, cradle, crib, bier, throne; bedstead B₂.
Serier el melic, the capital x.
(4) Sorra 2, 10, the navel.
Sirâr, umbilical cord x.
(5) Esêrier, lineaments, features.

سر Jörr, *va* tie up tight. *ger.* Jarr.
Jörra 10, a bundle; a purse.
iv. Ayurr cala', *vn* insist upon, persist in.
viii. Usturr, *vn* be overtight, as a shoe x.
Järr, binding, obligatory x.
Järra 12, an obligatory thing.
(2) Jurr, hoarfrost B.
(3) Jörr, *vn* grind (as the teeth), scratch (as a pen). *ger.* Jarier.
Jarrâr, scratchy, noisy, as a pen.
Jarriey, *adj.* clinking.

صرصر Jarrur, *vn* scratch (as pen), screech (as macaw).
Jarsara, *s.* scream of eagle.
Jarvar, Jörsöur, cricket, deathwatch.

اسر 'Eer, (leathern) strap; bundle? *fig.* entirety.
Bi'esrihi, in the bundle, in entirety, wholly.
Bi'esribim, every one of them.
'Eser Yesir, *va* strap together; take captive. *ger.* Isêr.
'Esier 8, captive of war.
ii. 'Esair, *va* strap tight.
v. Te'eaaer, and x. Istêsir, *vn* become captive.

SYR

سور Sour 4 B.; also 9; wall of castle, rampart.
Mosewwar, walled (town).
v. Tesewwar, *vn* climb up a wall.
(2) Siwâr 8, Iswar 11, bracelet.
ii. Sewwir, *va* adorn with bracelets.
v. Tesewwar, *vn* wear bracelets.
(3) Seura, *s.* trace, vestige c.

سور Usmir, *va* stun (the ears) B.
vii. Insawir, *vp* be stunned, deafened B.
(2) Jöura 10, form, aspect, image, effigy drawing.
Jöuratⁿ, in appearance.
Jaiyir, shapely, well moulded (horse).
ii. Jawwir, *va* form, draw, trace, paint.
Taswierêt, figures, images, paintings.
Mosawwir, painter, sculptor.
v. Tasawwar, *vp* of ii.; *vna* imagine.
Tasawwor, idea, conception.
(3) Jöur, Sour, Tyre.

سير Sier, *vn* proceed, move, glide (as ship, as affairs). *ger.* Mesier(a).
Sier, *s.* career, expedition.
Siera, course, route.
Seira, gait. Misyâr, route x.
Séyir, *partic.* moving, sailing.
Seyyâra, a planet.
ii. Seyyir, *va* put on route, send.
Tesyier, transport, mission.

SYR

iii. Sêyir, *va* keep pace with; *fig.* conciliate, humour; go along with, assent to.
Mosêyir, complaisant; *also,* communicative B.
(2) Seir 3, thong of leather.
(3) Sê'ir, the rest; *erroneously used for* all.

صير Juir, *en* become. *ger.* Jair. Jâr *is used for* It is.
Maynir, *s.* issue, result K.
ii. Jayyir, and iv. Ayuir, *va* cause to become, render.

سرو Serwa, *nu.* cypress; collectively Scrou.
(2) Sirwa, *su.* lizard's egg K. collectively Sirâ, spawn?
ii. Serri, *va* spawn.

سرى Iari, *en* pass (as rain through a coat, or as disease from one to another), find its way through, penetrate.
Sêri, *adj.* diffusive, contagious. Sirâya, contagion.
iv. Eari, *va* propagate contagion; cause (disease) to spread.
(2) Serâyâ, Serûya, Serâi, palace.

صرى Jâri 12, mast of a ship.

سرع Israc, *vn* hasten, speed. *ger.* Sirc.
Sories, speedy. Esrac, quicker.
Sorca, *s.* speed.
Sorcat⁻, in speed, speedily.
iv. Esric, *va* speed (another), hasten, press.

SRD

iii. Sêric, *va* vie in speed with.
vi. Tesêras, *or* d⁰ mutually.
Sircân, quick K. [K.
Misrus, habitually very prompt

صرع Jars, *ger.* a starting up, when suddenly waked or roused B. epilepsy.
Jaries, *pl.* Jarsa', thrown to the ground, as in epilepsy, or in wrestling.
Jurca, *s.* a wrestling.
Jurries, stout wrestler.
Marrous, epileptic.
Jöris, *ep* suffer epilepsy.
iii. Jûris, *va* wrestle with.
vi. Tayâras, *or* wrestle together.
vii. Ioyaris, *en* wake up with a start B.
(2) Muyrâs 11, one leaf of a folding door c. a hemistich c.

سرب Sirb, Sorba 4, a flock, swarm. [ranks K.
ii. Serrib, *va* drive a flock in
v. Teserrab, *en* form bands (as birds), flock together.
(2) Israb, *en* trickle K. But see Zrb. [desart.
(3) Scrûb, the mirage in the
(4) Sorâbâti, a nightman B.

سربل Serbel, sort of basket?

صربص Jarbuy, *va* wind on a reel B.

سرد Serd, *s.* coat of mail; but see Zerda. [troops B.
(2) Serd el sascir, review of
(3) Serroud 11, sort of basket?

SRD

سردب Serdâb 11, subterraneous apartment to live in during the extreme heat B₈.

سردق Sorâdiq 2, an awning.
Serdiq, *va* cover with an awning x.

صرف Osrof, *va* corrode, as worms in a tree. *ger*. Serf.
Sêrif, *adj*. corrosive B.
iv. Esrif, *va fig*. corrode (one's fortune), dissipate, lavish.
Mosrif, spend-thrift, prodigal.
Isrâf, prodigality.

صرف Osrof, *va or* Usrif; change (money), *also* spend (money); turn, convert, dispose of, sell (bank paper).
Usrif san, divert from. *ger*. Sarf 3, change; *pl*. vicissitudes.
Sarfa, change, small money.
Sarfeya, expenditure.
Sarrâf, money changer.
Sarrâfa, money drawer, till.
Sairafey 11, banker K.B.
Masrouf 11, expense.
Masrif, bill, account of expenses.
Saraf, *grammatical* change, inflection.
Sarfey, grammarian x.
ii. Sarrif, *va* inflect (words), decline, conjugate.
v. Tasarraf, *vn* be versatile; bi, dispose of, manage.
Tasarrof, versatility; disposal, management.

SRJ

Motasarrif, disposer, (arbitrary) ruler.
vii. Insarif san, *vn* turn oneself away from, retire.
Insarif, *vp* be changed; *esp*. affected, as health.
Insurâf, departure, impairing (of health). [with x.
iii. Sârif, *va* deal cunningly

سرح Sarall, *vn* go at large, roam as cattle; *also* as a lion F. (hence *dispersion* is not the fundamental idea, but *freedom*). *ger*. Soroull.
ii. Serrill, *va* set free, dishevel *the hair*; permit; send (cattle) to graze.
iv. Esrill, *va* set (cattle) free; divorce (a wife).
Mesrall 11, grazing ground, open prairie, lea.

صرح Sarlla, notoriety, publicity.
Sarllat^ᵘⁿ, openly.
Sariell, lucid of statement.
Sarálla, lucidity, distinctness.
ii. Sarrill bi, *vn* state clearly, expound unmistakeably.
iv. Asrill, d°.
vii. Insarill, *vp* of ii. and iv.

سرج Serj 3, military saddle.
Serrâj, saddler.
Sirâja, art and trade of d°.
ii. Serrij, *va* saddle (a horse).
(2) *Also*, Serrij, *va* card wool.
(3) Seiraj, oil from bush, oil of sesame AL B.

SRJ

Siráj, hand-lamp, adapted for common oil.
Misraja, any lamp; but *vulg.* Qandiel for foreign lamp.
iv. Esrij, *va* light a lamp? illumine?
(4) *Also* ii. Serrij, *va* whip *or* overcast in sewing.
Sirája, *ger.* whipping.

سرج Sarája, scrofula c.

سرخ Sérouk bâroud, a petard в.

سرخ Usrak, *vn* cry aloud, sound out, resound. *ger.* Sarka, call to prayer к.
Sarka, Sárika, a shout.
Sörák, *s.* outcry.
v. Tasarrak, *vn* shout one's best.
Sarrák, screamer, peacock.
vi. Tasârak, *vn* shout together.
x. Istasrik, *va* shout to (another) for aid к.

سرم Sirm, substance F. *See* Jirm.
(2) Sorm (*med. t.*), the rectum.

سرم Usrim, *va* prune sharply к.
Sárim, trenchant, severe, austere.
Saráma, severity, austerity.
(2) Sarmiya, principal of money в.
(3) Sarm, tanned leather.
Sarrám, dealer in tanned hides.
Sarma 10, *vulg.* Sarmáya 11, leather shoe.

SWS

سرمد Sermad, endless c.
Sermadaⁿ, perpetually, without end. [Samad.
Sermadiey, everlasting. *See*

سرك Seriec, shaft of a spear or column.
(2) Serci 11, promissory note.

سرق Isriq, *vn* steal. *ger.* Serij, Sorqa, theft.
Sériq 7, thief.
iii. Sériq, *va* do stealthily, *ila'* (a person).
Mosêraqa, furtive eying к.

سرسم Sersim, *va* infuriate.
Mosersem, infuriated.

سرت Serit, hard of mouth в.

سرط viii. Isterut, *va* devour F.
Istirât, voracity.
Mosterut, voracious.
Serarân, Cancer in the Zodiac; cancer (disease).

سرط Surât 10, direct road, correct road, route.

سوس Sous, liquorice root.
(2) Souse, *ɑw.* moth, worm.
Mosewwas, motheaten.
(3) Sous, *va* groom (a horse) в.
Séyis 5, an administrator, manager; *vulg.* a groom.
Siyáse, administration. [cal.
Siyásiey, administrative, politi-

سوس Sauy, covey of gamebirds.

SSN

سَنسِن Sensifl, *va* craze (the mind), enamour, overcome with love.

سَوسَن Sousen, the lily c.

سِتّ Sitt 2, lady (term of compliment).
Soteite, little lady, miss.
Soteitieya, lovebird, small dove.

اِسْت 'Ist, breech, rump.

وَسَط Wasat 4, middle, medium.
Wast, *prep.* in the midst of.
Wasiet, *adj.* middle, intermediate; *s.* mediator.
Ausat, midmost.
Wasatuiy, Wasrâni, midmost.
Wosta', middling c.
Wasut, Wasrâni, middling B.
Wasâta, mediocrity.
Wâsit, a go-between, marriage-broker.
Wâsita 11, means, medium.
v. Tewassat, *vn* mediate (between).
Motewassit, middle, central.
El baflr el motewassit, the Mediterranean sea.

سَوط Seut, *pl.* Siyât, whip, scourge.
(2) Miswat, spatula of druggist B.

صَوت Saut 4, voice.
Suit, renown, credit.
Suite, reputation.
Saiyit, *adj.* sounding.
Muywât, loud sounding?

STM

Mosayyit, having good credit.
ii. Sawwit, *vn* cry aloud.
v. Tasayyit, *vn* gain credit.

سَطو Satwa, assault x. prowess F. military superiority.
Esrâ, superior, first-rate F.

سَطَح Isras, *va* Istas bi, *vn* lay hand on, touch, reach B.
(2) Sérus, *adj.* brilliant (jewel), signal (proof).

سَطْبل Israbl, *pl.* Eserâbil, cow-house, stable.

سَتَذ 'Ostéd, 'Ostéa 11, artist, master, professor.

سَطَفَ Ayraufa, lutestring (lustring), a sort of braid or tape.

سَطَح Sarfl 3, flat roof of house.
ii. Sarrufl, *va* flatten, level.
v. Tesarrufl, *vn* lie flat.
vii. Insarufl, *vp* of ii.
Mesrafl, flat area.
Mosarrafl, *adj.* plane.

سَطَل Sarl 3, metal pot, metal pail, urn AL
(2) 'Osröul 11, squadron of ships F. *Gr.* στόλος.
(3) Isrul or Uyrul, *va* enchant, throw into trance.
Mesröul, ecstatic c.
vii. Insarul, *vp* be intoxicated by a certain herb K.

سَطَم Osröm, *va* temper (steel).

STR

سـتر Ostor, *va* veil, screen, protect. *ger.* Setr.
Sotra, a screen, *lit.* or *fig.*
Sitêra, Seltêra 11, a blind.
ii. Settir, *ca* hide by a curtain.
v. Tesetter *or* viii. Istetir, *vn* hide *oneself* behind a curtain.

سطر Ostör, *va* trace lines. *ger.* Satr 3, line (of writing).
Misrara, a ruler to rule lines with. [lines.
ii. Sarrar, *ca* rule with parallel
v. Teseirar, *vn* rule pedantically.
Teseirör, martinet rule.
(2) Sárünr 12, cook's large knife, butcher's knife.
(3) Mosrara 11, a sample; from Italian *mostra*.

T. T. Θ.

تا Tê! come! [*vulg.* used hortatively, as, Tê naronfl, let us go! *age eamus!*]
'Ete', he came. Yéti, he comes [but *vulgo* for locomotion, Já is used]. *ger.* Ityân, arrival.
'Eti, *partic.* coming (month, event).
iii. 'Eti, *va* go along with, agree with; *sala'*, concerning.
Mowéti, compatible?
v. Te'etté, *vn* come about, as an event.
vi. Te'etté, *vr* go along together, agree with one another, match as colours, etc., be in keeping.

TWΣ

بج Watt, *vn* Tewatwat, twitter, whimper, pule.
Watwat, a swallow, a bat (*see under* Tait).

وطي Wata' Yata', *vn* tread.
Maurâ', footprint.
Wâru, low (ground, voice).
Aura', lower.

لوا Tewa, Tewwa, *adv.* just now.

طوي Utwi, *ca* fold, roll up; *pop.* tuck in; *i.e.* gobble up. *ger.* Taiy.
Tuiya, a fold, plait.
Tawieya, bent, purpose, nature.
Marwa' 11, a fold, spire.
Marwi, a claspknife. [up.
ii. Tawwi, *va intens.* of i. wrap
(2) Tâwa, baking pan.
Töwaiya, d°· AL

توي Iθwi, *vn* sojourn, tarry.
Θiwaiy, a sojourner, an alien B.
Meθwa' 11, place of sojourning.
ii. Θewwi, *or* iv. Eθwi, *ca* entertain (a stranger).

تج Tertis, *va* jog about, push to and fro. *Also*, *vn* stammer. But see Tehtih.

طوع Töus li, *vn* obey. *ger.* Taus.
Táyis, obedient.
Tâsa, obedience.
ii. Tayyis (*modern*) *or* iv. Aruis, *va* reduce to obedience, subdue.
[Classically, iv. Aruis, *va* obey, which involves ambiguity.]

TWS

iii. Tâwiṡ, ɛɑ comply with.
Motâwiṡ, compliant.
(2) x. Istaruiṡ [common in modern literature], ɛn be able.
Istirâsa, ability.

تعب Tɛsb, s. toil, trouble.
Itɛab, ɛn toil, weary oneself. ger. Tɛsab.
Tesbân, weary.
iv. Etsub, ɛɑ tire, ennui.
Motsub, tiresome.

ثعب Θɑɛba, basilisk?
Θɑɛbân, huge serpent, boa.

طعج Tasj, boss of metal B.
Utɛaj, ɛɑ emboss in metal B.
vii. Intasuj, vp be embossed B. bulge as metal.

ثعلب Θeslab 11, fox.
Θosailab, fox's cub B.

طعم Utɛam, ɛɑ taste. ger.
Tasm, taste, appetite.
Tösma 10, taste of viands, a taste, a morsel.
Tasâm 8, food, bait for fish.
Taɛsâm, seller of cooked food.
Marsam 11, food.
ii. Tassum, ɛɑ bait (a hook); also, graft (a tree).
Tasma, Tarsuim, a graft.
Tarsuima, a bait for fish.
iv. Atsum, ɛɑ same as ii. also, feed, nourish.
Morsum, feeder.
Mursâm, hospitable.

TWB

viii. Irrasum, ɛn be savoury, as food; [be well educated x.]
Morrasum, savoury.
iii. Tâsum, ɛɑ attemper (steel).

طعن Ursan, ɛɑ pierce with a lance; oftener fig. impugn, revile. Tassân, censorious.
Tasna, a lunge with a foil.
vi. Terâsan, ɛn fence together in sport, with a foil.
Morâsana, tournament.
Tâsöun, the plague, pestilence.
Tâsöuniey, pestilential.
Marsöun, plague-stricken.

تعس Itɛas, ɛn fall heavily, perish, be ruined. ger. Toss, ruin, perdition.
Tesâse, dº. x.
iv. Etsas, ɛɑ ruin, cause to perish.

طب Tabb, ger. Tubb, be a physician.
Tubb, art of medicine.
Tubbicy, medicinal.
Tabieb 8, physician.
Tabieba, female dº.
Tabâyib, medical appliances.
iii. Tâbib, ɛɑ treat (a patient, a disease).
v. Terabbab, ɛn profess physic.
x. Isterubb, ɛɑ ask to be treated x.
(2) Tabrub li, ɛn wave the hand to; ɛɑ tap. [water x.]
Tabraba, sound of drum (of

توب Toub, ɛn repent of sin.
Touba, repentance.
Têyib, penitent.

TWB

طوب Töuba, *nu.* a brick.
Tawâba, brickfield.
Tawwâb, brickmaker.
(2) Tâba, ball of thread B.
Taub, Taup, cannon (*Turk.*).
Taubji, Tauptxi, cannoneer.
Taubajieya, artillery.

ثوب Θeub, *pl.* Θiyâb, garment, single gown; the sole essential of Arab dress.
Θiyâb, clothes, dress.
Θiyâbicy, keeper of clothes, chamberlain.
Θewwâb, clothes-seller.
(2) Θewâb, recompence (for good deeds), guerdon (*old style*).
ii. Θewwib *or* iv. EΘwib, *va* recompense.
v. TeΘewwab, *vn* earn recompense; do a work or say a prayer of "supererogation."
x. IsteΘwib, claim recompence.

طيب Tuib, *vn* be nice, pleasant.
Tâyib, ripe B.
Taiyib, good, nice. [*Also* alive and well AL]
Tuib, niceness, aroma.
Atyab, nicer, nicest.
Töuyâb, luscious.
ii. Tayyib, soften, sweeten, calm. Embalm (a dead body) c.
iv. Atuib, *va* improve.
x. Isteruib, *va* find nice.
Mosterâb, of approved flavour F.

TBS

ونب WeΘeb YeΘib sala', *vn* spring at, pounce on. *ger.* WeΘb.
WeΘba, *nu.* a spring, an assault.

تبع Itbas, *va* follow, *lit.* and *fig.*
Tobas, suite (of a prince).
Etbâs, good manners.
Tôbis, a follower, *pl.* Tebasa.
Tebisa 12, a consequence. *Also pl.* Tewâbis, appurtenances.
Tebasuiya, consequence, succession, result B.; subjection, obedience.
iii. Tebis, *va* follow in detail.
Tibâs, order of series E.
Motêbasa, close adherence.
Motêbis, continual.
v. Tetebbas, *va* follow diligently, track out.
vi. Telêbas, *vr* follow one another in series.
Tetêbos, continuity.
Motetêbis, successive. [suc.
viii. Ittebis, *va* follow up, pur-
iv. Etbis, *va* cause to follow, add (one thing to another).

طبع Urbas, *va* stamp, mark, print. *ger.* Tabs, stamp, mould, character.
Tabsuiy, natural, innate.
Tabiesa, Nature.
Tabiesuiy, natural.
Tâbis, printer. [printing.
Tubâsa, *ger.* printing, art of
Marbas, press. Dâr el Tubâsa, printing house.
Marbous, printed.

TBS

ii. Tabbis, *va* mould, train, educate. *Also* mark, spot.
[Tabis, muddy ᴇ. Tabsa, mud (Algiers) ᴇ.].
v. Terabbas *or* vii. Inrabis, *vn* be docile.
Monrabis, docile, impressible.

تبغ Tobus, tobacco.

طبخ Orbok, *va* cook (food), bake (brick). *ger.* Tabk.
Tubâka, cookery.
Tabbâk, a cook.
Tabick, a dish of cooked food.
Tabkâna 2, a *side* dish ?
Marbak 11, kitchen.
Murbak 11, cooking vessel.
vii. Inrabik, *vp* be cooked.

تبل Têbal, Têbil 12, spice, seasoning.
ii. Tebbil, *or* iii. Têbil, *also* Teubil, *va* spice, season.
(2) Toubâl, slag, scum of metals. *See* θofi.

طبل Tabla, *nu.* 3, 4, tambour, drum.
Tubâla, art of the timbrel.
Tabbâl, drummer, timbrel-player.

تبن Tibn, (chopped) straw.
Tibna, *nu.* a straw.
Tebbân, seller of chopped straw.

طبن Tâboun, hollow fireplace in the earth ᴇ. c.
(2) a bowing of the head ʙ.
v. Terabban, *vn* bow the head ʙ.

TBT

تبنج Tabanja, a pistol. *So* Tofenga, a musket.

طبق Tubq, *prep.* in accordance with.
Tabaqa 2, series, row, story of a house; class, rank.
Tabaq 8, a dish cover, flat dish, tray.
Tabicqieya, a meat tray. [ғ. Murbâqieya, tureen *or* ladle (!)
ii. Tabbiq, *va* apply, adjust (one thing on another).
iii. Tâbiq, *va* fit closely.
iv. Aʀbiq, *va* shut (a book), flap-to ; close (the hand).
v. Terabbaq, *vp* of ii.
vi. Terâbaq, *vr* fit in mutually, coincide.
vii. Inrabiq, *vp* of ii. Also, as *vp* of iv. to be shut in, to be confined (in doors).
Inʀubâq, the being shut up, or kept in doors (as by bad weather).
viii. Uʀʀabiq, *vp* of iv. ? *Also*, Orboq in i. same as iv.

تبر Tibr, precious ore.

طبر Tâbour, a legion, brigade, squadron of horse.

طبرزد Tabarzed, barley sugar.

طبس Tabai' 11, metal saucer for drinking on a journey. *But,* (Algiers, De Dr.) a plate.

تبت Têbout, ark of the covenant ; coffin.

ΘBT

ثبت Iθbit, *va* be steady, firm, certain. *ger.* Θobout.
— *cala'*, persist in.
Θêbit, firm, fixed (opinion).
Θêbits, a fixed (star), a constant quantity, in Algebra.
Θebiet, unflinching (soldier).
Θebât, constancy (of heart).
ii. Θebbit, iv. Eθbit, *va* corroborate (by argument). *Also*, iv. Eθbit, *va* fix, establish.

وتد Wetid 4, a stake, pale.
Weted Yetid, *va* drive in a stake.

وطر Warad Yarud, *vn* be stable.
ger. Warad, Tuda.
Waruid, *adj.* stable, solid.
Waráyid, *pl.* foundations of a house. *sing.* Waruida.
ii. Warrud, *va* consolidate.
v. Tewarrad, *vn* stand firm.

ندى Θedi, Θeda', *pl.* Eθdie, breast of any female.
Θodaiya, nipple of man?

تف Teftif, *vn* stammer. *See* Tehtib.

طف Taff, *va* leap across, clear (a ditch) в. *fig.* Taff cala', cast oneself upon (a person's aid).
Tafief, *adj.* general, incomplete (directions)? round, approximate (number)?

طوف Toúf, *vn* make a tour.
ii. Tawwif, *va* visit in official progress.

TFL

Morawwif, guide, cicerone.
v. Terawwaf, *vn* patrol.
(2) Tauf, a float, raft.
Toufána, *nu.* a deluge.
(3) Táyifa 12, tribe, people.

طيف Taif, *vn* appear in a dream. *ger.* Taif.
Táyif, *vulgo* Taif, an apparition, spectre. Taif el kayâl, d° в. x.

طفو Tufáwa, overboiling of a pot; halo round the moon. [See Urfall.]

طفى Tufi, *va* extinguish.
iv. Atfi, d° x.
Morfi, one who extinguishes c.
vii. Intafi, *vp* of i. *vn* go out, as fire.

نفي Oθfya 11, trivet, tripod c.

تف Toffáha, *nu.* apple.
Toffáll Armeniey, apricots.
Toffáll Farsiey, peaches.
Matfalla, apple orchard.

طف Urfall, *vn* be overfull, overflow. *ger.* Tôfoull.
Táfill, Tafllân, overfilled.
Tôfálla, overflow, surplus.
Tufall, plenitude, redundance c.
Murfalla, spoon to skim off the top of a fluid. [fill.
ii. Taffill, *or* iv. Arfill, *va* overviii. Urrafill, *va* skim (a fluid), take off the froth x.

نفل Tofl, spittle, froth.

ƟFL

نُفَل Ɵoſl. Ɵéfil, lees, dregs B.

طِفَل Tuſl 4, child, babe.
Töſoula c. Töſoulieya, infancy.
iv. ATſil, v. have a little one.
v. Tarafſul, vn sponge upon, come uninvited B. x.

تُفَنْكَ Toſeng, Toſenga, a musket; a war-rocket c.

طَفِق UTſaq fie, vn begin upon, set to work at.

نَفَر Ɵefar 4, vulg. Tafar 4, crupper to a saddle B.

طَفَر UTſir, spring, as goat; leap, as horse B.
Taſra, a leap. [leap.
iv. ATſir, va cause (a horse) to
(2) Taiſour, a certain small bird c.

طَفَش UTſix, vn disappear; play truant, rove, go out as colonist.
Tâfix, s. truant.

نُع Ɵeſθiſ, vn lisp.

طَفِى UTɣi, vn be rebellious.
Töɣyân, rebellion.
Taɣwa', d° impiety c. x.
Târi, rebellious, a rebel; pl. Töɣat c.
iv. ATɣi, va cause to rebel; instigate to infatuation.

نَفَر Ɵeɣou, vn bleat. ger. Ɵoɣû.

ƟHL

طُغْر Töɣra, royal signature.
(2) Tieɣâr, water jar, urn B.

نَغَر Ɵeɣr, fore-teeth c.; frontier of empire; gorge in mountains B.

تَج Tehtih, vn stammer.

طَڻ TöꞱꞱ, vn drop from the hand B.

طَحوِش TawwiꞱ, va rock (a cradle).
v. TarawwaꞱ, vn see-saw; balance oneself on a rope; gad to and fro x.

تِيَه Tieh (Touh), vn stray, lose one's way. ger. Tieh.
ii. TeyyiꞱ (Tewwih), iv. Etieh, va mislead, lead astray.

طِيح TuiꞱ (TöuꞱ), vn go astray, vanish, perish.

طَحَى OTHou, UTHê, va cook, bake.
Tahie, s. dish of cooked food B.
Tâhi (pl. Töhê¹ x.), cook, baker F.

تُحَف ToꞱfa, s. elegant article, TeꞱâyif, curiosities. [gift.
iv. EtꞱuf, va honour with an elegant present.
ii. TeꞱꞱuf, iv. EtꞱuf bi, va embellish, enrich with.

أَحَل Iɵhil, vn be cast away, cast forth. ger. Ɵehl.
Ɵêhil ɕala' el qâɕ, cast ashore.

THL

طَفَلْ Tafll, *s.* lees, dregs B.
Tafflul, muddy, turbid c.
(2) Tuflâl, *s.* the spleen; *pl.*
Taflal (Töflöl?) [loured.
Atflal, *adj.* livid, muddy co-

طَفْلَب Taflab, *s.* water-moss.
Motafllab, covered with water-moss.

تهم Ithem, *vs* slander, accuse.
(Perhaps from Wehm). *vp*
Tohim, be slandered.
Tohma, *s.* slander.
vi. Tetchem, *or* recriminate.

طَخَم Töbma, a surfeit, carouse, junketing.
ii. Tahhim, *vs* surfeit, disgust.
v. Tarahhem, *vn* feel disgust or antipathy.
Tarahhom, antipathy.

طَمْ Tafma, violence, impetuosity.
Tafflöum, *adj.* overpowering.

طَحَن Utflan, *vs* grind (corn) in a mill.
Tafluin, meal, flour.
Tafflân, a miller. [mill.
Tâflöuna 12, Mutflana 11, a
Tâfluna, a grinder, back-tooth c.

طَهَر Othor, *vn* be pure K. *ger.*
Tôhour. Tâhir, pure.
Tahêra, purity, ablution (water-closet, privy AL).
ii. Tabhir, *vs* purify.
iii. Tâhir, *vs* circumcise.

TK

v. Tarahher, *vs* purify oneself (affect purity K.).
Mather, purgatory.
Muthera, vessel or instrument of purification (as a toothpick K.).

تحت Teflt, *prep.* under.
Toflait, *adv.* a little below.
El toflöt, men of low rank K. underlings. [nether.
Teflteniey, *adj.* that is below;

تاج Têj 9, garland, crown; royal crown, diadem.
ii. Tewwij, *vs* crown (a king).
viii. Ittêj, *vp* of d°

تُج Teuj, *s.* bronze.

طاجن Tâjin 12, frying-pan.
ii. Tajjin, *vs* fry?
Motajjan, fried K.

تجر Têjir 7, merchant.
Tijûra, *s.* traffic, commerce, act of trafficking.
Matjar, commerce.
Matjara, place of commerce, market, exchange. *vulg.* Boure.
Also, a commercial country K.
iii. Têjir, *vn* traffic.
viii. Ittejir, *vn* act the merchant.
Probably from 'Ejr.

تك Tokk, *vn* rot, as wood B. become sour, as dough K. *ger.* Tokouka.

تك Tôkk, *vs* smash, crush?

TKM

خَتْم Tokm 3, limit (of a country), boundary (of fields).
Itkim, *va* limit, set a limit to x.
iii. Tèkim, *va* have a common boundary with; be contiguous to.
(2) Tokama, indigestion, from Wakiem.

نَخُنْ Ooknn, *vn* be thick, coarse. *ger.* θokouna.
θekan, thickness. [turbid.
θekien, thick, coarse, bulky,

تَخْتَ Tekt 3, bedstead, throne, seat (plank Bg.).
Tekt-a-rewân, palankeen, carried by mules, litter Al.
(2) Tekit, corpulent (*sic* B. *bis*). *Contrast* Xakit, thin, slim.

تَلّ Tell 3, 5, hill, hill country.
Tolail, little hill.

طَلّ Töll *cala'*, *vn* look out over, command with the eye, peer forth; *pop.* take a peep at, *i.e.* visit.
(2) Tall 5, dew Bg.
Tall, *va* bedew x.

نُول θoul, swarm of new bees.
v. Teθewwal, *vn* swarm in a bunch, as bees.

طُول Töul, length, longitude.
Töul, *vn* be long. *ger.* Taul.
Tawiel, long, tall.
Arwal, longer, taller.
Tuwal, a tether x.

TLS

ii. Tawwil *or* iv. Aruil, *va* lengthen out.
Tarwiel, diffuseness.
Urâla, prolongation.
iii. Tâwil, *va* put (a person) off, defer. [upon.
vi. Terâwal *cala'*, *vn* encroach
(2) Tâyil, Tâyila 12, advantage, avail.
Töul *calaibi bi*, *vn* anticipate him in kind offices B.; get advantage over him.
x. Istaruil *cala'*, *vn* get advantage over.
iii. Tâyil, *or* iv. Aruil, *va* avail (a person).
(3) Tâwola (*Ital.*), chess or draught table. *Also* (at Aleppo) any table.

تِيل Tiel, gold wire.

تَلُو Otlou, *vn* follow; *sep. fig.* peruse. *ger.* Tilâwa, perusal.
Têli, following (day) (words); *pl.* Tewâli, appurtenances, remnants. [succeed.
iii. Têli, *va* come next after,

طَلّى Urli, *va* besmear, anoint, embrocate; gild. *ger.* Urli c.
ii. Talli, *va* same as i.
Urrali, *sp* of d°
(2) Talâwa, grace, elegance c. x. [*Also*, a stud of horses B.]
vii. Inrali *cala'*, *vn* comport with.

طَلَع Urlas, *vn* come (go) out *or* up; come forth as a star.

TLS

ger. Tölous, rise of sun or star.
Tális 12, ascendant (in astrology), good fortune.
Talca, aspect, countenance.
Taliesa 11, van of army.
Matlas 11, place of a star's rising; opening of a poem, first distich.
ii. Tallus, va raise up, lift up, carry up.
Tailus, va pull out, push out в.
iii. Tâlus, va examine carefully, study.
Moralaса, examination, study of a thing, reading.
Morâlasât, pl. letters patent, edicts к.
v. Terallas, viii. Urralus, ғя look out, gaze; — sala', look at, consider; — ñe, look into.
Urralâs sala', survey of, knowledge of. [formed.
Morrálas, Morrálus, well-in-
iv. Arlus, va inform, acquaint.

نلع Θels, harrow; vulgo Mislafa, which also means Trowel.

نلب Iθlib, va fig. reproach with, censure severely. ger. Θelb.
Maθlaba 11, a censure, a rebuke.

نلب Toláb 11, scoria of metals.

طلب Orlob, va demand, require, inquire.
Talab, a request.
Matloub, thing claimed.

TLC

Matlab 11, dᵃ matter inquired into. [inquirer.
Tâlib (in Africa) 7, student,
iii. Tâlib, va call to account; pursue for vengeance, dun.

تلف Itlaf, ғя perish, waste.
ger. Telaf.
Tilf, dross, refuse, waste.
Telicñ, thing wasted к.
iv. Etlif, va waste (money, etc.).
Motlif, wasteful.
Mitlâf, prodigal.

تلن Telñ, Talñ, the mimosa tree.

طلن Tâliñ, wicked, ungodly; opp. of Sâliñ.
(2) Talñuiya, sheet of paper.

تلج Θelj 3, snow.
Θellâj, seller of ice.
Moθlaja 11, icehouse.
Θelij, icy-cold.
Θolújicy, snow-white.
Meθlouj, snowed over; cold-hearted.
iv. Eθlij, ғя pour forth snow.
Moθlij, snowy (day).

تلم Telam 4, a furrow.

تلم Iθlim, va chip, notch (edge of knife or china jar). ger. Θelm. [of i.
v. Teθellim, or vii. Inθelim, vp Eθlem, notched.

تلك Tile, f. that yonder. The masculine is Δélic.

TLC

(2) Tlc, Talq (*Pers.*), talc, a transparent stone.

طلق Uтlaq, *vn* be set free; be divorced (min). *ger.* Talâq.
Taliq, free, unshackled; acquitted (of crime); min', quit of.
Tulq, freedom, permission x.
Tŏloq el lisên, fluent of speech;
Tŏloq el yed, open-handed, generous (*rather* Taliq?).
Tâliq, *adj. partic.* set free, as an animal at large.
Talieq, free of bonds as a captive x. c.
Bi тalouq, *vulgo* gratis.
ii. Talliq, *va* divorce (a wife).
iv. Aтliq, *va* divorce (a wife). *Also*, discharge (a musket); set free (a beast, a captive); utter (a cry); remove conditions and exceptions, make absolute and universal.
Talqa', a discharge (of gun), a volley.
Uтlâq, *s.* зala' el Uтlâq, without exception, absolutely.
Moтlaqaⁿ, dº·
Moтlaq, absolute.
Solтân moтlaq, absolute king.
vii. Inтaliq, *vp* be dismissed, be discarded; *also*, *vn* take oneself off, depart x. c.
Inтaliq bi, go off with, carry off.

ثلث Θolθ, *s.* 4, a third part.
Θêliθ, third.
Θelâθe, *m.* Θelâθ *f.* three.
Θelâθoun(-θien), thirty, thirtieth

TM

Θelaθen, thrice.
Bil Θelâθe, three times.
[Θêliθoun, thirtieth x.]
Θolâθiey, tri-radical (word).
Θelouθ, Trinity. Telθieθ, dº·
Oθloθ, *va* divide in three.
ii. Θelliθ, *va* make triple.
Moθellaθ, triple (*also* triangular x.). *s.* a triangle.

طلس Tellies 11, white cement, plaster; (2) a large sack.

طلس Uтlis, *va* efface (writing). *ger.* Tals.
Maтlous, obtuse (intellect) B.
v. Taтallas, *vn* fade out, vanish (as writing).
Tuls 4, carte blanche, smooth page or tablet, free from writing.
Aтlas, *adj.* smooth, unwritten upon x. *s.* satin.
(2) Tailes, Tailisên, a portion of a certain head-dress which hangs on to the shoulders, especially worn by Persian dervishes.

طلسم Tulsem 2, 11, amulet or talisman. [x.
Talsim, *va* defend by an amulet

تم Timm, *vn* be finished, complete. Têmm, *adj.* complete.
Temâm, *adj.* complete, full moon.
Bil temâm, entirely.
Tcmâmaⁿ, dº· [ment.
Tзmâma, Tetemma, *s.* complement.
Tomâma, surplus.

TM

ii. Temmim, iv. Etimm, *va* finish, complete.
Tetmiem, pleonasm x.
Itmâm, *ger.* act of completing, completion, complete state.
Motemm, having received a surplus x.
vi. Tetômm, *vn* form a general union, combine into a complete whole.
(2) Temiema, *s.* amulet c.

طم Tömm, *va* smother, overwhelm; fill (a well) up to the brim.
vii. Intumm, *pp.* to be crammed full, choked up.

طمطم Tamtum, Temtim, *vn* stammer, stutter.

ثم Θomm(a), *adv.* next, thereupon.
(2) Timm, the gannet, seafowl.

أثم Iθem, *vn* be guilty.
ii. ʼEθθim, *va* criminate.
ʼIθm 4, guilt.
Mâθema, act of guilt.
ʼEθoum, ʼEθiem, criminal.
x. Istêθim, *va* count guilty, prosecute.

أتم ʼMê tem, *pl.* Meʼêtim, wailing s.
(2) ʼOtom, wild olive.

يتم Yetiem 4, 11, an orphan.
Yetm, Yetêma, orphanhood.

ΘMN

توم Toum, *s.* pearl, ostrich-egg x.
(2) Teum, *adj.* or *subs.* twin c.

طام Tâma, key (major or minor) in music b.

ثوم Θoum, garlic.
Θouma, *nu.* *Gr.* θύμον.

طمع Utmas, *v.* covet; hanker (after), with *fis* or *bi* of the thing, or with *en* before verb.
Tamas, covetousness.
Tammâs, covetous. Atmas, *comp.*

طمح Tammiñ, lift the two front feet into the air, in order to leap x. aspire towards?
Motammañ, an object to be leapt at?

تمل Temiela, species of wild cat in Arabia x.

طمل Otmol, *va* drench, impregnate x.
Tamiel, *adj.* imbued, steeped x.
Tamla, mud x. See Odmol.

طمن Tamn, tranquillity.
ii. Tammin, *va* recruit.
Utmienân, quietude.
Tömânieya, dº
Utmâʼn, *vn* tranquil.
Mormâin, Moterâmin, enjoying repose.
Mormân, trusted in x.

ثمن Θemen 8, price, cost.
Θemien, precious.

ΘMN

Eθman, more costly.
Moθmin(?), Moθemman x. costly.
iv. Eθmin, *va* pay a price x.
ii. θemmin, *va* appraise.
(2) θomn 4, *s*. an eighth part.
θemânia, *m*. θemâni *f*. eight.
θêmin, eighth. [ieth.
θemânoun (-ien), eighty, eight-
Moθemman, octagonal, octuple.

تومن Toumán, *s*. 2, 11, a Persian gold coin (worth 12 francs x.); a myriad, 10,000.

تمر Temra, *nu*. a date; *coll*.
Temr, *pl*. 2 (3, θ x.).
Temmâr, seller of dates.
Temr Hindiey, tamarind.
(2) ii. Temmir, Tammir, *va* groom, curry (a horse) B.

ثمر θemr, *s*. 4, 5, fruit, *lit*. or *fig*.
θemara, *nu*.
Meθmour, abundant, numerous (people).
iv. Eθmir, *vn* bear fruit.
Moθmir, fruit-bearing, fruitful (tree or country).
x. Isteθmir, *va* make fruitful.

طمر Urmir, *va* bury in the earth, inter, bury (corn).
Marmoura 11, subterraneous cellar for corn.
(2) Urmir, *vs* bound, leap.
But see Urfir.

طمس Urmis, *va* efface.
vii. Inramis, *vp*. See Urlis.
Tams, absorption in God (mystical phrase).

WTN

Tâmis, dead of heart x. [God.
v. Taramnes, *vp* be absorbed in

تمسح Timsêû 11, crocodile.

تمش v. Tetemmax, *vn* tryst; make rendezvous B.

تنن Tennien, the Dragon in astronomy.
Tennien, waterspout (meteoric phenomenon).

ثن θinn, dry plants; hay.
θonna 10, hair at horse's fetlock B.

طن Tunn, *vn* clank, ring, as metal; hum, as insect. *ger*.
Tanien, din, echo (of fame).
Tanrun, *vn* tinkle, jingle. *ger*.
Tanrana.

أتن 'Etên 10 (*pl*. 'Oton), sheass. [nace.
(2) Etoun (*also* Eθoun) 2, fur-

وثن Weθen 4, 10, idol, of wood or stone; from *Gr*. ἔθνη.
Weθeniey, idolatrous, pagan.

وطن Waran 4, home, native country. [cile.
Maurun 11, homestead, domi-
Warun Yarun, *vn* dwell x.; but commoner perhaps is,
v. Tewarran, *vn* reside, settle (fie, in).
iv. Aurun, *va* cause to dwell, plant (men) on the soil.

WTN

x. Istcuθin, ra choose one's residence, settle down.
'Ehl el istierân, the settled population x.

تون Teunieya, pl. Towan, a surplice.
(2) Meθêna, a bladder; is referred to root Mθn.

طون Tawân, ceiling.

تين Tiena, sw. a fig.
Towaiyina, beccafico, fig-eater, small bird like a snipe.

طين Tuin 4, clay, mud.
ii. Tayyin, es mould in clay.

تنو Tonwa, grounds of coffee B.

ثنى Iθni, ea double, bend; repeat.
Meθnicy, doubled, bent.
Θenieya, a doubling; hence, a ledge, a raised edge B. Also, 2, 14, a foretooth.
Iθnain (f. Θintein) two.
Θêni, second, double.
ii. Θenni, ea double numerically.
v. Teθennâ, ep of last.
Θenawiey, secondary F.
Θonâ'iey, biradical (word).
Θonyân, pl. Θinya x. secondary.
Θenâwi, twin, belonging to two
Θenwiya, dualism x. [x.
Teθniya, the dual.
vii. Inθeni, ep of i. be bent.
(2) Θenâ, pl. 8, Eθniya, salutation, praise.

TNC

Θenieya 2, 14, eulogium.
ii. Θenni, ea panegyric. (See also Θenni above.)
(3) x. Istiθni, make exception.
Istiθnâ, exception.
But Sifr el Istiθnâ, book of Repetition, i.e. Deutcronomy.
Moateθna', exceptional, unparalleled x.

تنب Tennoub, spruce fir.

تنبك Tonbec, zinc?
(2) Tenbec, damped and medicated Persian tobacco AL

طنب Urnib, ra be tight, as cord.
Tönob 4, tendon of neck. Also, Arnâb, pl. tent-ropes.
ii. Tannib, ea strain, tighten. fig. exaggerate, indulge rhetoric.
Moṭannab, highstrung; fig. overstrained, pompous.
Moṭnib, prolix(rather,excessive in rhetoric).
Urnâb, excess of rhetoric.

طنبر Tönbour 11, six-stringed guitâr.

طنف Tönaf 4, projecting roof?
(2) Tönfose, Tenfise 11, a carpet 11. From Gr. Lat. tapes?

طنجر Tanjara, Tenjara 11, metal stewpot AL

تنك Tonace, sw. tin AL

TNR

نَتر Tennour 11, round oven sunk in the earth. Forge for iron.

نَتب Tenour, the wood-pecker F.

طَطْبل Tantala, uvula of the throat B.

طَطْبر Tantônr, a peculiar head-covering; domino? hood?

تَكّ Tectic, *vn* crackle as salt in fire; simmer.

طق Taqtuq, *vn* rattle or clatter, as hoofs on pavement; crackle as the joints in shampooing. *ger.* Taqtaqa. [word] B.
Taqq, *vn* rattle, *for* die (coarse
(2) Taqrōuqa, a *belle* B.

وَثق Weθeq Yeθeq (ila', bi), *vn* confide in, rely on. *ger.* θiqa.
Weθieq, firm, fast.
Wiθêqa 2, a fastening, sure tie.
Weθicqa 11, firm resolution; letter of credit B.
Micθâq, *pl.* Mawêθiq, a compact c. x.
iii. Wêθiq, *va* bind in a compact.
ii. Weθθiq, *va* confirm, assure, set at rest.
iv. Auθiq, *va* tie fast x.
v. Teweθθuq, *vn* be steady (morally), have self-reliance.
x. Isteuθiq min, *vn* confide in.

وَطن Watâq, tabernacle, pavilion.

VOL. II.

θQF

توق Touq ila', long after. *ger.*
Touqân, hankering.
Tewwâq, vehement in desire.
Motewwaq, ardently desired x.
(2) Touqa [Teuqa?], door-catch B.; a clamp, a rivet?

طوق Tauq 4, collar, neckchain.
ii. Tawwiq, *va* adorn with collar.
Motawwaq, the ruff (a bird).
(2) Tâq 9, arched window.
(3) Tâq, *adj.* odd, not even c.
(4) Tâqa, power, ability.
iv. Atuiq ɛala', *vn* be able for.
Lâ otuiq ɛala', I cannot withstand, I cannot afford.
Lâ yotâq, unendurable.
vii. Lâ yentâq d°. B.
Utâqa, power, ability.

تَكي viii. Itteci, *vn* lean upon.
Mottecê, couch. [Root Weci.]
Tocêya, cushion.

تَقي Taqi! beware! c.
Taqi, pious. Etqa', more pious.
Taqwâ, Taqwa', piety.
Taqieya, piety x. [Root Wqy.]
(2) Taqâwa, Taqwiya 11, seed-corn.

تَقب Oθqob, *va* bore, drill.
θaqb, a hole bored through.
θâqib, penetrating, profound.
Eθqab, more penetrating.
Miθqab, an auger.

تَقف θaqif, θaqief, sharp, shrewd, subtle.
ii. θaqqif, *va* rectify, correct.

28

ΘCL

ثكل Iθcel, *vn vp* be bereaved of children. *ger.* Θocl.
Θecil, Θécil, Θecoul, Θeclân, bereaved of children.
Miθcél, totally bereaved.
iv. Eθcil, *va* bereave of children.

ثقل Oθqol *sala'*, *vn* be heavy upon. *ger.* Θiql 4, weight.
Θaqiel, heavy.
Θaqâla, *fig.* sullenness c.
Θaqal, Θaqala, heavy baggage, incumbrances.
ii. Θaqqil, *va* make heavy.
Θaqqil *sala'*, *vn* incommode, lay heavy burden upon.
iv. Eθqil, *va* load, lade, burden.
vi. Teθâqal, *vp* be encumbered.
x. Isteθqil, *va* count heavy к.
Miθqâl 11, weight to weigh with; piece of money, *shekel*.

طقم Taqm, a suit, set.
Tâqim, a soldier's uniform.

تقن Taqin, *adj.* consummate.
iv. Etqin, *va* do to perfection.
viii. Ittaqin, *vn* be perfect.
Mottaqin, *adj.* consummate.
[New root from Yaqin.]

طقس Taqs 3 (*Gr.* τάξις), order, rite, ceremony, liturgy.
Taqs el donyâ, state of weather.

تر Teterter, *vn* vacillate, totter; stammer? [quacity в. х.
Tertera, babbling, verbiage, lo-

ثرثر Θerθir, *vn* clack as a mill.

TWR

ط Törra, crest, comb of a bird.
(2) Tarr, *s.* free will, arbitrary power? teſlt тarr, (surrender) at discretion в.
(3) Tarröur, long pointed *cap;* also, a doctor's cloth *robe* ?
(4) Tararöur (*sic*), sauco ғ.
(5) Tarruir, tartar of wine.
(6) Törrör 11, silkworm.

أثر Eθr 4, footstep, trace, monument of the past.
'Eθeriey, traditionist к.
ii. 'Eθθir fie, *v.* impress.
v. Te'cθθer, viii. Ittcθir, *va* follow in the traces of.
(2) iii. 'Eθir, Wêθir, *va* frequent, haunt, prefer.
iv. Auθir, *va* d°. (as if from root Wθr). [ence.
x. Isteθir, *va* choose by prefer-

وثر Weθier, smooth and soft (bed).
ii. Weθθir, *va* shake up (a bed), make it soft and level.

وتر Woter 4, harpstring, bowstring.
ii. Wettir, *or* iv. Autir, *va* string (a bow), strain up (the lyre strings).
(2) vi. Towâter, *vn* follow in succession [for Tewâθer ?].
Motewâtir, successive.
(3) Witr, *adj.* odd (not even) в.

نور Toura, Teura, the law (of the Hebrews).
(2) Têra 2 (*or pl.* Tiyar к.), a turn, time. Têrateⁿ, once.

TWR

طور Taur 4, phase, species, type; *also*, a time (*Fr.* fois).
Târa, rim (of hat), border (of garment), ornamental edging.
Xaṃil el târa, embroider B.
Târatiey, embroiderer.
(2) Tauriya, bat used by washerwomen.

نار Θê'r, *en* retaliate. *ger.* Θê'r, retaliation. 'Eka Θê'r, taking of revenge.
Θêyir, avenger of blood.

نور Θour, *en* rise aloft, spring aloft, flame up. *ger.* Θeurân.
Θoura, a huff, an outburst.
Θêra, impetuosity.
Θêyira 12, tumult. [passion].
iv. AΘier, *va* kindle up (war, MoΘier, instigator. [Tauros.
(2) Θeur 9, a bull, *Gr. Lat.*

تير Teyyâr, torrent, surge; *esp. fig.* Tayyâr *or* Teyyâr B.

طير Tuir, *en* fly (as a bird), be flighty (as the mind). *ger.* Tairân. Târ saqli, my mind has taken flight, *i.e.* I am enraptured.
Tâyir, *vulgo* Tair 3, a bird.
Tairiey, belonging to a bird.
Töwair, little bird.
Tüyouriey, bird-seller.
Tayyâr, flying much; fleet (as horse). *Also*, *s.* reel to wind thread on B.
Tâyir, flighty, giddy.
Tayyariey, volatile.

TRB

Taira, flightiness, levity.
Tuira, bad omen.
Aṭyar, injudicious (person), ominous (event). [to fly.
ii. Tayyir, iv. Aṭuir, *va* cause v. Teṭayyar bi, min, *en* form an omen from, forebode by.
vi. Teṭâyar, *or* fly apart, as Mosteruir, volatile. [clouds.

نرا Θerâ, earth c. damp soil x.

نرو Θerwa, opulence.
MoΘri, opulent. Θeriey, d°·c.

ترى نرى Θorya, Teriɔya, lustre, hanging lamp.

طرى Tari, fresh, moist, extraordinary (expenditure) B.
Kobz ṭari, new bread.
Tarâwa, freshness.
Marâriya, a cooler.
ii. Tarri, *va* freshen.

ترع Torɛa 10, pond, pool r.

نرب IΘrib, *va* or with sala', *en* reproach, disdain. *See* IΘlib.

ترب Torâb 8, 9, mould, soil.
Torba 10, grave.
Torbâ, terrestrial globe x.
(2) Tirb 4, of same age.

طرب Uṭrab, *en* be touched in heart, *esp.* by music.
Tarab, keen emotion.
Taroub, susceptible.
Muṭrâb, very susceptible.

TRB

iv. Aᴛrib, *va* move, excite, fill with pathos. [rapturous.
Moᴛrib, *adj.* touching, affecting,

طرد Oᴛrod, *va* chase, drive out, cashier, banish. *ger.* Tard.
Tarieda, game, quarry.
Taried, persecuted.
Tarad naḍl, swarm of new bees.
iii. Târid, *va* pursue.
(2) viii. Uᴛᴛarid, *va* (in grammar) be regular.
Moᴛarrad, regular.
(3) x. Isᴛaᴛrid, *va* digress.
Isᴛuᴛrâd, digression.

طرف Taraf 4, side, edge, strip of country. [wink c.
Tarf(a), glance of the eye; a
v. Teᴛarraf, *va* lie along the edge, walk on edges ᴠ.
(2) Tarief, newly acquired.
Tariefa, a novelty ᴅ.

طرح Uᴛraḍ, *va* fling, throw down, *lit.* or *fig.* cast away, cast up, vomit. *ger.* Tarḍ.
Tarḍa, dangling lappet, scarf.
Tarieḍ, outcast, abject.
Törḍa, abortion, miscarriage.
Türrâḍa, undercloth of horse ᴀʟ. mattress.
Muᴛraḍa, mattress ᴀʟ
Maᴛraḍ 11, place (*esp.* ᴀʟ).
viii. Uᴛᴛariḍ, *va* reject.
(2) ii. Tarriḍ, iv. Aᴛriḍ, *va* carry up (a building) to a great height x.
iii. Târiḍ, *va* accost, make proposals to; moot a question x.

TRQ

ترجم Terjam, *va* interpret, translate. *ger.* Terjama.
Terjamân 11, interpreter.

ترلك Terliec, socks of carpet-material ᴀʟ.

طرنب Töromba, a pump.

ترمس Tormos(e), subterraneous apartment for hot weather. (Serdâb ʙₑ.) See Uᴛmir.
(2) Tormos (*Gr.*), lupin, a flower.

ترنج Toronj, Otrojja, citron.
Terinj, bitter orange ʙₑ.
Nârinj, sweet orange ʙₑ.

ترك Oᴛroc, *va* leave, quit; neglect, omit; forego; bequeath. *ger.* Terc.
Terice, Teriece, property left at death x.
iii. Téric, *va* leave (unmolested), let alone x. [tice.
Moᴛéroco, amnesty; *also*, armis-Terrêo, negligent x.
(2) Torc 4, Turk.
Torciey, Turkish.

طرق Tarieq 10, way, highway.
Tariaqa 11, way, mode, *fig.*
Tarqa 2, (*perhaps*) artificial footways in and round a city oɴ.
Törqa 10, file (of camels), series (of omnibuses).
Muᴛrâq, file (of troops).
ii. Tarriq, *va* open a road, guide (a person) to a road.

TRQ

vi. Terâraq, *vn* march in file.
vii. Intariq, *vn* be drawn out in file? Yantariq (used with relative understood), ductile в.
(2) Otroq, *va* knock down flat, strike (with tool or stick), knock (at the door), dash (face to the ground).
Törqa⁺ yed, *fig. coup de main.*
Mutraqa, sledge hammer, bat to beat (linen) with.
iv. Atriq, *va* cast (eyes on the ground).
(3) Turyâq [*but* Tiryâq к.], an antidote; *Gr. θηριακη.*

ترس Tors 4, buckler.
ii. Terris, *va* arm (another) with a buckler.
v. Teterras, *vn* assume a shield; shield oneself, *san*, from.
Terrâs, shield maker.
Tirâse, his art.
Torsêna, Tors-kâna, arsenal.

طرس Turs 3, 4, sheet of parchment, *esp.* palimpsest.
Utris, *va* scrape clean.

طرطق Tarraqa, clapper of bell.
Tarruq, *vn* clatter.

طرطش Tarrux, *va* bespatter, besprinkle. From Otrox.

طرش Otrox, Utrix, *va* cast out, cast up, vomit.
iv. Atrix, *va* cast, cast up.
(2) Atrax 9, 10, dull of hearing.

TΘ

Tarax, Tarxa, deafness.
Utrax, *vn* become deaf.
ii. Tarrix, *va* deafen.
vi. Terârax, *vn* pretend deafness.

طرشن Tarxaqn, a chink, cleft
в. *Compare* Darkoux.

طرز Tarz, Turâz, pattern (on carpet), *fig.* mode, type.
Turâz, anything embroidered к.
Utraz, *vn* be embroidered.
Tarrâz, embroidered.
ii. Tarriz, *va* embroider, work with a pattern.

طص Töyy, *va* discern, see in half-light. Mâ atöyy xni⁺, I can distinguish nothing.

طاس Tâsc, *nu.* 2, saucer, flat cup al к.
(2) ´Tâ⁺ous, *pl.* 12, Tawâwies, peacock. *Gr. ταως.*

تيس Tcis 3, he-goat; blockhead.

طبي iv. Atsi, *va* disgust в.

تسع Tisca, *m.* Tias *f.* nine.
Tissuin, ninety, ninetieth.
Tosca 4, ninth part.
Têsis, ninth.

تسم Têsouma 12, European shoe.

طث Taθθ, game of quoits.
Miraθθe, a quoit.

EθΘ

أنْث Eθėθ, gear, chattels (*old word?*). [hair].
Eθieθ, abundant, luxuriant (as

توت Tout, mulberries.
Tout el 'erḍ, strawberries.
Tout el söllieq, Tout el xauc, raspberries, or blackberries.
(2) Toutiya, antimony?

طيط Tuiᴛ, *vn* bellow as a camel ᴋ.
Aᴛuiᴛ, *s.* cry of camel ʙ.

طيطو Taiᴛᴀwie, the cuckoo ꜰ.

طّوِيت Taʀawiet, the peewit, tirwit, lapwing ꜰ.ʙ.ᴋ.

تتن Toton, dry tobacco ᴀʟ

طش Taxxa, *nu.* soft shower of rain; *fig.* a rumour, tattle.
Töxx, *va* rain upon gently.

طيش Tuix, *vn* be fickle, volatile. *ger.* Taix, Taixân.
Tâyix, Tayyâx, in constant movement, as an insect; flighty, giddy.

نشت [طشت *o.*] Taxt 3, a washbasin. *See* Doxt.

طوز iv. Aᴛwiz, *va* lop, dock.

طيز Taiz, the breech, buttock.

تزد Tézih, tender, soft ʙ. new (bread) ʙɢ.

ZYX
X.

شا Xâ', sheep, *pl. obsolete.*

شي Xai' 4, *pl.* Axyâ, a thing.
Xai'aⁿ, *adv.* somewhat.
Xowaiya, a little thing; *vulg. adv.* somewhat; gently.

شا Xâ, *obsolete verb*, hath willed.
In xâ 'llâḥ, if God will.
Xie'a, *s.* will; *obsol.* for Irâda.
Maxie'a, *s.* thing willed; *obsol.* for Morâd.

وشي Waxa' Yaxi, *va* variegate.
Xâya, dress-robe ʙ.
ii. Waxxi, *va* variegate; *also* colour (actions), misrepresent, slander; *with* bi, xala'.
(2) iv. Auxi, *va* heal.
viii. Ittexi, *vp* be healed; *vn* recover health.

شاي Xâi, Txâi, tea.
Xâidân, teapot.

شوي Ixwi, *va* broil.
Mexwiey, broiled meat.
Mixwâya, gridiron ᴋ. [of i. vii. Inxawi, or viii. Ixtewi, *vp*

شع Xaxâx, *s.* ray of the sun, *pl.* θ, Axixxa.
iv. Axixx, *va* radiate. [sa.
Xaxxix, *va* irradiate. *ger.* Xixxi-Texaxxas xala', d⁰.

شع Xier, *vn* spread (as news).
Xâyis, widespread (news), widely diffused (species).

XYS

iv. Axieς, ʋa spread news.
Oxieς, ʋp be bruited on.
Ixâsa, s. rumour on.
Moxâς, widely divulged.
Maxâsa, notoriety.
(2) Xiesa, a party or sect; *esp.* the sect which regards the 4th Khalif as the first legitimate. Xieςui, a Shiite, or member of this sect.
Xayyis, a partizan. [tizan of.
iii. Xâyis, ʋa be follower or par-

شـــب Ixsab, *vn* fork, as branches; stand apart. *ger.* Xasab.
Xasb, branch of a human family, large tribe, people; the *plebs*, the Commons.
Xosba 10, 5, a fork in branches, interval between two things that fork.
iii. Xâsub, ʋa separate (another) from oneself x.
v. Texassab, *vn* branch off; as boughs, people, river.
Moxassab, forked, branching.

شـــب Xasbara, escalade.
Texasbar, *vn* make escalade. Compare Texaslaq.

شـــور Xaswaac, jugglery s.
Moxaswis, juggler.

شـــعل Ixsal, ʋa kindle, light up.
Xosla, lighted match.
Xasuila, *nu.* 10, lighted wick.
Maxsal 11, lamp (more classical than Qandicl); night-lamp in the road.

XST

Maxsala 11, lantern.
Maxâsuliey, one who works by lanterns, a nightman.
v. Texassal, *vn* flame up.
vii. Inxasul, ʋp be kindled, *lit.* or *fig.* In chemistry, fulminate. viii. Ixtesul, ʋp d°.

شـــعلق Xaslaqa, escalade (military word; perhaps from Slq).
Texaslaq, *vn* make escalade. Compare Tesellaq, Texasbar.

شـــعن Xasnoun 11, twig B.

شـــعر Xasra, *nu.* 5, hair (*pl.* 3, 4, 5, in x.).
Xasrâni, very hairy.
Xasuir, bearded corn, barley.
Xasuira, a barleycorn.
(2) Ixsar bi, feel, be aware of, perceive. *ger.* Xosöur?
Xisr, poetry. Xâsur, poet.
iv. Axsur bi, ʋa cause (a person) to perceive, inform, warn of. (Distinguish it from Axhir.)
Moxsar bi, declaratory of.
(3) Ixsar, ʋa crack B. *ter.*
Maxsöur, cracked, crazy B.
(4) Xasrieya, voil for the head alone. [star.
(5) Xisra, the star Sirius, dog-

شـــت Xasliey, testy, touchy.
Maxsöut, queer (person) B.

شـــت ii. Xassuθ, ʋa dissipate, disperse.

شـــت Xaswur, ʋa scorch; same as Xalwur? *See also* Xayyur.

XB

شَبّ Xabb, alum.
(2) Xibâba (Xabbâba?), a flute.
(3) Xobb, *vn* curvet, as a horse.
Xibba, a curvet.
(4) Xâbb, *pl.* 9, Xobbân, man in prime. [woman.
Xâbba, *pl.* Xawâbb, young
Xabâb, youthful age.
Xababa, young people.
Xoboubieɣa, youthful prime.
ii. Xabbib, *va* court (a woman).

شوب Xoub, *va* mingle, dilute.
Xaib, grey hairs.
Xâyib, grey-haired. [wood).
Xaiba, elderhood (*also* worm-
(2) Xaub, scorching heat AL B.
ii. Xawwib, *va* scorch as the sun.

شبه Xibh bi 4, likeness to.
Xabieh bi, *adj.* like, resembling.
s. one's fellow.
Axbeh, more like.
iii. Xâbih, *va* resemble.
Moxâbahe, resemblance.
vi. Texâbeh, *vr* be alike, be easily mistaken, one for the other.
iv. Axbih bi, resemble, as iii.
Texbich, assimilation, comparison. [certitude.
(2) Xobhe 10, ambiguity, in-
ii. Xabbih, *va* make ambiguous or doubtful.
viii. Ixtebih, *vn* be ambiguous.
Moxabbeh, Moxtebih, obscure.

شبح Xabaḥ 3, 4, object seen dimly afar.

XBΘ

شبل Xibl 3, (lion's) cub.
Moxbil, (lioness) with cubs.
Maxboul, (land) full of beasts x.
(2) Xâbil, a shad (fish).

شبع Ixbac min, *vn* be satinted.
iv. Axbis, *va* satiate, saturate.
Xibc, satiety. Xabsân, satiated.
Xâbis, satiated, saturated.

شبن Xabiena, godmother c.

شبك Ixbec, fle, *vn* be caught in or on (as coat on a bush).
Xebece 10, 5, a net.
ii. Xabbic, *va* interlace, wattle.
Xobbâc(e) 11, a lattice; a window with frame, be interlaced.
v. Texabbec, vi. Texâbec, viii. Ixtebic, *vp* be interlaced, entangled (morally).
vii. Inxabic bi, viii. Ixtebic bi, *vp* be engaged in.

شبق Xoboq, Xoboc 2, pipe-stick (Txoboq, *Turk*).

شبر Xibr 4, a span.
ii. Xabbir, *va* span.
(2) ii. Xabbir, *va* gesticulate B.

شبث Xabbêθ, tongs x.
v. Texabbeθ bi, *vn* catch at, cling to; *fig.* be attached to
vii. Inxabiθ bi, *vn* clasp firmly.
[But in B. I find it spelt with т for θ.]

XBT

شبّوت Xabbout, carp (a fish).

شبط Xobât, February.
(2) Oxbot, ca rap c. See Oxmot.
(3) Xabier, perch, pole, measuring wand. See Xatb and Xoboq.

شدّ Xidd, ca tighten.
ii. Xâdid, ca strengthen.
Xiddn, tightness, intensity, severity.
Xadied, intense, severe.
iii. Xâdid, ca treat severely.
viii. Ixtidd, cn become intense.
Axadd, intenser.
Xadâyid, hardships.
Xodda 10, a packet.

شذّ Xoaa, cn be out of tune?
Xâaa, pl. 12, Xawâaa, singular, odd, irregular.
Xoaoua, singularity, oddity.

شيد ii. Xayyid, ca build up (morally), establish.

شدى Xâdi, actor in a play, singer, artist B.
Oxdou, cn recite (poetry), act in a play. ger. Xadou.

شذو Oxaou, cn be pungent in smell. ger. Xaaie, pungency.
Xâai, pungent.

شدخ Ixdak, ca crack open (a hollow thing). cn bend down as a tree.

شدق Xidq 4, corner of mouth.

XFQ

شذر Xaar 3, gold dust c. x.

شفّ Xiff, cn be transparent.
Xaffâf, transparent.

شفشف Xafxâf, hoarfrost.

شوف Xouf (vulgo), cn sco.

شأن Xâ'fa, ulcer x.

شفي Ixfi, ca heal. ger. Xifâ.
Xâfi, healing (adj.).
viii. Ixtefi, cn recover health.
Xafa, convalescence, a remedy. pl. Axfiya. Moxfi, healer.
Dâr el xafâ, hospital, infirmary.
(2) Xâfi, (in logic) definitive.
(3) Xafa, Xaffa, vulg. lip. (Xfh.)

شفع Xâfis, Xafies, intercessor (advocate c.).
v. Texaffas, intercede.
x. Istexfis, ask intercession.
Xifâea, intercession.
(2) Bi xifâaat, in addition to, over and above ox.

شفه Xafahe 5, lip, for which vulg. Xafa, pl. Xefawât, lip.
Xafahiey, labial (letter).
iii. Xâfih, ca address by lip.

شفن Xaufân, oats B.

شفق Ixfaq cala', cn pity, compassionate.
Xafaqa, compassion.
Xafouq, Xafieq, compassionate.
Moxnffaq, pitiable, insignificant (gift) x.

XFQ

Xafiq, contemptible, inferior (goods) x.
(2) Xafoq, evening twilight B.

شغر Xafour, hornet? [sarpo.
(2) Xafra, pruning hook. *Latin*

شفت ii. Xaffit, *va* exhaust (money, strength) B. exhaust (argument) B.

شغى Ixra', *vn* swarm, abound B. *Fourmiller*.

شغب Xarb, *s.* tumult.
Xârib, gone astray.
Xaroub, tumultuous.
Xarrâb, exciter of tumult.
ii. Xarrib, iv. Axrib, infest.
iii. Xârib, stir to tumult, excite.
Mixrâb, very turbulent.

شغف Xiraf, pericardium.
Ixraf, *va* draw into love.
vii. Inxarif bi, be enamoured of.
Xaraf, vehement love.
Maxrouf, passionately in love.

شغل Xorl 4, business, work.
ii. Xarril, *va* cause to work, put to work. Xarralt yedi, I set my hand to work. *Also*, ii. Xarril, *va* embroider B.
iv. Axril, d°.
iii. Xâril can, *va* divert (a person) from. [busy.
viii. Ixtaril, *vn* be occupied, be Maxroul, Moxteril, occupied, busy. [active.
Xarrâl, given to business, ever

XHW

شغر Xârir, camel's packsaddle.

شفت Xarte, aliminess (*glaire* B.), alimy or ropy matter.
Moxril, slimy, ropy.

شح Xoŭŭ, *s.* stinginess, avarice.
Xaŭuiŭ, avaricious.
Xiŭŭ, *vn* be stingy of.
iii. Xâŭuŭ, *va* treat stingily.
Xiŭŭa, a fit of avarice x.
vi. Texâŭŭ rala', *vn* compete greedily for.

وشح Wixâŭ, a sash, girdle.
viii. Ittexiŭ, *va* wear (sash).

شاه Xâh, king (*Pers.*).
Xâhin xâh, king of kings c.
Xâh zâdeh, king's son (*Pers.*).

شوه Ixwah, *vn* be ill-looking.
ii. Xawwih, *va* disfigure.
Axwah, Moxawwah, ugly.

شوح Xouŭa, a kite (bird).
(2) Xauŭuya 12, rafter, beam.

شيح Xiŭ 5, wormwood.

شهو Xahwa, *s.* desire, carnal desire. [desirable.
Xahiey, voluptuous, greedy (of), Exhe', more desirable.
Xehwâni, greedy, carnal.
viii. Ixtehi, *va* desire.
Ixtihê, appetite.
v. Texehhê, *va* hanker after.

XHB

شهب Axheb, *adj*. grey, brindled
Xohba, *s.* a grey hue.

شهب Xiñêb 10, meteor, bright star.

شهد Ixhed, *vn* bear witness. *ger.* Xohond.
Xêhid 7, *s.* eye-witness.
Xehied 6, *s.* martyr.
Xehêda, testimony, deposition.
iii. Xâhid, *va* be present at ĸ.
v. Texahhed, *vn* pronounce the creed.
iv. Axhid, x. Ixtehid, *va* summon as witness. Xohcda", in presence.
Mexhoud, attested by witnesses.
Maxhed 11, place of martyrdom, martyr's grave.
(2) Xohd 5, honeycomb with the honey.

شهذ Ixñas, *va* importune, act the beggar.
Xañña&, a beggar.
Xañâ&e, importunity, beggary.
ii. Xañnu&, *va* sharpen, make subtle в.

شهل Ixhel, *vn* glide swiftly?
ii. Xehhil, *va* dispatch (business) rapidly, expedite в.
iv. Axhil, *va* get ғ.
(2) Axhel, fallow coloured в.

شهلق Texañlaq, *vn* clamber, scale (a wall). Better perhaps Texaslaq.

XHR

شهم Xehim, Xehiem, strenuous.
Xehêma, energy, industry.

شهم Xañm 3, pulp, suet, tallow.
Xañum, pulpy (fruit).

شهن Xâhien 12, royal falcon.

شهنشين Xahnaxien, covered balcony в*.* (*Pers.*).

شهن Ixñan, *va* fill [not with liquid], lade, freight; man (a ship, castle). *ger.* Xañn.
Xiñna, garrison ĸ.
ii. Xañnun, *va* overlade.
Maxñöun, filled full.

شهنق Xehniq, *vn* bray as an ass. See the next.

شهنق Ixheq, *vn* sob, bray, hiccup.
Xahieq, *ger.* sobbing.
Xehqa, a sob, dying rattle.
(2) Xêbiq, lofty (mountain).

شهر Xehr, month; *pl.* Axhor.
Xahriey, monthly.
Moxêhera, monthly wage.
Xebrieya, d°
(2) Ixherbi, *vn* be celebrated for.
Xehier, famous, renowned.
Xohra, renown, notoriety.
Maxhour, well known, notorious.
iv. Axhir, *va* promulgate, make known.
Axber, more celebrated.

XHR

viii. Ixtehir, *vp vn* become known. Ixtihêr, celebrity. Moxtehar, famous.

خَشَرَ Xaŝŝâr B. Xoŝwâr c. soot.
Xaŝwir, *va* dapple, chequer.
Xaŝŝöur, Xoŝŝrour, blackbird.
(2) ii. Xaŝŝŝur, *vn* talk big (B. Denta.), show one's teeth, x. "open the mouth," in i.
(3) Xaŝŝr, a scar x. [scar.
Xaŝŝwir, *va* scar, mark with a Perhaps Xaŝŝr, εσχαρα and Scar are the same root. The Greek unites the idea to *a burning hearth*, as the Arabic to *soot.*

خَطَّ Ixŝŝat, *vn* trail,dangle c.B.
Xaŝŝra, line, trait (B. Filet).
Xaŝŝrut, *va lit.* draw, drag, tow. *fig.* attract, charm.
Xaŝŝrata, derangement, disorder (B. *sic*).

خَجَّ Xojj, *va* furrow (the waves).

خَوْج Waxiej, a sort of tree.

خَشَعَ Oxjou, *va* fill with emotion.
Xajiey, impassioned, pathetic.
Xajou, emotion.

خَجَس Xojâs, Xajies, courageous.
Xajâsa, courage.
ii. Xajjis, *va* encourage. [man.
v. Texajjas, *vn* play the brave

خَجَب Xajab, vexation.

XKB

Xâjib, vexed, dejected.
Oxjob, *va* condemn? Rom. ii. 1.
ii. Xajjib, *va* deject.

خَجَرَ Xajira, nu. a tree, *pl.* 4.
Maxjar, a grove, plantation.
Moxjir, wooded (country).
Mixjar, wooden horse for clothes (c.).
Moxajjar, (cloth) figured with trees; damask.
iv. Axjir, *v.* produce trees.
Xojaira, small tree, shrub.
Xijrieya, sapling. [dery B.
ii. Xajjir, *va* stitch with embroi-
(2) Xijr, gourd B_g.
(3) iii. Xâjir, *va* controvert.
vi. Texâjar, *vn* dispute.

خَكَّ Xakk, Xakxik, *vn* make urine (a coarse word).
(2) Xakxieka, child's coral with bells.

خَيَك Xaik 3, mature bearded man, elder, alderman; chief of a tribe; tutor to a young man, director.
Xaikouka, alderhood.
Maxâyik, elders (collectively).
Xaika, old lady.
Xiek, *vn* become elderly.
v. Texayyak, *vn* act the old man.

خَكَب Ixkab min, *vn fig.* flow from, be derived from.
x. Ixtexkib, *va* elicit (milk or blood).

XKR

شخر Ixkir, *vn* bray as an ass, snore. *ger*. Xakicr.
ii. Xakkir, *vn* bray, croak.

شخص Ixkay, *vn* stare at.
(2) Xakay 4, a person.
ii. Xakkuy, *va* personate, represent.

شخت Xakit, thin, alim в.

شخطر Xakṛōur 11, a barge.

شخشر Xakxour, light stuff trowsers.

شل Xilla, skein of thread.
Xaliel, distaff в.
ii. Xallil, *va* baste with thread.
Xallâl, cascade c.; water falling *in threads?*
Xalxil, *va* drip.
Xalxaliey, Moxalxil, drizzly.
Texalxal, *vn* drip (fall in threads?).

شال Xâla 2, 9, a shawl (of wool).

شول Axwal, lefthanded.
(2) Xaul, the desart AL
(3) Xoul, *vn* be raised (*esp.* as the tail?). (Δenaboh xâ-yil, his tail is raised г.)
iv. Xiel, *vulg. for*, Axiel (tolle), lift and *take away*; as, the plates, the dinner.
vii. Inxâl, *vp* be removed.
(4) Xawal (Jawâl), bag.

XEM

شلب Xelebiey (Txelebiey AL), refined and graceful.
Xelbana, gallantry to women в.

شلف Oxlof, *va* fling в. spurn c.

شلف Ixlafl, *va* pitch down, let drop (to another) AL
(2) Maxlafl, cloak of superior quality AL
(3) ii. Xallifl, *va* strip off AL

شلك Xalouc, S.E. wind в.

شلق Oxloq *va* [whip к.].
Xalqiey, a bully? в. Tapageur.
(2) viii. Ixteliq cala', *va* catch (a person) in the act в.; discover (a secret) в.

شلوط Xalwuṛ, *va* parch, roast. See Xaswuṛ.

شلش Xalix, Xaloux, awkward.
(2) Xalax, *vn* resound?

شم Xomm, Xamxim, *va* smell at.
Maxâmm, *pl.* odours.
Xamoum, sweet smelling.
Xammâma 2, a smell.
x. Isteximm, *va* smell out.
iv. Aximm, cause (another) to smell, give (to him) to smell.
Xamiom, fragrance c.
v. Texammam, *va* smell out.

شام Ix'em, *vn* be of evil augury (cala').
Max'oum, unlucky, *or vulgo.*
Maixoum, wilful.

XAM

شام Xâm, Damascus, Syria.
(2) Xâma, mole on the face.
(3) Xiema, habit, good disposition.
(4) Xaima, eddy or reverse of current? whirlpool?

شمع Xamɛ, wax. Xamɛa 3, *nw.* a (wax) candle.
Ximɛniy, waxen.
Xammâɛ, candleseller.
Mixmaɛa 11, candlestick?
Xamɛadân 2, *vulg.* candlestick.
ii. Xammiɛ, *to* wax over.
Moxammaɛ, waxed cloth, oil cloth.

شم Xâmik, *lit.* lofty; *fig.* haughty, *pl.* Xawâmik, lofty mountains, heights.
Ixmak, *vn fig.* be elated. *ger.* Xomouk.

شمل Ixmal, Oxmol fie, *vn* comprize. *ger.* Xaml.
Xaml, a parcel, a lot.
Xâmil, comprehensive.
Xamicla 11, innate excellence.
(2) Ximâl, north; left hand.
Ximâliey, northern.

شملل Xamloul, nimble, brisk.

شمن Xamandara, a buoy c.

شمر Ixmirmin, *vn* take offence at.
Xâmir, Ximmier, *adj.* trim, tight.
ii. Xammir, *to* tuck up the dress. Moxammar, in trim.

XAN

(2) ii. Xammir, *va* let (a ship) drift s.
v. Texammâr, *vn* drift as a ship.
(3) Xomra, Xammâr, the herb fennel.
(4) Ximrâk, cluster (of dates).

شمس Xams, *f.* 3, sun.
Xomaiɛe, little sun.
Xamɛiey, solar.
Xamɛieya, parasol.
Maxmiɛ, basking place. [sun.
ii. Xammiɛ, *ra* sun, expose to
Moxammaɛ, exposed to sun.
v. Texammaɛ, *vn* bask in sun.
(2) Xamous, *adj.* unruly.
(3) Xammâɛ 13, Christian deacon.

شمت Ixmet, *or* ii. Xammit, rejoice over another's loss. *Gr.* ἐπιχαίρω (with *accus.*).
ger. Xamâte, *also* riot, din.

شمط Oxmot, *va* whip, sweep away, filch, gobble up [all these senses in B.].
Also, Maxmout, dangling, as sword or tassel.

شمش Xamxa, brooch, clasp.

شن Mixanna, sort of basket.

شان Xân, *status* in life.
Fie xân, concerning F.
Li xân, because of, *commoner*,
Min xân, because of.

XWN

شون Xouna, Xiwan, barn, granary. [Xowan.
(2) Xauna, ship of war, *pl.*

شين Xien, *va* stain, dishonour.
Xaiyin, *adj.* disgraceful.
Maxâyin, *pl.* villanies.

شنع Xanies, loathsome, infamous. [pitude.
Xouɛa, Xanâsa, ugliness, turXanâyiɛ, *pl.* shameful deeds.
ii. Xannis, *va* defame.
v. Istexnis, *va* account disgraceful.

شنب Xanab 2, Xânib 12, moustache ʙ. See Xârib.

شنبر Xanbâr, kiyâr xanbar *or* janbar, cassia.

شند Xanada, cheese basket ʙ.

شنف Xanf 3, earring at *top* of the ear ɪ.
ii. Xannif, *va* attire with earrings, bedizen. *See* Xantif.
ɪ. Texannaf, *vn* wear earrings.

شنج Ixnaj, *vn* be in spasm. *ger.* Xanoj. vii. Inxanij, dᵒ Xanij, contracted by spasm.
ii. Xonnij, *va* contract.
v. Texannaj, *cp* of ii.
Texannoj, state of spasm.

شنخب Xinkâb, ridge of a horse's withers, ridge of mountain ?—ᴦârib.

XC

شنكل Xancêl, a hook ꜰ. commoner Jangêl.

شنلك Xanlec, public joy ? ʙ. rejouissance : *also*, Ḥarâqat xanlec, fireworks ʙ.

شنق Oxnoq, *va* strangle. *ger.* Maxnaqa, gallows. [Xanq.
iv. Axniq, *va fig.* pull up a horse rudely.

شنر ii. Xannir, *va* affront ɪ.
Xanyir, *va* treat rudely ʙ.
Xanâr, coarse insult.
Xinnier, malicious.

شنت Xintiyân, women's silk trowsers.
(2) Xinât, distraction ʙ.

شنط Xaniera, a running knot ʙ. Probably altered from Onxoura. *See* Xoura.

شنتف Xantif, *va* bedizen with jewels. See Xannif.
Xantefa, a trinket.
[Xontora, earclasp ɪ.]

شكك Xocc, *va* prick, gore. *See* Xouc.
(2) Xecc fîe, *vn* doubt of.
Xecc 3, doubt.
Xecouo, apt to doubt, (goods) of doubtful value.
Xocec, on credit ʙ.
ii. Xeccio, *va* cause to doubt.
v. Texeccec, *vn* be in doubt.
(3) Xecc wa lecc, zigzag ʙ.

XQ

شق Xoqq, *va* split. Xoqq sala', offend. vii. Inxiqq, *vp* of i.
Xâqq, *adj.* distressing.
Xiqqa, a half, split along; 10, a piece, strip of cloth, a para-
Moxaqqa, distress. [graph.
iii. Xâqiq, *va* quarrel with, separate from. Xiqâq, discord.
Xaqieq (*f.* -a), counterpart. [Uterine brother or sister x.] *Also*, red corn-poppy.
viii. Ixtiqq, be derived (as a word). Ixtiqâq, derivation.

شوك Xouc, *va* prick.
Xauce, *nu.* a thorn [*Also*, majesty, mightiness.]
Moxwic, thorny.

شوق Xauq, longing desire. *See* Touq.
Xauqiey, warm hearted.
ii. Xawwiq, *va* allure.
v. Texawwaq, *or* viii. Ixtêq, long after.
Ixtiyâq, *ger.* a longing.

شكى Xocêya, Xcewa, complaint.
Xâci, one who laments c.
viii. Ixteci, *en* complain (sala').
v. Texeccê, *en* dº.
Xcciey, querulous.
Motexcci, plaintive.

شقى Xaqâ, Xaqâwa, misery.
Xaqiey, wretched.
[Xâqq, Moxaqqa, *See* Xoqq.]

XCR

شكع Ixcec, *va* charm (*fig.*), pierce, touch, move the heart.
Yaxcec, romantic (country) B.
Xeciec, *adj.* moving ?

شقف Xaqf, *s.* potsherd.
Xoqfa 10, splinter, piece.
Xoqaf, small money AL
Xaqief, split in two, uterine brother. *See* Xuqicq.

شكل Xecl 4, *s.* shape.
Moxcccel, varied, motley.
iii. Xêcil, *va* resemble.
Moxêcil, apposite.
Moxêccla, plausibility B.
(2) Xicêl, *s.* horse tether, (surcinglo 5.) Xecel 5, dº.
Oxcol, *va* tether, hamper.
ii. Xcccil, *va* tie three feet.
iii. Xêcil, cavil, quibble.
Xocliey, disputatious B.
Moxcil, intricate, embarrassing. *s.* entanglement.
iv. Axcil, be embarrassing, obscure. *See* Xarcil.

شقل Oxqol, *va* carry, AL (= Onqol)?
Xuqoul, mason's plumbline.

شقلب Xaqlib, *va* upset, disorder. *See* Iqlib.

شقنق Xaqniq, *va* slice up. *See* Xaqq.

شكر Xocr, thanks.
Oxcor, *va* thank.
Xccour, grateful.
Xocrân, Moxêcera, gratitude.

XCR

(2) Xiceurieya, succory.
(3) Xauceràn, hemlock.

شَقَر Axqar, *adj.* pink, ruddy, fallow (deer) F. sorrel (horse) E. Axqarâni, russet.

شَقَرق Xaqrâq 11, the jackdaw? some species of pie.

شر Xarr, evil. Xirra, malice. Xarier, Xirrier, malicious.
(2) Xarar, hot embers.
Xarâra, spark.

شرشر Xarxour, a chaffinch.

أشر ii. 'Exxir, *va* sketch B. denote (formed from Ixâra in next?)

شور Xour salaihi bi, *v.* advertise him of.
iii. Xâwir, *va* consult.
vi. Texàwar, *vn* complot, deliberate together.
x. Istexior, consult, ask advice. Mostexûr, referee.
iv. Axier bi, point to.
Ixâra, a hint, indication.
Moxier, counsellor (of army).
El Xoura', the Council s.
Ehl ol xoura', d°
(2) Maxwâr, course, voyage, distance. See root Mxr.

شير Xiera, treacle of dates Bs.

شرى Xarya, *s.* a purchase.
Xàri, *s.* purchaser, customer.
Xirâ, *ger.* purchasing.

XRD

viii. Ixtori, *va* buy.
Moxterâ, a thing bought.
(2) Moxterie, planet Jupiter.
(3) Xari, *pl.* 4, Axrâ', pimple B.
(4) Xariyâu, artery, *pl.* Xarâyien.

شرع Ixras, *va* institute. *ger.*
Xarr, enacting, enactment, law.
Ixras fie, *v.* begin. *ger.* Xorous fie, beginning.
Xarsuiy, legal.
Xariesa, law 11.
Xâris 12, highway.
(2) Xirâs 2, sail of a ship, string of violin c.

شرب Ixrab, *va* drink, imbibe.
Xorb, *ger.* drinking.
Xorba, Xarba, draught, dose.
Xaràb, beverage, syrop, wine.
Xaroub, drinkable.
Xarrba, small jar.
Maxrab, temperament.
ii. Xarrib, *va* imbue.
v. Texarrab, *va* imbibe.
(2) Xârib 12, mustache.
Xarrâba 11, a tassel, tuft.

شربين Xarbien, larch tree.

شربك Xarbic, *va* entangle, hamper, embroil. *See* Ixbec and Orboo.

شرد Oxrod, *vn* flee.
Xârid, fugitive, timid (animal), wild (as lightning).
Xaroud, shy, habitually fugitive.
ii. Xarrid, iv. Axrid, *va* scare away.

XRD

v. Texarrad, *vp* be scared away, become shy.
Xaried, chased away — Taried x.

شرذم Xarᴀim, *va* mangle, slash, gash. *See* Xarrim.
Xirᴀima 11, a rag, tatter x. *modern*, a detachment (of troops).

شردق Xardiq, *va* choke (a person) in drinking ʙ.
ii. Texardaq, *vp* of d°. *See* Ixraq.

شرف Xaraf, elevation, nobility.
Xorfa, a pinnacle. Xorrâfa, d°
Xarief, lofty, noble.
Axraf, loftier, nobler.
Maxraf, an eminence.
Maxrafiey, foremost, chief in dignity.
Axrâfi 13, counter of gold ʙ.
ii. Xarrif, *va* dignify.
iv. Axrif aola', *vn* look down over, impend over, be on the point of (doing).
v. Texarraf, *vp* of ii. [outlook.
x. Istexrif, *vn* get a survey or

شرجل Texarjal, *vn* flounder; perhaps from Xarcil, entangle, for Texarcel.

شره Xarih, gluttonous.
Xaruh, Xarâhe, gluttony.
Ixrih, *vn* cala', ila', hunger after, crave.

شرح Xarfla, Xariefla, a slice.
Mixrafl, a fish-slice (knife).

XRC

ii. Xarrifl, *va* slice, carve (meat), dissect, anatomize.
Texriefl, anatomy.
Moxarrifl, anatomist.
(2) *fig*. Ixrafl, *va* lay open, expound, enunciate. *ger*. Xarfl, exposition.
Xarrâfl, expositor.
iv. Axrifl, *va fig*. open, enlarge (the heart), cause to breathe freely. (Compare Obsor.)
Moxrifl, delightful (country).
vii. Inxarifl, *vp* be relieved, receive pleasure.

شرول Xarwâl, trowsers.

شرم Oxrom, *va* slit. *ger*. Xarm.
ii. Xarrim, *va* slash, gash.

شرمط Xarmur, *va* mangle, tear, slash.
Xarmoura 11, a tatter.

شرن Xaryân 11, artery ʙ.
Xaran, d°. ʙ. (vowels uncertain).
Xaryâniey, arterial.
(2) Tixrien, first and second, October and November.

شرنق Xornoqa 11, cocoon of silkworm, chrysalis.
 Habb el xarâniq, millet.

شرك Ixrec fla, *vn* have a share in, partake in. *ger*. Xire.
viii. Ixteric fla, d°
vi. Texârec fla, d°. [said of copartners].

XRC

iii. Xâric, *va* take to oneself as partner.
iv. Axric, *va* cause to partake.
Xirco, Xarâce, partnership.
Xarâce, a company. [tion.
Xirc 4, a fellowship, participa-
Xariec 6, partner.
Moxâric, associate.
Moxârace, association.
Moxteric, shareholder? contributor (to a newspaper).
El flass el moxteric, common sense B.
(2) Xarec 2, 10 (*pl.* Xoroc), hunter's net. [latchet s.
Xirêc 10, 4, shoe-tie, shoe-

شرق Xarq, East.
Xarqiey, Eastern. [quarter.
Maxriq 11, Eastern place *or* Maxraqa, basking-place.
ii. Xarriq, *va* expose to the sun.
v. Texarraq, *va* bask.
iv. Axriq, *va* rise as the sun.
(2) Xarâqi, a fallow field B.
(3) Ixraq, *va* suffocate in drinking B. *See* Xardiq.

شركل Xarcil, *va* entangle, embarrass. *Compare* Oxcol and Xarec.

شرطـ Xarqut, crackle as salt in the fire B. (Qarqut.)

شرس Xaris, surly, fierce.
Xarâse, surliness.
iii. Xâris, *va* treat harshly.
vi. Texârs, *vr* squabble together. *See* Tehêrax.

XWS

شرصف Xarsouf, false rib.

شرت Oxrot, *va* shave with chisel. *See* Okrot.
Xarte, a splinter.

شرط Oxrot, *va* rend, tear B. crack C. [*See* Oqrot, Qarqut, Xarqut, Xarmut.]
Xarat 4, sign, mark x.
Xariet 8, Xariera 11, a strip? tape, ribbon, telegraphic cable.
Mixrât 11, surgical instrument for scarifying.
ii. Xarrut, *va medic.* scarify, gash, with small strokes.
(2) Oxrot, *va* [*lit.* cut a notch?] *fig.* stipulate.
Xarr 3, condition, bargain.
Xorruiy, stipulated.
Xariera 11, clause, stipulation.
iii. Xârut, *va* impose conditions on, engage; charter (a ship).
vi. Texârut, *vr* contract mutually, wager together.
viii. Ixterut cala' = iii.
(3) Xorra 10, the guard (*gens d'armes*), the police.
Xorruiy, soldier of the guard.

شرش Xarax, N.W. wind (*Syr.*)
(2) Xorx, Xolx 3, fibre of root, small root.

شرشف Xarxoufa, *nu.* a sheet.

شوس Axwes, *adj.* squinting.

شوص Xouya, Xaiya, *nu.* pang.

شسع Xâsi͑, distant, separate o.
(2) Xias 3, leathern thong of bootlace b.; shoe(?), shoe-latchet.

شسف Xâsif, shrivelled.

شت ii. Xattit, *va* disperse, disband.
v. Texattet, *vp* of d°·
Xatte', sundry, several.

شط Xutt fie, *vn* overdo.
Xetat, excess, exaggeration.
Moxutt, extravagant.
iii. Xâtut, *vn* extravagate.
iv. Axutt, *va* exceed.
(2) Xatt 4, riverside, wharf.
Xatt el Sarab, the river formed by the junction of the Euphrates and Tigris.

شوط Xaut, *s.* career, *fig.* s.
(2) Xouta, *vulg.* a running knot; corrupt for Onxouta.

شيت Xiet, calico.
ii. Xayyit, *va* card with comb.

شيط Xuit, *vp* be scorched.
ii. Xayyut, *va* scorch.
v. Texayyat, *vp* of ii. ; *fig.* flame out in rage.

شتو Xitâ, *pl.* θ, Axtiya, winter (winter-rain AL.).
Xctwa, winter AL
Xetewieya, winter season AL
Maxtê, Maxtêya, winter abode.
v. Texattê, *vn* pass the winter.
Texittê, *vn* rain AL

شط Xâtu 12, bank of river, shore of sea.

شطب Xatb, wand, switch, flexible withe.
Oxtôb, *va* cancel (by parallel lines across it).

شطف Oxtöf, *va* rinse b.
Textuif, a lotion c.

شطط Ixtaṭṭ, *vn* lie at full stretch.
v. Texattaṭṭ, d°· (*sic* b.). *See also* Istatt.

شطل Xetlo 3, blade (of corn), flaccid plant (as of melon).
ii. Xattil, *va* plant shrubs and herbs.

شتم Oxtom, *va* revile. *ger.*
Xetm, Xetima, contumely.
Xettêm, contumelious.
iii. Xêtim, *va* = Oxtom.

شطن Xairân 11, Satan, devil, tempter, rogue.
Xaitana, cunning malice.

شتر Ixtir, *va* wreck (a ship), wound, insult.

شطر Xâtur, clever.
Xatâra, cleverness.
(2) Xatt 3, one side of a thing c.
Xutta, a comma b.

شطرج Xatranj, game of chess; also Satranj.

XWX

شوش Xouxa, crest, tuft of bird, plume of cap, crest of Xâxa, *su.* muslin. [wave.
Xâxiya, muslin turban.
(2) Xawâx, disquiet, discord.
ii. Xawwix ṣala', *on* disturb.
Texwiex, disorder.

شيش Xiex, glass bottle B.

شثم Xaxma 10, jakes, privy B.

شثن Xaxna', specimen B.

شثر Xauxara, *s.* disorder.

شز Xezz, dry in style.
Xêzz, rugged (style) B.

شظى Xaʒuiya 14, splinter of bone or wood.
v. Texaʒʒâ, *ep* be splintered.

شزب Xêzib, shrivelled. *See* Xêsif.

شزر Ixzir, *ea* look askance at.
Xezr(a), side glance, sideway motion. [pleased at.
v. Texazzer ṣala', *ep* be dis-
vi. Texâzer, *er* be mutually displeased.

Z. 3.

زى Zeiy, *pl.* 4, Ezyâ, costume, fashion.
ii. Zeyyi, *ea* dress (another) in some special costume.

ZƐB

v. Tezeyyâ, *en* assume a garb.
(2) Mezieya 14, excellence, privilege.

ازا ʼIzê, *adv.* face to face.
Biʼizêi, face to face with.
iii. Wêzi, *ea* confront, compare with, compete with.
Mowêzi, corresponding.
vi. Tewêzê, *er* be side by side.
Motewêzi, parallel; collateral.

وز Wizz, Wezwiz, *ea* buzz. *ger.* Wezweze.
(2) Wezze, *nu.* a goose.
In literature also Iwezze, d°.
Wezz, geese collectively; *also,* a gander.

اوز Euz, *s.* compliment, ceremony B.

زوى Zêwiya 14, corner, *i.e.* innerangle; *also,* cell of monk·
v. Tezewwâ, *en* live in a corner, in retirement.

زز Zezzis, *ea* agitate. *ger.* Zezzeza, concussion.
Zozzez 11, gust (of wind).
(2) Zesâsa, a fief.

وزع ii. Wezziε, *ea* distribute.
Touzieε, distribution.

زوع ii. Zewwiε, *ea* dash a thing off, do hastily.

زعبر Zesbirsala', *on* juggle with.
Mozesbir, juggler.
Tezesbor, jugglery.

ZƐF

زعف‍ Zeɛâfa, a whisk, brush.
(2) Zeɛfarân, saffron.
Mozeɛfir, saffron coloured, red yellow.

زعج‍ Izɛaj, or iv. Azɛuj, va disquiet.
viii. Inzeɛuj, vp of i.
Inzɛâj, disquietude.

زعل‍ Izɛal, vn suffer ennui в.
Zeɛlân, Mozeɛɛal, ennuied.
ii. Zeɛɛul, va ennui в. disoblige c.
iv. Ezɛul, va discomfort.

زعم‍ Izɛam, va allege, pretend, make sure that. ger. Zeɛm, assertion, assumption.
Zeɛmiɛy, alleged, presumed.
Zeɛuim, apt to assume.
Mezɛam, matter of opinion, pl. Mezêɛum, various things opined.

زعن‍ Zeɛnifa 11, fin of fish.

ظعن‍ Uzɛan, vn travel in a camel's litter; or simply, migrate у. х. ger. 3aɛan.
Maʒɛan, departure, travel.

زعق‍ Izɛaq, va call aloud by name; vn clamour as a bird, cry as cuckoo. ger. Zeɛq.
Zeɛqa, nu. (bird's) cry.

زعر‍ ii Zeɛɛur, va crop (hair).

زب‍ Zebieb, raisins.
Zebiebiey, raisin-wine x.

ZBL

(2) Zebab, shag (horsehair? See Bebieb), shag on face.
Azebb, shaggy here and there. See Zeɛab.

وزب‍ Wezeb Yezib, vn flow x.
Miezêb 11, channel, gutter, duct of the body [x. calls it Persian. See Mizrâb.]

وظب‍ Wâʒub, adj. steady?
ii. Waʒʒub, va make (goods) steady, pack firmly.
iii. Wâʒub, vn persevere.
Mowâgaba, perseverance.
iv. Auʒub (el xoɛl), va (with double accus.) cause (men) to be steady (in) work; or (with single accus.) stick to (one's chamber).

ظبي‍ 3abie, f. 3abieya, the roebuck, dorcas.

زبع‍ Zeubaɛa 11, tempest.

زد‍ Zebâd, civet, odorous material, like musk.
Qurr el zebâd, civet cat.
(2) Zobda, nu fresh butter. fig. cream (best part) of a thing.
iv. Ezbid, vn foam.
Mozbid, foamy.
Mizbad, cream dish.

زبل‍ Zibl, s. dung, litter.
Zebbâl, dirt-box.
Zobâla, litter for a horse, of his own dung, dried in the sun.
Mezbal(a), dunghill.
ii. Zebbil, va manure в.

ZBN

زبن Izbin, *and* iii. Zêbin, *va* overreach in a bargain x. [*vulg.* Iṭbin.]
Zeboun, a dupe B.K.
(2) Zeboun, a customer B. F.
Zoubana, custom of shop.
ii. Zebbin, *va* bring custom to B.
iv. Ezbin bi, *va* supply (a customer?) with G.N.
Mozban bi, supplied with.
(3) Zebân, sting of insect B.
(4) Ziebonn, boddice, vest.

زبق Izbaq, *vn* glide in, creep in B.
(2) Ziebaq, quicksilver.

زبر Zibr 3, codex, sacred book. Compare Sifr. *pl.* Zobour, Canticles.
ii. Zebbir, *va* prune (trees).
Zebarjad (*Gr.* σμαραγδ), emerald? topaz? jasper s.

زبط Zebâra, *ns.* cluster (of dates).

زود Zewâda, victuals for a journey; *pl.* Ezwâd, Ezwida 4, 8.
Mizwad, wallet, provision-bag.
ii. Zewwid, *va* victual (a ship, etc.).
v. Tezewwad bi, *vn* victual oneself with.
(2) *Also* ii. Zewwid, *va* bid at an auction B. (*for* Zeyyid?).

زيد Zied *or* iv. Azied, *va* augment. *Also vn* Zied cala', surpass, exceed; bid at auction.
Ziyâda, surplus.

ZFR

Zêyid, redundant.
Ezyad, in excess, more.
Mezied, an augment.
Mezêd, a bid at an auction.
iii. Zêyid, *vn* bid at auction.
viii. Izdâd, *vp* be augmented.
Izdiyâd, augmentation.
Mostezêd, (word) augmented by auxiliary letters.

زدل Ezdal, skilful with both hands alike B.

Izdirâ, contempt. Root Zry.

زف Ziff, bird's down.
Ezeff, downy.
Zefzif, *vn* hover and flutter? (See Rafrif).

وظف Wazuifa 11, function, public duty, public post.
ii. Wazzuf, *va* invest with a public office. [tionary.
Mowazzaf, Motewazzuf, a func-

زوف Zouf, *vn* trail garment or wings, as pigeon?
(2) Zoufâ, hyssop.
(3) Zouf, *s.* plenty (B. *Foison*).
Bil Zêf, in plenty AG.

زيف ii. Zeyyif, *va* clip, pare (money).

زفر Zefar, rich food forbidden in Zefir, greasy, dirty. [Lent.
ii. Zeffir, *va* fatten up, manure; cram, fuddle.
v. Tezeffar, *vn* eat rich food, grow fat B.

3FR

ظفر Ʒufr 4, nail, claw.
Aʒfour 11, claw.
ii. Ʒaffir, *va* claw up.
viii. Uʒʒaɓir cala', *vn* pounce upon, seize. *Hence,*
(2) Uʒɓr bi, *vn* conquer. *ger.* Ʒafar, victory. [*oua.* Ʒâɓr, Ʒaɓer, Moʒaffir, victori- Ʒuffier, Muʒfâr, eminently victorious.

زفت Zift, pitch, resin.

وزغ Wezeɼ, small lizard *v. stellio.*

زاغ Zêɼ 9, the common or carrion crow. [Qâq is the genus, and Godâf the *rook* v.]

زيغ – زوغ Zouɼ, Ƶieɼ, *can, vn* swerve from, flinch from b.
Zéyiɼ, aslant.
iv. Eziɼ can, *va* disgust with.

زغي Zeɼâya, a bayonet.

زغب Zeɼab, downy board.
Zoɼaib, fine down.
Zoɼba, dormouse. *See* Zebab.

زغل Izɼil, *va* forge (money), garble.
Zeɼel, false coin, a counterfeit.
iii. Zêɼil, *va* counterfeit.
Mezɼil (lil rimâya) loophole for archery.
(2) Zeɼloul 11, young pigeon.
(3) Zeɼlil (el naẓar), *va* dazzle (the sight) b.

ZHD

زغر Zeɼr, Zeɼɼariey, boar-hound.

زج Zeɴziɴ, *va* stir.

زرح – زيح Zouɴ, Zieɴ, *vn* disappear. *ger.* Zeiɴân.
Zêɴ canni, it departed from me.
Ziɼâɴ 2, procession of priests b.
iv. Ezieɴ, *va* remove.

زهو Ozhou, *vn* be gay (of colour), vain (of dress).
Zêhi, gay, bright coloured; vain, dressed brightly.
Mezhou, self-vaunting, flaunting
Zehou, gaiety, brilliancy.
iv. Ezhi, *va* make gay.
viii. Izdahi, *va* disdain k. (See Izderi, under Zry).

زهب Zibêb, *pl.* stores, supplies.
ii. Zehhib, *va* stock, supply (bi).
v. Tezehheb, *vn* stock oneself, take in supplies.

زهد Zehd, Zehed 5, a dole, a scantlet, barely enough.
Zehied, scanty.
Izhed ɓe, *vn* be sparing in the use of. Izhed can, *vn* abstain from, lose taste for, have disgust for b. (*See* Izheq.)
Zêhid, abstemious, under a vow.
Zehêda, abstemiousness; *also,* scantiness?
v. Tezehhed, *vn* play the ascetic.
Tezehhod, ascetic life.
Mozhid, having slender means.
viii. Izdahid, *va* account insufficient.

ZHF

زحف; Izḥaf, vn glide, march.
Zeḥḥâf, creeping (as a plant?)
Ziḥâfa, troops on march, expeditionary corps.
ii. Zeḥḥuf, vs trail.
iv. Ezḥuf, vs push off, launch (a boat). [towards.
v. Tezeḥḥaf'ila', vn move gently

زحل; Izḥal, vn slip off behind, as saddle from mule B.
iv. Eaḥal, vs trail behind.
(2) Tezeḥḥaf, vn scud, as a sledge.
(3) Zoḥal, planet Saturn.
Zeḥḥiq, vn slip much, be slippery, as ground.
Zoḥḥouqa 11, sliding place, smooth sloping rock.

زحم; Zeḥm(a), Ziḥâm, pressure of a crowd.
iii. Zèḥum, vs crowd, crush.
vi. Tezèḥam, vn crowd one
Tezèḥòm, concourse. [another.
viii. Izdaḥum, as vi.
Izdiḥâm, pressure of crowd.

زهك; Zehic, adj. flabby, tasteless (fish).

زهق; Izheq, vn breathe with difficulty, choke B. vs take disgust for, loathe B. ger. Zehq, disgust (as, for study) B.
Zêhiq, out of heart.
ii. Zehhiq, vs choke, overfeed B. pop. bother (a person) by pettinesses B. dispirit.
[All from Bocthor.]

ZHR

زهر; Izher, vn be bright and fair. ger. Zohour.
Zêbir, bright, as colour, florid.
Ezher, brighter, fairer.
Zohra, brightness of beauty.
Zuhera, Zohra, planet Venus.
Zehráwiey, jovial in temperament.
Zehra 3, 4, a flower.
Zehriey, flowery.
Zoheira, a floweret.
ii. Zehhir, vn flower, blossom.
Mozhir, pleasant (place).

ظهر; Uẓher, vn appear. ger. Ẓôhour.
Ẓâhir, adj. apparent, external.
s. the outside, the surface.
Ẓâhiraⁿ, externally, apparently; also, evidently.
Ẓâhiriey, superficial.
Aẓher, plainer, more visible.
Ẓâhira, outside (better side) of a garment. Ẓuhêra, dⁿ
iv. Aẓhir, vs display.
Uẓhêr, demonstration, display.
Moẓher, manifested.
vi. Teẓâher, vn display oneself.
Teẓâhoraⁿ, by way of display.
Mostaẓhir, visible.
[Uẓher ɛala' is sometimes used for Uẓfar ɛala', conquer x.]
(2) In the following, ظ (3) is sounded as ض (Δ).
Ẓahr, s. back, rear, rearguard.
iii. Ẓâhir, vs back up, support.
vi. Teẓâher, vr aid one another.
Moẓâhera, succour.
x. Istaẓhir, ask aid.

ЗHR

(3) Зöhr, midday, noon.
Зahiera 11, d°

ج ز Zojj, va poise in the hand; brandish; fling, toss. *ger.*
Zejj(a). Zejzij, va dandle.
(2) Zojâj, glass. (*See* Qozèz).
Zojâja, *ms.* of d°
Zojâjiey, glassy; made of glass; a glass-dealer.
Zejjâj, a glazier.

ج ا ز Zéj, copperas; vitriol.

ج و ز Zeuj 4, a pair, couple; one of a pair; husband or Zeuja, a wife. [wife.
Ziwaja, married people x.
Zieja, Zewâj, marriage.
[Ziej, mason's rule c.]
Zeujieya, state of matrimony.
ii. Zewwij, va join in marriage.
v. Tezewwaj, va enter marriage.
viii. Izdawij, *vp* be married.
Izdiwâj, union (of a pair).

ز ج ل Zojla 10, tumult, noise of a crowd.
Izjel, *vn ger.* Zejel, be noisy, talk loud.

ز ج ر Ozjor, va scare by noise; drive (animals), drive (clouds and waves, as does the wind) s.; decry; scold ʙ.; prohibit c. *ger.* Zejr, Zijr c.

ز خ Zikk, va burst out, as rain fire, anger. *ger. ms.* Zikka.

ZL

Zekâk, outbursting, furious.
Matar zekâk, rain in torrents.

ز خم Izkam, va strike, propel, repel x. *ger.* Zekm, propulsion (of steam) ʏ.
Zekma, *plectrum,* bow or rod to strike musical strings x.
(2) Zekma 10, stirrup leather ʙ.

ز خر Izkar, *vn* be exuberant. *ger.* Zekr, state of overflow, redundance, luxuriance.
Zékir, Zekkâr, swollen (as sea), exuberant (in spirits).
Zokáriey, redundant.
Zekour, exuberant, swollen, blustering. [(plant).
Zekwar, thriving, vigorous v. Tezekkar, *vn* superabound.
Tezekwar bi, plume oneself upon.

ز خرف Zokrof, tinsel.
Zekrif, va decorate, gild. *ger.*
Zekrafa 11, a romance s.
Mozekraf, embellished, varnished up (as a false thing), bedizened.

ز ل Zill, *vn* make a false step; generally *fig.*
Zelle, a false step, slip of pen.
Zéll, defective (money), too
Zelel, defectiveness. [light.
Zelel, Zoll, *adj.* slippery (place).
iv. Ezill, va cause to slip, seduce [also as *vn* in ʙ.].
(2) Zolâl, limpid (water); perhaps for Зölâl.

ZL

(3) Ezell, agile K. Ezell, Zêlil, gaunt, haggard B. *Also* Zêlil, *pl.* Zêlla, restless (man), qui va et vient sans cesse [B. Ambulant]; *or* desperate, furious (case, man) [B. Désesperé]; desperado? mischievous vagabond [B. Bandit].
(4) Zelzele 11, earthquake.
Zelzil, *va* shake (the earth).
ii. Tezelzel, *vn* be in tremor, totter, suffer earthquake.
(5) Zillieya 11, shaggy rug K. *See* Zouliya.

ظل ; 3ull 5, shade; *fig.* screen, protection.
3ölla 10, awning.
[3ölel, water, which is always in the shade, and never made flat by the sun K. Is not this zolâl ?]
3ulâla, shadiness.
3aliel, shady place c.
ii. 3allil, *va* overshadow.
Mo3allal, shaded.
v. Te3allal, *vn* be under shade.
x. Istegull, *vn* seek the shade.
(2) 3all, *vn* continue to be. *ger.* 3öloul B. V. [place K. 3alla, prolonged sojourn in one 3aliel, constant.

أزل ; 'Ezel, eternity; esp. in the past.
'Ezeliey, eternal.
'Ezelieya, eternal existence.

وزل ; Wezêl, broom, a shrub.

ZLM

زال ; Zêl, *vn* leave off, cease. *ger.* Zeil. [Common with negation, Lem yezel, unfailing.]
Zêyil, fleeting, transitory.
iii. Zêyil, *va* abandon, leave.
(2) Zêyila 12, mule (*Algiers*).

زول ; Zoul, *vn* decline as the sun. *ger.* Zewâl.
ii. Zewwil *or* iv. Eziel, *va* cause to decline, lessen, calm.
(2) Zouliya, shaggy rug B. Perhaps better Zillieya 11.

زلع ; Zolca 10, amphora, peculiar urn or pitcher.

زلب ; Zolâbieya, fritter, pancake.

زلف ; Ozlof, *va* curl (hair).
Zêlif, a ringlet o.
[Quite different in K.]

ظلف ; 3ulf 4, cloven hoof.
3âlif 10, horny, hard.
Me3allaf, cloven-footed.

زلج ; Izlij, *vn* glide, slide (*vulg.* superseded by Izlaq).
Zelouj, *adj.* gliding, swift.
Mizlêj, a slider, *i.e.* a doorbolt; *vulg.* Mizlâq.

زلم ; Zelma, foot-soldier B. man, person AL.
(2) Zelouma, proboscis.
Zelema, hanging comb of turkey, etc. See Zenema.

ZLM

ظلم Zalm, Zalâma, iniquity, oppression. [tyrannical.
Zâlim, Zaloum, Zallâm, unjust,
Azlam, more tyrannical.
Mazlima, tyranny.
iii. Zâlim, *va* tyrannize over.
Mozâlama, tyranny.
v. Tezallam, *vn* act the oppressor. *Also*, complain r. x.
vii. Inzalim, *vp* be oppressed.
(2) In the following, ظ (z) is sounded ض (đ).
Zalam, *ger.* become dark.
Zalim, dark x.
Zôlma 2, Zalâm 10, darkness.
iv. Azlim, *va* be dark (as night).
Mozlim, dark (night, place).

زلط Zelṭ, nakedness?
Sala' el zelṭ, in a state of nakedness. [It may be slang, as we say, "in buff," for, with skin exposed.]
(2) Ozloṭ, *va* bolt down (food), *popular term* b.

زلطم Zelṭöum, snout. *Compare* Zelouma; *also* Barröum *and* Korröum.

زلق Izlaq, *vn* glide, slide, be slippery.
Mizlâq, a slider, *i.e.* a door-bolt.
Zellâqa, a slide, sliding-place.
Mezlaqa, slipperiness c.
Zaliq, Mozliq, slippery (place).
iv. Ezliq, *va* slide, cause to slide.
v. Tezallaq, *vn* slide for sport, skate.

ZMR

زمام Zimâm 8, sandal tie, bridle.
Zomm *or* ii. Zemmim, *va* bridle, generally *fig.*

زمزم Zemzim, *vn* simmer, seethe; mutter, rumble. *ger.* Zemzema.
Zemzem, a well at Mecca.

وزم iv. Mouzim, *adj.* instant, pressing (b. *sic.*) = Molzim?

زوم Zoum, gravy.

زمهرير Zemherier, intensity of (anger or) cold.
Mozmiherr, *adj.* intensely cold.

زمجّ Zimijja', Zimicce', root of the tail (in birds) b. x.

زمل Zêmila 12, packhorse b.g.
Zemiel 6 [*prop* one who rides on same horse], workfellow, colleague.

زمن Zeman 4, *or commoner* Zemân 8, (long) time.
Zemâniey, belonging to time.
Zemaniey, temporal (power of Pope).
Zomain, a short time x.
iv. Ezmin, *vn* last a long while [*va* inflame (passion) b.].
Mozmin, chronic (disease).

زمر Zemr, flute, musical instrument c.
Zemmâra, the double flute.
Zemmâr, a piper.

ZMR

Zimâra, art of flute-playing.
Izmar, *vn* pipe. *ger.* Zemr, Zemier.
(2) Ozmorfie, *vn* animadvert on.
(3) Zomra 10, troop of men, crew, gang.

زمرد Zomorrod, emerald c. a. *See* Zebarjad.

زمط Ozmot, *vn* decamp b.

زن Zinn, *vn* hum.
Zennân, hummingbird.

ظن 3önn, *v.* (*with* 'Enna) think, surmise. *ger.* 3önoun.
3ann, a thought, a notion.
3anoun, suspicious (person), apt to suspect. [to suspicion.
3anien, suspicious (thing), open
3unna, *pl.* 3anâyin, a suspicion x.; a surmise. [sumption.
Ma3unna, *pl.* Mo3ânn, a pre-

وزن Wezon Yezin, *va* weigh. *ger.* Wezn, Zina.
Wezn 4, weight.
Zinn, a weight.
Wezien, of just weight, weighty.
Auzen, heavier, weightier.
Wêzin, which weighs—*i.e.* is equivalent in weight to—.
iii. Wêzin, *va or with* bain, bi; compare, balance; *also va* compensate.
Wizên, counterpart x.
Mowêzena, rythmical balance of prose words x.
vi. Tewêzen, *or* balance mutually, be equal.

ZND

viii. Ittezin, *vn* be of equal weight.
Mauzoun, well weighed (counsel), well balanced (mind).
Miezên, instrument to weigh; a balance, *pl.* Mawêzien.
Miezênieya, balance of accounts, public budget.

زان Zên, beech tree.

زين Zêyin, *vulg.* Zein, fine, handsome; good Bg.
Ziena, ornament.
Zeyyân, beautifier, *i.e.* hairdresser, barber Bg.
Ziyâna, hairdresser's art.
ii. Zeyyin, *va* adorn; *esp.* dress hair, shave.
Mozeyyin, hairdresser AL

زنى Izni, *vn* commit sexual immorality. *ger.* Zinâ.
Zêni, adulterer, etc.
Zinwiey, bastard.
iii. Zêni, *va* debauch.

زنب Zenbiel 11, a frail, limber basket.
Zenbaq, lily, jasmine. [fly.
Zenbour 11, wasp, hornet, gadZenbareo, watchspring.
Zenbour, broccoli.

زند Zenâd, steel for striking light; cock of a musket.
Miznada, steel and flint.
(2) Zend, small bone of the arm, *radius.* Zend flarab, log of firewood b.
(3) Zindân, dungeon Bg.

ZND

Zendieq, Manichee.
Zendaqa, Manicheeism.

زنج ; Zinj, *coll.*; and *pl.* Zonouj, Ethiopians, gipsies, savages.
Zenjiey, Ethiopian.
(2) Zenjabiel, ginger.
Zenjifra, cinnabar, vermilion.
Zenjier 11, chain [*vulgo* Jen-Zenjir, *va* chain. [zier].
Zinjâr, verdigris, rust x.
Zinjâriey, rusty, greenish.

زنخ ; Iznak, *vn* be rancid.
Zenik, rancid.
Zinâka, rancidity.

زنم Zenema, dewlap.

زنك ; Zencêwa, stirrup AL
(2) Zence, a herring.

زنق ; Oznoq, Izniq, *va* compress, trammel B.
Zinâq, trammels, horse collar.
ii. Zenniq or iv. Ezniq, *va* constrict. [a stricture B.
Zenqa, narrow lane k.; *medic.*
Mozennaq, tight.

زنر ; Zonnâr 11, a belt; from modern *Gr.* ζωννάρι.
ii. Zennir, *va* belt.

زنطر ; Zenτara, caprice B.
Mozenτur, capricious.
(2) Zenτâria, a carbuncle (burning tumour).

زنز ; Zenzelakt, the acacia.

ZQL

زق ; Zoqq, *va* poke in (as bird into mouth of young one), *also pop.* punch, pummel B.
(2) Ziqq 4, waterskin.
(3) Zoqâq 8, narrow street, alley; *pl.* straits (of sea).
(4) Zeqâqiya, linnet.
(5) Zeqziq, *vn* creak as shoes.
(6) Zeqzâq, the ichneumon.

يزك or يزك Yezo, *s.* arrest of a soldier; detention?
ii. Yezzic *or* Yezziq, *va* detain, distrain goods by sale for debt; arrest, detain, confine (a soldier) B.

زوق ii. Zewwiq, *va* enamel, emblazon, gild; *fig.* adorn, style artificially. [lished.
Mozewwaq, elaborately embel-Zewwâq, emblazoner.
El ɣorâb el mozewwaq, the painted raven, *i.e.* the jay.

زيق Zieq, collar of a dress.

زكى ; Zeciey, pure, refined, chaste of colour, exquisite.
Zecêwa, purity, delicacy.
Izci, *vn* be pure, etc.
ii. Zecci, *va* purify, refine; *also* vindicate, justify.
Tezciya, vindication.
[*Contrast* Δeci, Δecêwa.]

زكب ; Zecieba, a sack.

زقل ; Zaqla, cudgel.

ZCM

زكم Izœm, *vn* run at the nose.
ger. Zocêm.
Mezœum, suffering catarrh.
ii. Zeccim, *va* give cold, catarrh, in head and nose.

زر Zirr 4, a bud.
Zorr, fetlock of horse.
Zorra 4, bud, button.
Zorr, Zerzir, *va* button. [tons.
iv. Ezirr, *va* furnish with but-
v. Tezerrar, *vn* bud, burgeon.
(2) Zorzour, starling (bird).

أزر Iezêr, woman's white shroud. Miezêr, apron.

أزر Iz'er, *vn* roar, as a lion.
ger. Ze'ier.
iv. Ez'ir, v. Tezê'er, dᵃ x.

زور Zour, obliquity, falsehood.
Zeura, obliquity, crookedness.
Ezwar, awry. [a leer.
Izwar cala', *vn* leer at.
ii. Zewwir, *va* slouch? falsify, forge, garble. Mozewwar, oblique, slouching, falsified.
(2) Zeur, force, violence; corrupt from Jaur.
(3) Zour, *va* visit, pay a visit of respect or of pilgrimage.
ger. Ziyâra, a visit.
Zêyir 1, *or pl.* Zowwâr, visitor, pilgrim.
Mezêr 2, visit, place visited.
iv. Ezier, *va* cause to visit.
(4) Zuur, thicket ᴀʟ Bg.
(5) Mizwar, a prop? (B. chevalet, supplice).

ZRB

(6) Zewar, top of breast, bottom of throat, *esp.* in beast and bird ꜰ. Zewariey, jugular.
Izwar, *vn* stuff oneself, choke (fill one's crop?) B.
Zêra, Zêwira, bird's gizzard x.
(7) Mêzour, kingfisher.

زير Zier 4, a jar.

زري Izri cala', *vn* blame.
Zêri, one who blames.
Mizrâ, censorious.
v. Tezerrâ cala', *vn* as i.
viii. Izderi, *va* disparage, disdain, despise (*Popular*).
iv. Ezri, *va* despise?
Mozri, despiser ꜰ.

زرع Izras, *va* sow, plant.
Zêris, sower, planter.
Zerrâs, agriculturist.
Zerr 3, seed. Zeries, sown.
Zersuiy, of seed.
Zerrâsa, sown land.
Mezêries, sown fields.
ii. Zetris, *vn* sprout B.
viii. Mozdarisa, sown land.

زرب Israb, *vn* leak B. flow x.
Zirba, watercourse x.
Zerab, flux of the body? Zerab el barn, diarrhœa? [*But* Δerab B. x.]
Mizrâb 11, gutter, shoot down which rain pours.
(2) Zerieba, fence, paling.
ii. Zerrib, *va* fence in.
(3) Mizraba, mallet; corrupt for Mirzeba?

ZRB

(4) Zerboul 11, heavy shoo.
(5) Zerboun, red perch (fish).

زربن Ꜯarbàn, polecat, skunk.
(2) Teꜯarban, *vn* revolt, rebel ʙ.

زرد Zerd, Zerdieya, coat of mail.
Zerda, *nu.* a single ring of d⁰
Ozrod, *v.* work chain armour.
(2) Zard, zebra ʙ. [honey.
(3) Zerda, rice with saffron and
(4) Zerdawá, genet; animal akin to the ferret ʀ.

زرف Ziráfa, giraffe, camelopard.

ظرف Ꜯarf 8, utensil, vessel; a case. *But pl.* 3, a condition, limitation, limit of time; *also,* an adverb.
Ꜯörfa, external coffee cup-holder.
Maꜯrouf, contained in a vessel. *s.* ware.
(2) Ꜯarief, delicate, elegant.
Ꜯaráfa, delicacy and elegance.
Oꜯrof, *vn* be elegant. [to.
v. Teꜯarraf bi, play the gallant

زرم Iꜯram, *vn* stop short, hold up (as tears), be cut short, run suddenly dry. *ger.* Zoram.
[Ozrom, *ger.* Zerm, *va* cut away (*fig.* ʀ.)]
iv. Ezrim, *va* cut short, interrupt, deprive of; restrain.

ZZQ

Mozrim, circumspect, prudent ɪ.
vii. Inzerim, *cp* of iv.

زرق Ezraq, *adj.* Zorqa, *s.* blue.
Sadou ezraq, bitter enemy.
Ozeiriq, Mozriqq, bluish.
Mozerraq, made blue.
(2) Ozroq bi, *vn* fling with.
Zerûqa, Mizrâq 11, a dart.
See Irxaq.
(3) Zeuraq 11, a shallop.
(4) Zorrâq 11, goshawk.
(5) Abou zericq, magpie.

زركش Zereix, *va* embroider (with gold). Zercex, brocade.

زرزم Zerzemieya, cool subterraneous apartment, summer cellar ʙ. (=Serdâb, Tormose.)

زرت Zitt, *va* fling horizontally ʙ₉.

زيت Zeit, olive-oil. Zeitoun, olive. Zeitouna, olive-tree.
Zeyyêt, oilman.
Ziet, *va* enrich (food) with oil.

زى Zier, *vn* shout, scream. *ger.* Ziyàt. · Zeyyàt, shouter.

زوز Zouz, marrow.

زيزفن Zeizefrân, linden-tree.

ززق Zeuziq, *va* embellish. See Zewwiq.

END OF VOL. II.

LIST OF WORKS
BY
F. W. NEWMAN,
PUBLISHED BY
TRÜBNER & CO., 8 AND 60, PATERNOSTER ROW.

THE ODES OF HORACE translated into unrhymed metre, with Introduction and ample Notes. 8vo., cloth. Price 6s.

THE ILIAD OF HOMER faithfully translated into unrhymed metre. Second Edition. Royal 8vo., cloth. 1871. Price 10s. 6d.

HOMERIC TRANSLATION: a reply to Professor MATTHEW ARNOLD. Price 2s. 6d.

THE TEXT OF THE IGUVINE INSCRIPTIONS, with Interlinear Latin Translations and Notes. 8vo. Price 2s.

HIAWATHA: rendered into Latin, with abridgement. 12mo. Price 2s. 6d.

TRANSLATIONS OF ENGLISH POETRY INTO LATIN VERSE. Crown 8vo., cloth, pp. xiv. and 202. Price 6s.

ORTHOËPY; or, a Simple Mode of Accenting English, for the advantage of Foreigners and all Learners. Price 1s.

A HANDBOOK OF MODERN ARABIC, consisting of a Practical Grammar, with numerous examples, dialogues, and newspaper extracts, in a European type. In one vol., crown 8vo., pp. 212, cloth. Price 6s.

"This manual is peculiarly adapted to render the earlier stages in the acquisition of the Arabic language much easier than they are ordinarily proved to be. For by an exact system of transliteration of that alphabet into easy equivalents, it saves the student the double perplexity of having to contend, at once, with a strange language and a strange character; and while familiarising him with the sound of the more common words and constructions, it insensibly leads him to the knowledge of the original mode of writing them. To those who wish to acquire and speak modern Arabic, this work, by the singular pains taken to define and enforce the exact sounds of the spoken language, offers advantages very far surpassing those of the most celebrated grammars of the learned idioms."—Dr. J. NICHOLSON, Penrith.

www.ingramcontent.com/pod-product-compliance
Lightning Source LLC
Chambersburg PA
CBHW022113300426
44117CB00007B/695